10th Workshop on Argument Mining (ArgMining 2023)

Singapore and Online
7 December 2023

ISBN: 978-1-7138-8595-5

Printed from e-media with permission by:

Curran Associates, Inc.
57 Morehouse Lane
Red Hook, NY 12571

CURRAN ASSOCIATES INC.
proceedings
.com

Some format issues inherent in the e-media version may also appear in this print version.

Association for Computational Linguistics
209 N. Eighth Street
Stroudsburg, Pennsylvania 18360

Phone: 1-570-476-8006
Fax: 1-570-476-0860

acl@aclweb.org

Additional copies of this publication are available from:

Curran Associates, Inc.
57 Morehouse Lane
Red Hook, NY 12571 USA
Phone: 845-758-0400
Fax: 845-758-2633
Email: curran@proceedings.com
Web: www.proceedings.com

EMNLP 2023

The 10th Workshop on Argument Mining (ArgMining 2023)

Proceedings of the Workshop

December 7, 2023
Online and in Singapore

Order copies of this and other ACL proceedings from:

Association for Computational Linguistics (ACL)
209 N. Eighth Street
Stroudsburg, PA 18360
USA
Tel: +1-570-476-8006
Fax: +1-570-476-0860
acl@aclweb.org

Introduction

Argument mining (also known as "argumentation mining") is a gradually maturing research area within computational linguistics. At its heart, argument mining involves the automatic identification of argumentative structures in free text, such as the conclusions, premises, and inference schemes of arguments as well as their interrelations and counter-considerations. To date, researchers have investigated argument mining on genres such as legal documents, product reviews, news articles, online debates, user-generated web discourse, Wikipedia articles, scholarly data, persuasive essays, tweets, and dialogues. Aside from mining argumentative components, the field focuses on studying argument quality assessment, argument persuasiveness, and the synthesis of argumentative texts.

Argument mining gives rise to various practical applications of great importance. In particular, it provides methods that can find and visualize the main pro and con arguments in a text corpus — or even in an argument search on the web — towards a topic or query of interest. In instructional contexts, written and diagrammed arguments represent educational data that can be mined for conveying and assessing students' command of course material. Moreover, debate technologies like IBM Project Debater that drew a lot of attention recently rely heavily on argument mining tasks.

While solutions to basic tasks such as component segmentation and classification slowly become mature, many tasks remain largely unsolved, particularly in more open genres and topical domains. Success in argument mining requires interdisciplinary approaches informed by NLP technology, theories of semantics, pragmatics and discourse, knowledge of discourse in application domains, artificial intelligence, information retrieval, argumentation theory, and computational models of argumentation.

The ArgMining community is constantly growing, as demonstrated by the increasing number of submissions on argument mining being accepted at top level international conferences in the fields of NLP and AI. This year's 10th edition of the workshop had 40 valid submissions (30 in 2020, 39 in 2021, and 37 in 2022). Among the submitted papers, there were 13 long papers, 13 short papers, and 1 demo paper. We accepted 8 long papers and 3 short papers (41% acceptance rate). In addition, the workshop features 13 shared-task papers. The submissions came from institutions in 17 countries. All accepted papers are included in the proceedings at hand. We would like to thank our Program Committee members as well as the members of our Best Paper Selection Committee: Claire Cardie (Cornell University), Naoya Inoue (JAIST) and Benno Stein (Bauhaus-Universität Weimar).

The one-day workshop was conducted in hybrid format. We were delighted to have Noam Slonim from IBM Research AI as the keynote speaker, on the topic of "Project Debater and argument mining - a historical and somewhat personal perspective". In celebration of the 10th anniversary of the workshop series, a panel of distinguished researchers in the field, including Khalid Al Khatib (University of Groningen), Yufang Hou (IBM Research AI), Diane Litman (University of Pittsburgh), Chris Reed (University of Dundee), and Henning Wachsmuth (Leibniz Universität Hannover), reflected on the past and the future of argument mining. ArgMining 2023 also hosted two shared tasks, namely the First Shared Task in Multimodal Argument Mining (ImageArg 2023) and the First Shared Task on Pragmatic Tagging of Peer Reviews (PragTag 2023).

We would like to express our gratitude to our sponsors, IBM and Naver. Their support allowed the workshop program to feature a best paper award, chosen by an independent committee. Awards are announced on the official workshop website: https://argmining-org.github.io/2023/index.html.

Thanks to everyone who supported and made this workshop possible!

Milad Alshomary, Chung-Chi Chen, Smaranda Muresan, Joonsuk Park, and Julia Romberg
(ArgMining 2023 co-chairs)

Organizing Committee

Milad Alshomary, Leibniz Universität Hannover
Chung-Chi Chen, National Institute of Advanced Industrial Science and Technology
Smaranda Muresan, Columbia University & AWS AI Labs
Joonsuk Park, University of Richmond
Julia Romberg, Heinrich-Heine-Universität Düsseldorf

Program Committee

Rodrigo Agerri, University of the Basque Country
Yamen Ajjour, Leibniz Universität Hannover
Khalid Al Khatib, University of Groningen
Tariq Alhindi, King Abdulaziz City for Science and Technology (KACST)
Emily Allaway, Columbia University
Safi Eldeen Alzi'abi, Isra University
Ozkan Aslan, Afyon Kocatepe University
Roy Bar-Haim, IBM Research AI
Miriam Butt, University of Konstanz
Elena Cabrio, Université Côte d'Azur, CNRS, Inria, I3S
Claire Cardie, Cornell University
Jonathan Clayton, University of Sheffield
Johannes Daxenberger, summetix
Lorik Dumani, Trier University
Roxanne El Baff, German Aerospace Center (DLR)
Ivan Habernal, Paderborn University
Shohreh Haddadan, University of Luxembourg
Yufang Hou, IBM Research AI
Xinyu Hua, Bloomberg AI
Lea Kawaletz, Heinrich-Heine-Universität Düsseldorf
Christopher Klamm, University of Mannheim
Gabriella Lapesa, University of Stuttgart
John Lawrence, University of Dundee
Beishui Liao, Zhejiang University
Simon Parsons, University of Lincoln
Georgios Petasis, NCSR Demokritos, Athens
Olesya Razuvayevskaya, University of Sheffield
Chris Reed, University of Dundee
Patrick Saint-Dizier, IRIT, CNRS
Robin Schaefer, University of Potsdam
Jodi Schneider, University of Illinois Urbana-Champaign
Gabriella Skitalinskaya, Leibniz Universität Hannover
Manfred Stede, University of Potsdam
Benno Stein, Bauhaus-Universität Weimar
Simone Teufel, University of Cambridge
Serena Villata, Université Côte d'Azur, CNRS, Inria, I3S
Henning Wachsmuth, Leibniz Universität Hannover
Vern R. Walker, Hofstra University
Timon Ziegenbein, Leibniz Universität Hannover

Shared Task Organizers

Zhexiong Liu, University of Pittsburgh
Mohamed Elaraby, University of Pittsburgh

Yang Zhong, University of Pittsburgh
Diane Litman, University of Pittsburgh
Nils Dycke, Technical University of Darmstadt
Ilia Kuznetsov, Technical University of Darmstadt

Best Paper Selection Committee

Claire Cardie, Cornell University
Naoya Inoue, JAIST
Benno Stein, Bauhaus-Universität Weimar

Table of Contents

Conference Program

Thursday, December 7, 2023

09:00–09:10 **Opening Remarks**

09:10–10:10 **Panel Session**

10:10–10:34 **Paper Session I**

Dimensionality Reduction for Machine Learning-based Argument Mining
Andrés Segura-Tinoco and Iván Cantador

Argument Detection in Student Essays under Resource Constraints
Omid Kashefi, Sophia Chan and Swapna Somasundaran

10:34–11:00 **Break**

11:00–12:30 **Paper Session II**

On the Impact of Reconstruction and Context for Argument Prediction in Natural Debate
Zlata Kikteva, Alexander Trautsch, Patrick Katzer, Mirko Oest, Steffen Herbold and Annette Hautli-Janisz

Unsupervised argument reframing with a counterfactual-based approach
Philipp Heinisch, Dimitry Mindlin and Philipp Cimiano

Legal Argument Extraction from Court Judgements using Integer Linear Programming
Basit Ali, Sachin Pawar, Girish Palshikar, Anindita Sinha Banerjee and Dhirendra Singh

Teach Me How to Argue: A Survey on NLP Feedback Systems in Argumentation
Camelia Guerraoui, Paul Reisert, Naoya Inoue, Farjana Sultana Mim, Keshav Singh, Jungmin Choi, Irfan Robbani, Shoichi Naito, Wenzhi Wang and Kentaro Inui

Detecting Argumentative Fallacies in the Wild: Problems and Limitations of Large Language Models
Ramon Ruiz-Dolz and John Lawrence

Thursday, December 7, 2023 (continued)

Constituency Tree Representation for Argument Unit Recognition
Samuel Guilluy, Florian Mehats and Billal Chouli

Mind the Gap: Automated Corpus Creation for Enthymeme Detection and Reconstruction in Learner Arguments (Findings Paper)
Maja Stahl, Nick Düsterhus, Mei-Hua Chen and Henning Wachsmuth

Automatic Analysis of Substantiation in Scientific Peer Reviews (Findings Paper)
Yanzhu Guo, Guokan Shang, Virgile Rennard, Michalis Vazirgiannis and Chloé Clavel

12:30–14:00 Lunch

14:00–15:00 Shared Task Session

Overview of ImageArg-2023: The First Shared Task in Multimodal Argument Mining
Zhexiong Liu, Mohamed Elaraby, Yang Zhong and Diane Litman

Overview of PragTag-2023: Low-Resource Multi-Domain Pragmatic Tagging of Peer Reviews
Nils Dycke, Ilia Kuznetsov and Iryna Gurevych

15:00–16:00 Poster Session (Shared Task Papers + Main Workshop Papers)

15:30–16:00 Break

16:00–17:00 Keynote Speech

17:00–17:52 Paper Session III

Towards Fine-Grained Argumentation Strategy Analysis in Persuasive Essays
Robin Schaefer, René Knaebel and Manfred Stede

Using Masked Language Model Probabilities of Connectives for Stance Detection in English Discourse
Regina Stodden, Laura Kallmeyer, Lea Kawaletz and Heidrun Dorgeloh

Thursday, December 7, 2023 (continued)

Stance-Aware Re-Ranking for Non-factual Comparative Queries
Jan Heinrich Reimer, Alexander Bondarenko, Maik Fröbe and Matthias Hagen

Unveiling the Power of Argument Arrangement in Online Persuasive Discussions (Findings Paper)
Nailia Mirzakhmedova, Johannes Kiesel, Khalid Al Khatib and Benno Stein

High-quality argumentative information in low resources approaches improves counter-narrative generation (Findings Paper)
Damián Furman, Pablo Torres, José Rodríguez, Diego Letzen, Maria Vanina Martinez and Laura Alonso Alemany

18:00–18:15 Closing Remarks + Best Paper Award

Detecting Argumentative Fallacies *in the Wild*: Problems and Limitations of Large Language Models

Ramon Ruiz-Dolz and **John Lawrence**
Centre for Argument Technology (ARG-tech)
University of Dundee
United Kingdom
{rruizdolz001,j.lawrence}@dundee.ac.uk

Abstract

Previous work on the automatic identification of fallacies in natural language text has typically approached the problem in constrained experimental setups that make it difficult to understand the applicability and usefulness of the proposals in the real world. In this paper, we present the first analysis of the limitations that these data-driven approaches could show in real situations. For that purpose, we first create a validation corpus consisting of natural language argumentation schemes. Second, we provide new empirical results to the emerging task of identifying fallacies in natural language text. Third, we analyse the errors observed outside of the testing data domains considering the new validation corpus. Finally, we point out some important limitations observed in our analysis that should be taken into account in future research in this topic. Specifically, if we want to deploy these systems *in the Wild*.

1 Introduction

In the field of the automatic analysis of natural language argumentative discourse, the identification of fallacies plays an important role since it can be a determining feature to measure the *quality* of argumentation (Wachsmuth et al., 2017). Furthermore, the automatic identification of fallacies can also be helpful for the development of disinformation detection systems and critical thinking tools (Visser et al., 2020). Studied since the times of the ancient Greece by Aristotle (Aristotle, 1978), a fallacy was seen as an argumentation strategy used to deceive an opponent in a debate and unfairly get the reason. This definition evolved with time (Van Eemeren and Grootendorst, 1984; Hamblin, 1970) extending the instrumental notion of the Aristotelian fallacy to more modern theories of logic and mathematics. A more recent (and complete) definition was provided by Walton (1995), where fallacies are defined as "*important, baptizable types of errors or deceptive tactics of argumentation that tend to fool or trip up participants in argumentation in various kinds of everyday discussions*". This definition is less constrained and more accurate to the natural language challenges we may face these days.

Detecting a piece of fallacious reasoning, however, is not trivial and requires knowledge in a broad number of areas that make this task challenging. First, it is important to be able to analyse the logical reasoning underlying natural language arguments. For that purpose, it is required to distil the abstract and formal components from the informal natural language argument. This first case is that of *formal* fallacies (Oliver, 1967). Second, solid knowledge on the domain of discussion is of utmost importance. An argument can be logically sound but still fallacious, such is the case of *informal* fallacies (Walton, 1987). Therefore, only with a complete analysis is it possible to determine if a natural language argument is a fallacy or not, as well as the underlying reasons why it is fallacious. A consistent way to conduct this analysis is to rely on validated models of argument which capture the notion of fallacy. Different models have been proposed and studied in the literature; such is the case of the pragma-dialectic theory of argumentation (Van Eemeren and Grootendorst, 2016) in which the authors define ten rules to guide argumentative discussions. The fulfilment of these rules allows to create a fruitful discussion, but an argument that breaks any of these rules is considered a fallacy. Another good example of these models is the argumentation schemes proposed by Walton (Walton et al., 2008). An argumentation scheme combines the abstract representation of the underlying logic of a natural language argument with a set of critical questions that must be successfully answered to prove the validity of an argument. The argumentation scheme model is very interesting w.r.t. fallacy analysis, since an argument being fallacious is not determined by belonging to a specific class, but depending on the answers provided to the set of

Proceedings of the 10th Workshop on Argument Mining, pages 1–10
December 7, 2023. ©2023 Association for Computational Linguistics

critical questions. For example, a natural language argument belonging to the *Ad Hominem* scheme is not a fallacy per se, but it must be structured as follows:

Character Attack Premise: a is a person of bad character.

Conclusion: a's argument α should not be accepted.

And it is only considered to be fallacious if any of the following critical questions cannot be successfully answered,

- CQ1: How well supported by evidence is the allegation made in the character attack premise?
- CQ2: Is the issue of the character relevant in the type of dialogue in which the argument was used?
- CQ3: Is the conclusion of the argument that α should be rejected, or is the conclusion that α should be assigned a reduced weight of credibility?

Therefore, with the argumentation scheme paradigm, it is possible to partially dissociate the natural language and the logic of the argument, allowing for a more informed analysis of the reasons of an argument being fallacious.

In this paper, we integrate the concept of argumentation schemes in the evaluation of machine learning and Transformer-based language models for the automatic detection of fallacies in natural language arguments. It is our objective to understand the way these models, as they have been proposed in most of the previous work in this topic, are able to *learn* the reasons behind a fallacy and generalise to data outside of the training domain. Our contribution is therefore threefold: (i) we create a fallacy validation corpus consisting of natural language argumentation schemes; (ii) we provide new empirical results for the emerging task of identifying fallacies in natural language text; and (iii) we analyse the observed errors inside and outside of the testing data domains considering the argumentation scheme validation corpus, and point out some of the main limitations of relying exclusively on LLMs when addressing complex natural language reasoning problems.

2 Related Work

The automatic detection of fallacies in natural language texts is an emerging topic of research within the area of Natural Language Processing. One of the first efforts in developing a database of fallacies was done in (Habernal et al., 2017) creating "*Argotario*", an educative platform where participants could improve their debating skills. Through gamification, the authors collected fallacies registered by the participants belonging to one of the following five classes: *ad hominem*, appeal to emotion, red herring, hasty generalisation, irrelevant authority. A direct continuation of this work was presented in (Habernal et al., 2018a), where the resulting corpus from the use of "*Argotario*" containing 430 annotated arguments was released. In that work, arguments belonging to the previous five classes plus a *no fallacy* set of arguments were compiled, and a set of preliminary results of experiments with a Support Vector Machine (SVM) and a Bidirectional Long Short-Term Memory (BiLSTM) neural network were reported.

Aimed at better understanding the linguistic features underlying the *Ad Hominem* argument, Habernal et al. developed a corpus from user discussions in the *Change My View* subreddit on the Reddit social network (Habernal et al., 2018b). For that purpose they retrieved the comments that were removed by the administrators because they were labelled as rude or hostile by the community, matching one of the non breakable rules proposed in (Van Eemeren and Grootendorst, 2016) as part of the pragma-dialectic theory of argumentation. The authors also reported a set of fallacy detection experiments with a Convolutional Neural Network (CNN) in which they used this corpus consisting of 7,242 samples balanced between non-fallacious and *ad hominem* classes.

The automatic identification of argumentative fallacies has also been studied from the propaganda viewpoint in (Da San Martino et al., 2019), where the authors annotate news articles containing up to 18 propaganda techniques and report a series of experiments on propaganda classification. This perspective on fallacious argumentation was continued in a shared task organised for the SemEval forum (Da San Martino et al., 2020) aimed at the automatic classification of natural language propaganda.

Based on the pragma-dialectic theory (Van Eemeren and Grootendorst, 2016) eight classes of fallacious arguments were annotated in a corpus of informal fallacies in online discussions by Sahai et al. (2021). More than 1,700 fallacious comments retrieved from Reddit were annotated into the classes of Appeal to authority, Appeal to majority, Appeal to nature, Appeal to tradition, Appeal to worse problems, Black-or-white, Hasty generalisation, and Slippery slope fallacies. Furthermore, the authors report results on the binary task of classifying natural language text as fallacious or not, and on the 8-class classification problem of determining the type of fallacy to which each fallacious comment belongs to. For the experiments, the authors consider more advanced models based in the Transformer architecture, and the granularity network that performed the best in (Da San Martino et al., 2019).

A simplified version of the task is presented in (Goffredo et al., 2022), where another corpus of fallacious argumentation is released. In this paper, the annotation of fallacious arguments is done from the transcripts of 31 political debates of the U.S. Presidential Campaigns. The authors annotate six different types of fallacy: *Ad Hominem*, Appeal to Emotion, Appeal to Authority, Slippery Slope, False Cause, and Slogans. In addition to these classes, 11 sub-classes are also annotated, providing additional information of the fallacious arguments. In their experiments, the best results are reported with a Transformer-based architecture that combines natural language with argumentative features. The experimental results reported in that work are exclusively focused on the task of classifying fallacies, assuming that the fallacy has already been detected.

Recently, (Alhindi et al., 2022) al explores the use of multitask instruction-based prompting to dectect 28 different fallacies across five datasets. The authors compare the use of T5 (Raffel et al., 2020) and GPT-3 (Brown et al., 2020) for prompt-based fallacy classification, and a fine-tuned BERT (Devlin et al., 2018) model for a more classic baseline. From their results, it is possible to observe how the multitask instruction-based prompting with T5 achieves a significant increase in performance compared to the GPT-3 and BERT baselines. However, the methodology applied in this paper is similar to the one followed in previous work, in which the fallacy type of a text sequence is determined by only taking the natural language of the sequence into account.

Finally, one of the most recent papers in the automatic detection of logical fallacies proposes a new task for pre-training language models based on the structure of arguments (Jin et al., 2022). For that purpose, the authors release a corpus consisting of 2,449 argumentative samples labelled into one of 13 different fallacy types. A set of experiments comparing Large Language Models (LLMs) as zero-shot classifiers with Transformer-based models fine-tuned on the corpus is reported, emphasising on the importance of looking at structural reasoning features for this type of classification problems.

We can observe how, in the past years, a varied set of relatively small corpora have been annotated and publicly released. Most of them, however, share a similar paradigm for addressing the automatic identification of argumentative fallacies. Short spans of text are labelled with one of the corresponding fallacy labels, but no attention is given to the underlying logic that makes the argument fallacious or not. Furthermore, all the reported experiments are done in a similar way, the natural language text is used as the input to learn a set of N classes (varying from one corpus to another) directly from the text, and no in-depth error analyses are reported in most of these works. These limitations might raise some concerns, such as the impact of non-fallacious arguments being labelled as fallacious (false positives) while they are not, just because they share similar words or natural language patterns. To have a better understanding of these cases, and the potential problems of relying only in deep learning algorithms for addressing a complex problem such as the identification of natural language fallacies, the argumentation scheme model of arguments presents itself as a promising alternative to the models considered in the literature.

3 Data

In order to validate our hypothesis and to provide an evaluation outside of the training domain, we decided to use two different corpora in our experiments. First, the fallacy detection corpus, which consists of a partial combination of the data described in (Sahai et al., 2021) and (Goffredo et al., 2022). Second, the argumentation scheme validation dataset, a small collection of natural language argumentation schemes that we created in this work in order to evaluate the inferences done by the predictive models to detect a natural language fallacy outside of the domains considered during training. With this second dataset, it is our objective to observe how well the model generalises when detecting natural language fallacies following a different model or structure than the one considered in the data used for training, similar to what would happen when deploying the predictive models *in the Wild.*

As depicted in Table 1, the fallacy detection corpus used in this work consists of four fallacy classes and the non-fallacious class. We selected the fallacy classes of Appeal to Authority, Appeal to Majority, Slippery Slope and *Ad Hominem* since they represent the majority of the natural language fallacies commonly used in human dialogues and debates.

Since the annotation in both corpora was based on similar fallacy theory, our fallacy detection corpus combines some of the natural languages fallacies annotated in U.S. presidential debates (Goffredo et al., 2022), with some others annotated in social media discussions (Sahai et al., 2021) and the non-fallacious class. The decision of combining both corpora is twofold. First, we wanted to address the automatic detection of natural language fallacies (not just classifying them as done in (Goffredo et al., 2022)) so non-fallacious samples were needed. The assumption done in (Goffredo et al., 2022) of knowing beforehand that some piece of natural language is fallacious represents a significant limitation of the contribution since knowing the fallacious condition of an input is not trivial, and represents an important challenge in the area. The second reason to combine both corpora is to have a more balanced distribution of samples when comparing fallacious to non-fallacious samples, and to expand the natural language domains in which fallacies can be observed during training.

A sample in our fallacy detection corpus consists of a short snippet of text where the fallacious (or not) reasoning has been identified, a natural language context in which the fallacy has been detected (a paragraph in the case of the debates, and the previous comment of the text snippet in the case of the social media discussions), and the annotated label. In order to homogenise the natural language context in data belonging to both corpora, for the samples extracted from the debate corpus we considered as the context only the sentences before and after the text snippet.

Aimed at validating the performance of machine learning and deep learning systems to detect natural language fallacies, we developed a small

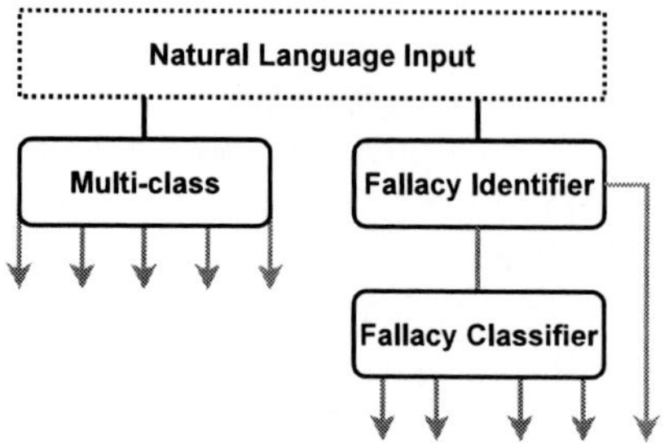

Figure 1: Multi-class and cascaded approaches.

dataset containing natural language argumentation schemes (Walton et al., 2008). In this dataset, we included seven different types of argumentation schemes matching the fallacy classes included in the fallacy detection corpus: Argument from Expert Opinion (AFEO), Argument from Position to Know (AFPK), Argument from Popular Practice (AFPP), Argument from Popular Opinion (AFPO), Slippery Slope Argumentation Scheme (SSAS), Generic *Ad Hominem* (GAH), and Circumstantial *Ad Hominem* (CAH). This way, we can easily relate each argumentation scheme with one of the four fallacy classes included in the fallacy detection corpus, the Appeal to Authority with AFEO and AFPO, the Appeal to Majority with AFPP and AFPO, the Slippery Slope with the SSAS, and the *Ad Hominem* with the GAH and CAH. It is important to remember that, argumentation schemes are not fallacious by definition as they are the fallacy classes used to annotate previous corpora, but they can only be considered as fallacious if and only if some of the critical questions cannot be successfully answered. Taking this into consideration, in our argumentation scheme validation dataset, we included two natural language instances of each scheme, one in which all the critical questions can be answered (i.e., valid reasoning), and another that fails in some aspect (i.e., fallacy). Therefore, our argumentation scheme validation dataset consists of fourteen natural language arguments specifically designed to validate the inference process of the predictive models in the task of automatically detecting natural language fallacies. These natural language argumentation schemes have been compiled in Table 2.

Samples	Appeal to Authority	Appeal to Majority	Slippery Slope	Ad Hominem	Fallacy Total	Non-fallacious
(Sahai et al., 2021)	212	196	228	-	636	1650
(Goffredo et al., 2022)	208	-	48	146	402	-
Total	420	196	276	146	1038	1650

Table 1: Class distribution of the fallacy detection corpus.

4 Experiments

4.1 Method

To extend the experimental results previously reported in the literature, we consider the two different approaches to the automatic detection of argumentative fallacies depicted in Figure 1. First, we consider a multi-class classification problem in which fallacy classes and the non-fallacious class are considered in the same level. In this case, we will be facing a five-class classification problem. Second, we consider a cascaded approach in which we first try to discriminate fallacies from valid reasoning. For that purpose, we combine a two-class classifier in charge of detecting fallacies, with a four-class classification model that determines the specific type of the fallacy (i.e., Authority, Majority, Slipepry Slope, and *Ad Hominem*).

4.2 Experimental Setup

In our experiments, we have considered three different implementations of the fallacy classifiers proposed in our method. Aimed at covering some of the state-of-the-art general approaches in NLP, we used a Support Vector Machine combined with natural language embeddings (eSVM), a fine-tuned RoBERTa for sequence classification, and zero-shot prompting GPT-3.5-TURBO and GPT-4 without any additional training. We also considered two versions of each input in our experiments: (i) we used as our input the text snippet only, and (ii) we combined the snippet with its context.

Regarding the eSVM, the best results were obtained with the radial basis function kernel, a *gamma* equal to one divided by the number of features, and C equal to 1000. On the other hand, for fine-tuning the RoBERTa model, we trained the model for 20 epochs with a learning rate of 1e-5 and a weight decay of 0.01. Finally, the prompt used in our experiments with GPT-3.5-TURBO and GPT-4 to automatically detect and classify natural language fallacies was designed in three sequential messages as follows:

- *You task is to detect a fallacy in the Text Snippet. The label can be "Slippery Slope", "Appeal to Authority", "Ad Hominem", "Appeal to Majority" or "None".*
- *Text Snippet:* [SAMPLE]
- *Label:*

The first paragraph of the prompt was adapted for each of the different situations proposed in our method. For example by removing *"None"* for fallacy classification (4-class), and grouping the fallacy labels into *"Fallacy"* for fallacy identification (2-class).

In all of our experiments, we considered an 80-10-10 split of our data into train, development, and test respectively. Furthermore, we removed all the duplicated text snippets from the U.S. presidential debates corpus to prevent the occurrence of the same natural language snippets in train and test at the same time, as happened in the experiments reported in (Goffredo et al., 2022). The best performing hyperparameters described above were selected based on the best performance in the development split. The code and the data used in our experiments can be publicly accessed at `https://github.com/raruidol/ArgumentMining23-Fallacy`.

5 Results

We have grouped the analysis of our results into two sections. First, we evaluate our models on the test split of the fallacy detection corpus. Second, we evaluate these same models when used to detect or classify fallacies *in the Wild* (i.e., outside of the training/testing data domain), for which purpose we use the argumentation scheme validation dataset.

5.1 Experimental Evaluation

Regarding the experimental evaluation, we measured the performance of the models by calculating the precision, recall, and macro f1 of the predictions done over the test samples. Table 3 contains the results of the multi-class classification experiments, Table 4 contains the results of the fallacy

Arg. Scheme	CQs	Natural Language Argumentation Schemes
AFEO	✓	*Major Premise*: "Prof Whittaker is a professor of virology at the Cornell University College" *Minor Premise*: "Prof Whittaker said that viruses can be spread by sneezing" *Conclusion*: "Viruses can be spread by sneezing"
AFEO	✗	*Major Premise*: "Stephen Hawking was an expert on AI" *Minor Premise*: "Stephen Hawking said that AI could spell the end of the human race" *Conclusion*: "AI could spell the end of the human race"
AFPK	✓	*Major Premise*: "Alice lives in New York" *Minor Premise*: "Alice says that New York City Hall is in Lower Manhattan" *Conclusion*: "New York City Hall is in Lower Manhattan"
AFPK	✗	*Major Premise*: "David is a cab driver in London" *Minor Premise*: "David says that the best way to get to Tower Bridge is by cab" *Conclusion*: "The best way to get to Tower Bridge is by cab"
AFPP	✓	*Major Premise*: "Most people wear black clothes at a funeral" *Minor Premise*: "If most people wear black clothes at a funeral, that is acceptable to do" *Conclusion*: "It is acceptable to wear black clothes at a funeral"
AFPP	✗	*Major Premise*: "Most people drive at least 10 miles per hour over the speed limit" *Minor Premise*: "If most people drive at least 10 miles per hour over the speed... ...limit, that is acceptable to do" *Conclusion*: "It is acceptable to drive at least 10 miles per hour over the speed limit"
AFPO	✓	*General Acceptance Premise*: "The majority of climate scientists agree that humans... ...are causing global warming and climate change" *Presumption Premise*: "If the majority of climate scientists agree that humans... ...are causing global warming and climate change, there is a reason to believe that is true" *Conclusion*: "There is reason to believe that humans... ...are causing global warming and climate change"
AFPO	✗	*General Acceptance Premise*: "The majority of people we asked agreed that the Earth may be flat " *Presumption Premise*: "If the majority of people we asked agreed that the Earth... ...may be flat, there is a reason to believe that is true" *Conclusion*: "There is reason to believe that the Earth may be flat"
SSAS	✓	*First Step Premise*: "I should go out with my friends rather than study for the exam" *Recursive Premise*: "If I don't pass the exam, this might affect my GPA, which... ...in turn might impact my chances of going to a good college" *Bad Outcome Premise*: "Not going to a good college would be a disaster" *Conclusion*: "I should not go out with my friends rather than study for the exam"
SSAS	✗	*First Step Premise*: "We should lower the legal drinking age from 21 to 18 in line with other countries" *Recursive Premise*: "If we lower it to 18, next it will be 17, then 16, 15, etc. " *Bad Outcome Premise*: "If we lower the legal drinking age, we'll have ten-year-olds getting drunk in bars!" *Conclusion*: "We should not lower the legal drinking age "
GAH	✓	*Character Attack Premise*: "Steve has cheated on a number of past exams" *Conclusion*: "We should doubt Steve's claim that someone else copied his work in this exam"
GAH	✗	*Character Attack Premise*: "The CEO was convicted of a DUI in college" *Conclusion*: "We should doubt the CEO's sales report"
CAH	✓	*Argument Premise*: "The car salesman argued that I should buy a gas car because... ...they are more reliable than electric cars" *Inconsistent Commitment Premise*: "The car salesman chose to drive an electric car" *Credibility Questioning Premise*: "The car salesman is not credible in this case" *Conclusion*: "The car salesman's argument that I should buy a gas car is not valid"
CAH	✗	*Argument Premise*: "Mark argued that you should not take illegal drugs as they can have dangerous side effects" *Inconsistent Commitment Premise*: "Mark has taken illegal drugs in the past" *Credibility Questioning Premise*: "Mark is not credible in this case" *Conclusion*: "Mark's argument that you should not take illegal drugs is not valid"

Table 2: Argumentation Scheme validation dataset. A (✓) indicates that the argument successfully answers its critical questions. A (✗) indicates that some of the critical questions cannot be successfully answered and thus, the argument is a fallacy.

Model	Precision	Recall	Macro-F1
RB	21.6	24.6	18.6
eSVM	68.3	55.8	60.3
RoBERTa	**68.2**	**65.3**	**66.5**
GPT-3.5-TURBO	59.0	46.2	45.5
GPT-4	53.5	55.0	51.7
eSVM+[*ctx*]	67.3	50.0	54.4
RoBERTa+[*ctx*]	62.0	58.4	59.9
GPT-3.5-TURBO+[*ctx*]	50.2	32.1	35.8
GPT-4+[*ctx*]	54.4	51.2	50.8

Table 3: Precision, Recall and Macro-F1 results of the 5-class fallacy detection task. [*ctx*] represents the contextual information added to the input of each model.

detection (i.e., 2-class classification) experiments, and Table 5 contains the results of the fallacy (i.e., 4-class) classification experiments. We have also included the random baseline (RB) in order to relativise the results with respect to the class complexity of each instance of the task. From all these results, we have identified two interesting patterns.

First of all, for a corpus of this size (i.e., ~2000 samples) and distribution, the best results were consistently achieved by fine-tuning the RoBERTa architecture. The eSVM model performed slightly worse and the worst performing approach was the zero-shot prompts for the GPT-3.5-TURBO and GPT-4 model. It is important to mention that in the zero-shot prompting experiments, no parameters were specifically fine-tuned for our data, and taking this into account, the results were surprisingly good compared to a random or a majority baseline. Furthermore, we could observe an important difference between GPT-3.5-TURBO and GPT-4 when prompted to detect and classify fallacies in natural language. We found out that in all of the fallacy detection and classification tasks GPT-4 significantly outperformed GPT-3.5-TURBO. Specifically in the cascaded approach, GPT-4 was able to outperform GPT-3.5-TURBO in more than a 20% with respect to macro F1 reaching a maximum improvement of a 58% in the fallacy classification task. After removing the negative samples, the GPT-4 model is able to focus on more relevant linguistic aspects of the text snippets than its predecessor, resulting in a significant improvement in this task (see Table 5). Finally, we were also able to observe that in general, better results were achieved by the cascaded approach. Therefore, when addressing a fallacy identification problem, given the linguistic complexity of this task, it is better to do it by separating the detection and the classification than doing both tasks at the same time.

The second pattern that we were able to observe is that, including the context as we did in our experiments was not helpful at all. Adding more contextual information to the text snippet resulted in redundant information that made the task more difficult for the predictive models. Given the generalised bad performance of the models when just including the adjacent text of the snippet to the input, we consider that argumentative context should be brought into consideration from a different perspective (e.g., explicitly modelling the underlying reasoning of the argument). Since the detection of fallacious reasoning is a task that involves the analysis of finer grained reasoning and logical aspects of natural language, it might be a better idea to support the natural language input with some structural and argumentative features in the line of what was proposed in (Jin et al., 2022), rather than just including the adjacent text. However, we could not integrate such features in our experiments since part of the fallacy detection corpus did not contain such annotations. Finally, we would also like to point out that from the consistent drop of performance observed between all of our experiments with and without context, the development of an effective segmentation algorithm that focuses on the relevant linguistic aspects of the text is of utmost importance when addressing a high linguistic complexity task such as the automatic detection of argumentative fallacies.

5.2 Evaluation *in the Wild*

In order to validate the behaviour of these models when making predictions outside of the training domains, we have used the validation dataset created on the basis of the argumentation scheme model of argument (see Table 2). For this validation *in the Wild*, we have selected the best model of the experimental evaluation considering both fine-tuning and prompt-based models independently. As depicted in Table 6, we have evaluated the RoBERTa and GPT-4 models considering both the multi-class and the fallacy identification tasks (i.e., 5-class and 2-class classification problems respectively) proposed at the beginning of this paper.

Firstly, looking at the 5-class classification re-

Model	Precision	Recall	Macro-F1
RB	47.1	47.0	46.4
eSVM	77.8	77.5	77.7
RoBERTa	**79.8**	**79.6**	**79.6**
GPT-3.5-TURBO	41.7	46.2	40.6
GPT-4	53.2	53.2	51.1
eSVM+[*ctx*]	76.8	74.0	74.8
RoBERTa+[*ctx*]	78.0	78.8	78.3
GPT-3.5-TURBO+[*ctx*]	47.1	48.8	43.5
GPT-4+[*ctx*]	56.6	56.7	54.1

Table 4: Precision, Recall and Macro-F1 results of the 2-class fallacy detection task. [*ctx*] represents the contextual information added to the input of each model.

Model	Precision	Recall	Macro-F1
RB	22.9	22.1	22.4
eSVM	69.6	65.5	67.1
RoBERTa	75.4	**78.0**	**76.2**
GPT-3.5-TURBO	51.7	46.4	44.6
GPT-4	60.4	60.0	58.3
eSVM+[*ctx*]	**79.7**	72.1	74.8
RoBERTa+[*ctx*]	72.3	72.6	72.3
GPT-3.5-TURBO+[*ctx*]	45.9	38.1	35.1
GPT-4+[*ctx*]	58.7	57.0	55.7

Table 5: Precision, Recall and Macro-F1 results of the 4-class fallacy classification task. [*ctx*] represents the contextual information added to the input of each model.

Arg. Scheme	CQs	RoBERTa		GPT-4	
		5-class	2-class	5-class	2-class
AFEO	✓	Authority	Fallacy	None	None
AFEO	✗	Authority	Fallacy	Authority	Fallacy
AFPK	✓	None	Fallacy	None	None
AFPK	✗	Authority	Fallacy	Authority	Fallacy
AFPP	✓	None	Fallacy	Majority	None
AFPP	✗	None	Fallacy	Majority	Fallacy
AFPO	✓	Majority	Fallacy	Authority	None
AFPO	✗	Majority	Fallacy	Majority	Fallacy
SSAS	✓	None	Fallacy	Slippery Slope	None
SSAS	✗	Slippery Slope	Fallacy	Slippery Slope	Fallacy
GAH	✓	None	None	Ad Hominem	Fallacy
GAH	✗	Ad Hominem	Fallacy	Ad Hominem	Fallacy
CAH	✓	None	None	Ad Hominem	Fallacy
CAH	✗	None	None	Ad Hominem	Fallacy

Table 6: Evaluation *in the Wild* of the fallacy detection LLMs.

sults, we can observe different behaviour between RoBERTa and GPT-4. In the case of RoBERTa, it failed to distinguish the fallacious aspects of the underlying logic of four argumentation schemes. We can see this problem with both AFEO that are classified as an authority fallacy, both AFPP that are classified as non-fallacious while both AFPO are labelled as an appeal to majority fallacy, and both CAH that are classified as non-fallacious. This behaviour can be attributed to the fact that they look too similar to the samples labelled as fallacious (in the case of AFEO and AFPO) or non-fallacious (in the case of AFPP and CAH) in the training corpora. Only for three out of the seven argumentation schemes was the model able to correctly distinguish between fallacious and non-fallacious instances of the same scheme, this is the case of AFPK, SSAS, and GAH. Differently, GPT-4 only managed to correctly distinguish between an instance of the same argumentation scheme being fallacious or not in the AFEO and AFPO. All the rest of the argumentation schemes were labelled as fallacious belonging to each of its respective fallacy classes. It is interesting to mention that GPT-4 also failed to identify the fallacy type in the valid AFPO, since the word "*scientist*" appeared, the model predicted that it was an appeal to authority fallacy, being it not a fallacy and being structured as a popular opinion scheme, meaning that the authority was not a relevant aspect in the argumentative reasoning.

Secondly, looking at the 2-class classification results, the observed behaviour between RoBERTa and GPT-4 was also significantly different. In the case of RoBERTa, except for the *Ad Hominem* schemes, all the other argumentation schemes were labelled as fallacious regardless of their logic. The model was also not able to correctly discriminate a fallacy in the case of CAH arguments, where both of them were labelled as non-fallacious. Only the natural language GAH schemes were correctly discriminated between fallacious or not. On the other hand, GPT-4 performed surprisingly well in this instance of the task. All the schemes apart from the *Ad Hominem* ones were correctly classified as fallacious or not. However, both GAH and CAH schemes were labelled as fallacious, regardless of the actual reasons (e.g., critical questions) of being fallacious.

6 Discussion

In this paper, we present the first analysis of the limitations of approaching the fallacy detection problem with LLMs. For that purpose, we provide a new viewpoint to the existing work done in the automatic identification of natural language fallacies through the use of the argumentation scheme model of arguments. The argumentation scheme model allows us to partially dissociate the logic of the argument from the natural language of it, evidencing the limitation that LLMs have when used to approach complex natural language tasks where logical reasoning is involved. For that purpose, we first ran a set of experiments training a machine learning and a deep learning algorithm plus prompting two LLMs on existing annotated corpora for fallacy identification, resulting in new baselines for this task. Second, we evaluated the best performing models on a specifically created argumentation scheme validation dataset that helped us to understand how well were these models able to identify fallacies based on the logic of the argument rather than over-fitting to a natural language pattern not relevant for the definition of a fallacy. From our findings we have been able to observe that there is still much more work to do in this area, and that relying exclusively on LLMs to approach such a challenging task *in the Wild* may not be the best option.

Acknowledgements

This work has been supported by the 'AI for Citizen Intelligence Coaching against Disinformation (TITAN)' project, funded by the EU Horizon 2020 research and innovation programme under grant agreement 101070658, and by UK Research and innovation under the UK governments Horizon funding guarantee grant numbers 10040483 and 10055990.

References

Tariq Alhindi, Tuhin Chakrabarty, Elena Musi, and Smaranda Muresan. 2022. Multitask instruction-based prompting for fallacy recognition. In *Proceedings of the 2022 Conference on Empirical Methods in Natural Language Processing*, pages 8172–8187, Abu Dhabi, United Arab Emirates. Association for Computational Linguistics.

Aristotle. 1978. *De Sophisticis Elenchis (On Sophistical Refutations)*. Harvard University Press.

Tom Brown, Benjamin Mann, Nick Ryder, Melanie Subbiah, Jared D Kaplan, Prafulla Dhariwal, Arvind Neelakantan, Pranav Shyam, Girish Sastry, Amanda Askell, et al. 2020. Language models are few-shot learners. *Advances in neural information processing systems*, 33:1877–1901.

G Da San Martino, Alberto Barrón-Cedeno, Henning Wachsmuth, Rostislav Petrov, and Preslav Nakov. 2020. Semeval-2020 task 11: Detection of propaganda techniques in news articles. *arXiv preprint arXiv:2009.02696*.

Giovanni Da San Martino, Seunghak Yu, Alberto Barrón-Cedeno, Rostislav Petrov, and Preslav Nakov. 2019. Fine-grained analysis of propaganda in news article. In *Proceedings of the 2019 conference on empirical methods in natural language processing and the 9th international joint conference on natural language processing (EMNLP-IJCNLP)*, pages 5636–5646.

Jacob Devlin, Ming-Wei Chang, Kenton Lee, and Kristina Toutanova. 2018. Bert: Pre-training of deep bidirectional transformers for language understanding. *arXiv preprint arXiv:1810.04805*.

Pierpaolo Goffredo, Shohreh Haddadan, Vorakit Vorakitphan, Elena Cabrio, and Serena Villata. 2022. Fallacious argument classification in political debates. In *Thirty-First International Joint Conference on Artificial Intelligence {IJCAI-22}, International Joint Conferences on Artificial Intelligence Organization*, pages 4143–4149.

Ivan Habernal, Raffael Hannemann, Christian Pollak, Christopher Klamm, Patrick Pauli, and Iryna Gurevych. 2017. Argotario: Computational argumentation meets serious games. In *Proceedings of the 2017 Conference on Empirical Methods in Natural Language Processing: System Demonstrations*, pages 7–12.

Ivan Habernal, Patrick Pauli, and Iryna Gurevych. 2018a. Adapting serious game for fallacious argumentation to german: Pitfalls, insights, and best practices. In *Proceedings of the Eleventh International Conference on Language Resources and Evaluation (LREC 2018)*.

Ivan Habernal, Henning Wachsmuth, Iryna Gurevych, and Benno Stein. 2018b. Before name-calling: Dynamics and triggers of ad hominem fallacies in web argumentation. In *Proceedings of the 2018 Conference of the North American Chapter of the Association for Computational Linguistics: Human Language Technologies, Volume 1 (Long Papers)*, pages 386–396.

Charles L Hamblin. 1970. *Fallacies*. Advanced Reasoning Forum.

Zhijing Jin, Abhinav Lalwani, Tejas Vaidhya, Xiaoyu Shen, Yiwen Ding, Zhiheng Lyu, Mrinmaya Sachan, Rada Mihalcea, and Bernhard Schoelkopf. 2022. Logical fallacy detection. In *Findings of the Association for Computational Linguistics: EMNLP 2022*, pages 7180–7198, Abu Dhabi, United Arab Emirates. Association for Computational Linguistics.

James Willard Oliver. 1967. Formal fallacies and other invalid arguments. *Mind*, 76(304):463–478.

Colin Raffel, Noam Shazeer, Adam Roberts, Katherine Lee, Sharan Narang, Michael Matena, Yanqi Zhou, Wei Li, and Peter J Liu. 2020. Exploring the limits of transfer learning with a unified text-to-text transformer. *The Journal of Machine Learning Research*, 21(1):5485–5551.

Saumya Sahai, Oana Balalau, and Roxana Horincar. 2021. Breaking down the invisible wall of informal fallacies in online discussions. In *Proceedings of the 59th Annual Meeting of the Association for Computational Linguistics and the 11th International Joint Conference on Natural Language Processing (Volume 1: Long Papers)*, pages 644–657.

Frans H Van Eemeren and Rob Grootendorst. 1984. *Speech acts in argumentative discussions*. Dordrecht: Foris Publications.

Frans H Van Eemeren and Rob Grootendorst. 2016. *Argumentation, communication, and fallacies: A pragma-dialectical perspective*. Routledge.

Jacky Visser, John Lawrence, and Chris Reed. 2020. Reason-checking fake news. *Communications of the ACM*, 63(11):38–40.

Henning Wachsmuth, Nona Naderi, Ivan Habernal, Yufang Hou, Graeme Hirst, Iryna Gurevych, and Benno Stein. 2017. Argumentation quality assessment: Theory vs. practice. In *Proceedings of the 55th Annual Meeting of the Association for Computational Linguistics (Volume 2: Short Papers)*, pages 250–255.

Douglas Walton, Christopher Reed, and Fabrizio Macagno. 2008. *Argumentation schemes*. Cambridge University Press.

Douglas N Walton. 1987. *Informal fallacies*, volume 4. John Benjamins Publishing.

Douglas N. Walton. 1995. *A pragmatic theory of fallacy*. Studies in rhetoric and communication. University of Alabama Press, Tuscaloosa.

Using Masked Language Model Probabilities of Connectives for Stance Detection in English Discourse

Regina Stodden[1], **Laura Kallmeyer**[1], **Lea Kawaletz**[2] and **Heidrun Dorgeloh**[2]
[1] Institute of Linguistics; [2] Institute of English and American Studies
Heinrich Heine University
Düsseldorf, Germany
{firstname.secondname}@hhu.de

Abstract

This paper introduces an approach which operationalizes the role of discourse connectives for detecting argument stance. Specifically, the study investigates the utility of masked language model probabilities of discourse connectives inserted between a claim and a premise that supports or attacks it. The research focuses on a range of connectives known to signal support or attack, such as *because, but, so,* or *although.* By employing a LightGBM classifier, the study reveals promising results in stance detection in English discourse. While the proposed system does not aim to outperform state-of-the-art architectures, the classification accuracy is surprisingly high, highlighting the potential of these features to enhance argument mining tasks, including stance detection.

1 Introduction

The task this paper addresses is argument stance detection in English discourse. More concretely, based on the definition of *argument* following established terminology (Stab and Gurevych, 2017; Stede and Schneider, 2018), where an argument consists of a *claim*, a controversial statement, and a *premise*, a statement supporting or attacking the claim, we want to automatically decide whether the premise supports (label: 1) or attacks (label: 0) the claim. This task has been modeled in a number of approaches already (Schiller et al., 2021; Hardalov et al., 2021). In contrast to these approaches, we aim at operationalizing the role of connectives with the following simple idea: We insert one-word connectives, i.e., linking words such as *because, but, so,* or *although*, between the claim and the candidate premise and use a language model (LM) to quantify acceptability. Connectives include coordinators (such as *and*, or *but*), subordinators (such as *because*, or *while*), as well as linking adverbs (such as *therefore*, or *however*; Dorgeloh and Wanner 2022). They can express support, attack, or other types of relations. The underlying hypothesis is that features obtained from an LM's probability for inserting certain connectives between a claim and premise can improve stance detection. Put differently, our research question is whether we can verify whether a premise is a support for or an attack against a given claim based on explicit discourse connectives. We show that using probabilities of connectives as features, we obtain a significant improvement in stance detection compared to a majority and a random baseline. This indicates that, although we do not aim at a competitive argument mining system in this paper, integrating these features into argument mining has the potential to improve existing approaches. We use English data but we assume that a similar approach should also work for other languages.[1]

2 Motivation and Related Work

The expression of stance is linked closely to argumentative structures in discourse since arguments by definition involve stance, and stance markers are known to facilitate the processing of argumentative relations (Stein and Wachsmuth, 2019; Wei et al., 2021). Besides a variety of other stance markers (Gray and Biber, 2014), connectives play a crucial role in that respect. Work on various languages has shown that the discourse function of connectives is closely related to that of other linguistic elements expressing stance or subjectivity in their role for argumentative discourse. In particular, there seems to be a "division of labor," where the presence of stance markers makes an explicit connective less expected while fewer stance markers make the use of specific connectives more likely (Wei et al. 2020). Such a trade-off between connectives and other cues for stance suggests that markers of one kind may be omitted if there are cues in the context that make the information of those markers

[1]The code and results are available at https://github.com/rstodden/stance-detection.

Proceedings of the 10th Workshop on Argument Mining, pages 11–18
December 7, 2023. ©2023 Association for Computational Linguistics

already predictable (Uniform Information Density Hypothesis; Torabi Asr and Demberg 2015), which motivates here our expectation that discourse connectives also mark argument stance.

Masked LMs (MLMs), e.g., BERT (Devlin et al., 2019) or RoBERTa (Liu et al., 2019), are bidirectional encoders which are mostly trained on massive data to solve the task of *language modeling*. The intention of language modeling is similar to a cloze test; the model is trained on extensive unlabeled data, wherein random tokens (at any position of a sequence) are masked, enabling the model to learn how to predict them (Devlin et al., 2019). The pre-trained MLMs return probabilities for any word of the vocabulary at the position of the masked token; the higher the probability the more suitable the word in the sequence. In recent years, MLMs are also often used for stance detection.[2] Following Schiller et al. (2021), the current state-of-the-art model (called MT-DN$_{MDL}$) across multiple stance detection datasets is a BERT model (bert-large-uncased with an additional classification layer; Devlin et al. 2019), initially fine-tuned on the GLUE benchmark (Wang et al., 2018) and subsequently fine-tuned concurrently on several stance detection datasets . In contrast to MT-DN$_{MDL}$ and related models, in our approach we do not predict the stance based on the weights of an MLM but make use of the knowledge of MLMs with respect to connectives as stance markers.

Methodologically, the present study builds on existing approaches which tackle the problem of classifying implicit discourse relations by using masked LMs to *explicitate* the relations. Specifically, the models predict how likely a given connective is in sentence pairs without an overtly expressed discourse relation. For example, Kishimoto et al. (2020) experiment with additionally pre-training and fine-tuning MLMs on texts with masked connectives (called *connective prediction task*), finding that only the first technique provides gain. Kurfalı and Östling (2021) use a pipeline approach to classify unlabeled, implicit discourse relations, where explicit data – a set of 65 candidate connectives – is concatenated with two sequences and then fed into an explicit discourse relation classifier. Recently, Zhou et al. (2022) have tackled the problem by using a prompt learning method. Given a template that arises from natural language use (e.g. 'Arg1: *Arg1*. Arg2: *Arg2*. The conjunction between Arg1 and Arg2 is <mask>.'), they select the most frequent and least ambiguous predicted connective as the answer word to replace the mask token. We do not use prompting or causal LMs as we are interested in the probabilities of the connectives. Masked LMs, in contrast to generative LMs, are capable of giving the probabilities of a word at any position of a sequence based on the left and right context (and not only at the end of a sequence). To the best of our knowledge, our work is the first approach to use probabilities of discourse connectives of masked LMs as features and to combine them with stance detection.

3 Methods

Our method comprises four components:

1. the concatenation of claims and premises with a masked token (see subsection 3.2),
2. an LM that estimates the likelihood of a given connective in the concatenated sequence (see subsection 3.1 and subsection 3.3),
3. a feature vector which comprises all the probabilities of the connectives (see subsection 3.3),
4. and a binary classifier which, based on the feature vector, learns whether the premise supports or attacks the claim (see subsection 3.4).

We hypothesize that the LMs have learned argumentative structures and the usage of connectives. Therefore, we anticipate that the model will assign higher probabilities to support connectives and lower probabilities to attack connectives for support premises, and vice versa for attacks. For example, in Example 1, the premise attacks the claim, and we expect lower probabilities for support connectives like *because* or *since* as they would render the argument incoherent. For attack connectives like *but* or *although* we expect higher probabilities as they are in line with the attack relation.

(1) [Masking should be mandated]$_{C}$ `[MASK]` [it infringes on personal freedoms.]$_{P}$

3.1 Connectives

We selected connectives from DimLex-Eng (Das et al., 2018), a lexicon of discourse markers which contains 100 connectives from the Penn Discourse Treebank (PDTB; Prasad et al. 2008) plus 42 from RST-SC (Das and Taboada, 2018), all annotated with discourse relations. Out of all 79 single-token connectives, we selected

[2]For an overview of existing stance detection datasets and approaches see Schiller et al. (2021); Hardalov et al. (2021).

those with relevant PDTB relations[3]: For the support relation we chose connectives marked with `Contingency.Cause.Result` or `Contingency.Cause.Reason` (n=18, e.g. *therefore*, *because*), since relations in the contingency class "involve an implication relation, and hence can be classified as causal" (Sanders et al., 2021, 21). For the attack relation we chose `Comparison.Contrast` and `Expansion.Alternative.Disjunctive` (n=30, e.g. *but*, *however*), as they correlate with the attack relations of *undercut* and *rebut* (Hewett et al. 2019). Finally, some connectives were excluded as the LMs tokenized them into subwords (e.g., *however*: *how* and *ever*).[4] Table 1 summarizes the resulting 12 support-indicating and 18 attack-indicating connectives for which probabilities could be extracted.[5] Six connectives are labeled with the relations of both groups.

For more information on the connectives, we calculated how often a connective is tagged with the chosen PDTB relations divided by the number of all occurrences of the connective in DimLex-Eng. Based on this percentage, we grouped the connectives as follows: *Group 1*: all attack/support connectives (>0%, n=24), *Group 2*: not predominatly attack/support connectives (>34%, n=12), i.e., those which were used in up to 66% of occurrences in some other PDTB relation, and *Group 3*: predominantly attack/support connectives (>66%, n=5), i.e., those which were used in up to 34% of occurrences in some other PDTB relation.

3.2 Data & Preprocessing

In comparison to Hardalov et al. (2021) and Schiller et al. (2021), we reduce the selection of corpora to the following three corpora: `ibmcs` (Bar-Haim et al., 2017), `perspectrum` (Chen et al., 2019), and `argmin` (Stab et al., 2018).[6] All corpora (except `argmin`) have full sentences as claims (= topics) and have (balanced) binary stance labels.[7] For `argmin`, we changed the one-word topics to sentences (e.g., for topic *"cloning"*: *"cloning should be permitted."*).

attack				support			
conn.	**order**	**%**	**G**	**conn.**	**order**	**%**	**G**
unless	C-LW-P	98.95	1,2,3	for	C-LW-P	100.0	1,2,3
but	*C-LW-P*	*73.28*	*1,2,3*	so	P-LW-C	100.0	1,2,3
while	C-LW-P	52.50	1,2	because	C-LW-P	99.53	1,2,3
yet	P-LW-C	52.48	1,2	with	C-LW-P	60.00	1,2
still	P-LW-C	50.53	1,2	since	C-LW-P	52.17	1,2
although	C-LW-P	47.87	1,2	given	C-LW-P	33.33	1
though	C-LW-P	47.50	1,2	*as*	*C-LW-P*	*28.53*	*1*
rather	P-LW-C	23.53	1	*and*	*C-LW-P*	*2.17*	*1*
except	C-LW-P	10.00	1	*when*	*C-LW-P*	*2.02*	*1*
nor	C-LW-P	3.23	1	*then*	*C-LW-P*	*1.47*	*1*
instead	C-LW-P	2.68	1	*if*	*C-LW-P*	*0.08*	*1*
until	C-LW-P	1.85	1	*but*	*C-LW-P*	*0.03*	*1*
or	C-LW-P	1.02	1				
and	*C-LW-P*	*0.70*	*1*				
if	*C-LW-P*	*0.41*	*1*				
then	*C-LW-P*	*0.29*	*1*				
when	*C-LW-P*	*0.20*	*1*				
as	*C-LW-P*	*0.13*	*1*				

Table 1: Connectives with their order (*claim-connective-premise* or *premise-connective-claim*) and usage in PDTB as attack (left) or support (right). `G` shows the group of the connectives for the analysis. Connectives in italics are both attack as well as support.

During preprocessing, we remove any given punctuation mark at the end of the first argument component and lower-case the beginning of the second part. We then concatenate each pair of premise and claim with a masked token, e.g., "<mask>," that indicates the place for a potential connective. For every argument, we create the concatenation in the following two orders, because not all connectives require the same order of claim and premise (see Table 1): i) claim - masked token - premise (order C-LW-P), or ii) premise - masked token - claim (order P-LW-C). Some examples of the concatenated sequences are provided in the Appendix, Table 5. We do not tokenize the data or do any other preprocessing beyond what has already been mentioned (or is provided in the original corpus).

3.3 Feature Extraction

We then use these concatenated sequences as input for a masked LM, e.g., BERT (Devlin et al., 2019). As output, the LM returns word-probability pairs, where words with higher probabilities are more likely to be a suitable fit within the sequence.

We use the pipeline `fill-mask` of the Python package `transformers` (Wolf et al., 2020) to extract the probabilities of the connectives for

[3] We excluded all multi-token connectives as the applied fill-mask pipeline can predict only one token at a time.

[4] We do not employ Huggingface's fallback strategy, which is using subwords instead of the full word, as it could result in overly general word fragments (e.g., *how* for *however*).

[5] We also extracted all connectives which do not belong to any of the groups (n=13), henceforth called *other*. For DistilBERT and BERT, probabilities of more connectives could be extracted. However, we found out that using the probabilities of more connectives (n=42) of both LMs as features could not outperform using fewer connectives of RoBERTa or XLM-RoBERTa. Hence, we only report results on the reduced connective set (n=24) for all LMs.

[6] An overview of the datasets' meta data can be found in Table 1 and 2 of Hardalov et al. (2021).

[7] For our experiments, we used the original train, validation, and test splits provided by the authors of the datasets.

the following large LMs: i) *DistilBERT-base-uncased* (Sanh et al., 2019), ii) *BERT-base-uncased & -large* (Devlin et al., 2019), iii) *RoBERTa-base & -large* (Liu et al., 2019), as well as iv) *xlm-RoBERTa-base & -large* (Conneau et al., 2020).

The probabilities of either one of those LMs or of all LMs were then used as features for a classifier.[8] The LMs were not explicitly trained on argumentative data or structures and they were not fine-tuned on any other data or task; rather, we use them in their original form as provided on HuggingFace (Wolf et al., 2020).

3.4 Classifier

To find the best classifier and its best parameters for stance detection on all three datasets, we built up a search space of parameters[9] and applied methods of the `optuna` package (Akiba et al., 2019) to find the best hyperparameter combination for each validation set. Based on the best parameter combination for all probabilities of all LMs with all attack and support connectives, we averaged the parameters per validation set. The resulting parameters were then used for all experiments on the test sets. LightGBM turned out to be the best classifier out of six classifiers[10], hence, we are reporting only the results with LightGBM using the best hyperparameter setting (see Appendix A).

3.5 Evaluation

For the evaluation protocol, we mostly follow Schiller et al. (2021); Hardalov et al. (2021): We evaluate our approaches by calculating the macro F1-Score, and we report a majority baseline (always returns the most frequent label) and a random baseline (randomly returns one label of the two labels). As further comparison, we also report results of four state-of-the-art models (SOTA): i) BERT-large with a classification head (BERT_{SDL}), ii) BERT fine-tuned on GLUE benchmark with a classification head (MT-DNN_{SDL}), iii) MT-DNN_{SDL} additionally trained on ten stance detection data sets (MT-DNN_{MDL}; Schiller et al. 2021), and iv) RoBERTa-base with domain expert functions and a classification head (MoLe; Hardalov et al. 2021).

[8]An example of probabilities for given sequences is provided in the Appendix, Table 5.

[9]For the entire search space per classifier see the code.

[10]We have also experimented with the following classifiers and search spaces for them:i) a support vector machine, ii) a decision tree classifier, iii) a random forest classifier, iv) a neural multi-layer perceptron, and v) a XGBoost classifier.

4 Results

We first validated our main assumption by measuring Spearman's correlation coefficient ρ between the probabilities of the connectives and the stance per each sample of each dataset. Appendix B summarizes all correlations and significance levels. For all three datasets, we found that the probabilities of nearly all connectives significantly correlate with stance (p-level at least < 0.1; all except *with*, *if*, and *when*). As expected, the probabilities of the attack connectives show a negative correlation, whereas those of the support connectives show a positive correlation, and the ambiguous connectives show a mixed picture. However, most correlations are weak (i.e., $\rho < 0.3$) except for five moderate (i.e., $0.3 \leq \rho < 0.5$; *except*, *unless*, *until*, *yet*, and three strong ones (i.e., $\rho \geq 0.5$; *although*, *though*, *but*). To sum up, our assumption was validated across all three datasets. Therefore, we can now turn to our results on stance detection based on the connectives' probabilities.

All our models using all connectives (Group 1) can outperform the two baselines. The best model with all probabilities (Group 1) of only one LM is RoBERTa-large (see bold row in the third part of Table 2). As expected, DistilBERT achieves the worst results compared to all other LMs, and all large versions outperform their base versions. We can infer that the larger the model and the more data the model was trained on, the more knowledge it has about connectives and, therefore, the more valuable the connective features are for stance detection and, hence, the higher the macro F1-Score. However, the multi-lingual data on which xlm-RoBERTa is trained seems to reduce the score, which might be due to its larger vocabulary size and less distinct probabilities for the connectives. Further analysis is required to justify this finding. Overall, combining the probabilities of all 24 connectives (Group 1) of all LMs achieves a higher macro F1-Score than using the Group 1 probabilities of only one LM (see bold row in the last part of Table 2). This model outperforms all SOTA models on `argmin` and is on par with the SOTA model on the other two datasets. Comparing all models based on BERT-large (i.e., BERT_{SDL}, MT-DNN_{SDL}, MT-DNN_{MDL}, and our BERT-large), our model achieves similar scores as the other models on the `argmin` dataset, although it classifies just on the probabilities of 24 connectives of neither fine-tuned nor otherwise preprocessed LMs.

models	argmin	ibmcs	perspectrum
majority	0.3383	0.3406	0.3466
random	0.4998	0.4864	0.5011
BERT$_{SDL}$	0.6167	0.5347	0.8012
MT-DNN$_{SDL}$	0.6019	0.7066	0.8480
MT-DNN$_{MDL}$	0.6174	0.7772	0.8374
MoLe	**0.6373**	**0.7938**	**0.8527**
DistilBERT	0.5233	0.5499	0.6079
BERT-base	0.5718	0.5500	0.6442
BERT-large	0.6104	0.5810	0.6828
RoBERTa-base	0.6218	0.5961	0.6890
RoBERTa-large	**0.7204**	**0.7633**	**0.8274**
xlm-RoBERTa-base	0.5830	0.5456	0.6130
xlm-RoBERTa-large	0.6601	0.7247	0.7475
all-LMs (Group 1, n=24)	**0.7467**	**0.7885**	0.8314
all-LMs (Group 2, n=12)	0.7218	0.7638	0.8185
all-LMs (Group 3, n=5)	0.6861	0.7449	0.7897
all-LMs (other, n=12)	0.6792	0.6676	0.7539
all-LMs (random, n=24)	0.7286	0.7710	0.8286
all-LMs (all, n=36)	0.7423	0.7850	**0.8456**

Table 2: First part baselines, second SOTA, third own models per LM features (Group 1), and last combination of all feature groups of all LMs. Results of SOTA are copied from corresponding paper. F1 macro scores.

Further, we analyzed the ablation of some ambiguous connectives (see results of Group 2), e.g., *and* or *when*, and not predominant connectives, e.g., *instead* or *given* (see results of Group 3).

As can be seen in the last six lines of Table 2 (or also for all other LMs in the Appendix, Table 6), the ablations reduce the scores. The more support and attack connectives (or features), the better the result. It can be argued that not only distinctive connectives, such as *because* or *yet*, are helpful for stance detection, but also the presence of other connectives. Yet, adding additionally the probabilities of all *other* connectives (n=12), slightly reduces the F1-Score on `argmin` and `ibmcs` (see last row in Table 2), whereas it increases the score on `perspectrum`. Hence, the selection of the connectives is also important. For example, replacing the 24 support and attack connectives by 24 randomly chosen connectives (12 *other* and 12 randomly chosen support or attack connectives) the score drops on average of 5 runs. Further, including only the probabilities of the *other* connectives (n=12) reduces the score even more.

Also, the combination of attack and support connectives seems to be helpful for stance detection (see Appendix C). For all datasets, the F1-Score drops when removing support connectives (by less than 0.01 points) as well as, more noticeably, when removing attack connectives (between 0.01 and 0.35 points). When using only connectives which are in both lists (n=6), the score even drops by one more 0.01 point. This effect might be due to the decreasing number of features, as the analysis of the connectives of Group 3 with the same number of features (i.e., connectives most often used for attack or support, n=5) also show a clear drop in performance. An additional observation is that some connectives (e.g., *and, when*) appear in both groups, indicating that their interpretation as support or attack is inferred. This highlights that the role of connectives in signaling stance does not necessarily demand the explicit expression of the semantics of the claim-premise relation.

5 Conclusion and Future Work

In this paper, we performed stance detection based only on the masked LM probabilities of discourse connectives that are assumed to indicate support or attack. The classifiers we trained on these features performed surprisingly well, given that the aim was not at all to develop a competitive argument mining system. From our results one can conclude that connectives, i.e. different kinds of linking words, can help to automatically verify if a premise is related to a given claim and, with that, also aid stance detection. Connectives should thus play an even more prominent role in argument mining.

In future work, we plan to also experiment with additional punctuation marks between the first part and the linking word. This is a promising avenue because some connectives occur more naturally at a sentence beginning and not between two clauses, e.g., *therefore*, or require a preceding comma, e.g., *but*. Furthermore, we plan to integrate features based on the MLM probabilities of connectives, as used in this paper, with state-of-the-art approaches to stance detection that use input embeddings representing the actual text of claim and premise. Finally, we will investigate whether additional preprocessing of the LMs in the form of fine-tuning on argumentative data or data with explicit connectives before extracting the MLM probabilities increases stance detection performance.

Acknowledgments

We would like to thank the anonymous reviewers for their helpful comments. We would also like to thank NVIDIA for access to GPUs, which enabled a fast calculation of the probabilities.

References

Takuya Akiba, Shotaro Sano, Toshihiko Yanase, Takeru Ohta, and Masanori Koyama. 2019. Optuna: A next-generation hyperparameter optimization framework. In *Proceedings of the 25th ACM SIGKDD International Conference on Knowledge Discovery & Data Mining*, KDD '19, page 2623–2631, New York, NY, USA. Association for Computing Machinery.

Roy Bar-Haim, Indrajit Bhattacharya, Francesco Dinuzzo, Amrita Saha, and Noam Slonim. 2017. Stance classification of context-dependent claims. In *Proceedings of the 15th Conference of the European Chapter of the Association for Computational Linguistics: Volume 1, Long Papers*, pages 251–261, Valencia, Spain. Association for Computational Linguistics.

Sihao Chen, Daniel Khashabi, Wenpeng Yin, Chris Callison-Burch, and Dan Roth. 2019. Seeing things from a different angle:discovering diverse perspectives about claims. In *Proceedings of the 2019 Conference of the North American Chapter of the Association for Computational Linguistics: Human Language Technologies, Volume 1 (Long and Short Papers)*, pages 542–557, Minneapolis, Minnesota. Association for Computational Linguistics.

Alexis Conneau, Kartikay Khandelwal, Naman Goyal, Vishrav Chaudhary, Guillaume Wenzek, Francisco Guzmán, Edouard Grave, Myle Ott, Luke Zettlemoyer, and Veselin Stoyanov. 2020. Unsupervised cross-lingual representation learning at scale. In *Proceedings of the 58th Annual Meeting of the Association for Computational Linguistics*, pages 8440–8451, Online. Association for Computational Linguistics.

Debopam Das, Tatjana Scheffler, Peter Bourgonje, and Manfred Stede. 2018. Constructing a lexicon of English discourse connectives. In *Proceedings of the 19th Annual SIGdial Meeting on Discourse and Dialogue*, pages 360–365, Melbourne, Australia. Association for Computational Linguistics.

Debopam Das and Maite Taboada. 2018. RST Signalling Corpus: A Corpus of Signals of Coherence Relations. *Language Resources and Evaluation*, 52(1):149–184.

Jacob Devlin, Ming-Wei Chang, Kenton Lee, and Kristina Toutanova. 2019. BERT: Pre-training of deep bidirectional transformers for language understanding. In *Proceedings of the 2019 Conference of the North American Chapter of the Association for Computational Linguistics: Human Language Technologies, Volume 1 (Long and Short Papers)*, pages 4171–4186, Minneapolis, Minnesota. Association for Computational Linguistics.

Heidrun Dorgeloh and Anja Wanner. 2022. *Discourse Syntax: English Grammar Beyond the Sentence*. Cambridge University Press.

Bethany Gray and Douglas Biber. 2014. Stance markers. In Karin Aijmer and Christoph Rühlemann, editors, *Corpus Pragmatics: A Handbook*, chapter 8, page 219–248. Cambridge University Press.

Momchil Hardalov, Arnav Arora, Preslav Nakov, and Isabelle Augenstein. 2021. Cross-domain label-adaptive stance detection. In *Proceedings of the 2021 Conference on Empirical Methods in Natural Language Processing*, pages 9011–9028, Online and Punta Cana, Dominican Republic. Association for Computational Linguistics.

Freya Hewett, Roshan Prakash Rane, Nina Harlacher, and Manfred Stede. 2019. The utility of discourse parsing features for predicting argumentation structure. In *Proceedings of the 6th Workshop on Argument Mining*, pages 98–103, Florence, Italy. Association for Computational Linguistics.

Yudai Kishimoto, Yugo Murawaki, and Sadao Kurohashi. 2020. Adapting BERT to implicit discourse relation classification with a focus on discourse connectives. In *Proceedings of the Twelfth Language Resources and Evaluation Conference*, pages 1152–1158, Marseille, France. European Language Resources Association.

Murathan Kurfalı and Robert Östling. 2021. Let's be explicit about that: Distant supervision for implicit discourse relation classification via connective prediction. In *Proceedings of the 1st Workshop on Understanding Implicit and Underspecified Language*, pages 1–10, Online. Association for Computational Linguistics.

Yinhan Liu, Myle Ott, Naman Goyal, Jingfei Du, Mandar Joshi, Danqi Chen, Omer Levy, Mike Lewis, Luke Zettlemoyer, and Veselin Stoyanov. 2019. Roberta: A robustly optimized BERT pretraining approach. *CoRR*, abs/1907.11692.

Rashmi Prasad, Nikhil Dinesh, Alan Lee, Eleni Miltsakaki, Livio Robaldo, Aravind Joshi, and Bonnie Webber. 2008. The Penn Discourse TreeBank 2.0. In *Proceedings of the Sixth International Conference on Language Resources and Evaluation (LREC'08)*, Marrakech, Morocco. European Language Resources Association (ELRA).

Ted J.M. Sanders, Vera Demberg, Jet Hoek, Merel C.J. Scholman, Fatemeh Torabi Asr, Sandrine Zufferey, and Jacqueline Evers-Vermeul. 2021. Unifying dimensions in coherence relations: How various annotation frameworks are related. *Corpus Linguistics and Linguistic Theory*, 17(1):1–71.

Victor Sanh, Lysandre Debut, Julien Chaumond, and Thomas Wolf. 2019. DistilBERT, a distilled version of BERT: smaller, faster, cheaper and lighter. In *5th Workshop on Energy Efficient Machine Learning and Cognitive Computing @ NeurIPS 2019*.

Benjamin Schiller, Johannes Daxenberger, and Iryna Gurevych. 2021. Stance detection benchmark: How robust is your stance detection? *KI - Künstliche Intelligenz*, 35(3-4):329–341.

Christian Stab and Iryna Gurevych. 2017. Parsing Argumentation Structures in Persuasive Essays. *Computational Linguistics*, 43(3):619–659.

Christian Stab, Tristan Miller, Benjamin Schiller, Pranav Rai, and Iryna Gurevych. 2018. Cross-topic argument mining from heterogeneous sources. In *Proceedings of the 2018 Conference on Empirical Methods in Natural Language Processing*, pages 3664–3674, Brussels, Belgium. Association for Computational Linguistics.

Manfred Stede and Jodi Schneider. 2018. *Argumentation Mining*. Synthesis Lectures on Human Language Technologies. Morgan & Claypool Publisher.

Benno Stein and Henning Wachsmuth, editors. 2019. *Proceedings of the 6th Workshop on Argument Mining*. Association for Computational Linguistics, Florence, Italy.

Fatemeh Torabi Asr and Vera Demberg. 2015. Uniform surprisal at the level of discourse relations: Negation markers and discourse connective omission. In *Proceedings of the 11th International Conference on Computational Semantics*, pages 118–128, London, UK. Association for Computational Linguistics.

Alex Wang, Amanpreet Singh, Julian Michael, Felix Hill, Omer Levy, and Samuel Bowman. 2018. GLUE: A multi-task benchmark and analysis platform for natural language understanding. In *Proceedings of the 2018 EMNLP Workshop BlackboxNLP: Analyzing and Interpreting Neural Networks for NLP*, pages 353–355, Brussels, Belgium. Association for Computational Linguistics.

Yipu Wei, Jacqueline Evers-Vermeul, and Ted J.M. Sanders. 2020. The use of perspective markers and connectives in expressing subjectivity: Evidence from collocational analyses. *Dialogue & Discourse*, 11:62–88.

Yipu Wei, Jacqueline Evers-Vermeul, Ted M. Sanders, and Willem M. Mak. 2021. The Role of Connectives and Stance Markers in the Processing of Subjective Causal Relations. *Discourse Processes*, 58(8):766–786.

Thomas Wolf, Lysandre Debut, Victor Sanh, Julien Chaumond, Clement Delangue, Anthony Moi, Pierric Cistac, Tim Rault, Remi Louf, Morgan Funtowicz, Joe Davison, Sam Shleifer, Patrick von Platen, Clara Ma, Yacine Jernite, Julien Plu, Canwen Xu, Teven Le Scao, Sylvain Gugger, Mariama Drame, Quentin Lhoest, and Alexander Rush. 2020. Transformers: State-of-the-art natural language processing. In *Proceedings of the 2020 Conference on Empirical Methods in Natural Language Processing: System Demonstrations*, pages 38–45, Online. Association for Computational Linguistics.

Hao Zhou, Man Lan, Yuanbin Wu, Yuefeng Chen, and Meirong Ma. 2022. Prompt-based connective prediction method for fine-grained implicit discourse relation recognition. In *Findings of the Association for Computational Linguistics: EMNLP 2022*, pages 3848–3858, Abu Dhabi, United Arab Emirates. Association for Computational Linguistics.

A Hyperparameter of classifiers

Best hyperparameter: {"classifier": "LightGBM", "lambda_l1": 0.0001, "lambda_l2": 0.002, "num_leaves": 220, "feature_fraction": 0.9, "bagging_fraction": 0.8, "bagging_freq": 2}

B Correlation Connectives' Probabilities and Stance

	argmin	ibmcs	perspectrum
although	-0.24***	**-0.54*** **	**-0.53*** **
except	-0.26***	-0.49***	-0.44***
instead	-0.13***	-0.36***	-0.28***
nor	-0.15***	-0.23***	-0.24***
or	-0.04***	-0.12***	-0.10***
rather	-0.14***	-0.18***	-0.22***
still	-0.20***	-0.27***	-0.22***
though	-0.22***	**-0.53*** **	**-0.52*** **
unless	-0.2***	-0.35***	-0.36***
until	-0.18***	-0.34***	-0.32***
while	-0.11***	-0.37***	-0.21***
yet	-0.29***	-0.45***	-0.41***
because	+0.04***	+0.17***	+0.08***
for	+0.07***	+0.07***	+0.13***
given	+0.02*	+0.07**	+0.04***
since	+0.07***	+0.18***	+0.06***
so	+0.08***	+0.05*	+0.03***
with	+0.00	-0.13***	+0.01
and	+0.09***	-0.13***	+0.09***
as	+0.06***	+0.14***	+0.12***
but	-0.32***	**-0.54*** **	**-0.58*** **
if	-0.01	-0.09***	-0.08***
then	-0.02*	-0.21***	-0.12***
when	-0.02	-0.28***	-0.13***

Table 3: First block attacking connectives, second supporting connectives, and third which are classified as both. The asterisks indicate the level of significance (*: $p < 0.1$, **: $p < 0.05$, ***: $p < 0.01$). The bold face numbers indicate a strong, significant correlation ($\rho \geq 0.5$), underlining a moderate, significant correlation ($\rho \geq 0.3$) and the gray numbers are not significant.

C Results per Connective Type

	argmin	ibmcs	perspectrum
attack+support (n=24)	**0.7467**	**0.7885**	**0.8314**
attack (n=18)	0.7305	0.7872	0.8288
support (n=12)	0.7265	0.7531	0.8164
both (n=6)	0.7132	0.7513	0.8058

Table 4: Results per connective set for all LMs.

ID	stance	claim-connective-premise	because	but	premise-connective-claim	so	yet
Train-23	0	[Nuclear energy should be permitted]$_C$ [MASK] [it should be banned from Australia. If terrorists come they can target the power plant and it would kill heaps of people .]$_P$	0.000010 <	0.009026	[It should be banned from Australia. If terrorists come they can target the power plant and it would kill heaps of people]$_P$ [MASK] [nuclear energy should be permitted]$_C$	0.002439 <	0.00033800
Train-2874	1	[Nuclear energy should be permitted]$_C$ [MASK] [nuclear plants also provide stability to the electrical grid , as their output is constant and reliable .]$_P$	0.000584 >	0.000067	[Nuclear plants also provide stability to the electrical grid , as their output is constant and reliable]$_P$ [MASK] [Nuclear energy should be permitted .]$_C$	0.000018 >	0.00000037
Train-9125	0	[Cloning should be permitted]$_C$ [MASK] [when we consider cloning , we must not blindly overlook its negative implications .]$_P$	0.000005 <	0.002498	[When we consider cloning , we must not blindly overlook its negative implications]$_P$ [MASK] [cloning should be permitted .]$_C$	0.000014 <	0.00001765
Train-7226	1	[Cloning should be permitted]$_C$ [MASK] [a cloned child could actually enhance the family relationship for otherwise childless couples .]$_P$	0.000880 >	0.000026	[A cloned child could actually enhance the family relationship for otherwise childless couples]$_P$ [MASK] [cloning should be permitted .]$_C$	0.000061 >	0.00000006

Table 5: Cherry-picked examples of the argmin dataset including masking input and probabilities of connectives in both claim-premise orders. The $<$ and $>$ signs show the expected relation between the support and attack connectives in examples with positive and negative stance. The examples represent the opinions of the annotators and not necessarily those of the authors of this paper.

	Group 1 (n=24)			Group 2 (n=12)			Group 3 (n=5)		
	argmin	**ibmcs**	**perspectum**	**argmin**	**ibmcs**	**perspectum**	**argmin**	**ibmcs**	**perspectum**
DistilBERT	0.5233	0.5499	0.6079	0.5120	0.5373	0.5753	0.5006	0.5331	0.5690
BERT-base	0.5718	0.5500	0.6442	0.5448	0.5314	0.5939	0.5213	0.5316	0.5593
BERT-large	0.6104	0.5810	0.6828	0.5705	0.5898	0.6366	0.5610	0.5494	0.6154
RoBERTa-base	0.6218	0.5961	0.6890	0.6019	0.5842	0.6508	0.5757	0.5709	0.6152
RoBERTa-large	0.7204	0.7633	0.8274	0.7080	**0.7670**	0.8021	0.6683	0.7422	0.7677
xlm-RoBERTa-base	0.5830	0.5456	0.6130	0.5678	0.5473	0.5899	0.5455	0.5530	0.5608
xlm-RoBERTa-large	0.6601	0.7247	0.7475	0.6171	0.7082	0.7287	0.6070	0.6921	0.7149
all_LMs	**0.7467**	**0.7885**	**0.8314**	**0.7218**	0.7638	**0.8185**	**0.6861**	**0.7449**	**0.7897**

Table 6: Results per LM and feature set.

Teach Me How to Argue: A Survey on NLP Feedback Systems in Argumentation

Camélia Guerraoui[1,2,3] Paul Reisert[4] Naoya Inoue[5,2] Farjana Sultana Mim[6]
Keshav Singh[7] Jungmin Choi[1,2] Irfan Robbani[5]
Shoichi Naito[1,2,8] Wenzhi Wang[1,2] Kentaro Inui[9,1,2]
[1]Tohoku University [2]RIKEN [3]INSA Lyon [4]Beyond Reason
[5]JAIST [6]Tufts University [7]CTW Inc. [8]Ricoh Company, Ltd. [9]MBZUAI
{guerraoui.camelia.kenza.q4, naito.shoichi.t1, wang.wenzhi.r7}@dc.tohoku.ac.jp, beyond.reason.sp@gmail.com, naoya-i@jaist.ac.jp
farjana.mim@tufts.edu, keshav.singh29@gmail.com, jungmin.choi@riken.jp, robbaniirfan@jaist.ac.jp, kentaro.inui@tohoku.ac.jp

Abstract

The use of argumentation in education has shown improvement in students' critical thinking skills, and computational models for argumentation have been developed to further assist this process. Although these models are useful for evaluating the quality of an argument, they often cannot explain why a particular argument score was predicted, i.e., why the argument is good or bad, which makes it difficult to provide constructive feedback to users, e.g., students, so that they can strengthen their critical thinking skills. In this survey, we explore current NLP feedback systems by categorizing each into four important dimensions of feedback (Richness, Visualization, Interactivity and Personalization). We discuss limitations for each dimension and provide suggestions to enhance the power of feedback and explanations to ultimately improve user critical thinking skills.

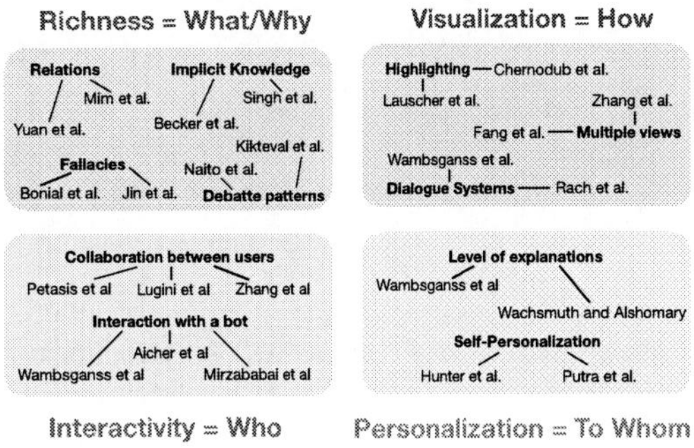

Figure 1: Overview of some NLP feedback systems categorized into our feedback dimensions.

1 Introduction

Argumentation is the field of elaborating and presenting arguments to engage in debate, convince others, and eventually reach agreements. In this context, *an argument* is made of a conclusion (i.e., a claim) supported by reasons (i.e., premises) (Toulmin, 1958). *Computational argumentation* emerged as a way to support argumentation. It is a subfield of natural language processing (NLP) that deals with the automated representation, evaluation, and generation of arguments. It includes tasks such as mining arguments (Al-Khatib et al., 2016), assessing arguments' quality (El Baff et al., 2018), reconstructing implicit assumptions in arguments (Habernal et al., 2018) or even providing constructive feedback for improving arguments (Naito et al., 2022), to name a few.

In education, learning how to argue (e.g., writing argumentative essays, debates, etc.) has been shown to improve students' critical thinking skills (Pithers and Soden, 2000; Behar-Horenstein and Niu, 2011). To further improve critical thinking skills, several researchers have been working on computational argumentation and specifically argumentative feedback systems to provide support and to assist learners in improving the quality of their arguments (Habernal et al., 2017; Wachsmuth et al., 2017; Lauscher et al., 2022).

Although argumentative feedback systems are proven to assist students' learning and reduce teachers' workload (Twardy, 2004; Wambsganß et al., 2021), such systems still lack the ability to *deeply explain* how an argument can be improved; i.e., not only providing a holistic label or score, but explaining particularly *why* this result was given by automatic evaluation rubrics. Such explanations as feedback can ultimately *explain and visualize the results comprehensively* for the users so that users can understand and improve their argumentation skills. The lack of ability in current systems to provide deep explanations as feedback motivated our interest in investigating the current state of argumentative feedback generation.

In this survey, we focus on different kinds of feedback given to learn how to argue. Inspired by the sections *Tutorial Feedback* and *Architecture and Technology* mentioned in Scheuer et al. (2010), we combine features of feedback systems,

Proceedings of the 10th Workshop on Argument Mining, pages 19–34
December 7, 2023. ©2023 Association for Computational Linguistics

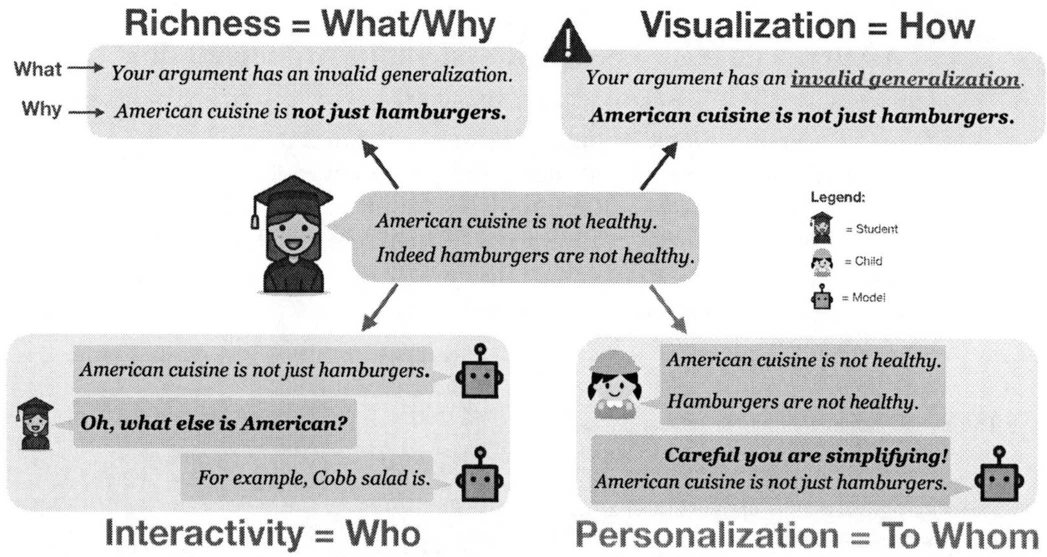

Figure 2: Example of four feedback for each dimension (*Richness*, *Visualization*, *Interactivity* and *Personalization*).

formulate four distinct dimensions and categorize existing papers into these dimensions (Figure 1):

- *Richness*: Level of feedback details given by a model, i.e., *what* is the error identified by the model and *why* it is an error.
- *Visualization*: Model's ability to present feedback, i.e., *how* the feedback is shown to the end user.
- *Interactivity*: Model's ability to allow the user to communicate with other users or the model itself, i.e., with *whom* the user is talking.
- *Personalization*: Model's ability to adapt the feedback to the users' background, i.e., *to whom* the feedback is given.

Figure 2 shows four different dimensions of feedback (*Richness*, *Visualization*, *Interactivity*, and *Personalization*), for a given argument consisting of two claims and one premise. In this example, in the *Richness* dimension, a faulty generalization in the argument is identified (cf. What) and explained (cf. Why). *Visualization* would add symbols and highlight important feedback elements to make it more understandable. *Interactivity* would allow the user to ask for more explanations to the model. *Personalization* would consider that the user is a child and provide appropriate feedback on that basis.

Towards better argumentative feedback, this survey aims to give an overview of argumentative feedback systems. We explore work that provide feedback answering one or multiple questions among the types: *What/Why* (§4), *How* (§5), *Who* (§6), and *To Whom* (§7). Finally, we discuss remaining challenges and potential ways to overcome them (§8) in order to develop systems that provide feedback or detailed explanations in a way so that learners can improve their critical thinking skills. We believe this survey can aid researchers in understanding current explanations in argumentation and broaden their horizon on argumentative feedback.[1]

2 Related Work

Several surveys have been done in the field of argumentation (Ke and Ng, 2019; Habernal and Gurevych, 2016; Lawrence and Reed, 2020; Wang et al., 2022) and explainability (Danilevsky et al., 2020; Islam et al., 2021; Hartmann and Sonntag, 2022). As we would like to focus on how well a model can explain its results as a type of feedback for learners, we present here recent surveys related to feedback or explainability in argumentation.

Beigman Klebanov and Madnani (2020) present the progress in automated writing evaluation, using Page (1966) to frame the presentation. In this survey, the succinct feedback section enumerates different systems for writing assistant and highlights the inconclusiveness of research on effectiveness

[1]For more details, papers mentioned in this survey are categorized at `https://kmilia.github.io/teach_me_how_to_argue/`.

of automated writing evaluation.

Vassiliades et al. (2021) highlights the potential of argumentation in explainable AI systems. They provide an exhaustive overview of argumentation systems by grouping them based on domain, such as law. For each domain, papers are compared by tasks (e.g., argument classification). Despite the extensiveness of their survey, some topics to improve explanations in argumentative systems received little attention. For example, frameworks that include arguments with commonsense knowledge and diverse attack relations between them have rarely been discussed, even though they can enhance the model's explainability (Saha et al., 2021).

Čyras et al. (2021) focus on the different frameworks, types, and forms of explanations. They distinguish intrinsic approaches (i.e., models using argumentative methods) from post-hoc approaches (i.e., non-argumentative models that provide complete or partial explanations). They discuss multiple forms of argumentation, such as dialogue. Their final roadmap covers the need to focus more on properties and computational aspects of argumentation-based explanations. Whereas they focus on how argumentation can be used to enhance the explainability of models, our work discusses what kind of feedback (i.e., explanations) on argumentation models can provide.

Moreover, our work distinguishes itself from the surveys previously mentioned by giving an overview of automatized feedback on argumentation from the angle of *rich* (§4), *visual* (§5), *interactive* (§6), and *personalized* (§7) explanations inspired by Scheuer et al. (2010).

3 Pedagogy

Before discussing the four dimensions mentioned a priori, it is essential to know the pedagogy used to teach argumentation and adopted by computational models. This section presents some standard pedagogical methods used in teaching how to argue.

Toulmin model The Toulmin model (Toulmin, 1958), often seen as the foundation of teaching argumentation, is a popular framework for constructing, analyzing and evaluating arguments, and can contribute to the improvement of students' argumentative writing (Rex et al., 2010; Yeh, 1998) as well as critical thinking skills (Giri and Paily, 2020). This approach deconstructs an argument into six elements (Appendix, Figure 4), and students are taught to identify each element within an argument. By identifying elements from the Toulmin model, models can provide users with *rich* feedback.

Rhetorical structure theory Based on Mann and Thompson (1988), the rhetorical structure theory was originally developed in the context of computer-based text generation in order to attribute a formal structure to a text (Hou et al., 2020). This theory employs graphical representations, such as mind maps or graphs, to illustrate the relationships between different components of the text's architecture. This visual approach can help students visualize the connections between different concepts and enhance their understanding of complex topics (Matsumura and Sakamoto, 2021). The advent of tools like Tiara (Putra et al., 2020) has given rise to the deployment of the rhetorical structure theory, i.e. the generation of *visual* feedback.

Collaborative argumentation In collaborative argumentation-based learning, also described as CABLE by Baker et al. (2019), individuals work together to construct, refine, and evaluate arguments on a particular topic or issue. The main goal of collaborative argumentation is to foster constructive dialogue, critical thinking, and the exploration of different perspectives. Weinberger and Fischer (2006) differentiate four dimensions of CABLE:

- *Participation*: Do learners participate at all? Do they participate on an equal basis?
- *Epistemic*: Are learners engaging in activities to solve the task (on-task discourse) or rather concerned with off-task aspect?
- *Argumentative*: Are learners following the structural composition of arguments and their sequences?
- *Social*: To what extent do learners refer to the contributions of their learning partners? Are they gaining knowledge by asking questions?

Veerman et al. (2002); Baker et al. (2019) show CABLE's positive effects on students' argumentation development. Nevertheless, they also highlight the challenges of this method, as not every dialogue can be predicted. By using CABLE, models can generate *interactive* feedback.

Socratic questioning The Socratic questioning is a common teaching strategy, described in Schauer (2012); Abrams (2015). With this method, the student is guided through reflexive questions towards solving a problem on their own, instead of receiving directly a solution. The user receives feedback which is tailored to their background, i.e., *personalized* feedback.

Recently, this method has been integrated into large language models (LLMs) to more effectively adhere to user-provided queries (Ang et al., 2023; Pagnoni et al., 2023), to enhance the ability of such models in generating sequential questions (Shridhar et al., 2022), and also to enhance the explainability of these models (Al-Hossami et al., 2023).

Nevertheless, the Socratic questioning is now raising debates among researchers focusing on pedagogy in argumentation. Indeed, Kerr (1999) and Christie (2010) pointed out its inefficiency and abusiveness as students are forced to give imperfect answers in a hurry and endure criticism.

4 Richness - What is an Error and Why?

To improve students' critical thinking skills, we first need to evaluate their argumentative texts, i.e., identify argumentative errors. In this section, we focus on models providing shallow explanations, i.e., models that identify *what* should be corrected in the arguments. We discuss relevant works that identify properties such as the structure of arguments which is helpful in this process.

Components Identifying argumentative components is one of the fundamental tasks in argumentation (Teufel, 1999; Stab and Gurevych, 2014; Jo et al., 2020). Such works primarily focus on identifying components such as *claims* and *premises*. More recently, the usefulness of identifying such components can be seen in tasks such as counter-argument generation. For example, in Alshomary et al. (2021), weak premises are identified and ranked to generate counter-arguments.

Relations After identifying the different components of an argumentative text, it is necessary to distinguish the multiple relations between them, ultimately to assert the arguments' quality. Indeed, supporting or refuting a claim is made of complex logical moves, such as promoting, contradicting, or acknowledging a fact. To identify the different relations patterns, Yuan et al. (2021) focus on finding interactive argument pairs, whereas Mim et al. (2022) enables annotating complex attack relations.

Schemes In addition to components and relations, Walton et al. (2008) proposed a set of roughly 80 logical argumentation schemes to categorize the underlying logic. Each scheme has a set of critical questions which provide a template to assess the strength of the argument depending upon the associated scheme. Since the first work on automatically detecting argumentation schemes in argumentative texts (Feng and Hirst, 2011), the use of such schemes has been explored in tasks such as essay scoring (Song et al., 2014).

Fallacies Although a good structure with a claim and premises is necessary for a good argument, it is not sufficient. An argument has more complex properties, such as its logical, dialectical, and rhetorical aspects. A fallacy is a logical error or deceptive argument that undermines the validity of a conclusion or reasoning, which poses a substantial issue due to its propensity to generate miscommunication. Towards teaching students to avoid making errors in logical reasoning, logical fallacies have received attention (Habernal et al., 2017; Bonial et al., 2022; Zhivar et al., 2023; Nakpih and Santini, 2020). Motivated by the gamification method made by Habernal et al. (2017), Bonial et al. (2022) aimed to capture similar fallacy types for news articles, but the low distribution of fallacy types in the wild makes identification challenging. However, most natural texts do not have recurrent specific patterns, compared to current datasets, like the Logic and LogicClimate datasets (Jin et al., 2022). Moreover, given the large number of logical fallacies that exist (over 100 types), long arguments can be grouped into multiple fallacies, resulting in difficulties in classification (Goffredo et al., 2022).

Debate patterns In a case of a debate, an opponent is willing to give a counter-argument synchronously and interactively. Analyzing and evaluating a debate is a difficult task as we need to retrieve not only the argumentation structure of each opponent but also the relations between them. Bao et al. (2022) focuses on argument pair extraction (APE), which consists of finding two interactive arguments from two argumentative passages of a discussion. Although the APE task gives insights into relations between different argumentative texts, it does not indicate complex relations (i.e., how claims, supports, attacks and the intention of the speakers are interrelated). To palliate this issue, Hautli-Janisz et al. (2022) identified and analyzed the dialogical argumentative structure of debates using Inference Anchoring Theory (IAT) (Budsziyska et al., 2014). Following the same IAT theory, Kikteva et al. (2022) showed that the type of questions (e.g., pure, assertive, and rhetorical questions) leads to different argumentative discourse. Focused more on the opponent's side, Naito et al. (2022) propose diagnostic comments for assessing the quality of counter-arguments by providing expressive, informative and unique templates. The feedback is then written by template selection and slot filling.

In-Depth Explanations Although identifying such argumentative structures (components, relations, and schemes) and properties (fallacies and debate patterns) is important, it has limitations in terms of effective feedback. Identifying a missing claim or a wrong premise is insufficient to understand how to improve the argumentation properly. Thus, we relate the identification of structure and properties to shallow explanations in the sense that users can still benefit from the output of the models.

Shallow explanations can be difficult to understand, especially for beginners, as they tend to be minimalist and lack guidance. To explain more effectively the errors in an argument, a model should go a step further, hence by providing *in-depth* explanations, which attempt to identify the argument's implicit components to explain *why* it is an error in a particular argument. In Figure 2, we implicitly know that hamburgers belong to the American cuisine, as same as the Cobb salad, a healthy garden salad from California. Therefore, if the model is able to reason out this implicit knowledge, it can better explain the invalid generalization in Figure 2.

Implicit Knowledge and Reasoning in Arguments To provide *in-depth* explanations, we need to know how to refine the argument, i.e., how to identify implicit information. Recently, many works have focused their attention on this aim. The main goal of such studies is to make the structure and reasoning of arguments explicit to explain the arguments for humans better. Additionally, this focus can eventually help build robust argumentation machines that can be enriched with language understanding capacity. Following the pioneer works of Razuvayevskaya and Teufel (2017), the ExpLAIN project (Becker et al., 2021) and Jo et al. (2021) are one such example that focuses extensively on reconstructing implicit knowledge in arguments by relying on knowledge graphs among others. Taking a step further in this direction, Heinisch et al. (2022) and Saadat-Yazdi et al. (2023) proposed to utilize such implicit information to bridge the implicit reasoning gap in arguments to help students explain their arguments better.

Large annotated corpora are required to improve implicit reasoning detection for models. To address this need, various studies have proposed methods for annotating implicit knowledge, leading to the development of multiple datasets (Becker et al., 2020; Singh et al., 2021, 2022). In Singh et al. (2021), semi-structured warrants, i.e. links between a claim and evidence (c.f. Appendix Figure 4), were annotated via crowdsourcing, whereas Becker et al. (2020) focus on reconstructing omitted information, semantic clause types, and commonsense knowledge relations through expert annotation. Corpora can be dedicated to a specific domain or sentence patterns. For example, (Singh et al., 2022) focused on domain-specific knowledge using six topics. However, implicit knowledge may take various forms, such as warrants, causal relations, facts, beliefs, or assumed-known arguments. Thus, revealing implicit knowledge in an unknown text through annotated datasets can be challenging.

In recent years, LLMs have made significant progress in exhibiting reasoning abilities. A comprehensive overview of the current state of reasoning abilities in LLMs is provided in the survey Huang and Chang (2023). The increasing interest in LLMs and implicit reasoning prompted the first ever workshop on natural language reasoning and structured explanations in 2023 (Dalvi Mishra et al., 2023). This workshop discussed that while LLMs have demonstrated good capabilities to find implicit components within an argument, they often cannot correctly explain the logical reasons behind their responses. To bridge this gap, a novel category of explanation techniques has arisen, playing a vital role in shaping the logical reasoning of models. One such example is the chain-of-thought prompting (Wei et al., 2022; Wang et al., 2023a), which employs explanations as a means for LLMs to emulate human reasoning procedures. While the references Huang and Chang (2023) and Dalvi Mishra et al. (2023) do not primarily focus on argumentative tasks, they can be a valuable source of inspiration in argumentation.

5 Visualization - How to Show the Error?

The effectiveness of any argument does not solely rely on its content but also on its presentation. This is where visualization of argumentative feedback emerges as a crucial factor. Visualizing feedback empowers individuals to perceive the intricacies of an argument in a more comprehensive manner. By using visual aids like graphs, feedback becomes more accessible and engaging, fostering constructive discussions. In this section, we discuss how visualization impacts argumentative feedback.

Highlights A simple approach to visualization is highlighting, i.e., application of visual emphasis on a specific pattern with the intention of drawing the viewer's attention to this specific pattern. For example, Lauscher et al. (2018) identify the argument component (Claim, background, data) and visualizes them by highlighting the text in different colors. Similarly, Chernodub et al. (2019) allow the user to choose the model to use and the components to highlight. Wambsganss et al. (2022b) take a step further by highlighting and presenting scores that give a quick overview of users' skills.

Highlighting serves as an essential key step in the cognitive input process, enabling viewers to quickly identify crucial argumentative structures. However, its use should be complemented with other visualization techniques to ensure a more profound exploration and comprehension of complex explanations. Studies conducted by Lauscher et al. (2018); Chernodub et al. (2019); Wambsganss et al. (2022b) shed light on the potentials and limitations of highlighting, paving the way for future advancements in data visualization methodologies.

Multiple views To overcome the shallowness of highlighting, several researchers add to their system other views, such as diagrams showing the argumentative structure. For example, to compare two drafts of an essay, Zhang et al. (2016); Afrin et al. (2021) use a revision map made of color-coded tiles, whereas Putra et al. (2021) rely on a tree to reorder arguments.

Based on the work of Wambsganß et al. (2020), Xia et al. (2022) and Wambsganss et al. (2022a) use a text editor which highlights components, a graph view which shows the argumentative structure, and a score view showing the user's performance. Based on the classroom-setting evaluation, students using such systems wrote texts with a better formal quality of argumentation compared to the ones using the traditional approach.

Nevertheless, the current accuracy of such systems' feedback still leaves a large improvement space in order for users to be motivated to use them. More recent work such as Zhang et al. (2023) incorporate feedback generated by state-of-the-art LLMs in their graphical systems. Nonetheless, factual inaccuracies, as well as inconsistent or contradictory statements, are still generated, exposing the user to confusion and leaving room for improvement.

Dialogue Systems In the realm of visualization, a novel approach gaining attraction is the integration of dialogue systems to enhance the interaction between users and visual representations. Dialogue systems, commonly known as chatbots like ChatGPT, have been increasingly explored for their potential to facilitate information comprehension (Rach et al., 2020; Wambsganß et al., 2021).

This kind of representation is challenging in terms of user-friendliness. Particularly, in a pedagogical context, users may have difficulties visualizing their previous feedback and progress. Indeed, users may be lost in the discussion flow and struggle to keep track of the ongoing discussions, lessons, or feedback because the representation does not provide clear signposts or structure. Students may forget a specific lesson and want to verify some information, or they simply need to reread their lessons and exercises. However, finding specific information in a chat discussion may take much effort. Thus, it is important (i) to have a chat session per lesson, exercise or test and (ii) to keep structured notes of the issues users face and how these issues can be solved. Eventually, a personal dashboard showing a user's progress through time could be beneficial not only for students but also for teachers. Indeed, with a dashboard, teachers can see if a specific student needs more attention. Moreover, teachers sometimes need to compare students among them, specifically during a test. Therefore, we believe that to improve the user-friendliness of pedagogical dialogue systems, other visual elements should be used.

Despite the growing popularity of both graphs and chatbots in data visualization, limited work has directly compared their effectiveness in improving critical thinking skills. Further research is needed to provide more nuanced insights on the comparison on one hand between both approaches and on the other between works among the same approach.

The importance of visualization lies in its ability to enhance the understanding of complex ideas. In this section, we highlighted the potential of the visualization of argumentative feedback and how it can improve students' learning process.

6 Interactivity - Who Talks to the User?

Teaching how to argue is a multifaceted task that demands more than the dissemination of theoretical knowledge; it requires fostering interactive learning environments that facilitate active engagement and practice. The traditional approach to teaching argumentation often centers on lecturing and one-way communication, where instructors impart information to students. While didactic methods have their place in education, a more interactive pedagogical approach, one that encourages learners to actively participate, can be used. In this section, we will see in which ways current argumentative computational models enable a form of interaction.

Interaction between different users NLP systems mostly allow communication between a user and a conversational agent. Nonetheless, some works chose to apply the CABLE pedagogy (§3) by allowing a user to dialog with *other users*. Following the footsteps of Petasis (2014), Lugini et al. (2020) track real-time class discussions and help teachers annotate and analyze them. Recent works such as Zhang et al. (2023) plan to add a collaborative setting in their future work.

The collaboration between multiple users within NLP systems is promising. Nevertheless, only a few works focus on the CABLE pedagogy. It is essential to acknowledge that some challenges and barriers have hindered its use in NLP, possibly due to the difficulty of designing and evaluating such tools, as human resources in a real-class setting (e.g., students, teachers) are required.

Interaction with a conversational agent As seen in §5, several research papers have showcased the feasibility of employing current conversational agents for educational purposes (Lee et al., 2022; Macina et al., 2023; Wang et al., 2023b). Often based on state-of-the-art language models, these agents have shown great capabilities in understanding and generating human-like responses. They can engage in dynamic and contextually relevant conversations, making them potentially valuable tools for educational purposes.

The use of conversational agents as dialog tutors has been explored outside of argumentation (Wambsganß et al., 2021; Mirzababaei and Pammer-Schindler, 2022; Aicher et al., 2022). For instance, in Mirzababaei and Pammer-Schindler (2022), an agent examines arguments to determine a claim, a warrant, and evidence, identifies any missing elements, and then assists in completing the argument accordingly. Wambsganß et al. (2021) create an interactive educational system that uses interactive dialogues to teach students about the argumentative structure of a text. The system not only provides feedback on the user's texts but also learning sessions with different exercises.

Research on chatbots in education is still preliminary due to the limited number of studies exploring the application of effective learning strategies using chatbots. This indicates a significant opportunity for further research to facilitate innovative teaching methods using conversational agents (Hwang and Chang, 2021). However, extraction and classification of useful data remain challenging, as the data collected are noisy and much effort still has to be made to make it trainable (Lin et al., 2023). Researchers must also continue to account for ethical considerations, including biased representations and data privacy safeguards, to ensure that their chatbots positively impact users (Kooli, 2023).

Overall, integrating interaction in teaching how to argue is not merely a pedagogical choice but an essential requirement to cultivate adept arguers who can navigate the intricacies of argumentation. Therefore, we encourage researchers to consider this dimension in their future pedagogical systems.

7 Personalization - To Whom is it For?

Even if the feedback mentioned in §4 are a step towards good guidance, they are static, which can be problematic. Beginners and professionals in argumentation do not need the same amount of feedback. A child and an adult have different levels of understanding and knowledge. Therefore, it is essential that a model knows *to whom* it should explain the errors and hence how to adapt its output by providing *personalized* explanations.

Levels of explanations A first approach to personalization is to discretize different users' proficiency levels in argumentation into a small number of categories. For instance, with the system described in Wambsganß et al. (2020) and Wambsganss et al. (2022a), users can select their own level among the following categories: Novice, Advanced, Competent, Proficient, Expert.

Although Wambsganß et al. (2020) and Wambsganss et al. (2022a) propose different granularity levels of explanations, their study is restrained to students from their university. Having end-users from different backgrounds may imply the need for new levels of explanations. Wachsmuth and Alshomary (2022) show that the explainee's age affects the way an explainer explains the topic at hand. Thus, we consider that information such as the learner's age should be considered in future interactive argumentative feedback systems, where terminology such as *fallacy* and their existence would require different explanation approaches for younger students (i.e., elementary) compared to older students.

Self-personalization For more personalized feedback, systems such as Hunter et al. (2019) and Putra et al. (2020) rely on user's inputs. They allow users to make their custom tags or to choose their preferences among a set of rubrics. Nevertheless, manually personalizing the system can be overwhelming and time-consuming for users.

Next directions Hunter et al. (2019) argue that the next direction for personalized argumentative feedback would be to develop argumentation chatbots for persuasion and infer the user's stance based on the discussion. Chatbots' personalization capabilities enable them to tailor their responses to individual learners' needs and learning styles, potentially enhancing the effectiveness of the tutoring process (Lin et al., 2023). However, bridging the gap among personalized chatbots (Qian et al., 2021; Ma et al., 2021), personalized educational methods (González-González et al., 2023; Ismail et al., 2023; Liu et al., 2020) and argumentation has remained unexplored. Thus, we think researchers should focus in the future on providing more *personalized* explanations (i.e., precisely adjusted by considering the learner's background) to improve the users' critical thinking skills efficiently.

8 Discussions

Teaching how to argue through NLP systems holds significant promise for enhancing students' learning process. However, existing research in this area presents various open issues. In this section, we explore some difficulties in designing and evaluating computational models for argumentation and discuss some methods for mitigating them.

Evaluating different systems The evaluation of NLP systems often relies on human assessment, which is insightful. However, this reliance makes it hard to reproduce the evaluation and to compare different systems. To the best of our knowledge, no research has focused on comprehensive comparative studies of different end-to-end systems. The lack of direct comparisons between similar systems hampers the understanding of their relative advantages and limitations. As researchers and educators, it becomes overwhelming to discern which system best fits specific pedagogical objectives. A possible reason for this issue resides in the restricted access to various tools. Indeed, many systems may not be accessible, limiting researchers to test them. Additionally, the lack of guidelines to evaluate systems for learning argumentation exacerbates the difficulty in evaluating these systems in a systematic manner. Current systems' performance is evaluated with metrics such as coherence. Nevertheless, new evaluation methods such as the ones described in Heuer and Buschek (2021) should be explored. Therefore, we should promote open-source projects and the research of standard guidelines.

Domain Adaptation Towards effectively explaining output to improve critical thinking skills of users, future systems must be capable of understanding the topic of discussion in a way that argumentation errors (e.g., fallacies) can be identified. In a pedagogical setting, teachers have the ability to choose new topics of discussion annually; hence, systems must also be capable of adapting to various domains. Recent works have focused on domain adaptation for tasks such as short answer scoring (Funayama et al., 2023), which focus on training models for several tasks to learn common properties helpful in evaluating unseen topics. We must also adopt such strategies for computational argumentation to ensure the most reliable feedback is given to the user.

Collaboration NLP researchers and pedagogical researchers generally conduct their research independently, thus creating a gap. We suggest that researchers from both fields must come together to ensure that appropriate and sufficient explanations are provided to learners. Ideally, a system for linking various educational schools and providers with artificial intelligence researchers could significantly help assist with ensuring systems can be properly evaluated.

Ethics Tailoring a constructive feedback system to each user's background and current worldview would benefit the user significantly. Nevertheless, the creation of such a system presents significant challenges in navigating ethical issues (Hovy et al.,

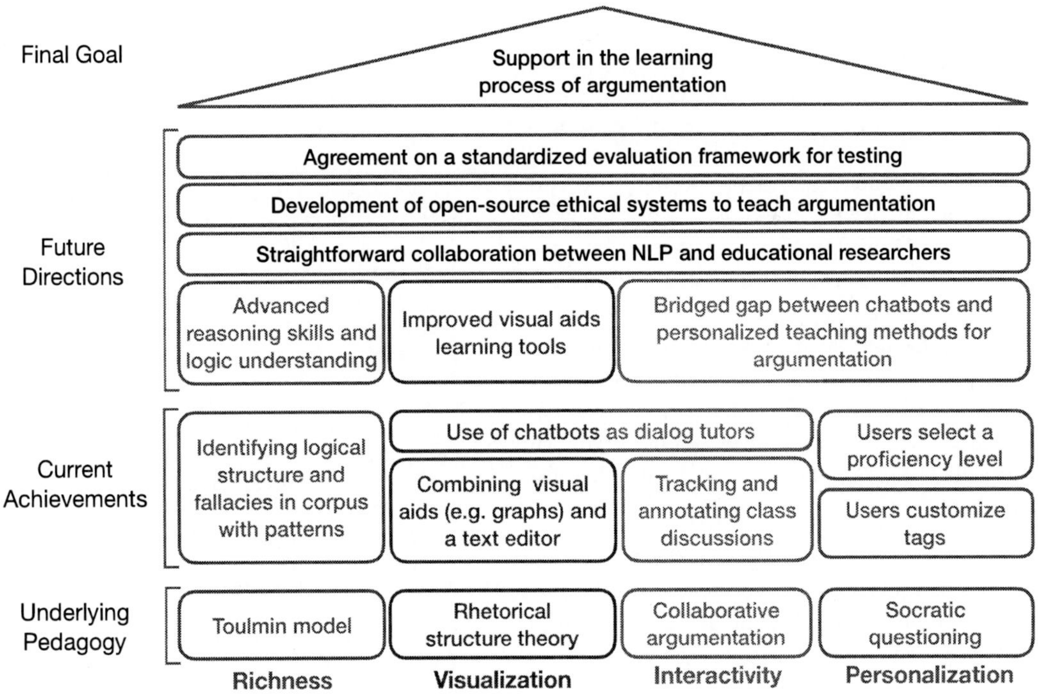

Figure 3: Current and future directions of teaching argumentation with NLP systems. Boxes with a specific color correspond to a specific dimension, whereas the ones in black are general directions.

2017; Trust et al., 2023). Hence, conceiving novel systems with an *ethics by design* approach remains important (Leidner and Plachouras, 2017). *Ethics by design* is a concept that emphasizes the integration of ethical considerations and principles into the design and development of products, systems, technologies, and processes from the very beginning. It promotes the idea that ethical considerations should be a fundamental part of the design process rather than added as an afterthought or compliance requirement. This approach aims to prevent and mitigate potential ethical issues, such as privacy violations, bias, discrimination, and lack of transparency, by building ethical principles and values into the core of a project. In order to add this principles in a project, Leidner and Plachouras (2017) suggest an Ethics Review Board (ERB) for companies and research institutions, as well as a list of remedies that researchers can consider when facing ethical dilemmas.

9 Conclusion

In our survey, we explored several works providing feedback in argumentation, following various dimensions: *Richness* (§4), *Visualization* (§5), *Interactivity* (§6), and *Personalization* (§7). Figure 3 summarizes the pedagogy, current achievements and potential future directions of each dimension.

As potential areas for improvement to enhance the quality of educational argumentative systems, we highlighted the following points: (1) generate accurate, constructive feedback for a real-life input(§4-5), (2) tailor the output based on the user's background (§6-7), (3) evaluate and compare end-to-end systems more deeply(§8), (4) improve models' abilities to adapt to unknown topics(§8), (5) collaborate with pedagogical teams and actual students(§8), and finally (6) take into consideration ethical issues(§8). For instance, in challenge (2), the use of conversational agents becomes increasingly frequent. However, such systems still leave room for improvement, particularly their ability to tailor discussions based on the user's background.

We hope our survey contributes to enriching the research community focused on argumentation with a comprehensive understanding of current perspectives in NLP systems for teaching how to argue. In our future work, we will focus further on real-life and end-to-end systems (Challenges (1) and (3)). We plan to prototype a system to measure the effects of different feedback on users and evaluate it in actual classrooms (Appendix, Figure 5).

Limitations

This survey offers an overview of NLP feedback systems in argumentation. Despite our best efforts, some limitations may still exist in this research.

Paper selection Our survey primarily focuses on argumentative feedback systems in the context of NLP and human-machine interaction, but there may be valuable insights from other feedback systems that could be applied to argumentation. For instance, feedback systems for grammatical errors, such as (Liang et al., 2023), could inspire new argumentative feedback systems. Moreover, we excluded non-English articles in our survey and prioritized works dedicated to students rather than teachers (e.g., Datta et al., 2021).

Categorization Based on our understanding and subjective opinions, we have categorized the works into four dimensions. It could be relevant to have external opinions on this categorization.

Descriptions The descriptions provided in this survey are generally concise to ensure comprehensive coverage within the constraints of page limits. We hope this survey can be a reference, directing readers to more detailed information in the respective works.

Experiments It is important to note that this survey is purely informational and lacks experimental data or empirical results. Conducting comparative experiments with different feedback systems could offer more substantial guidance. However, this aspect is left for future research.

Acknowledgements

This work was supported by JSPS KAKENHI Grant Number 22H00524 and by JST CREST Grant Number JPMJCR20D2, Japan.

References

Jamie Abrams. 2015. Reframing the socratic method. *Journal of Legal Education*, 64(4):562–585.

Tazin Afrin, Omid Kashefi, Christopher Olshefski, Diane Litman, Rebecca Hwa, and Amanda Godley. 2021. Effective interfaces for student-driven revision sessions for argumentative writing. In *Proceedings of the 2021 CHI Conference on Human Factors in Computing Systems (CHI 2021)*. ACM.

Annalena Aicher, Nadine Gerstenlauer, Isabel Feustel, Wolfgang Minker, and Stefan Ultes. 2022. Towards building a spoken dialogue system for argument exploration. In *Proceedings of the Thirteenth Language Resources and Evaluation Conference*, pages 1234–1241, Marseille, France. European Language Resources Association.

Erfan Al-Hossami, Razvan Bunescu, Ryan Teehan, Laurel Powell, Khyati Mahajan, and Mohsen Dorodchi. 2023. Socratic questioning of novice debuggers: A benchmark dataset and preliminary evaluations. In *Proceedings of the 18th Workshop on Innovative Use of NLP for Building Educational Applications (BEA 2023)*, pages 709–726, Toronto, Canada. Association for Computational Linguistics.

Khalid Al-Khatib, Henning Wachsmuth, Matthias Hagen, Jonas Köhler, and Benno Stein. 2016. Cross-domain mining of argumentative text through distant supervision. In *Proceedings of the 2016 Conference of the North American Chapter of the Association for Computational Linguistics: Human Language Technologies*, pages 1395–1404, San Diego, California. Association for Computational Linguistics.

Milad Alshomary, Shahbaz Syed, Arkajit Dhar, Martin Potthast, and Henning Wachsmuth. 2021. Counter-argument generation by attacking weak premises. In *Findings of the Association for Computational Linguistics: ACL-IJCNLP 2021*, pages 1816–1827, Online. Association for Computational Linguistics.

Beng Heng Ang, Sujatha Das Gollapalli, and See-Kiong Ng. 2023. Socratic question generation: A novel dataset, models, and evaluation. In *Proceedings of the 17th Conference of the European Chapter of the Association for Computational Linguistics*, pages 147–165, Dubrovnik, Croatia. Association for Computational Linguistics.

Michael Baker, Jerry Andriessen, and Baruch Schwarz. 2019. *Collaborative Argumentation-Based Learning*, pages pp. 76–88. Routledge.

Jianzhu Bao, Jingyi Sun, Qinglin Zhu, and Ruifeng Xu. 2022. Have my arguments been replied to? argument pair extraction as machine reading comprehension. In *Proceedings of the 60th Annual Meeting of the Association for Computational Linguistics (Volume 2: Short Papers)*, pages 29–35, Dublin, Ireland. Association for Computational Linguistics.

Maria Becker, Katharina Korfhage, and Anette Frank. 2020. Implicit knowledge in argumentative texts: An annotated corpus. In *Proceedings of the Twelfth Language Resources and Evaluation Conference*, pages 2316–2324, Marseille, France. European Language Resources Association.

Maria Becker, Siting Liang, and Anette Frank. 2021. Reconstructing implicit knowledge with language models. In *Proceedings of Deep Learning Inside Out (DeeLIO): The 2nd Workshop on Knowledge Extraction and Integration for Deep Learning Architectures*, pages 11–24, Online. Association for Computational Linguistics.

Linda Behar-Horenstein and Lian Niu. 2011. Teaching critical thinking skills in higher education: A review of the literature. *Journal of College Teaching and Learning*, 8.

Beata Beigman Klebanov and Nitin Madnani. 2020. Automated evaluation of writing – 50 years and counting. In *Proceedings of the 58th Annual Meeting of the Association for Computational Linguistics*, pages 7796–7810, Online. Association for Computational Linguistics.

Claire Bonial, Austin Blodgett, Taylor Hudson, Stephanie M. Lukin, Jeffrey Micher, Douglas Summers-Stay, Peter Sutor, and Clare Voss. 2022. The search for agreement on logical fallacy annotation of an infodemic. In *Proceedings of the Thirteenth Language Resources and Evaluation Conference*, pages 4430–4438, Marseille, France. European Language Resources Association.

Kasia Budsziyska, Mathilde Janier, Chris Reed, Patrick Saint-Dizier, Manfred Stede, and Olena Yakorska. 2014. A model for processing illocutionary structures and argumentation in debates. In *Proceedings of the 9th International Conference on Language Resources and Evaluation (LREC 2014)*, volume 14, pages electronic–medium. European Language Resources Association (ELRA).

Artem Chernodub, Oleksiy Oliynyk, Philipp Heidenreich, Alexander Bondarenko, Matthias Hagen, Chris Biemann, and Alexander Panchenko. 2019. TARGER: Neural argument mining at your fingertips. In *Proceedings of the 57th Annual Meeting of the Association for Computational Linguistics: System Demonstrations*, pages 195–200, Florence, Italy. Association for Computational Linguistics.

Christie A. Linskens Christie. 2010. What critique have been made of the socratic method in legal education. *European Journal of Law Reform*, 12.

Bhavana Dalvi Mishra, Greg Durrett, Peter Jansen, Danilo Neves Ribeiro, and Jason Wei, editors. 2023. *Proceedings of the 1st Workshop on Natural Language Reasoning and Structured Explanations (NLRSE 2023)*. Association for Computational Linguistics, Toronto, Canada.

Marina Danilevsky, Kun Qian, Ranit Aharonov, Yannis Katsis, Ban Kawas, and Prithviraj Sen. 2020. A survey of the state of explainable ai for natural language processing.

Debajyoti Datta, Maria Phillips, James P. Bywater, Jennifer Chiu, Ginger S. Watson, Laura Barnes, and Donald Brown. 2021. Virtual pre-service teacher assessment and feedback via conversational agents. In *Proceedings of the 16th Workshop on Innovative Use of NLP for Building Educational Applications*, pages 185–198, Online. Association for Computational Linguistics.

Roxanne El Baff, Henning Wachsmuth, Khalid Al-Khatib, and Benno Stein. 2018. Challenge or empower: Revisiting argumentation quality in a news editorial corpus. In *Proceedings of the 22nd Conference on Computational Natural Language Learning*, pages 454–464, Brussels, Belgium. Association for Computational Linguistics.

Vanessa Wei Feng and Graeme Hirst. 2011. Classifying arguments by scheme. In *Proceedings of the 49th Annual Meeting of the Association for Computational Linguistics: Human Language Technologies*, pages 987–996, Portland, Oregon, USA. Association for Computational Linguistics.

Hiroaki Funayama, Yuya Asazuma, Yuichiroh Matsubayashi, Tomoya Mizumoto, and Kentaro Inui. 2023. Reducing the cost: Cross-prompt pre-finetuning for short answer scoring. In *Lecture Notes in Computer Science*, page 78–89, Berlin, Heidelberg. Springer-Verlag.

Vetti Giri and M. U. Paily. 2020. Effect of scientific argumentation on the development of critical thinking. *Science & Education*, 29.

Pierpaolo Goffredo, Shohreh Haddadan, Vorakit Vorakitphan, Elena Cabrio, and Serena Villata. 2022. Fallacious argument classification in political debates. In *Proceedings of the 31st International Joint Conference on Artificial Intelligence IJCAI 2022*, pages 4143–4149. International Joint Conferences on Artificial Intelligence Organization. Main Track.

Carina González-González, Vanesa Muñoz-Cruz, Pedro Antonio Toledo-Delgado, and Eduardo Nacimiento-García. 2023. Personalized gamification for learning: A reactive chatbot architecture proposal. *Sensors*, 23(1).

Ivan Habernal and Iryna Gurevych. 2016. Argumentation mining in user-generated web discourse. *CoRR*, abs/1601.02403.

Ivan Habernal, Raffael Hannemann, Christian Pollak, Christopher Klamm, Patrick Pauli, and Iryna Gurevych. 2017. Argotario: Computational argumentation meets serious games. In *Proceedings of the 2017 Conference on Empirical Methods in Natural Language Processing: System Demonstrations*, pages 7–12, Copenhagen, Denmark. Association for Computational Linguistics.

Ivan Habernal, Henning Wachsmuth, Iryna Gurevych, and Benno Stein. 2018. The argument reasoning comprehension task: Identification and reconstruction of implicit warrants. In *Proceedings of the 2018 Conference of the North American Chapter of the Association for Computational Linguistics: Human Language Technologies, Volume 1 (Long Papers)*, pages 1930–1940, New Orleans, Louisiana. Association for Computational Linguistics.

Mareike Hartmann and Daniel Sonntag. 2022. A survey on improving nlp models with human explanations.

Annette Hautli-Janisz, Zlata Kikteva, Wassiliki Siskou, Kamila Gorska, Ray Becker, and Chris Reed. 2022. QT30: A corpus of argument and conflict in broadcast debate. In *Proceedings of the Thirteenth Language Resources and Evaluation Conference*, pages 3291–3300, Marseille, France. European Language Resources Association.

Philipp Heinisch, Anette Frank, Juri Opitz, and Philipp Cimiano. 2022. Strategies for framing argumentative conclusion generation. In *Proceedings of the 15th International Conference on Natural Language Generation*, pages 246–259, Waterville, Maine, USA and virtual meeting. Association for Computational Linguistics.

Hendrik Heuer and Daniel Buschek. 2021. Methods for the design and evaluation of HCI+NLP systems. In *Proceedings of the First Workshop on Bridging Human–Computer Interaction and Natural Language Processing*, pages 28–33, Online. Association for Computational Linguistics.

Shengluan Hou, Shuhan Zhang, and Chaoqun Fei. 2020. Rhetorical structure theory: A comprehensive review of theory, parsing methods and applications. *Expert Systems with Applications*, 157:113421.

Dirk Hovy, Shannon Spruit, Margaret Mitchell, Emily M. Bender, Michael Strube, and Hanna Wallach, editors. 2017. *Proceedings of the First ACL Workshop on Ethics in Natural Language Processing*. Association for Computational Linguistics, Valencia, Spain.

Jie Huang and Kevin Chen-Chuan Chang. 2023. Towards reasoning in large language models: A survey. In *Findings of the Association for Computational Linguistics: ACL 2023*, pages 1049–1065, Toronto, Canada. Association for Computational Linguistics.

Anthony Hunter, Lisa Chalaguine, Tomasz Czernuszenko, Emmanuel Hadoux, and Sylwia Polberg. 2019. Towards computational persuasion via natural language argumentation dialogues. In *KI 2019: Advances in Artificial Intelligence*, pages 18–33, Cham. Springer International Publishing.

Gwo-Jen Hwang and Ching-Yi Chang. 2021. A review of opportunities and challenges of chatbots in education. *Interactive Learning Environments*, 0(0):1–14.

Sheikh Rabiul Islam, William Eberle, Sheikh Khaled Ghafoor, and Mohiuddin Ahmed. 2021. Explainable artificial intelligence approaches: A survey.

Heba Ismail, Nada Hussein, Saad Harous, and Ashraf Khalil. 2023. Survey of personalized learning software systems: A taxonomy of environments, learning content, and user models. *Education Sciences*, 13(7).

Zhijing Jin, Abhinav Lalwani, Tejas Vaidhya, Xiaoyu Shen, Yiwen Ding, Zhiheng Lyu, Mrinmaya Sachan, Rada Mihalcea, and Bernhard Schoelkopf. 2022. Logical fallacy detection. In *Findings of the Association for Computational Linguistics: EMNLP 2022*, pages 7180–7198, Abu Dhabi, United Arab Emirates. Association for Computational Linguistics.

Yohan Jo, Jacky Visser, Chris Reed, and Eduard Hovy. 2020. Extracting implicitly asserted propositions in argumentation.

Yohan Jo, Haneul Yoo, JinYeong Bak, Alice Oh, Chris Reed, and Eduard Hovy. 2021. Knowledge-enhanced evidence retrieval for counterargument generation. In *Findings of the Association for Computational Linguistics: EMNLP 2021*, Online. Association for Computational Linguistics.

Zixuan Ke and Vincent Ng. 2019. Automated essay scoring: A survey of the state of the art. In *Proceedings of the 28th International Joint Conference on Artificial Intelligence IJCAI 2019*, pages 6300–6308. International Joint Conferences on Artificial Intelligence Organization.

Orin Kerr. 1999. The decline of the socratic method at harvard. *Nebraska law review*, 78:113.

Zlata Kikteva, Kamila Gorska, Wassiliki Siskou, Annette Hautli-Janisz, and Chris Reed. 2022. The keystone role played by questions in debate. In *Proceedings of the 3rd Workshop on Computational Approaches to Discourse*, pages 54–63, Gyeongju, Republic of Korea and Online. International Conference on Computational Linguistics.

Chokri Kooli. 2023. Chatbots in education and research: A critical examination of ethical implications and solutions. *Sustainability*, 15:5614.

Anne Lauscher, Goran Glavaš, and Kai Eckert. 2018. ArguminSci: A tool for analyzing argumentation and rhetorical aspects in scientific writing. In *Proceedings of the 5th Workshop on Argument Mining*, pages 22–28, Brussels, Belgium. Association for Computational Linguistics.

Anne Lauscher, Henning Wachsmuth, Iryna Gurevych, and Goran Glavaš. 2022. Scientia potentia Est—On the role of knowledge in computational argumentation. *Transactions of the Association for Computational Linguistics*, 10:1392–1422.

John Lawrence and Chris Reed. 2020. Argument Mining: A Survey. *Computational Linguistics*, 45(4):765–818.

Mina Lee, Percy Liang, and Qian Yang. 2022. CoAuthor: Designing a human-AI collaborative writing dataset for exploring language model capabilities. In *Proceedings of the 2022 CHI Conference on Human Factors in Computing Systems (CHI 2022)*. ACM.

Jochen L. Leidner and Vassilis Plachouras. 2017. Ethical by design: Ethics best practices for natural language processing. In *Proceedings of the First ACL Workshop on Ethics in Natural Language Processing*, pages 30–40, Valencia, Spain. Association for Computational Linguistics.

Kai-Hui Liang, Sam Davidson, Xun Yuan, Shehan Panditharatne, Chun-Yen Chen, Ryan Shea, Derek Pham, Yinghua Tan, Erik Voss, and Luke Fryer. 2023. ChatBack: Investigating methods of providing grammatical error feedback in a GUI-based language learning chatbot. In *Proceedings of the 18th Workshop on Innovative Use of NLP for Building Educational Applications (BEA 2023)*, pages 83–99, Toronto, Canada. Association for Computational Linguistics.

Chien-Chang Lin, Anna Huang, and Stephen Yang. 2023. A review of ai-driven conversational chatbots implementation methodologies and challenges (1999–2022). *Sustainability*, 15:4012.

Haochen Liu, Zitao Liu, Zhongqin Wu, and Jiliang Tang. 2020. Personalized multimodal feedback generation in education. In *Proceedings of the 28th International Conference on Computational Linguistics*, pages 1826–1840, Barcelona, Spain (Online). International Committee on Computational Linguistics.

Luca Lugini, Christopher Olshefski, Ravneet Singh, Diane Litman, and Amanda Godley. 2020. Discussion tracker: Supporting teacher learning about students' collaborative argumentation in high school classrooms. In *Proceedings of the 28th International Conference on Computational Linguistics: System Demonstrations*, pages 53–58, Barcelona, Spain (Online). International Committee on Computational Linguistics (ICCL).

Zhengyi Ma, Zhicheng Dou, Yutao Zhu, Hanxun Zhong, and Ji-Rong Wen. 2021. One chatbot per person: Creating personalized chatbots based on implicit user profiles. In *Proceedings of the 44th International ACM SIGIR Conference on Research and Development in Information Retrieval (SIGIR 2021)*. ACM.

Jakub Macina, Nico Daheim, Lingzhi Wang, Tanmay Sinha, Manu Kapur, Iryna Gurevych, and Mrinmaya Sachan. 2023. Opportunities and challenges in neural dialog tutoring.

William Mann and Sandra Thompson. 1988. Rhetorical structure theory: Toward a functional theory of text organization. *Text - Interdisciplinary Journal for the Study of Discourse*, 8(3):243–281.

Kana Matsumura and Teruyo Sakamoto. 2021. A structure analysis of japenese efl students' argumentative paragraph writings with a tool for annotating discourse relations. *Bulletin of the JACET Kansai Branch Writing Guidance Study Group*, 14:pp. 31–50.

Farjana Sultana Mim, Naoya Inoue, Shoichi Naito, Keshav Singh, and Kentaro Inui. 2022. LPAttack: A feasible annotation scheme for capturing logic pattern of attacks in arguments. In *Proceedings of the Thirteenth Language Resources and Evaluation Conference*, pages 2446–2459, Marseille, France. European Language Resources Association.

Behzad Mirzababaei and Viktoria Pammer-Schindler. 2022. Learning to give a complete argument with a conversational agent: An experimental study in two domains of argumentation. In *Educating for a New Future: Making Sense of Technology-Enhanced Learning Adoption*, pages 215–228, Cham. Springer International Publishing.

Shoichi Naito, Shintaro Sawada, Chihiro Nakagawa, Naoya Inoue, Kenshi Yamaguchi, Iori Shimizu, Farjana Sultana Mim, Keshav Singh, and Kentaro Inui. 2022. TYPIC: A corpus of template-based diagnostic comments on argumentation. In *Proceedings of the Thirteenth Language Resources and Evaluation Conference*, pages 5916–5928, Marseille, France. European Language Resources Association.

Callistus Ireneous Nakpih and Simone Santini. 2020. Automated discovery of logical fallacies in legal argumentation. *International Journal of Artificial Intelligence & Applications*.

Ellis Page. 1966. The imminence of... grading essays by computer. *The Phi Delta Kappan*, 47(5):238–243.

Artidoro Pagnoni, Alex Fabbri, Wojciech Kryscinski, and Chien-Sheng Wu. 2023. Socratic pretraining: Question-driven pretraining for controllable summarization. In *Proceedings of the 61st Annual Meeting of the Association for Computational Linguistics (ACL 2023)*, pages 12737–12755, Toronto, Canada. Association for Computational Linguistics.

Georgios Petasis. 2014. Annotating arguments: The nomad collaborative annotation tool. In *Proceedings of the 9th International Conference on Language Resources and Evaluation (LREC 2014)*, Reykjavik, Iceland. European Language Resources Association (ELRA).

R.T. Pithers and Rebecca Soden. 2000. Critical thinking in education: a review. *Educational Research*, 42(3):237–249.

Jan Wira Gotama Putra, Kana Matsumura, Simone Teufel, and Takenobu Tokunaga. 2021. Tiara 2.0: an interactive tool for annotating discourse structure and text improvement. *Language Resources and Evaluation*, 57:5 – 29.

Jan Wira Gotama Putra, Simone Teufel, Kana Matsumura, and Takenobu Tokunaga. 2020. TIARA: A tool for annotating discourse relations and sentence reordering. In *Proceedings of the Twelfth Language Resources and Evaluation Conference*, pages 6912–6920, Marseille, France. European Language Resources Association.

Hongjin Qian, Xiaohe Li, Hanxun Zhong, Yu Guo, Yueyuan Ma, Yutao Zhu, Zhanliang Liu, Zhicheng Dou, and Ji-Rong Wen. 2021. Pchatbot: A large-scale dataset for personalized chatbot.

Niklas Rach, Yuki Matsuda, Johannes Daxenberger, Stefan Ultes, Keiichi Yasumoto, and Wolfgang Minker. 2020. Evaluation of argument search approaches in the context of argumentative dialogue systems. In *Proceedings of the Twelfth Language Resources and Evaluation Conference*, pages 513–522, Marseille, France. European Language Resources Association.

Olesya Razuvayevskaya and Simone Teufel. 2017. Finding enthymemes in real-world texts: A feasibility study. *Argument Computation.*

Lesley Rex, Ebony Thomas, and Steven Engel. 2010. Applying toulmin: Teaching logical reasoning and argumentative writing. *The English Journal*, 99.

Ameer Saadat-Yazdi, Jeff Z. Pan, and Nadin Kokciyan. 2023. Uncovering implicit inferences for improved relational argument mining. In *Proceedings of the 17th Conference of the European Chapter of the Association for Computational Linguistics*, pages 2484–2495, Dubrovnik, Croatia. Association for Computational Linguistics.

Swarnadeep Saha, Prateek Yadav, Lisa Bauer, and Mohit Bansal. 2021. ExplaGraphs: An explanation graph generation task for structured commonsense reasoning. In *Proceedings of the 2021 Conference on Empirical Methods in Natural Language Processing*, pages 7716–7740, Online and Punta Cana, Dominican Republic. Association for Computational Linguistics.

Frederick Schauer. 2012. *Thinking like a Lawyer.* Harvard University Press.

Oliver Scheuer, Frank Loll, Niels Pinkwart, and Bruce Mclaren. 2010. Computer-supported argumentation: A review of the state of the art. *I. J. Computer-Supported Collaborative Learning*, 5:43–102.

Kumar Shridhar, Jakub Macina, Mennatallah El-Assady, Tanmay Sinha, Manu Kapur, and Mrinmaya Sachan. 2022. Automatic generation of socratic subquestions for teaching math word problems. In *Proceedings of the 2022 Conference on Empirical Methods in Natural Language Processing*, pages 4136–4149, Abu Dhabi, United Arab Emirates. Association for Computational Linguistics.

Keshav Singh, Naoya Inoue, Farjana Sultana Mim, Shoichi Naito, and Kentaro Inui. 2022. IRAC: A domain-specific annotated corpus of implicit reasoning in arguments. In *Proceedings of the Thirteenth Language Resources and Evaluation Conference*, pages 4674–4683, Marseille, France. European Language Resources Association.

Keshav Singh, Farjana Sultana Mim, Naoya Inoue, Shoichi Naito, and Kentaro Inui. 2021. Exploring methodologies for collecting high-quality implicit reasoning in arguments. In *Proceedings of the 8th Workshop on Argument Mining*, pages 57–66, Punta Cana, Dominican Republic. Association for Computational Linguistics.

Yi Song, Michael Heilman, Beata Beigman Klebanov, and Paul Deane. 2014. Applying argumentation schemes for essay scoring. In *Proceedings of the First Workshop on Argumentation Mining*, pages 69–78, Baltimore, Maryland. Association for Computational Linguistics.

Christian Stab and Iryna Gurevych. 2014. Identifying argumentative discourse structures in persuasive essays. In *Proceedings of the 2014 Conference on Empirical Methods in Natural Language Processing (EMNLP)*, pages 46–56, Doha, Qatar. Association for Computational Linguistics.

Simone Teufel. 1999. *Argumentative Zoning: Information Extraction from Scientific Text.* Ph.D. thesis, University of Edinburgh.

Stephen Toulmin. 1958. *The Uses of Arguments*, 1 edition. Cambridge University Press.

Torrey Trust, Jeromie Whalen, and Chrystalla Mouza. 2023. Editorial: Chatgpt: Challenges, opportunities, and implications for teacher education. *Contemporary Issues in Technology and Teacher Education*, 23(1):1–23.

Charles Twardy. 2004. Argument maps improve critical thinking. *Teaching Philosophy*, 27.

Alexandros Vassiliades, Nick Bassiliades, and Theodore Patkos. 2021. Argumentation and explainable artificial intelligence: a survey. *The Knowledge Engineering Review*, 36:e5.

Arja Veerman, Jerry Andriessen, and Gellof Kanselaar. 2002. Collaborative argumentation in academic education. *Instructional Science*, 40(3).

Henning Wachsmuth and Milad Alshomary. 2022. "mama always had a way of explaining things so I could understand": A dialogue corpus for learning to construct explanations. In *Proceedings of the 29th International Conference on Computational Linguistics*, pages 344–354, Gyeongju, Republic of Korea. International Committee on Computational Linguistics.

Henning Wachsmuth, Nona Naderi, Yufang Hou, Yonatan Bilu, Vinodkumar Prabhakaran, Tim Alberdingk Thijm, Graeme Hirst, and Benno Stein. 2017. Computational argumentation quality assessment in natural language. In *Proceedings of the 15th Conference of the European Chapter of the Association for Computational Linguistics: Volume 1, Long Papers*, pages 176–187, Valencia, Spain. Association for Computational Linguistics.

Douglas Walton, Christopher Reed, and Fabrizio Macagno. 2008. *Argumentation schemes.* Cambridge University Press.

Thiemo Wambsganss, Andrew Caines, and Paula Buttery. 2022a. ALEN app: Argumentative writing support to foster English language learning. In *Proceedings of the 17th Workshop on Innovative Use of NLP for Building Educational Applications (BEA 2022)*, pages 134–140, Seattle, Washington. Association for Computational Linguistics.

Thiemo Wambsganss, Andreas Janson, Tanja Käser, and Jan Marco Leimeister. 2022b. Improving students argumentation learning with adaptive self-evaluation nudging. *Proceedings of the ACM on Human-Computer Interaction (PACMHCI 2022)*, 6(520):1–31.

Thiemo Wambsganß, Tobias Kueng, Matthias Söllner, and Jan Marco Leimeister. 2021. Arguetutor: An adaptive dialog-based learning system for argumentation skills. In *Proceedings of the 2021 CHI Conference on Human Factors in Computing Systems (CHI 2021)*, pages 1–13.

Thiemo Wambsganß, Christina Niklaus, Matthias Cetto, Matthias Söllner, Siegfried Handschuh, and Jan Marco Leimeister. 2020. Al: An adaptive learning support system for argumentation skills. In *Proceedings of the 2021 CHI Conference on Human Factors in Computing Systems (CHI 2020)*.

Boshi Wang, Sewon Min, Xiang Deng, Jiaming Shen, You Wu, Luke Zettlemoyer, and Huan Sun. 2023a. Towards understanding chain-of-thought prompting: An empirical study of what matters. In *Proceedings of the 61st Annual Meeting of the Association for Computational Linguistics (ACL 2023)*, pages 2717–2739, Toronto, Canada. Association for Computational Linguistics.

Lingzhi Wang, Mrinmaya Sachan, Xingshan Zeng, and Kam-Fai Wong. 2023b. Strategize before teaching: A conversational tutoring system with pedagogy self-distillation.

Xinyu Wang, Yohan Lee, and Juneyoung Park. 2022. Automated evaluation for student argumentative writing: A survey.

Jason Wei, Xuezhi Wang, Dale Schuurmans, Maarten Bosma, Brian Ichter, Fei Xia, Ed Chi, Quoc V Le, and Denny Zhou. 2022. Chain-of-thought prompting elicits reasoning in large language models. In *Advances in Neural Information Processing Systems*, volume 35, pages 24824–24837. Curran Associates, Inc.

Armin Weinberger and Frank Fischer. 2006. A framework to analyze argumentative knowledge construction in computer-supported collaborative learning. *Computers & Education*, 46(1):71–95. Methodological Issues in Researching CSCL.

Meng Xia, Qian Zhu, Xingbo Wang, Fei Nie, Huamin Qu, and Xiaojuan Ma. 2022. Persua: A visual interactive system to enhance the persuasiveness of arguments in online discussion. *Proceedings of the 25th ACM Conference On Computer-Supported Cooperative Work And Social Computing (CSCW 2022)*, 6(CSCW2):1–30.

Stuart Yeh. 1998. Empowering education: Teaching argumentative writing to cultural minority middle-school students. research in the teaching of english. *Research in the Teaching of English*, 33(1):49–83.

Jian Yuan, Zhongyu Wei, Donghua Zhao, Qi Zhang, and Changjian Jiang. 2021. Leveraging argumentation knowledge graph for interactive argument pair identification. In *Findings of the Association for Computational Linguistics: ACL-IJCNLP 2021*, pages 2310–2319, Online. Association for Computational Linguistics.

Fan Zhang, Rebecca Hwa, Diane Litman, and Homa B. Hashemi. 2016. ArgRewrite: A web-based revision assistant for argumentative writings. In *Proceedings of the 2016 Conference of the North American Chapter of the Association for Computational Linguistics: Demonstrations*, pages 37–41, San Diego, California. Association for Computational Linguistics.

Zheng Zhang, Jie Gao, Ranjodh Singh Dhaliwal, and Toby Jia-Jun Li. 2023. Visar: A human-ai argumentative writing assistant with visual programming and rapid draft prototyping.

Sourati Zhivar, Ilievski Filip, Sandlin Hông-Ân, and Mermoud Alain. 2023. Case-based reasoning with language models for classification of logical fallacies.

Kristijonas Čyras, Antonio Rago, Emanuele Albini, Pietro Baroni, and Francesca Toni. 2021. Argumentative xai: A survey.

A Appendix

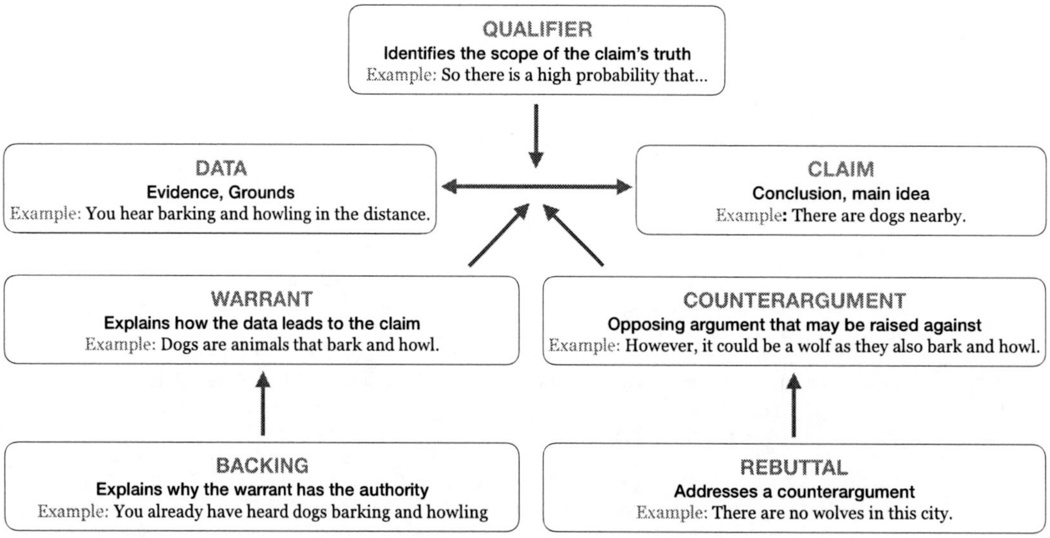

Figure 4: Six elements of the Toulmin's model.

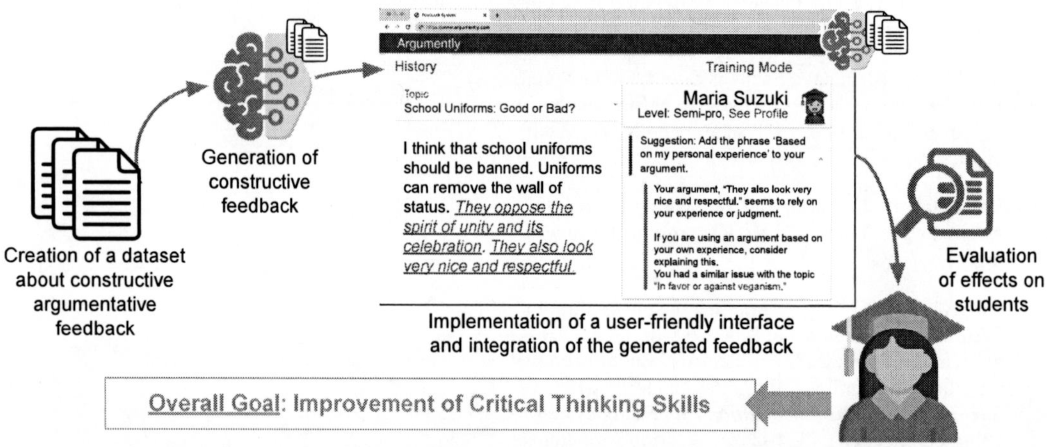

Figure 5: Preliminary sketch design of an end-to-end system to learn argumentation.

Constituency Tree Representation for Argument Unit Recognition

Samuel Guilluy
Univ Rennes 1 - IRMAR
Rennes, France
samuel.guilluy@univ-rennes1.fr

Florian Mehats
Ravel Technologies on leave from Univ Rennes
Rennes, France
florian.mehats@univ-rennes1.fr

Billal Chouli
Headmind AI & Blockchain
Paris, France
bchouli812@headmind.com

Abstract

The conventional method of extracting arguments from sentences solely relies on word proximity, disregarding the syntactic structure of the sentence. This approach often leads to inaccuracies, especially when identifying argumentative span boundaries. In this research, we investigate the benefits of utilizing a constituency tree representation of sentences to predict Argument Discourse Units (ADUs) at the token level. We first evaluate the effectiveness of utilizing the constituency tree representation for capturing the structural attributes of arguments within sentences. We demonstrate empirically that the constituency structure surpasses simple linear dependencies among neighboring words in terms of effectiveness. Our approach involves leveraging graph neural networks in conjunction with the constituency tree, adapting it specifically for argument unit recognition. Through extensive evaluation, our model outperforms existing approaches in recognizing argument units at the token level. Furthermore, we employ explainability methods to assess the suitability of our model architecture, providing insights into its performance.

1 Introduction

Argument identification within documents serves as the initial step in studying rhetorical speech processes, student essays, or political debates. The objective is to accurately identify Argument Discourse Units (ADUs), defined as minimal analysis units, within sentences, and predict their stance and relation to each other.

Previous works on token-level argument analysis (Trautmann, 2020) have employed language models such as Bidirectional Encoder Representations from Transformers (BERT) (Devlin et al., 2019), in conjunction with probabilistic models like Conditional Random Field (CRF) (Lafferty et al., 2001). This combination enhances overall prediction coherence with constrained fine-tuning.

The study of arguments and discourse has been approached from a grammatical perspective, including frameworks such as Rhetorical Structure Theory (Mann and Thompson, 1987), one of the conclusion from the annotation guideline (Stede and Taboada) is the use of syntax to better identify the Elementary Discourse Units (EDU). Building grammatical parsers is a complex task that has received extensive research attention. The results achieved thus far are promising and can serve as a foundation for various applications.

In this research, we investigate the benefits of incorporating grammatical structure into a BERT-CRF model for argument unit recognition, with a specific focus on the constituency tree representation of sentences (as illustrated in Figure 1). This representation consists of a tree where interior nodes represents the grammatical structure of the sentence, along with leaf nodes (nodes without children) corresponding to the words within the sentence.

The primary objectives of this paper are:

- Evaluate the potential benefits of using the constituency tree for argument unit recognition and develop rules to modify the constituency tree into a structure better suited for identifying argument structure (Section 3).
- Assess the effectiveness of Graph Neural Network (GNN) models combined with a CRF layer in leveraging the syntactic information encoded in the constituency tree representation (Sections 4, 5, and 6).

2 Related Works

Argumentation Theory The precise definition of the concept of argument is an important step when creating dataset annotation rules. The identification of argument is strongly related to the discourse structure of the text and the identification

Proceedings of the 10th Workshop on Argument Mining, pages 35–44
December 7, 2023. ©2023 Association for Computational Linguistics

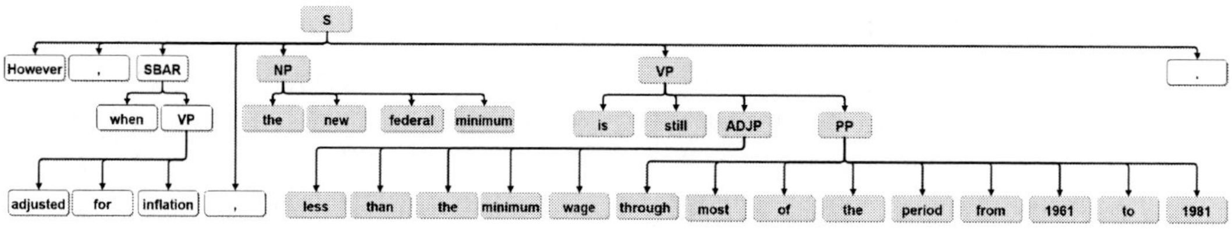

Figure 1: Constituency tree representation of the sentence, according to the Universal POS tags categories (where we limit the depth of the tree to 3): *"However, when adjusted for inflation, the new federal minimum is still less than the minimum wage through most of the period from 1961 to 1981."* from the AURC dataset. The green nodes represents words or spans with "PRO" label and the grey nodes represents words and spans with "NON" label.

of Elementary Discourse Units. As introduced in the Rhetorical Structure Theory (RST) by Mann and Thompson (1987), the Elementary Discourse Units (EDU) refers to a minimal unit of meaning within a larger discourse or conversation. It represents a self-contained piece of information that contributes to the overall structure and coherence of a discourse. A non-elementary Discourse Unit (DU) is called a complex discourse unit (CDU). The structure of a document is the set of linked DUs. As presented by Jo et al. (2019), Argument Discourse Unit (ADU) are units of meaning that contribute to the development and presentation of an argumentative structure. ADUs typically contain propositions, claims, evidence, or reasoning that support or challenge a particular standpoint or claim.

In practical applications, while certain studies rely on the annotator's judgment to determine the boundary of an ADU, many studies prefer to utilize a set of syntactic rules as a foundation (Stede and Taboada). This approach is favored because employing syntactic structure for annotating a sizable corpus at the token level is comparatively easier (Carlson and Marcu).

Tree Structure Representation in Natural Language Processing (NLP) Substantial evidence (Crain and Nakayama, 1987) supports the hypothesis that semantic interpretation of sentences by humans involves a tree-structured, hierarchical computation, where smaller constituents recursively combine into larger constituents, until we reach the full sentence.

In NLP, pioneer work (Gildea and Palmer, 2002) presenting the benefits of using constituency tree representation has failed to scale into production. According to the authors, this is caused by the lack of a reliable model to generate constituency tree representation of the sentences. However, recent promising results (Zhang, 2020) were made in consistency and dependency parsing.

Other papers have recently studied the use of tree structure to incorporate syntactic information to their models. Marcheggiani and Titov (2017) uses Graph Convolutional Networks (GCNs) based on the dependency tree structure of the sentence for semantic role labeling. Beck et al. (2018) uses GNNs for generation tasks from abstract meaning representation. Recently, Murty et al. (2022) demonstrate that for some tasks, transformers models become more "tree-like" over the course of training and in some cases unsupervisedly recovering the same trees as supervised parsers. Showing the importance of constituency tree in the learning process of the Transformers models.

Segmentation of argumentative units in texts has been explored in Ajjour et al.. The research indicates that both structural and semantic features are pivotal for segmenting argument units across various domains. However, within specific domains, semantic features stand out as the most effective for identifying the boundaries of these units.

3 Evaluation of the node similarity

In the subsequent section, we evaluate the effectiveness of utilizing the constituency tree representation for capturing the structural attributes of arguments within sentences. In Subsection 3.2, we introduce three metrics to assess the proximity of nodes in the tree concerning their argumentative label. Additionally, in Subsection 3.3, we propose modifications to the tree to enhance its suitability for argument recognition.

3.1 Experimental Setup

Our experimental setup involves the utilization of four argument datasets: ARG2020 (Alhindi and Ghosh, 2021), AURC (Trautmann et al., 2020), CDCP (Park and Cardie, 2018), and UKP (Stab and Gurevych, 2014) (detailed in subsection 5.1). These datasets share a common characteristic, as they are all annotated at the token level, meaning that each word in the sentences is assigned a label. To represent the sentences in the datasets as constituency trees, we employ the Berkeley Neural Parser (BENEPAR) (Kitaev and Klein, 2018), which is introduced in subsection 5.2. As a brief reminder, in the context of a constituency tree, a node without any children is referred to as a "leaf," while an "Interior Node (IN)" is a node that has child nodes.

As the labels for the interior nodes (IN) of the constituency tree were not initially provided, we made the decision to annotate these interior nodes following the same labeling rules utilized in the AURC (presented in 5.1) for sentence labeling. Our approach prioritizes the "no argument" label as less significant compared to the others, selecting the more predominant label among the remaining options. This strategy enables us to effectively learn the representation of IN nodes while ensuring consistency with the sentence-level labeling annotations.

3.2 Label proximity computation

One of the main advantages of adding a constituency tree to argument identification methods is the greater proximity of words that belong to the same grammatical class. In this section, we aim to validate the intuition that words belonging to the same grammatical class have more often the same label than words that are only neighbours in the sense of the linear representation of the sentence.

We have established three metrics to evaluate the suitability of employing the constituency tree representation for argument unit recognition. The three proportions computed, summarized in Table 1 and illustrated in Figure 2, are the following.

- **Leaf-Leaf similarity metric**: This refers to the ratio of nodes in a linear chain sentence (Table 1 column 3) representation that have both the same label and are adjacent to each other. In the cases where a constituency tree representation is available (Table 1 columns 4, 5, 6), we further narrow down this set of nodes to those that not only share the same label but also have the same parent node (illustrated in color red of Figure 2).
- **Leaf-IN similarity metric**: Only when a constituency tree representation is available (Table 1 columns 4, 5, 6), this indicates the proportion of leaf nodes that share the same label as their corresponding parent node (illustrated in color blue of Figure 2).
- **IN-IN similarity metric**: Only when a constituency tree representation is available (Table 1 columns 4, 5, 6), this measures the ratio of interior nodes that are connected by an edge and have the same label (illustrated in color orange of Figure 2).

The Leaf-Leaf metric tends to favor deeper trees, as deeper trees contain neighboring nodes that belong to finer grammatical categories and the same Argumentative Discourse Unit (ADU). However, an excessively deep tree is not desirable as it reduces the proximity between parent and child nodes. Metrics 2 and 3 are used to address this bias.

Indeed, regarding the Leaf-Leaf metric, we observe a stronger proximity between neighboring words within the same grammatical class compared to neighboring words when the grammatical structure is not considered. Additionally, the constituency tree with a maximum depth of 4 exhibits greater node similarity than the tree with a maximum depth of 2 or 3. As for the other two metrics, when the tree becomes too deep, the distance between words of the same grammatical class may become longer than that between words of different grammatical classes. This leads us to impose a limit on the maximum allowed tree depth. Setting a depth cap at 4 may not necessarily be the best choice, as the constituency tree with a maximum depth of 3 demonstrates better results concerning grammatical class similarity. In conclusion, these findings prompt us to experiment with a maximum depth of 3 for our models.

3.3 Fine grained stats

In this section, we explore the possibility of transforming the constituency tree to better align it with grammatical structures, with the aim of reducing tree complexity while maintaining its ability to segment into Argumentative Discourse Units (ADUs). To achieve this, we consider the grammatical class of nodes and identify those that exhibit higher coherence with the ADU segmentation. In practical terms, this involves examining the grammatical labels of linked nodes to determine whether parent and child nodes share the same label or differ in nature.

Metrics	Dataset	No tree	Depth 2	Depth 3	Depth 4
With Constituency tree					
Leaf-Leaf similarity	ARG2020	95.4 %	97.9%	98.2 %	**98.6 %**
	AURC	97.1 %	98.3%	98.4%	**98.6 %**
	CDCP	97.8 %	99.6 %	99.7 %	**99.7 %**
	UKP	91.9 %	97.9%	97.9%	**98.3 %**
Leaf-IN similarity	ARG2020	//	91.8%	**92.9 %**	59.2%
	AURC	//	90.2%	**91.3%**	84.2%
	CDCP	//	98.1%	**98.7 %**	68.9%
	UKP	//	89.2 %	**89.7 %**	49.8%
IN-IN similarity	ARG2020	//	91.7%	**95.1%**	88.3%
	AURC	//	88.5%	**93.3%**	92.9%
	CDCP	//	96.4%	**97.8%**	90.4%
	UKP	//	85.1 %	**92.1%**	84.3%
With reduced Constituency tree					
Leaf-Leaf similarity	ARG2020	//	//	98.2 %	**98.6%**
	AURC	//	//	98.4%	**98.6%**
	CDCP	//	//	**99.8%**	99.7%
	UKP	//	//	97.8%	**98.3%**
Leaf-IN similarity	ARG2020	//	//	**93 %**	59.2%
	AURC	//	//	**91.4%**	84.2%
	CDCP	//	//	**98.8%**	68.7%
	UKP	//	//	**90%**	50%
IN-IN similarity	ARG2020	//	//	**95 %**	88.3%
	AURC	//	//	**93.4%**	92.9%
	CDCP	//	//	**97.8%**	90.1%
	UKP	//	//	**92.1%**	84.4%

Table 1: Assessment of three measures to evaluate the suitability of the constituency tree representation. The first section of the table examines the evaluation of the constituency tree with varying the maximum depths allowed for the tree, while the second section focuses on the assessment of the tree reduction method from Subsection 3.3.

Table 2 provides a snapshot of the statistics observed in the datasets for the most common grammatical classes present in the constituency trees. We observe significant differences across the studied datasets. The argumentation structure in the AURC and CDCP datasets align more closely with the syntactic structure, compared to the UKP and ARG2020 datasets. This is consistent with the fact that the CDCP and AURC datasets are both online feedback datasets and UKP and ARG2020 are both student essays datasets.

When a particular constituency class consistently shares the same grammatical label as its children, it indicates coherence with the grammatical structure. In such cases, our reduction method involves simplifying the tree structure by grouping all its children and removing the intermediate interior node. In practice, we establish a threshold. If the ratio of identical labels exceeds this threshold as outlined in Table 2, we simplify the structure at this level. This adjustment reduces tree complexity while preserving the fact that words sharing the same parent node are more likely to have the same grammatical label.

For a tangible illustration based on Table 2, consider the AURC dataset where the tag "NML", representing nominal modifiers, has a ratio of 97%. This indicates that 97% of the time, its child elements bear the same labels. Given that a nominal modifier is a noun that adjusts another noun (effectively functioning as an adjective) it makes sense for them to share the same labels. Therefore, simplifying the structure to retain only the parent node "NML" and treating all the leaf nodes below it as its direct children appears to be an effective strategy.

The latter part of Table 1 illustrates the updated proximity statistics after the tree transformation. We observe that the three metrics are preserved

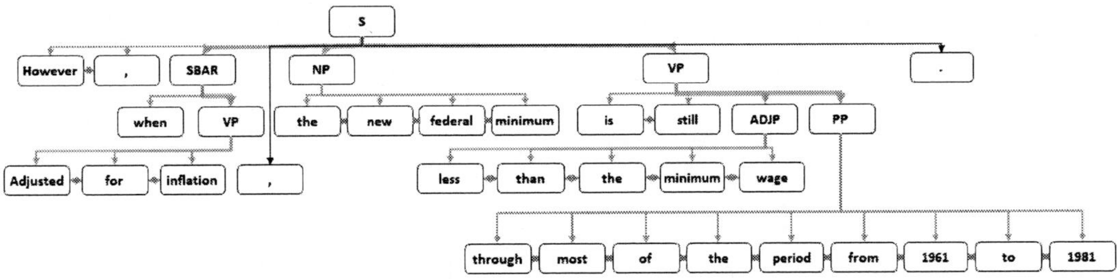

Figure 2: Visualization of the label proximity metrics on the constituency tree representation of the sentence: *"However, when adjusted for inflation, the new federal minimum is still less than the minimum wage through most of the period from 1961 to 1981."* from the AURC dataset. The blue arrows represent the edges analyzed for the Leaf-IN metric, the orange arrows for the IN-IN metric, and the red arrows for the Leaf-Leaf metric.

across all four datasets. We can thus reduce the complexity of the constituency tree in order the accelerate the training process of the models while hoping to preserve its capacity. We will evaluate this assumption in Section 5 and 6.

4 Presentation of our Model

In this section, we present a detailed overview of the architecture and components of our proposed model for argument unit recognition.

4.1 Baseline: Linear chain approach

The reference model, to which our model will be compared, has been introduced by Trautmann et al. (2020). It is composed of two modules. In the first module, the sentence is tokenized following the BERT tokenizer and the BERT model is fine-tuned for token classification, where the output of the last layer matches the number of classes of the dataset. In the second module, a linear chain Conditional Random Field (Lafferty et al., 2001) is applied to estimate the probability of each label class. The main intuition of this model is to leverage the BERT LLM "semantic knowledge" and then to improve the results by incorporating a linear chain dependency structure for the syntactic part. This takes advantage of neighbours dependency relations between words. The good results of this model lead us to use it as a competitive benchmark for our approach based on constituency trees as input representations of sentences.

4.2 Our model: Graph Neural Network approach

A major difficulty in choosing a graph neural layer architecture is that each sentence has a different tree representation. Hence, the model needs to be agnostic to the lack of completeness of the tree structures from the dataset. The message passing design enables to share the model weights among the network nodes, thus the results do not depend on the upfront global tree structure access. The Graph Attention Layer (GAT) (Veličković et al., 2018) allows to combine the attention mechanism with the graph structure in a message passing design, preserving the syntactic structural information of the sentence. In order to improve the model stability, adding multi-head attention layers is beneficial to the training step. The different heads are then aggregated in order to provide the next hidden states of the neural network. To leverage the dependency structure of the sentence, we integrate a multi-layer GAT (Graph Attention Network) model between the BERT module and the linear chain CRF. For the CRF, we use the implementation from (Gardner et al., 2017), which was present in the baseline model. The idea behind this architecture is the following. The GAT model outputs the probability of each label for each node in the graph. When subsequently employing a linear chain CRF, we retain only the leaf nodes to represent the sentence in a traditional linear chain format. As illustrated in Figure 3, first, the BERT language model outputs the sentence hidden representation. Next, the information is spread to the graph neighbours at each iteration. In that way, we expect to reach a better consistency between neighbour nodes when we train on a restricted dataset.

5 Experimental Setup

In the next sections, we present a comprehensive evaluation of our proposed model for argument unit recognition using constituency tree representations and GNNs with a CRF layer. We compare the performance of our model against existing approaches and analyze its effectiveness in capturing syntactic

Dataset	Parent node type	Number of same labels	Number of different labels	ratio
ARG2020	VP	25710	13911	65 %
	NP	18414	9767	65 %
	S	28169	14325	66%
	PP	9744	4097	68 %
	SBAR	8545	5099	63 %
	ADJP	1293	753	63 %
	NML	182	101	64%
	ADVP	344	211	62 %
AURC	VP	30342	3274	90 %
	NP	29792	2279	93 %
	S	28202	9181	75 %
	PP	12878	1173	92 %
	SBAR	9474	2517	79 %
	ADJP	2316	269	90 %
	NML	638	22	97 %
	ADVP	411	58	88 %
CDCP	VP	4112	1623	72 %
	NP	2608	840	76 %
	S	3960	1371	74 %
	PP	1253	386	76 %
	SBAR	1607	725	69 %
	ADJP	202	49	80 %
	NML	48	13	79 %
	ADVP	81	27	75 %
UKP	VP	25266	15789	61 %
	NP	17147	12534	57 %
	S	29179	23857	55 %
	PP	8952	7265	55 %
	SBAR	8210	6498	56 %
	ADJP	1400	1276	52 %
	NML	106	94	53 %
	ADVP	519	440	54 %

Table 2: Extracts from the metrics of Evaluation of fine grained stats. We present only the parent nodes that appear most frequently in the training dataset.

information from the constituency tree.

First, we describe the experimental setup and datasets used for evaluation

5.1 Data Source

ARG2020 (Alhindi and Ghosh, 2021) is an argument mining corpus annotated with argumentative structure composed of "claims" and "premises". It is composed of 145 English argumentative essays selected through the Writing Mentor Educational App. It is based on middle school students writing. The claims is defined as a potentially arguable statement that indicates a person is arguing for or arguing against something. The premises is defined as the reasons given by either for supporting or attacking the claims.

Argument Unit Recognition and Classification (AURC) (Trautmann et al., 2020) is a corpus for argument mining that includes annotations for argumentative structure information, capturing the polarity of arguments on a given topic. The corpus consists of 8000 sentences, evenly distributed across 8 topics. The authors distinguished between PRO (supporting), CON (opposing) arguments, and NON (non-argumentative) words for each topic, in order to construct sentence-level labels. Their labeling rule is as follows: if only NON words occur, the sentence is labeled as NON. If both NON and

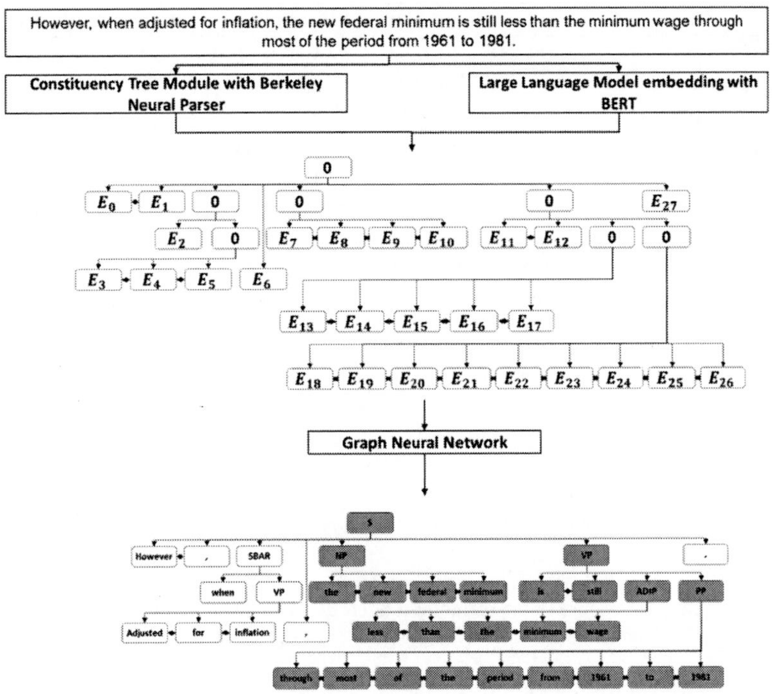

Figure 3: Illustration of the model architecture on an example of a sentence. We present the three distinct modules composing the model with their associated input/output. The colored node after the Graph Neural Network refers to the nodes where the label predicted in "PRO", this phrase is taken from the AURC dataset. The E_x refers to the embeddings from the BERT model, the interior nodes are initialized with the 0 vector.

only PRO (or only CON) words occur, the label PRO (or CON) is assigned. If both PRO and CON words occur, the label that appears more frequently is assigned. In (Trautmann et al., 2020), the authors distinguish between "in-domain" settings, where the domain of the arguments is present in both the training and test datasets, and "cross-domain" settings, where the domains in the test dataset are not found in the training dataset. In our experiments, we focus solely on the "in-domain" scenario.

The Cornell eRulemaking Corpus (CDCP) (Park and Cardie, 2018) is a corpus for argument mining that includes annotations for argumentative structure information, specifically capturing the evaluability of arguments. The corpus comprises 731 user comments on the Consumer Debt Collection Practices rule issued by the Consumer Financial Protection Bureau. The resulting dataset contains a total of 4931 elementary unit annotations and 1221 support relation annotations.

Argument Annotated Essays corpus (UKP) consists of a collection of persuasive essays gathered by (Stab and Gurevych, 2014). This essay corpus is equipped with annotations of argument components at the clause level, as well as argumentative relations. Specifically, it includes annotations for major claims, claims, and premises, which are interconnected through argumentative support and attack relations. The corpus was annotated by three raters, achieving an inter-annotator agreement of alpha = 0.72 for argument components and alpha = 0.81 for argumentative relations. In total, the corpus consists of 90 essays containing 1673 sentences.

The models are trained individually on each of the four datasets, conforming to the respective label schemes they offer. For comparison with the baseline, we adhere to the train-test splits presented in the original datasets' experiments when available. In cases where these are not provided, we employ a random sampler to allocate 20% of the sentences for testing and 80% for training. Subsequently, the sentences are segmented into chunks of 64 tokens each.

5.2 Constituency tree construction

One of the main advantages of incorporating a constituency tree into traditional methods is the

	Test Intervals	Best values	Relative parameters importance
Learning rate	10^{-5} to 10^{-3}	$2.8 \cdot 10^{-5}$	30 %
Maximum gradient allowed	10^{-1} to 10^{2}	9.7	49 %
Number of GAT layers	1 to 3	2	2 %
Number of unit per GAT layers	50 to 300	290 and 100	2 %
Number of heads per GAT layers	1 to 3	3 and 3	7 %
Number of linear layers	1 to 3	2	5 %
Number of unit per linear layers	50 to 250	100 and 100	5 %

Table 3: Feature importance of the BERT-GAT-CRF model with Constituency Tree evaluate on the AURC evaluation dataset.

	AURC	CDCP	ARG2020	UKP
BERT	68 %	80 %	75 %	81 %
BERT - CRF	69 %	81 %	75.5 %	81.6 %
BERT - GAT	64 %	75.5 %	75.2 %	79.3 %
BERT - GAT - CRF with Constituency Tree	72.8 %	81.5 %	**76.1 %**	**82.8 %**
BERT - GAT - CRF with Reduced Constituency Tree	**73.2 %**	**83.1 %**	75.9 %	81.4 %

Table 4: F1-score of the different models at token level on the test dataset.

increased proximity of words belonging to the same grammatical class compared to words that are merely adjacent in a linear sentence representation. This can be further illustrated by referring to the constituency tree depicted in Figure 1. In this sentence, the distribution of ADUs aligns with the grammatical structure of the sentence. For instance, although the words "inflation" and "the" are neighboring words in the sentence, they are positioned further apart in the constituency tree structure. This leads to improved identification of boundaries between ADUs.

For our preprocessing step, we employed a neural network model called the Berkeley Neural Parser (BENEPAR) (Kitaev and Klein, 2018), which has been trained on 11 different languages and is available with Spacy and works with GPUs. We utilized the weights provided by the model's development team for our experimentation.

5.3 Hyperparameters Optimization

The BERT-GAT-CRF model has a significantly larger number of hyperparameters compared to the BERT-CRF model. This is primarily attributed to the extensive hyperparameters associated with the GAT, such as the number of layers, units per layer, and number of heads. To determine the optimal hyperparameters for this model, we employed the Optuna library (Akiba et al., 2019). Optuna is a framework specifically designed for efficient hyperparameter optimization. To evaluate the relative importance of different hyperparameters in our model, we conducted experiments on the AURC dataset and presented the results in Table 3. Notably, we observed that the most influential hyperparameters are the learning rate and the maximum gradient value allowed. Empirically, we found that unconstrained gradients led the model to converge to a local optimum, where the label "NO" was assigned to every word. This local optimum emerges due to the dataset's imbalance, which tends to favor the absence of arguments.

6 Models Evaluation

6.1 Results Presentation

While the original paper by Trautmann et al. (2020) introduced metrics such as token level, span level, and sentence level, our focus lies primarily on improving argument border recognition rather than argument stance identification. Consequently, our model excels in token-level performance, showcasing superior results. However, our model achieves comparable outcomes at the sentence and span levels.

The results pertaining to token-level classification are outlined in Table 4. In accordance with the insights from Table 1, we computed our models with a maximum depth of 3. Our best-performing model consists of BERT-GNN-CRF with Reduced Constituency Tree. These outcomes highlight the significant advancements achieved by our proposed model in argument unit recognition. By leveraging the constituency tree representation, integrating GNNs and CRF, and incorporating reduced constituency trees, our model excels in capturing the intricacies of argument structures.

7 Conclusion

In conclusion, this research study introduces a novel method for identifying the boundary of ADUs using the sentence constituent tree representation. Our model effectively spreads information across the graph and achieves promising results on a small dataset.

Previously identified errors in these datasets include the incorrect recognition of argumentative segment spans and inaccurate classification of stances. In this study, we focus on improving the span detection problem and successfully enhance the method for identifying ADU boundaries.

However, it is worth noting that some argument mining datasets does not strictly adhere to grammatical correctness, as noted in (Trautmann et al., 2020). This limitation arises from sentences where subjects are absent, which hampers the performance of models relying solely on grammatical structure. This issue could be resolved by devising annotation rules that more strictly align with the syntactic structure of sentences. Furthermore, the second type of error, which pertains to position identification, is primarily attributed to the limitations of the BERT model. The dataset only provides sentences with a maximum length of 64, thereby restricting the available context for ADUs and impeding our model's capability. Many arguments require deeper domain knowledge to fully comprehend the underlying issues.

References

Yamen Ajjour, Wei-Fan Chen, Johannes Kiesel, Henning Wachsmuth, and Benno Stein. Unit segmentation of argumentative texts. In *Proceedings of the 4th Workshop on Argument Mining*, pages 118–128. Association for Computational Linguistics.

Takuya Akiba, Shotaro Sano, Toshihiko Yanase, Takeru Ohta, and Masanori Koyama. 2019. Optuna: A Next-generation Hyperparameter Optimization Framework. In *Proceedings of the 25th ACM SIGKDD International Conference on Knowledge Discovery & Data Mining*, KDD '19, pages 2623–2631, New York, NY, USA. Association for Computing Machinery.

Tariq Alhindi and Debanjan Ghosh. 2021. "Sharks are not the threat humans are": Argument Component Segmentation in School Student Essays. In *Proceedings of the 16th Workshop on Innovative Use of NLP for Building Educational Applications*, pages 210–222, Online. Association for Computational Linguistics.

Daniel Beck, Gholamreza Haffari, and Trevor Cohn. 2018. Graph-to-Sequence Learning using Gated Graph Neural Networks. In *Proceedings of the 56th Annual Meeting of the Association for Computational Linguistics (Volume 1: Long Papers)*, pages 273–283, Melbourne, Australia. Association for Computational Linguistics.

Lynn Carlson and Daniel Marcu. Discourse Tagging Reference Manual. page 87.

Stephen Crain and Mineharu Nakayama. 1987. Structure Dependence in Grammar Formation. *Language*, 63(3):522–543. Publisher: Linguistic Society of America.

Jacob Devlin, Ming-Wei Chang, Kenton Lee, and Kristina Toutanova. 2019. BERT: Pre-training of Deep Bidirectional Transformers for Language Understanding. In *Proceedings of the 2019 Conference of the North American Chapter of the Association for Computational Linguistics: Human Language Technologies, Volume 1 (Long and Short Papers)*, pages 4171–4186, Minneapolis, Minnesota. Association for Computational Linguistics.

Matt Gardner, Joel Grus, Mark Neumann, Oyvind Tafjord, Pradeep Dasigi, Nelson F. Liu, Matthew Peters, Michael Schmitz, and Luke S. Zettlemoyer. 2017. Allennlp: A deep semantic natural language processing platform.

Daniel Gildea and Martha Palmer. 2002. The Necessity of Parsing for Predicate Argument Recognition. In *Proceedings of the 40th Annual Meeting of the Association for Computational Linguistics*, pages 239–246, Philadelphia, Pennsylvania, USA. Association for Computational Linguistics.

Yohan Jo, Jacky Visser, Chris Reed, and Eduard Hovy. 2019. A Cascade Model for Proposition Extraction in Argumentation. In *Proceedings of the 6th Workshop on Argument Mining*, pages 11–24, Florence, Italy. Association for Computational Linguistics.

Nikita Kitaev and Dan Klein. 2018. Constituency Parsing with a Self-Attentive Encoder. In *Proceedings of the 56th Annual Meeting of the Association for Computational Linguistics (Volume 1: Long Papers)*, pages 2676–2686, Melbourne, Australia. Association for Computational Linguistics.

John D. Lafferty, Andrew McCallum, and Fernando C. N. Pereira. 2001. Conditional Random Fields: Probabilistic Models for Segmenting and Labeling Sequence Data. In *Proceedings of the Eighteenth International Conference on Machine Learning*, ICML '01, pages 282–289, San Francisco, CA, USA. Morgan Kaufmann Publishers Inc.

William Mann and Sandra Thompson. 1987. *Rhetorical Structure Theory: A Theory of Text Organization.*

Diego Marcheggiani and Ivan Titov. 2017. Encoding Sentences with Graph Convolutional Networks for Semantic Role Labeling. In *Proceedings of the 2017 Conference on Empirical Methods in Natural Language Processing*, pages 1506–1515, Copenhagen, Denmark. Association for Computational Linguistics.

Shikhar Murty, Pratyusha Sharma, Jacob Andreas, and Christopher D. Manning. 2022. Characterizing Intrinsic Compositionality in Transformers with Tree Projections. ArXiv:2211.01288 [cs].

Joonsuk Park and Claire Cardie. 2018. A Corpus of eRulemaking User Comments for Measuring Evaluability of Arguments. In *Proceedings of the Eleventh International Conference on Language Resources and Evaluation (LREC 2018)*, Miyazaki, Japan. European Language Resources Association (ELRA).

Christian Stab and Iryna Gurevych. 2014. Annotating Argument Components and Relations in Persuasive Essays. In *Proceedings of COLING 2014, the 25th International Conference on Computational Linguistics: Technical Papers*, pages 1501–1510, Dublin, Ireland. Dublin City University and Association for Computational Linguistics.

Manfred Stede and Maite Taboada. Annotation Guidelines for Rhetorical Structure.

Dietrich Trautmann. 2020. Aspect-Based Argument Mining. In *Proceedings of the 7th Workshop on Argument Mining*, pages 41–52, Online. Association for Computational Linguistics.

Dietrich Trautmann, Johannes Daxenberger, Christian Stab, Hinrich Schütze, and Iryna Gurevych. 2020. Fine-Grained Argument Unit Recognition and Classification. *Proceedings of the AAAI Conference on Artificial Intelligence*, 34(05):9048–9056. Number: 05.

Petar Veličković, Guillem Cucurull, Arantxa Casanova, Adriana Romero, Pietro Liò, and Yoshua Bengio. 2018. Graph Attention Networks.

Meishan Zhang. 2020. A Survey of Syntactic-Semantic Parsing Based on Constituent and Dependency Structures. *arXiv:2006.11056 [cs]*. ArXiv: 2006.11056.

Stance-Aware Re-Ranking for Non-factual Comparative Queries

Jan Heinrich Reimer and **Alexander Bondarenko** and **Maik Fröbe** and **Matthias Hagen**
Friedrich-Schiller-Universität Jena

Abstract

We propose a re-ranking approach to improve the retrieval effectiveness for non-factual comparative queries like 'Which city is better, London or Paris?' based on whether the results express a stance towards the comparison objects (London vs. Paris) or not. Applied to the 26 runs submitted to the Touché 2022 task on comparative argument retrieval, our stance-aware re-ranking significantly improves the retrieval effectiveness for all runs when perfect oracle-style stance labels are available. With our most effective practical stance detector based on GPT-3.5 (F_1 of 0.49 on four stance classes), our re-ranking still improves the effectiveness for all runs but only six improvements are significant. Artificially "deteriorating" the oracle-style labels, we further find that an F_1 of 0.90 for stance detection is necessary to significantly improve the retrieval effectiveness for the best run via stance-aware re-ranking.

1 Introduction

Argument retrieval is the task of identifying and ranking text passages or documents based on their topical relevance to an argumentative query and based on their argumentativeness (i.e., the presence and quality of arguments). Current argument search engines like args.me (Wachsmuth et al., 2017) or ArgumenText (Stab et al., 2018) mainly focus on retrieving pro and con arguments on socially relevant and potentially controversial topics like 'nuclear energy' or 'plastic bottles' but they do not directly target to find pros and cons for the different options in "everyday" non-factual comparisons like 'Which city is better, London or Paris?'.

Such information needs were in the focus of the comparative argument retrieval task at the Touché 2022 lab (Bondarenko et al., 2022b). Given a query with two comparison objects (e.g., the London vs. Paris example), the goal was to retrieve results that contain arguments for or against either object. Many participants of the task improved over a BM25 baseline (Robertson et al., 1994) by using neural (re-)ranking models like ColBERT (Khattab and Zaharia, 2020) or mono- and duoT5 (Pradeep et al., 2021), and by taking estimated argument quality into account. Still, none of the participants successfully exploited stance information for the ranking (i.e., whether a result expresses a stance on the comparison objects or not) even though stance detection was also offered as a subtask at Touché.

We close this gap and, as our first contribution, suggest a simple stance-aware re-ranking approach that can be applied to the retrieval results for any comparative query: rank documents that do not express a stance on the comparison objects below any documents that do. In an evaluation on the 26 runs submitted to the Touché 2022 task, we find that our re-ranking significantly improves the retrieval effectiveness of all runs when using the task's official ground truth stance labels (i.e., assuming a "perfect" oracle-style stance detector). When instead using the participants' stance predictions, hardly any run's effectiveness can be improved as the participants' stance detectors are not effective enough ($F_1 \leq 0.31$ on the four classes 'pro first object', 'pro second object', 'both equal', and 'no stance').

As our second contribution, we thus target a better practical stance detection effectiveness and compare three approaches: (1) a fine-tuned sentiment-prompted RoBERTa model (Liu et al., 2019), (2) a zero-shot stance detector based on a pre-trained Flan-T5 model (Chung et al., 2022), and (3) GPT-3.5 (Brown et al., 2020) with few-shot prompting. Among these, the GPT-3.5-based stance detector is the most effective with an F_1 of 0.49. Using the stances detected with GPT-3.5, our stance-aware re-ranking can again improve the retrieval effectiveness of all 26 runs but only 6 of the improvements (23%) are significant. In further experiments, we artificially perturb the ground truth stance labels to analyze what stance detection effectiveness is necessary to significantly improve

Proceedings of the 10th Workshop on Argument Mining, pages 45–51
December 7, 2023.

the retrieval effectiveness of the best run via stance-aware re-ranking and find that an F_1 of 0.90 is required. Our code and data are publicly available.[1]

2 Re-Ranking Scenario: Touché 2022

Our re-ranking scenario is that of the Touché 2022 shared task on comparative argument retrieval. Given one of 50 non-factual comparative queries, relevant text passages from a collection of about one million passages should be retrieved and ranked, and (optionally) their stances be detected. For our experiments, we use the 26 runs (ranked lists of results) submitted to the task, as well as the relevance + quality assessments and the stance labels that the task organizers provided (Bondarenko et al., 2022b). In the task, the retrieval effectiveness of the submitted runs was evaluated using nDCG@5 (Järvelin and Kekäläinen, 2002) for topical relevance and for argument quality, and the stance detection effectiveness was evaluated using macro-avg. F_1 on the four stance classes.

3 Stance-Aware Re-Ranking

Interestingly, none of the Touché participants successfully used stance information in their retrieval approaches. This is somewhat surprising as, intuitively, helpful retrieval results for non-factual comparative queries should express some stance towards the comparison objects (either favoring one of the objects or stating that both are equal). Our suggested re-ranking approach thus simply moves all results that do not express a stance to the end of a ranking (i.e., below any result that expresses a stance), while preserving the relative order of the documents that express a stance. Table 1 shows a respective example for a top-5 re-ranking. We have implemented this stance-aware re-ranking approach in the PyTerrier framework (Macdonald et al., 2021) as a module that expects a ranking and stances for the individual results as inputs.

4 Initial Re-Ranking Experiments

In our initial experiments, we re-rank the top-5 results of each of the 26 runs submitted to Touché based on the task's ground truth stance labels (i.e., assuming "perfect" oracle-style stance detection) or based on the participants' detected stances. Following the Touché setup, we report nDCG@5 scores for relevance and for quality and refer to the runs by their team names (e.g., Aldo Nadi or Captain L.).

[1]Code and data: github.com/webis-de/ArgMining-23

Table 1: Example of our stance-aware re-ranking. Results with no stance ('$\perp$') are moved below all results with a stance ('$O_{1/2}$': pro first / second object; '=': both equal) that keep their original relative ordering.

Approach	**Rank**				
	1	2	3	4	5
Original run	$\perp$	O_1	$\perp$	$=$	O_2
Our re-ranking	O_1	$=$	O_2	$\perp$	$\perp$

4.1 Oracle-Style Stances

To demonstrate the potential of our stance-aware re-ranking, we first re-rank based on "perfect" stances from the Touché ground truth. The results in column 'Oracle' of Table 2 show that our re-ranking then significantly improves almost all nDCG@5 scores—only the improvement of the quality score of the quality-wise best run (Aldo Nadi A) is not significant. Interestingly, the scores of the oracle-style re-ranking often are close to a run's hypothetical optimal top-5 re-ranking (column 'Opt.').

Comparing a run's rank in the original leaderboard (column '#' in 'Touché') to the potential rank if the oracle-style re-ranking was applied to only that run ('#' in 'Oracle'; 'Δ' indicates the rank change), one can, for instance, observe that the relevance-wise top-3 runs each could reach rank 1.

4.2 Touché Participants' Detected Stances

When we re-rank based on the participants' detected stances, the effectiveness of hardly any run can be improved (column 'Orig.' in Table 2); some even get worse (e.g., Captain L. B). Compared to the oracle scenario, the participants' stance detection is not effective enough ($F_1 \leq 0.31$). We thus aim to improve the practical stance detection.

5 Improving the Stance Detection

Targeting better practical stance detection, we compare three approaches: (1) a fine-tuned sentiment-prompted RoBERTa model (Liu et al., 2019), (2) a zero-shot stance detector based on a pre-trained Flan-T5 model (Chung et al., 2022), and (3) GPT-3.5 (Brown et al., 2020) with few-shot prompting. Following Touché, we use macro-avg. F_1 to compare the detection effectiveness (class distribution: 'pro first object' 19%, 'pro second object' 13%, 'both equal' 20%, 'no stance' 48%).

For the RoBERTa-based detector, we fine-tune a RoBERTa model using the sentiment-prompting

Table 2: Effectiveness (as nDCG@5) of the runs submitted to the Touché 2022 task on comparative argument retrieval (referred to by their Touché team names) and with our stance-aware re-ranking; originally submitted ('Touché'), best achievable when re-ranking the top-5 ('Opt.'), and after stance-aware re-ranking of the top-5 with: ground truth stance labels ('Oracle'), simulated labels with an F_1 of about 0.75 ('Simul.'), stance detected with GPT-3.5, Flan-T5, or RoBERTa, and with a team's original detection approach (two teams did not detect stance; grayed out). The '#' columns denote an approach's rank in the task leaderboard; for re-rankings, these columns give the rank the re-ranking would have achieved if all other runs would stay as submitted to Touché. Differences in effectiveness or rank compared to the originally submitted run are shown in the 'Δ' columns; statistically significant effectiveness differences are bold-faced (Student's t-test, $\alpha = 0.05$, Bonferroni correction for the multiple tests).

Run	Touché		Opt.	Oracle (F_1=1.00)				Simul. ($F_1 \approx$0.75)				GPT-3.5 (F_1=0.49)				Flan-T5 (F_1=0.39)				RoBERTa (F_1=0.34)				Orig. ($F_1 \leq$0.31)			
	Score	#	Score	Score	Δ	#	Δ	Score	Δ	#	Δ	Score	Δ	#	Δ	Score	Δ	#	Δ	Score	Δ	#	Δ	Score	Δ	#	Δ
Topical relevance																											
Captain L. B	0.76	1	0.81	**0.79**	(+0.03)	1	(0)	0.78	(+0.02)	1	(0)	0.78	(+0.02)	1	(0)	0.76	(±0.00)	1	(0)	0.77	(+0.01)	1	(0)	0.75	(−0.01)	2	(↓1)
Captain L. A	0.76	2	0.82	**0.79**	(+0.03)	1	(↑1)	0.77	(+0.01)	1	(↑1)	0.78	(+0.02)	1	(↑1)	0.76	(±0.00)	1	(↑1)	0.76	(±0.00)	1	(↑1)	0.75	(−0.01)	3	(↓1)
Captain L. D	0.75	3	0.81	**0.78**	(+0.03)	1	(↑2)	0.77	(+0.02)	1	(↑2)	0.77	(+0.02)	1	(↑2)	0.76	(+0.01)	1	(↑2)	0.75	(±0.00)	3	(0)	0.75	(±0.00)	3	(0)
Captain L. E	0.73	4	0.79	**0.75**	(+0.02)	4	(0)	0.74	(+0.01)	4	(0)	0.74	(+0.01)	4	(0)	0.72	(−0.01)	4	(0)	0.73	(±0.00)	4	(0)	0.73	(±0.00)	4	(0)
Captain L. C	0.72	5	0.78	**0.75**	(+0.03)	4	(↑1)	0.75	(+0.03)	4	(↑1)	0.74	(+0.02)	4	(↑1)	0.72	(±0.00)	5	(0)	0.73	(+0.01)	5	(0)	0.72	(±0.00)	5	(0)
Aldo Nadi E	0.71	6	0.77	**0.74**	(+0.03)	4	(↑2)	0.73	(+0.02)	4	(↑2)	0.72	(+0.01)	6	(0)	0.71	(±0.00)	6	(0)	0.71	(±0.00)	6	(0)	0.71	(±0.00)	6	(0)
Aldo Nadi A	0.70	7	0.75	**0.73**	(+0.03)	4	(↑3)	0.72	(+0.02)	6	(↑1)	0.70	(±0.00)	7	(0)	0.71	(+0.01)	6	(↑1)	0.70	(±0.00)	7	(0)	0.70	(±0.00)	7	(0)
Aldo Nadi D	0.67	8	0.73	**0.70**	(+0.03)	7	(↑1)	0.69	(+0.02)	8	(0)	0.68	(+0.01)	8	(0)	0.68	(+0.01)	8	(0)	0.68	(+0.01)	8	(0)	0.67	(±0.00)	8	(0)
Aldo Nadi C	0.64	9	0.70	**0.67**	(+0.03)	8	(↑1)	**0.67**	(+0.03)	9	(0)	0.65	(+0.01)	9	(0)	0.64	(±0.00)	9	(0)	0.63	(−0.01)	9	(0)	0.64	(±0.00)	9	(0)
Katana A	0.62	10	0.69	**0.65**	(+0.03)	9	(↑1)	**0.64**	(+0.02)	9	(↑1)	**0.65**	(+0.03)	9	(↑1)	0.63	(+0.01)	10	(0)	0.62	(±0.00)	10	(0)	0.62	(±0.00)	10	(0)
Katana C	0.60	11	0.67	**0.64**	(+0.04)	9	(↑2)	**0.63**	(+0.03)	10	(↑1)	**0.62**	(+0.02)	10	(↑1)	0.61	(+0.01)	11	(0)	0.60	(±0.00)	11	(0)	0.60	(±0.00)	11	(0)
Captain T. A	0.57	12	0.64	**0.61**	(+0.04)	11	(↑1)	**0.61**	(+0.04)	11	(↑1)	0.59	(+0.02)	12	(0)	0.58	(+0.01)	12	(0)	0.58	(+0.01)	12	(0)	0.57	(±0.00)	12	(0)
Captain T. B	0.57	13	0.64	**0.61**	(+0.04)	11	(↑2)	0.59	(+0.02)	12	(↑1)	0.58	(+0.01)	12	(↑1)	0.57	(±0.00)	13	(0)	0.57	(±0.00)	13	(0)	0.57	(±0.00)	13	(0)
Captain T. C	0.56	14	0.62	**0.59**	(+0.03)	12	(↑2)	0.58	(+0.02)	12	(↑2)	0.57	(+0.01)	13	(↑1)	0.57	(+0.01)	14	(0)	0.56	(±0.00)	15	(↓1)	0.56	(±0.00)	14	(0)
Katana B	0.56	15	0.63	**0.60**	(+0.04)	11	(↑4)	**0.59**	(+0.03)	12	(↑3)	0.58	(+0.02)	12	(↑3)	0.56	(±0.00)	16	(↓1)	0.56	(±0.00)	15	(0)	0.56	(±0.00)	15	(0)
Captain T. E	0.56	16	0.64	**0.60**	(+0.04)	12	(↑4)	**0.59**	(+0.03)	12	(↑4)	0.58	(+0.02)	12	(↑4)	0.57	(+0.01)	14	(↑2)	0.56	(±0.00)	16	(0)	0.56	(±0.00)	16	(0)
Aldo Nadi B	0.55	17	0.61	**0.58**	(+0.03)	12	(↑5)	**0.57**	(+0.02)	14	(↑3)	0.56	(+0.01)	16	(↑1)	0.55	(±0.00)	17	(0)	0.55	(±0.00)	17	(0)	0.55	(±0.00)	17	(0)
Captain T. D	0.54	18	0.61	**0.58**	(+0.04)	12	(↑6)	0.56	(+0.02)	16	(↑2)	0.56	(+0.02)	16	(↑2)	0.54	(±0.00)	18	(0)	0.54	(±0.00)	18	(0)	0.54	(±0.00)	18	(0)
Olivier A. A	0.48	19	0.57	**0.55**	(+0.07)	17	(↑2)	**0.53**	(+0.05)	19	(0)	**0.52**	(+0.04)	19	(0)	0.50	(+0.02)	19	(0)	**0.51**	(+0.03)	19	(0)	0.49	(+0.01)	19	(0)
Puss in B. A	0.47	20	0.55	**0.52**	(+0.05)	19	(↑1)	**0.50**	(+0.03)	19	(↑1)	0.49	(+0.02)	19	(↑1)	0.47	(±0.00)	20	(0)	0.47	(±0.00)	20	(0)	0.47	(±0.00)	20	(0)
Grimjack E	0.42	21	0.48	**0.46**	(+0.04)	21	(0)	**0.45**	(+0.03)	21	(0)	0.44	(+0.02)	21	(0)	0.42	(±0.00)	21	(0)	0.43	(+0.01)	21	(0)	0.42	(±0.00)	21	(0)
Grimjack C	0.38	22	0.46	**0.44**	(+0.06)	21	(↑1)	**0.41**	(+0.03)	22	(0)	**0.41**	(+0.03)	22	(0)	0.39	(+0.01)	22	(0)	0.40	(+0.02)	22	(0)	0.38	(±0.00)	22	(0)
Grimjack B	0.38	23	0.46	**0.44**	(+0.06)	21	(↑2)	**0.42**	(+0.04)	22	(↑1)	**0.41**	(+0.03)	22	(↑1)	0.39	(+0.01)	22	(↑1)	0.40	(+0.02)	22	(↑1)	0.38	(±0.00)	23	(0)
Grimjack D	0.35	24	0.41	**0.38**	(+0.03)	22	(↑2)	0.36	(+0.01)	24	(0)	0.36	(+0.01)	24	(0)	0.35	(±0.00)	24	(0)	0.35	(±0.00)	24	(0)	0.35	(±0.00)	24	(0)
Grimjack A	0.34	25	0.43	**0.40**	(+0.06)	22	(↑3)	**0.38**	(+0.04)	22	(↑3)	**0.38**	(+0.04)	22	(↑3)	0.37	(+0.03)	24	(↑1)	0.37	(+0.03)	24	(↑1)	0.34	(±0.00)	25	(0)
Asuna A	0.26	26	0.34	**0.32**	(+0.06)	26	(0)	**0.30**	(+0.04)	26	(0)	0.28	(+0.02)	26	(0)	0.27	(+0.01)	26	(0)	0.27	(+0.01)	26	(0)	0.26	(±0.00)	26	(0)
Argument quality																											
Aldo Nadi A	0.77	1	0.83	0.80	(+0.03)	1	(0)	0.78	(+0.01)	1	(0)	0.78	(+0.01)	1	(0)	0.78	(+0.01)	1	(0)	0.78	(+0.01)	1	(0)	0.77	(±0.00)	1	(0)
Aldo Nadi C	0.76	2	0.81	**0.79**	(+0.03)	1	(↑1)	0.78	(+0.02)	1	(↑1)	0.77	(+0.01)	2	(0)	0.76	(±0.00)	2	(0)	0.76	(±0.00)	2	(0)	0.76	(±0.00)	2	(0)
Aldo Nadi E	0.75	3	0.80	**0.77**	(+0.02)	2	(↑1)	**0.77**	(+0.02)	2	(↑1)	0.75	(±0.00)	3	(0)	0.74	(−0.01)	3	(0)	0.75	(±0.00)	3	(0)	0.75	(±0.00)	3	(0)
Captain L. B	0.74	4	0.82	**0.77**	(+0.03)	2	(↑2)	**0.77**	(+0.03)	2	(↑2)	**0.77**	(+0.03)	2	(↑2)	0.76	(+0.02)	3	(↑1)	0.75	(+0.01)	3	(↑1)	0.74	(±0.00)	5	(↓1)
Captain L. A	0.74	5	0.82	**0.77**	(+0.03)	2	(↑3)	**0.77**	(+0.03)	2	(↑3)	**0.77**	(+0.03)	2	(↑3)	**0.76**	(+0.02)	3	(↑2)	0.75	(+0.01)	3	(↑2)	0.74	(±0.00)	5	(0)
Captain L. D	0.73	6	0.79	**0.75**	(+0.02)	4	(↑2)	0.74	(+0.01)	4	(↑2)	**0.75**	(+0.02)	3	(↑3)	**0.75**	(+0.02)	4	(↑2)	0.73	(±0.00)	6	(0)	0.73	(±0.00)	6	(0)
Captain L. E	0.71	7	0.76	**0.73**	(+0.02)	7	(0)	0.72	(+0.01)	7	(0)	0.72	(+0.01)	7	(0)	0.72	(+0.01)	7	(0)	0.71	(±0.00)	7	(0)	0.71	(±0.00)	7	(0)
Captain L. C	0.70	8	0.77	**0.72**	(+0.02)	7	(↑1)	0.71	(+0.01)	7	(↑1)	**0.72**	(+0.02)	7	(↑1)	0.70	(±0.00)	8	(0)	0.70	(±0.00)	8	(0)	0.70	(±0.00)	8	(0)
Aldo Nadi D	0.66	9	0.73	**0.69**	(+0.03)	9	(0)	0.68	(+0.02)	9	(0)	0.68	(+0.02)	9	(0)	0.67	(+0.01)	9	(0)	0.68	(+0.02)	9	(0)	0.66	(±0.00)	9	(0)
Katana C	0.64	10	0.71	**0.67**	(+0.03)	9	(↑1)	**0.68**	(+0.04)	9	(↑1)	0.66	(+0.02)	9	(↑1)	0.66	(+0.02)	10	(0)	0.65	(+0.01)	10	(0)	0.64	(±0.00)	10	(0)
Katana A	0.64	11	0.72	**0.68**	(+0.04)	9	(↑2)	**0.67**	(+0.03)	9	(↑2)	**0.67**	(+0.03)	9	(↑2)	0.66	(+0.02)	10	(↑1)	0.65	(+0.01)	10	(↑1)	0.64	(±0.00)	11	(0)
Katana B	0.64	12	0.70	**0.67**	(+0.03)	9	(↑3)	**0.66**	(+0.02)	9	(↑3)	0.66	(+0.02)	10	(↑2)	0.64	(±0.00)	12	(0)	0.64	(±0.00)	11	(↑1)	0.64	(±0.00)	12	(0)
Captain T. E	0.60	13	0.67	**0.63**	(+0.03)	13	(0)	**0.62**	(+0.02)	13	(0)	**0.62**	(+0.02)	13	(0)	0.61	(+0.01)	13	(0)	0.60	(±0.00)	13	(0)	0.60	(±0.00)	13	(0)
Captain T. B	0.59	14	0.65	**0.62**	(+0.03)	13	(↑1)	0.61	(+0.02)	13	(↑1)	0.61	(+0.02)	13	(↑1)	0.60	(+0.01)	13	(↑1)	0.59	(±0.00)	14	(0)	0.59	(±0.00)	14	(0)
Captain T. A	0.59	15	0.65	**0.62**	(+0.03)	13	(↑2)	**0.62**	(+0.03)	13	(↑2)	0.61	(+0.02)	13	(↑2)	0.60	(+0.01)	14	(↑1)	0.59	(±0.00)	15	(0)	0.59	(±0.00)	15	(0)
Captain T. C	0.58	16	0.64	**0.61**	(+0.03)	13	(↑3)	0.60	(+0.02)	13	(↑3)	0.60	(+0.02)	13	(↑3)	0.59	(+0.01)	15	(↑1)	0.58	(±0.00)	16	(0)	0.58	(±0.00)	16	(0)
Olivier A. A	0.57	17	0.65	**0.62**	(+0.05)	13	(↑4)	**0.61**	(+0.04)	13	(↑4)	**0.61**	(+0.04)	13	(↑4)	0.59	(+0.02)	16	(↑1)	0.59	(+0.02)	15	(↑2)	0.58	(+0.01)	17	(0)
Aldo Nadi B	0.57	18	0.63	**0.60**	(+0.03)	13	(↑5)	0.58	(+0.01)	16	(↑2)	0.58	(+0.01)	17	(↑1)	0.58	(+0.01)	17	(↑1)	0.58	(+0.01)	16	(↑2)	0.57	(±0.00)	18	(0)
Captain T. D	0.57	19	0.65	**0.61**	(+0.04)	13	(↑6)	**0.60**	(+0.03)	13	(↑6)	**0.59**	(+0.02)	15	(↑4)	0.58	(+0.01)	17	(↑2)	0.57	(±0.00)	17	(↑2)	0.57	(±0.00)	19	(0)
Puss in B. A	0.48	20	0.54	**0.51**	(+0.02)	20	(0)	0.49	(+0.01)	20	(0)	0.49	(+0.01)	20	(0)	0.49	(+0.01)	20	(0)	0.50	(+0.02)	20	(0)	0.48	(±0.00)	20	(0)
Grimjack E	0.40	21	0.47	**0.44**	(+0.04)	21	(0)	0.42	(+0.02)	21	(0)	**0.42**	(+0.02)	21	(0)	0.41	(+0.01)	21	(0)	**0.43**	(+0.03)	21	(0)	0.40	(±0.00)	21	(0)
Grimjack D	0.37	22	0.42	**0.39**	(+0.02)	22	(0)	0.38	(+0.01)	22	(0)	0.38	(+0.01)	22	(0)	0.38	(+0.01)	22	(0)	0.37	(±0.00)	22	(0)	0.37	(±0.00)	22	(0)
Grimjack C	0.36	23	0.44	**0.41**	(+0.05)	21	(↑2)	**0.40**	(+0.04)	22	(↑1)	**0.39**	(+0.03)	22	(↑1)	**0.39**	(+0.03)	22	(↑1)	**0.40**	(+0.04)	22	(↑1)	0.36	(±0.00)	23	(0)
Grimjack B	0.36	24	0.44	**0.41**	(+0.05)	21	(↑3)	**0.40**	(+0.04)	22	(↑2)	**0.39**	(+0.03)	22	(↑2)	**0.39**	(+0.03)	22	(↑2)	**0.40**	(+0.04)	22	(↑2)	0.36	(±0.00)	24	(0)
Grimjack A	0.34	25	0.42	**0.39**	(+0.05)	22	(↑3)	**0.38**	(+0.04)	22	(↑3)	**0.38**	(+0.04)	22	(↑3)	**0.38**	(+0.04)	22	(↑3)	0.36	(+0.02)	25	(0)	0.34	(±0.00)	25	(0)
Asuna A	0.33	26	0.42	**0.38**	(+0.05)	22	(↑4)	**0.37**	(+0.04)	22	(↑4)	0.35	(+0.02)	25	(↑1)	0.35	(+0.02)	25	(↑1)	0.35	(+0.02)	25	(↑1)	0.33	(±0.00)	26	(0)

idea and data of Bondarenko et al. (2022a). For the Flan-T5-based detector, we let Flan-T5 predict stances for each sentence in a passage (to avoid truncation at 512 tokens) using 4 zero-shot prompts (one per comparison object and pro/con) and then aggregate the stances (prompts and aggregation: Appendix A). Finally, for the GPT-3.5-based detector, we few-shot prompt GPT-3.5[2] with four examples (one per stance) that consist of a comparative query, two comparison objects, a text passage, and a stance + short explanation (prompt: Appendix B).

Using GPT-3.5-based stances (with an F_1 of 0.49, it is our most effective practical stance detector), our re-ranking approach can improve all nDCG@5 scores, but only 6 of the relevance-wise (23%) and 12 of the quality-wise improvements (46%) are significant (column 'GPT-3.5' in Table 2). The relevance-wise top-3 runs each would reach rank 1 after re-ranking, while the quality-wise best run cannot be "dethroned". The Flan-T5-based stances (F_1 of 0.39) also suffice to move the relevance-wise top-3 runs to rank 1 (column 'Flan-T5' in Table 2), while for the RoBERTa-based stances (F_1 of 0.34) only the relevance-wise second run could make it to the top (column 'RoBERTa' in Table 2).

6 Testing Limits with Simulated Stances

To analyze the (potential) impact of stance detectors that are more effective than our currently most effective practical approach (GPT-3.5-based; F_1 of 0.49), we gradually artificially deteriorate the ground truth stances as follows. From the passages with ground truth stance labels, we iteratively randomly select one without replacement and sample a stance label from the ground truth label distribution (O_1: 19%, O_2: 13%, =: 20%, $\perp$: 48%; a sampled label for a passage could be the same as in the ground truth) until the F_1 of the perturbed ground truth falls below a desired stopping threshold. Using this process, we simulate "stance detectors" with F_1 scores of 0.95, 0.9, 0.85, ..., 0.25, 0.2. For each threshold, we run the process ten times with different random seeds to obtain ten perturbed ground truths per target F_1 score. The ten perturbed ground truths are then each used to re-rank a run's retrieval results and the resulting ten nDCG@5 scores are averaged—to somewhat smooth out possible randomization effects.

[2]Accessed via its API on January 19, 2023; default parameters (model: text-davinci-003, temp.: 0.0, max tokens: 64, top-p: 1.0, frequency penalty: 0.0, presence penalty: 0.0).

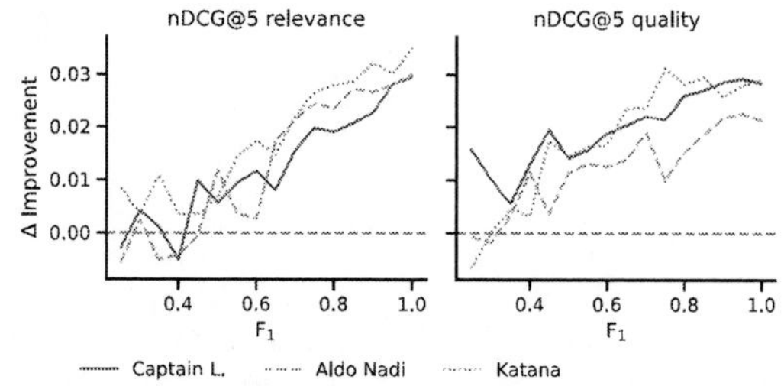

Figure 1: Effectiveness improvements of the top-3 teams' best runs when re-ranked with stance labels of the simulated target F_1 scores. For each target F_1 score, the improvement is averaged over the re-rankings with the ten simulated ground truths of that F_1 score. The 16 actually discrete improvement values per run are connected as line plots for a better visual discriminability.

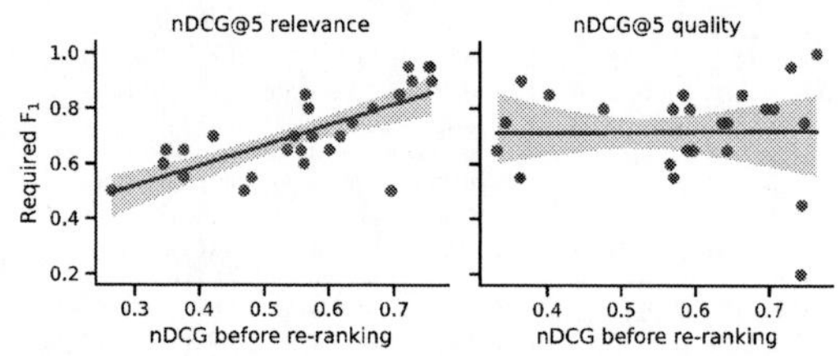

Figure 2: Minimum simulated stance detection F_1 scores for which the stance-aware re-ranking significantly improves an original Touché run (given by their nDCG@5 score before re-ranking). For each F_1 score, the improvement is averaged over the re-rankings with the ten simulated ground truths of that F_1 score.

As an example, column 'Simul.' in Table 2 shows the effects of a simulated stance detection with an F_1 of 0.75—midst of the perfect oracle and our currently best practical detector (GPT-3.5-based). One can observe that the $F_1 = 0.75$-based re-ranking improves the effectiveness scores of all runs, as is the case with GPT-3.5-based stances, and that a few more of the differences are significant—none of the relevance-wise top-8, though.

To clarify whether there is a relationship between stance detection F_1 and retrieval effectiveness improvement, Figure 1 shows the effectiveness scores when re-ranking the top-3 teams' best runs with the perturbed ground truths of different target stance detection F_1 scores. One can clearly observe that an increasing stance detection F_1 yields increased retrieval effectiveness improvements (relevance and quality; trends similar for other runs and teams).

The minimally needed stance detection F_1 so that the respective stance-aware re-ranking significantly improves an original run is shown in Figure 2 (runs given by their initial nDCG@5 scores). As for the relevance-wise improvements, one can observe a clear trend that runs with a better initial effectiveness require better stance detection to yield significant improvements. For the relevance-wise best runs, even almost perfect stance detection F_1 scores of 0.9 or 0.95 are needed to yield significant relevance-wise improvements.

As for the quality-wise improvements, no clear trend is observable. Two "outliers" of runs with a good initial effectiveness only require some rather low stance detection F_1 for significant improvements, but many runs with quite different initial quality-wise effectiveness require pretty high F_1 scores. Interestingly, the quality-wise best run Aldo Nadi A can never be significantly improved, even with perfect oracle-style stance labels.

7 Conclusion

We have proposed a simple stance-aware re-ranking approach for non-factual comparative queries that just moves results that do not express a stance on the comparison objects below any results that do. For all 26 runs submitted to the Touché 2022 task on comparative argument retrieval, our re-ranking can significantly improve the retrieval effectiveness when using the official Touché stance labels (i.e., assuming a "perfect" oracle-style stance detector). Then again, re-ranking based on the stances detected by the task participants ($F_1 \leq 0.31$) hardly improves any run. We thus experimented with other stance detectors to achieve better practical stance effectiveness. Using our most effective detector (GPT-3.5-based; F_1 of 0.49), the re-ranking can again improve the retrieval effectiveness for all 26 runs but only 6 of the relevance-wise and 12 of the quality-wise improvements are significant. In a final experiment with controlled perturbation of the ground truth stances, we found that better stance detection effectiveness tends to yield better re-ranking effectiveness and that a stance detection F_1 of 0.90 is necessary to significantly improve the relevance-wise most effective run.

Substantially improving the practical stance detection effectiveness thus is an interesting direction for future work that could also be the basis for a diversified result presentation: splitting the results into three separate lists for 'pro first object', 'pro second object', and 'both equal'. Besides, our re-ranking approach does not yet consider any potential confidence scores of a stance detection model and also no potentially predicted stance "magnitude". Developing stance detectors that assign a confidence or stance magnitude might actually be helpful to further improve the stance-aware re-ranking (e.g., to rank results with high-confidence stances above the ones with low confidence).

Acknowledgments

This work has been partially supported by the DFG (German Research Foundation) through the project "ACQuA 2.0: Answering Comparative Questions with Arguments" (project 376430233) as part of the priority program "RATIO: Robust Argumentation Machines" (SPP 1999).

References

Alexander Bondarenko, Yamen Ajjour, Valentin Dittmar, Niklas Homann, Pavel Braslavski, and Matthias Hagen. 2022a. Towards understanding and answering comparative questions. In *Proceedings of WSDM 2022*, pages 66–74.

Alexander Bondarenko, Maik Fröbe, Johannes Kiesel, Shahbaz Syed, Timon Gurcke, Meriem Beloucif, Alexander Panchenko, Chris Biemann, Benno Stein, Henning Wachsmuth, Martin Potthast, and Matthias Hagen. 2022b. Overview of Touché 2022: Argument retrieval. In *Proceedings of CLEF 2022*, pages 311–336.

Tom B. Brown, Benjamin Mann, Nick Ryder, Melanie Subbiah, Jared Kaplan, Prafulla Dhariwal, Arvind Neelakantan, Pranav Shyam, Girish Sastry, Amanda Askell, Sandhini Agarwal, Ariel Herbert-Voss, Gretchen Krueger, Tom Henighan, Rewon Child, Aditya Ramesh, Daniel M. Ziegler, Jeffrey Wu, Clemens Winter, Christopher Hesse, Mark Chen, Eric Sigler, Mateusz Litwin, Scott Gray, Benjamin Chess, Jack Clark, Christopher Berner, Sam McCandlish, Alec Radford, Ilya Sutskever, and Dario Amodei. 2020. Language models are few-shot learners. In *Proceedings of NeurIPS 2020*.

Hyung Won Chung, Le Hou, Shayne Longpre, Barret Zoph, Yi Tay, William Fedus, Eric Li, Xuezhi Wang, Mostafa Dehghani, Siddhartha Brahma, Albert Webson, Shixiang Shane Gu, Zhuyun Dai, Mirac Suzgun, Xinyun Chen, Aakanksha Chowdhery, Sharan Narang, Gaurav Mishra, Adams Yu, Vincent Y. Zhao, Yanping Huang, Andrew M. Dai, Hongkun Yu, Slav Petrov, Ed H. Chi, Jeff Dean, Jacob Devlin, Adam Roberts, Denny Zhou, Quoc V. Le, and Jason Wei. 2022. Scaling instruction-finetuned language models. arXiv 2210.11416.

Kalervo Järvelin and Jaana Kekäläinen. 2002. Cumulated gain-based evaluation of IR techniques. *ACM Trans. Inf. Syst.*, 20(4):422–446.

Omar Khattab and Matei Zaharia. 2020. ColBERT: Efficient and effective passage search via contextualized late interaction over BERT. In *Proceedings of SIGIR 2020*, pages 39–48.

Yinhan Liu, Myle Ott, Naman Goyal, Jingfei Du, Mandar Joshi, Danqi Chen, Omer Levy, Mike Lewis, Luke Zettlemoyer, and Veselin Stoyanov. 2019. RoBERTa: A robustly optimized BERT pretraining approach. arXiv 1907.11692.

Craig Macdonald, Nicola Tonellotto, Sean MacAvaney, and Iadh Ounis. 2021. PyTerrier: Declarative experimentation in Python from BM25 to dense retrieval. In *Proceedings of CIKM 2021*, pages 4526–4533.

Ronak Pradeep, Rodrigo Nogueira, and Jimmy Lin. 2021. The expando-mono-duo design pattern for text ranking with pretrained sequence-to-sequence models. arXiv 2101.05667.

Stephen E. Robertson, Steve Walker, Susan Jones, Micheline Hancock-Beaulieu, and Mike Gatford. 1994. Okapi at TREC-3. In *Proceedings of TREC 1994*, pages 109–126.

Christian Stab, Johannes Daxenberger, Chris Stahlhut, Tristan Miller, Benjamin Schiller, Christopher Tauchmann, Steffen Eger, and Iryna Gurevych. 2018. ArgumenText: Searching for arguments in heterogeneous sources. In *Proceedings of NAACL-HLT 2018*, pages 21–25.

Henning Wachsmuth, Martin Potthast, Khalid Al Khatib, Yamen Ajjour, Jana Puschmann, Jiani Qu, Jonas Dorsch, Viorel Morari, Janek Bevendorff, and Benno Stein. 2017. Building an argument search engine for the Web. In *Proceedings of ArgMining@EMNLP 2017*, pages 49–59.

A Flan-T5 Prompts and Aggregation

Positive prompt:
<sentence>
Is this sentence pro <object O_x>? yes or no

Negative prompt:
<sentence>
Is this sentence against <object O_x>? yes or no

On these prompts, Flan-T5 usually generates some longer answer text. We derive object stance scores st_{O_x} for the objects O_1 and O_2 based on whether the outputs contain some "trigger" terms like yes, no, pro, or con (left table below). Afterwards, we map the object stance scores to sentence stance scores st_s (right table below).

A passage's stance is the average of all contained sentences' stances (ignoring sentences without stance) mapped to: > 0 'pro first obj.', < 0 'pro second obj.', 0 'both equal', $\perp$ 'no stance'.

Flan-T5 output contains		Stance	Sentence Stance		
Pos. prompt	Neg. prompt	st_{O_x}	st_{O_1}	st_{O_2}	st_s
(yes∨pro)∧¬no	(yes∨con)∧¬no	0	$\perp$	$\perp$	$\perp$
(yes∨pro)∧¬no	(¬yes∧¬con)∨no	1	a	a	0
(¬yes∧¬pro)∨no	(yes∨con)∧¬no	0	a	$\perp$	a
(¬yes∧¬pro)∨no	(¬yes∧¬con)∨no	$\perp$	$\perp$	a	$-a$
			a	b	$a-b$

B GPT-3.5 Prompt (Few-Shot)

You will be shown a text passage that compares two objects. Decide if the passage provides arguments pro first object, pro second object, both equal, or no stance is given. First, we start with examples and definitions. Please read them carefully.

Question: Apple vs Microsoft: Which is better?
Answer passage: I switched from PC to Mac about 2 years ago, after becoming familiar with Macs using my sister's computer. I will NEVER go back to PCs. I also like that Macs are simplified for basic things such as photos, music, internet, and e-mail. Truthfully, the only programs I have issues with are Microsoft applications like Word and IE. I think Apple's superiority comes from the fact that Macs are inherently more stable systems.
First object: Apple, second object: Microsoft.
Explanation: The answer provides a strong pro argument (opinion) for MAC (which is referred to as Apple). Note, that the text passage may not use the same object names as the question, e.g., it can contain synonyms or abbreviations or just mention only one object. Stance: pro first object.

Question: Is it better to dual-boot or run a VM?
Answer passage: Dual boot is a waste of time. I describe it to people as the 5-minute alt-tab. [...] I avoid dual boot like the plague. VM all the way. Or, just use a single OS that does what you want. Windows with Cygwin provides a lot of the Unixy stuff that people need.
First object: to dual-boot, second object: run a VM.
Explanation: The answer provides a strong opinion that a VM is better than a dual-boot. Note, that the text passage may not use the same object names as the question, e.g., it can contain synonyms or abbreviations or just mention only one object. Stance: pro second object.

Question: Who would win in a battle, a squirrel or a bird?
Answer passage: First of all, it depends on the bird's size. The bird has the initial advantage of flying away. [...] But if it is small, it would fly

away. And you know, the winner never runs away from the battlefield.
First object: squirrel, second object: bird.
Explanation: The answer suggests that under some condition a bird would win, but without the condition a squirrel would. This means both could win a fight, and they are equal. Stance: both equal.

Question: Which to choose a pie or a tart?
Answer passage: Generally speaking, a pie refers to a pastry covered with a lid, like a typical apple pie. A tart is open-topped, like a quiche, or a French tartes aux pommes. [...] Regional variations also apply.
First object: pie, second object: tart.
Explanation: The answer does not provide any pro or con arguments or opinions. The answer simply describes what a pie and a tart are. According to the definition of stance (see above), there is no stance in the passage. Stance: no stance.

Also, select "no stance" if the text passage does not contain arguments / opinions toward the objects (that is neither the first nor second object nor their synonyms are in the text).

Now, I have a question comparing first object: <first object> and second object: <second object>:
Question: <question>
Identify whether the following text is "pro first object", "pro second object", "both equal", or "no stance". Please, answer only with "pro first object", "pro second object", "both equal", or "no stance":
Answer passage: <passage>
Stance:

Legal Argument Extraction from Court Judgements using Integer Linear Programming

Basit Ali[1], **Sachin Pawar**[1], **Girish K. Palshikar**[1], **Anindita Sinha Banerjee**[1]
Dhirendra Singh[2]
[1]TCS Research, Tata Consultancy Services Limited, India.
[2]CFILT, Indian Institute of Technology Bombay, India.
{ali.basit, sachin7.p, gk.palshikar, anindita.sinha2}@tcs.com
dhirendra.singh@iitb.ac.in

Abstract

Legal arguments are one of the key aspects of legal knowledge which are expressed in various ways in the unstructured text of court judgements. A large database of past legal arguments can be created by extracting arguments from court judgements, categorizing them, and storing them in a structured format. Such a database would be useful for suggesting suitable arguments for any new case. In this paper, we focus on extracting arguments from Indian Supreme Court judgements using minimal supervision. We first identify a set of certain sentence-level *argument markers* which are useful for argument extraction such as whether a sentence contains a *claim* or not, whether a sentence is argumentative in nature, whether two sentences are part of the same argument, etc. We then model the legal argument extraction problem as a text segmentation problem where we combine multiple *weak evidences* in the form of argument markers using Integer Linear Programming (ILP), finally arriving at a global document-level solution giving the most optimal legal arguments. We demonstrate the effectiveness of our technique by comparing it against several competent baselines.

1 Introduction

In the field of argument mining, extraction of legal arguments from court judgements has been receiving increasing attention (Poudyal et al., 2020; Grundler et al., 2022; Habernal et al., 2023). Most of these approaches are supervised in nature in the sense that they need a significantly large corpus of documents from a specific area (e.g., ECHR - European Court of Human Rights) which are annotated with legal arguments. In this paper, we focus on extracting legal arguments from Indian Supreme Court judgements using minimal supervision. Our goal is to construct a large database of past legal arguments by extracting legal arguments from court judgements, categorizing them, and storing them in a structured format. Such a database would be useful in building a high-level legal decision support system where some of its features could be – i) suggesting suitable arguments given a new case description, ii) learning to estimate the strength of a new argument based on the similar past arguments that helped to win the case.

In this paper, we focus specifically on extraction of legal arguments and to the best of our knowledge, this is the first such attempt for – i) legal argument extraction without any in-domain supervision and ii) argument extraction from Indian court judgements. For categorizing the arguments, we propose to simply map them to the *statute facets* which were recently proposed in our previous work (Pawar et al., 2023). A statute facet is any important specific aspect of an Act which can be potentially used in legal arguments in a case related to the Act. For example, following are statute facets from India's Industrial Disputes Act – *workman*, *illegal strikes*, and *notice of retrenchment.*

We consider a *legal argument* as *a sequence of contiguous sentences in a court judgement which constitute a complete and coherent argument.* A legal argument generally consists of a sentence containing a major *claim* (or conclusion) and other sentences acting as sufficient *premises* for that claim. Table 1 shows a few examples of such legal arguments where the statute facets from India's Industrial Disputes Act (1947) are also underlined.

A major challenge in legal argument extraction from Indian court judgements is the unavailability of a training dataset where the legal arguments are annotated by human experts. Hence, we first propose to identify certain *argument markers* within sentences of a court judgement which are *weak* indicators of presence of a legal argument. Here, we refer to these argument markers as weak evidences because individually any marker is not a strong enough indicator of a legal argument and it is also not possible to automatically identify these

Proceedings of the 10th Workshop on Argument Mining, pages 52–63
December 7, 2023.

Arguments
- There were different systems of dearness allowance for the operators and the clerical and subordinate staff in the appellant company.
- That such a different system of dearness allowance for employees working under the same employer is not warranted is clear from the decisions of this Court in the cases of Greaves Cotton & Co. and Bengal Chemical & Pharmaceutical Works Ltd.
- Therefore the Tribunal was justified in devising a uniform scale of dearness allowance applicable to all the employees of the appellant. (**claim**)
- It is therefore clear that the claim for bonus can be made by the employees only if as a result of the joint contribution of capital and labour the industrial concern has earned profits. (**claim**)
- If in any particular year the working of the industrial concern has resulted in loss there is no basis nor justification for a demand for bonus.
- Bonus is not a deferred wage, because if it were so it would necessarily rank for precedence before dividends.
- The dividends can only be paid out of profits and unless and until profits are made no occasion or question can also arise for distribution of any sum as bonus amongst the employees.
- If the industrial concern has resulted in a trading loss, there would be no profits of the particular year available for distribution of dividends, much less could the employees claim the distribution of bonus during that year.

Table 1: Examples of legal arguments from court judgements related to Industrial Disputes Act.

Argument Marker	What does it indicate for a sentence S?
Claim sentence (C)	whether S makes any claim or draw some conclusion
Argumentative sentence (A)	whether S is argumentative in nature, i.e., is it either a claim or a premise of some argument
Sentence pair relation (SP)	whether S and its previous sentence belong to the same argument
Statute Facets (F)	the statute facets mentioned in S
Discourse connectors (D)	whether S has a discourse relation with its previous sentence through a causal discourse marker such as *therefore* or *hence*
Argument agent (AA)	whether S has a different argument agent (i.e., entity making the argument) than its previous sentence
Subjectivity score (SS)	whether S is a subjective sentence

Table 2: List of various argument markers used

argument markers with high accuracy. Table 2 shows the list of various argument markers used and it can be observed that the statute facets are also used as one of the argument markers. Each argument marker is identified either by using linguistic rules/patterns (for C, F, D, AA) or, by learning a classifier using training data from another area – ECHR (for AS and SP), or by using an off-the-shelf library (for SS). We then use Integer Linear Programming (ILP) to combine the weak evidences provided by these argument markers to arrive at a final document-level solution leading to identification of legal arguments. The ILP framework also enables us to represent various domain rules in the form of constraints and objectives. The main contributions of this work are:

- **Argument markers**: Techniques for identifying various argument markers (Section 3.1).
- **ArgExt-ILP**: An ILP-based technique for legal argument extraction (Section 3.3).
- **Dataset**: A dataset of 10 court judgements from Indian Supreme Court containing 127 arguments, which is the first such arguments-annotated dataset for Indian court judgements (Section 5.1).
- **Evaluation metrics**: A set of evaluation metrics for comparing the predicted arguments with the gold-standard arguments (Section 5.3).

2 Problem Definition

The problem is formally defined as follows:
Input: (i) A court judgement document J (sequence of N sentences $S_1, S_2, \cdots, S_N$), and (ii) A set of statute facets $f_1, f_2, \cdots, f_k$ for an Act A
Output: A set of extracted arguments where any i^{th} argument is a tuple (i_s, i_e) such that all the contiguous sentences starting from S_{i_s} to S_{i_e} constitute the argument.
Scope and assumptions: If there are multiple arguments present in J, they must be mutually exclusive, i.e., no sentence is common between any two such arguments. Also, another simplifying assumption is that an argument consists of contiguous sentences which may not be always true[1]. Extending our techniques to extract non-contiguous arguments is to be tackled as a part of future work.

3 Proposed Techniques

In this section, we describe identification of various argument markers and our proposed argument extraction techniques which use these markers.

[1]In ECHR corpus (Poudyal et al., 2020), almost 50% arguments consist of contiguous text

3.1 Argument Markers

3.1.1 Claim sentences (C)

As any legal argument must contain at least one claim sentence, it becomes one of the most important argument markers. It is very challenging to identify claim sentences without any direct supervision. We attempted to train sentence classifiers to identify claims using training data from ECHR corpus as well as using zero-shot text classification using open source LLMs like falcon-7b-instruct (Almazrouei et al., 2023). However, these attempts were not successful. Therefore, we designed a set of linguistic rules/patterns by observing the claim sentences in court judgements.

LR1: If a sentence contains a copula verb which is modified by a causal discourse marker (e.g., *therefore, hence*) as an adverbial modifier then it may be a claim. E.g., *Therefore, he was not a workman.*

LR2: If a sentence contains a non-copula verb which is modified by a causal discourse marker as an adverbial modifier and also modified by a modal verb (e.g., *would, could*) then it may be a claim. E.g., *Therefore, as Ram was not a workman his case would not be covered by the IDA...*

LR3: We prepared a list[2] of nouns and verbs which indicate some kind of claim, conclusion, view, or opinion. Examples of such nouns/verbs are *opinion, conclusion, contended, concluded,* etc. If a sentence contains any of these followed by a complement clause containing actual claim/conclusion/opinion then it may be a claim. For example, consider the following sentences where such noun/verb and the complement clause are highlighted – *We are of the opinion that the High Court erred in not awarding compensation to the appellant., The learned counsel contended that the respondent was denied a fair hearing.*

LR4: We also prepared a list of adjectives and adverbs with positive or negative sentiment, e.g., *erroneous, incorrectly, valid, wrongly, illegally.* If a sentence contains any one of these words to evaluate something or to express an opinion about something, then it may be a claim. Following are example sentences – *The order of the Labour Court deciding the reference against the respondent-workman is illegal., The said stand of the workers union is not consistent with the nature of the complaint.*

[2]The complete lists of words used in these patterns are provided in Appendix A.

3.1.2 Argumentative sentences (AS)

Identification of argumentative sentences has been studied in many domains (e.g., essays, debates, legal, etc.) and the techniques employed are mostly supervised in nature (Poudyal et al., 2020). Argumentative sentences can be thought of as a superset of claim sentences in the sense that both claims as well as their premises are part of argumentative sentences. We used a BERT-based sentence classifier which combines the [CLS] representation of a sentence and attention weighted average of the other tokens to get the overall representation of the sentence. It is trained using training data from multiple sources (e.g., ECHR corpus, essay corpus, rhetorical role corpus, and Indian judgements corpus) as described in Ali et al. (2022).

3.1.3 Sentence pair relation (SP)

The goal here is to predict whether any two sentences belong to the same argument or not. For this, we used a BERT-based sentence pair classifier (where two sentences are separated by a [SEP] token) which is trained using the ECHR corpus (Poudyal et al., 2020). The positive training examples (10418) are created by taking all the pairs present within an argument whereas the equal number of negative pairs are chosen randomly such that the sentences in each pair are not part of the same argument. We used this classifier for each pair of contiguous sentences in a court judgement to predict the probability that these sentences belong to the same argument.

3.1.4 Statute facets (F)

We considered all the noun phrase facets extracted from Industrial Disputes Act[3] using the technique described in previous work (Pawar et al., 2023). We matched each facet with each sentence in a court judgement ensuring that morphological variations are handled (e.g., *employer* and *employers*). The intuition is that if a facet is present in a sentence then it is more likely to be argumentative in nature. Moreover, presence of a common facet across most sentences in an argument is also a weak measure of coherence. E.g., in the first argument of Table 1, the facet *dearness allowance* is present in all its sentences. Hence, even though *statute facets* are not strong indicators of a legal argument on their own, they may help as weak argument markers (see ablation results in Section 5.4).

[3]Because all our test files are chosen to be related to IDA.

3.1.5 Discourse connectors (D)

If a sentence is connected with its previous sentence through a causal discourse connector (e.g., *therefore, consequently*) then it is a strong indication of coherence between the two sentences. Moreover, it is also a weak indication of the current sentence being a claim. Hence, we identify this information about discourse connectors using the rules described in Ali et al. (2022).

3.1.6 Argument agent (AA)

An argument agent is the entity who is putting forward any argument such as *appellant, lower court*, or *respondent*. If argument agents of the two contiguous sentences are different then it is a good indicator of non-cohesion between them. Hence, for each sentence, we identify whether its argument agent is different from its previous sentence using the rules described in Ali et al. (2022).

3.1.7 Subjectivity score (SS)

We compute subjectivity score for each sentence in a court judgement using TextBlob library[4]. Here, the intuition is that if a sentence is subjective then it is more likely to be an opinion or a claim.

Data: J: court judgement with N sentences $\{S_1, \cdots S_N\}$, C: binary array of length N s.t. $C[i] = 1$ if i^{th} sentence contains a claim, P: array of length N s.t. $P[i]$ indicates paragraph number, D: binary array of length N s.t. $D[i] = 1$ if i^{th} sentence is connected to its previous sentence through a causal discourse marker, SP: real-valued array of length N s.t. $SP[i]$ indicates the probability that i^{th} and $(i-1)^{th}$ sentences are part of the same argument, F: set of statute facets from act A
Result: $Args$: set of arguments extracted from J

```
Args := {}
for S_i ∈ J do
    if C[i] == 1 then
        R_1 := {S_i}; j := i − 1
        while S_j exists AND S_j contains at least one facet from F AND P_j == P_i do
            R_1 := R_1 ∪ {S_j}; j := j − 1
        R_2 := {S_i}; j := i + 1
        while S_j exists AND S_j contains at least one facet from F AND P_j == P_i do
            R_2 := R_2 ∪ {S_j}; j := j + 1
        if D[i] == 1 then Args := Args ∪ R_1 ;
        else
            PR_1 := Avg pairwise SP values in R_1
            PR_2 := Avg pairwise SP values in R_2
            if PR_1 > PR_2 then
                Args := Args ∪ R_1 ;
            else Args := Args ∪ R_2 ;
return Args
```

Algorithm 1: Algorithm for ArgExt-Rules

3.2 ArgExt-Rules

We propose a simple rule-based technique which uses the information about argument markers in a court judgement to extract legal arguments from it. Algorithm 1 describes this technique in detail. Intuitively, this technique simply tries to extract a set of coherent and complete arguments without using any optimization technique, ensuring that either the first or last sentence in each argument is a claim sentence along with some additional constraints. It expands each claim sentence (say S_i for which $C[i] = 1$) in either forward or backward direction to identify a complete argument. While expanding the argument in either of the directions, it adds a new sentence to the argument only if that sentence mentions at least one facet from F and it lies in the same paragraph as that of S_i. A new sentence may still be added even if it does not mention any facet but at most one such sentence is allowed in an argument only as an intermediate sentence. As S_i is expanded in both forward and backward directions, the above process results in two candidate arguments – R_1 (where S_i is expanded backward) and R_2 (where S_i is expanded forward), where only one of them has to be selected. If S_i contains a discourse marker which connects it to its previous sentence (i.e., if $D[i] = 1$) then R_1 is selected as a more coherent argument. Otherwise, average sentence pair similarity score is computed for both R_1 and R_2 and the one with higher score is selected. The algorithm may result in overlapping arguments which are resolved as follows. For each pair of overlapping arguments, we discard that argument which contains lesser number of argumentative sentences than the other.

3.3 ArgExt-ILP

We now describe our principal technique ArgExt-ILP which uses Integer Linear Programming (ILP) for combining multiple weak evidences provided by argument markers to extract actual arguments. ILP provides a suitable framework where the constraints and the objective can incorporate – (i) the information about argument markers (e.g., *each argument should start or end with a claim sentence*) and (ii) various types of domain knowledge about legal arguments (e.g., *an argument is unlikely to cross paragraph boundaries*). Thus, an optimal solution to an ILP program leads to a set of predicted arguments which conform to the argument markers

[4]https://textblob.readthedocs.io/en/dev/

and satisfy these domain rules as much as possible.

Tables 3 and 4 show our ILP formulation in detail. For each input document (i.e., court judgement J), an ILP program is prepared using the information about various argument markers in that document. The ILP program is then solved to obtain the predicted arguments from that document. The information about argument markers is provided to ILP through various input parameters such as C (claim sentences), AS (argumentative sentences), SP (sentence pair relations) as described in Table 3. The decision variables X and Y are binary variables. They are designed to represent the output (i.e., the predicted arguments) in such a way that the jth column of the matrix $X - Y$ contains 1's in only those rows which correspond to sentences constituting the jth argument (see Table 3). In other words, $(X[i,j] - Y[i,j])$ equals 1 if and only if i^{th} sentence is part of the jth argument. The constraints C_1 to C_5 ensure that the extracted arguments are non-overlapping and correspond to contiguous sentences only. The constraint C_6 ensures that each extracted argument contains a claim sentence as its first or last sentence. For any j, $(X[i,j] - X[i-1,j])$ is 1 for only one i (because of the constraint C_1) which corresponds to the first sentence of the jth argument. Similarly, for any j, $(Y[i+1,j] - Y[i,j])$ is 1 only for one i (because of the constraint C_2) which corresponds to the last sentence of the jth argument. Hence, the left hand side of C_6 is at least 1 if and only if j^{th} argument contains a claim sentence as its first or last sentence. Also, the right hand side of C_6, i.e., $X[N,j]$ is 1 only if j^{th} argument exists, otherwise it is 0. Similarly, other constraints C_7 to C_9 are added to conform to other domain knowledge based rules as described in Table 3. Table 4 describes the objective which is minimized. The overall objective consists of 3 terms. The first term Obj_1 attempts to minimize the number of claim, subjective, and argumentative sentences which are not part of any extracted argument. Obj_2 ensures that as far as possible, the sentence pairs on argument boundaries are not related to each other. Obj_3 tries to maximize the overall number of facets which are part of the extracted arguments.

4 Related Work

Extraction of legal arguments: We discuss some of the most relevant techniques for extraction of legal arguments here. Poudyal (2016) identified the argumentative sentences and used soft clustering technique to form an argument which consists of premises and claims. They automatically identified the premise/claim structure within an argument using multiple features such as lexical, syntactic (tree kernel), dependency, n-gram, etc. The top n features are selected using gain-ratio for both classifying argumentative and premise/claim type sentences. Wei et al. (2017) proposed to use ILP to jointly solve multiple sub-tasks in argument mining such as argumentation component type classification and relation classification. We are also using ILP in our proposed technique, but we have modelled argument extraction differently as a text segmentation problem. One of the most significant work in legal argument extraction is by Poudyal et al. (2020) where they released an arguments-annotated corpus of 42 judgements of European Court of Human Rights (ECHR). They also presented BERT-based baseline techniques for three key tasks in argument extraction – argument clause recognition, clause relation prediction, and premise/conclusion recognition. Grundler et al. (2022) released *Demosthenes* which is a corpus of 40 judgements of the Court of Justice of the European Union on matters of fiscal state aid. The corpus contains annotations for three hierarchical levels of information – the argumentative elements, their types, and their argument schemes. Recently, Habernal et al. (2023) proposed an interesting alternate perspective that rather than simplifying arguments into generic premises and claims, it is more important to capture rich typology of arguments for gaining insights into the particular case and applications of law in general. They proposed a new annotation scheme accordingly for capturing 16 argument types and 5 argument actors for each argument, where an argument is a text span. The text span of an argument was allowed to cross sentence boundaries but not paragraph boundaries. They released a large corpus of 373 annotated court decisions and also proposed sequence labelling techniques for identifying argument text spans. We have used their model as one of the baselines. Other techniques for legal argument extraction are (Mochales and Moens, 2011; Trautmann, 2020; Xu and Ashley, 2023; Zhang et al., 2023; Santin et al., 2023).

Text Segmentation: This task is relevant for our work because we have modelled argument extraction as a text segmentation problem. Some generic

Input parameters:

N: No. of sentences in the court judgement J

M: Maximum no. of arguments in any court judgement

K: Total no. of facets in the Act A

C: Binary array of length N such that $C[i] = 1$ iff i^{th} sentence contains any *claim*. (Section 3.1.1)

D: Binary array of length N such that $D[i] = 1$ iff i^{th} sentence contains support indicating discourse markers such as *therefore* and *consequently* which link it to the $(i-1)^{th}$ sentence. (Section 3.1.5)

AS: Binary array of length N such that $AS[i] = 1$ iff i^{th} sentence is argumentative in nature. (Section 3.1.2)

AA: Binary array of length N such that $AA[i] = 1$; iff i^{th} sentence's argument agent (such as *appellant, respondent, lower court, judge*) is different from the previous sentence's agent. (Section 3.1.6)

F: Binary matrix of size $N \times K$ such that $F[i,k] = 1$ iff i^{th} sentence contains k^{th} facet and $F[i,k] = 0$ otherwise (Section 3.1.4)

P: Binary array of length N such that $P[i] = 1$; iff i^{th} sentence belongs to a new (different) paragraph as compared to the $(i-1)^{th}$ sentence.

SP: Real-valued array of length N such that $SP[i] =$ the probability that the ith sentence and the $(i-1)^{th}$ sentence belong to the same argument. (Section 3.1.3)

SS: Real-valued array of length N such that $SS[i] =$ the subjectivity score of the ith sentence. (Section 3.1.7)

Decision variables:

X: Binary matrix of size $N \times M$ such that $X[i,j] = 1, \forall_{i \geq k}$ iff j^{th} argument starts at the kth sentence. $X[i,j] = 0, \forall_{i<k}$

Y: Binary matrix of size $N \times M$ such that $Y[i,j] = 1, \forall_{i > k}$ iff j^{th} argument ends at the kth sentence. $Y[i,j] = 0, \forall_{i \leq k}$

Constraints:

C_1: For a fixed j, $X[:,j]$ should be monotonically increasing. $X[i-1,j] \leq X[i,j]; \;\forall_{i,j} \; s.t. \; 2 \leq i \leq N, 1 \leq j \leq M$

C_2: For a fixed j, $Y[:,j]$ should be monotonically increasing. $Y[i-1,j] \leq Y[i,j]; \;\forall_{i,j} \; s.t. \; 2 \leq i \leq N, 1 \leq j \leq M$

C_3: The start of an argument should be before its end. $X[i,j] \geq Y[i,j]; \;\forall_{i,j} \; s.t. \; 1 \leq i \leq N, 1 \leq j \leq M$

C_4: j^{th} argument should start only after $(j-1)^{th}$ argument ends. $Y[i,j-1] \geq X[i,j]; \;\forall_{i,j} \; s.t. \; 1 \leq i \leq N, 2 \leq j \leq M$

C_5: Any argument should contain at least one sentence.

$$\sum_{i=1}^{N-1}((i+1) \cdot (Y[i+1,j] - Y[i,j])) - \sum_{i=2}^{N}(i \cdot (X[i,j] - X[i-1,j])) \geq X[N,j]; \;\forall_j \; s.t. \; 1 \leq j \leq M$$

C_6: At least one of the first sentence or the last sentence of any argument should contain a claim.

$$\sum_{i=2}^{N}(C[i] \cdot (X[i,j] - X[i-1,j])) + \sum_{i=1}^{N-1}(C[i] \cdot (Y[i+1,j] - Y[i,j])) \geq X[N,j]; \;\forall_j \; s.t. \; 1 \leq j \leq M$$

C_7: Any argument should not start with a sentence containing discourse connector to its previous sentence.

$$\sum_{i=2}^{N} D[i] \cdot (X[i,j] - X[i-1,j]) \leq 0; \;\forall_j \; s.t. \; 1 \leq j \leq M$$

C_8: If a sentence contains an argument agent which is different from the previous sentence then such sentence can either be the first sentence in some argument or it may not be part of any argument.

$$\sum_{j=1}^{M}(X[i,j] - Y[i,j]) - \sum_{j=1}^{M}(X[i,j] - X[i-1,j]) + AA[i] \leq 1; \;\forall_i \; s.t. \; 2 \leq i \leq M$$

C_9: Any argument should not be spread across multiple paragraphs.

$$(X[i,j] - Y[i,j]) - (X[i,j] - X[i-1,j]) + P[i] \leq 1; \;\forall_{i,j} \; s.t. \; 2 \leq i \leq N, 1 \leq j \leq M$$

Table 3: Input parameters, decision variables and constraints used in ArgExt-ILP

Objective: Minimize $Obj_1 + Obj_2 - Obj_3$

Obj_1: Minimize the number of claim, argumentative, and subjective sentences which are not part of any extracted argument.

$$Obj_1 = \sum_{i=1}^{N}(C[i] + SS[i] + AS[i]) \cdot \left(1 - \left(\sum_{j=1}^{M}(X[i,j] - Y[i,j])\right)\right)$$

Obj_2: Minimize the average of probability scores that i^{th} and $(i-1)^{th}$ sentences belong to the same argument when they occur on an argument boundary.

$$Obj_2 = \sum_{j=1}^{M} \frac{1}{2}\left(\sum_{i=2}^{N} SP[i] \cdot (X[i,j] - X[i-1,j]) + \sum_{i=1}^{N-1} SP[i+1] \cdot (Y[i+1,j] - Y[i,j])\right)$$

Obj_3: Maximize the total number of facets mentioned within the extracted arguments.

$$Obj_3 = \sum_{j=1}^{M}\left(\sum_{i=1}^{N}\left(\sum_{k=1}^{K} F[i,k]\right) \cdot (X[i,j] - Y[i,j])\right)$$

Table 4: Objectives used in ArgExt-ILP

text segmentation techniques have been proposed like C99 algorithm (Choi, 2000) which identifies optimal segments, semantic segmentation technique (Alemi and Ginsparg, 2015) which incorporates semantic word embedding while identifying the segments. Some recent work using deep learning for text segmentation is by Lattisi et al. (2022) where they are using BERT model's Next Sentence Prediction (NSP) probability as a coherence score between sentences in their objective. Moro and Ragazzi (2022) employs self-segmentation technique to extract the semantic chunks from a long legal documents, where they fine-tuned the Legal-BERT model with metric learning setup to incorporate the segment semantics. Our technique is motivated by the work of Palshikar et al. (2019) which also uses the ILP framework for identifying certain types of sections in a document.

5 Experiments

5.1 Annotated Dataset for Evaluation

We identified 10 court judgements related to industrial disputes from the Supreme Court of India[5]. These judgements were annotated manually with gold-standard legal arguments[6] These 10 judgements contain 1524 sentences spread across 418 paragraphs overall. The total of 127 gold-standard arguments were identified during the manual annotation process. Each argument is represented by its start and end sentence numbers where each sentence in between is considered as a part of the argument. Annotators were also asked to identify a sentence for each argument which contains its major claim. To estimate the inter-annotator agreement (IAA), we used the pygamma-agreement library (Titeux and Riad, 2021) which is based on (Mathet et al., 2015). We used the positional dissimilarity based γ statistic for comparing the arguments identified by two annotators and the average value of γ was observed to be 0.405. As another estimate for IAA, we also used the same evaluation metrics (described in Section 5.3) which we use to evaluate the predicted arguments. The F1-scores for the IAA were observed as follows: Arg-exact=0.3, Arg-subset=0.47, Arg-overlap=0.56, and Arg-sentences=0.59. The IAA scores are not very strong which indicates the difficulty level and subjective nature of the task.

For training the classifiers needed for identifying the argument markers AS and SP, we used the ECHR corpus as it is similar to our dataset in the sense that it is also a corpus of court judgements which is annotated for legal arguments by lawyers. However, this corpus did not help in identifying claims with reasonable accuracy by training a classifier, hence we had to rely on the linguistic rules. This shows that even though this corpus is similar to our dataset, there are some differences, especially the language used for claim sentences.

5.2 Baselines

Baseline-TextSeg: We use C99 algorithm (Choi, 2000) for segmenting the court judgements. We retain only those text segments as legal arguments which contain at least one claim sentence, and discard all the remaining text segments.

Baseline-RhetoricalRoles: We obtained rhetorical roles for each sentence in each judgement using the opennyai python package[7] based on the work of Kalamkar et al. (2022). Each sequence of contiguous sentences which is labelled by the same argument indicating rhetorical role (ARG_RESPONDENT or ARG_PETITIONER) is identified as a legal argument.

Baseline-LegalArgs: This baseline is based on the technique proposed by Habernal et al. (2023) where a paragraph is given as an input to a sequence labelling model which labels each token in the paragraph with appropriate argument type using BIO encoding. For making it comparable with our problem setting, we merged all their 16 argument types into a single type, re-trained the *roberta-large* model on their training dataset, and used the model to infer the argument labels on each paragraph in our evaluation dataset. We also extended the token level classification output to sentence level, i.e., even if a subset of tokens in a sentence is labelled as part of an argument by the model, we consider the entire sentence as a part of the argument.

5.3 Evaluation Metrics

For evaluating the predicted arguments, we propose a set of new metrics. These are in the form of traditional precision, recall and F1-score scores only but they differ from each other in how true positives (TP), false positives (FP), and false negatives (FN) are computed based on when two arguments are

[5]Downloaded from `http://www.liiofindia.org/in/cases/cen/INSC/`

[6]The annotation guidelines are shared in Appendix C. The dataset would be shared upon request.

[7]`https://pypi.org/project/opennyai/`

Metric	Technique	With predicted claims			With gold-standard claims		
		P	R	F1	P	R	F1
Arg-exact	Baseline-LegalArgs (Habernal et al., 2023)	0.206	0.055	0.087	0.296	0.063	0.104
	Baseline-RhetoricalRoles Kalamkar et al. (2022)	0.012	0.016	0.014	0.031	0.016	0.021
	Baseline-TextSeg (Choi, 2000)	0.029	0.047	0.036	0.058	0.047	0.052
	ArgExt-Rules	0.088	0.094	0.090	0.257	0.142	0.183
	ArgExt-ILP	0.145	0.197	**0.167**	0.330	0.283	**0.305**
Arg-subset	Baseline-LegalArgs (Habernal et al., 2023)	0.417	0.118	0.184	0.576	0.150	0.238
	Baseline-RhetoricalRoles Kalamkar et al. (2022)	0.160	0.205	0.179	0.351	0.213	0.265
	Baseline-TextSeg (Choi, 2000)	0.251	0.433	0.318	0.434	0.441	0.438
	ArgExt-Rules	0.223	0.165	0.190	0.684	0.205	0.315
	ArgExt-ILP	0.380	0.551	**0.450**	0.641	0.661	**0.651**
Arg-overlap	Baseline-LegalArgs (Habernal et al., 2023)	0.500	0.134	0.211	0.667	0.142	0.234
	Baseline-RhetoricalRoles Kalamkar et al. (2022)	0.243	0.205	0.222	0.385	0.157	0.223
	Baseline-TextSeg (Choi, 2000)	0.251	0.409	0.311	0.447	0.362	0.400
	ArgExt-Rules	0.294	0.315	0.304	0.486	0.268	0.345
	ArgExt-ILP	0.427	0.575	**0.490**	0.690	0.598	**0.641**
Arg-sentences	Baseline-LegalArgs (Habernal et al., 2023)	0.470	0.129	0.203	0.739	0.140	0.235
	Baseline-RhetoricalRoles Kalamkar et al. (2022)	0.521	0.259	0.346	0.624	0.218	0.323
	Baseline-TextSeg (Choi, 2000)	0.403	0.708	0.514	0.529	0.616	0.569
	ArgExt-Rules	0.594	0.331	0.425	0.901	0.263	0.407
	ArgExt-ILP	0.506	0.768	**0.610**	0.758	0.752	**0.755**

Table 5: Evaluation results for argument extraction by various techniques

With predicted claims:				
Objective	**Arg-Exact**	**Arg-Subset**	**Arg-Overlap**	**Arg-Sentences**
$Obj_1 + Obj_2 - Obj_3$	0.167	0.450	0.490	0.610
Without Obj_1	0.106	0.352	0.397	0.525
Without Obj_2	0.168	0.427	0.474	0.606
Without Obj_3	0.173	0.448	0.502	0.612
With gold-standard claims:				
Objective	**Arg-exact**	**Arg-subset**	**Arg-overlap**	**Arg-sentences**
$Obj_1 + Obj_2 - Obj_3$	0.305	0.651	0.641	0.755
Without Obj_1	0.197	0.527	0.535	0.660
Without Obj_2	0.340	0.659	0.694	0.764
Without Obj_3	0.287	0.638	0.647	0.762

Table 6: Ablation study for objectives in ArgExt-ILP (F1-scores)

considered to be "matching" with each other. If a gold-standard argument "matches" with a predicted argument, then a TP is counted, otherwise a FN is counted. Further, if a predicted argument does not "match" with any gold-standard argument, then a FP is counted. The following metrics correspond to different ways of "matching":

Arg-exact: A predicted argument is considered to be "matching" with a gold-standard argument if their start and end sentence indices are same.

Arg-subset: A gold-standard argument is considered to be "matching" with a predicted argument if the set of sentence indices within the gold-standard argument is a proper subset of the set of sentence indices of the predicted argument.

Arg-overlap: Two arguments are considered to be "matching" with one another if Jaccard similarity between the sets of sentence indices within the two arguments is greater than or equal to 0.5.

Arg-sentences: Unlike the above metrics where TP/FP/FN are counted at argument-level, in this metric, these are counted at a sentence level. A sentence in any predicted argument is considered a TP if it is also part of some gold-standard argument, otherwise it is considered as a FP. Similarly, a sentence in a gold-standard argument is considered as a FN if it is not part of any predicted argument.

5.4 Evaluation Results

Table 5 shows the comparative performance of our proposed argument extraction techniques with respect to the baselines. It can be observed that ArgExt-ILP outperforms all other techniques across all evaluation metrics. Even though ArgExt-ILP and ArgExt-Rules are based on the same argument markers, ArgExt-ILP consistently outperforms ArgExt-Rules. This shows that the ILP framework is helpful in combining multiple weak evidences in the form of argument markers and potentially conflicting domain rules in a more princi-

With predicted claims:				
Constraints	**Arg-exact**	**Arg-subset**	**Arg-overlap**	**Arg-sentences**
All constraints in Table 3	0.167	0.450	0.490	0.610
Without C_6	0.080	0.418	0.416	0.530
Without C_7	0.147	0.423	0.450	0.601
Without C_8	0.157	0.459	0.472	0.604
Without C_9	0.060	0.548	0.244	0.540
With gold-standard claims:				
Constraints	**Arg-exact**	**Arg-subset**	**Arg-overlap**	**Arg-sentences**
All constraints in Table 3	0.305	0.651	0.641	0.755
Without C_6	0.086	0.435	0.422	0.535
Without C_7	0.352	0.641	0.656	0.746
Without C_8	0.347	0.679	0.694	0.772
Without C_9	0.132	0.649	0.395	0.598

Table 7: Ablation study of the constraints in ArgExt-ILP (F1 scores)

pled manner than a rule-based logic. However, the performance of ArgExt-ILP is still far from being perfect and this highlights the challenging nature of the task. The error analysis shows that there are mainly two sources of errors - (i) incorrect identification of claim sentences and (ii) incorrect boundary identification of the arguments. In order to estimate the effect of the first source, we re-run all the techniques assuming gold-standard claim sentences are known. Table 5 shows the detailed results in this setting in the last 3 columns. Again, ArgExt-ILP outperforms all other techniques and also improves significantly over its own performance with predicted claim sentences. This shows that there still scope for improvement in identification of argument markers like claims so as to improve the end-to-end argument extraction. More implementation details for ArgExt-ILP are provided in Appendix B.

Ablation Studies for ArgExt-ILP: Table 6 shows the results of ablation for the multiple objectives used in ArgExt-ILP. It can be observed that the objective Obj_1 is the most important one as the performance drops the most if we remove it. The objective Obj_2 is contributing when we are using predicted claim sentences which is a more practical setting, whereas the objective Obj_3 has mixed results across various metrics. Similarly, Table 7 shows the results of ablation studies for the multiple constraints used in ArgExt-ILP. The constraints C_6 and C_9 are the most significant ones as removing them results in reduced performance consistently.

Argument Markers Identification Accuracy: Table 8 shows the accuracy with which individual argument markers C, AS and SP are identified. It can be observed that individually these markers are not identified with very high accuracy and hence we are considering them as *weak evidences*.

Argument Marker	P	R	F1
C (linguistic rules)	0.422	0.724	0.533
AS ($prob \geq 0.5$)	0.356	0.612	0.450
SP ($prob \geq 0.2$)	0.577	0.653	0.613

Table 8: Evaluation results for argument markers

6 Conclusions and Future Work

We proposed a technique to extract legal arguments from Indian Supreme Court judgements by first identifying a set of certain *argument markers* and then incorporating them in an Integer Linear Programming (ILP) framework with domain knowledge based constraints. Individually, these argument markers are weak indicators of arguments mentioned in the text of a judgement, but the information from multiple such markers gets combined effectively in our ArgExt-ILP technique. We annotated a small dataset of 10 court judgements containing 127 legal arguments and evaluated our techniques on it along with multiple competent baselines. We demonstrated that ArgExt-ILP outperforms other baselines across multiple evaluation metrics. To the best of our knowledge, this is the first attempt to extract legal arguments from Indian court judgements and also a first arguments-annotated dataset for the same. As part of future work, our argument extraction techniques need to be improved further in multiple aspects – (i) the accuracy of identifying individual argument markers needs to be improved further which will automatically improve ArgExt-ILP's performance, (ii) we plan to do away with some of our simplifying assumptions to also extract overlapping and non-contiguous arguments, and (iii) we plan to evaluate our techniques on a wider variety of court judgements such as judgements other than industrial disputes and also from other geographies than India.

References

Alexander A Alemi and Paul Ginsparg. 2015. Text segmentation based on semantic word embeddings. *arXiv preprint arXiv:1503.05543.*

Basit Ali, Sachin Pawar, Girish Palshikar, and Rituraj Singh. 2022. Constructing a dataset of support and attack relations in legal arguments in court judgements using linguistic rules. In *Proceedings of the Thirteenth Language Resources and Evaluation Conference*, pages 491–500, Marseille, France. European Language Resources Association.

Ebtesam Almazrouei, Hamza Alobeidli, Abdulaziz Alshamsi, Alessandro Cappelli, Ruxandra Cojocaru, Merouane Debbah, Etienne Goffinet, Daniel Heslow, Julien Launay, Quentin Malartic, Badreddine Noune, Baptiste Pannier, and Guilherme Penedo. 2023. Falcon-40B: an open large language model with state-of-the-art performance.

Freddy YY Choi. 2000. Advances in domain independent linear text segmentation. *arXiv preprint cs/0003083.*

Giulia Grundler, Piera Santin, Andrea Galassi, Federico Galli, Francesco Godano, Francesca Lagioia, Elena Palmieri, Federico Ruggeri, Giovanni Sartor, and Paolo Torroni. 2022. Detecting arguments in cjeu decisions on fiscal state aid. In *Proceedings of the 9th Workshop on Argument Mining*, pages 143–157.

Ivan Habernal, Daniel Faber, Nicola Recchia, Sebastian Bretthauer, Iryna Gurevych, Indra Spiecker genannt Döhmann, and Christoph Burchard. 2023. Mining legal arguments in court decisions. *Artificial Intelligence and Law*, pages 1–38.

Prathamesh Kalamkar, Aman Tiwari, Astha Agarwal, Saurabh Karn, Smita Gupta, Vivek Raghavan, and Ashutosh Modi. 2022. Corpus for automatic structuring of legal documents. In *Proceedings of the Language Resources and Evaluation Conference*, pages 4420–4429, Marseille, France. European Language Resources Association.

Tiziano Lattisi, Davide Farina, and Marco Ronchetti. 2022. Semantic segmentation of text using deep learning. *Computing and Informatics*, 41(1):78–97.

Yann Mathet, Antoine Widlöcher, and Jean-Philippe Métivier. 2015. The unified and holistic method gamma (γ) for inter-annotator agreement measure and alignment. *Computational Linguistics*, 41(3):437–479.

Raquel Mochales and Marie-Francine Moens. 2011. Argumentation mining. *Artificial Intelligence and Law*, 19:1–22.

Gianluca Moro and Luca Ragazzi. 2022. Semantic self-segmentation for abstractive summarization of long documents in low-resource regimes. In *Proceedings of the AAAI Conference on Artificial Intelligence*, volume 36, pages 11085–11093.

Girish K Palshikar, Sachin Pawar, Rajiv Srivastava, and Mahek Shah. 2019. Identifying repeated sections within documents. *Computación y Sistemas*, 23(3):819–828.

Sachin Pawar, Basit Ali, Girish Palshikar, Ramandeep Singh, and Dhirendra Singh. 2023. Extraction and classification of statute facets using few-shots learning. In *19th International Conference on Artificial Intelligence and Law (ICAIL).*

Prakash Poudyal. 2016. Automatic extraction and structure of arguments in legal documents. *Sarah A. Gaggl, Matthias Thimm (Eds.)*, page 19.

Prakash Poudyal, Jaromír Šavelka, Aagje Ieven, Marie Francine Moens, Teresa Goncalves, and Paulo Quaresma. 2020. Echr: Legal corpus for argument mining. In *Proceedings of the 7th Workshop on Argument Mining*, pages 67–75.

Piera Santin, Giulia Grundler, Andrea Galassi, Federico Galli, Francesca Lagioia, Elena Palmieri, Federico Ruggeri, Giovanni Sartor, Paolo Torroni, et al. 2023. Argumentation structure prediction in cjeu decisions on fiscal state aid. In *ICAIL'23: Proceedings of the Nineteenth International Conference on Artificial Intelligence and Law*, pages N–A.

Hadrien Titeux and Rachid Riad. 2021. pygamma-agreement: Gamma γ measure for inter/intra-annotator agreement in python. *Journal of Open Source Software*, 6(62):2989.

Dietrich Trautmann. 2020. Aspect-based argument mining. *arXiv preprint arXiv:2011.00633.*

Zhongyu Wei, Chen Li, and Yang Liu. 2017. A joint framework for argumentative text analysis incorporating domain knowledge. *arXiv preprint arXiv:1701.05343.*

Huihui Xu and Kevin Ashley. 2023. Argumentative segmentation enhancement for legal summarization. *arXiv preprint arXiv:2307.05081.*

Gechuan Zhang, Paul Nulty, and David Lillis. 2023. Argument mining with graph representation learning.

A Details about linguistic rules

Following are the complete details about various list of words used in by the linguistic rules for identification of claim sentences.

List of causal discourse markers used in LR1 and LR2: *therefore, thus, hence, consequently, moreover, furthermore, similarly, likewise, accordingly, thereby*

List of nouns used in LR3: *opinion, belief, impression, indication, judgement, assessment, estimation, position, argument, argumentation, submission, contention, objection, justification, conclusion, claim, clarification.*

List of verbs used in LR3: *sustain, contend, argue, debate, assert, conclude, assess, believe, maintain, submit, show, demonstrate, prove, appear, seem, clear, justify, conclude, claim, affirm, arrogate, indicate, clarify, hold, opine*. Also note that the list contains only the base forms of these verbs but while matching in the sentence, we consider all the morphological variations such as *conclude* $\Rightarrow$ *concluded, concluding, concludes*.
List of negative adjectives used in LR4: *unfair, erroneous, incorrect, wrong, inaccurate, inexact, imprecise, invalid, fallacious, misleading, illogical, unsound, faulty, flawed, spurious, unfounded, unjustified, illegal, inappropriate, inconsistent, unsustainable, unwarranted*
List of positive adjectives used in LR4: *correct, accurate, exact, precise, valid, logical, justified, warranted, consistent, sustained, fair, legal, appropriate, permitted, maintainable.*
List of negative adverbs used in LR4: *inconsistently, unfairly, erroneously, incorrectly, wrongly, mistakenly, illegally, inappropriately, spuriously.*
List of positive adverbs used in LR4: *consistently, fairly, correctly, legally, appropriately.*

B Implementation Details

For solving ILP programs in ArgExt-ILP, we used the glpk solver[8] through Python's pyomo library[9]. For better running time efficiency, we split each judgement into two parts, solve two separate ILP programs, and later merge their solutions to get the final output. We used $M = 10$ so that at most 20 arguments can be extracted from each judgement. Also while splitting a judgement, we make sure that it is always split at a paragraph boundary. As there is a constraint (C_9) which ensures that no extracted argument can cross paragraph boundaries, we believe that this is a reasonable approximation.

C Annotation Guidelines

The following guidelines were shared with the annotators.
Goal: To identify legal arguments mentioned in court judgements. We assume each legal argument to be a chunk of contiguous sentences in the court judgement such that each chunk corresponds to a complete and coherent argument.
Annotation format: For each coherent and complete argument (consisting of a chunk of k contiguous sentences), the the following details are noted – **Filename** (file name of the court judgement), **StartSentNo** (sentence number of the first sentence of an argument), **EndSentNo** (sentence number of the last sentence of the argument), **ClaimSentNo** (sentence number of the sentence which contains the key claim/conclusion of the argument).

General guidelines:
1. Only contiguous sentences should be identified as an argument.
2. No overlapping arguments should be identified.
3. Each identified argument should be "complete" (as self-sufficient as possible to understand it) and "coherent" (should be mainly related to only one topic or legal point).
4. There should be at least one sentence in an argument which contains some "claim" being made or some "conclusion" being arrived at or some legal point be argued about. It also includes some opinion being expressed or some decision (or evaluation of lower court decision) that judge/court arrives at. Generally, the ultimate "claim" in an argument occurs either as the first sentence or the last sentence within the contiguous sentences identified as a legal argument. Some examples of "claims" are as follows:
• *the leniency shown by the Labour Court is clearly unwarranted and would in fact encourage indiscipline* (**evaluation of lower court decision**)
• *The finding is based on surmises* (**opinion**)
• *the petitioner who is working as an Area Sales Executive is not a workman within the meaning of Section 2(s) of the Industrial Disputes Act, 1947.* (**conclusion or legal point**)
Some examples of sentences which DO NOT contain any "claim":
• *A review application, however, was filed inter alia on the premise that the workmen were not entitled to claim any bonus.* (**a past event or fact**)
• *Section 12 of the Act provides the duties of the Conciliation Officer.* (**referring to a statute**)
• *This Court while allowing the appeal directed the respondent No.2 the Labour Commissioner, Chandigarh to make a reference under Section 12 of the Act.* (**direction by a court**)
Please note that the above are just some types of sentences which are not "claims" such as a past event, fact, direction by a court, or reference to a statutes, etc. There may be several additional types of sentences which are not "claims".
5. There should be at least one sentence in an argument which contains supporting facts, statements, evidences, or any other premises including prior

[8]https://www.gnu.org/software/glpk/
[9]https://pypi.org/project/Pyomo/

cases, statutes etc. which support the major "claim" or "conclusion" in the argument.
6. An argument may consist of a single sentence, i.e., both "claim" and its supporting premises are present in the single sentence.
7. Even if we are using the terminology "argument", the argument need not be made only by the contesting parties (appellant/plaintiff and respondent/defendant). The argument may correspond to reasoning given by lower court / current court to arrive at certain conclusion.
8. There can be multiple "claims" in an argument. But there exists only one major claim which may be supported by intermediate claims.
9. Opinion of any court (judge) can be considered as a claim. E.g., *the order of Labour Court as affirmed by High Court can not be sustained*
10. An argument can be found within sentences which are quoted from some prior case. That means the sentences are not about the current case but show why certain argument was made or decision was taken in a prior case.

Argument Detection in Student Essays under Resource Constraints

Omid Kashefi, Sophia Chan, Swapna Somasundaran
Educational Testing Service (ETS)
660 Rosedale Rd, Princeton, NJ, USA
{okashefi,schan,ssomasundaran}@ets.org

Abstract

Learning to make effective arguments is vital for the development of critical-thinking in students and, hence, for their academic and career success. Detecting argument components is crucial for developing systems that assess students' ability to develop arguments. Traditionally, supervised learning has been used for this task, but this requires a large corpus of reliable training examples which are often impractical to obtain for student writing. Large language models have also been shown to be effective few-shot learners, making them suitable for low-resource argument detection. However, concerns such as latency, service reliability, and data privacy might hinder their practical applicability. To address these challenges, we present a low-resource classification approach that combines the intrinsic entailment relationship among the argument elements with a parameter-efficient prompt-tuning strategy. Experimental results demonstrate the effectiveness of our method in reducing the data and computation requirements of training an argument detection model without compromising the prediction accuracy. This suggests the practical applicability of our model across a variety of real-world settings, facilitating broader access to argument classification for researchers spanning various domains and problem scenarios.

1 Introduction

In today's educational landscape, the development of critical thinking and persuasive writing skills holds significant importance. The ability to construct compelling arguments is essential for effective communication and argumentative writing enables students to express ideas clearly, present clear evidence, and address counterarguments effectively. These skills are vital for academic success, professional growth, and civic engagement (Farra et al., 2015; Bertling et al., 2015). Therefore, having a system to analyze and detect argumentation in students' writing would be essential for educators to assess and provide feedback on students' argumentative skills and foster continuous growth in their argumentative writing skills. Furthermore, by using the tool to evaluate their writing, students can identify any weaknesses or gaps in their arguments and make necessary revisions independently. This promotes self-reflection and empowers students to take ownership of their learning, improving their critical thinking and communication skills.

However, the task of detecting arguments within students' essays poses several challenges due to the nuanced nature of argumentation. Constructing an argument involves presenting a *"claim"* and supporting it with *"premises."* However, claims can take various forms, ranging from explicit statements to implicit assertions that require inferential reasoning. Similarly, premises may be stated explicitly or indirectly implied, further complicating the process of argument detection.

Traditional supervised models for argument analysis often rely on large amounts of training data to achieve satisfactory performance. Collecting and annotating such data can be time-consuming and resource-intensive, making it challenging to build large training datasets that cover the diverse range of argumentative patterns and structures present in student essays. Moreover, the practical deployment of large language models such as GPT (Radford et al., 2019; Brown et al., 2020) and PaLM (Chowdhery et al., 2022) can be hindered by cost, latency, and data privacy concerns.

To address these challenges, we introduced an argument classification approach that combines the inherent linguistic characteristics of argumentation with advanced machine learning techniques. We showed the efficacy of exploiting the natural language inference (NLI) relationship between argument components to prime a pre-trained language model for the argument detection task. By merging this with a well-suited prompt-tuning strategy, we

Proceedings of the 10th Workshop on Argument Mining, pages 64–75
December 7, 2023.

established a streamlined architecture that effectively reduces the data and computation requirements of training an argument detection model without compromising the prediction accuracy.

We evaluate the performance and generalizability of our approach across two scenarios: one characterized by availability of reliable training data, and the other representing a resource-constrained noisy domain more akin to real-world settings. In both cases, our approach yielded competitive results, often surpassing the performance of resource-intensive alternatives in classifying argument components. This suggests the practical viability of our model across a variety of real-world settings. We believe that our approach has the potential to make argument classification accessible to a wider range of researchers and problem domains.

2 Argumentation as Entailment

Automated argument detection systems have the potential to help teachers and students by offering a consistent and objective means of evaluating students' work, providing them with timely feedback to enhance their critical thinking and argumentative skills. By automating the process of identifying argument components like claims and premises, educators can redirect their efforts toward other crucial aspects of teaching and providing personalized support to students. However, developing a reliable and accurate automatic system poses certain challenges. Natural language processing algorithms must be sophisticated enough to comprehend the nuances of human language, including various writing styles and levels of proficiency. The system must also recognize context and cultural differences to avoid misinterpretations.

To address these challenges, we propose leveraging semantic relationships between argument elements by framing the argument detection task as natural language inference (NLI). NLI involves discerning the semantic connection between two sentences, where one sentence logically follows (entails) from the other (van Benthem, 2008; MacCartney and Manning, 2009). This notion of entailment and contradiction serves as a foundation for enhancing the semantic representation of various natural language understanding (NLU) problems, including parsing, coreference resolution, and reasoning tasks (Bowman et al., 2015). Similarly, we argue that the NLI framework can be effectively extended to capture the semantic relationships between different components within argumentation. For instance, a counter-claim may contradict the main claim of an argument, or a supportive premise might entail the corresponding claim (Cabrio and Villata, 2013).

We believe that this formulation allows NLP models to leverage their inherent understanding of semantic relationships between logical elements to recognize whether a sentence provides the necessary support or context for a given argument component, and facilitate the development of argument component classification systems, even with a limited volume of training examples. However, employing the entailment paradigm for argument classification requires (a small set of) reliable labeled training data and careful consideration of complex structure of argumentation to ensure accurate and robust results.

3 Proposed Approach

Given that a primary emphasis of this research lies in addressing the challenges posed by resource-limited and noisy conditions in student essay argument detection, we naturally lean towards the utilization of zero-shot/few-shot classification methodologies. In Section 3.1, we discuss how to leverage the inherent structure of zero-shot classification to improve the performance of argument-detection models, and in Section 3.2, we discuss an approach based on efficiently tuning prompts for argument component classification using a small set of training examples.

3.1 Entailment Tuning (ARG-NLI)

Zero-shot classification is a machine learning approach that allows a model to classify instances belonging to classes it has never seen during training. Zero-shot classification in NLP is often approached as an NLI problem, where the goal is to determine the relationship between two sentences: a *premise* (not to be confused with the premise in argumentation) and a *hypothesis*, categorized as "entailment," "contradiction," or "neutral". This framework can be extended to zero-shot classification by casting the classification task as an entailment problem, where the input serves as the premise, and the hypothesis corresponds to a descriptive representation of the target class (Yin et al., 2019).

As we mentioned in Section 2, the relation between argument components can be represented as entailment relations:

- a *premise* **"entails"** the corresponding *claim* ($premise \rightarrow claim$)
- a *claim* **"entails"** the *stance* of the essay ($claim \rightarrow stance$)
- a *counter-claim* **"contradicts"** the *stance* and *claims* of the essay ($counter\text{-}claim \perp stance$)
- *unrelated* argument components are **"neutral"** to each other

We believe further fine-tuning a zero-shot classifier (i.e., a pre-trained transformer-based model trained for NLI task (Bowman et al., 2015; Williams et al., 2018)) on a small set of argumentative training data orchestrated as the entailment task (we refer to this as **ARG-NLI**) would help the model better understand the semantic relationship between different argument components (i.e., between premise and claim, between claim and stance, and between counter-claim and claims/stances). By fine-tuning zero-shot models through ARG-NLI, we anticipate improvements in performance of such models on the task of argument component classification.

3.2 Prompt-Based Tuning (Bart-PEPT)

Large pre-trained language models like GPT (Radford Alec et al., 2018) and BERT (Devlin et al., 2019) have achieved impressive results in NLP benchmarks. However, fine-tuning these models on downstream tasks requires a large dataset of labeled data, which may be a barrier for many NLP tasks. In-context learning is an alternative approach that allows large language models (**LLMs**) to learn new tasks from a few examples, where a single pre-trained model with fixed parameters is shared across all downstream tasks (Radford et al., 2019). This approach works by providing the model with a prompt design for a given task. A prompt is a hand-crafted piece of text that describes or provides examples of the task, usually in natural language. For example, to condition a model for sentiment analysis, one could attach the prompt, "Is the following sentence positive or negative" before the input sequence, "No reason to watch."

Le Scao and Rush (2021) show that a prompt may be worth 100 conventional data points, suggesting that prompts can bring a giant leap in sample efficiency; sharing the same frozen model across tasks also greatly simplifies serving and allows for efficient mixed-task inference. However, task performance can be highly dependent on the prompt design; seemingly trivial changes to the prompt may affect the results. Prompt tuning is an emerging research area that aims to address the limitations posed by manually crafted prompts. Instead of relying on fixed prompts, this approach leverages tunable prompts that are dynamically generated from a small set of training examples. Prompt tuning can improve sample efficiency and enable the seamless integration of mixed tasks, facilitating more effective and versatile inference processes (Schick and Schütze, 2020; Gao et al., 2020; Qin and Eisner, 2021; Zhong et al., 2021; Li and Liang, 2021; Liu et al., 2021; Zhao et al., 2021).

In addition to natural language prompts, LLMs can also be primed by *soft prompts*. These soft prompts are learnable vectors rather than preexisting vocabulary items (Qin and Eisner, 2021; Zhong et al., 2021; Han et al., 2022). This mechanism allows for end-to-end optimization over a training dataset, and for the prompt to serve as a mechanism for condensing information from large datasets (Lester et al., 2021).

Parameter efficient prompt tuning (**PEPT**) (Lester et al., 2021) is a (soft) prompt tuning approach that focuses on optimizing only a small subset of the model's parameters, specifically the prompt, while keeping the rest of the parameters fixed. PEPT was initially introduced in the context of the T5 model (Raffel et al., 2019) for text-to-text problems. Lester et al. (2021) show that by just tuning the prompt rather than fine-tuning the entire model, T5 can achieve comparable performance on generation and NLU tasks.

Inspired by this, we adapted a version of PEPT to utilize Bart (Lewis et al., 2019) as the core transformer model and made slight modification by incorporating a linear classification head. This model serves as our approach for few-shot classification using smaller language models (**SLMs**). The overarching architecture of PEPT is illustrated in Figure 1. PEPT operates by attaching a tunable vector of numbers to the beginning of the (encoded) input, which functions as the prompt. During the training process, the model parameters are frozen, and gradient updates are only applied to this (soft) prompt vector. Subsequently, the trained prompt is concatenated to the beginning of each input during inference to generate predictions.

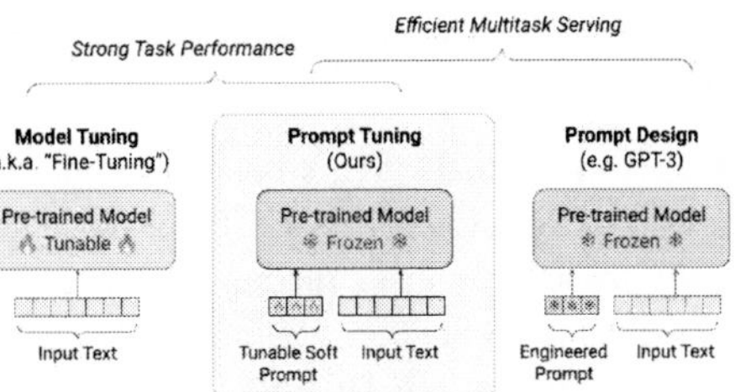

Figure 1: PEPT Model Structure (Lester et al., 2021)

4 Evaluation Methodology

In order to examine the practical viability of our proposed low-resource argument classification approach in a variety of real-world settings, we evaluate the performance and generalizability of our methods in two different scenarios: (i) a problem domain characterized by an abundance of reliable training data (Section 5.1), wherein the availability of the data allows for training traditional *supervised* models, and (ii) a resource-constrained noisy domain more akin to real-world conditions (Section 5.2), wherein *LLMs* as an effective low-resource alternative to supervised training, may seem a more suitable option to approach the problem. While we were able to carry out a small annotation project to collect data for the middle school domain, such annotations may not be feasible, especially if we wish to adapt the system to multiple new domains.

Further information about these problem domains can be found in Section 4.1. The detailed overview of the baseline models we established for both the supervised and zero-shot/few-shot LLM training approaches, as well as the details of our proposed low-resource argument classification methods, are discussed in Section 4.2.

4.1 Problem Domains

4.1.1 Abundance of Reliable Data

In our first set of experiments we use the dataset from Stab and Gurevych (2017), which we refer to as **SG17** in this work. This is a well-known, reliable dataset of argumentation annotations containing essays from "essayforum.com", a site where users submit their academic essays for feedback.

By leveraging this dataset, we can train traditional supervised models as benchmarks for topline performance for the argument classification problem and allows us to assess the comparative effectiveness of our proposed approach against these traditional methods in an ideal scenario where reliable training data is available.

	SG17		ARG	
	train	test	train	test
Claim	1,800	457	64	202
Premise	3,023	809	64	799

Table 1: Total number of samples in each class for sentence-level datasets for Experiment 1 (SG17) and Experiment 2 (ARG).

The statistics of class distribution of examples in SG17 dataset is shown in Table 1. For simplicity, we project the label of the clauses onto sentences and use the dataset at sentence level in all of our experiments. It's important to highlight that there are sentences that contain multiple clauses with different labels (e.g., "*CLAIM because PREMISE*"). However, these cases are comprising only about 2% of the dataset, wherein we assign the label of the minority class to theses sentences to enhance the diversity of the class distribution within our sentence-level dataset.

4.1.2 Limited Noisy Data

A second set of experiments was conducted on an in-house dataset of students' essays, which we refer to as **ARG**. We consider this our low-resource and noisy domain and use these experiments to demonstrate that our approach is suitable for such real-world settings.

This dataset comprises of essays written by students in grades 5 through 9 who reside in the United States. These essays, along with the prompt, were presented to eight annotators as part of the annotation project. Annotators were asked to provide a score along four different persuasive dimensions (*claim*, *counter-claim*, *premise*, and *persuasive strategy*), and to select a text span as the rationale for that score. We consider these *rationales* as our argument components, and used a remapping heuristic to project them to the binary $\{Claim, Premise\}$ classes (see Appendix A for more details).

4.2 Argument Classification Models

In this section, we present the technical details of our proposed low-resource argument classification approaches. Furthermore, we outline the supervised, SLM, and LLM-based baselines that we have established as alternative methods.

4.2.1 Supervised Models

We establish two supervised argument classifier baselines as follows:

Bert-Sequence We use the HuggingFace (Wolf et al., 2019) `bert-base-uncased` (Devlin et al., 2018) model with a classification head to predict whether a sentence is either a `Claim`, or a `Premise`.

Bert-BIO We adopt the model architecture introduced by Alhindi and Ghosh (2021), which employs a BIO classification scheme to identify and classify argument components. We use `bert-base-uncased` as the base transformer model and train a token-level classifier head on top. This baseline aims to label each token as `B-claim`, `I-claim`, `B-premise`, `I-premise`, or `O`. For consistency in our evaluation, we incorporate a label projection heuristic to map BIO prediction to sentence-level labels, as discussed in Appendix B.

4.2.2 Large Language Models

To establish our LLM-based baselines, we utilize the OpenAI GPT-3 models in zero-shot and few-shot settings. In the zero-shot configuration, the model relies solely on its pretrained knowledge without any task-specific fine-tuning. In the latter setup, we provide the model with a limited amount of task-specific examples to adapt it to our argument detection task. It's also important to note that at the time of conducting this study, the newer GPT-4 model was not publicly accessible, restricting our experiments to the utilization of the GPT-3 version.

GPT3:Zero-shot We use `text-davinci-001` via the OpenAI Completion endpoint[1] with the following prompt:

```
Classify the text as
{claim_label} or {premise_label}.
Text: {sentence}
Label:
```

For each sentence in the test set, we replace the placeholder in the prompt with that sentence and feed it to the completion endpoint. We experiment with a couple different values for `claim_label` ($\{Claim|Idea\}$) and `premise_label` ($\{Premise|Support\}$) due to a trait of generative models that "causes probability to be rationed between different valid strings, even ones that differ trivially" (Holtzman et al., 2021). We then pick and report the result of the combination that performs best within each experiment and problem domain.

GPT3:Fine-tuned The extensive pretrained knowledge of LLMS enables them to adapt efficiently to specific tasks or domains, even with a relatively small number of training examples, making them a potentially suitable low-resource baseline for argument detection tasks. Accordingly, we fine-tuned a GPT3-DaVinci model via the OpenAI endpoint using 64 randomly sampled sentences from each class and obtained predictions from the completions endpoint.

4.2.3 Smaller Language Models

Bart-MNLI:Zero-shot We use the HuggingFace port of `facebook/bart-large-mnli` out of the box as our zero-shot baseline. This is a checkpoint for the Bart-large model (Lewis et al., 2019) after training on the MultiNLI (MNLI) dataset (Williams et al., 2018). Similar to the `GPT3:Zero-shot` baseline, we used a simple prompt template of:

```
This sentence is {label}
```

Again, we experiment with a couple different values for `claim_label` ($\{Claim|Idea\}$) and `premise_label` ($\{Premise|Support\}$). Our experiments revealed that employing the labels $\{Idea|Support\}$ yielded the the most promising and robust results, so we present and discuss the results of this label configuration in this study.

Adjustment for Bias. The language models, including our `Bart-MNLI:Zero-shot` baseline, may exhibit biases towards certain values within the answer space. For example, there could be an imbalance in the training data, resulting in a higher likelihood of predicting certain answers, such as "positive", over others like "negative".

To address this issue of prompting bias, we implemented a threshold adjustment strategy as suggested by Sun et al. (2022). We initiated this process by determining the probability of an empty input ($x =$ "") being classified as "claim" by querying the model with the prompt:

$[x]$ `is an idea`

This probability value serves as the basis for establishing the threshold used to categorize inputs as claims. For instance, if the probability of being claim for the empty input be 0.63, any input with

[1] `https://openai.com/blog/openai-api`

a probability of lower than 0.63 would no longer be classified as a claim, whereas any value above 0.5 would have been categorized as such prior to the bias adjustment. This strategy has the potential to enhance the fairness, accuracy, and reliability of our zero-shot baselines, making them more equitable and dependable classifiers.

4.2.4 Our Proposed Models

ARG-NLI In order to investigate the effectiveness of using the entailment formulation of argument classification problem as we proposed in Section 3.1, we randomly picked a few essays from the training datasets and created the entailment pairs for the premises and related claims, and claims and major claims. The SG17 dataset (Section 4.1.1) contains relation annotations in the form of (source, target) tuples, where the source claim/premise either supports or attacks the target claim/premise. An attacking claim is also known as a counter-claim. In addition to claims and premises, major claims that express the writer's stance towards the prompt are also annotated. We used this information to create the NLI representation of argumentative annotation of claim and premises in SG17, as follows:

- claims **entail** major claims in the same essay
- premises **entail** their related claim
- counter-claims **contradict** their related major claim
- premises of an essay are **neutral** towards the claims of other essays

Our in-house ARG dataset (Section 4.1.2) does not have the relation annotations so we used a simple heuristic to relate the argument components:

- claims within an essay **entail** one another
- premises **entail** claims within the same paragraph
- counter-claims **contradict** all the claims in the same essay
- premises of an essay are **neutral** towards the claims of other essays

After creating the NLI representation of argumentation datasets (pair of sentences with appropriate entailment label), we use them to fine-tune the same `Bart:MNLI:Zero-shot` we used in Section 4.2.3. We then used the fine-tuned model in zero-shot classification fashion– feed in a *single* sentence and prompt the model to determine whether the input sentence is a `claim`, or a `premise`?

Bart-PEPT As mentioned in Section 3.2, we developed a modified version of the model introduced by Lester et al. (2021) to operate on `facebook/bart-large-mnli` of HuggingFace for "classification" tasks as our approach for few-shot classification using SLMs.

ARG-NLI + Bart-PEPT This variation of Bart-PEPT uses the argument-NLI finetuned version of the Bart we developed (a.k.a, `ARG-NLI`) as the core transformer model; a prompt is then tuned on top of this base model.

5 Experiments

5.1 Exp. 1: Large Reliable Training Data

In this experiment, we use the SG17 dataset described in Section 4.1.1 to evaluate our model in a scenario where a large corpus of reliable training data with argument annotation is available.

The anticipation is that supervised models will excel in the task of *distinguishing between "claim" and "premise" sentences* within this context. Therefore, our main objective of this is *to explore the comparative capabilities of our proposed low-resource alternative models in relation to the well-established supervised training paradigm.*

We trained all argument classifier models on the SG17 train set described in Table 1. The `Bert-Sequence`, and `Bert-BIO` baselines are trained on the entire training set of the SG17, which consists of 4.8K sentences with 115K tokens. The zero-shot baselines (`GPT3:Zero-shot` and `Bart-MNLI:Zero-shot`) are not exposed to any training examples. The `GPT3:Finetuned` and `Bart-PEPT` models are trained with 64 claim examples and 64 premise examples from the training set. For entailment tuning for `ARG-NLI` model, we randomly picked 20 essays from the train set and created the argument component pairs of "entailment" and "contradiction" examples.

Overall, we fine-tune the Bart-MNLI model with 700 argumentative entailment examples and evaluated that as a zero-shot classifier on the test set of SG17. For more details on our argumentative entailment dataset please refer to Appendix D.

Model	SG17	ARG
Supervised		
Bert-Sequence	72%	66%
Bert-BIO	69%	62%
L(arge)LM		
GPT3:Zero-shot	61%	56%
GPT3:Finetuned	66%	62%
S(mall)LM		
Bart-MNLI:Zero-shot	52%	51%
Our approach		
ARG-NLI	61%	59%
Bart-PEPT	70%	72%
ARG-NLI + Bart-PEPT	**73%**	**77%**

Table 2: Macro-F1 scores for argument classification across various models and training paradigms for Experiment 1 (SG17) and Experiment 2 (ARG). The boldfaced numbers indicate the best performing models.

5.1.1 Results

Table 2 shows the macro-F1 score of our models in classifying 1.3K argument-related sentences of the SG17 test set as either "claim", or "premise". As expected, both supervised baselines are capable of reliably predicting the correct label for the argument components within this dataset, with the sequence classifier baseline (F1 = 72%) performs better than the token classifier baseline (F1 = 69%).

Both zero-shot baselines yield sub-par performance compared to their counterparts. Also in line with our expectations, the LLM-based baseline outperformed the SLM-based baseline (61% versus 52%). These results highlight the challenging nature of argument classification, indicating that distinguishing between claims and premises involves subtleties beyond what can be achieved through simply prompting pre-trained transformers. Incorporating argument entailment tuning (`ARG-NLI`) leads to a substantive 9% enhancement over the SLM zero-shot baseline (61% vs. 52%), indicating that priming models with the entailment relationship between argument components can make them better zero-shot learners for the task.

Fine-tuning LLM on the task with 128 training examples led to a 6% performance increase compared to the baseline achieved by the zero-shot LLM. However, with the same number of training examples, our `Bart-PEPT` approach achieved a remarkable F1 performance of 70%, trails the best-performing supervised alternative by only 2%, even though the latter is trained on a corpus over 35 times larger. Furthermore, once we combined our argument NLI fine-tuned model with PEPT (`ARG-NLI + Bart-PEPT`), we achieve a substantial 21% improvement over the SLM zero-shot baseline and 3% over our Bart-PEPT model. This model surpasses the top-performing supervised model in terms of F1 performance, despite using only a fraction of the training data.

5.2 Exp. 2: Limited Noisy Training Data

In this experiment, we evaluate our model on the ARG dataset (described in Section 4.1.2), a scenario more akin to real-world conditions, wherein a large corpus of reliable training data is not available. In this setting, we annotate about 1.2K argumentative sentences of student's essays. We used 128 of these examples for training the models and held-out the remainders for testing.

Since there is not enough data to train a robust supervised model, we anticipate that traditional supervised models will fail to accurately distinguish between "claim" and "premise" sentences in this experiment. Therefore, this experiment would help us to assess the applicability of our proposed low-resource argument classifier approaches as an alternative to data and resource intensive supervised and LLM baselines.

We trained the `Bert-Sequence`, `GPT3:Finetuned` and `Bart-PEPT` models on the 64 claim examples and 64 premise examples of our in-house argumentative student writing dataset ARG. The `Bert-BIO` baseline a variation of ARG dataset with token-level annotation, containing 68 claim and 96 premise entities. Appendix C presents the BIO statistics of ARG dataset. The zero-shot baselines (`GPT3:Zero-shot` and `Bart-MNLI:Zero-shot`) are not exposed to any training examples. In addition, we used the ARG training essays to create 700 argument component pairs with entailment labels. We then leverage this dataset to finetune our proposed `ARG-NLI` model.

5.2.1 Results

The numbers under the ARG column of Table 2 are showing the macro-F1 score of different models in classifying 1K argument-related sentences of our ARG test set as either "claim" or "premise".

Although both the sequence and BIO supervised classifier baselines are still performing in a reasonable range (62% and 66%, respectively), we observe a noticeable drop (5% on average) in performance compared to the previous experiment, which was conducted on a larger training dataset. These outcomes corroborate that supervised approaches rely heavily on access to high-quality training data, a requirement that does not consistently align with resources available for various real-world NLP problems.

Consistent with previous experiments, zero-shot baselines continue to show relatively poor performance on this dataset (51% and 56% for SLM and LLM zero-shot baselines respectively). This outcome, however, is inline with expectations, as these baselines are not trained with examples from the target domain. Our proposed argumentative entailment fine-tuning approach (ARG-NLI) exhibits an 8% improvement over the SLM zero-shot baseline (59% vs. 51%). These consistent observations from both of our experiments demonstrates the effectiveness of pre-training (smaller) foundational models with the inherent entailment structure of argument elements. This approach helps models comprehend the semantic structure of argumentation more thoroughly, leading to improved performance as zero-shot learners for the task.

Fine-tuning LLMs with domain-specific training data shows certain performance enhancements compared to their zero-shot counterparts (62% vs. 56%). However, similar to the previous experiment, these improvements remain limited. Despite the relatively high costs associated with using LLMs, their performance as a low-resource solution still falls short of being viable for production deployment in the argument classification task.

As shown in Table 2, our prompt-based tuning approach Bart-PEPT outperformed all other methods in this low-resource setting (F1=72%). Moreover, once it uses our ARG-NLI model as the core foundation models, we observe an additional 5% performance boost. These outcomes underscore the suitability of our proposed approach as a reliable and accurate method for argument classification in low-resource domains. Our approach achieves results on par with data and resource-intensive supervised and LLM alternatives within resource-abundant contexts, while outperforming them in problem domains lacking such extensive training corpora. This positions our approach as a versatile choice for a broader range of problems.

5.3 Latency Analysis

While LLMs can yield reasonable results with a small number of training examples, fine-tuning them demands extensive parameter updates, consuming substantial time and computation. For instance, the fine-tuning of the GPT-3 "davinci" model entails updating over 170B parameters, whereas our Bart-PEPT model requires modifying only 40K parameters within the prompt (the model parameters frozen). This raises practical concerns regarding the latency when working with these models. Therefore, we conducted a comparison of inference latency among the methods discussed in this study, as shown in Table 3.

Models	Latency (ms)
Bert-Sequence	0.66
Bert-BIO	22.46
GPT3:Finetuned	19.74
Bart-PEPT	7.6

Table 3: Average inference time of selected argument classifier models.

Latency measurements were conducted on the ARG test set, comprising 1K sentences with an average of 17 tokens per sentence. For transformer-based models, we use a single Tesla K20Xm GPU with 22.5 GiB of RAM and a batch size of 32. For GPT-3 we batched up to 20 requests, the current maximum allowed by the completion endpoint.

6 Conclusion

In this work, we introduced an argument classification strategy that effectively leverages the logical entailment relationship within argument components, along with a parameter efficient prompt-tuning technique. Our approach demonstrates remarkable efficiency in reducing data and computational requirements for training while maintaining high prediction accuracy. Its robust performance across diverse scenarios highlights its practical applicability in real-world settings, making argument classification more accessible to researchers across various domains. Notably, the model's ability to achieve competence with a minimal number of examples per class sets it apart from traditional data-intensive supervised alternatives.

Additionally, unlike expensive and time-intensive LLM-based solutions, our proposed approach can reliably operate on smaller foundation models such as Bart, offering expedited training and inference, making it a cost-effective and efficient solution suitable for in-house deployment and enjoying the added benefits of data privacy.

Limitation

The focus of this study lies in argument component classification. A more practical application would entail a pipeline system that initially distinguishes argumentative sentences from non-arguments—potentially through a separate predictive model. Then, our approach in this study could offer fine-grained insights into the usage and developmental stages of argumentation within student writing at the claim and premise levels. It is also important to note that while our method streamlines requirements, it still requires a small amount of data for model tuning.

As future work, we intend to expand our efforts towards multi-class prediction, incorporating the "*none-argument*" category as a potential label. This expansion necessitates re-annotating our in-house dataset using an argumentative annotation scheme, as we suspect that rationale-based annotation schemes tend to classify argumentative elements as non-arguments, inviting the need for a more specific annotation guideline.

Furthermore, our company's data privacy policy prohibits us from publicly releasing student-written essays. Unfortunately, we are unable to make our in-house argument dataset (ARG) mentioned in this work available to the public.

Ethics Statement

While we strive to contribute positively to the field of argument detection, we are fully aware of the ethical dimensions and potential challenges associated with deployment of AI models, particularly in education domain. We recognize the potential for representational harm (Suresh and Guttag, 2021), which is complex and often challenging to quantify. Biases can emerge from multiple sources, including annotators, system designers, and the data itself, and it can shape how claims, premises, and arguments are defined and interpreted (Gaskins, 2023). Despite our efforts to source a diverse range of student essays and annotators, biases within the data are possible. We are also aware of well-documented biases in language models like Bert and GPT (Monarch and Morrison, 2020). These biases could inadvertently manifest in our system's output, potentially perpetuating and amplifying inequalities.

To mitigate these risks, we have taken several steps. Our primary intention is to assist students in becoming better writers and reduce the burden on teachers, fostering formative assessment. We require teacher approval before presenting feedback to students, thereby minimizing representational harm by ensuring that feedback aligns with educational objectives. Additionally, we commit to avoiding the use of our system in high-stakes testing or consequential decisions, thereby reducing allocational harm. We remain committed to continuous evaluation, refinement, and transparent communication of the ethical considerations in our work, with the ultimate goal of fostering responsible and equitable AI adoption in education.

References

Tariq Alhindi and Debanjan Ghosh. 2021. "Sharks are not the threat humans are": Argument Component Segmentation in School Student Essays. In *Proceedings of the 16th Workshop on Innovative Use of NLP for Building Educational Applications*, pages 210–222, Online. Association for Computational Linguistics.

Maria Bertling, G. Tanner Jackson, Andreas Oranje, and V. Elizabeth Owen. 2015. Measuring argumentation skills with game-based assessments: Evidence for incremental validity and learning. *Lecture Notes in Computer Science (including subseries Lecture Notes in Artificial Intelligence and Lecture Notes in Bioinformatics)*, 9112:545–549.

Samuel R. Bowman, Gabor Angeli, Christopher Potts, and Christopher D. Manning. 2015. A large annotated corpus for learning natural language inference. *Conference Proceedings - EMNLP 2015: Conference on Empirical Methods in Natural Language Processing*, pages 632–642.

Tom B Brown, Benjamin Mann, Nick Ryder, Melanie Subbiah, Jared Kaplan, Prafulla Dhariwal, Arvind Neelakantan, Pranav Shyam, Girish Sastry, Amanda Askell, Sandhini Agarwal, Ariel Herbert-Voss, Gretchen Krueger, Tom Henighan, Rewon Child, Aditya Ramesh, Daniel M Ziegler, Jeffrey Wu, Clemens Winter, Christopher Hesse, Mark Chen, Eric Sigler, Mateusz Litwin, Scott Gray, Benjamin Chess, Jack Clark, Christopher Berner, Sam Mccandlish, Alec Radford, Ilya Sutskever, and Dario Amodei. 2020. Language Models are Few-Shot Learners. *Advances in Neural Information Processing Systems*, 33:1877–1901.

Elena Cabrio and Serena Villata. 2013. Detecting Bipolar Semantic Relations among Natural Language Arguments with Textual Entailment: a Study. In *Joint Symposium on Semantic Processing. Textual Inference and Structures in Corpora*, pages 24–32.

Aakanksha Chowdhery, Sharan Narang, Jacob Devlin, Maarten Bosma, Gaurav Mishra, Adam Roberts, Paul Barham, Hyung Won Chung, Charles Sutton,

Sebastian Gehrmann, Parker Schuh, Kensen Shi, Sasha Tsvyashchenko, Joshua Maynez, Abhishek Rao, Parker Barnes, Yi Tay, Noam Shazeer, Vinodkumar Prabhakaran, Emily Reif, Nan Du, Ben Hutchinson, Reiner Pope, James Bradbury, Jacob Austin, Michael Isard, Guy Gur-Ari, Pengcheng Yin, Toju Duke, Anselm Levskaya, Sanjay Ghemawat, Sunipa Dev, Henryk Michalewski, Xavier Garcia, Vedant Misra, Kevin Robinson, Liam Fedus, Denny Zhou, Daphne Ippolito, David Luan, Hyeontaek Lim, Barret Zoph, Alexander Spiridonov, Ryan Sepassi, David Dohan, Shivani Agrawal, Mark Omernick, Andrew M. Dai, Thanumalayan Sankaranarayana Pillai, Marie Pellat, Aitor Lewkowycz, Erica Moreira, Rewon Child, Oleksandr Polozov, Katherine Lee, Zongwei Zhou, Xuezhi Wang, Brennan Saeta, Mark Diaz, Orhan Firat, Michele Catasta, Jason Wei, Kathy Meier-Hellstern, Douglas Eck, Jeff Dean, Slav Petrov, and Noah Fiedel. 2022. PaLM: Scaling Language Modeling with Pathways. *Computing Research Repository, ArXiv:2204.02311*.

Jacob Devlin, Ming-Wei Chang, Kenton Lee, and Kristina Toutanova. 2019. BERT: Pre-training of Deep Bidirectional Transformers for Language Understanding. In *NAACL*, pages 4171–4186.

Jacob Devlin, Ming-Wei Chang, Kenton Lee, and Kristina Toutanova. 2018. BERT: Pre-training of Deep Bidirectional Transformers for Language Understanding. *Computing Research Repository*.

Noura Farra, Swapna Somasundaran, and Jill Burstein. 2015. Scoring Persuasive Essays Using Opinions and their Targets. *10th Workshop on Innovative Use of NLP for Building Educational Applications, BEA 2015 at the 2015 Conference of the North American Chapter of the Association for Computational Linguistics: Human Language Technologies, NAACL-HLT 2015*, pages 64–74.

Tianyu Gao, Adam Fisch, and Danqi Chen. 2020. Making Pre-trained Language Models Better Few-shot Learners. *ACL-IJCNLP 2021 - 59th Annual Meeting of the Association for Computational Linguistics and the 11th International Joint Conference on Natural Language Processing, Proceedings of the Conference*, pages 3816–3830.

Nettrice Gaskins. 2023. Interrogating Algorithmic Bias: From Speculative Fiction to Liberatory Design. *TechTrends : for leaders in education & training*, 67(3):417–425.

Xu Han, Weilin Zhao, Ning Ding, Zhiyuan Liu, and Maosong Sun. 2022. PTR: Prompt Tuning with Rules for Text Classification. *AI Open*, 3:182–192.

Ari Holtzman, Peter West, Vered Shwartz, Yejin Choi, and Luke Zettlemoyer. 2021. Surface form competition: Why the highest probability answer isn't always right. In *Proceedings of the 2021 Conference on Empirical Methods in Natural Language Processing*, pages 7038–7051, Online and Punta Cana, Dominican Republic. Association for Computational Linguistics.

Jan-Christoph Klie, Michael Bugert, Beto Boullosa, Richard Eckart de Castilho, and Iryna Gurevych. 2018. The INCEpTION platform: Machine-assisted and knowledge-oriented interactive annotation. In *Proceedings of the 27th International Conference on Computational Linguistics: System Demonstrations*, pages 5–9, Santa Fe, New Mexico. Association for Computational Linguistics.

Teven Le Scao and Alexander M. Rush. 2021. How Many Data Points is a Prompt Worth? *NAACL-HLT 2021 - 2021 Conference of the North American Chapter of the Association for Computational Linguistics: Human Language Technologies, Proceedings of the Conference*, pages 2627–2636.

Brian Lester, Rami Al-Rfou, and Noah Constant. 2021. The Power of Scale for Parameter-Efficient Prompt Tuning. *EMNLP 2021 - 2021 Conference on Empirical Methods in Natural Language Processing, Proceedings*, pages 3045–3059.

Mike Lewis, Yinhan Liu, Naman Goyal, Marjan Ghazvininejad, Abdelrahman Mohamed, Omer Levy, Ves Stoyanov, and Luke Zettlemoyer. 2019. BART: Denoising Sequence-to-Sequence Pre-training for Natural Language Generation, Translation, and Comprehension. *Proceedings of the Annual Meeting of the Association for Computational Linguistics*, pages 7871–7880.

Xiang Lisa Li and Percy Liang. 2021. Prefix-Tuning: Optimizing Continuous Prompts for Generation. *ACL-IJCNLP 2021 - 59th Annual Meeting of the Association for Computational Linguistics and the 11th International Joint Conference on Natural Language Processing, Proceedings of the Conference*, pages 4582–4597.

Xiao Liu, Yanan Zheng, Zhengxiao Du, Ming Ding, Yujie Qian, Zhilin Yang, and Jie Tang. 2021. GPT Understands, Too. *Computing Research Repository*.

Bill MacCartney and Christopher D. Manning. 2009. An extended model of natural logic. In *Eight International Conference on Computational Semantics*, pages 140–156.

Robert Monarch and Alex Morrison. 2020. Detecting Independent Pronoun Bias with Partially-Synthetic Data Generation. *Conference on Empirical Methods in Natural Language Processing (EMNLP)*, pages 2011–2017.

Guanghui Qin and Jason Eisner. 2021. Learning How to Ask: Querying LMs with Mixtures of Soft Prompts. *NAACL-HLT 2021 - 2021 Conference of the North American Chapter of the Association for Computational Linguistics: Human Language Technologies, Proceedings of the Conference*, pages 5203–5212.

Alec Radford, Jeffrey Wu, Rewon Child, David Luan, Dario Amodei, and Ilya Sutskever. 2019. Language models are unsupervised multitask learners. *OpenAI*.

Radford Alec, Narasimhan Karthik, Salimans Tim, and Sutskever Ilya. 2018. Improving language understanding by generative pre-training. Technical report, OpenAI.

Colin Raffel, Noam Shazeer, Adam Roberts, Katherine Lee, Sharan Narang, Michael Matena, Yanqi Zhou, Wei Li, and Peter J. Liu. 2019. Exploring the Limits of Transfer Learning with a Unified Text-to-Text Transformer. *Journal of Machine Learning Research*, 21:1–67.

Timo Schick and Hinrich Schütze. 2020. It's Not Just Size That Matters: Small Language Models Are Also Few-Shot Learners. *Conference of the North American Chapter of the Association for Computational Linguistics: Human Language Technologies (NAACL-HLT)*, pages 2339–2352.

Christian Stab and Iryna Gurevych. 2017. Parsing Argumentation Structures in Persuasive Essays. *Computational Linguistics*, 43(3):619–659.

Yi Sun, Yu Zheng, Chao Hao, and Hangping Qiu. 2022. NSP-BERT: A Prompt-based Few-Shot Learner through an Original Pre-training Task —— Next Sentence Prediction. In *COLING*, pages 3233–3250.

Harini Suresh and John Guttag. 2021. A Framework for Understanding Sources of Harm throughout the Machine Learning Life Cycle. *ACM International Conference Proceeding Series*.

Johan van Benthem. 2008. A Brief History of Natural Logic. Technical report, ILLC Amsterdam.

Adina Williams, Nikita Nangia, and Samuel R. Bowman. 2018. A Broad-Coverage Challenge Corpus for Sentence Understanding through Inference. *NAACL HLT 2018 - 2018 Conference of the North American Chapter of the Association for Computational Linguistics: Human Language Technologies - Proceedings of the Conference*, 1:1112–1122.

Thomas Wolf, Lysandre Debut, Victor Sanh, Julien Chaumond, Clement Delangue, Anthony Moi, Pierric Cistac, Tim Rault, Rémi Louf, Morgan Funtowicz, et al. 2019. Huggingface's transformers: State-of-the-art natural language processing. *arXiv preprint arXiv:1910.03771*.

Wenpeng Yin, Jamaal Hay, and Dan Roth. 2019. Benchmarking Zero-shot Text Classification: Datasets, Evaluation and Entailment Approach. *EMNLP-IJCNLP 2019 - 2019 Conference on Empirical Methods in Natural Language Processing and 9th International Joint Conference on Natural Language Processing, Proceedings of the Conference*, pages 3914–3923.

Tony Z. Zhao, Eric Wallace, Shi Feng, Dan Klein, and Sameer Singh. 2021. Calibrate Before Use: Improving Few-Shot Performance of Language Models. In *ICML*.

Zexuan Zhong, Dan Friedman, and Danqi Chen. 2021. Factual Probing Is [MASK]: Learning vs. Learning to Recall. *NAACL-HLT 2021 - 2021 Conference of the North American Chapter of the Association for Computational Linguistics: Human Language Technologies, Proceedings of the Conference*, pages 5017–5033.

A ARG Annotation

We conducted the annotation study on the Inception platform (Klie et al., 2018). In total, eight annotators double-annotated 300 essays after completing a calibration exercise that involved annotating 30 essays. Annotators gave each essay a score along four persuasive dimensions (*claim*, *counter-claim*, *premise*, and *persuasive strategy*). For each dimension, the annotators selected text spans that served as the rationale or explanation for their score, and we take these spans to be our argument components. A span was counted if it was selected by any annotator, and spans were combined when more than 10% tokens overlap.

After the annotation was completed, one of the authors examined ten essays and created rules to map rationale labels to the binary $\{Claim, Premise\}$ classes. In addition, based on our review of the data, we decided to only count double-annotated premise spans and remove any essays that contain no claims. The rules for remapping are as follows:

- *claim* $\rightarrow$ *claim*
- *counter-claim* $\rightarrow$ *premise*
- *claim, premise* $\rightarrow$ *claim*
- *persuasive strategy* $\rightarrow$ discard

B BIO Label Projection

In the `Bert-Sequence` baseline every sentence receives only one label (either claim or premise), while the BIO baseline can predict different segments of the sentence as different argument components. To ensure a uniform sentence-level prediction scheme across baselines, we incorporate a label projection policy as follows:

- when all predicted argument components within a sentence are classified as the same class, we project that prediction to the entire sentence

- if a sentence contains argument components with different classes, we label the sentence with the label of the minority class (in our experiments, the "claim" class)

C Token-Level Annotation

Table 4 shows the token-level class distribution of the SG17 and ARG examples, used to train the supervised token classifier baseline.

To make the token-level dataset for our low-resource ARG examples comparable to the sentence-level dataset described in Table 1, we included a similar amount of claims and premises. The sentence-level dataset contains 64 claims and 64 premises, while the BIO dataset contains 68 claim and 96 premises entities. For both SG17 and ARG, we excluded O spans from the test set, as only claims and premises are included in the sentence-level experiments.

Label	SG17		ARG	
	train	test	train	test
B-claim	1.8k	573	62	527
I-claim	25k	6.2k	1.1k	3.8k
B-premise	3k	833	87	585
I-premise	50k	10.6k	1.8k	7.5k
O	35k	-	1.4k	-

Table 4: Total number of samples in each class for BIO datasets for Experiment 1 (SG17) and Experiment 2 (ARG).

D Entailment Argument Dataset

Table 5 shows the class distribution of the 700 NLI examples we created from SG17 and ARG datasets, used to train our ARG-NLI fine-tuned zero-shot model.

Label	SG17		ARG	
	train	dev	train	dev
Entails	263	56	225	56
Contradicts	17	4	27	7
Neutral	280	60	308	77
Total	560	140	560	140
	700		700	

Table 5: Total number of argument entailment samples in each class for Experiment 1 (SG17) and Experiment 2 (ARG).

E Hyperparameters

We used the default settings of HuggingFace transformers and OpenAI for most of the parameters except the following:

- Bert-Sequence
  - eps=1e-8
  - lr = 2e-5
  - max_length = 256
- Bert-BIO
  - lr = 5e-5
  - max_seq_length = 512
- LLM zero-shot
  - temperature = 0
  - top_p = 1
  - max_tokens = 16
- LLM fine-tuned
  - temperature = 0
  - top_p = 1
  - max_tokens = 2
- Our approach (Bart-PEPT)
  - model_max_length = 1024
  - prompt length = 20 tokens
  - lr = 2e-5 (significantly different from the value Lester et al. (2021) used)

Towards Fine-Grained Argumentation Strategy Analysis in Persuasive Essays

Robin Schaefer and **René Knaebel** and **Manfred Stede**
Applied Computational Linguistics
University of Potsdam
14476 Potsdam, Germany
{robin.schaefer|rene.knaebel|stede}@uni-potsdam.de

Abstract

We define an *argumentation strategy* as the set of rhetorical and stylistic means that authors employ to produce an effective, and often persuasive, text. First computational accounts of such strategies have been relatively coarse-grained, while in our work we aim to move to a more detailed analysis. We extend the annotations of the Argument Annotated Essays corpus (Stab and Gurevych, 2017) with specific types of claims and premises, propose a model for their automatic identification and show first results, and then we discuss usage patterns that emerge with respect to the essay structure, the "flows" of argument component types, the claim-premise constellations, the role of the essay prompt type, and that of the individual author.

1 Introduction

The field of Argument Mining (AM), which has grown into a productive area of research during the last decade (Stede and Schneider, 2018; Lawrence and Reed, 2020), focuses on the tasks of automatic identification and extraction of argumentation in natural language. This includes the detection of argument components, like claims (Daxenberger et al., 2017; Schaefer et al., 2022) and premises (Rinott et al., 2015), and the relations between them (Carstens and Toni, 2015). Research has been conducted on different text domains ranging from more edited texts, e.g. editorials (Al-Khatib et al., 2016) or Wikipedia texts (Rinott et al., 2015), to social media, e.g. Change My View (Hidey et al., 2017) or Twitter (Schaefer and Stede, 2022).

A so far relatively understudied area of interest is the identification of argumentation strategies, i.e., the decisions that authors make on linearizing their argumentation and on marking it with linguistic expressions for persuasive effect (Al-Khatib et al., 2017; El Baff et al., 2019). Effectiveness, which can be described as one dimension of argumentation quality (Wachsmuth et al., 2017), depends (inter alia) on using the "right" arguments for the audience, their arrangement, and their linguistic formulation. This is also the case for persuasive essays, which already have been extensively used in AM research (Stab and Gurevych, 2014b; Wachsmuth et al., 2016), but to the best of our knowledge not much for modeling underlying strategies. To contribute to filling this gap we utilize our own claim and premise type annotations to extract semantic "flow patterns" from the Argument Annotated Essays (AAE) corpus (Stab and Gurevych, 2017). We argue that these types and flow patterns are fine-grained and informative to shed more light on the strategies authors of persuasive essays apply to structure their texts.

The contributions of this paper are: 1) We provide a dataset with claim and premise *type* annotations for the full AAE corpus (Sct. 3) by revising and extending the prior work of Carlile et al. (2018); 2) we trained classification models on our annotations and present first promising results (Sct. 4); 3) we contribute to argumentation strategy modeling by (i) extracting flow patterns of the argument component types, also in relation to the essay structure (roles of different paragraphs), (ii) examining the patterns of claim and supporting premise w.r.t. their types, and (iii) looking into the influences of essay prompt as well as the individual author of the text (Sct. 5).

2 Related Work

Argument Mining in Essays. Stab and Gurevych (2014a) presented the first edition of the AAE corpus, which consisted of 90 persuasive essays annotated for argument components and relations. Later, it was extended to 402 essays (Stab and Gurevych, 2017). This corpus has been repeatedly used for component detection (Stab and Gurevych, 2014b; Schaefer et al., 2022) and as a starting point for component type

Proceedings of the 10th Workshop on Argument Mining, pages 76–88
December 7, 2023.

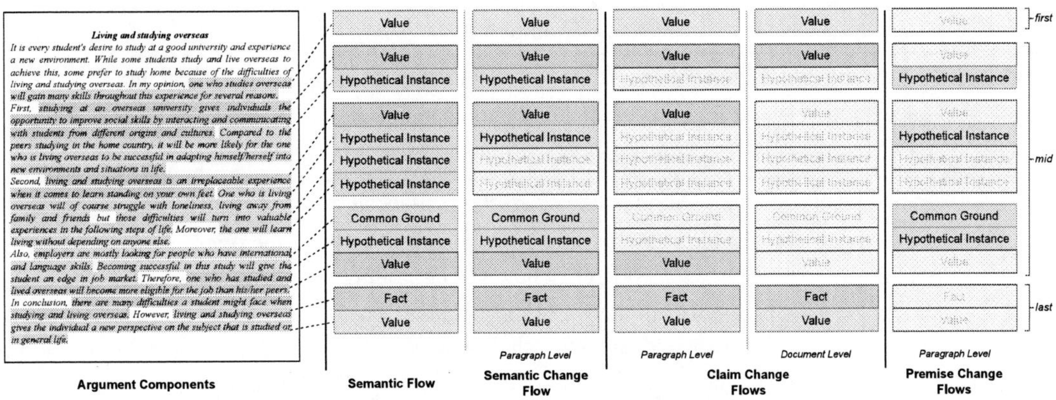

Figure 1: Overview: Essay #5 (Stab and Gurevych, 2017) with argument component types: major claim (blue), claim (red), and premise (green). Based on our semantic types, different variants of semantic flows are demonstrated.

annotations (Carlile et al., 2018).

Considerable work has been dedicated to automated essay quality scoring (Ke and Ng, 2019). While essays often were assigned only holistic scores, more recently research has shifted towards the investigation of individual dimensions of essay quality, e.g., coherence or persuasiveness (Nguyen and Litman, 2018). While argument patterns and strategies are related to essay quality, in this paper we do not specifically investigate the implications for quality but leave that to future work.

Argument Component Types. Type tagsets have been proposed for different argument components and data domains. In more formal texts like Wikipedia articles (Rinott et al., 2015), news editorials (Al-Khatib et al., 2016) or argumentative essays (Carlile et al., 2018) premises are categorized as *study/statistics*, *expert/testimony*, *anecdote* and/or *common knowledge/common ground*, among others. Hua and Wang (2017) annotated the types *study*, *factual*, *opinion*, and *reasoning* in idebate.org texts. With respect to claims, Carlile et al. (2018) assigned the types *fact*, *value*, and *policy*, as well as Aristotle's modes of persuasion *logos*, *pathos*, and *ethos* (Higgins and Walker, 2012). Recently, Chen et al. (2022) annotated argumentative units in Amazon reviews with the types *fact*, *testimony*, *policy*, and *value* in order to enable review helpfulness prediction.[1]

For Twitter, Addawood and Bashir (2016) applied a set of premise types to *news media accounts*, *blog posts*, or *pictures*. Dusmanu et al. (2017) annotated argumentative tweets according to them being *factual* or *opinionated*. More recently, Schaefer and Stede (2022) used the premise types *reason* and *external/internal evidence* and annotated claims for their *un/verifiability* (Park and Cardie, 2014). Other relevant social media platforms include the subreddit Change My View. Hidey et al. (2017) assign a rather unique set of types to claims, consisting of *interpretation*, *evaluation-rational*, *evaluation-emotional*, and *agreement/disagreement*, while annotating premises with *logos*, *pathos*, and *ethos*.

In our work, we use a modified set of claim and premise types for annotation, which has been derived from the annotation guidelines applied by Al-Khatib et al. (2016) and Carlile et al. (2018).

Argument Patterns. Wachsmuth et al. (2016) experiment with argumentative discourse unit (ADU) flows. They train models on argumentative essays in AAE (Stab and Gurevych, 2014a) to automatically identify argument components in the larger ICLE corpus (Granger et al., 2020). In contrast to their work, we use more fine-grained semantic classes instead of the argument component types themselves. We expect more informative patterns for describing the writing strategies in student essays. Al-Khatib et al. (2017) adapt previous work, extract evidence types (*statistics*, *testimony*, *anecdote*) in argumentative newspaper editorials, and show differences across automatically classified topics.

3 Corpus & Annotation

In this section, we briefly describe the corpus we use, i.e. the AAE corpus (Stab and Gurevych, 2017). In addition, we present our annotation scheme, the procedure, and results.

[1]While their vocabulary overlaps with Carlile et al. (2018), their definitions (except for *policy*) are notably different.

	Examples	Type
1)	[...] we should attach more importance to cooperation during primary education.	P
2)	[...] keeping the cultural traditions in the destination countries is tremendous important.	V
3)	[...] teachers teach us knowledge but also the skills to tell right from wrong.	F
4)	Frank Zappa once said, "Mind is like a parachute, it doesn't work if its not open"	T
5)	The waste products and harmful gases produced by these factories cause a significant amount of air pollution.	S
6)	[...] if there are no animals in the world, the balance of nature will broke down, and we, human, will die out as well.	HI
7)	[...] tourism makes up one-third of the Czech Republic's economy.	RE
8)	Nowadays, time is the most valuable thing in life with increased pace.	CG

Table 1: Examples of semantic type annotations. Abbreviations: P (policy), V (value), F (fact), T (testimony), S (statistics), HI (hypothetical-instance), RE (real-example), CG (common-ground). Linguistic errors in the original text have not been corrected.

3.1 The Argument Annotated Essays Corpus

The AAE corpus (Stab and Gurevych, 2017) consists of 402 persuasive student essays, which were written in response to a prompt (e.g. *International tourism is now more common than ever before. Some feel that this is a positive trend, [...]. What are your opinions on this?*). The essays have been annotated for the core components of argumentation, i.e., (major) claim and premise. Persuasive essays tend to exhibit a rather rigid structure, which is reflected in the actual usage of the components.

An essay starts with an introduction, which usually contains the *major claim*. The major claim is the author's main stance regarding the essay's topic, i.e., the prompt. The introduction is followed by several paragraphs in which the actual argumentation unfolds. Each paragraph contains one or more arguments, consisting of a *claim* and at least one *premise*, the latter of which supports or attacks the former. The claim bears a stance toward the major claim. Thus, a unit's argument role depends on its position in the argumentative tree; e.g., a unit directly relating to a major claim is a claim.

In this work, we add another annotation layer to the corpus, claim types and premise types. While Carlile et al. (2018) annotated semantic types for only 102 essays, we applied our modified annotation scheme to the full corpus of 402 essays.

3.2 Annotation Scheme

We derived and modified our annotation scheme from the schemes created by Carlile et al. (2018) and Al-Khatib et al. (2016). We annotate three claim types (*policy*, *value* and *fact*) and five premise types (*testimony*, *statistics*, *hypothetical-instance*, *real-example* and *common-ground*).[2] We motivate our decision to apply a new annotation scheme as follows: 1) In our initial experiments, annotating the dataset using the guidelines by Carlile et al. (2018) was challenging and repeatedly led to low IAA. 2) Some types were rarely annotated (analogy, definition) or difficult to define (warrant). These were removed from our set. 3) Some types were also used in other studies (e.g., testimony and statistics; Al-Khatib et al. (2016)) and allow for a potential comparison across corpora. See Table 1 for annotation examples.

Claim Types. We annotated the same claim types as Carlile et al. (2018) but modified their definitions in order to facilitate the annotation process. All types are defined with a focus on the author's argumentative intention, i.e., what they argue for. As this is usually left somewhat implicit, the annotator needs to take into account the context of the essay to understand the author's reasoning.

A *policy* claim is used to argue towards some action to be taken or not to be taken, while a *value* claim attaches a certain value to a target, e.g., good/bad or important/unimportant. Importantly, this often is achieved using implicit means, which complicates the annotation procedure. Finally, a *fact* claim is used to argue in favor or against some target statement being true or false, i.e., it asserts

[2] Our data and annotation guidelines can be found here: `https://github.com/discourse-lab/arg-essays-semantic-types`.

something to (not) hold in the world. Crucially, a *fact* claim does not need to state an actual truth in the world (fact checking is a separate issue) but is used to convince the audience of the target's assumed truthfulness or falseness. As these classes semantically overlap to a certain degree, we apply a claim annotation hierarchy: policy > value > fact.

Premise Types. The premise types were initially derived from those of Carlile et al. (2018). However, as testing the guidelines in early annotation sessions did not yield promising results, we refined our guidelines using the evidence type definitions of Al-Khatib et al. (2016).

A *testimony* unit gives evidence by stating or quoting that a proposition was made by an expert, authority, group, or similar. The expert can be explicitly named, but a more general usage is also accepted, such as "Scientists suggest that...". *Statistics* states the results of quantitative research or studies, and also includes more general phrasings that refer to quantitative analyses and dependencies. The latter focuses on proportions, aggregations like the mean, correlations, or similar dimensions.

We apply two *example* categories, viz. *real-example* and *hypothetical-instance*. A *real-example* describes either a real (historical) event, that can be located in space and/or time, or a specific statement about the world. The event or statement can be "proven" by an external source, which does not need to be given. While the author's personal experiences are treated as *real-example*, usually described using 1st person pronouns, statements adopting any 3rd person perspective are treated as *testimony*. A *hypothetical-instance* is similar to a *real-example*, but as it is hypothetical it was conceived merely by the author and thus cannot be verified by an external source.

A *common-ground* unit includes statements being depicted as common knowledge or self-evident fact. In other words, the author presents them as being accepted without evidence by most readers. In contrast with the example categories, *common-ground* refers to general issues, not to specific events or statements. Finally, we use an *other* class to allow for the annotation of units that the annotator is uncertain about. We apply the following premise annotation hierarchy: testimony > statistics > hypothetical-instance > real-example > common-ground > other.

Annotation Class	Krippendorff's α
Policy	0.78
Value	0.52
Fact	0.34
Claim Type	*0.52*
Testimony	-
Statistics	0.16
Hypothetical-Instance	0.70
Real-Example	0.58
Common-Ground	0.42
Other	-
Premise Type	*0.53*

Table 2: Inter-annotator agreement.

3.3 Annotation Procedure

Three annotators, one of whom is a co-author of this paper, were trained to annotate the data. On a paragraph-by-paragraph basis the annotation task consists of 1) annotating the types of all claims and 2) annotating the types of all premises.

Annotators were trained in an iterative manner. A first draft of the guidelines was tested by two annotators in an initial round of 20 essays. Afterward, IAA was calculated, and feedback was given by the annotators leading to revised guidelines. These steps were repeated until acceptable IAA scores were obtained. Then, the third annotator was trained using the final annotation guidelines and another set of 20 essays. Once all annotators were able to complete the task, they labeled the same set of 40 essays, i.e., 10% of the corpus, in order to calculate the final IAA scores. Finally, two annotators continued labeling until the whole corpus was annotated (with one single judgement).

3.4 Annotation Results

We evaluate our annotation guidelines in terms of Krippendorff's α (Artstein and Poesio, 2008). In addition to the IAA by component (claim and premise) we calculate alpha for individual semantic types by using a binary "class vs. not class" distinction. See Table 2 for the IAA.

With respect to claim types, annotators obtained the best results for the policy class (0.78). *Value* yielded a score of 0.52, while the fact class obtained a score of 0.34. Calculating IAA on the set of all claim type annotations received a score of 0.52.

Considering premise type annotation, the best results were obtained for hypothetical-instance (0.70) and real-example (0.58), which are both example classes. Common-Ground achieved a score of 0.42. The statistics class posed a challenge for annota-

Annotation Class	Counts	Proportion
Policy	344	0.15
Value	1,502	0.67
Fact	411	0.18
Testimony	22	0.01
Statistics	400	0.10
Hypothetical-Instance	917	0.24
Real-Example	717	0.19
Common-Ground	1774	0.46
Other	2	0.00

Table 3: Annotation statistics: counts and proportions.

tors (0.16). As our set of 40 essays did not provide enough testimony to calculate IAA, we cannot present results for this class. Altogether, annotators achieved a score of 0.53 for the set of all premise types.

3.5 Corpus Statistics

In this work, we provide another annotation layer for the AAE corpus. Hence, all basic corpus statistics were obtained from the originally published dataset.[3] The corpus consists of 402 essays with a mean token count of 357 (min: 207; max: 550) and a mean sentence count of 17 (min: 8; max: 33). On average the essays consist of five paragraphs (min: 3; max: 7), including the introduction and the final paragraph. The paragraphs have a mean ADU count of 3 (min: 1; max: 12).

Our annotations show a notable class imbalance (see Table 3). *Value* is the dominant claim type with a proportion of 0.67, followed by *fact* (0.18) and *policy* (0.15). With respect to premise types, *common-ground* was annotated most frequently (0.46). The *example* categories *hypothetical-instance* and *real-example* show a comparable proportion (0.24 vs 0.19), while *statistics* has been identified more rarely (0.10). *Testimony* shows a small proportion of 0.01. *Other* only has been annotated twice and will be ignored in the following sections.

4 Classification of Semantic ADU Types

We fine-tune a pre-trained language model, the *roberta-base* architecture (Liu et al., 2019), to predict semantic types. As input we use solely the argument component span, without further context. See Appendix A for details on hyper-parameters. Our complete classification results are also provided there; in the following, we mention the main points.

We train the semantic type classifiers separately for the different ADU types (major claim, claim, premise), and in addition with the variant of combining the two claim types (major claim and claim). Per run, the data is randomly divided into train/dev/test with proportions 80/10/10. The results that we report are averaged over 10 runs.

Previous State of the Art. To allow for comparison with previous research by Ke et al. (2018), we first train our neural model on their originally annotated 102 essays (henceforth referred to as PREVIOUS). While they provide only accuracy (micro-average) results, we will below, in contrast, present a more detailed report with a per-class evaluation. Our accuracy for claim type predictions is better, with 76.9% compared to 69.5% reported by Ke et al. (2018). For premise types, we achieved 70.1% accuracy, compared to 31.2%.

The main contribution to our increase in performance is probably due to the pre-trained language model. A closer look at the premises' macro F1 scores reveals that the only class that is well-predicted is *common-ground* (81.5 F1), followed by *real-example* (65.6 F1) and *statistics* (30.3 F1). Three out of eight classes (*analogy*, *testimony*, and *definition*) have no predictions at all, due to the imbalanced class distribution.

Baseline. As a baseline for the experiments with our own annotations on the full corpus (402 texts), we take the simple prediction of the most frequent (majority) semantic type observed in the training data per ADU type. This yields macro scores for major claims and claims of 26.2 F1 and 26.9 F1, respectively, while for premises it amounts to only 13.5 F1, in part due to the higher number of classes.

Results. Trained on our annotation, the neural model clearly outperforms the baselines. For both major claim types (75.9 F1) and claim types (77.2 F1), we achieved very good results. In comparison to PREVIOUS, our claim predictions increased by 12.4 F1. While we perform better on *value* and *policy* classification, PREVIOUS has higher scores on *fact*, which is probably due to different label distributions: Two-thirds of the claim labels in the data of Carlile et al. (2018) are facts. Unexpectedly, training with a fused class of the two claim types has not led to an improved performance. While the F1 score for *fact* is marginally better, the

[3]We use the Trankit Toolkit (Nguyen et al., 2021) for data preprocessing.

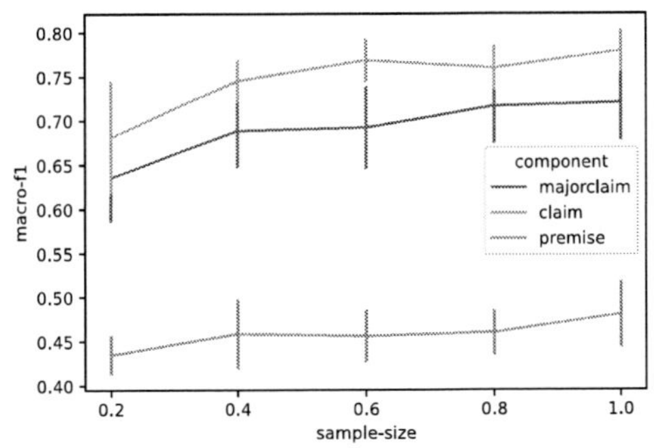

Figure 2: Learning curve with respect to sample size.

performance of the other two classes (*value* and *policy*) does not improve. Here, the results are just in between the separately trained models.

For the premise predictions, we achieve similar performance (70.2%) as PREVIOUS in terms of accuracy. However, the higher macro-average of our model (56.6 F1) compared to PREVIOUS (25.0 F1) indicates a better balance of our per-class predictions. The complete results are shown in Appendix A.

Data Size Learning Curve. We study how our additionally annotated data affects the performance of our neural model. We run the same experiments, but after splitting the test set we use only a subsample for training and development.[4]

Figure 2 shows the varying performance of our models with different portions (20% to 100%) of training data. While the increase for semantic types of premises is not particularly high, a larger increase in performance is evident for the two other ADU classes, claim and major claim. This shows that the effort of additional annotation is justified.

5 Pattern Extraction and Analysis

Argumentative essays have a very specific structure, as described in Section 3. Following previous works on argument component types (Wachsmuth et al., 2016) and argumentation strategies (Al-Khatib et al., 2017), we hypothesize finding similar patterns of semantic argument types in the essays.

First, we linearize the semantic types and order them by their textual positions. In Figure 1, for example, the essay starts with a value-based major claim in the first paragraph, followed by a value claim and a premise with semantic type *hypothetical-instance*. The full sequence of semantic types is referred to as the *semantic flow* of the essay. We further abstract over semantic repetitions, thus resulting in so-called *semantic change flows*. For example, in the previous flow, multiple consecutive *hypothetical-instances* are reduced to a single occurrence. This abstraction leads to more reliable/general patterns (Al-Khatib et al., 2017). Similar to Wachsmuth et al. (2016), we use the natural structure of argumentative essays and split them into paragraphs, as individual arguments are fully contained in single paragraphs. This reduces the length of extracted patterns and their variance.

Additionally, we also study differences in the semantic change flows of component types. For claim change flows, besides paragraphs we study their change flow on full documents, too. As claims should only relate to the major claim, we assume document-level change flows should summarize the global structure of an essay quite well. For premises, we restrict our study to the paragraph level, as premises should not be connected to the premises of other paragraphs.

Argument components show different distributions across paragraphs, with major claims only appearing in the first and last, and premises predominantly being used in the middle paragraphs. This has an effect on the semantic flows. See Table 4 for our semantic change flow results.

Regarding the change flows of claim types (see Table 4 (a)), the first paragraph often only contains flows consisting of a single unit, usually a major claim (value: 0.35; policy: 0.18; fact: 0.07). If a flow of two units can be found, a major claim usually precedes a claim. This pattern deviates from the last paragraph, where the major claim is reformulated. It is common for a change flow to start or end with a major claim. The middle paragraphs are dominated by individual claim types (value: 0.65; fact: 0.23; policy: 0.09), while changes from one type to another occur more rarely. With respect to claim change flows over full essays, changes between types most prominently occur 2-4 times. Usually two major claim types are combined with 1-3 claim types. The value type is most commonly applied, which is reflected by the distribution of type annotations. Individual combinations of value and fact types are a more common pattern than other claim type combinations.

Considering the change flows of premise types (see Table 4 (b)) *common-ground* is the most common type, It is used either as an individual flow or

[4]We make sure that the different component models use the same test split across varying sample ratios.

Level	#	Change Flow	Freq
par-first	1	(M:Value)	0.35
	2	(M:Policy)	0.18
	3	(C:Value)	0.11
	4	(M:Fact)	0.07
	5	(M:Value, C:Value)	0.06
	6	(C:Value, M:Value)	0.04
	7	(C:Fact)	0.03
	8	(M:Policy, C:Value)	0.03
	9	(C:Policy)	0.02
	10	(M:Value, C:Fact)	0.02
par-mid	1	(C:Value)	0.65
	2	(C:Fact)	0.23
	3	(C:Policy)	0.09
	4	(C:Fact, C:Value)	0.01
	5	(C:Value, C:Fact)	0.01
par-last	1	(M:Value)	0.23
	2	(M:Value, C:Value)	0.14
	3	(C:Value, M:Value)	0.14
	4	(M:Policy)	0.08
	5	(M:Policy, C:Value)	0.08
	6	(C:Value, M:Policy)	0.04
	7	(C:Fact, M:Value)	0.03
	8	(M:Fact)	0.03
	9	(M:Value, C:Fact)	0.03
	10	(M:Value, C:Policy)	0.02
full	1	(M:Value, C:Value, M:Value)	0.09
	2	(M:Value, C:Value, M:Value, C:Value)	0.05
	3	(M:Value, C:Value, C:Fact, M:Value)	0.04
	4	(C:Value, M:Value)	0.03
	5	(M:Value, C:Fact, C:Value, M:Value)	0.03
	6	(M:Value, C:Value, C:Fact, C:Value, M:Value)	0.02
	7	(M:Value, C:Fact, C:Value, M:Value, C:Value)	0.01
	8	(M:Policy, C:Value, M:Policy, C:Value)	0.01
	9	(C:Value, C:Fact, M:Value)	0.01
	10	(C:Value, M:Value, C:Value)	0.01

(a) Claim change flows.

Level	#	Change Flow	Freq
par-mid	1	(CG)	0.20
	2	(CG, HI)	0.11
	3	(HI)	0.07
	4	(CG, RE)	0.06
	5	(CG, HI, CG)	0.04
	6	(S, CG)	0.04
	7	(RE)	0.03
	8	(HI, CG)	0.03
	9	(S)	0.03
	10	(CG, S)	0.02

(b) Premise change flows.

Level	#	Change Flow	Freq
par-mid	1	(C:Value, CG)	0.08
	2	(C:Value, HI)	0.04
	3	(C:Value, CG, HI)	0.03
	4	(CG, C:Value)	0.03
	5	(C:Fact, CG)	0.03
	6	(C:Value, RE)	0.02
	7	(C:Value, S, CG)	0.02
	8	(CG, HI, C:Value)	0.02
	9	(C:Value, CG, RE)	0.02
	10	(C:Value, CG, HI, CG)	0.02
	11	(C:Value, HI, CG)	0.01
	12	(C:Policy, CG)	0.01
	13	(CG, C:Value, CG)	0.01
	14	(C:Fact, CG, HI)	0.01
	15	(C:Value, S)	0.01
	16	(CG, C:Fact)	0.01
	17	(CG, RE, C:Value)	0.01
	18	(C:Value, HI, RE)	0.01
	19	(C:Value, CG, HI, CG, HI)	0.01
	20	(C:Value, RE, CG)	0.01

(c) Claim and premise change flows.

Table 4: Most common change flows of semantic types for different argument components. The letters M and C followed by a colon refer to major claim and claim, respectively. For premise types, we use the abbreviations: CG (common-ground), HI (hypothetical-instance), RE (real-example), and S (statistics).

in combination with other types, the latter of which most often starts with *common-ground*. The most prominent change flow consisting of three types is *(CG, HI, CG)*. A combination of the two example types *hypothetical-instance* and *real-example* is not among the most frequent change flows. *Statistics* most often co-occurs with *common-ground*.

Finally, the claim and premise change flows by paragraph (see Table 4 (c)) reveal that a middle paragraph most often begins with a value claim followed by at least one premise of a certain type. More complex change flows contain *common-ground* and *hypothetical-instance* (e.g. (C:Value, CG, HI); (C:Value, CG, HI, CG)). Flows including fact claims are slightly more frequent than flows including policy claims.

Patterns of Claim-Premise Pairs. In addition to the extraction of semantic type flows we are interested in analyzing the patterns of claims with their direct premise dependents (see Table 5). While the former is focusing on linear order, the latter is hierarchical in nature.

All claim types exhibit the same order of types among their direct premise dependents, i.e., *common-ground* is the most dominant type, followed by *hypothetical-instance*, *real-example*, *statistics*, and *testimony*. This order is reflected by annotation proportions. However, differences between claim types can be observed with respect to the distribution of premise types. Policy claims are associated with a notably larger proportion of *common-ground* (0.59 vs. 0.47/0.43) and a smaller proportion of *real-example* (0.11 vs. 0.19/0.17), while also showing the largest difference between *common-ground* and the following premise type *hypothetical-instance*. Fact claims are supported by the largest proportion of *statistics* (0.15 vs. 0.09/0.10). *Hypothetical-instance* is rather equally distributed with a small drop for policy claims.

Effects of Prompt Type and Author. As the argumentative essays were written in response to prompts, we are interested in identifying their po-

Claim Type	Premise Type	Proportion
Policy	Common-Ground	0.59
	Hypothetical-Instance	0.20
	Real-Example	0.11
	Statistics	0.09
	Testimony	0.01
Value	Common-Ground	0.47
	Hypothetical-Instance	0.24
	Real-Example	0.19
	Statistics	0.10
	Testimony	<0.01
Fact	Common-Ground	0.43
	Hypothetical-Instance	0.25
	Real-Example	0.17
	Statistics	0.15
	Testimony	<0.01
	other	<0.01

Table 5: Claim heads and their direct premise dependents. Only support relations are considered.

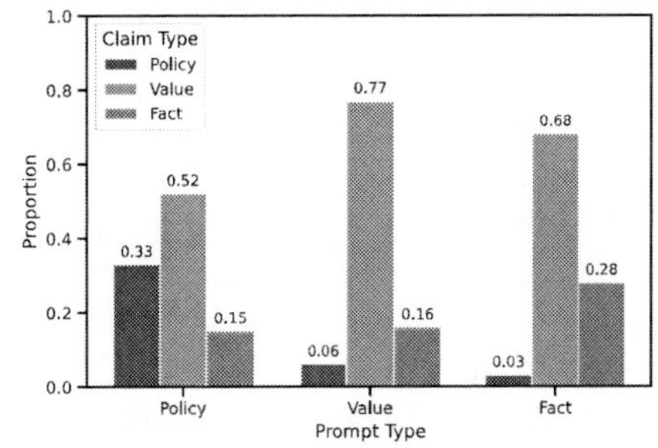

Figure 3: Claim type proportions by prompt type.

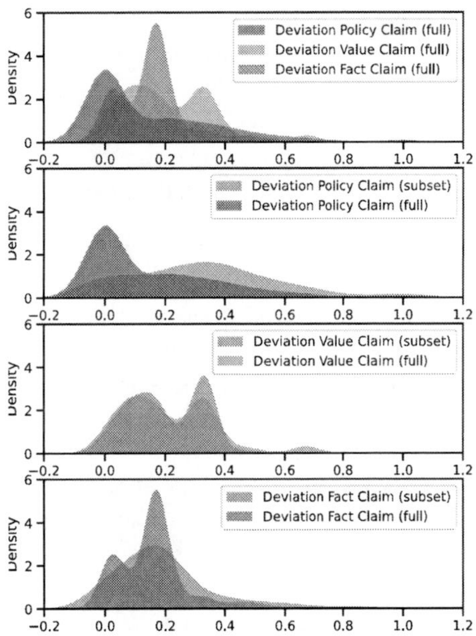

Figure 4: Density plots of absolute deviation from proportion median by claim type for full dataset (plot 1) and by prompt type subset (*policy*: plot 2; *value*: plot 3; *fact*: plot 4).

tential effect on the claim type distribution. To achieve this we annotated each prompt with a type from our set of claim types. As the whole *prompt* can consist of multiple propositions, we only consider its central message in combination with the actual prompting sentence, which is often phrased as a question. Consider the prompt example shown in Section 3.1: *International tourism is now more common than ever before. Some feel that this is a positive trend, [...]. What are your opinions on this?*. While this *prompt* bears some complexity, it primarily asks the author to present their opinion on whether the growth of international tourism represents a positive or negative trend. Thus, this prompt is labeled with type *value*.

After the prompt annotation, we calculated the claim type class distribution by prompt type.[5] Due to duplicates among the prompts we only consider 370 individual prompts in our analysis (see Figure 3). While value claims are dominant across all prompts, it is notable that the prompt type has an effect. Policy prompts elicit essays with a rather high policy claim proportion (0.33) while essays in response to value and fact prompts rarely show *policy*. Furthermore, essays written in response to fact prompts show the highest proportion of fact claims (0.28 vs. 0.15/0.16) while value prompts elicit essays with the highest proportion of value claims (0.77 vs. 0.52/0.68).

Another potential factor of interest is the author, i.e., the usage of argument types may depend on the person writing the essay. In order to investigate this question we calculated each essay's absolute deviation from the median proportion by claim type. The median was calculated using the 370 essays elicited by individual prompts. We use density plots to show the distribution of absolute deviation (see Figure 4, plot 1). The analysis reveals a substantial difference in distribution by claim type. While the deviation from the median of the policy proportion is positively skewed, the deviation of the value annotations shows a bimodal distribution. The fact annotations' deviation also show a bimodal distribution, albeit with a stark difference in density between major and minor modes. While being differently distributed, all claim types show

[5]Prompt types are distributed as follows: policy: 0.37; value: 0.48; fact: 0.15.

a notable deviation from the respective proportion median.

While both prompt and author may have an independent effect, they may interact with each other (see Figure 4, plots 2-4; see Appendix B for a full analysis). We show the effect of prompt type by splitting the dataset accordingly and individually comparing the distribution of deviation per claim type with the respective distribution of the full dataset. Plot 2 reveals that the deviation of policy claim annotations in the policy prompt subset is more broadly spread than in the full dataset. In the fact prompt subset, the deviation distribution of fact claim annotations resembles a normal distribution, while it is bimodal in the full dataset (plot 4). However, the distributions of deviation of value claim annotations appear to be similar in both the value prompt subset and the full dataset (plot 3).

6 Discussion

Our change flow analysis reveals several frequently occurring patterns. To begin with, an essay usually starts with a major claim (most frequently of type *value* or *policy*) which is sometimes followed by a claim. The final paragraph, however, shows more flexibility regarding the ordering of both claim variants, which shows that some authors choose to end with a major claim, i.e., the essay's central claim. Moreover, middle paragraphs either contain a single claim (a single argument) or several claims of the same type, which may show an author's tendency to not switch between claim types within a paragraph. Then, while both major claims and claims are most frequently of type *value*, we found a notable difference in the usage of policy and fact types. While *policy* more often occurs in major claim flows, i.e., in the first and last paragraphs, *fact* is more prominently applied as a claim type in the middle paragraphs. Thus, an essay's central claim is more often arguing towards some action being taken, while the argumentation unfolding in the essay's body more often focuses on the question if a target is true or not.

Regarding the usage of premise types we observe the frequent pattern of flows starting with *common-ground* and ending with a different type, or, alternatively, of *common-ground* framing another type. Hence, authors tend to begin their flow of premises with a general statement, followed, e.g., by an example. Less often, *common-ground* is applied to end a flow, while being rarely used in-between types. This may be indicative of a strategy to begin (and end) with a general observation while more concrete statements are placed in-between.

In this work, we explore the effect of two potential factors on the constellation of claim types, prompt type and author, and their potential interaction. Our prompt type analysis provides evidence that the prompt's phrasing has indeed an effect on the usage of claim types, as all prompt types elicit essays with a higher proportion of the respective claim type. Thus, authors adapt their argumentation strategy to the task at hand. We also show that authors exhibit a substantial variance in their usage of claim types, which is further dependent on the essay's prompt type. We argue that this is indicative of the task's role in choosing the most efficient argumentation strategy.

7 Conclusion

In this work, we analyzed patterns of claim and premise types in persuasive essays to shed light on underlying argumentation strategies. We extended the annotations of the AAE corpus with a layer of semantic types, which we used for automatic type classification, pattern extraction both on the level of change flows and argument relations, and the analysis of prompt and author effects on argumentation strategies.

We show that semantic types of argument components are an appropriately fine-grained level of analysis to investigate argumentation strategies. Several common patterns of semantic type flows could be identified. Furthermore, we provide evidence for the effect of author and, especially, prompt type on the adoption of argumentation strategies.

In the future, we would like to extend our scope of analysis. Further research can include the relation between prompt type and semantic flows and the effect of prompt type on the usage of premise types. We are also interested in investigating the effect of semantic flows on essay quality. Finally, we want to apply our analysis to other corpora, both in-domain (the ICLE dataset (Granger et al., 2020)) and out-of-domain (e.g., the subreddit Change My View).

Limitations

In this work, we use a corpus that consists of learner essays that exhibit a rather wide range of language levels. This may influence the distribution of patterns, as presumably the argumentation will be of different complexity.

Furthermore, while being a standard corpus in AM research, the AAE corpus offers only a limited amount of data. This is reflected in some classes being rarely represented (e.g., testimony) and affects the success of the semantic type classification. Thus, applying the framework to different data such as the ICLE dataset becomes important for getting a better impression of used patterns in persuasive essays.

Further limitations concern our analyses. So far we have not investigated the relation between prompts and semantic flows, which could yield important insights on differences in argument patterns with respect to the task. We also concentrated on the effect of prompt type and author on the usage of claim types, while ignoring their effect on the premise type distribution.

Ethics Statement

Our annotations are based on the publicly available AAE corpus. We point out that information about the essays' authors is not known for this corpus. Thus it is not possible to assess whether these essays are well distributed and representative of a broader audience.

Acknowledgements

This research has been supported by the German Research Foundation (DFG) with grant number 455911521, project "LARGA" in SPP "RATIO". We would like to thank Sophia Rauh and Hugo Meinhof for their annotation efforts, and the anonymous reviewers for their valuable feedback.

References

Aseel Addawood and Masooda Bashir. 2016. "what is your evidence?" a study of controversial topics on social media. In *Proceedings of the Third Workshop on Argument Mining (ArgMining2016)*, pages 1–11, Berlin, Germany. Association for Computational Linguistics.

Khalid Al-Khatib, Henning Wachsmuth, Matthias Hagen, and Benno Stein. 2017. Patterns of argumentation strategies across topics. In *Proceedings of the 2017 Conference on Empirical Methods in Natural Language Processing*, pages 1351–1357, Copenhagen, Denmark. Association for Computational Linguistics.

Khalid Al-Khatib, Henning Wachsmuth, Johannes Kiesel, Matthias Hagen, and Benno Stein. 2016. A news editorial corpus for mining argumentation strategies. In *Proceedings of COLING 2016, the 26th International Conference on Computational Linguistics: Technical Papers*, pages 3433–3443, Osaka, Japan. The COLING 2016 Organizing Committee.

Ron Artstein and Massimo Poesio. 2008. Inter-Coder Agreement for Computational Linguistics. *Comput. Linguist.*, 34(4):555–596.

Winston Carlile, Nishant Gurrapadi, Zixuan Ke, and Vincent Ng. 2018. Give me more feedback: Annotating argument persuasiveness and related attributes in student essays. In *Proceedings of the 56th Annual Meeting of the Association for Computational Linguistics (Volume 1: Long Papers)*, pages 621–631, Melbourne, Australia. Association for Computational Linguistics.

Lucas Carstens and Francesca Toni. 2015. Towards relation based argumentation mining. In *Proceedings of the 2nd Workshop on Argumentation Mining*, pages 29–34, Denver, CO. Association for Computational Linguistics.

Zaiqian Chen, Daniel Verdi do Amarante, Jenna Donaldson, Yohan Jo, and Joonsuk Park. 2022. Argument mining for review helpfulness prediction. In *Proceedings of the 2022 Conference on Empirical Methods in Natural Language Processing*, pages 8914–8922, Abu Dhabi, United Arab Emirates. Association for Computational Linguistics.

Johannes Daxenberger, Steffen Eger, Ivan Habernal, Christian Stab, and Iryna Gurevych. 2017. What is the essence of a claim? cross-domain claim identification. In *Proceedings of the 2017 Conference on Empirical Methods in Natural Language Processing*, pages 2055–2066, Copenhagen, Denmark. Association for Computational Linguistics.

Mihai Dusmanu, Elena Cabrio, and Serena Villata. 2017. Argument mining on Twitter: Arguments, facts and sources. In *Proceedings of the 2017 Conference on Empirical Methods in Natural Language Processing*, pages 2317–2322, Copenhagen, Denmark. Association for Computational Linguistics.

Roxanne El Baff, Henning Wachsmuth, Khalid Al Khatib, Manfred Stede, and Benno Stein. 2019. Computational argumentation synthesis as a language modeling task. In *Proceedings of the 12th International Conference on Natural Language Generation*, pages 54–64, Tokyo, Japan. Association for Computational Linguistics.

Sylviane Granger, Maïté Dupont, Fanny Meunier, Hubert Naets, and Magali Paquot. 2020. *International Corpus of Learner English. Version 3*. Presses universitaires de Louvain.

Christopher Hidey, Elena Musi, Alyssa Hwang, Smaranda Muresan, and Kathy McKeown. 2017. Analyzing the semantic types of claims and premises in an online persuasive forum. In *Proceedings of the 4th Workshop on Argument Mining*, pages 11–21,

Copenhagen, Denmark. Association for Computational Linguistics.

Colin Higgins and Robyn Walker. 2012. Ethos, logos, pathos: Strategies of persuasion in social/environmental reports. *Accounting Forum*, 36(3):194–208. Analyzing the Quality, Meaning and Accountability of Organizational Communication.

Xinyu Hua and Lu Wang. 2017. Understanding and detecting supporting arguments of diverse types. In *Proceedings of the 55th Annual Meeting of the Association for Computational Linguistics (Volume 2: Short Papers)*, pages 203–208, Vancouver, Canada. Association for Computational Linguistics.

Zixuan Ke, Winston Carlile, Nishant Gurrapadi, and Vincent Ng. 2018. Learning to give feedback: Modeling attributes affecting argument persuasiveness in student essays. In *Proceedings of the Twenty-Seventh International Joint Conference on Artificial Intelligence, IJCAI-18*, pages 4130–4136. International Joint Conferences on Artificial Intelligence Organization.

Zixuan Ke and Vincent Ng. 2019. Automated essay scoring: A survey of the state of the art. In *Proceedings of the Twenty-Eighth International Joint Conference on Artificial Intelligence, IJCAI-19*, pages 6300–6308. International Joint Conferences on Artificial Intelligence Organization.

John Lawrence and Chris Reed. 2020. Argument Mining: A Survey. *Computational Linguistics*, 45(4):765–818.

Yinhan Liu, Myle Ott, Naman Goyal, Jingfei Du, Mandar Joshi, Danqi Chen, Omer Levy, Mike Lewis, Luke Zettlemoyer, and Veselin Stoyanov. 2019. Roberta: A robustly optimized BERT pretraining approach. *CoRR*, abs/1907.11692.

Ilya Loshchilov and Frank Hutter. 2019. Decoupled weight decay regularization. In *7th International Conference on Learning Representations, ICLR 2019, New Orleans, LA, USA, May 6-9, 2019*. OpenReview.net.

Huy Nguyen and Diane Litman. 2018. Argument mining for improving the automated scoring of persuasive essays. *Proceedings of the AAAI Conference on Artificial Intelligence*, 32(1).

Minh Van Nguyen, Viet Dac Lai, Amir Pouran Ben Veyseh, and Thien Huu Nguyen. 2021. Trankit: A lightweight transformer-based toolkit for multilingual natural language processing. In *Proceedings of the 16th Conference of the European Chapter of the Association for Computational Linguistics: System Demonstrations*, pages 80–90, Online. Association for Computational Linguistics.

Joonsuk Park and Claire Cardie. 2014. Identifying appropriate support for propositions in online user comments. In *Proceedings of the First Workshop on Argumentation Mining*, pages 29–38, Baltimore, Maryland. Association for Computational Linguistics.

Ruty Rinott, Lena Dankin, Carlos Alzate Perez, Mitesh M. Khapra, Ehud Aharoni, and Noam Slonim. 2015. Show me your evidence - an automatic method for context dependent evidence detection. In *Proceedings of the 2015 Conference on Empirical Methods in Natural Language Processing*, pages 440–450, Lisbon, Portugal. Association for Computational Linguistics.

Robin Schaefer, René Knaebel, and Manfred Stede. 2022. On selecting training corpora for cross-domain claim detection. In *Proceedings of the 9th Workshop on Argument Mining*, pages 181–186, Online and in Gyeongju, Republic of Korea. International Conference on Computational Linguistics.

Robin Schaefer and Manfred Stede. 2022. GerCCT: An annotated corpus for mining arguments in German tweets on climate change. In *Proceedings of the Thirteenth Language Resources and Evaluation Conference*, pages 6121–6130, Marseille, France. European Language Resources Association.

Christian Stab and Iryna Gurevych. 2014a. Annotating argument components and relations in persuasive essays. In *Proceedings of COLING 2014, the 25th International Conference on Computational Linguistics: Technical Papers*, pages 1501–1510, Dublin, Ireland. Dublin City University and Association for Computational Linguistics.

Christian Stab and Iryna Gurevych. 2014b. Identifying argumentative discourse structures in persuasive essays. In *Proceedings of the 2014 Conference on Empirical Methods in Natural Language Processing (EMNLP)*, pages 46–56, Doha, Qatar. Association for Computational Linguistics.

Christian Stab and Iryna Gurevych. 2017. Parsing argumentation structures in persuasive essays. *Computational Linguistics*, 43(3):619–659.

Manfred Stede and Jodi Schneider. 2018. *Argumentation Mining*, volume 40 of *Synthesis Lectures in Human Language Technology*. Morgan & Claypool.

Henning Wachsmuth, Khalid Al-Khatib, and Benno Stein. 2016. Using argument mining to assess the argumentation quality of essays. In *Proceedings of COLING 2016, the 26th International Conference on Computational Linguistics: Technical Papers*, pages 1680–1691, Osaka, Japan. The COLING 2016 Organizing Committee.

Henning Wachsmuth, Nona Naderi, Yufang Hou, Yonatan Bilu, Vinodkumar Prabhakaran, Tim Alberdingk Thijm, Graeme Hirst, and Benno Stein. 2017. Computational argumentation quality assessment in natural language. In *Proceedings of the 15th Conference of the European Chapter of the Association for Computational Linguistics: Volume 1, Long Papers*, pages 176–187, Valencia, Spain. Association for Computational Linguistics.

A Hyper-Parameters & Experimental Results

For argument component classification, we use RoBERTa (Liu et al., 2019) for sequence classification. In particular, we choose the *roberta-base* architecture implemented by HuggingFace.[6] We freeze the first half of the model and only fine-tune the second half in order to reduce the computational effort.

For optimization, we use AdamW (Loshchilov and Hutter, 2019) with $5e^{-5}$ learning rate. The batch size is set to 16 throughout our experiments. We train for 10 epochs and linearly reduce the learning rate over the number of training steps.

The best model is chosen based on the best average loss during validation. Each component type's samples are randomly divided into three parts, train/dev/test with portions 80/10/10, respectively. All experiments are repeated 10 times and the reported results cover mean and standard deviation.

ADU	Semantic-Type	Precision	Recall	F1
MAJORCLAIM	fact	$0.457_{0.218}$	$0.475_{0.149}$	$0.448_{0.159}$
	value	$0.910_{0.034}$	$0.918_{0.040}$	$0.914_{0.031}$
	policy	$0.937_{0.056}$	$0.898_{0.074}$	$0.915_{0.049}$
	micro avg			$\mathbf{0.881}_{0.043}$
	macro avg	$0.768_{0.079}$	$0.763_{0.065}$	$0.759_{0.049}$
CLAIM	fact	$0.592_{0.069}$	$0.581_{0.089}$	$0.583_{0.067}$
	value	$0.857_{0.037}$	$0.862_{0.032}$	$0.859_{0.023}$
	policy	$0.871_{0.071}$	$0.882_{0.059}$	$0.874_{0.047}$
	micro avg			$\mathbf{0.800}_{0.030}$
	macro avg	$0.773_{0.032}$	$0.775_{0.031}$	$0.772_{0.020}$
(MAJOR-)CLAIM	fact	$0.626_{0.069}$	$0.556_{0.095}$	$0.587_{0.081}$
	value	$0.871_{0.021}$	$0.901_{0.021}$	$0.885_{0.015}$
	policy	$0.893_{0.030}$	$0.874_{0.052}$	$0.882_{0.030}$
	micro avg			$\mathbf{0.836}_{0.016}$
	macro avg	$0.796_{0.025}$	$0.777_{0.026}$	$0.786_{0.020}$
PREMISE	hypothetical-instance	$0.694_{0.065}$	$0.699_{0.052}$	$0.695_{0.049}$
	common-ground	$0.739_{0.025}$	$0.759_{0.034}$	$0.749_{0.024}$
	real-example	$0.785_{0.066}$	$0.731_{0.051}$	$0.756_{0.048}$
	statistics	$0.435_{0.050}$	$0.433_{0.063}$	$0.431_{0.042}$
	testimony	$0.208_{0.315}$	$0.233_{0.335}$	$0.193_{0.264}$
	micro avg			$\mathbf{0.702}_{0.030}$
	macro avg	$0.572_{0.054}$	$0.571_{0.060}$	$0.566_{0.048}$

Table 6: Class specific results (Ours) across argument components and the combination of claims and major claims.

ADU	Semantic-Type	Precision	Recall	F1
CLAIM	fact	$0.848_{0.069}$	$0.872_{0.053}$	$0.857_{0.042}$
	value	$0.584_{0.189}$	$0.556_{0.158}$	$0.538_{0.115}$
	policy	$0.579_{0.293}$	$0.645_{0.380}$	$0.549_{0.288}$
	micro avg			$\mathbf{0.769}_{0.061}$
	macro avg	$0.670_{0.104}$	$0.691_{0.106}$	$0.648_{0.098}$
PREMISE	common-knowledge	$0.744_{0.070}$	$0.911_{0.063}$	$0.815_{0.044}$
	warrant	$0.058_{0.118}$	$0.058_{0.118}$	$0.058_{0.118}$
	invented-instance	$0.250_{0.344}$	$0.154_{0.238}$	$0.164_{0.221}$
	real-example	$0.771_{0.089}$	$0.596_{0.177}$	$0.656_{0.120}$
	analogy	$0.000_{0.000}$	$0.000_{0.000}$	$0.000_{0.000}$
	testimony	$0.000_{0.000}$	$0.000_{0.000}$	$0.000_{0.000}$
	statistics	$0.467_{0.476}$	$0.242_{0.270}$	$0.303_{0.319}$
	definition	$0.000_{0.000}$	$0.000_{0.000}$	$0.000_{0.000}$
	micro avg			$\mathbf{0.701}_{0.055}$
	macro avg	$0.286_{0.087}$	$0.245_{0.066}$	$0.250_{0.065}$

Table 7: Class specific results (PREVIOUS) of our model on the 102 essays annotated by Carlile et al. (2018).

[6]www.huggingface.com

B Density Plots: Effects of Prompt Type and Author

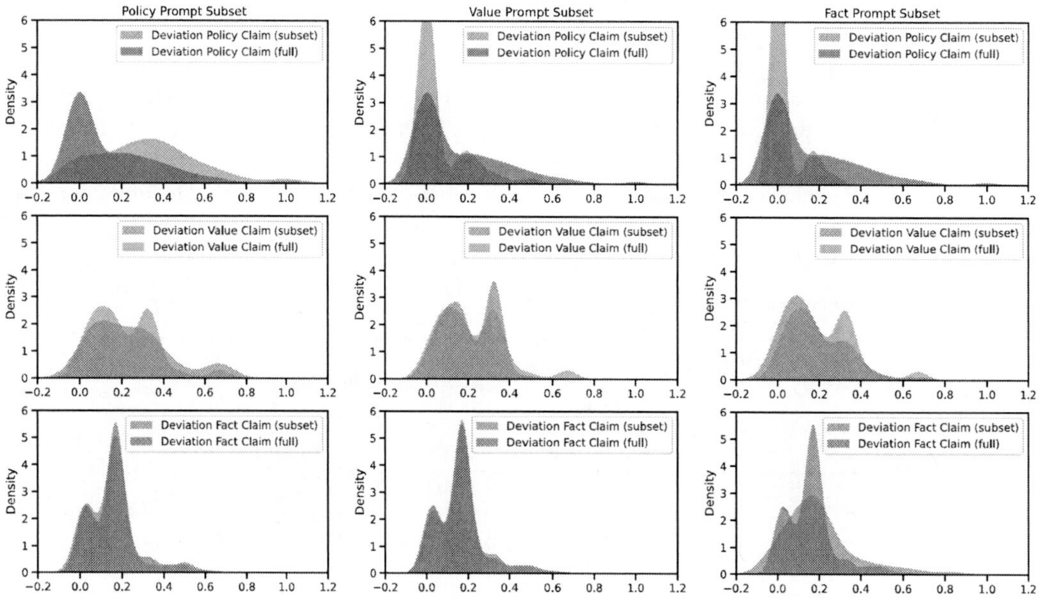

Figure 5: Comparison of density plots of absolute deviation from proportion median by claim type between full dataset and prompt type subsets. The rows are split by claim type. The columns are split by prompt type.

Dimensionality Reduction for Machine Learning-based Argument Mining

Andrés Segura-Tinoco and **Iván Cantador**
Universidad Autónona de Madrid, Madrid, Spain
andres.segurat@uam.es, ivan.cantador@uam.es

Abstract

Recent approaches to argument mining have focused on training machine learning algorithms from annotated text corpora, utilizing as input high-dimensional linguistic feature vectors. Differently to previous work, in this paper, we preliminarily investigate the potential benefits of reducing the dimensionality of the input data. Through an empirical study, testing SVD, PCA and LDA techniques on a new argumentative corpus in Spanish for an underexplored domain (e-participation), and using a novel, rich argument model, we show positive results in terms of both computation efficiency and argumentative information extraction effectiveness, for the three major argument mining tasks: argumentative fragment detection, argument component classification, and argumentative relation recognition. On a space with dimension around 3-4% of the number of input features, the argument mining methods are able to reach 95-97% of the performance achieved by using the entire corpus, and even surpass it in some cases.

1 Introduction

Since its origins in the late 2000s, the argument mining (AM) field has witnessed significant advances on the problem of automatically extracting structured argumentative information from text corpora (Lytos et al., 2019; Lawrence and Reed, 2020), which commonly entails three tasks: the identification of argumentative fragments in an input text, the split or classification of such fragments into argument components (e.g., *claims* and *premises*), and the recognition of relations (e.g., *support* and *attack*) between pairs of argument components.

In particular, previous research has led to the development of effective approaches based on machine learning (ML) (Lippi and Torroni, 2015, 2016) with results almost equal to those obtained with more complex approaches, such as those based on deep learning. Hence, argumentative fragment detection (Mochales Palau and Moens, 2009a, 2011; Poudyal et al., 2016), argument component classification (Habernal and Gurevych, 2017; Du et al., 2017), and argument relation recognition (Du et al., 2017) have been modeled as *sequence labeling* problems, where, in general, each sentence[1] is represented as a vector of real-valued linguistic features and has associated certain label or class, e.g., *argumentative* vs. *non-argumentative*, and *claim* vs. *premise*. ML algorithms are thus trained with sets of labeled sentence vectors in order to predict the class of new sentences.

In this context, a variety of features have been considered –ranging from lexical and morphological, to structural and syntactic, and semantic and discourse features (Stab and Gurevych, 2014; Aker et al., 2017; Habernal and Gurevych, 2017)– and, in general, approaches have dealt with feature vectors of high dimensionality.

To the best of our knowledge, only a few research attempts have been made to use a subset of features (Poudyal et al., 2016; Du et al., 2017). Motivated by this fact and the increasing need for more efficient (i.e., less resource-consuming) AM model building, in this paper, instead of exploring new argument-related classification algorithms, we investigate the potential benefits of reducing the dimensionality of the input data space.

As an innovative research in the AM field, we report experiments conducted with the well known SVD (Beltrami, 1973; Stewart, 1993), PCA (Hotelling, 1933) and LDA (Fisher, 1936) dimensionality reduction techniques on a novel corpus in Spanish with electronic (online) citizen participation discussions, which represent an underexplored domain in the field.

Considering a rich argument model with several argument relations, and addressing the argumenta-

[1]The majority of feature-based AM approaches consider the sentence as the argumentative unit. However, there are models that also exploit other text fragments, such as the previous and next sentences to the current sentence (Habernal and Gurevych, 2017).

Proceedings of the 10th Workshop on Argument Mining, pages 89–99
December 7, 2023.

tive fragment detection, argument component classification, and argument relation recognition tasks, we evaluate a number of ML algorithms trained with labeled data without and with dimensionality reduction, achieving favorable results in terms of both computation efficiency and argumentative information extraction effectiveness. With around 3-4% of the number of input features, the argument mining methods are able to reach 95-97% of the performance achieved by using the entire corpus, and even surpass it in some cases.

We thus claim the following contributions of our ongoing work:

- Building a new argumentative corpus in Spanish, on an underexplored, but highly relevant domain: e-participation, and more specifically, e-participatory budgeting.
- Proposing a new argument model, which includes a variety of fine-grained types of argumentative relations.
- Developing and evaluating machine learning-based methods for the main tasks of the argument mining pipeline.
- Testing the effects of dimensionality reduction on the efficiency and effectiveness of the argument mining methods.

Moreover, we make the generated argument model, corpus, annotation tool, software code, and empirical results publicly available[2].

Before presenting our experiments (Section 5) and conclusions (Sections 6 and 7), we next survey related work on feature-based machine learning AM (Section 2), and describe the addressed case study and created corpus (Section 3) and the used dimensionality reduction techniques (Section 4).

2 Related work

In this section, we survey previous work on applying feature-based machine learning for AM. We discard deep learning approaches, since they are appropriate to very large amounts of input data[3].

Feature-based ML methods model AM tasks as sequence labeling problems. They have been proposed to separately address the argumentative fragment detection (Mochales Palau and Moens, 2009a, 2011; Poudyal et al., 2016; Kunaefi and Aritsugi, 2020; Alhamzeh et al., 2021), argument component classification (Mochales Palau and Moens, 2009a, 2011; Habernal and Gurevych, 2017; Burhan ud Din Tahir, 2017), and argument relation recognition (Du et al., 2017) tasks.

The surveyed methods consider the sentence as the argument unit, and exploit its linguistic features to classify it. Only Habernal and Gurevych (2017) also exploited feature information from the previous and next sentences to the target sentence. In all cases, however, the used features are manifold, as we will detail in Section 4.1.

From our survey, only Du et al. (2017) addressed the argument relation recognition task. This is not the case in recent word embedding-based deep learning methods, which deal with the three tasks as *sequence tagging* problems, by commonly following the BIO tagging format, e.g., (Deguchi and Yamaguchi, 2019; Mayer et al., 2020).

With respect to the used ML algorithms, published work has focused on logistic regression (Du et al., 2017; Kunaefi and Aritsugi, 2020), naive Bayes (Mochales Palau and Moens, 2009a, 2011; Burhan ud Din Tahir, 2017), maximum entropy (Mochales Palau and Moens, 2009a, 2011), decision trees (Burhan ud Din Tahir, 2017; Du et al., 2017), random forests (Poudyal et al., 2016; Burhan ud Din Tahir, 2017; Du et al., 2017; Kunaefi and Aritsugi, 2020), and support vector machines (Mochales Palau and Moens, 2009a, 2011; Poudyal et al., 2016; Burhan ud Din Tahir, 2017; Du et al., 2017; Kunaefi and Aritsugi, 2020; Alhamzeh et al., 2021).

Additionally, as done in deep learning works, the surveyed papers have focused on the traditional domains and corpora of the AM field, such as the Persuasive Student Essays corpus (Burhan ud Din Tahir, 2017; Du et al., 2017; Alhamzeh et al., 2021), the legal texts ECHR (Mochales Palau and Moens, 2009a, 2011; Poudyal et al., 2016) and AraucariaDB (Mochales Palau and Moens, 2009a, 2011) corpora, and the Web Discourse corpus (Alhamzeh et al., 2021), which are mostly in English.

To the best of our knowledge, in the AM research literature, only Poudyal et al. (2016) and Du et al. (2017) have explored feature selection using information gain, reducing the input feature vector space. In this context, a traditional pre-learning di-

[2]Data and code are available at `https://github.com/argrecsys/arg-classifier`

[3]Experimenting with some deep neural network architectures, we did not achieve better performance results than those reported in this paper with traditional machine learning algorithms.

mensionality reduction approach, such as the ones we evaluate here, has not been explored yet.

Differently from (Poudyal et al., 2016; Kunaefi and Aritsugi, 2020; Alhamzeh et al., 2021), we do not only focus on classifying a sentence as *argumentative* or *non-argumentative*, but also aim to classify the type of argumentative component of a text span, i.e., a *premise* or a *claim*, and to recognize the existence of a relation between a pair of components and its type.

Finally, motivated by the need for addressing other domains and dealing with corpora in languages distinct to English, in our work we explore a novel domain in AM and provide a new corpus in Spanish, which are described next.

3 Case study

In this section, we introduce the case study for which we have built our argumentative corpus and have implemented and evaluated the machine learning-based argument mining methods with and without dimensionality reduction techniques.

Citizen participation refers to the active involvement of citizens in influencing on public opinion and being part of democratic decision and policy making processes. It represents one of the most widespread forms of open government, and historically has been conducted through physical interactions like assemblies, meetings and working groups (Gramberger, 2001).

Nowadays, under the umbrella of e-participation (Boudjelida et al., 2016), it often occurs on the internet, via online digital tools, in which citizens' opinions and contributions are easily shared, thus generating new opportunities for communication, consultation and collaboration at a large scale (Held, 2006).

The majority of current e-participation platforms are based on web forums where citizens upload comments, forming large conversation threads. This makes the processing of the underlying debates challenging and sometimes overwhelming. Without functionalities to support critical thinking and argumentation, it is usually very difficult and time-consuming for users to achieve a well-formed view of existing problems and proposed solutions.

In our work, we focus our attention on one of such platforms, Decide Madrid[4], which is an online web portal created by the City Council of Madrid (Spain) to support its annual participatory budgets since September 2015. Every year, the city residents use the platform to freely post proposals to address issues and problems in the city, and comment and vote others' proposals. Those citizen proposals that receive a certain number of votes and are technically and economically feasible are funded and implemented by the city government. In 2021-2022, the municipal budget allocated to such proposals has been 50 million euro.

Figures 1 and 2 show an example of a citizen proposal and its comment threads in Decide Madrid.

Figure 1: Screenshot of a Decide Madrid webpage showing a citizen proposal that suggests having more tree areas close to M-30, one of the principal motorways in Madrid.

Figure 2: Screenshot of a Decide Madrid webpage showing the comment threads of a citizen proposal.

Both proposal descriptions and comments are rich on argumentative information, which may be very valuable for citizens and government stakeholders, and which we aim to extract in our work. For this purpose, we consider the Decide Madrid dataset used by Cantador et al. (2017, 2020), which contains information about 21,744 citizen proposals —classified into 30 categories and 325 topics, geolocated in 21 city districts, and annotated with controversy scores—, and 62,838 comments.

From this dataset, we selected the 40 most controversial proposals, and collaboratively searched for and annotated the arguments given by citizens

[4]Decide Madrid, `https://decide.madrid.es`

in the proposals descriptions and comments, generating a first version of a corpus that we make publicly available[5]. To ease the manual argument annotation process, and store the identified arguments in a formal, structured format –including the components and relations of the arguments–, we used ARGAEL (Segura-Tinoco and Cantador, 2023), an easy-to-use, configurable desktop tool that we have developed to assist with the argument annotation and evaluation task, and which can be freely downloaded[6].

Our corpus is composed of 3,254 propositions annotated with 922 claims and 538 premises interconnected, and to the best of our knowledge, ours is one of the first argumentative corpora in Spanish in the AM field.

The underlying argument model is configured in ARGAEL and, going beyond the traditional *support* and *attack* argumentative links, it includes the following categories of relations between argument components (claims c and premises p):

- *Cause*, stating the *reason* or *condition* for an argument, e.g., "[The pollution levels in the city center are very high]$_c$ because [most people use the car to get around]$_p$," "[If the government wants to favor tourism]$_p$, [it must offer free tourist information]$_c$."

- *Clarification*, introducing a *conclusion*, *exemplification*, *restatement*, or *summary* of an argument, e.g., "As a conclusion, [we suggest the government to authorize this initiative]$_c$," "In short, [we have to wait for the results of the elections so that they can start to do something]$_c$."

- *Consequence*, evidencing an *explanation*, *goal*, or *result* of an argument, e.g., "[The use of public transport should be facilitated]$_p$ to [avoid pollution in the downtown area]$_c$," "[I have not seen garbage trucks for a week]$_p$, hence [the bins are full, and people have to throw the garbage in the streets]$_c$."

- *Contrast*, conflicting with an argument by giving *alternatives*, doing *comparisons*, making *concessions*, or providing *oppositions*, e.g., "On the other hand, [we must think about the costs that this work will cause due to its maintenance]$_c$," "[Restricting the access of private vehicles to the downtown area helps in mitigating noise]$_c$, but [it is still insufficient due to the presence of buses, taxis, etc.]$_c$"

- *Elaboration*, introducing an argument that provides details about another one, entailing *addition*, *precision*, or *similarity* issues, e.g., "[The asphalt of the streets is in very bad conditions]$_c$, moreover, [the sidewalks have holes]$_c$," "[The youth unemployment rate has increased compared to last year]$_c$, specifically, [it has gone from 23% to 28%]$_c$."

This taxonomy is a compendium of relations used in the AM literature (Knott and Dale, 1994; Mochales Palau and Moens, 2009b; Wei Feng and Hirst, 2011; Stab and Gurevych, 2014, 2017), and represent a fine-grained representation of argumentative structures, which entails addressing the argument relation recognition as a multi-class classification problem.

Specifically, in our corpus, we annotated 538 argument relations distributed by category as: 77 relations belonging to the *Cause* category, 64 to *Clarification*, 76 to *Consequence*, 120 to *Contrast*, and 201 to *Elaboration*. Figure 4 shows additional details about the number of argument relations by subcategory in the corpus.

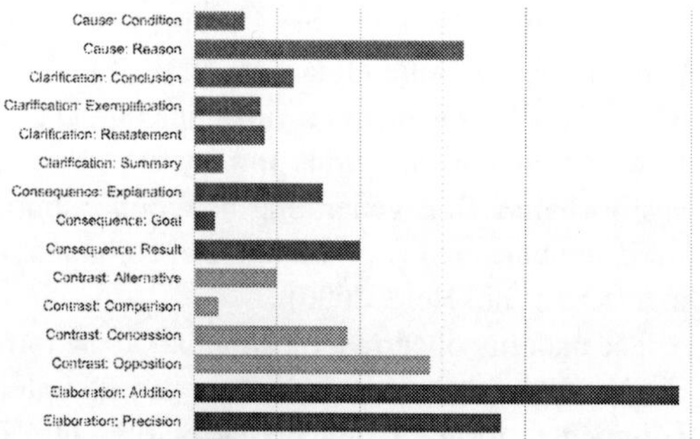

Figure 4: Number of argument relations by subcategory in our corpus.

4 Dimensionality Reduction

In this section, we introduce the linguistic features of the vector representations exploited by the evaluated ML models to AM, and the vector dimensionality reduction techniques applied before building such models.

[5]Decide Madrid corpus, `https://github.com/argrecsys/decide-madrid-2019-annotations`

[6]ARGAEL, `https://github.com/argrecsys/argael`

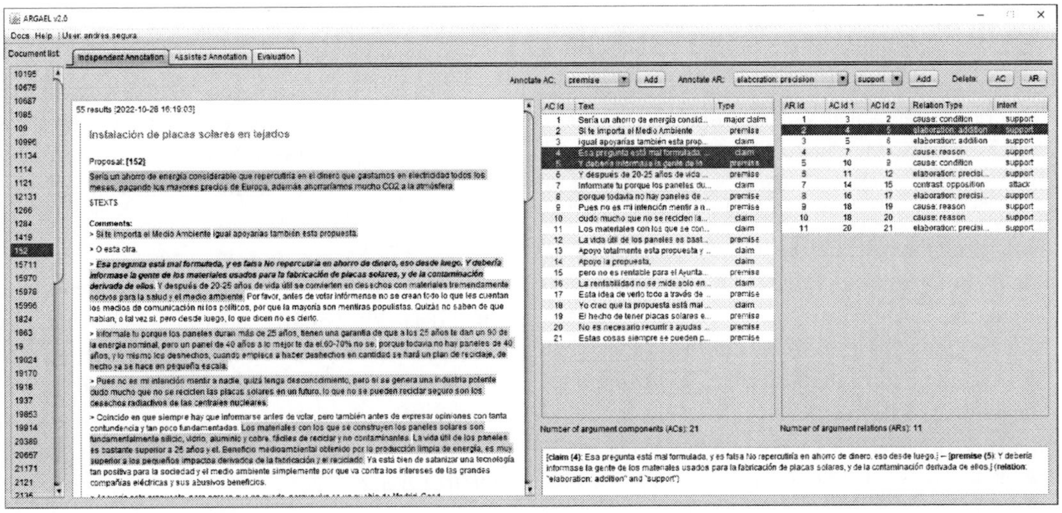

Figure 3: Screenshot of the ARGAEL tool, whose graphical user interface allows, among other things, marking argument components and relations in a set of input texts, according to a given argument model.

4.1 Linguistic Features

Researchers have considered different types of features for the AM sequence labeling tasks (Stab and Gurevych, 2014; Aker et al., 2017; Du et al., 2017; Habernal and Gurevych, 2017).

Almost all the surveyed ML-based works on argumentative fragment detection, argument component classification, and argument relation recognition make use of some well-known structural, lexical, morphosyntactic and discourse-associated features. Only Habernal and Gurevych (2017) explore the use of word embedding features (sum up the first 300 embeddings of each word, resulting in a single vector for the entire sentence) with good results in cross-domain scenarios.

Therefore, in this work we have considered the following features at sentence level:

- *Structural features*: sentence length, relative position in paragraph, average word length, number of tokens, and punctuation marks.
- *Lexical features*: bag of words 1-3 grams, TF-IDF weighted nouns, verbs and adverbs, modal auxiliaries, and named entities.
- *Morphosyntactic features*: part-of-speech 1-3 grams, depth and number of subclauses of the sentence constituency tree.
- *Discourse features*: keywords representing argumentative linkers (made publicly available with the created corpus, see Section 3).

We discard topic and sentiment features because we aimed to investigate with domain-independent features. They together with semantic and word embedding features could be explored in the future.

4.2 Dimensionality Reduction Techniques

In statistics and machine learning, dimensionality reduction is the process of reducing the number of random variables (features) under consideration, obtaining a new set of informative variables, commonly referred to as principal components.

Three of the main techniques for dimensionality reduction are Singular Value Decomposition, SVD (Beltrami, 1973; Stewart, 1993), Principal Components Analysis, PCA (Hotelling, 1933), and Linear Discriminant Analysis, LDA (Fisher, 1936).

They search for linear combinations of the features that best explain the input data, but they differ on the fact that LDA is a supervised technique that also classifies the data, and SVD and PCA are unsupervised techniques that ignore class labels.

Specifically, SVD obtains a factorization USV^t of the feature matrix A, where the diagonal entries of the small, inner matrix S are called singular values, correspond to the root of the positive eigenvalues of AA^t, and can be used as a reduced set of new variables that produce optimal low rank approximation of A with minimal reconstruction error. PCA derives new feature variables that are linear combinations of the original variables and are uncorrelated, by capturing the direction of maximum variation in the dataset, and without paying attention to the underlying class structure. Finally, LDA focuses on finding a feature subspace that maximizes the separability of classes, i.e., finding directions (components) of maximum variance.

As shown by Martínez and Kak (2001), although it is generally believed that algorithms based on LDA are superior to those based on PCA, this is not always the case. On the image recognition field, the authors concluded that if the target dataset is small, PCA can outperform LDA, being less sensitive to the used training set. In fact, as we shall show in the experimental section, LDA degraded the addressed AM tasks since its resultant components are determined by the number of classes to predict: 2 for the argumentative fragment detection task, 3 for the argument component classification task, and 6 for the argument relation recognition task.

5 Experiments

In this section, we describe the methodology used to evaluate a number of machine learning models for the three target AM tasks (i.e., *argumentative fragment detection*, *argument component classification* and *argument relation recognition*), and report their performance results with and without dimensionality reduction of the input data.

5.1 Evaluation Methodology

We approached the *argumentative fragment detection* and *argument component classification* tasks as binary classification problems –*argumentative* vs. *non-argumentative*), and *premise* vs. *claim*, respectively–, and the *argument relation recognition* as a multi-class classification problem, with a total of six relation types (classes): *cause*, *consequence*, *contrast*, *elaboration*, *clarification*, and *none* (in absence of relation).

The *argument component classification* task (task 2) was tested on those feature vectors that corresponded to text fragments previously identified as argumentative (task 1).

The *argument relation recognition* task (task 3) was tested on vectors obtained by concatenating each pair of argumentative text fragment vectors (from task 1), considering their order. That is, given two argument components c_1 and c_2, task 3 was fed with two vectors $u = (c_1, c_2)$ and $v = (c_2, c_1)$. If the argument components were linked via a relation r, e.g., (c_2, r, c_1), one of such vectors (v in the example) was assigned with a class that correspond to the type of r, whereas the other vector was assigned with the *none* class.

Considering the surveyed related work of Section 2, the ML algorithms we selected for the above tasks are: naive Bayes (NB), logistic regression (LR), support vector machine (SVM), and gradient boosting (GB).

For all tasks, we split the dataset into 80% for training and 20% for testing. We followed a stratified data split with respect to the label to be predicted, and used the 10-fold cross-validation technique on the training data to find the best hyperparameters for the ML algorithms. Before splitting, we normalized the input values of each feature to the [0,1] range.

The optimal values of the hyperparameters of the classification models and the SVD/PCA/LDA techniques were obtained by grid search with respect to the micro-F1 score. As future work, we leave the use of other more efficient model training optimization methods, such as Optuna, presented by Akiba et al. (2019). Table 1 shows the hyperparameters configurations tested, and their optimal values obtained for each ML algorithm and AM task.

In each ML algorithm training configuration, we tested several numbers of principal components for the dimensionality reduction techniques, in order to explore whether horizontal reduction of the input feature space improved classification performance. Specifically, for SVD and PCA, we tested 20 different numbers of components, from 25 up to 500 (with increment steps of 25). In the case of LDA, for each AM task, the number of dimensions was reduced to the number of target classes minus 1.

For the tested number of principal components, figures 5, 6 and 7 show the effects of the SVD and PCA dimensionality reduction techniques on the performance (in terms of micro-F1 score values) of the tested ML algorithms in the three AM tasks. As it can be seen, in general, the ML algorithms outperformed their counterparts operating on reduced feature spaces and, as expected, the F1 tends to increase with the number of components. We discuss the maximum performance values for all approaches in the next subsection. More details are given in Appendix A.

5.2 Classification Results

Tables 2, 3 and 4 show the best performance results of the evaluated approaches, for *argumen-*

Algorithm	Hyperparameter	Tested values	Task 1	Task 2	Task 3
NB	alpha	{0.0001, 0.001, 0.01, 0.1, 1}	1	1	1
	fit prior	{true, false}	false	false	false
	solver	{newton-cg, lbfgs, liblinear, saga}	liblinear	saga	saga
LR	C	{0.001, 0.01, 0.1, 1, 10, 100}	0.1	1	1
	penalty	{none, elasticnet, L1, L2}	L2	L2	L1
	kernel	{linear, rbf}	rbf	linear	rbf
SVM	C	{100, 10, 1, 0.1, 0.01, 0.001}	10	0.1	10
	gamma	{1, 0.1, 0.01, 0.001, 0.0001}	0.01	-	0.1
	learning rate	{0.15, 0.1, 0.05, 0.02, 0.01}	0.1	0.1	0.1
	n estimators	{150, 175, 200, 225, 250}	200	200	150
GB	max depth	{2, 3, 4, 5, 6}	3	3	5
	min samples leaf	{1, 2, 5, 7}	5	5	1
	min samples split	{2, 3}	2	2	2

Table 1: Tested hyperparameter values and obtained best performing hyperparameters for each ML algorithm and AM task: argument detection (task 1), argument component classification (task 2), and argument relation recognition (task 3). The names of the hyperparameters are those used by the Python Scikit-learn library. NB, LR, SVM and GB stand for Naive Bayes, Logistic Regression, Support Vector Machine, and Gradient Boosting, respectively.

tative fragment detection, *argument component classification* and *argument relation recognition*, respectively. They report the accuracy (acc), precision (p), recall (r) and micro-F1 score (F1) values of the ML algorithms on the original feature spaces and on the principal component spaces obtained by SVD and PCA. The results of LDA are not reported because they were relatively low. This supervised technique degraded the resultant component space, whose dimension was determined by the number of classes in the target AM tasks.

The results show that reducing the dimensionality of the corpus feature space –composed of a total of 12,593 lexical, morphosyntactic, structural and discourse-associated features extracted from each sentence–, did not impact drastically on the classification accuracy of the evaluated ML models. Applying dimensionality reduction, the best reached F1 was similar to the best F1 achieved by using the entire feature space: on average, 97% for task 1, 95% for task 2, and 107% for task 3. In some cases (which are underlined in the tables), the F1 values achieved by the ML algorithm on a reduced space were greater than the entire space ones.

In particular, we observe that the first 400-500 components of SVD and PCA provided the best relative performance on the *Logistic Regression* and *Support Vector Machine* algorithms. This represents around 3-4% of the number of dimensions in the entire input feature space. Thus, in terms of training time, we found remarkable improvements for the three tasks, reducing on average the time required to train the ML algorithms by 77.58%, 84.29% and 82.31%, respectively for tasks 1, 2 and 3. This finding, although expected, is significant, as it would allow testing a larger hyperparameter set and fast experimenting with new algorithmic solutions, while reducing the well-known carbon footprint generated by massive ML model training.

As shown in the tables, when no dimensionality reduction was applied, GB was consistently the best performing algorithm, achieving decreasing maximum F1 values for the three consecutive tasks: 0.729, 0.624 and 0.554 (marked in bold in the tables). These values reflect the increasing difficulty of the underlying classification problems.

In the *argumentative fragment detection* (binary classification) task, GB achieved the best performance (F1=0.729), closely followed by NB (F1=0.726). SVM was the worst performing ML algorithm. However, this algorithm took benefit from the dimensionality reduction techniques, especially from SVD, with which it was able to increase its F1 value to 0.725, using its first n=500 components (4% of the total number of original dimensions).

For the *argument component classification* (multiclass) task, GB and SVM again were respectively the best and worst performing ML algorithms, with maximum F1 values equal to 0.624 and 0.584. In this case, LR was the algorithm whose performance improved the most with the help of the dimensionality reduction techniques; specifically, it reached an F1 value of 0.620 with the first n=400 principal components of PCA, representing 3% of the number of original features.

Finally, with respect to the *argument relation recognition* (multiclass) task, GB –with an F1 value of 0.554– was followed in performance by approaches that made use of dimensionality reduction

Approach	acc	p	r	F1
NB	.727	.726	.727	.726
NB + SVD (n=250)	.647	.656	.647	.647
NB + PCA (n=425)	.633	.649	.633	.632
LR	.717	.717	.717	.715
LR + SVD (n=400)	.708	.708	.708	.705
LR + PCA (n=350)	.708	.708	.708	.705
SVM	.711	.711	.711	.708
SVM + SVD (n=500)	.727	.726	.727	.725
SVM + PCA (n=475)	.719	.718	.719	.717
GB	.730	.729	.730	**.729**
GB + SVD (n=325)	.719	.721	.719	.714
GB + PCA (n=350)	.710	.711	.710	.705

Table 2: Achieved results on the argumentative fragment detection task.

Approach	acc	p	r	F1
NB	.624	.589	.624	.587
NB + SVD (n=200)	.499	.573	.499	.521
NB + PCA (n=150)	.518	.594	.518	.539
LR	.633	.603	.633	.607
LR + SVD (n=500)	.636	.612	.636	.615
LR + PCA (n=400)	.642	.618	.642	.620
SVM	.621	.586	.621	.584
SVM + SVD (n=400)	.624	.608	.624	.570
SVM + PCA (n=425)	.627	.612	.627	.573
GB	.648	.631	.648	**.624**
GB + SVD (n=100)	.604	.577	.604	.556
GB + PCA (n=125)	.594	.556	.594	.551

Table 3: Achieved results on the argument component classification task.

Approach	acc	p	r	F1
NB	.490	.363	.490	.355
NB + SVD (n=500)	.455	.472	.455	.462
NB + PCA (n=475)	.470	.488	.470	.477
LR	.555	.537	.555	.489
LR + SVD (n=500)	.555	.483	.555	.490
LR + PCA (n=300)	.545	.456	.545	.470
SVM	.570	.643	.570	.472
SVM + SVD (n=225)	.525	.474	.525	.482
SVM + PCA (n=275)	.535	.488	.535	.490
GB	.615	.594	.615	**.554**
GB + SVD (n=350)	.550	.510	.550	.482
GB + PCA (n=125)	.555	.552	.555	.490

Table 4: Achieved results on the argument relation classification task.

for all the reminder ML algorithms. Thus, this task, despite being the most complex of the three main AM tasks, was the one that took the most advantage from using the unsupervised SVD and PCA techniques.

6 Conclusions

Although the conducted experiments can be considered preliminary, they have shown promising results about the potential benefits of selecting informative linguistic features and reducing dimensionality in ML-based approaches to AM. For the three major AM tasks (i.e., argumentative fragment detection, argument component classification, and argument relation recognition), and for almost all the ML algorithms used in the AM literature, working on feature spaces of much lower dimensionality generated by SVD and PCA has entailed not only improvements in training efficiency, but also consistent classification performance of the algorithms, especially logistic regression and support vector machines.

In addition to these issues, our work contributes to the AM field through the publication of a new argumentative corpus in Spanish on e-participation, a novel and relevant domain for the AM community. We plan to increase the size and quality of the corpus, and hope it will be of interest for researchers and practitioners. Regardless of the impact of dimensionality reduction, the developed AM methods and their performance results on our corpus could be of reference for future improvements.

Moreover, we believe that the corpus may be exploited in different argumentative scenarios. In particular, it could be used to extract argumentative threads from online political discussions (Lawrence et al., 2017) and parliamentary debates, whose transcripts are available as open government datasets.

7 Limitations

As previous work on machine learning-based AM, a limitation of our study is the fact that we have aimed to extract argumentative units at sentence level. However, a single sentence may contain several units, such as a claim and an associated premise, and an argumentative unit could encompass several, generally two, consecutive sentences (Habernal and Gurevych, 2017).

Moreover, to draw robust and generalizable conclusions about the advantages of applying dimensionality reduction, we need to make further experiments not only with more data, but also considering other types of features (e.g., word embeddings) and several domains and corpora, which may be in languages distinct to Spanish (Lawrence and Reed, 2020).

We could further research which are the most relevant features in each of the AM tasks, and focus on and boost them with ad hoc algorithms. In this context, we could also consider topic, sentiment, debate structure, and domain (or language) dependent features that may be valuable to identify argumentative fragments and their components and relations (Lawrence and Reed, 2020).

Finally, we should compare our results with those achieved by of recent deep learning approaches to argument extraction (Eger et al., 2017; Reimers et al., 2019), in order to properly analyze the benefits and drawbacks of using a simple technique with respect to much more complex and computational costly methods. For such purpose, we have to extend our corpus, so that deep learning architectures for AM could be fine-tuned with existing large language models, such as BETO (Cañete et al., 2020) for the Spanish language.

Acknowledgements

This research was supported by the Spanish Ministry of Science and Innovation: Grant PID2019-108965GB-I00 and Grant PID2022-139131NB-I00, funded by MCIN/AEI/10.13039/501100011033 and by "ERDF A way of making Europe." We sincerely thank the anonymous reviewers of the paper for their valuable comments and suggestions.

References

Ahmet Aker, Alfred Sliwa, Yuan Ma, Ruishen Lui, Niravkumar Borad, Seyedeh Ziyaei, and Mina Ghobadi. 2017. What works and what does not: Classifier and feature analysis for argument mining. In *Proceedings of the 4th Workshop on Argument Mining*, pages 91–96.

Takuya Akiba, Shotaro Sano, Toshihiko Yanase, Takeru Ohta, and Masanori Koyama. 2019. Optuna: A next-generation hyperparameter optimization framework. In *Proceedings of the 25th ACM SIGKDD International Conference on Knowledge Discovery & Data Mining*, page 2623–2631. Association for Computing Machinery.

Alaa Alhamzeh, Mohamed Bouhaouel, Előd Egyed-Zsigmond, Jelena Mitrović, Lionel Brunie, and Harald Kosch. 2021. A stacking approach for cross-domain argument identification. In *Proceedings of the 32nd International Conference on Database and Expert Systems Applications*, pages 361–373. Springer.

Eugenio Beltrami. 1973. Sulle funzioni bilineari. *Giornale di matematiche ad Uso degli Studenti Delle Università*, 11:98–106. An English translation by D. Boley is available at the Department of Computer Science of University of Minnesota, Minneapolis, MN, Technical Report 90-37, 1990.

Abdelhamid Boudjelida, Sehl Mellouli, and Jungwoo Lee. 2016. Electronic citizens participation: Systematic review. In *Proceedings of the 9th International Conference on Theory and Practice of Electronic Governance*, pages 31–39.

Syed Burhan ud Din Tahir. 2017. Comparative analysis of supervised learning approaches for argument identification. In *Proceedings of the 20th International Multi-topic Conference*, pages 1–5. IEEE.

José Cañete, Gabriel Chaperon, Rodrigo Fuentes, Jou-Hui Ho, Hojin Kang, and Jorge Pérez. 2020. Spanish pre-trained BERT model and evaluation data. In *Proceedings of the 2020 Workshop on Practical ML for Developing Countries*, volume 2020, pages 1–10.

Iván Cantador, Alejandro Bellogín, María E Cortés-Cediel, and Olga Gil. 2017. Personalized recommendations in e-participation: Offline experiments for the 'decide madrid' platform. In *Proceedings of the International Workshop on Recommender Systems for Citizens*, pages 1–6. CEUR Workshop Proceedings.

Iván Cantador, María E Cortés-Cediel, and Miriam Fernández. 2020. Exploiting open data to analyze discussion and controversy in online citizen participation. *Information Processing & Management*, 57(5):102301.

Mamoru Deguchi and Kazunori Yamaguchi. 2019. Argument component classification by relation identification by neural network and TextRank. In *Proceedings of the 6th Workshop on Argument Mining*, pages 83–91. ACL.

Yang Du, Minglan Li, and Mengxue Li. 2017. Joint extraction of argument components and relations. In *Proceedings of the 2017 International Conference on Asian Language Processing*, pages 1–4. IEEE.

Steffen Eger, Johannes Daxenberger, and Iryna Gurevych. 2017. Neural end-to-end learning for computational argumentation mining. In *Proceedings of the 55th Annual Meeting of the Association for Computational Linguistics*, page 11–22. ACL.

Ronald A Fisher. 1936. The use of multiple measurements in taxonomic problems. *Annals of Eugenics*, 7(2):179–188.

Marc Gramberger. 2001. *Citizens as partners. OECD Handbook on Information, Consultation and Public Participation in Policy-making*. OECD Publishing.

Ivan Habernal and Iryna Gurevych. 2017. Argumentation mining in user-generated web discourse. *Computational Linguistics*, 43(1):125–179.

David Held. 2006. *Models of Democracy*. Polity.

Harold Hotelling. 1933. Analysis of a complex of statistical variables into principal components. *Journal of Educational Psychology*, 24(6):417.

Alistair Knott and Robert Dale. 1994. Using linguistic phenomena to motivate a set of coherence relations. *Discourse Processes*, 18(1):35–62.

Anang Kunaefi and Masayoshi Aritsugi. 2020. Characterizing user decision based on argumentative reviews. In *Proceedings of the 2020 IEEE/ACM International Conference on Big Data Computing, Applications and Technologies*, pages 161–170. IEEE.

John Lawrence, Joonsuk Park, Katarzyna Budzynska, Claire Cardie, Barbara Konat, and Chris Reed. 2017. Using argumentative structure to interpret debates in online deliberative democracy and eRulemaking. *ACM Transactions on Internet Technology*, 17(3):1–22.

John Lawrence and Chris Reed. 2020. Argument mining: A survey. *Computational Linguistics*, 45(4):765–818.

Marco Lippi and Paolo Torroni. 2015. Argument mining: A machine learning perspective. In *Proceedings of the 3rd International Workshop on Theory and Applications of Formal Argumentation*, pages 163–176. Springer.

Marco Lippi and Paolo Torroni. 2016. Argumentation mining: State of the art and emerging trends. *ACM Transactions on Internet Technology*, 16(2):1–25.

Anastasios Lytos, Thomas Lagkas, Panagiotis Sarigiannidis, and Kalina Bontcheva. 2019. The evolution of argumentation mining: From models to social media and emerging tools. *Information Processing & Management*, 56(6):102055.

Aleix M Martínez and Avinash C Kak. 2001. PCA versus LDA. *IEEE Transactions on Pattern Analysis and Machine Intelligence*, 23(2):228–233.

Tobias Mayer, Elena Cabrio, and Serena Villata. 2020. Transformer-based argument mining for healthcare applications. In *Proceedings of the 24th European Conference on Artificial Intelligence*, pages 2108–2115. IOS Press.

Raquel Mochales Palau and Marie-Francine Moens. 2009a. Argumentation mining: The detection, classification and structure of arguments in text. In *Proceedings of the 12th International Conference on Artificial Intelligence and Law*, pages 98–107. ACM.

Raquel Mochales Palau and Marie-Francine Moens. 2009b. Argumentation mining: The detection, classification and structure of arguments in text. In *Proceedings of the 12th International Conference on Artificial Intelligence and Law*, pages 98–107. ACM.

Raquel Mochales Palau and Marie-Francine Moens. 2011. Argumentation mining. *Artificial Intelligence and Law*, 19(1):1–22.

Prakash Poudyal, Teresa Goncalves, and Paulo Quaresma. 2016. Experiments on identification of argumentative sentences. In *Proceedings of the 10th International Conference on Software, Knowledge, Information Management & Applications*, pages 398–403. IEEE.

Nils Reimers, Benjamin Schiller, Tilman Beck, Johannes Daxenberger, Christian Stab, and Iryna Gurevych. 2019. Classification and clustering of arguments with contextualized word embeddings. In *Proceedings of the 57th Annual Meeting of the Association for Computational Linguistics*, pages 567–578. ACL.

Andrés Segura-Tinoco and Iván Cantador. 2023. ARGAEL: ARGument Annotation and Evaluation tooL. *SoftwareX*, 23:101410.

Christian Stab and Iryna Gurevych. 2014. Identifying argumentative discourse structures in persuasive essays. In *Proceedings of the 2014 Conference on Empirical Methods in Natural Language Processing*, pages 46–56.

Christian Stab and Iryna Gurevych. 2017. Parsing argumentation structures in persuasive essays. *Computational Linguistics*, 43(3):619–659.

Gilbert W Stewart. 1993. On the early history of the singular value decomposition. *SIAM review*, 35(4):551–566.

Vanessa Wei Feng and Graeme Hirst. 2011. Classifying arguments by scheme. In *Proceedings of the 49th Annual Meeting of the Association for Computational Linguistics*, pages 987–996. ACL.

A Effects of the Dimensionality Reduction

Figures 5, 6 and 7 show the effects of the 3 dimensionality reduction techniques used on the performance (in terms of micro-F1 score values) of the tested ML algorithms, in the *argumentative fragment detection*, *argument component classification* and *argument relation recognition* tasks, respectively.

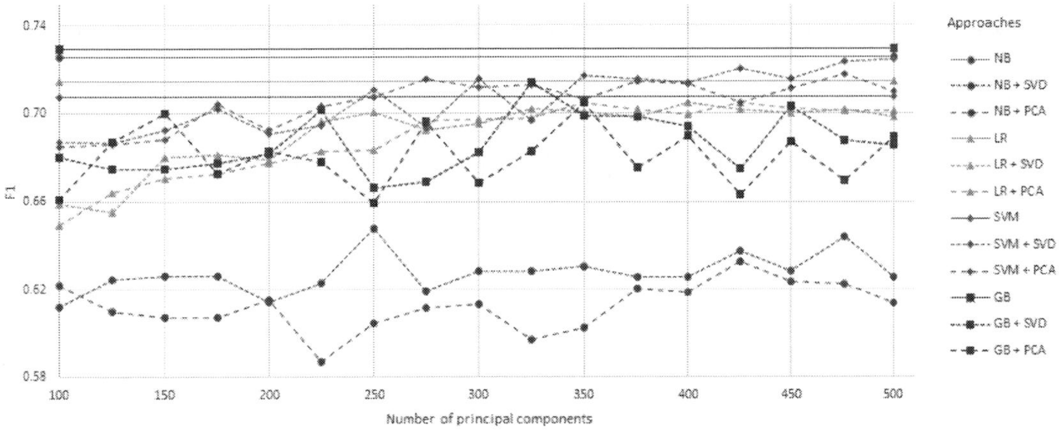

Figure 5: Micro-F1 score values achieved on the *argumentative fragment detection* task on training sets. NB, LR, SVM and GB stand for Naive Bayes, Logistic Regression, Support Vector Machines, and Gradient Boosting, respectively.

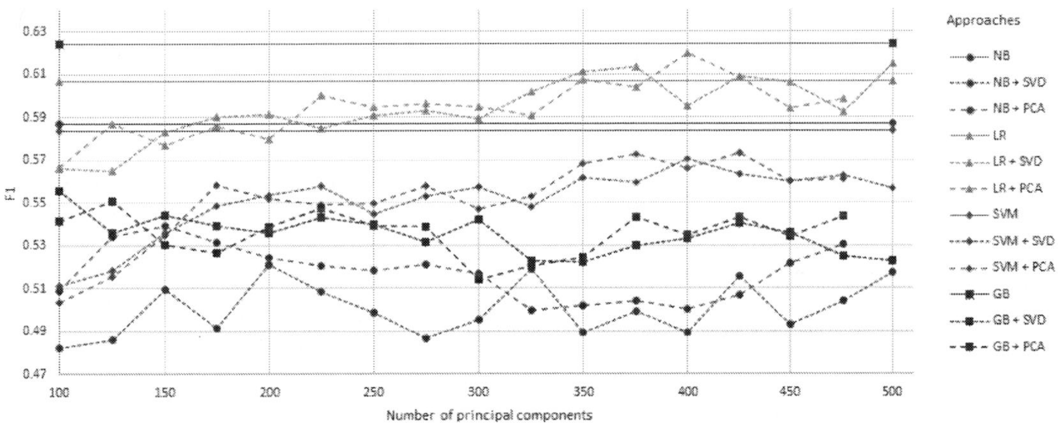

Figure 6: Micro-F1 score values achieved by the tested approaches on the *argument component classification* task on training sets. NB, LR, SVM and GB stand for Naive Bayes, Logistic Regression, Support Vector Machines, and Gradient Boosting, respectively.

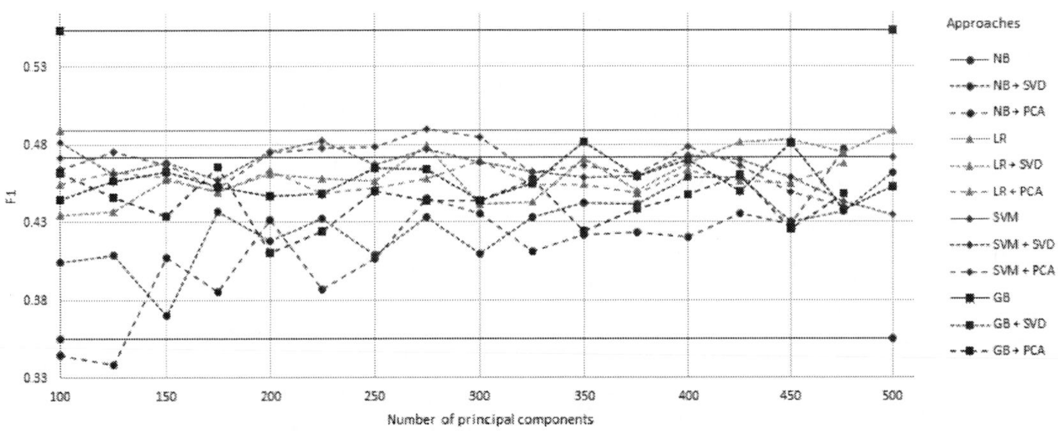

Figure 7: Micro-F1 score values achieved by the tested approaches on the *argument relation recognition* task on training sets. NB, LR, SVM and GB stand for Naive Bayes, Logistic Regression, Support Vector Machines, and Gradient Boosting, respectively.

On the Impact of Reconstruction and Context for Argument Prediction in Natural Debate

Zlata Kikteva Alexander Trautsch Patrick Katzer Mirko Oest
Steffen Herbold Annette Hautli-Janisz
Faculty of Computer Science and Mathematics
University of Passau
`firstname.lastname@uni-passau.de`

Abstract

Debate naturalness ranges on a scale from small, highly structured, and topically focused settings to larger, more spontaneous and less constrained environments. The more unconstrained a debate, the more spontaneous speakers act: they build on contextual knowledge and use anaphora or ellipses to construct their arguments. They also use rhetorical devices such as questions and imperatives to support or attack claims. In this paper, we study how the reconstruction of the actual debate contributions, i.e., utterances which contain pronouns, ellipses and fuzzy language, into full-fledged propositions which are interpretable without context impacts the prediction of argument relations and investigate the effect of incorporating contextual information for the task. We work with highly complex spontaneous debates with more than 10 speakers on a wide variety of topics. We find that in contrast to our initial hypothesis, reconstruction does not improve predictions and context only improves them when used in combination with propositions.

1 Introduction

Spontaneous natural debate is anything but easy to track: it contains anaphora, elliptical constructions, fragments, a fuzzy linguistic surface and a wide variety of rhetorical structures. The waters get even murkier when 10+ speakers contribute, multiple, possibly divergent, topics are covered in one debate, the stakes of the interlocutors are high, and debate constraints are low.

So far, debates at this scale of naturalness have been largely ignored in computational argumentation: either the number of participants was restricted and debates were highly constrained (Visser et al., 2020), there was only one topic per debate (Lawrence et al., 2018), or the setting was structured and consisted of monological speaker utterances (Mirkin et al., 2018a).

Most striking is the difference in the underlying data: argument mining on natural debate has either taken propositions as argumentative units of analysis, i.e., fully reconstructed records of speaker contributions that do not need context for interpretation (Gemechu and Reed, 2019; Ruiz-Dolz et al., 2021) or like Lavee et al. (2019) removed claims that contain, for instance, unresolved demonstratives. Another common approach, however, is to take transcripts as is, without any edits or restrictions (Haddadan et al., 2019). Our hypothesis is that using fully reconstructed material, i.e., propositions, increases the performance of argument relation prediction. In the case of locutions, where for instance anaphora and ellipses are not reconstructed, we assume that some of the information relevant to reconstruction is contained within the preceding context, like in an example from the corpus[1] where an anaphoric pronoun *'she'* from the location *'She's looking at what happened'* can be resolved as *'Sue Grey'* in a proposition *'Sue Gray is looking at what happened'* using preceding context *'Sue Grey is doing this investigation'*.

However, the task of completely reconstructing propositions from locutions, i.e., the actual, skeletal contributions in the debate, is costly: manual reconstruction requires an extensive amount of effort (Hautli-Janisz et al., 2022; Visser et al., 2020), while automatic approach struggles with unresolved non-personal anaphora and omitted verb phrases (Jo et al., 2019, 2020).

Our contributions in this paper are as follows: (1) we provide more insight into model performance in a realistic debate mining setting where only skeletal locutions and not fully reconstructed propositions are available, using the best-performing model on a dataset that is closest in nature to the debates here. Our results indicate that despite the notable structural differences between locutions and propositions, we achieve comparable performance in argument relation prediction for both. (2) We perform a

[1]Node set ID 28238, access via `http://ova3.arg.tech`

Proceedings of the 10th Workshop on Argument Mining, pages 100–106
December 7, 2023. ©2023 Association for Computational Linguistics

detailed error analysis and show that performance across argument relations varies noticeably and that context does not help in solving the issue of using only skeletal locutions but improves the predictions when used in combination with propositions.

2 Related work

In computational argumentation in the debate genre, one strand of research focuses on mostly monological speech, either produced by professional debaters (Mirkin et al., 2018a,b; Lavee et al., 2019; Orbach et al., 2020) or by political actors (Menini et al., 2018). A slightly different variety of debate concerns heavily structured Oxford-style debates (Zhang et al., 2016) where conversational flow is important.

In the case of more natural but still highly moderated debates, the focus is mostly on the political genre with some work on the identification of the central and divisive elements of the debate (Lawrence and Reed, 2017) and prediction of the argument relations using support and attack annotation scheme (Gemechu and Reed, 2019) as well as more complex categories (Ruiz-Dolz et al., 2021). There is more research on the US 2016 elections (Haddadan et al., 2019) as well as the UK Prime-ministerial elections from 2015 (Lippi and Torroni, 2016) with both papers focusing on the detection of argument components such as claims and premises/evidence.

In terms of segmentation, we are similar to most other work in debate mining: Lippi and Torroni (2016) and Haddadan et al. (2019) also assume sentential (or potentially sub-sentential) segments between which argument relations can hold, in contrast to Menini et al. (2018) who seem to take utterances to be the minimal units of analysis. Given the significant amount of argument relations within one utterance, we are confident that the former approach is what captures this genre most appropriately.

3 Empirical basis

3.1 Data

This paper is based on debates in 'Question Time' (QT), a political talk show in the UK broadcasted on BBC1. QT is significantly less structured than debate datasets in previous work, for instance, by Mirkin et al. (2018a,b). In QT, the audience challenges a panel of political figures regarding current topics who then respond and freely discuss the issues with each other. As the participants are different in each episode, their rhetorical skills vary considerably. Topics discussed within and across episodes range from UK-specific and time-sensitive ones such as extension of the lockdowns during the height of the COVID pandemic to more general ones like racism and climate change.

The data is annotated with Inference Anchoring Theory (IAT) (Budzynska et al., 2014, 2016). IAT is a framework that captures how arguments evolve and are reacted to in dialogue, anchoring argument structure in dialogue structure by way of illocutionary connections. The pairs of argumentative units and their relation that are used in this paper have not been annotated in isolation, but have been annotated together with all surrounding material. For the purpose of this paper, we only extract the pairs and their relation (plus the immediately preceding context). Arguments in QT30 comprise inferences ('Inference', supports – serial, divergent, convergent) conflicts ('Conflict', attacks – undercutting, rebutting, undermining) and rephrases ('Rephrase', reformulations of previous content). We extract those argument relations and also include 'No relation' instances (between adjacent units) due to a large number of unconnected contributions in natural debate (see Table 1 for details).

The training data is taken from QT30 (Hautli-Janisz et al., 2022), which comprises analyses of 30 episodes of QT. With 19,842 locutions (plus their propositional counterparts), 280,000 words and more than 10,000 arguments, QT30 is three times larger than the dataset that is most closely related in genre and annotation scheme (Visser et al., 2020). For testing, we use an additional ten episodes of QT on topics that are different than those seen in training (the training data aired between May 2020 and November 2021, test data aired between December 2021 and July 2022). Overall, this leaves us with a training/test split of about 80/20.

Table 1: Number of argument relations of different types and 'No relation' for training and testing

	Training	Test	Total
Inferences	3,223	845	4,068
Conflicts	697	315	1,012
Rephrases	3,634	1,085	4,719
No relation	4,558	1,052	5,610

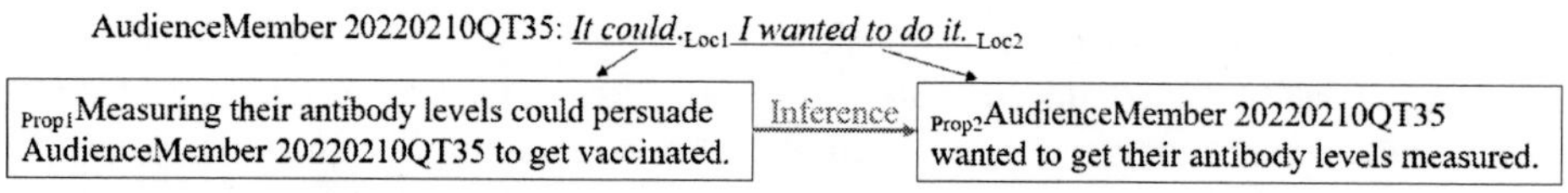

Figure 1: Example with locutions ($_{Loc1}$ and $_{Loc2}$) and propositions ($_{Prop1}$ and $_{Prop2}$)

3.2 Locutions vs. propositions

Locutions are the actual, skeletal speaker contributions in a debate. Propositions are their fully reconstructed equivalents: anaphora and ellipses are reconstructed, fragments are transformed into grammatical structures and fuzzy language is resolved. In Figure 1, the locutions of the speaker (an audience member) do not specify what they want to do and why [2]. The manually reconstructed propositions contain this information, namely that the speaker is discussing measuring their antibody levels to inform their decision to get vaccinated. Also, the pronoun *'I'* is reconstructed to *'AudienceMember 20220210QT35'*.

Data extraction We extract the pairs of locutions and matching propositions corresponding to argumentative discourse units (ADUs) which make up an argument (inference, conflict or rephrase) or a 'No relation'. For the 'No relation' category we extract adjacent ADUs which are not connected via an argumentative relation of inference, conflict or rephrase. We also extract the locution and corresponding proposition preceding the first element of the pair – this is what we consider context. This can be an adjacent unit or the one that is dialogically or content-wise preceding the argumentative pair, for instance, in the case of interruptions, the text segment before the interruption is extracted. We end up with a total of 15,409 locution (and the same number of corresponding proposition) triplets.

Structural comparison Locutions and propositions vary consistently in their structure: the average locution length is 11.72 words, propositions tend to be longer with 14.02 words per unit (average Levensthein distance is 19.86, normalized word-level distance is 0.83). For locutions, the average number of pronouns is 1.17 per unit, for propositions it drops significantly to 0.79 per unit. The remaining pronouns in the propositions are either instances where the antecedent of the anaphora is within the same unit (e.g. in *'Boris Johnson lied in his speech about X'*) or cases where their resolution would result in overinterpretation (e.g., *'we need to take care of the older people in care homes')*. Pointing to a similar trend, there are on average 0.37 named entities per locution, compared to 0.76 per proposition.

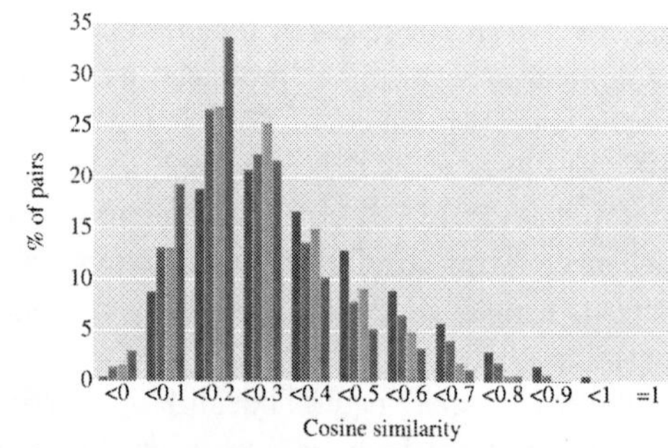

(a) Locutions

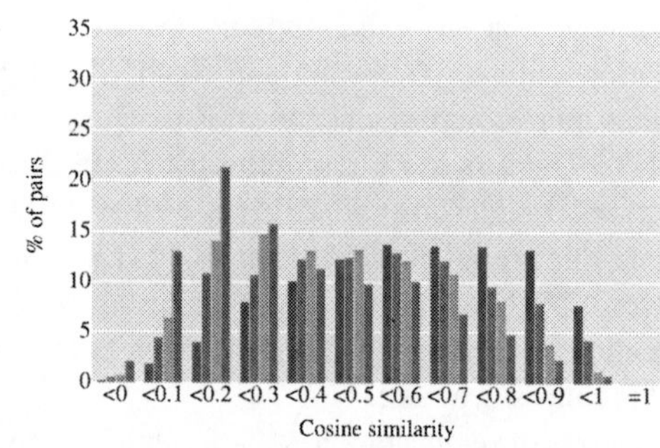

(b) Propositions

Figure 2: Cosine similarity between units in argument relations that are locutions (a) and propositions (b). Rephrases are indicated in blue, conflicts in red, inferences in green, 'No relation' in purple.

Embedding space comparison Given that we use BERT-based prediction for argument relations, we also investigate the impact that the reconstruction has on the embedding space. We calculate the cosine similarity between the first and the second element of the arguments and 'No relation' pairs. We do this for both propositions and locutions us-

[2] Node set ID 27967, access via `http://ova3.arg.tech`

ing SentenceTransformers with BERT embeddings (the all-MiniLM-L6-v2 model). The results are plotted in Figure 2. The distribution of the cosine similarity in the graphs suggests the following: (1) the model sees very different input in the location-versus proposition-driven model, as the overall semantic similarity is lower for locutions than propositions while the similarity for propositions is more equally distributed. (2) The semantic space representations can be indicative of the type of relation. Propositions in rephrase relations are more similar than those in conflict or inference ones. The 'No relation' propositions are most dissimilar. Interestingly, units in conflict relations tend to be more similar than inference units.

4 Argument type prediction

4.1 Models

LSTM (baseline) We use softmax activation with categorical cross-entropy as a loss function and the Adam optimizer with a batch size of 32, a maximum sequence length of 200 trained over 4 epochs.

BERT-Based We use pre-trained RoBERTa-large-cased (Liu et al., 2019), the best model identified by Ruiz-Dolz et al. (2021), who worked with the same categories as we do though for more constrained debate settings (fewer topics and speakers, more moderation). In order to compare with a more common BERT model, we also include results for BERT-large-cased. For both models, finetuning is performed on the QT30 data. We use 20% of the training data for validation. For the evaluation, we use 10 extra QT episodes. We train for 6 epochs and choose the best-performing epoch checkpoint on the test data. We use the Adam optimizer with a learning rate of 1e-05, epsilon of 1e-08, a batch size of 32 and a maximum sequence length of 200 which fits our data. In addition, we use 120 warmup steps and a warmup ratio of 0.06. The hyperparameters are taken from Ruiz-Dolz et al. (2021).

4.2 Results

As expected, RoBERTa outperforms the BERT and significantly outperforms the LSTM models [3].

Our best-performing model (Propositions+context) (we use macro F_1-score, as in related work, see Table 2) is still lower in comparison to Ruiz-Dolz et al. (2021), who use the same four-way distinction as we did and achieve the performance of 0.70. However, the corpus they use contains both written discussions as well as transcripts of the US presidential debates which is much more constrained than the debates used here. In comparison to other related work, our results seem to indicate that the less constrained debates are, the lower the performance of the model is. This is supported by the results in earlier work: Menini et al. (2018) who use monological speeches with a binary distinction into inferences and attacks, achieve an F_1-score of 0.82, while Gemechu and Reed (2019) achieve an F_1-score of 0.64 when using a political debate corpus with multiple speakers with the same categories.

Table 2: Macro F_1-scores across models and data

	LSTM	BERT large cased	RoBERTa large cased
Loc	0.25	0.41	0.54
Loc+cont	0.25	0.40	0.53
Prop	0.25	0.41	0.54
Prop+cont	0.24	0.41	**0.56**

Surprisingly, the results indicate that the use of propositions does not improve the performance of the model when compared to the locutions and that context does not help the prediction of relations between locutions, but increases performance when used with propositions. We will reflect on this in the following section. This pattern also holds for the predictions with BERT except for lack of improvement in the case of propositions with context; LSTM also exhibits different kind of behaviour in terms of context but the F_1-scores are too low to be able to draw any meaningful conclusions from them.

5 Error analysis

Context only helps sometimes A closer inspection of the results (for details see Appendix A, Table 3) shows that, with context, the model tends to predict the 'No relation' more often, both in terms of true and false positives. We hypothesize that context locutions in some cases provide information beyond the one relevant for the identification of argument relations thus leading to an increase in the number of predicted 'No relations'.

When we compare the results for propositions with and without context (for details see Appendix A, Table 4), we see that the model is better at pre-

[3]Code available at https://github.com/ZlataKikteva/argmining2023-reconstr

dicting the class of 'Conflict' if context is given, as well as reducing the number of misclassified 'Inference', in particular, inferences misclassified as 'No relation'. With the introduction of context for propositions, we still observe a tendency to over-predict the 'No relation' category, however, this tendency is not as strong as in the case with locutions and context. This can be explained by the fact that due to the reconstruction, the units of the proposition pairs are more likely to have a higher semantic similarity, making it slightly easier for the model to identify the argumentative relations as opposed to 'No relation'.

Reconstruction improves predictions of inferences and rephrases While the F_1-scores of the models based on locutions and propositions are the same, the confusion matrices for the two settings show that the underlying predictions are quite different (the confusion matrices for RoBERTa predictions are attached in Appendix B). The overall tendency when using propositions is leaning towards identifying inferences and rephrases at the cost of 'No relation' (for details see Appendix A, Table 5). Specifically, while the number of correctly predicted 'No relation' propositions went down about 15%, the improvement in the prediction of both rephrases and inferences is about 8%. The example in Figure 1 illustrates the issue: without heavy reconstruction, the model cannot correctly predict the inference and instead goes for 'No relation'. The reconstruction leads to the increased similarity of the embeddings in a number of cases, which makes the prediction of 'Rephrase' and 'Inference' easier while losing out on 'No relation'. In addition to that, this kind of tendency also comes at the cost of misclassifying 'No relation' as inferences.

6 Conclusion

Contrary to our expectations, the reconstruction of skeletal locutions into full-fledged propositions does not necessarily improve the overall performance of the models. What we observe, however, is that the model trained and evaluated on propositions is better at identifying argumentative relations at the cost of the 'No relation' category. In addition, context seems to be beneficial only in the case of propositions as it improves the prediction of conflicts and inferences.

Acknowledgements

The work reported on in this paper was partially funded by the VolkswagenStiftung under grant Az. 98544 'Deliberation Laboratory'.

References

Katarzyna Budzynska, Mathilde Janier, Juyeon Kang, Chris Reed, Patrick Saint-Dizier, Manfred Stede, and Olena Yaskorska. 2014. Towards argument mining from dialogue. In *Proceedings of the Fifth International Conference on Computational Models of Argument (COMMA 2014)*, pages 185–196. IOS Press.

Katarzyna Budzynska, Mathilde Janier, Chris Reed, and Patrick Saint Dizier. 2016. Theoretical foundations for illocutionary structure parsing. *Argument & Computation*, 7(1):91–108.

Debela Gemechu and Chris Reed. 2019. Decompositional argument mining: A general purpose approach for argument graph construction. In *Proceedings of the 57th Annual Meeting of the Association for Computational Linguistics*, pages 516–526, Florence, Italy. Association for Computational Linguistics.

Shohreh Haddadan, Elena Cabrio, and Serena Villata. 2019. Yes, we can! mining arguments in 50 years of US presidential campaign debates. In *Proceedings of the 57th Annual Meeting of the Association for Computational Linguistics*, pages 4684–4690, Florence, Italy. Association for Computational Linguistics.

Annette Hautli-Janisz, Zlata Kikteva, Wassiliki Siskou, Kamila Gorska, Ray Becker, and Chris Reed. 2022. QT30: A corpus of argument and conflict in broadcast debate. In *Proceedings of the Thirteenth Language Resources and Evaluation Conference*, pages 3291–3300, Marseille, France. European Language Resources Association.

Yohan Jo, Jacky Visser, Chris Reed, and Eduard Hovy. 2019. A cascade model for proposition extraction in argumentation. In *Proceedings of the 6th Workshop on Argument Mining*, pages 11–24, Florence, Italy. Association for Computational Linguistics.

Yohan Jo, Jacky Visser, Chris Reed, and Eduard Hovy. 2020. Extracting implicitly asserted propositions in argumentation. In *Proceedings of the 2020 Conference on Empirical Methods in Natural Language Processing (EMNLP)*, pages 24–38, Online. Association for Computational Linguistics.

Tamar Lavee, Matan Orbach, Lili Kotlerman, Yoav Kantor, Shai Gretz, Lena Dankin, Michal Jacovi, Yonatan Bilu, Ranit Aharonov, and Noam Slonim. 2019. Towards effective rebuttal: Listening comprehension using corpus-wide claim mining. In *Proceedings of the 6th Workshop on Argument Mining*, pages 58–66, Florence, Italy. Association for Computational Linguistics.

John Lawrence and Chris Reed. 2017. Using complex argumentative interactions to reconstruct the argumentative structure of large-scale debates. In *Proceedings of the 4th Workshop on Argument Mining*, pages 108–117, Copenhagen, Denmark. Association for Computational Linguistics.

John Lawrence, Jacky Visser, and Chris Reed. 2018. Bbc moral maze: Test your argument. In *7th International Conference on Computational Models of Argument, COMMA 2018*, pages 465–466. IOS Press.

Marco Lippi and Paolo Torroni. 2016. Argument mining from speech: Detecting claims in political debates. In *Proceedings of the AAAI conference on artificial intelligence*, volume 30.

Yinhan Liu, Myle Ott, Naman Goyal, Jingfei Du, Mandar Joshi, Danqi Chen, Omer Levy, Mike Lewis, Luke Zettlemoyer, and Veselin Stoyanov. 2019. Roberta: A robustly optimized bert pretraining approach.

Stefano Menini, Elena Cabrio, Sara Tonelli, and Serena Villata. 2018. Never retreat, never retract: Argumentation analysis for political speeches. In *Proceedings of the AAAI Conference on Artificial Intelligence*, volume 32.

Shachar Mirkin, Michal Jacovi, Tamar Lavee, Hong-Kwang Kuo, Samuel Thomas, Leslie Sager, Lili Kotlerman, Elad Venezian, and Noam Slonim. 2018a. A recorded debating dataset. In *Proceedings of the Eleventh International Conference on Language Resources and Evaluation (LREC 2018)*, Miyazaki, Japan. European Language Resources Association (ELRA).

Shachar Mirkin, Guy Moshkowich, Matan Orbach, Lili Kotlerman, Yoav Kantor, Tamar Lavee, Michal Jacovi, Yonatan Bilu, Ranit Aharonov, and Noam Slonim. 2018b. Listening comprehension over argumentative content. In *Proceedings of the 2018 Conference on Empirical Methods in Natural Language Processing*, pages 719–724, Brussels, Belgium. Association for Computational Linguistics.

Matan Orbach, Yonatan Bilu, Assaf Toledo, Dan Lahav, Michal Jacovi, Ranit Aharonov, and Noam Slonim. 2020. Out of the echo chamber: Detecting countering debate speeches. In *Proceedings of the 58th Annual Meeting of the Association for Computational Linguistics*, pages 7073–7086, Online. Association for Computational Linguistics.

Ramon Ruiz-Dolz, Jose Alemany, Stella M. Heras Barberá, and Ana García-Fornes. 2021. Transformer-based models for automatic identification of argument relations: A cross-domain evaluation. *IEEE Intelligent Systems*, 36(6):62–70.

Jacky Visser, Barbara Konat, Rory Duthie, Marcin Koszowy, Katarzyna Budzynska, and Chris Reed. 2020. Argumentation in the 2016 US presidential elections: annotated corpora of television debates and social media reaction. *Language Resources and Evaluation*, 54(1):123–154.

Justine Zhang, Ravi Kumar, Sujith Ravi, and Cristian Danescu-Niculescu-Mizil. 2016. Conversational flow in Oxford-style debates. In *Proceedings of the 2016 Conference of the North American Chapter of the Association for Computational Linguistics: Human Language Technologies*, pages 136–141, San Diego, California. Association for Computational Linguistics.

A Differences in class assignments (RoBERTa-large-cased predictions)

We generate these tables based on the class predictions from the confusion matrices.

Table 3: Difference in class assignments between locutions and locutions with context (in percentage)

	Inference	Conflict	Rephrase	No rel.
Inference	-6.75%	0.36%	-0.59%	6.98%
Conflict	-8.57%	-1.59%	-0.63%	10.79%
Rephrase	-1.94%	0.09%	-2.58%	4.42%
No rel.	-5.32%	-0.48%	-1.24%	7.03%

Table 4: Difference in class assignments between propositions and propositions with context (in percentage)

	Inference	Conflict	Rephrase	No rel.
Inference	-1.30%	-0.83%	-0.12%	2.25%
Conflict	-6.67%	1.90%	-2.54%	7.30%
Rephrase	-2.86%	-0.28%	-0.65%	3.78%
No rel.	-10.17%	-0.57%	3.14%	7.60%

Table 5: Difference in class assignments between locutions and propositions (in percentage)

	Inference	Conflict	Rephrase	No rel.
Inference	7.69%	-1.18%	2.96%	-9.47%
Conflict	7.30%	1.27%	2.86%	-11.43%
Rephrase	-0.09%	0.28%	8.48%	-8.66%
No rel.	14.16%	0.19%	0.86%	-15.21%

B Confusion matrices (RoBERTa-large-cased predictions)

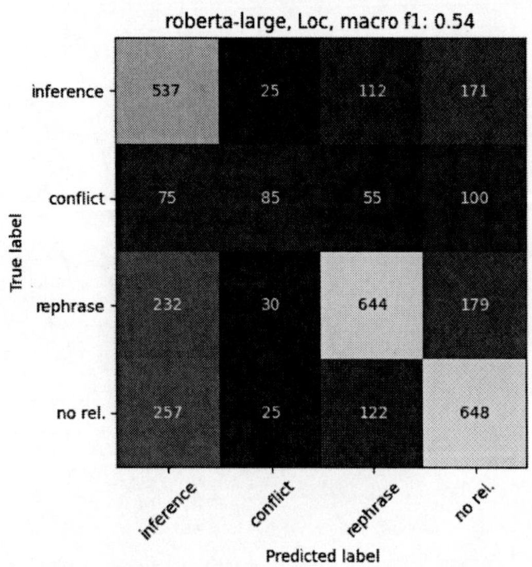

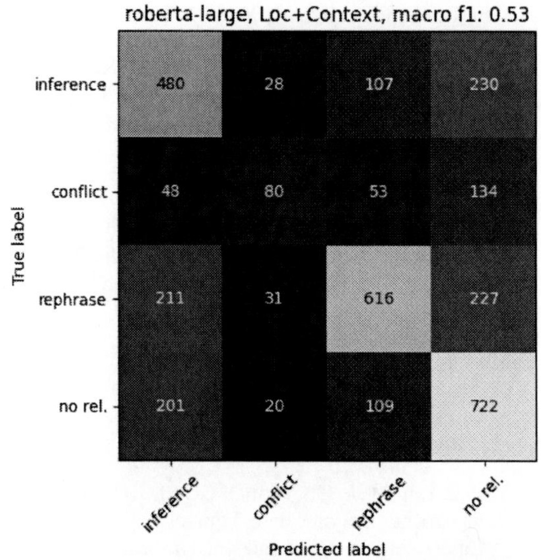

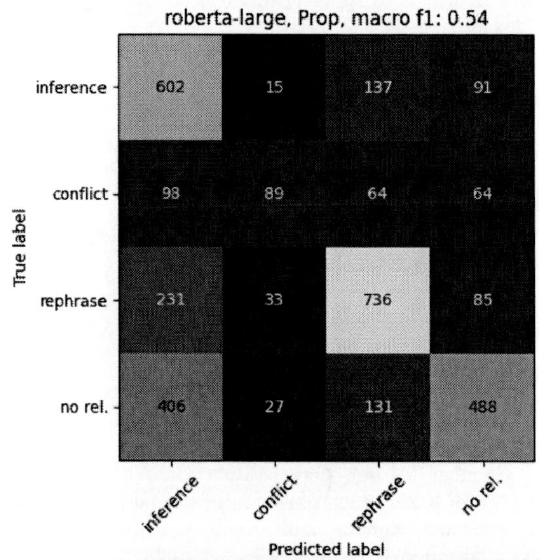

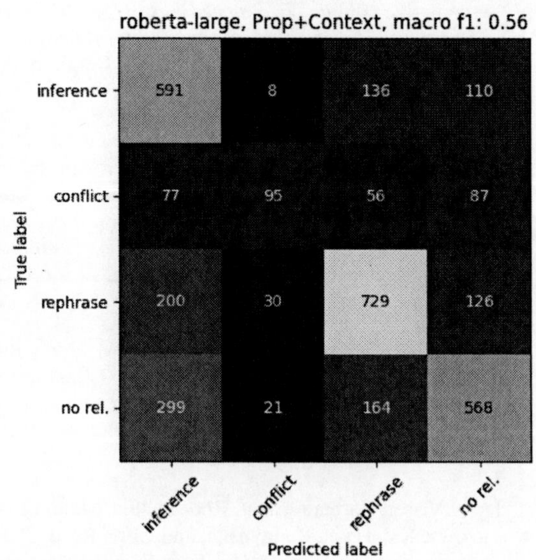

Unsupervised argument reframing with a counterfactual-based approach

Philipp Heinisch
Bielefeld University
pheinisch@techfak.uni-bielefeld.de

Dimitry Mindlin
Bielefeld University
dimitry.mindlin@uni-bielefeld.de

Philipp Cimiano
Bielefeld University
cimiano@techfak.uni-bielefeld.de

Abstract

Framing is an important mechanism in argumentation, as participants in a debate tend to emphasize those aspects or dimensions of the issue under debate that support their standpoint. The task of reframing an argument, that is changing the underlying framing, has received increasing attention recently. We propose a novel unsupervised approach to argument reframing that takes inspiration from counterfactual explanation generation approaches in the field of eXplainable AI (XAI). We formalize the task as a mask-and-replace approach in which an LLM is tasked to replace masked tokens associated with a set of frames to be eliminated by other tokens related to a set of target frames to be added. Our method relies on two key mechanisms: framed decoding and reranking based on a number of metrics similar to those used in XAI to search for a suitable counterfactual. We evaluate our approach on three topics using the dataset by Ruckdeschel and Wiedemann (2022). We show that our two key mechanisms outperform an unguided LLM as a baseline by increasing the ratio of successfully reframed arguments by almost an order of magnitude.

1 Introduction

Framing is an important mechanism in argumentation, as participants in a debate tend to emphasize those aspects or dimensions of the topic under debate that support their standpoint (Misra et al., 2016; Mou et al., 2022). In this context, reframing is a task that has recently received increased attention, consisting in switching the underlying framing of an argument (Chakrabarty et al., 2021; Chen et al., 2021).

In our conceptualization of the problem, there are frames to be deleted, D, and frames to be added, A, to an argument. Our approach essentially masks the tokens that belong to frame D and uses a language model to regenerate the tokens so that ideally they belong to A. Instead of rewriting complete sentences as in previous work (Chen et al., 2021), our approach aims to maximize the change in framing by minimal precise and controlled intervention into the argument. This "mask-and-replace" approach circumvents the need to fine-tune a language model for the specific task and is thus unsupervised.

Consider the following argument debating "nuclear energy" that emphasizes aspects related to *safety*: *"While geothermal, solar, and wind are safe, nuclear energy is not"*. A minimal change to the argument that changes the frame from focusing on safety aspects towards emphasizing economic aspects could yield the following argument: *"While geothermal, solar, and wind are affordable, nuclear energy is not"*.

In this paper, we draw inspiration from current eXplainable AI (XAI) approaches to propose a novel reframing approach that is based on counterfactual explanation generation to explain the decision of a classifier (Wachter et al., 2017). A counterfactual can plainly speaking be seen as an answer to the question: *How would an example have to be different to belong to a different class?* We transfer this idea to the task of reframing arguments, coming up with a "counterfactual" that answers the question: *How would the argument need to be changed to have a different frame?* Counterfactual generation can be seen as a search in the space of possible changes to a given example or argument that switches the class or respective frame. Different metrics have been proposed to constrain and guide the search in the space of possible counterfactuals. As two examples, approaches have used the following metrics: *proximity*, which measures the similarity of the generated instance to the initial instance, and *data manifold closeness*, which measures how well the generated counterfactual fits within the target data distribution (Verma et al., 2020).

Our approach in particular works on the token

Proceedings of the 10th Workshop on Argument Mining, pages 107–119
December 7, 2023. ©2023 Association for Computational Linguistics

level, assuming that each frame-relevant token of an argument is assigned to a frame class. The task of frame classification on the token level of an argument has been proposed by Ruckdeschel and Wiedemann (2022). Given the feasibility of this task, we build on this representation and use the models by Ruckdeschel and Wiedemann (2022) as a starting point for our reframing approach.

Our contributions are:

- We present an unsupervised approach to argument reframing that relies on a mask-and-replace approach on the token level, relying on a language model to replace tokens associated with a set of frames to be deleted by other tokens denoting a set of target frames to be added.

- The approach in particular relies on a frame-guided decoding and reranking strategy inspired by the metrics used in counterfactual generation. Concerning the reranking strategy, we transfer existing metrics used in counterfactual explanation generation and adapt them for the case of the reframing task.

- We conduct a comprehensive analysis and evaluation on three controversial topics (nuclear energy, minimum wage, and marijuana), demonstrating the impact of our reranking and framed decoding strategies. We show in particular that these two mechanisms are effective, increasing the ratio of appropriately reframed arguments from 2% to 18% compared to a baseline in our manual evaluation, corresponding to an improvement of almost an order of magnitude. In addition, we analyze the influence of the number of generated candidates as well as of LLM size.

The manual annotations, spanning over 600 reframed arguments as well as our code are available on GitHub[1].

2 Related work

The automatic analysis of frames in texts has been pioneered by Boydstun et al. (2014) and Card et al. (2015), who applied it to the analysis of newspaper articles. Frames help to organize and structure text and arguments but are also used to bias discussions (Mou et al., 2022) or tailor arguments to specific audiences (de Vreese, 2005; Ajjour et al., 2019; Chen et al., 2021).

The task of reframing arguments, as we consider, has been tackled before by Chen et al. (2021), who used the generic frame classes defined by Card et al. (2015) and relied on fine-tuned language models to rewrite complete sentences, using two surrounding sentences as context.

Similar to our goal of minimal changes, Chakrabarty et al. (2021) extended this approach to generate a reframed argument that is closely related the original one. They propose an approach that first identifies parts of the original argument to be replaced and then relies on a fine-tuned BART model to generate replacement candidates, picking the candidate that has the highest score of being entailed by the original argument according to an entailment model.

In contrast to the above-mentioned previous work on reframing that relies on models fine-tuned for the task, our approach is unsupervised.

Beyond the inventory of 15 generic frames proposed by Boydstun et al. (2014), recent work has made a strong case for more fine-granular and topic-specific framesets. Ajjour et al. (2019) have for example explored an approach by which frame labels can be derived bottom-up by clustering, and Mou et al. (2022) have demonstrated that the transferability of frames across topics is limited. Reimers et al. (2019) have made the case that arguments rarely only evoke one frame and that often multiple aspects are emphasized. In alignment with this observation, Schiller et al. (2021) have operationalized the assignment of frames as a span extraction task rather than as a document classification task. Following up on this, Ruckdeschel and Wiedemann (2022) present a dataset with topic-specific frame classes annotated on token-level.

We directly build on the work of Schiller et al. (2021) and Ruckdeschel and Wiedemann (2022) as a starting point and rely on an argument in which each token is labeled with a corresponding topic-specific frame. This allows us to select the token/spans that have to be modified to switch the frame.

Our proposed approach is inspired by research in XAI, which uses counterfactuals to explain classifier decisions. In the context of XAI, counterfactuals are explanations rooted in counterfactual reasoning. This process entails pinpointing the specific features that, if altered, would result in

[1] `https://github.com/phhei/counterfactualREframing`

different outcomes or predictions (Miller, 2019). Given this, applying counterfactual approaches to reframing feels intuitive, since changing the frame is conceptually similar to changing a classifier's prediction.

From the literature on counterfactuals, we adopt the idea that suitable metrics can be used to guide the search in the space of potential counterfactuals. Common metrics for selecting an appropriate counterfactual are validity and proximity. A recent paper catalogued up to eight such metrics from contemporary XAI research on generating and evaluating counterfactuals (Verma et al., 2020). In our work, we reuse the metrics related to validity, proximity, and data manifold closeness that are explained in section 3.2.

Counterfactual methods in natural language processing have primarily been used to explain and evaluate sentiment classifiers (Wu et al., 2021; Madaan et al., 2021) or to uncover dataset artifacts (Ross et al., 2021). To our knowledge, their application in the context of reframing is novel, marking a primary contribution of our paper.

3 Methodology

We model the task of reframing as a generative mask-and-replace approach. Given an argument and its frameset $\mathcal{S}$, called source frameset, and a target frameset $\mathcal{T}$, the task is to shift the aspects covered by the argument towards this target frameset $\mathcal{T}$ by rewriting it. Hence, the goal is to remove n_d frames contained in set D to be deleted and add n_a new frames in a set A that are not contained in $\mathcal{S}$. The frameset of the rewritten argument is thus expected to be identical with the target frameset $\mathcal{T} = (\mathcal{S} \setminus D) \cup A$.

Our unsupervised approach is described in Figure 1. In particular, given an argument to be reframed, we apply a sequence tagging model to classify each token into its corresponding frame, relying on the approach proposed by Ruckdeschel and Wiedemann (2022). We then mask each token that has been assigned a frame label that is in the set D. For each masked span, a language model generates an alternative text span which is placed in the corresponding spot, resulting in a new text that is a mixture of original text spans and newly generated text spans.

In order to guide the replacement of a masked span by a span related to set A, we rely on two strategies to increase the ratio of successfully reframed arguments: framed decoding and various output reranking strategies based on the field of counterfactual explanations. We explain these strategies in more detail in what follows.

3.1 Framed Decoding

We follow the proposal of Heinisch et al. (2022) to increase the probability of generating tokens of the target frames to the given argument. In our introductory example, for instance, our goal would be to increase the probability of generating tokens related to an economic frame, such as *affordable* in the example.

For a given frame f, we compute $p(f|v)$, that is the (conditional) probability that if v occurs, it occurs in a text position labeled with frame f. This measures the specificity of v for frame f. At inference time, we modify the logit for each vocabulary element l_v for each target frame $f_t \in \mathcal{T}$ to be added as follows:

$$\tilde{l_v} = l_v + \lambda(\max(l) - \min(l))\; p(f_t|v) \quad (1)$$

where λ is a hyperparameter controlling the degree to which vocabulary elements related to the frames to be targeted are boosted. While a small value of λ yields only a weak boost, a high value strongly boosts tokens related to the frames to be added, potentially leading to output that is unrelated to the input. In order to avoid the repetition of frame-exclusive vocabularies and to aim for frame diversity when multiple frames are applied, we set the repetition penalty to $1 + \lambda$ as proposed by Keskar et al. (2019).

3.2 Reranking strategies

We decode the model using beam search to yield n rewrites of the original sentence. We then apply a re-ranking strategy to select sentences that best align with a quartet of metrics. The first three metrics derive inspiration from the collection presented by Verma et al. (2020) for counterfactuals: i) Frame-Validity, ii) Proximity, iii) Data Manifold Closeness. The fourth metric, iv) Grammaticality and Fluency, is tailored to our specific requirements.

Equation 2 shows how the metrics are aggregated to obtain the final score, which is used to rerank

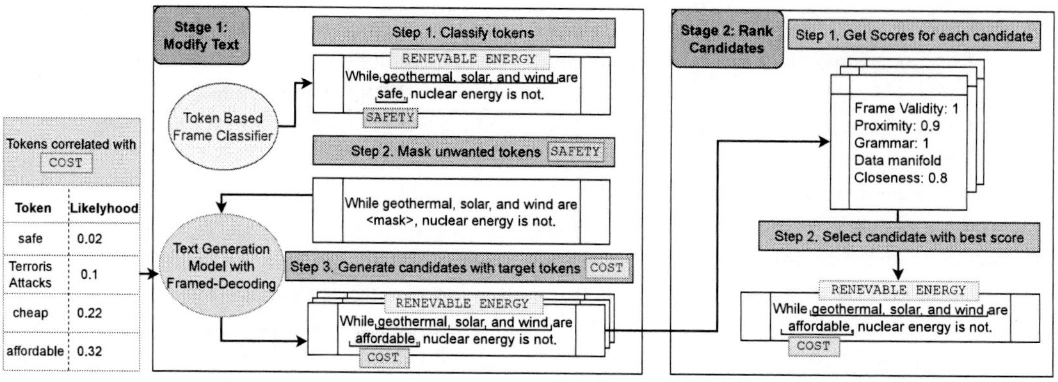

Figure 1: Proposed Reframing Method with Reranking Strategy via Counterfactual Properties

the rewrites in descending order:

$$\begin{aligned} \text{score} &= \omega_{\text{validity}} \cdot \text{frame-validity} \\ &+ \omega_{\text{proximity}} \cdot \text{proximity} \\ &+ \omega_{\text{closeness topic}} \cdot \text{data\_manifold\_closeness}_{\text{topic}} \\ &+ \omega_{\text{closeness frame}} \cdot \text{data\_manifold\_closeness}_{\text{frame}} \\ &+ \omega_{\text{grammar}} \cdot \text{grammar} \end{aligned} \tag{2}$$

with ω_m as a weight hyperparameter for metric m.

Frame-Validity The aim of our approach is to generate a rewriting of the given argument that evokes the frames to be targeted. In analogy to the criterion of validity that is used in counterfactual explanation generation to measure the degree to which generated counterfactuals switch a classifiers' prediction, we introduce the analogous *frame-validity* metric that indicates whether the reframing has been successful. For this, we compute a weighted Jaccard similarity between the target frames $\mathcal{T}$ and the frames predicted by the sequence labeling approach $\mathcal{P}$ for the reframed argument, where the weights correspond to the probabilities of the predicted frames:

$$\frac{\sum_{f \in \mathcal{P} \cap \mathcal{T}} p(f)}{\#\mathcal{T} + \sum_{f \in \mathcal{P} \setminus \mathcal{T}} p(f)} \tag{3}$$

Proximity Proximity is used to ensure that the generated counterfactual is semantically close to the original example in counterfactual explanation generation approaches. As we aim for a minimal modification of the argument that effectively reframes the argument, we apply a similar metric in our approach. We aim to maximize the proximity of the generated argument to the original argument, computed by using a Sentence-Bert-model (Reimers and Gurevych, 2019) to embed both sentences and calculate the cosine similarity between them.

Data Manifold Closeness Counterfactual explanation generation approaches aim to generate 'realistic' counterfactuals with a high probability of originating from the actual data distribution. The same holds for reframed arguments, so we transfer the *Data Manifold Closeness* used in counterfactual explanation generation approaches to the reframing task. We aim for reframed arguments to have a strong relation to the desired frames as well as to the issue/topic under discussion. To compute the similarity to the frame and topic, we take the top-k Sentence-Bert embedded neighbors and take the average cosine similarity between those.

Grammaticality and Fluency An important goal is to ensure the grammaticality and fluency of the reframed arguments, so that as a further metric we compute the acceptability of the sentence according to the corpus of linguistic acceptability (CoLA) by Warstadt et al. (2019).

4 Experiment Design

4.1 Dataset

We use the Argument Aspect Corpus (AAC) by Ruckdeschel and Wiedemann (2022) that features manually annotated frame labels for token spans within argumentative sentences. These sentences were drawn from the UKP Sentential Argument Mining Corpus by Reimers et al. (2019), expressing a stance on three major political topics: *m*inimum wage, *n*uclear energy, and *m*arijuana legalization. Since the dataset offers slightly above 1,000 annotated sentences for each topic on the token level, it fits our token-based reframing setting.

4.2 Experimental Settings

As our approach relies on a model that can assign a frame to each token of a given sentence, we reproduce the model proposed by Ruckdeschel and Wiedemann (2022), using the exact same hyperparameters and dataset. We consider the best variant based on `roberta-large` with a sequence tagging head, using the best-performing fine-tuned model on the test data across 5 runs. On the token level, we yield micro-averaged F1 scores across all 12 to 13 frame classes (the topic-specific framesets are defined by Ruckdeschel and Wiedemann (2022)) of 0.63, 0.6, and 0.69 for "nuclear energy", "minimum wage", and "marijuana", respectively.

For the language model generating rewritings for the masked tokens, we rely on the pretrained T5-model variants `t5-small` (60 million parameters) and `t5-large` (770 million parameters) (Raffel et al., 2020) as implemented in the `transformers`-library by Wolf et al. (2020). We mask all token spans with a predicted frame belonging to the frames to be deleted D with placeholders that were used in the masked language pretraining objective of T5. For each placeholder in an incrementing order, T5 generates alternative text spans which we replaced with the placeholders then. Note that T5 does not repeat the input argument while generating. We generate between 4 and 25 tokens per reframed argument candidate, sampling with a temperature of 1.25. To receive n different candidates, we apply beam search with $2n$ beams.

For reranking the candidates, we apply the automatic metrics as proposed in Section 3.2. As the Sentence-BERT model, we rely on `all-MiniLM-L6-v2` (or the more complex model `all-MiniLM-L12-v2` in experiments where `t5-large` was used). For the Data Manifold Closeness, we chose $k = 5$. For the grammar score, we rely on the model `textattack/roberta-base-CoLA` provided by Morris et al. (2020).

Determining the Target Frameset $\mathcal{T}$ Given the frameset $\mathcal{F}$ defined for the debated topic of the argument (Ruckdeschel and Wiedemann, 2022) and the set of all frames $\mathcal{S}$ contained in the argument as predicted by the frame classifier, we randomly delete $n_d \in \{0, 1, 2\}$ frame classes D from $\mathcal{S}$ and randomly add $n_a \in \{0, 1, 2\}$ frame classes from $\mathcal{F} \setminus \mathcal{S}$. In our primarily evaluated reframing setting, we select $n_d = n_a = 1$, exchanging a single frame class in the set of frame classes emphasized by an argument.

Manual study In order to evaluate the reframed arguments beyond using the automatic frame predictions and measurements as proposed in Section 3.2, we conduct a manual study involving three paid annotators, students from the field of (computational) social science.

For the assessment of frames, we use the original well-explored and reviewed guidelines by Ruckdeschel and Wiedemann (2022), including the definition and examples (when given) for each specific frame. In order to ensure a fair evaluation, we hide the original frames of the argument as well as the target frames. Annotators were thus asked to select none or up to five relevant frames evoked by the reframed argument. This is in contrast to studies that ask annotators to confirm whether the reframed argument fits the target frame as a choice between yes, partial, and no (Chen et al., 2021).

For the assessment of grammar and fluency, each annotator had to rate the reframed argument on a Likert scale between 1 (broken/unfinished text) to 5 (perfect fluency and grammar). For the assessment of meaning, each annotator provided two binary labels: one for the preservation of meaning in relation to the original argument and another for the plausibility of the proposed argument as a valuable contribution to the discussion.

On the task of indicating the relevant frames, we obtain a fair inter-annotator-agreement of $\alpha_\kappa = 0.32$ according to Krippendorff's alpha measure, which is comparable to other tasks in the field of argumentation. While we observe an almost perfect agreement in frames that are directly mentioned in the text, e.g. fossil fuels in the first example of Table 3, disagreement occurs in cases of implicit concepts or weakly related implications such as reliable energy when only "special needs by industry" is mentioned. The agreement on the tasks of labeling fluency and grammaticality ($\alpha_\kappa = 0.15$[2]) and meaning ($\alpha_\kappa = 0.16$) are lower due to the subjectivity of these tasks. However, we observe common trends. In terms of grammaticality, we receive constant low grammar scores for obviously broken sentences. Higher deviations are mostly caused by irregular punctuation in which different perspectives are acceptable. In terms of the binary categories related to the meaning, we observe dis-

[2]aligning the annotator-specific mean score across the annotators

agreement on borderline examples and different penalizations of tautologies and repetitions. For example, while all annotators agree regarding the plausibility of the first example in Table 3, they disagree whether the reframed argument is still related to the original argument. Further details on the manual study are provided in Appendix B.

5 Results

We analyze the appropriateness of our reframed arguments along different dimensions. First of all, we evaluate the reframing success of our approach, that is the success of fitting the target frameset $\mathcal{T}$. For this, we compare the frames covered by the reframed argument ($\mathcal{P}$) with the target frames $\mathcal{T}$. Note that $\mathcal{P}$ is predicted by the model of Ruckdeschel and Wiedemann (2022) in the case of the automatic evaluation and annotated by humans in the case of the manual evaluation. We present results with respect to the frames towards three criteria: i) FIT measuring the *target-set-fit ratio*, that is the ratio of instances where $\mathcal{P} = \mathcal{T}$, ii) REM measures the ratio of instances where the unwanted frames are successfully removed, i.e. $\mathcal{P} \cap D = \varnothing$, and iii) ADD measures the ratio of successfully added frames $A \subseteq \mathcal{P}$. These three metrics allow us to judge the reframing validity of our approach. The automatic results covering three topics are presented in Section 5.1. In Section 5.2 we broaden the perspective by also including further metrics that measure other relevant aspects of the reframed argument beyond frame-validity, considering the other automatic metrics introduced in Section 3.2. In addition, we present the results of our manual study in Section 5.3, adding the criteria of meaning preservation and plausibility, evaluating the impact of reranking and framed decoding as well as the impact of the model size of the text-generating model (Section 5.3.1) and the impact of the edit distance between the source frameset $\mathcal{S}$ and the target frameset $\mathcal{T}$ (Section 5.3.2).

We conducted further experiments regarding the impact of the number of rewritings per argument in Appendix A.

5.1 Evaluating Reframing Success

This section evaluates the reframed arguments using `t5-small` by automatically retrieving frames from the rewritten arguments with the task of removing one frame and adding a new frame. In order to exclusively focus on the contained frames while reranking, we set the weights of all counterfactual metrics to 0 in Equation 2 except $\omega_{\text{validity}} = 1$. The automatic results are provided in Table 1. Regarding yielding the target frameset $\mathcal{T}$ as the predicted frameset (FIT), we see an improvement of approximately 4 times by using reranking among 10 rewrites across all three topics. Using nuclear energy as an example topic, the ratio of successful reframing increased from 2.1 to 8.6. Activating framed decoding ($\lambda = 0.5$) improves again the ratios by approximately 6 times (more than an order of magnitude compared to the baseline using a vanilla language model without reranking), yielding ratios of 53.9, 40.1, and 50.9 for nuclear energy, minimum wage, and marijuana. With respect to the ability of the model to remove the frames to be deleted as measured by REM, we observe the same trends but with only comparable minor gains. Vanilla language models are already good at generating replacements that do not share the same frame, having success ratios between 82.6% and 89.7%. Reranking (gaining between 1.9% and 4.4%) as well as framed-decoding (gaining between 6.4% and 11.7%) increases the ratio further, ending with an almost guaranteed frame removal (e.g. 98% for marijuana). Looking at the success rate of adding frames as measured by ADD, we observe major gains using reranking and framed decoding comparable to the FIT analyses, yielding ratios between 45.8% (minimum wage) and 63.4% (nuclear energy).

Note that the results are worse for all topics when decreasing the strength of framed decoding (λ-value) from 0.5 to 0.1, showing the importance of a higher boost of frame-related tokens.

The following example illustrates a common pattern using a high value of $\lambda = 0.5$: Reframing the argument against nuclear energy *"Italy, Belgium, Spain and Switzerland have also principally decided to become nuclear energy-free"* emphasizing the aspect of energy policy ($\mathcal{S}$) towards an argument emphasizing renewable energy ($\mathcal{T}$) results in *"It is essential solar panels wind farms concentrated concentrated in hydro biomass farms to become nuclear energy-free."*, which is barely understandable. The text mentions several technologies for renewable energies to maximize the probability of this particular frame and avoids any names of countries or decision processes to minimize the probability of being labeled with energy policy. This example shows that beyond successfully switching the

	Nuclear energy			Minimum wage			Marijuana		
	REM	ADD	FIT	REM	ADD	FIT	REM	ADD	FIT
MLM (T5small)	84.0	2.9	2.1	82.6	2.5	1.3	89.7	3.0	2.5
⌞**+rerank (10)**	88.4 ‡	10.9 ‡	8.6 ‡	85.1 ‡	9.5 ‡	6.8 ‡	91.6 ‡	12.2 ‡	9.7 ‡
⌞**+frame-dec**$_{\lambda=0.1}$	89.9	20.4 ‡	15.9 ‡	84.1	10.8	8.3	93.0	21.2 ‡	17.8 ‡
⌞**+frame-dec**$_{\lambda=0.5}$	**95.8** ‡	**63.4** ‡	**53.9** ‡	**96.8** ‡	**45.8** ‡	**40.1** ‡	**98.0** ‡	**55.7** ‡	**50.9** ‡

Table 1: Ratios in % of evaluating the reframing success. (‡) significant improvement to the method above with $p < 0.005$ according to the approximate randomization test with 10.000 resampling steps.

	Nuclear energy		
	∅	FIT	Gram.
MLM (T5small)	56.7	2.1	73.8
⌞**+rerank (10)**	61.1 ‡	8.3 ‡	**85.6** ‡
⌞**+frame-dec**$_{\lambda=0.1}$	62.9 ‡	15.9 ‡	85.3
⌞**+frame-dec**$_{\lambda=0.2}$	**65.7** ‡	38.1 ‡	80.1
⌞**+frame-dec**$_{\lambda=0.5}$	62.7	**53.4** ‡	39.3

Table 2: Scores (0-100) for the different model variants on nuclear energy: Average of all metrics, target-set-fit (FIT), and Grammaticality.

frame, grammaticality and preserving topicality are crucial, so we evaluate our arguments with respect to further criteria in the following section.

5.2 Evaluation including other Reframing Aspects

In order to analyze the appropriateness of reframed arguments beyond the reframing success, we evaluate them with respect to all other metrics introduced in Section 3.2 by introducing an unweighted average of those five (∅), scaling each metric from 0 to 100. However, for reranking, while still regarding frame-validity as the most important metric, we compute an aggregate involving all metrics with weights ω as follows[3]: $\omega_{\text{validity}} = 4$, $\omega_{\text{proximity}} = 1$, $\omega_{\text{closeness topic}} = 1$, $\omega_{\text{closeness frame}} = 0.5$, and $\omega_{\text{grammar}} = 2$ (Equation 2)

The results of the automatic evaluation using again `t5-small` exchanging exactly one frame are provided in Table 2. We observe that the reranking improves every single metric and, hence, the average score. In the case of the topic of nuclear energy, the improvement is 3.4 points, increasing from 56.7 to 61.1. While looking at the different rewrites, we notice that arguments with shorter replacements are preferred on average in order to avoid hallucination and therefore optimize proximity and data manifold closeness while ensuring a high frame-validity. Introducing framed decoding shows a tradeoff between target-set-fit (favoring high λ) and grammaticality/proximity (favoring low λ). The highest target-set-fit ratio (53.4%) is achieved at $\lambda = 0.5$ at the expense of a lower grammaticality (39.3). Conversely, deactivating framed decoding yielded the highest score in terms of grammaticality (85.6) but lowered target-set-fit (8.3%). Thus, framed decoding enforces the target frameset but decreases the (linguistic) coherence, moving the reframed argument away from the original. We find the optimal λ value at 0.2 with a 38.1% ratio of fitting target framesets and a grammaticality score of 80.1. Table 3 shows examples using this setting, containing one successfully reframed argument and two examples of failing to introduce the added frame in the target set.

5.3 Manual Evaluation

To explore the trade-off between target-set fit and linguistic acceptance further, we conducted a manual study with 50 randomly selected arguments derived from the debate on nuclear energy. Once, we exchanged one frame without framed decoding and twice with framed decoding ($\lambda = [0.1, 0.2]$). We automatically selected the best-reframed sentence out of 10 each using the proposed weights in Section 5.2. Table 4 presents the results of the 150 annotated arguments, incorporating the majority vote for frames and meaning and mean values for grammaticality/fluency.

The results of the manual evaluation generally confirm the results of the automatic evaluation. Deactivating framed decoding results in a low target-set-fit (8% of the generated arguments add the new frame, 64% of them remove the deleted frame, and 4% fit the target frameset exactly). However, these arguments have only minor grammaticality/fluency flaws with an average of 3.9, every second preserv-

[3]In an application case such as a dashboard with sliders, a user of the system could select an individual weighting of the different metrics to get different reranked lists.

	w/o λ	$\lambda = 0.1$	$\lambda = 0.2$
Success of reframing (%)			
REM	64	82	**82**
ADD	8	8	**26**
FIT	4	4	**18**
Grammar/ Fluency (1-5)			
∅	**3.9**	**3.9**	3.7
Meaning (%)			
Preservation	**50**	48	40
Plausibility	60	**68**	60

Table 4: Results of manual evaluation (t5-small + rerank (10)), debating *nuclear energy*

	t5-small (10)		t5-large (10)	
	w/o λ	$\lambda = 0.2$	w/o λ	$\lambda = 0.2$
Frame-FIT (%)	4	**18**	6	**18**
Grammar (1-5)	3.9	3.7	4.1	**4.1**
Preservation (%)	50	40	**62**	60
Plausibility (%)	60	60	70	**72**

Table 5: Results of the manual study considering two model variants, debating *nuclear energy*

Original argument	Reframed argument
Just to maintain the current world production of nuclear power, either the oldest, creakiest plants need to be relicensed or a veritable orgy of nuclear construction needs to begin. [RELIABILITY]	*There is a need for fossil oil*, either the oldest, creakiest plants need to be relicensed or a veritable orgy of nuclear construction needs to begin. [FOSSIL FUELS]
The support of nuclear power by government results from special pleading lobbying by the industry. [ENERGY POLICY]	The support of nuclear power by the *industry* results from special *needs by the industry.* [RELIABILITY]
Prospects for nuclear energy as an option are limited, the report found, by four unresolved problems: (1) high relative costs; (2) perceived adverse safety, environmental, and health effects; (3) potential security risks stemming from proliferation; and (4) unresolved challenges in long-term management of nuclear wastes. [COSTS], [ACCIDENTS/SECURITY], [ENVIRONMENTAL IMPACT], [HEALTH EFFECTS], [WASTE]	Prospects for nuclear energy as an option are limited, the report found, by four unresolved problems: (1) high relative costs; (2) perceived adverse safety, *safety*, and health effects; (3) potential security risks stemming from proliferation; and (4) unresolved challenges in long-term management of nuclear wastes. [COSTS], [ACCIDENTS/SECURITY], [HEALTH EFFECTS], [WASTE], [TECHNOLOGICAL INNOVATION]

Table 3: Examples using t5-small+rerank (10) with framed decoding ($\lambda = 0.2$), removing and adding one frame class

ing the meaning of the original argument, and 60% of which are plausible. Activating the framed decoding again shows a similar λ influence with a sweat-spot of $\lambda = 0.2$, yielding a high target-set-fit (18%) and generating well-formulated arguments (3.7) while preserving meaning (40%) and plausibility (60%).

In comparison to the automatic evaluation results shown in Table 2, we notice a significant drop by $\approx 50\%$ in the target-set-fit ratio. This discrepancy can be primarily attributed to the use of the same classifier for both the automatic evaluation and the classification of tokens with frames. This classifier plays a crucial role in identifying the text segments that need to be replaced to achieve a new target frameset. As a consequence of this setup, incorrect frame predictions that occur outside the replaced text segments go unnoticed in the automatic evaluation but are detected in the manual evaluation.

5.3.1 Impact of model size

To analyze the impact of using a larger model (namely `t5-large`), we expanded our manual annotation study by 50 reframed arguments for each hyperparameter setting. Table 5 shows the results.

Regarding the target-set-fit ratio, we observe similar performances, yielding only 4% and 6% for `t5-small` and `t5-large`, respectively, without framed decoding. While `t5-small` is better in avoiding the removed frame class (64%) but not successful and targeting the added frame class (8%), t5-large is worse in removing (58%) but better in adding (16%). Due to the higher model complexity, t5-large is better at generating context-fitting replacements, having a higher chance to restore the masked text part but also to uncover new aspects, while t5-small tends to generate more general and debate-unspecific replacements, resulting in less meaning preservation (dropping from 62 to 50%) and plausibility (from 70% to 60%).

Nevertheless, activating the framed decoding process with $\lambda = 0.2$ reduces the impact of model size regarding the framing. Both text-generating models produce a target-set-fit ratio of 18%, demonstrating the success of our decoding strategy being insensitive to model size. However, t5-large shows a better performance on selecting linguistically fitting tokens which leads to comparable ratings in grammaticality (∅4.1), meaning preservation (60%) and plausibility (72%). Here, t5-small starts to generate clearly ungrammatical or unfitting text replacements in some cases.

5.3.2 Evaluating reframing on multiple frames

Up to this point, our focus has been on the task of reframing involving the replacement of a single frame class within an argument in a multilabel setting. Next, we experimented with removing and adding none or multiple frame classes simultaneously, exclusively relying on arguments covering at least two frame classes. Due to the increasing complexity, we used t5-large with activated framed decoding ($\lambda = 0.2$), again reranking among 10 candidates per argument. The manual analysis incorporated 50 reframed arguments, once for removing 1 frame class (deframing) and once for exchanging 2 frame classes (extended reframing).

Increasing the edit distance between the source frameset $\mathcal{S}$ and target frameset $\mathcal{T}$ increases the task difficulty. With deframing, we achieve a target-set-fit of 24% (yielding 66% reframed arguments without the removed target frame). By exchanging 1 target frame class we measure a target-set-fit of 18% while finally dropping to 8% by exchanging 2 target frame classes due to the major changes needed to achieve the complex changes between $\mathcal{S}$ and $\mathcal{T}$. The challenge of this extended reframing is also reflected by the other three manual metrics but still yielding an average grammar score of 3.9, a ratio of 42% in meaning preservation, and a ratio of 64% in terms of plausibility.

6 Conclusion

We have proposed an unsupervised approach to argument reframing, which takes inspiration from approaches to counterfactual explanation generation in the sense that we transfer and adapt metrics used in counterfactual generation to implement a reranking strategy for reframed arguments. We use an LLM to replace text spans that were tagged by a token classifier with a frame to be deleted by tokens that are associated with the frame to be added.

Our automatic and manual evaluation demonstrates that the combination of framed decoding and reranking, utilizing metrics such as frame-validity, proximity, data manifold closeness, and grammaticality, outperforms a vanilla LLM baseline by nearly an order of magnitude in terms of reframing success. Furthermore, by showing a tradeoff between tailoring the rewritten argument to the target frameset and yielding a plausible and grammatically correct argument, we identified a sweet spot in the strength of framed decoding yielding across two different language generation model sizes.

Acknowledgements

This work has been funded by DFG within the project ACCEPT, which is part of the priority program "Robust Argumentation Machines" (RATIO), and the project B01 within the TRR 318 "Constructing Explainability".

References

Yamen Ajjour, Milad Alshomary, Henning Wachsmuth, and Benno Stein. 2019. Modeling frames in argumentation. In *Proceedings of the 2019 Conference on Empirical Methods in Natural Language Processing and the 9th International Joint Conference on Natural Language Processing (EMNLP-IJCNLP)*, pages 2922–2932, Hong Kong, China. Association for Computational Linguistics.

Amber E. Boydstun, Dallas Card, Justin Gross, Paul Resnick, and Noah A. Smith. 2014. Tracking the development of media frames within and across policy issues.

Dallas Card, Amber E. Boydstun, Justin H. Gross, Philip Resnik, and Noah A. Smith. 2015. The media frames corpus: Annotations of frames across issues. In *Proceedings of the 53rd Annual Meeting of the Association for Computational Linguistics and the 7th International Joint Conference on Natural Language*

Processing (Volume 2: Short Papers), pages 438–444, Beijing, China. Association for Computational Linguistics.

Tuhin Chakrabarty, Christopher Hidey, and Smaranda Muresan. 2021. ENTRUST: Argument reframing with language models and entailment. In *Proceedings of the 2021 Conference of the North American Chapter of the Association for Computational Linguistics: Human Language Technologies*, pages 4958–4971, Online. Association for Computational Linguistics.

Wei-Fan Chen, Khalid Al Khatib, Benno Stein, and Henning Wachsmuth. 2021. Controlled neural sentence-level reframing of news articles. In *Findings of the Association for Computational Linguistics: EMNLP 2021*, pages 2683–2693, Punta Cana, Dominican Republic. Association for Computational Linguistics.

Claes de Vreese. 2005. News framing: Theory and typology. *Information Design Journal*, 13:51–62.

Philipp Heinisch, Anette Frank, Juri Opitz, and Philipp Cimiano. 2022. Strategies for framing argumentative conclusion generation. In *Proceedings of the 15th International Conference on Natural Language Generation*, pages 246–259, Waterville, Maine, USA and virtual meeting. Association for Computational Linguistics.

Nitish Shirish Keskar, Bryan McCann, Lav R. Varshney, Caiming Xiong, and Richard Socher. 2019. CTRL: A conditional transformer language model for controllable generation. *CoRR*, abs/1909.05858.

Nishtha Madaan, Inkit Padhi, Naveen Panwar, and Diptikalyan Saha. 2021. Generate your counterfactuals: Towards controlled counterfactual generation for text. In *Thirty-Fifth AAAI Conference on Artificial Intelligence, AAAI 2021, Thirty-Third Conference on Innovative Applications of Artificial Intelligence, IAAI 2021, The Eleventh Symposium on Educational Advances in Artificial Intelligence, EAAI 2021, Virtual Event, February 2-9, 2021*, pages 13516–13524. AAAI Press.

Tim Miller. 2019. Explanation in artificial intelligence: Insights from the social sciences. *Artif. Intell.*, 267:1–38.

Amita Misra, Brian Ecker, and Marilyn Walker. 2016. Measuring the similarity of sentential arguments in dialogue. In *Proceedings of the 17th Annual Meeting of the Special Interest Group on Discourse and Dialogue*, pages 276–287, Los Angeles. Association for Computational Linguistics.

John Morris, Eli Lifland, Jin Yong Yoo, Jake Grigsby, Di Jin, and Yanjun Qi. 2020. TextAttack: A framework for adversarial attacks, data augmentation, and adversarial training in NLP. In *Proceedings of the 2020 Conference on Empirical Methods in Natural Language Processing: System Demonstrations*, pages 119–126, Online. Association for Computational Linguistics.

Xinyi Mou, Zhongyu Wei, Changjian Jiang, and Jiajie Peng. 2022. A two stage adaptation framework for frame detection via prompt learning. In *Proceedings of the 29th International Conference on Computational Linguistics*, pages 2968–2978, Gyeongju, Republic of Korea. International Committee on Computational Linguistics.

OpenAI. 2023. Gpt-4 technical report.

Colin Raffel, Noam Shazeer, Adam Roberts, Katherine Lee, Sharan Narang, Michael Matena, Yanqi Zhou, Wei Li, and Peter J. Liu. 2020. Exploring the limits of transfer learning with a unified text-to-text transformer. *J. Mach. Learn. Res.*, 21(1).

Nils Reimers and Iryna Gurevych. 2019. Sentence-bert: Sentence embeddings using siamese bert-networks. In *Proceedings of the 2019 Conference on Empirical Methods in Natural Language Processing and the 9th International Joint Conference on Natural Language Processing, EMNLP-IJCNLP 2019, Hong Kong, China, November 3-7, 2019*, pages 3980–3990. Association for Computational Linguistics.

Nils Reimers, Benjamin Schiller, Tilman Beck, Johannes Daxenberger, Christian Stab, and Iryna Gurevych. 2019. Classification and clustering of arguments with contextualized word embeddings. In *Proceedings of the 57th Annual Meeting of the Association for Computational Linguistics*, pages 567–578, Florence, Italy. Association for Computational Linguistics.

Alexis Ross, Ana Marasović, and Matthew Peters. 2021. Explaining NLP models via minimal contrastive editing (MiCE). In *Findings of the Association for Computational Linguistics: ACL-IJCNLP 2021*, pages 3840–3852, Online. Association for Computational Linguistics.

Mattes Ruckdeschel and Gregor Wiedemann. 2022. Boundary detection and categorization of argument aspects via supervised learning. In *Proceedings of the 9th Workshop on Argument Mining*, pages 126–136, Online and in Gyeongju, Republic of Korea. International Conference on Computational Linguistics.

Benjamin Schiller, Johannes Daxenberger, and Iryna Gurevych. 2021. Aspect-controlled neural argument generation. In *Proceedings of the 2021 Conference of the North American Chapter of the Association for Computational Linguistics: Human Language Technologies*, pages 380–396, Online. Association for Computational Linguistics.

Sahil Verma, Varich Boonsanong, Minh Hoang, Keegan E Hines, John P Dickerson, and Chirag Shah. 2020. Counterfactual explanations and algorithmic recourses for machine learning: A review. *arXiv preprint arXiv:2010.10596*.

Sandra Wachter, Brent D. Mittelstadt, and Chris Russell. 2017. Counterfactual explanations without opening the black box: Automated decisions and the GDPR. *CoRR*, abs/1711.00399.

Alex Warstadt, Amanpreet Singh, and Samuel R. Bowman. 2019. Neural network acceptability judgments. *Transactions of the Association for Computational Linguistics*, 7:625–641.

Thomas Wolf, Lysandre Debut, Victor Sanh, Julien Chaumond, Clement Delangue, Anthony Moi, Pierric Cistac, Tim Rault, Remi Louf, Morgan Funtowicz, Joe Davison, Sam Shleifer, Patrick von Platen, Clara Ma, Yacine Jernite, Julien Plu, Canwen Xu, Teven Le Scao, Sylvain Gugger, Mariama Drame, Quentin Lhoest, and Alexander Rush. 2020. Transformers: State-of-the-art natural language processing. In *Proceedings of the 2020 Conference on Empirical Methods in Natural Language Processing: System Demonstrations*, pages 38–45, Online. Association for Computational Linguistics.

Tongshuang Wu, Marco Tulio Ribeiro, Jeffrey Heer, and Daniel Weld. 2021. Polyjuice: Generating counterfactuals for explaining, evaluating, and improving models. In *Proceedings of the 59th Annual Meeting of the Association for Computational Linguistics and the 11th International Joint Conference on Natural Language Processing (Volume 1: Long Papers)*, pages 6707–6723, Online. Association for Computational Linguistics.

A Analysing the impact of the number of generated candidates for reframing

This section presents a concise analysis of how the quantity of rewrites impacts the quality of the best-reframed argument considering the automatic reranking with weights proposed in Section 5.2, measured by the target-set-fit ratio and the average score of the reranking metrics.

Investigating the debate of "nuclear energy", Figure 2 illustrates a pattern wherein an increasing number of rewrites monotonously increases both metrics across all models since additional rewrites potentially outperform the choice among fewer rewrites, but can not worsen the metrics based on the best argument after reranking. However, the curves flatten with an increasing number of rewrites, representing a stochastic principle of sampling from an ordered distribution. Since we apply sampling at decoding time itself, every language model has the capability to generate every text that maximizes the automatic metrics (100%). Hence, our distribution contains this optimal text which has to be sampled assuming access to infinite rewrites. However, this is not practicable, raising the question of the probability mass of the "good" rewrites. Here, we observe that framed decoding shifts the

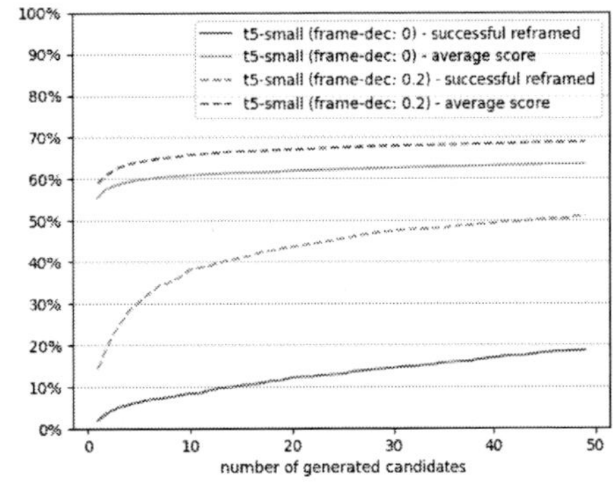

Figure 2: Influence of the number of rewrites debating "Nuclear energy" (`t5-small`)

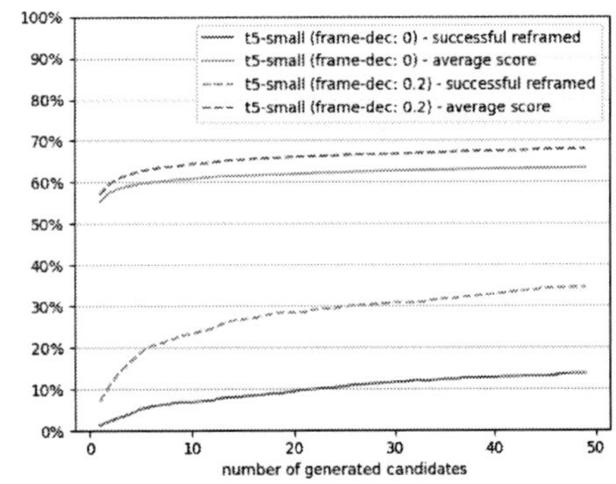

Figure 3: Influence of the number of rewrites debating "Minimum wage" (`t5-small`)

probability mass significantly, leading to better solutions at fewer rewrites compared to instances where framed decoding is not employed.

The observation holds for other topics as well. Figure 3 for the topic "minimum wage" shows a similar relation between the metrics and number rewrites, having only a smaller slope of increment. Looking at Table 1, we see that this topic yields the smallest ratio of successfully reframed arguments on average, suggesting more complex frame classes. Nevertheless, the same stochastic principles apply here, observing the same trends.

B User Interface of the Manual study

Figure 4 shows the user interface of our manual study. Annotators were shown one argument at a time and were asked to rate the mentioned frames, the fluency, and the meaning. Each frame class is

Frame	α_κ
Accidents/security	0.361
Costs	0.462
Energy policy	0.133
Environmental impact	0.362
Fossil fuels	0.286
Health effects	0.498
Public debate	0.107
Reliability/efficiency	0.173
Renewables	0.386
Technological innovation	0.209
Waste	0.454
Weapons	0.457
Overall	0.324

Table 6: Inter-annotator agreements (Krippendorff's Alpha) of the manual user study, topic *Nuclear energy*

described adapting the original descriptions[4], once by hovering the frames and once in the guidelines at the bottom of the page, containing examples as well. The annotators answered the questions sample by sample independently from each other.

C Replacing T5 with larger prompt-based Large Language Models

Recent advancements in prompt-based Large Language Models, such as chatGPT or the successor GPT-4 (OpenAI, 2023), show wide applicability for many NLP tasks in a few- or even zero-shot setting. To test the potential for usage as reframing models, we used a prompt[5] to test the performance of GPT-4 on some selected examples shown in Table 3:

1. Just to maintain the current world consumption of fossil fuels, either the oldest, most depleted fields need to be rejuvenated or a significant surge in new drilling needs to begin."
2. "The support of nuclear power by the government results from its reliability in the industry.
3. "Prospects for nuclear energy as an option are limited, the report found, by four unresolved problems: high relative costs; perceived adverse safety and technological challenges; health effects; potential security risks stemming from proliferation; and unresolved challenges in long-term management of nuclear wastes."

While the first look at the reformed arguments is promising (introducing related phrases towards the frame class which should be added in all arguments), we see critical drawbacks using GPT-4. Although the parts marked as "fit the target frame set" of the reframed arguments align with the original argument, GPT-4 failed to keep them completely unchanged and, hence, perform more changes than necessary, leading to less controllability. Furthermore, with respect to the automatic frame class prediction, GPT-4 often fails to reframe successfully. In the presented examples, GPT-4 successfully added only once the new frame class and failed two times to remove the frame class that should have been discarded. GPT-4 shows also a dependency on descriptions of the frame classes, e.g. to guide the second example towards "reliable energy" rather than "reliability" in general. All in all, GPT-4 alone without further guidance as provided by framed decoding or reranking is not suited to support the type of minimalistic reframing that we are targeting. However, using these two techniques to introduce framing capabilities in an unsupervised manner, we require only a general language understanding of the underlying generative language model. Using a much larger prompt-based model with more capabilities is not necessarily beneficial here. In order to keep the requirements for the computational resources realistic, especially with respect to a beam search using up to 100 beams in order to yield a comprehensive search space for counterfactual reranking, we consider T5 as the model of choice for this paper.

[4] `https://zenodo.org/record/7525183/files/AAC_NE_Guidelines.md?download=1`

[5] You are an assistant for reframing sentences that are tagged with specific aspects. The current topic is nuclear energy and the tags show which aspects of the topic the tokens belong to. You will be given a sentence with a set of initial aspects and your task is to perform minimal changes on the sentence to reframe it into a new target set of aspects, without changing words that are not labeled to an aspect that needs to be removed. The new aspects are general topics and not the words that need to be included.

This is a tagged sentence with the aspects [SOURCE SET] and the target set is [TARGET SET]

[Sentence with annotated labels]

Now perform minimal changes to this sentence to achieve a reframed sentence that has the target set as annotated aspects. Try to keep the sentence as close to the original one and change only what is necessary. The fewer changes the better. Keep the tokens that are not related to the reframing the same, i.e. don't remove unnecessary tokens if they are not related to an aspect that needs to be removed. Write the new sentence without aspect classifications but just as a plain sentence.

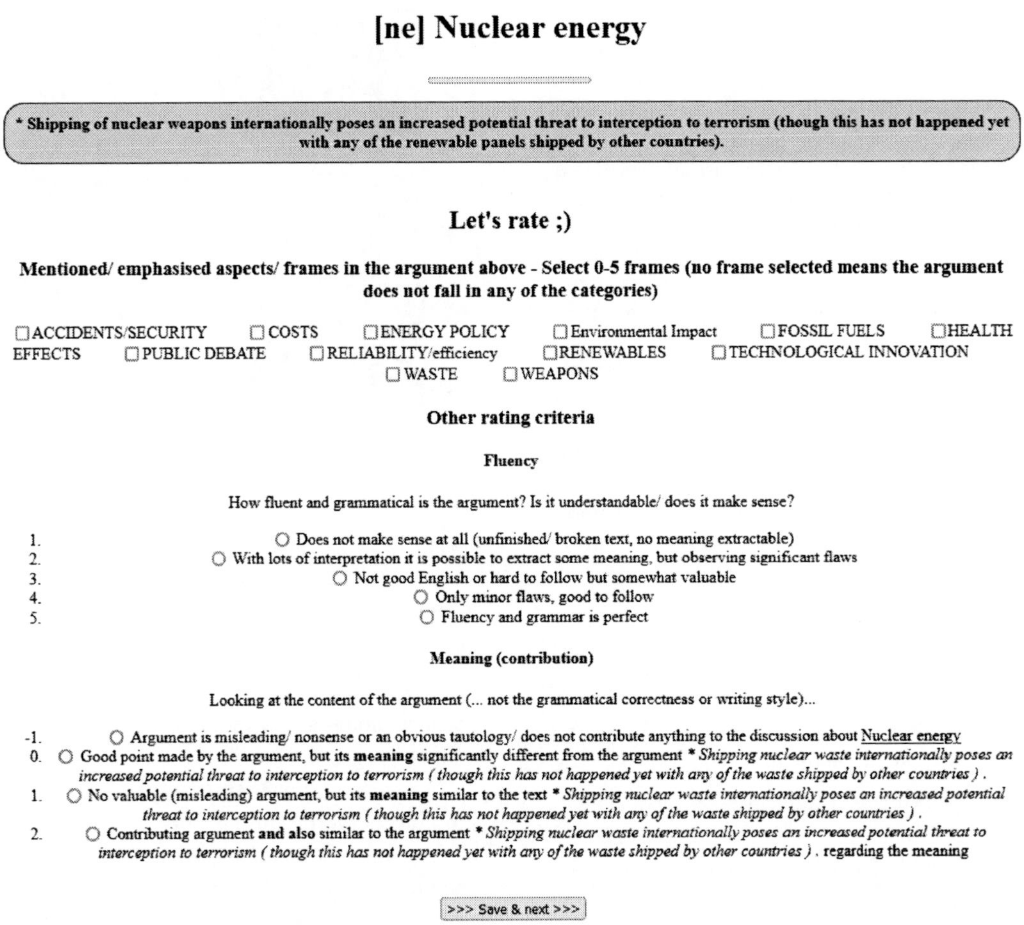

Figure 4: Screenshot of part of the annotator interface of the manual study

Overview of ImageArg-2023: The First Shared Task in Multimodal Argument Mining

Zhexiong Liu, Mohamed Elaraby*, Yang Zhong*, Diane Litman
Department of Computer Science
University of Pittsburgh, Pittsburgh, PA 15260 USA
{zhexiong.liu, mse30, yaz118, dlitman}@pitt.edu

Abstract

This paper presents an overview of the *ImageArg* shared task, the first multimodal Argument Mining shared task co-located with the 10th Workshop on Argument Mining at EMNLP 2023. The shared task comprises two classification subtasks - (1) Subtask-A: Argument Stance Classification; (2) Subtask-B: Image Persuasiveness Classification. The former determines the stance of a tweet containing an image and a piece of text toward a controversial topic (e.g., gun control and abortion). The latter determines whether the image makes the tweet text more persuasive. The shared task received 31 submissions for Subtask-A and 21 submissions for Subtask-B from 9 different teams across 6 countries. The top submission in Subtask-A achieved an F1-score of 0.8647 while the best submission in Subtask-B achieved an F1-score of 0.5561.

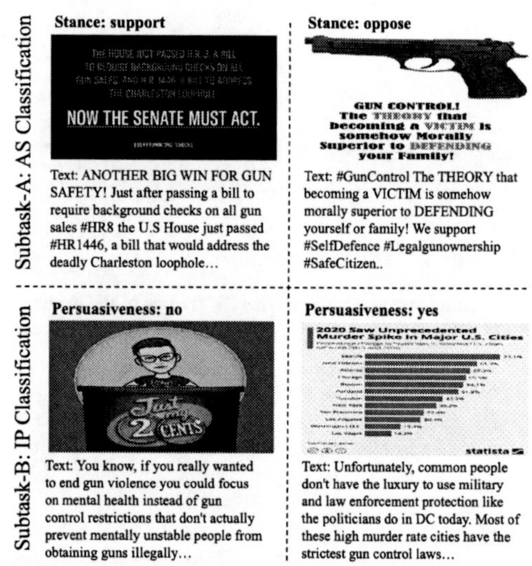

Figure 1: Examples of Subtask-A: Argument Stance (AS) Classification and Subtask-B: Image Persuasiveness (IP) Classification.

1 Introduction

Research in Argument Mining (AM) typically centers around the examination of an author's argumentative position, achieved through the automated identification of argument structures. This research has predominantly concentrated on domains presented in textual formats, encompassing endeavors such as mining persuasiveness in essays (Stab and Gurevych, 2014) and user-generated web discourse (Habernal and Gurevych, 2017). Recently, there has been a growing recognition of the need for multimodality in AM research. A noteworthy development in this regard is the *Retrieval for Argument* shared task (Carnot et al., 2023). This task is designed to retrieve images related to a controversial topic that aligns with the textual stance, whether it supports or contradicts the topic. In a related context, Liu et al. (2022) introduced the *ImageArg* corpus, which is designed to investigate multimodal persuasiveness within tweets. This corpus represented an advancement in the field of automated persuasive text identification (Duthie et al., 2016) by introducing a new modality through the inclusion of images.

This paper introduces the *ImageArg* shared task[1], building upon the groundwork laid by Liu et al. (2022) and conducted as a part of the 10th Workshop on Argument Mining[2]. The shared task comprises two subtasks that center around two highly controversial topics (gun control and abortion):

- Subtask-A: Argument Stance (AS) Classification. The primary objective is to determine, for each of these topics, whether a given tweet text and its accompanying image express either support or opposition. This subtask addresses the research question: how to identify an argument stance of the tweet that contains a piece of text and an image?

* These authors contributed equally to this work.

[1] https://imagearg.github.io/
[2] https://argmining-org.github.io/2023/

Proceedings of the 10th Workshop on Argument Mining, pages 120–132
December 7, 2023.

- Subtask-B: Image Persuasiveness (IP) Classification. The goal is to assess whether the image associated with a tweet makes the tweet text more persuasive or not. This subtask addresses the research question: does the tweet image make the tweet text more persuasive?

Figure 1 shows examples of the two subtasks. The upper left tweet expresses a strong stance towards supporting gun control by indicating a house bill about the requirement of background checks for all gun sales. The upper right tweet opposes gun control because it is inclined to self-defense. The lower left tweet has an image irrelevant to the gun control topic. It does not improve the persuasiveness of the tweet text (and its stance) that argues to focus on mental health instead of gun restriction. The lower right tweet makes the tweet text (and its stance) more persuasive because it provides strong evidence to show the statistics of the murder rate in major U.S. cities due to restrictive gun control laws, so citizens cannot easily arm themselves.

The shared task received 31 submissions for Subtask-A and 21 submissions for Subtask-B from 9 diverse teams, comprising both academic experts from various universities and industry researchers, across 6 different countries. In general, the submissions that utilized text information from tweet images and performed data augmentation yielded favorable results for Subtask-A. The submissions that utilized unified multimodal models also achieved good performance in Subtask-B. The highest Subtask-A F1-score of 0.8647 was attained by **Team KnowComp** (Zong et al., 2023), while the leading Subtask-B F1-score of 0.5561 was attained by **Team feeds** (Torky et al., 2023). Details about task submissions are described in Section 4.

2 Related Work

Multimodal Learning Recently, there has been increasing attention to assessing the ability of artificial intelligence models to process and understand multimodal input signals that occur in real-world applications (Zhang et al., 2018; Alwassel et al., 2020). In the vision-language domain, tasks are primarily designed to evaluate the capacity of models to comprehend visual data and articulate reasoning in language (Goyal et al., 2017; Hudson and Manning, 2019). In addition, Zheng et al. (2021) are interested in the discourse relations between text and its associated images in recipes, while Kruk et al. (2019) explores the multimodal document intent of Instagram posts. More recently, Liu et al. (2022) introduce *ImageArg*, the first multimodal learning corpus for argument mining. However, the size of the *ImageArg* corpus is small, which motivates our construction of an extension of the original corpus. Regarding multimodal modeling, researchers have developed methods to derive strong representations for each modality and implement fusion techniques (Tsai et al., 2018; Hu et al., 2019; Tan and Bansal, 2019; Lu et al., 2020). Although several shared tasks in machine translation (Specia et al., 2016; Barrault et al., 2018) and argument retrieval (Carnot et al., 2023) have revealed the effectiveness of multimodal learning, none of them focused on argument persuasiveness. Therefore, this shared task provides opportunities to benchmark the new multimodal argument persuasiveness corpus by utilizing various image and text encoders along with effective fusion strategies.

Computational Persuasiveness While classical argument mining primarily focuses on the identification of argumentative components and their corresponding relationships (Stab et al., 2014, 2018; Lawrence and Reed, 2020), researchers have also focused on argument persuasiveness (Chatterjee et al., 2014; Park et al., 2014; Lukin et al., 2017; Carlile et al., 2018; Chakrabarty et al., 2019). Furthermore, while Riley (1954), O'Keefe (2015), and Wei et al. (2016) investigated the ranking of debate arguments on the same topic, they did not focus on discovering factors contributing to the persuasiveness of these arguments. In addition, Lukin et al. (2017) and Persing and Ng (2017) investigate how audience personality influences persuasiveness through diverse argument styles, such as factual versus emotional arguments. However, their work only focuses on the textual modality. In contrast, Higgins and Walker (2012) and Carlile et al. (2018) focus their attention on persuasion strategies, e.g., Ethos (credibility), Logos (reason), and Pathos (emotion), within the context of reports and student essays. Building upon their work designed for textual corpora, Liu et al. (2022) extend the annotation schemes to include the image modality. Although Park et al. (2014), Joo et al. (2014), and Huang and Kovashka (2016) employ facial expressions and bodily gestures to analyze persuasiveness within the realm of social multimedia, their investigations remain limited to human portraits and fail to generalize across diverse image domains. While prior work does explore persuasive advertisements

Confidence	Abortion	Gun control
>= L5	0.8437	0.7434
>= L4	0.7842	0.6697
>= L3	0.7824	0.6551
>= L2	0.7820	0.6516
>= L1	0.7807	0.6487

Table 1: Krippendorff's alpha for abortion and gun control topics with respect to different confidence levels.

in a multimodal fashion (Hussain et al., 2017; Guo et al., 2021), it is important to note that their focus is on sentiment analysis, intent reasoning, and persuasive strategies tailored specifically for advertisements. In contrast, our shared task is interested in argument mining, marking an aligned goal to the *ImageArg* work (Liu et al., 2022), offering substantial value to multimodal computational social science.

3 Corpus

We extended the *ImageArg* corpus (Liu et al., 2022) by following its annotation protocol to annotate new data on abortion and gun control topics. Specifically, we annotated 1141 new abortion tweets and 301 new gun control tweets. Parts of the new gun control tweets were used to replace 131 out of the original 1003 gun control tweets in the *ImageArg* corpus which were no longer available due to deletions or account suspensions. The other extras were annotated to ensure gun control and abortion tweets have close data distributions. Therefore, we obtained 1173 gun control tweets in total. In addition to using the original annotation protocol (Liu et al., 2022), we required annotators to score confidence levels, which was designed to improve the inter-annotation agreement. Confidence was divided into 5 levels: L5-Extremely confident (understood and answered all annotations carefully), L4-Quite confident (tried to understand and answered most annotations carefully), L3-Somewhat confident (confused about some annotations), L2-Not very confident (did not understand some annotations), and L1-Not confident (mostly educated guesses).

In the annotation process, each tweet was annotated by three annotators on Amazon Mechanical Turk (AMT)[3] who had done more than 5,000 approved annotations with at least 95% approved rates in their historical hits. Annotators were required to pass a qualification exam that annotated

[3]https://www.mturk.com/

Topic	Split	AS		IP		Total
		Sup.	Opp.	Yes	No	
Gun control	train	475	448	251	672	923
	dev	54	46	33	67	100
	test	85	65	53	97	150
Abortion	train	244	647	278	613	891
	dev	19	81	26	74	100
	test	33	117	53	97	150

Table 2: The data statistics for Subtask-A and Subtask-B for gun control and abortion topics.

pilot examples with at least 0.7 accuracy. Table 1 shows AS annotation agreements in terms of Krippendorff's alpha (Krippendorff, 2011) and confidence levels. We observed that annotations with high confidence levels had high agreements but dropped more annotations. To make the trade-off between annotation costs and agreements, we disregarded annotations with confidence levels less than L4 for abortion and less than L5 for gun control. The remaining new AS annotations for abortion and gun control have alpha scores of 0.78 and 0.74, respectively. The new IP annotations were also inherited from the *ImageArg* protocol. First, annotators annotated two persuasiveness scores: one for tweet text (s_t), another for tweet text and image (s_{it}). Then we computed a score difference $\Delta s_i = max(s_{it} - s_t, 0)$ as a persuasiveness gain from adding a tweet image. The final image persuasiveness score for each tweet was the average of persuasiveness gains from three annotators. To interpret image persuasiveness, we used the same threshold (0.5) in *ImageArg* to split them into binary labels, indicating whether the image made the tweet text more persuasive or not.

We split the corpus into train, development, and test sets in the shared task, which obtained 1814 train, 200 development, and 300 test samples for both subtasks[4]. The data statistics are shown in Table 2 for Subtask-A and Subtask-B, respectively. We released the train and development data splits for model development and the test set without labels before the task submission deadline. We shared the complete test set with labels after completing the shared task. The full corpus can be downloaded from the GitHub repository[5].

[4]We removed one abortion tweet in the test set when we evaluated team submissions for the leaderboard because the tweet was no longer available during the task submission phase so a few teams were unable to download the full 300 test samples.

[5]https://github.com/ImageArg/ImageArg-Shared-Task

ID	System	Score	Modality	Model	Notes
1*	KnowComp-4	0.8647	I+T	ResNet50 + DeBERTa	Augment Text with Back Translation + WordNet
2	KnowComp-5	0.8571	I+T	ResNet50 + DeBERTa	Augment Text with Translation + WordNet + Semantic SimilarityAttention
3	KnowComp-1	0.8528	I+T	ResNet101 + DeBERTa	Augment Text with Translation + WordNet
4*	Semantists-4	0.8506	T+E		Ensemble of All Models
5	Semantists-3	0.8462	T+E	BERTweet	OCR on Image
6	Semantists-5	0.8417	T+E	BERT	Dual Contrastive Loss + OCR on Image
7	Semantists-1	0.8365	T+E	BERT	Contrastive Loss + OCR on Image
8	Semantists-2	0.8365	T+E	T5	OCR on Image
9	KnowComp-2	0.8365	I+T	ResNet50 + DeBERTa	Augment Text with Translation + WordNet + Semantic SimilarityAttention
10	KnowComp-3	0.8346	I+T	LayoutLMv3 + DeBERTa	Augment Text with Translation + WordNet
11*	Mohammad Soltani-2	0.8273	I+T	CLIP32	AdaBoost for Abortion + Xgboost for Gun Control
12*	Pitt Pixel Persuaders-2	0.8168	T		Emsemble All The Model
13	Mohammad Soltani-1	0.8142	I+T	CLIP32	AdaBoost for Abortion and Gun Control
14	Mohammad Soltani-4	0.8093	I+T	CLIP32	Xgboost for Abortion and Gun Control
15*	GC-HUNTER-2	0.8049	T	XLMRoberta	
16	Mohammad Soltani-3	0.8000	I+T	CLIP32	AdaBoost for Abortion + RUSBoost for Gun Control
17	Pitt Pixel Persuaders-1	0.7910	T	BLOOM-560m	
18	Mohammad Soltani-5	0.7782	I+T	CLIP32	SVM-Poly for Abortion and Gun Control
19	GC-HUNTER-1	0.7766	T	BERT	
20*	IUST-1	0.7754	T+E	BERTweet	Augment Text with ChatGPT paraphraser + OCR on image
21	IUST-2	0.7752	T+E	RoBERTa	Augment Text with ChatGPT paraphraser + OCR on image
22	Pitt Pixel Persuaders-4	0.7710	T	Bloom-1B	
23	Pitt Pixel Persuaders-5	0.7415	T	XLNet	
24*	KPAS-1	0.7097	I+T	CLIP	
25*	ACT-CS-4	0.6325	I+T+E+C	ViT+BERT	Cross-Attention
26	ACT-CS-3	0.6178	I+T+E	ViT+BERT	Cross-Attention
27	ACT-CS-2	0.6116	I+T	ViT+BERT	Cross-Attention
28	ACT-CS-1	0.5863	I+T	ViT+BERT	Simple Concatenation of features
29	IUST-3	0.5680	I+T+E	CLIP+BERT	Augment Text with ChatGPT paraphraser + OCR on image
30	Pitt Pixel Persuaders-3	0.5285	I+T	ViLT	
31*	feeds-1**	0.4418	T	BERT	

Table 3: The Subtask-A submission results. The System column refers to the Team name and submission attempt number connected by "-". Each Team has at most five submissions. The scores are positive F1 scores. The T, I, E, and C represent text, image, extracted text from image, and image caption modality, respectively. Rows with **bold** ID and marked with * refer to the best system for each participating team. ** Team feeds submitted results for one topic by the submission deadline, so only partial results are evaluated.

4 Submission Results

We provide summaries about Subtask-A (Sec. 4.1) and Subtask-B (Sec. 4.2) submissions for all the teams. In cases where a team did not submit a description paper, we include their results and provide a brief description based on the survey completed by the team at the time of submission.

4.1 Subtask-A: AS Classification

Initially, we observed that models utilizing multimodal features (I+T or T+E) displayed higher performances, where I denotes tweet images, T denotes tweet text, and E denotes the text extracted from images. Table 3 illustrates that the top-performing submissions (top 10) employed two primary strategies: they either fused features extracted from both image and text encoders separately, or used pretrained language models finetuned on text extracted from images and tweets, which gave an additional textual context to the original tweet. This innovative method improved model performance compared to the ones that only used tweet text data in general[6]. Also, the last column shows that data augmentation exhibited promise, given the limited annotated data in this shared task.

4.1.1 System Descriptions

We describe representative methods from leading teams while summarizing the approaches from the remaining teams as follows:

Team KnowComp introduced a unified Framework for Text, Image, and Layout Fusion in Argument Mining, TILFA (Zong et al., 2023). They highlighted the need for better image encoding with textual information. To tackle the problem of unbalanced data, they augmented the tweet texts with backtranslation and synonym replacements.

Team Semantists (Rajaraman et al., 2023) submitted five system runs for task A, focusing mainly on the text-based approaches. To harness the information from the images, they extract text from the tweet image through an OCR system and concatenate it with the tweet texts. Pretrained language models such as T5 NLI (Raffel et al., 2020) and BERTTweet are applied for label predictions. The team also adopts a Multi-task Contrastive Learning Framework similar to Chen et al. (2022) with the label aware augmentation for contrastive learning.

Team Mohammad Soltani (Soltani and Romberg, 2023) experimented with CLIP (Radford et al., 2021) to extract the textual and visual modality features. They then combined features from both modalities by concatenating them along the last dimension according to an early fusion strategy, followed by traditional machine learning classifiers such as AdaBoostClassifier and SVM-Poly.

Team Pitt Pixels Persuaders (Sharma et al., 2023) fine-tuned multiple text-based pre-trained models such as XLNet (Yang et al., 2019) and BLOOM (Scao et al., 2022) on the corpus. **Team IUST** (Nobakhtian et al., 2023) did data augmentation using GPT to paraphrase tweet text and extracted text from images and finetuned text-based models. **Team feeds** (Torky et al., 2023) and **Team GC-Hunter** (Shokri and Levitan, 2023) only fine-tuned pre-trained language models on the tweet text. Both **Team ACT-CS** (Zhang et al., 2023) and **Team KPAS** studied multimodal feature fusions.

4.1.2 Method Discussions

Table 3 reveals that the most successful submissions utilized pretrained language models such as DeBERTa, BERT, and BERTweet (Nguyen et al., 2020). Furthermore, the integration of data augmentation techniques, such as backtranslation and word substitution using WordNet, was observed to enhance performance, as depicted in Figure 2. This boost in performance can be attributed to the inherent reliance on textual information in the stance detection task. Augmenting the relatively limited annotated corpus with these techniques appears to be advantageous. Additionally, leveraging features from the visual modality, whether through image representations or image-text representations, further improved performance, ultimately leading to the highest overall scores, as demonstrated in Table 3 (rows 1 to 10).

On the other hand, the methods that utilized multimodal techniques like CLIP performed relatively lower than those that employed separate encoders for text and visual modalities. This is evident when referencing Table 3, where the system achieving the highest performance using CLIP as the joint encoder, namely the submission by Mohammad Soltani-2, is ranked 11th on the leaderboard. Additionally, it's noteworthy that only a limited number of teams explored the use of Large Language Models (LLMs). This might be attributed to our

[6]Results may vary depending on the model training details and experimental setups across participating teams

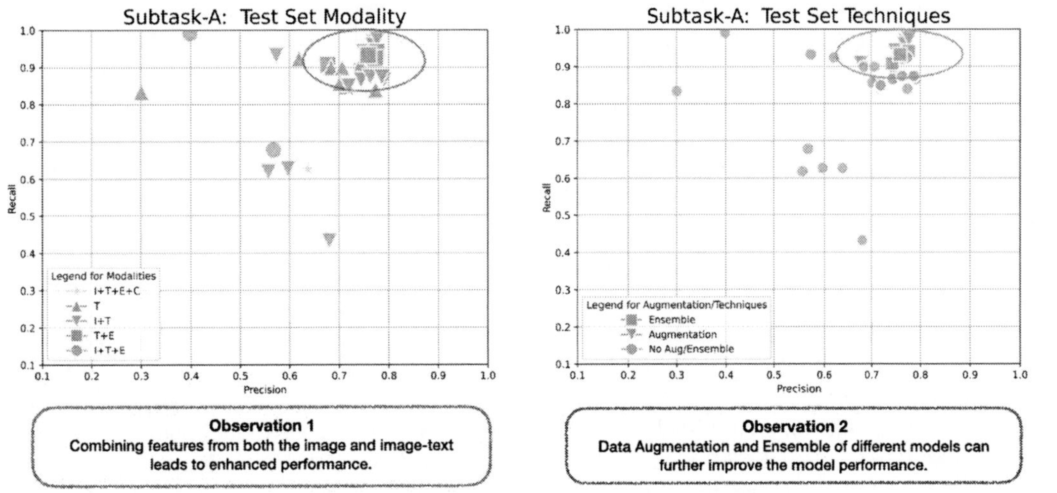

Figure 2: Subtask-A: system performance in relation to the computation approaches (left: modalities, right: techniques). We grouped systems based on the modalities used by the model (left) and computational techniques (right). The T, I, E, and C represent text, image, extracted text from image, and image caption modality, respectively.

initial guidelines[7], which indicated that the utilization of commercial APIs like chatGPT[8] would not contribute to the final ranking. Nevertheless, submissions that leveraged open-source LLMs, such as BLOOM-1B (row 22), exhibited lower performance compared to other submissions using pretrained language models. This opens up opportunities for further research into exploring the capabilities of LLMs in understanding argumentation, especially in multimodal contexts.

4.1.3 Error Analysis

Figure 3 categorized the systems based on the modalities they incorporate and evaluated their respective success rates. Our analysis focused on system' ability to make accurate predictions, quantified by the number of successful systems out of 31 systems. We found that systems that incorporated both image and text modalities (I+T) generally yielded reasonable predictions, with at least one system in this category correctly identifying the label. Additionally, models that combined text and extracted text from images (T+E) displayed particularly strong performance, especially for data of intermediate difficulty. In these cases, the success rate for these systems exceeded 60%, with at least 19 out of the 31 systems making correct predictions.

In a qualitative analysis of the 299 valid tweets

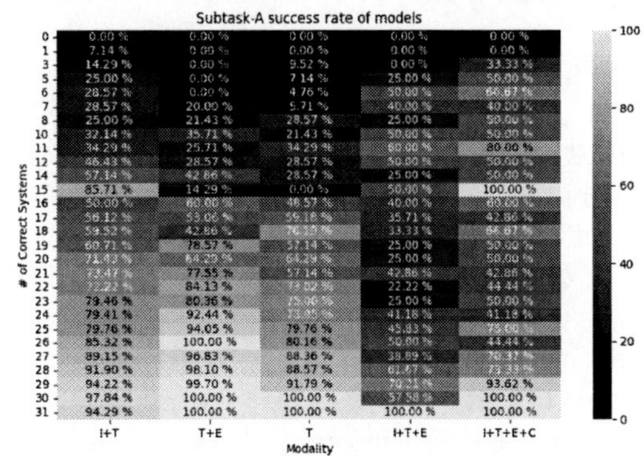

Figure 3: Average rate of correct predictions for Subtask-A systems (grouped by modalities) across tweet difficulties: the y-axis represents the number of systems making correct predictions out of 31 systems.

in the test set, we found that 160 tweets (53%) were accurately predicted by a majority of systems (>= 26 out of 31 systems). Among the subset of tweets (86) exhibiting intermediate difficulty (where 6-20 teams failed to predict the correct labels), we manually sampled ten tweets for label analysis and provided potentially correct labels. Our findings indicate that these tweets often encompass cynicism or sarcasm regarding a specific topic (3 cases), are heavily reliant on the image contents/charts (3 cases), or can be traced back to annotation noise or contents unrelated to the provided topic. Detailed insights are shown in Table 5 in Appendix A. For instance, the first example associates "pro-life" with "Abortion Law", suggesting the tweets favor

[7] https://imagearg.github.io/

[8] https://platform.openai.com/docs/guides/gpt/chat-completions-api

abortion. In the second example, a deep understanding of the text embedded within images is crucial for providing accurate labels. These observations underscore the complexities in multimodal argument mining tasks and highlight the critical role of cross-modal information fusion.

4.2 Subtask-B: IP Classification

In contrast to Subtask-A, participating teams made fewer submission attempts for Subtask-B (a total of 21 compared to 31 for Subtask-A). Notably, all submissions in Subtask-B employed approaches that incorporated multiple modalities, as this task inherently requires an integration of visual and textual information to assess image persuasiveness.

As shown in Table 4, utilizing CLIP (Radford et al., 2021) model is evident to be the most effective technique in extracting multimodal features, which yields the best results (top-4 systems leveraged CLIP). This indicates that a unified encoder can better model the cross-modal information fusion, compared to employing individual models (i.e., ViT (Dosovitskiy et al., 2020) for image and BERT (Devlin et al., 2019) for text) for feature extractions. Moreover, three teams utilized off-the-shelf Optical Character Recognition (OCR) tools to extract image text content. This extracted text was then combined with the original tweet texts to fine-tune pre-trained language models, which suggests that users could include arguments through texts embedded in the images.

4.2.1 System Descriptions

We describe systems from the top-performing teams and briefly summarize the remaining teams:[9]

Team feeds (Torky et al., 2023) made 2 submissions (Table 4 rows 1 and 3). The team utilized the CLIP model to encode the image and text and use a simple concatenation to fuse the two modalities, then trained a neural network on the concatenated features. They carefully cleaned tweet texts by recovering common abbreviations with their full forms (such as "I'm to I am") and also removed content such as URLs, emails, and phone numbers.

Team KPAS did not submit a system demonstration paper. However, their submission notes showed that they also employed the CLIP model to extract multimodal features.

Team Mohammad Soltani (Soltani and Romberg, 2023) made a total of 5 submissions (Table 4 rows 4, 7, 8, 9, and 12). Notably, they adopted a topic-specific approach, tailoring their strategies to each topic separately. For the "Abortion" topic, they integrated visual features extracted from the CLIP model and utilized them as inputs for a classifier. Conversely, when tackling the "gun control" topic, their most successful model was crafted by combining features from Reformer (Kitaev et al., 2019), ELECTRA (Clark et al., 2019), and LayoutLM (Xu et al., 2020).

Similar to the systems in Subtask-A, **Team Semantists** (Rajaraman et al., 2023) extracted texts from images and fine-tuned pretrained Language models such as T5 NLI and StancyBERT (Popat et al., 2019) on the corpus. **Team ACT-CS** (Zhang et al., 2023) and **Team KnowComp** (Zong et al., 2023) used separate models to encode the visual and textual information individually, then fine-tuned classifiers based on the fused features. **Team IUST** (Nobakhtian et al., 2023) (Table 4 row 11) leveraged the MultiModal Bit Transformer to extract features from both image and text sources concurrently. **Team GC-Hunter** (Shokri and Levitan, 2023) chose to concatenate text content from both tweets and OCR outputs to fully leverage textual information, complemented by image features extracted from a separately trained ViLT model. Finally, **Team Pitt Pixel Persuaders** (Sharma et al., 2023) (Table 4, row 21) did not include the details of their Subtask B submission in their system description paper. However, their submission notes reveal that they also relied on CLIP, which proved to be less successful in their case.

4.2.2 Method Discussion

Figure 4 illustrates that, unlike Subtask A, the application of data augmentation techniques which primarily concentrated on augmenting the text modality exclusively obtained only modest improvements in classification performance. Notably, none of the participating teams explored augmentation for the visual modalities, which presents an opportunity for further research into the impact of image augmentation on enhancing persuasiveness detection.

Additionally, Table 4 indicates that none of the submissions integrated LLMs into their systems. This observation can also be attributed to the task's primary emphasis on both visual and textual modalities and the guidelines we enforced, which limited the use of LLMs to open-source models. These open-source models have received less attention within the context of multimodal tasks, providing

[9]While Team KPAS was among the top-performing teams, they did not submit a system description paper.

ID	System	Scores	Modality	Model	Notes
1*	feeds-1	0.5561	I+T	CLIP	Cleaned Text
2*	KPAS-2	0.5417	I+T	CLIP	
3	feeds-2	0.5392	I+T	CLIP	Uncleaned Text
4*	Mohammad Soltani-5	0.5281	I+T	CLIP32+REL +Convnext	
5*	Semantists-1	0.5045	T+E	T5	OCR on Image
6*	ACT-CS-1	0.5000	I+T	Vit+BERT	
7	Mohammad Soltani-1	0.4875	I+T	CLIP32	SVM-Poly for Abortion LogisticReg for Gun Control
8	Mohammad Soltani-4	0.4778	I+T	CLIP32+REL +Convnext	SGD for Abortion LogisticReg for Gun Control
9	Mohammad Soltani-3	0.4762	I+T	CLIP_L_14	SVM-Poly for Abortion and Gun Control
10	Semantists-5	0.4659	T+E		Emsemble with majority vote
11*	IUST-1	0.4609	I+T	CLIP+BERT	Augment Text with ChatGPT paraphraser + OCR on image
12	Mohammad Soltani-2	0.4545	I+T	CLIP32	SGD for Abortion and Gun Control
13	ACT-CS-4	0.4432	I+T+E+C	Vit+BERT	Cross Attention
14	ACT-CS-3	0.4348	I+T+E	Vit+BERT	Cross Attention
15	Semantists-4	0.4222	T+E		Emsemble with consistency loss
16	Semantists-2	0.4141	T+E	Stancy BERT	
17*	KnowComp-1	0.3922	I+T	LayoutLMv3 +DeBERTa	Augment Text with Translation + WordNet
18*	GC-HUNTER-1	0.3832	I+T+E	ViLT	OCR on Image
19	ACT-CS-2	0.3125	I+T	Vit+BERT	Cross Attention
20	Semantists-3	0.2838	I+T+E	ALBEF	
21*	Pitt Pixel Persuaders-1	0.1217	I+T	CLIP	

Table 4: The Subtask-B submission results. Each Team is allowed at most 5 submissions. The scores are positive label F1. The T, I, E, and C, represent text, image, extracted text from image, and image caption modality, respectively. Rows with **bold** ID and marked with * refer to the best system for each participating team.

an explanation for their absence in the submissions.

4.2.3 Error Analysis

Figure 5 categorizes the systems based on the modalities they incorporate and their respective success rates. Our analysis focused on the models' ability to make accurate predictions, quantified by the number of successful systems out of the 21 total systems. We found that systems incorporating both image and text modalities (I+T) consistently produced accurate predictions across data points with varying levels of difficulty. Interestingly, systems that combined text, text on images, images, and captions (I+T+E+C) demonstrated strong performance, particularly for data with high difficulty levels (as indicated by rows where only 4/5 systems made correct predictions). As reported by Soltani and Romberg (2023), these systems tended to classify images showing only text as persuasive. Further analysis on the data illustrated different argumentation techniques, such as cases, consequences, or outcomes related to the textual argument, further highlighting the complexity and diversity of approaches employed in this shared task.

5 Conclusion

In this paper, we introduced the *ImageArg* shared task, marking a significant milestone as the inaugural shared task in multimodal argument mining, co-located with the 10th Argument Mining Workshop at EMNLP 2023. A total of 9 teams from 6 different countries enthusiastically participated in this task, collectively submitting 31 systems for Subtask-A Argument Stance (AS) classification and 21 systems for Subtask-B Image Persuasiveness (IP) classification. The results reveal that

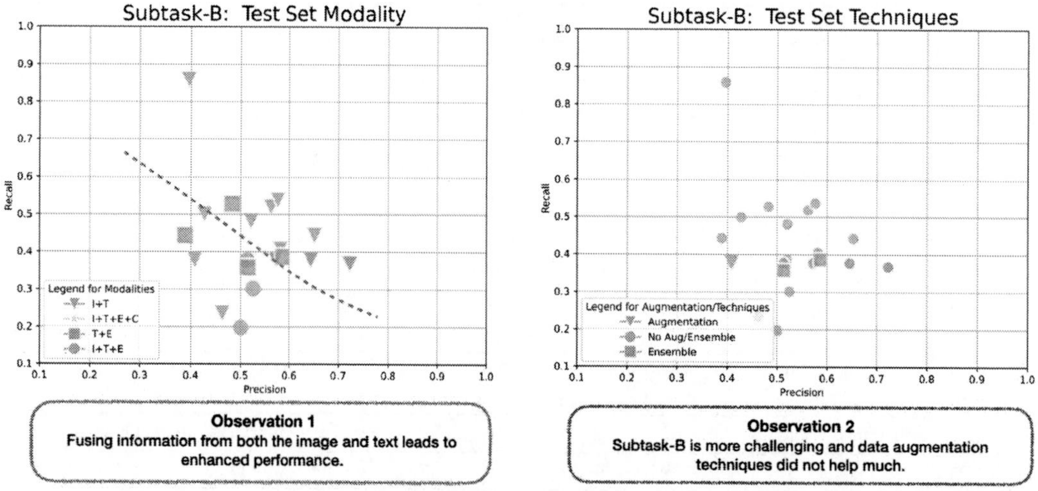

Figure 4: Subtask-B: system performance in relation to the computation approaches (left: modalities, right: techniques). We grouped systems based on the modalities used by the model (left) and computational techniques (right). The T, I, E, and C represent text, image, extracted text from image, and image caption modality, respectively.

Subtask-A is comparatively more predictable than Subtask-B. Models that utilized both textual information and the text embedded within images demonstrated considerable performance in Subtask-A. Furthermore, the strategic use of data augmentation and ensemble methods further enhanced the models' effectiveness. In contrast, Subtask-B witnessed the predominant adoption of CLIP for feature extraction from both images and texts, a technique that exhibited significant promise. The two subtasks offered valuable opportunities for participants to actively engage and foster fruitful exchanges in multimodal argument mining research.

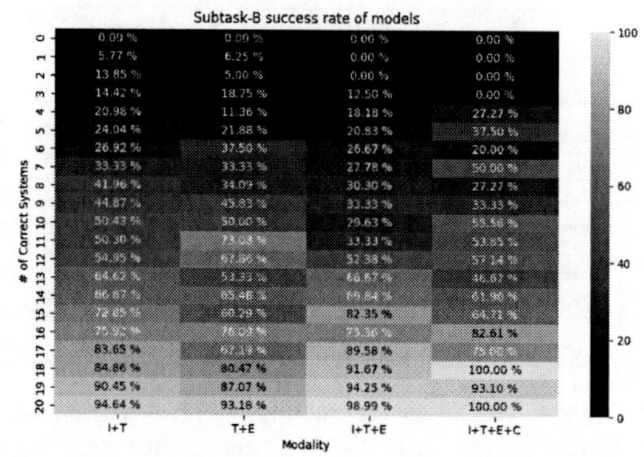

Figure 5: Average rate of correct predictions for Subtask-B systems (grouped by modalities) across tweet difficulties: the y-axis represents the number of systems making correct predictions out of 21 systems.

6 Limitations

In this section, we discuss the limitations of our work from multiple perspectives. First, the datasets utilized in this task may not sufficiently cover a broad range of multimodal data, possibly leaning toward social media content related to two specific topics: gun control and abortion. The language of data included in the paper is English, which is limited and should be extended to other languages for argument mining. Meanwhile, as demonstrated in Section 4.1.3, the label annotations may exhibit inconsistencies or inaccuracies, given the inherent complexity of the task. Also, the use of rhetorical devices, especially in addressing challenges like sarcasm detection, remains an underexplored area. The evaluation metrics employed may not fully encompass the nuanced performance aspects crucial for multimodal argument mining. Lastly, it's important to acknowledge that participating systems may encounter challenges when attempting to generalize their approaches across diverse data types, domains, or modalities.

Regarding the analysis of the results, it's important to acknowledge that since we mainly collected final predictions for both subtasks, the interpretability of the systems might remain unclear, presenting challenges in gaining insights into their decision-making processes. The intricate nature of multimodal argument mining can lead to multiple valid interpretations, potentially affecting the clarity of the ground truth.

7 Ethics

We acknowledge that there are privacy and ethical considerations in the collection and utilization of social media data. It's possible that biases within the dataset or system outputs may not have been fully mitigated. Given that our data originates from Twitter and the annotators predominantly come from English-speaking countries, it's inevitable that cultural biases are inherent in the data. However, we have implemented several measures to mitigate potential risks. To address privacy concerns, we have chosen to publicly share only the tweet IDs with the research community, which aligns with Twitter Developer Policy[10].

References

Humam Alwassel, Dhruv Mahajan, Bruno Korbar, Lorenzo Torresani, Bernard Ghanem, and Du Tran. 2020. Self-supervised learning by cross-modal audio-video clustering. *Advances in Neural Information Processing Systems*, 33:9758–9770.

Loïc Barrault, Fethi Bougares, Lucia Specia, Chiraag Lala, Desmond Elliott, and Stella Frank. 2018. Findings of the third shared task on multimodal machine translation. In *Proceedings of the Third Conference on Machine Translation: Shared Task Papers*, pages 304–323, Belgium, Brussels. Association for Computational Linguistics.

Winston Carlile, Nishant Gurrapadi, Zixuan Ke, and Vincent Ng. 2018. Give me more feedback: Annotating argument persuasiveness and related attributes in student essays. In *Proceedings of the 56th Annual Meeting of the Association for Computational Linguistics (Volume 1: Long Papers)*, pages 621–631.

Miriam Louise Carnot, Lorenz Heinemann, Jan Braker, Tobias Schreieder, Johannes Kiesel, Maik Fröbe, Martin Potthast, and Benno Stein. 2023. On stance detection in image retrieval for argumentation.

Tuhin Chakrabarty, Christopher Hidey, Smaranda Muresan, Kathleen Mckeown, and Alyssa Hwang. 2019. Ampersand: Argument mining for persuasive online discussions. In *Proceedings of the 2019 Conference on Empirical Methods in Natural Language Processing and the 9th International Joint Conference on Natural Language Processing (EMNLP-IJCNLP)*, pages 2933–2943.

Moitreya Chatterjee, Sunghyun Park, Han Suk Shim, Kenji Sagae, and Louis-Philippe Morency. 2014. Verbal behaviors and persuasiveness in online multimedia content. In *Proceedings of the Second Workshop on Natural Language Processing for Social Media (SocialNLP)*, pages 50–58.

[10]https://developer.twitter.com/en/developer-terms/policy

Qianben Chen, Richong Zhang, Yaowei Zheng, and Yongyi Mao. 2022. Dual contrastive learning: Text classification via label-aware data augmentation. *arXiv preprint arXiv:2201.08702*.

Kevin Clark, Minh-Thang Luong, Quoc V Le, and Christopher D Manning. 2019. Electra: Pre-training text encoders as discriminators rather than generators. In *International Conference on Learning Representations*.

Jacob Devlin, Ming-Wei Chang, Kenton Lee, and Kristina Toutanova. 2019. Bert: Pre-training of deep bidirectional transformers for language understanding. In *Proceedings of the 2019 Conference of the North American Chapter of the Association for Computational Linguistics: Human Language Technologies, Volume 1 (Long and Short Papers)*, pages 4171–4186.

Alexey Dosovitskiy, Lucas Beyer, Alexander Kolesnikov, Dirk Weissenborn, Xiaohua Zhai, Thomas Unterthiner, Mostafa Dehghani, Matthias Minderer, Georg Heigold, Sylvain Gelly, et al. 2020. An image is worth 16x16 words: Transformers for image recognition at scale. In *International Conference on Learning Representations*.

Rory Duthie, Katarzyna Budzynska, and Chris Reed. 2016. Mining ethos in political debate. In *Computational Models of Argument: Proceedings from the Sixth International Conference on Computational Models of Argument (COMMA)*, pages 299–310. IOS Press.

Yash Goyal, Tejas Khot, Douglas Summers-Stay, Dhruv Batra, and Devi Parikh. 2017. Making the v in vqa matter: Elevating the role of image understanding in visual question answering. In *Proceedings of the IEEE conference on computer vision and pattern recognition*, pages 6904–6913.

Meiqi Guo, Rebecca Hwa, and Adriana Kovashka. 2021. Detecting persuasive atypicality by modeling contextual compatibility. In *Proceedings of the IEEE/CVF International Conference on Computer Vision*, pages 972–982.

Ivan Habernal and Iryna Gurevych. 2017. Argumentation mining in user-generated web discourse. *Computational Linguistics*, 43(1):125–179.

Colin Higgins and Robyn Walker. 2012. Ethos, logos, pathos: Strategies of persuasion in social/environmental reports. In *Accounting forum*, volume 36, pages 194–208. Elsevier.

Di Hu, Chengze Wang, Feiping Nie, and Xuelong Li. 2019. Dense multimodal fusion for hierarchically joint representation. In *ICASSP 2019-2019 IEEE International Conference on Acoustics, Speech and Signal Processing (ICASSP)*, pages 3941–3945. IEEE.

Xinyue Huang and Adriana Kovashka. 2016. Inferring visual persuasion via body language, setting, and deep features. *2016 IEEE Conference on Computer*

Vision and Pattern Recognition Workshops (CVPRW), pages 778–784.

Drew A Hudson and Christopher D Manning. 2019. Gqa: A new dataset for real-world visual reasoning and compositional question answering. In *Proceedings of the IEEE/CVF conference on computer vision and pattern recognition*, pages 6700–6709.

Zaeem Hussain, Mingda Zhang, Xiaozhong Zhang, Keren Ye, Christopher Thomas, Zuha Agha, Nathan Ong, and Adriana Kovashka. 2017. Automatic understanding of image and video advertisements. In *Proceedings of the IEEE Conference on Computer Vision and Pattern Recognition (CVPR)*.

Jungseock Joo, Weixin Li, Francis F Steen, and Song-Chun Zhu. 2014. Visual persuasion: Inferring communicative intents of images. In *Proceedings of the IEEE conference on computer vision and pattern recognition*, pages 216–223.

Nikita Kitaev, Lukasz Kaiser, and Anselm Levskaya. 2019. Reformer: The efficient transformer. In *International Conference on Learning Representations*.

Klaus Krippendorff. 2011. Computing krippendorff's alpha-reliability.

Julia Kruk, Jonah Lubin, Karan Sikka, Xiao Lin, Dan Jurafsky, and Ajay Divakaran. 2019. Integrating text and image: Determining multimodal document intent in instagram posts. In *Proceedings of the 2019 Conference on Empirical Methods in Natural Language Processing and the 9th International Joint Conference on Natural Language Processing (EMNLP-IJCNLP)*, pages 4622–4632.

John Lawrence and Chris Reed. 2020. Argument mining: A survey. *Computational Linguistics*, 45(4):765–818.

Zhexiong Liu, Meiqi Guo, Yue Dai, and Diane Litman. 2022. ImageArg: A multi-modal tweet dataset for image persuasiveness mining. In *Proceedings of the 9th Workshop on Argument Mining*, pages 1–18, Online and in Gyeongju, Republic of Korea. International Conference on Computational Linguistics.

Jiasen Lu, Vedanuj Goswami, Marcus Rohrbach, Devi Parikh, and Stefan Lee. 2020. 12-in-1: Multi-task vision and language representation learning. In *Proceedings of the IEEE/CVF Conference on Computer Vision and Pattern Recognition*, pages 10437–10446.

Stephanie Lukin, Pranav Anand, Marilyn Walker, and Steve Whittaker. 2017. Argument strength is in the eye of the beholder: Audience effects in persuasion. In *Proceedings of the 15th Conference of the European Chapter of the Association for Computational Linguistics: Volume 1, Long Papers*, pages 742–753.

Dat Quoc Nguyen, Thanh Vu, and Anh Tuan Nguyen. 2020. BERTweet: A pre-trained language model for English Tweets. In *Proceedings of the 2020 Conference on Empirical Methods in Natural Language Processing: System Demonstrations*, pages 9–14.

Melika Nobakhtian, Ghazal Zamaninejad, Erfan Moosavi Monazzah, and Sauleh Eetemadi. 2023. Iust at imagearg: The first shared task in multimodal argument mining. In *Proceedings of the 10th Workshop on Argument Mining*, Online and in Singapore. Association for Computational Linguistics.

Daniel J O'Keefe. 2015. *Persuasion: Theory and research*. Sage Publications.

Sunghyun Park, Han Suk Shim, Moitreya Chatterjee, Kenji Sagae, and Louis-Philippe Morency. 2014. Computational analysis of persuasiveness in social multimedia: A novel dataset and multimodal prediction approach. In *Proceedings of the 16th International Conference on Multimodal Interaction*, pages 50–57.

Isaac Persing and Vincent Ng. 2017. Why can't you convince me? modeling weaknesses in unpersuasive arguments. In *Proceedings of the 26th International Joint Conference on Artificial Intelligence*, pages 4082–4088.

Kashyap Popat, Subhabrata Mukherjee, Andrew Yates, and Gerhard Weikum. 2019. Stancy: Stance classification based on consistency cues. In *Proceedings of the 2019 Conference on Empirical Methods in Natural Language Processing and the 9th International Joint Conference on Natural Language Processing (EMNLP-IJCNLP)*, pages 6413–6418.

Alec Radford, Jong Wook Kim, Chris Hallacy, Aditya Ramesh, Gabriel Goh, Sandhini Agarwal, Girish Sastry, Amanda Askell, Pamela Mishkin, Jack Clark, Gretchen Krueger, and Ilya Sutskever. 2021. Learning transferable visual models from natural language supervision. In *Proceedings of the 38th International Conference on Machine Learning, ICML 2021, 18-24 July 2021, Virtual Event*, volume 139 of *Proceedings of Machine Learning Research*, pages 8748–8763. PMLR.

Colin Raffel, Noam Shazeer, Adam Roberts, Katherine Lee, Sharan Narang, Michael Matena, Yanqi Zhou, Wei Li, and Peter J. Liu. 2020. Exploring the limits of transfer learning with a unified text-to-text transformer. *Journal of Machine Learning Research*, 21(140):1–67.

Kanagasabai Rajaraman, Hariram Veeramani, Saravanan Rajamanickam, Adam Maciej Westerski, and Jung-Jae Kim. 2023. Semantists at imagearg-2023: Exploring cross-modal contrastive and ensemble models for multimodal stance and persuasiveness classification. In *Proceedings of the 10th Workshop on Argument Mining*, Online and in Singapore. Association for Computational Linguistics.

Matilda White Riley. 1954. Communication and persuasion: psychological studies of opinion change.

Teven Le Scao, Angela Fan, Christopher Akiki, Ellie Pavlick, Suzana Ilić, Daniel Hesslow, Roman Castagné, Alexandra Sasha Luccioni, François Yvon,

Matthias Gallé, et al. 2022. Bloom: A 176b-parameter open-access multilingual language model. *arXiv preprint arXiv:2211.05100*.

Arushi Sharma, Abhibha Gupta, and Maneesh Bilalpur. 2023. Argumentative stance prediction: An exploratory study on multimodality and few-shot learning. In *Proceedings of the 10th Workshop on Argument Mining*, Online and in Singapore. Association for Computational Linguistics.

Mohammad Shokri and Sarah Ita Levitan. 2023. Gc-hunter at imagearg shared task: Multi-modal stance and persuasiveness learning. In *Proceedings of the 10th Workshop on Argument Mining*, Online and in Singapore. Association for Computational Linguistics.

Mohammad Soltani and Julia Romberg. 2023. A general framework for multimodal argument persuasiveness classification of tweets. In *Proceedings of the 10th Workshop on Argument Mining*, Online and in Singapore. Association for Computational Linguistics.

Lucia Specia, Stella Frank, Khalil Sima'an, and Desmond Elliott. 2016. A shared task on multimodal machine translation and crosslingual image description. In *Proceedings of the First Conference on Machine Translation: Volume 2, Shared Task Papers*, pages 543–553, Berlin, Germany. Association for Computational Linguistics.

Christian Stab and Iryna Gurevych. 2014. Annotating argument components and relations in persuasive essays. In *Proceedings of COLING 2014, the 25th international conference on computational linguistics: Technical papers*, pages 1501–1510.

Christian Stab, Christian Kirschner, Judith Eckle-Kohler, and Iryna Gurevych. 2014. Argumentation mining in persuasive essays and scientific articles from the discourse structure perspective. In *ArgNLP*, pages 21–25.

Christian Stab, Tristan Miller, Benjamin Schiller, Pranav Rai, and Iryna Gurevych. 2018. Cross-topic argument mining from heterogeneous sources. In *Proceedings of the 2018 Conference on Empirical Methods in Natural Language Processing*, pages 3664–3674.

Hao Tan and Mohit Bansal. 2019. Lxmert: Learning cross-modality encoder representations from transformers. In *Proceedings of the 2019 Conference on Empirical Methods in Natural Language Processing and the 9th International Joint Conference on Natural Language Processing (EMNLP-IJCNLP)*, pages 5103–5114.

Islam Torky, Simon Ruth, Shashi Sharma, Mohamed Salama, Krishna Chaitanya, Tim Gollub, Johannes Kiesel, and Benno Stein. 2023. Team feeds @ imagearg 2023: Embedding-based stance and persuasiveness classification. In *Proceedings of the 10th Workshop on Argument Mining*, Online and in Singapore. Association for Computational Linguistics.

Yao-Hung Hubert Tsai, Paul Pu Liang, Amir Zadeh, Louis-Philippe Morency, and Ruslan Salakhutdinov. 2018. Learning factorized multimodal representations. In *International Conference on Learning Representations*.

Zhongyu Wei, Yang Liu, and Yi Li. 2016. Is this post persuasive? ranking argumentative comments in online forum. In *Proceedings of the 54th Annual Meeting of the Association for Computational Linguistics (Volume 2: Short Papers)*, pages 195–200.

Yiheng Xu, Minghao Li, Lei Cui, Shaohan Huang, Furu Wei, and Ming Zhou. 2020. Layoutlm: Pre-training of text and layout for document image understanding. In *Proceedings of the 26th ACM SIGKDD International Conference on Knowledge Discovery & Data Mining*, KDD '20, page 1192–1200, New York, NY, USA. Association for Computing Machinery.

Zhilin Yang, Zihang Dai, Yiming Yang, Jaime Carbonell, Russ R Salakhutdinov, and Quoc V Le. 2019. Xlnet: Generalized autoregressive pretraining for language understanding. *Advances in neural information processing systems*, 32.

Jing Zhang, Shaojun Yu, Xuan Li, Jia Geng, Zhiyuan Zheng, and Joyce Ho. 2023. Split: Stance and persuasion prediction with multi-modal on image and textual information. In *Proceedings of the 10th Workshop on Argument Mining*, Online and in Singapore. Association for Computational Linguistics.

Mingda Zhang, Rebecca Hwa, and Adriana Kovashka. 2018. Equal but not the same: Understanding the implicit relationship between persuasive images and text. In *Proceedings of the British Machine Vision Conference (BMVC)*.

Hanzhong Zheng, Zhexiong Liu, and Dejia Shi. 2021. Image-text discourse coherence relation discoveries on multi-image and multi-text documents. *Journal of Physics: Conference Series*, 1948(1):012013.

Qing Zong, Zhaowei Wang, Baixuan Xu, Tianshi Zheng, Haochen Shi, Weiqi Wang, Yangqiu Song, Ginny Wong, and Simon See. 2023. Tilfa: A unified framework for text, image, and layout fusion in argument mining. In *Proceedings of the 10th Workshop on Argument Mining*, Online and in Singapore. Association for Computational Linguistics.

A Appendix

Image	**Text**	Annotations
	'Abortion law is pro-life. It saves 'mother over 'growing fetus in unwanted pregnancy due to rape, psychological trauma, social stigma, etc. It stops back-alley abortions that kill. Counseling & transition homes can lessen 'need for abortion.	**Topic:** Abortion **Annotated Label:** Oppose **System Predictions:** {'Oppose': 19, 'Support':12} **Potentially Correct Label:** Support **Rationale:** The human annotation is inaccurate, super interesting on the usage of 'pro-life', to advocate for abortion.
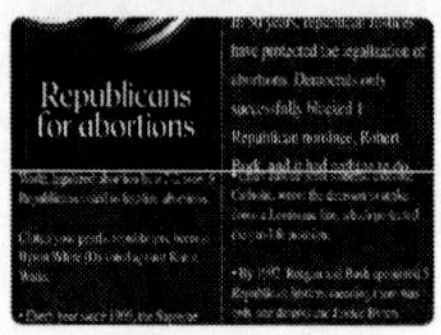	How Pro-Life is the Republican party and Justices? Facts matter here the answer, they're not. Thanks to their rulings, women have been able to safely have abortions. #RoeVWade #Republicans #SCOTUShearings #Constitution #prochoice #ProLife #Facts	**Topic:** Abortion **Annotated Label:** Support **System Predictions:** {'Oppose': 20, 'Support':11} **Potentially Correct Label:** Support **Rationale:** This tweet uses sarcasm, and is hard to annotate (republicans are in general not supporting legal abortion). Here the contents are image-dependent.

Table 5: Manually checked data with controversial scenarios for Subtask-A, where nearly half of the systems failed to predict the correct label. We sampled a few tweets and provided a potential correct label based on our manual inspections. The first example redefines a widely used anti-abortion term, pro-life, and advocates for abortion instead. The second is a complicated one that requires the comprehension of texts embedded in the image.

IUST at ImageArg: The First Shared Task in Multimodal Argument Mining

Melika Nobakhtian, Ghazal Zamaninejad, Erfan Moosavi Monazzah, Sauleh Eetemadi
Iran University of Science and Technology
{melika.nobakhtian2000@gmail.com, gh_zamaninejad, moosavi_m@comp.iust.ac.ir, sauleh@iust.ac.ir

Abstract

ImageArg is a shared task at the 10th ArgMining Workshop at EMNLP 2023. It leverages the ImageArg dataset to advance multimodal persuasiveness techniques. This challenge comprises two distinct subtasks: 1) Argumentative Stance (AS) Classification: Assessing whether a given tweet adopts an argumentative stance. 2) Image Persuasiveness (IP) Classification: Determining if the tweet image enhances the persuasive quality of the tweet. We conducted various experiments on both subtasks and ranked sixth out of the nine participating teams.

1 Introduction

Argumentation mining, a task in Natural Language Processing (NLP), aims to automatically detect argumentative structures in a document (Green et al., 2014). This process unveils not only people's viewpoints but also the reasons behind their beliefs (Lawrence and Reed, 2019). It offers valuable insights across a wide spectrum of fields, ranging from predicting financial market trends to public relations. However, prior research in this field mainly concentrates on text and does not exploit multimodal data.

ImageArg, a multimodal dataset introduced by Liu et al. (2022), is designed to bridge this gap. It includes persuasive tweets accompanied by images and its goal is to identify the image's stance towards the tweet and assess its persuasiveness score on specific topics.

ImageArg constitutes a collaborative challenge (Liu et al., 2023) tailored to advance multimodal persuasive techniques, using the ImageArg dataset. It is made of two subtasks: Argumentative Stance (AS) Classification and Image Persuasiveness (IP) Classification which will be further discussed in subsection 3.1 and subsection 3.2 respectively.

The whole system architecture is shown in Fig.1. We make three experiments on the AS subtask.

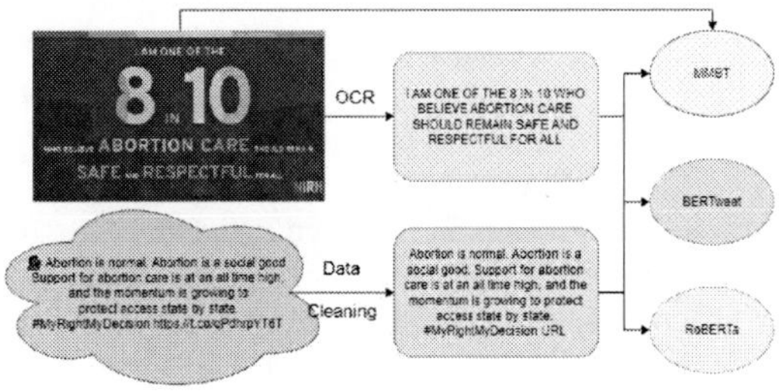

Figure 1: Our System Architecture

While in two of them, we only used the text as input data, in the third, we adopted a multimodal approach, considering both image and text inputs. In the former, we utilize BERTweet (Nguyen et al., 2020) in one experiment and RoBERTa (Liu et al., 2019) in the other. For our final experiment, we employed the Multimodal Bitransformer (MMBT) architecture (Kiela et al., 2020), harnessing tweets' text, text within images, and the images themselves. Our first approach, which leveraged BERTweet, achieved the highest F1-score compared to the two other methods.

For the IP task, we conducted a single experiment employing the MMBT model. We employed tweets' text, text extracted from images, and the images themselves as inputs.

2 Related Work

Persuasiveness Mining: Persuasiveness mining has been the subject of many recent studies (Chatterjee et al. (2014); Park et al. (2014); Lukin et al. (2017); Carlile et al. (2018); Chakrabarty et al. (2019)) but they do not provide the factors that make an argument persuasive. Liu et al. (2022) provides a framework to assign numerical score to the persuasiveness of an image based on its content type. They also determine the mode of persuasiveness for their images which can be based on reason, emotion, or ethics. In this work, we are going to use the dataset provided by Liu et al. (2022) for de-

Proceedings of the 10th Workshop on Argument Mining, pages 133–138
December 7, 2023. ©2023 Association for Computational Linguistics

	Topic	Split	Original Pos	Original Neg	Original Total	Processed Pos	Processed Neg	Processed Total
Argumentative Stance	Gun Control	Train	475	448	923	470	442	912
		Dev	54	46	100	52	45	97
		Test	85	65	150	85	65	150
	Abortion	Train	244	647	891	**729**	644	**1373**
		Dev	19	81	100	19	81	100
		Test	33	117	150	33	117	150
Image Persuasiveness	Gun Control	Train	251	672	923	**747**	663	**1410**
		Dev	33	67	100	31	66	97
		Test	53	97	150	53	97	150
	Abortion	Train	278	613	891	**556**	609	**1165**
		Dev	26	74	100	26	74	100
		Test	53	97	150	53	97	150

Table 1: Statistics for the Original and Processed (Cleaning & Paraphrasing) Datasets. The 'Pos' class corresponds to 'Yes' and 'Support', while the 'Neg' class corresponds to 'No' and 'Oppose'. Numbers modified due to data augmentation are highlighted in bold.

termining image persuasiveness and argumentative mining.

Multimodal Learning: The recent surge in attention towards AI models lies in their capability to handle and comprehend inputs from multiple sources, thanks to the complementary nature of these multimodal signals in real-world applications (Aytar et al. (2016); Zhang et al. (2018); Alwassel et al. (2020)). Within the field of vision and language, tasks primarily revolve around assessing the models' proficiency in both grasping visual data and articulating reasoning through language (Agrawal et al. (2016); Goyal et al. (2017); (Hudson and Manning, 2019)). Although some research diverges from this mainstream which explores the connection between images and text: Alikhani et al. (2019) delve into annotating discourse relations between textual and accompanying visual elements in recipe instructions, while Kruk et al. (2019) delve into understanding multimodal document intent in Instagram posts.

3 Task and Data

ImageArg Shared Task includes two subtasks: Argumentative Stance (AS) Classification and Image Persuasiveness (IP) Classification. The dataset provided for this task encompasses two distinct topics of societal significance, namely abortion and gun control. Within the training subset of the dataset[1], a total of 912 examples are allocated to the domain of gun control, while 887 examples pertain to the topic of abortion. In the development subset, there are 100 data entries related to abortion and 97 data records related to gun control. In the testing partition, both the abortion and gun control categories are represented equally, each comprising 150 examples.

In the following parts, we will provide more details about subtasks and statistics related to the data specified for each subtask.

3.1 Argumentative Stance Classification

In this subtask, a tweet consisting of an image and text is given and the task is to predict whether this tweet supports or opposes a certain topic. It is considered a binary classification task; the proposed topics are abortion and gun control.

According to the data distribution shown in Fig.2 in the gun control section, we deal with a dataset that is approximately balanced and there is no need to worry about imbalanced classes. On the other hand, the abortion topic has different conditions; unfortunately, the dataset is imbalanced in both the train and dev sections. Over 70% of the data has been specified to the "Oppose" class.

3.2 Image Persuasiveness Classification

Like the previous subtask, a tweet composed of an image and text is given to a model as input and it will predict if the image beside the tweet text makes it more persuasive or not. The scenario is the same as the first subtask, a binary classification problem with the mentioned topics.

[1]We observed that we had data inconsistency according to the ImageArg statistics.

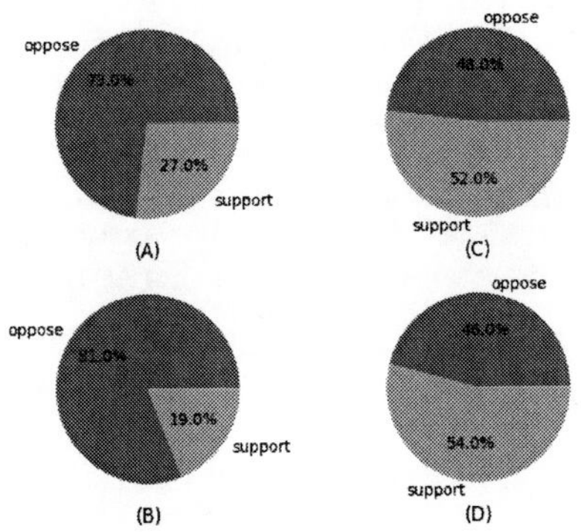

Figure 2: Data distribution in Argumentative Stance Classification. (A) Abortion Train. (B) Abortion Dev. (C) Gun Control Train. (D) Gun Control Dev.

As shown in Fig. 3, the dominant class label in both topics is "No", indicating that a significant portion of images does not enhance the persuasiveness of the tweet text. More than 65% of tweets on gun control and abortion belong to the "No" class.

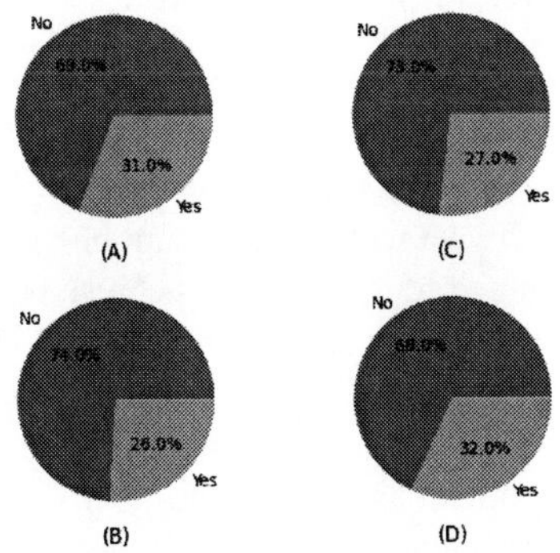

Figure 3: Data distribution in Image Persuasiveness Classification. (A) Abortion Train. (B) Abortion Dev. (C) Gun Control Train. (D) Gun Control Dev.

4 Methods

We first present preprocessing techniques used for both subtasks, as well as some ideas to make the performance of both tasks better before training models. Next, we introduce models developed for the argumentative stance followed by image persuasiveness models.

4.1 Preprocessing

Initially, we undertook text processing enhancements for the tweet content, incorporating various modifications to enhance their overall quality. In the preprocessed tweet corpus, all URLs were systematically substituted with the designated keyword "URL". A similar substitution approach was employed for mentions, seamlessly replaced by the keyword "MENTION". Given the inherent limitations of numerous text-processing models in deciphering emojis, a pragmatic approach of substituting them with the term "EMOJI" was adopted. Lastly, non-English characters were transcoded into their corresponding ASCII representations, subsequently utilized to supplant these characters within the text.

After inspecting the data instances, we found that many images have some text in their background. We assumed that including this text as an additional feature in the dataset, would improve our ability to develop more effective models for detecting valuable concepts. To achieve this, we used an OCR API[2] to extract text from images if it is available. It was the best tool that we came across in the variety of approaches.

OCR will bring many advantages to our approach. Firstly OCR can extract text from images that would otherwise be unavailable to the model. This can be especially useful for social media posts and other types of online content that often include images. Secondly, OCR can help to improve the performance of the model on multimodal data, where the image and the text are both relevant to the task.

In the preceding section, we examined the distribution of classes, revealing the presence of an imbalanced dataset issue. While diverse approaches exist to address this concern, our strategy is centered on employing oversampling techniques. Specifically, we chose to implement an oversampling methodology by augmenting the minority class instances independently for each subtask and topic. To achieve this equilibrium, we employed a paraphrasing technique facilitated by the ChatGPT paraphraser (Vladimir Vorobev, 2023) , harnessed from the foundational T5 model (Raffel et al., 2020). Tailored to each unique class ratio within varying contexts, a variable count of paraphrased samples was generated for each instance within the dataset. In the table 1 you can see the dataset statistics before and after applying pre-processing and paraphrasing techniques. Our primary objective was to approximate a balanced class distribution across diverse scenarios.

[2] `https://ocr.space`

4.2 Argumentative Stance Classification

We employed two different approaches for this subtask: One of them solely relies on text and the second method utilizes both images and text from tweets.

To ascertain the stance of tweets, it appears that placing trust in the textual content alone would suffice, given that images are unlikely to provide supplementary information. As a result, our first approach depends exclusively on text-based analysis. Within this approach, we used two distinct models for text classification, RoBERTa and BERTweet.

While RoBERTa leverages both the textual content of tweets and text extracted from accompanying images to infer stance, BERTweet focuses solely on training with tweet text. These models have undergone training on the entire dataset, encompassing gun control and abortion topics.

Our third approach capitalizes on a multimodal classification framework by integrating both textual content and images sourced from tweets. To realize this objective, we adopted the Multimodal Bitransformer (MMBT) architecture (Kiela et al., 2020), designed specifically to address image-and-text classification challenges. The MMBT model merges insights from text and image encoders. While the original configuration employs BERT (Devlin et al., 2019) as the text encoder and ResNet (He et al., 2015) as the image encoder, Inspired by (Neskorozhenyi, 2021) we replaced the image encoder with diverse iterations of the CLIP (Radford et al., 2021) model. CLIP, or Contrastive Language-Image Pre-Training, emerges as a neural network fine-tuned on (image, text) pairs, yielding feature representations that exhibit greater richness and applicability to the task at hand. Our exploration encompassed a spectrum of image encoders, loss functions, and optimizers within this framework, pursued to secure optimal outcomes for each distinct topic.

4.3 Image Persuasiveness Classification

Due to time limitations, we focused our efforts on presenting a singular methodology for this particular subtask. This approach harnesses the MMBT architecture, as detailed in the preceding section. This subtask similarly involves a multimodal classification challenge, entailing the utilization of both tweet images and text as inputs to the model. We undertook the development of separate models tailored to each individual topic, thereby enabling optimization specific to the nuances of each topic's content and characteristics.

Model	Topic	Precision	Recall	F1-score
BERTweet	All data	0.9068	0.6772	**0.7754**
	Abortion	0.8778	**0.5777**	**0.6824**
	Gun Control	0.9176	0.7358	0.8168
RoBERTa	All data	0.8475	**0.7143**	0.7752
	Abortion	0.8485	0.5600	0.6747
	Gun Control	0.8471	**0.8000**	**0.8229**
MMBT	All data	**0.9915**	0.3980	0.5680
	Abortion	**0.9697**	0.2222	0.3616
	Gun Control	**1.0000**	0.5667	0.7234

Table 2: Argumentative Stance classification results on test data

Model	Topic	Precision	Recall	F1-score
MMBT	All data	0.5000	0.4274	0.4609
	Abortion	0.5094	0.4030	0.4500
	Gun Control	0.4906	0.4561	0.4727

Table 3: Image Persuasiveness classification results on test data

5 Experiments and Results

First, we discuss our results of the first subtask, which is summarised in Tab.2. Our first and best submission for argumentative stance classification was BERTweet which is a variant of BERT specifically trained for tweets. We achieved 0.7754 F1-score on test data and we stand out as the 6-th team among others. BERT-based models are known for their strong performance in various NLP tasks, and this experiment confirms their utility for Argumentative Stance classification in tweets.

RoBERTa was the second submission and its result was highly close to BERTweet, with a score of 0.7752 based on F1. It suggests that incorporating text from images did not notably enhance the model's performance, which is an interesting finding. It is possible that the text within images may not have provided much additional useful information for this specific task. Both BERTweet and RoBERTa were trained for 10 epochs with batch-size of 8, using AdamW as optimizer (Loshchilov and Hutter, 2019).

MMBT was the last approach and it did not perform as well as the two first approaches. It yielded a noticeably lower F1-score of 0.5680 compared to the text-only models. Although we employed separate models for each topic, the image encoder was the same and we utilized CLIP-RN50x4 for this purpose. In addition, weighted Binary Cross

Entropy (BCE) was used as a loss function and we specified a weight according to class distribution for each topic for a better performance. The drop in performance could indicate that the addition of image information did not help and may have even introduced noise or complexity into the model. It's important to note that multimodal models can be challenging to train and may require a substantial amount of data and careful tuning to outperform text-only models in specific tasks.

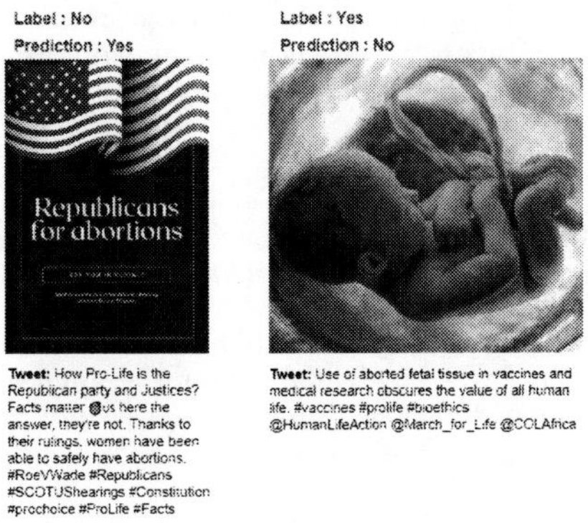

Figure 4: Examples of Image Persuasiveness subtask that were misclassified

Figure 5: Examples of Image Persuassieveness that were classified correctly

In the second subtask, the only approach we followed was MMBT. The specified model for the gun control topic employed CLIP-RN101 as its image encoder whereas the abortion model used CLIP-RN50x16. These models were trained for 10 epochs with batch-size of 32. Its result is shown in Tab.3. While the model's performance may not be exceptionally high, it demonstrates some capability in assessing the persuasiveness of tweets with both text and image content. Some instances of the dataset with the model's predictions are shown in Fig.4 and Fig.5.

6 Conclusion

In this paper, we presented our approach in the ImageArg shared task which was the first shared task in Multimodal Argument Mining. We proposed three methods for the first subtask. These models have different varieties from models solely dependent on text to multimodal pre-trained models. We also had only one submission for the second subtask and we achieved 6-th place in both tasks among other groups that participated.

References

Aishwarya Agrawal, Jiasen Lu, Stanislaw Antol, Margaret Mitchell, C. Lawrence Zitnick, Dhruv Batra, and Devi Parikh. 2016. Vqa: Visual question answering.

Malihe Alikhani, Sreyasi Nag Chowdhury, Gerard de Melo, and Matthew Stone. 2019. CITE: A corpus of image-text discourse relations. In *Proceedings of the 2019 Conference of the North American Chapter of the Association for Computational Linguistics: Human Language Technologies, Volume 1 (Long and Short Papers)*, pages 570–575, Minneapolis, Minnesota. Association for Computational Linguistics.

Humam Alwassel, Dhruv Mahajan, Bruno Korbar, Lorenzo Torresani, Bernard Ghanem, and Du Tran. 2020. Self-supervised learning by cross-modal audio-video clustering.

Yusuf Aytar, Carl Vondrick, and Antonio Torralba. 2016. Soundnet: Learning sound representations from unlabeled video.

Winston Carlile, Nishant Gurrapadi, Zixuan Ke, and Vincent Ng. 2018. Give me more feedback: Annotating argument persuasiveness and related attributes in student essays. In *Proceedings of the 56th Annual Meeting of the Association for Computational Linguistics (Volume 1: Long Papers)*, pages 621–631, Melbourne, Australia. Association for Computational Linguistics.

Tuhin Chakrabarty, Christopher Hidey, Smaranda Muresan, Kathy McKeown, and Alyssa Hwang. 2019. AMPERSAND: Argument mining for PERSuAsive oNline discussions. In *Proceedings of the 2019 Conference on Empirical Methods in Natural Language Processing and the 9th International Joint Conference on Natural Language Processing (EMNLP-IJCNLP)*, pages 2933–2943, Hong Kong, China. Association for Computational Linguistics.

Moitreya Chatterjee, Sunghyun Park, Han Suk Shim, Kenji Sagae, and Louis-Philippe Morency. 2014. Verbal behaviors and persuasiveness in online multimedia content. In *Proceedings of the Second Workshop on Natural Language Processing for Social Media*

(SocialNLP), pages 50–58, Dublin, Ireland. Association for Computational Linguistics and Dublin City University.

Jacob Devlin, Ming-Wei Chang, Kenton Lee, and Kristina Toutanova. 2019. Bert: Pre-training of deep bidirectional transformers for language understanding.

Yash Goyal, Tejas Khot, Douglas Summers-Stay, Dhruv Batra, and Devi Parikh. 2017. Making the v in vqa matter: Elevating the role of image understanding in visual question answering.

Nancy Green, Kevin Ashley, Diane Litman, Chris Reed, and Vern Walker, editors. 2014. *Proceedings of the First Workshop on Argumentation Mining*. Association for Computational Linguistics, Baltimore, Maryland.

Kaiming He, Xiangyu Zhang, Shaoqing Ren, and Jian Sun. 2015. Deep residual learning for image recognition.

Drew A. Hudson and Christopher D. Manning. 2019. Gqa: A new dataset for real-world visual reasoning and compositional question answering.

Douwe Kiela, Suvrat Bhooshan, Hamed Firooz, Ethan Perez, and Davide Testuggine. 2020. Supervised multimodal bitransformers for classifying images and text.

Julia Kruk, Jonah Lubin, Karan Sikka, Xiao Lin, Dan Jurafsky, and Ajay Divakaran. 2019. Integrating text and image: Determining multimodal document intent in Instagram posts. In *Proceedings of the 2019 Conference on Empirical Methods in Natural Language Processing and the 9th International Joint Conference on Natural Language Processing (EMNLP-IJCNLP)*, pages 4622–4632, Hong Kong, China. Association for Computational Linguistics.

John Lawrence and Chris Reed. 2019. Argument mining: A survey. *Computational Linguistics*, 45(4):765–818.

Yinhan Liu, Myle Ott, Naman Goyal, Jingfei Du, Mandar Joshi, Danqi Chen, Omer Levy, Mike Lewis, Luke Zettlemoyer, and Veselin Stoyanov. 2019. Roberta: A robustly optimized BERT pretraining approach. *CoRR*, abs/1907.11692.

Zhexiong Liu, Mohamed Elaraby, Yang Zhong, and Diane Litman. 2023. Overview of ImageArg-2023: The first shared task in multimodal argument mining. In *Proceedings of the 10th Workshop on Argument Mining*, Online and in Singapore. Association for Computational Linguistics.

Zhexiong Liu, Meiqi Guo, Yue Dai, and Diane Litman. 2022. ImageArg: A multi-modal tweet dataset for image persuasiveness mining. In *Proceedings of the 9th Workshop on Argument Mining*, pages 1–18, Online and in Gyeongju, Republic of Korea. International Conference on Computational Linguistics.

Ilya Loshchilov and Frank Hutter. 2019. Decoupled weight decay regularization.

Stephanie Lukin, Pranav Anand, Marilyn Walker, and Steve Whittaker. 2017. Argument strength is in the eye of the beholder: Audience effects in persuasion. In *Proceedings of the 15th Conference of the European Chapter of the Association for Computational Linguistics: Volume 1, Long Papers*, pages 742–753, Valencia, Spain. Association for Computational Linguistics.

Rostyslav Neskorozhenyi. 2021. How to get high score using mmbt and clip in hateful memes competition. https://towardsdatascience.com/how-to-get-high-score-using-mmbt-and-clip-in-hateful-memes-competition-90bfa65cb117. Accessed: 2023-08-31.

Dat Quoc Nguyen, Thanh Vu, and Anh Tuan Nguyen. 2020. Bertweet: A pre-trained language model for english tweets. *CoRR*, abs/2005.10200.

Sunghyun Park, Han Suk Shim, Moitreya Chatterjee, Kenji Sagae, and Louis-Philippe Morency. 2014. Computational analysis of persuasiveness in social multimedia: A novel dataset and multimodal prediction approach. In *Proceedings of the 16th International Conference on Multimodal Interaction*, ICMI '14, page 50–57, New York, NY, USA. Association for Computing Machinery.

Alec Radford, Jong Wook Kim, Chris Hallacy, Aditya Ramesh, Gabriel Goh, Sandhini Agarwal, Girish Sastry, Amanda Askell, Pamela Mishkin, Jack Clark, Gretchen Krueger, and Ilya Sutskever. 2021. Learning transferable visual models from natural language supervision.

Colin Raffel, Noam Shazeer, Adam Roberts, Katherine Lee, Sharan Narang, Michael Matena, Yanqi Zhou, Wei Li, and Peter J. Liu. 2020. Exploring the limits of transfer learning with a unified text-to-text transformer.

Maxim Kuznetsov Vladimir Vorobev. 2023. A paraphrasing model based on chatgpt paraphrases.

Mingda Zhang, Rebecca Hwa, and Adriana Kovashka. 2018. Equal but not the same: Understanding the implicit relationship between persuasive images and text.

TILFA: A Unified Framework for Text, Image, and Layout Fusion in Argument Mining

Qing Zong[1], Zhaowei Wang[2], Baixuan Xu[2], Tianshi Zheng[2], Haochen Shi[2], Weiqi Wang[2], Yangqiu Song[2], Ginny Y. Wong[3], Simon See[3]

[1]Harbin Institute of Technology (Shenzhen), Guangdong, China

[2]Department of Computer Science and Engineering, HKUST, Hong Kong SAR, China

[3]NVIDIA AI Technology Center (NVAITC), NVIDIA, Santa Clara, USA

zongqing0068@gmail.com, {bxuan, tzhengad, hshiah}@connect.ust.hk, {zwanggy, wwangbw, yqsong}@cse.ust.hk

Abstract

A main goal of Argument Mining (AM) is to analyze an author's stance. Unlike previous AM datasets focusing only on text, the shared task at the 10*th* Workshop on Argument Mining introduces a dataset including both text and images. Importantly, these images contain both visual elements and optical characters. Our new framework, **TILFA**[1] (A Unified Framework for **T**ext, **I**mage, and **L**ayout **F**usion in **A**rgument Mining), is designed to handle this mixed data. It excels at not only understanding text but also detecting optical characters and recognizing layout details in images. Our model significantly outperforms existing baselines, earning our team, **KnowComp**, the **1*st*** place in the leaderboard[2] of Argumentative Stance Classification subtask in this shared task.

Tweet Image:

Tweet Text: Background checks save lives. Full stop. We deserve #MoreThanThoughtsAndPrayers from our elected leaders to end gun violence.
Topic: gun control
Stance: support

Tweet Image:

Tweet Text: A child deserves a chance at life. A child deserves a future. A child deserves to be loved. We will always fight for the innocent unborn. #ProLife
Topic: abortion
Stance: oppose

Figure 1: Examples of positive (support) and negative (oppose) tweets of different topics. The images also contain a lot of information crucial to stance identification.

1 Introduction

Argument mining (AM) aims to automatically analyze the structure and components of arguments in text. Persuasiveness analysis is a crucial aspect of it, which has gained significant attention in the NLP community (Habernal and Gurevych, 2017; Carlile et al., 2018). However, previous works focus solely on text, overlooking other modalities like images which can also impact an argument's persuasiveness. To fill this gap, Liu et al. (2022) introduces **ImageArg**, a dataset going beyond text to include also images. It features tweets centered on contentious topics like gun control and abortion. These associated images contain not only objects but also optical characters (e.g., slogans, tables).

The 10*th* Workshop on Argument Mining in EMNLP 2023 introduces a shared task (Liu et al., 2023b) called ImageArg Shared Task 2023, centering around this dataset. It is divided into two subtasks: Argumentative Stance (AS) Classification and Image Persuasiveness (IP) Classification. We primarily focus on the former, which aims to identify the stance of a given tweet towards a specific topic. Examples can be found in Fig. 1.

After scrutinizing the dataset, we found several challenges: (1) Imbalanced data distribution (Ratio of positive to negative examples on abortion topic is about 1 : 2.65); (2) Limited data size (Neither of the two topics has more than 1000 entries); (3) Presence of both objects and optical characters in images (They are difficult to be handled by a single model at the same time). To address these challenges, we have made the following contributions:

- To tackle data imbalance, we employ back-translation to enrich data in the fewer class, as described by Yu et al. (2018); Wieting and Gimpel (2018).
- For data augmentation, we utilize WordNet (Miller, 1994) with GlossBERT (Huang et al., 2019) to create additional data by replacing synonyms of nouns in original instances.
- We introduce **TILFA** which can understand both text and image well, especially adept at detecting optical characters and discerning layout details in images.

[1]The code and data are available at https://github.com/HKUST-KnowComp/TILFA.

[2]https://imagearg.github.io/

Proceedings of the 10th Workshop on Argument Mining, pages 139–147
December 7, 2023. ©2023 Association for Computational Linguistics

2 Related work

Data Augmentation: Data augmentation enhances a model's performance and increases its generalization capabilities in Natural Language Processing (NLP). At the word level, Wang et al. (2019) used databases like WordNet (Miller, 1994), to replace certain words with their synonyms, while Rizos et al. (2019) implemented embedding replacement to find contextually fitting words; At the document level, Yu et al. (2018) used back-translation, translating data to another language and then back to the source one.

Document AI: Document AI refers to the extraction and comprehension of information from scanned documents, web pages, ads, posters, or images with textual content. Previous works like Hao et al. (2016); Liu et al. (2019) all missed the integrated pre-training of text and layout details, which are vital for document image comprehension. To fix this, Xu et al. (2020) proposed LayoutLM. Its updated versions, LayoutLMv2 (Xu et al., 2021) and LayoutLMv3 (Huang et al., 2022), encapsulated text, layout and also image interactions within a unified multimodal framework.

3 Methods

We employ back-translation (Yu et al., 2018) to address data imbalance and apply WordNet (Miller, 1994) for data augmentation, assisted by GlossBERT (Huang et al., 2019). Our new framework, **TILFA**, uses DeBERTa (He et al., 2021) as the text encoder and LayoutLMv3 (Huang et al., 2022) as the image encoder, thus excels at not only understanding text but also detecting optical characters and recognizing layout details in images. We also experiment with several multimodal fusion mechanisms. Consequently, we achieve the **highest** F1-score in the Argumentative Stance Classification subtask of the ImageArg Shared Task 2023.

3.1 Addressing Data Imbalance

Label imbalance is serious in the training set, particularly concerning the abortion topic (The ratio of positive to negative examples is about $1 : 2.65$). To address this, we preprocess the data through bask-translation (Yu et al., 2018). We translate the English tweet text belonging to the underrepresented label (e.g., positive in abortion topic) to a random language (e.g., French, German) and then back to English. This maintains the tweet's meaning and thus the stance label. The translated text is finally paired with its original image.

3.2 Data Augmentation

More data usually leads to better model performance (Bayer et al., 2022; Fang et al., 2022). We employ data augmentation methods since our ImageArg training set is limited: only 918 entries for gun control and 888 for abortion. We first utilize spaCy to tokenize the tweet text and extract the nouns in it. Then we find all their synonym sets in WordNet (Miller, 1994). We determine these nouns' meanings in context by Word Sense Disambiguation (WSD) using GlossBERT (Huang et al., 2019), thus getting their correct synonym set. Finally, we replace these nouns with their synonyms to create new data.

3.3 Model

To solve this task, we introduce a model: **TILFA** (A Unified Framework for **T**ext, **I**mage, and **L**ayout **F**usion in **A**rgument Mining). The structure of **TILFA** is illustrated in Fig. 2, comprising three components: Image Encoder, Text Encoder, and Multimodal Fusion. We will discuss details of them one by one.

Image Encoder: As highlighted by Liu et al. (2022), traditional image encoders like ResNet50, ResNet101 (He et al., 2016), VGG (Simonyan and Zisserman, 2015) are good at identifying objects but fall short in recognizing optical characters in images, which may hurt performance. However, as shown in Fig. 1, many of the images in our dataset contain significant amount of characters. So we reasonably believe that using models which can capture the text in the images will have better results. And we notice that those characters with more prominent position and larger size are relatively more important. So considering the importance of this layout information of characters in images, we employ LayoutLMv3 (Huang et al., 2022)) to encode the images, favoring it over sole OCR tools.

Text Encoder: To encode tweet texts, we employ DeBERTa (He et al., 2021). It has shown great performance in various NLP tasks . Our experimental results confirm its effectiveness in the ImageArg task as well.

Multimodal Fusion: We explore three multimodal fusion methods, illustrated in Fig. 2. The

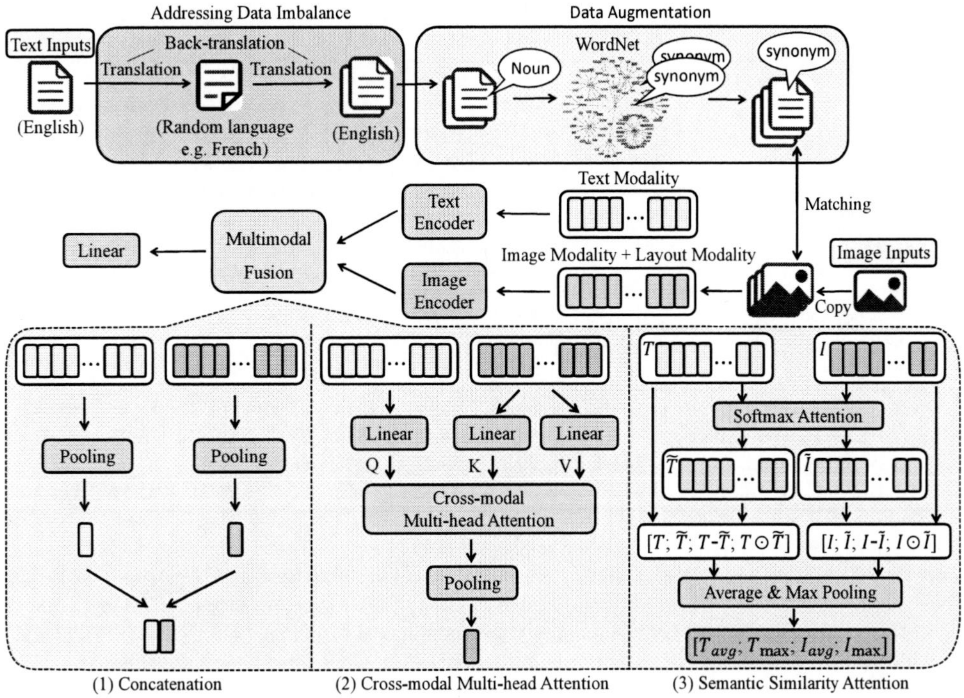

Figure 2: Our model, **TILFA**, includes three main parts: a text encoder, an image encoder, and a multimodal fusion module. In this fusion module, we experiment with three different methods: (1) Concatenation; (2) Cross-modal Multi-head Attention; (3) Semantic Similarity Attention.

first simply concatenates the hidden states from text and image inputs. The second method, named cross-modal multi-head attention, is adapted from Yu et al. (2021). And the third is a new approach adapted from ESIM (Chen et al., 2017). ESIM is a sequential natural language inference model used to predict the logic relationship between two sentences. We adapt it for text and image fusion, and name our version: Semantic Similarity Attention.

4 Experiments

4.1 Experiment Settings

Metrics: We use F1 score, Macro F1, AUC (Area Under Curve) and accuracy scores to evaluate baselines and our models. Models with the best F1-score on validation set are chosen.

Baselines: For images, we use ResNet50, ResNet101, VGG16, and LayoutLMv3. For text, we use DeBERTa. For combined image and text input, DeBERTa serves as text encoder, while ResNet50, ResNet101, and VGG16 act as image encoder. All models use the original dataset.

Implementation Details: To be more specific, we report scores within topics. Since the hyperparameters have a non-negligible effect on the scores, we conduct the experiments at a learning rate of 1e-4, 1e-5, 5e-6 and a batch size of 16, 8, 4. More implementation details can be found in Appendix A.

4.2 Results and Analysis

Table 1 shows the results on both topics in ImageArg dataset. (Experimental results of more models can be seen in Appendix B.)

Our model, **TILFA**, outperforms the baselines (those above the double horizontal line) on all the four evaluation metrics by a large margin. Also, our model achieves the SOTA performance on the leaderboard of Argumentative Stance Classification subtask in ImageArg Shared Task 2023, which demonstrate the effectiveness of our methods.

For combined text and image inputs, models utilizing LayoutLMv3 for image encoding perform much better than those using traditional ones, which verifies our belief in Section 3.3 that a better understanding of the text in images is beneficial.

Back-translation and WordNet also greatly improve performance across all metrics (e.g. an improvement of 1.68 on gun control and 3.98 on abortion for **TILFA** in F1-score), confirming the value

Models	Modality	Gun Control F1	Gun Control Ma-F1	Gun Control AUC	Gun Control Acc	Abortion F1	Abortion Ma-F1	Abortion AUC	Abortion Acc
ResNet50	I	65.00	62.50	62.90	62.67	35.71	60.42	59.55	75.84
ResNet101	I	67.43	60.91	60.86	62.00	38.89	59.71	60.44	70.47
VGG16	I	67.44	61.85	61.81	62.67	38.46	58.32	59.80	67.79
LayoutLMv3	I+L	56.98	46.67	46.92	48.67	39.47	59.38	60.66	69.13
DeBERTa	T	86.32	81.34	80.54	82.67	71.43	80.11	86.40	83.89
DeBERTa+ResNet50	T+I	**88.04**	**84.54**	**83.80**	**85.33**	70.59	79.43	85.97	83.22
DeBERTa+ResNet101	T+I	87.50	82.64	81.72	84.00	73.17	81.49	87.26	85.23
DeBERTa+VGG16	T+I	87.96	83.43	82.49	84.67	**74.07**	**82.20**	**87.70**	**85.91**
DeBERTa+ResNet50	T+I $^{+}$	**90.32**	**87.27**	**86.33**	**88.00**	75.95	83.64	88.56	87.25
DeBERTa+ResNet101	T+I $^{+}$	87.43	83.89	83.21	84.67	70.73	79.81	85.32	83.89
DeBERTa+VGG16	T+I $^{+}$	89.73	86.60	85.75	87.33	**77.50**	**84.62**	**90.07**	**87.92**
TILFA (DeBERTa+LayoutLMv3)	t1 T+I+L	89.13	85.94	85.16	86.67	76.54	83.89	89.64	87.25
TILFA (DeBERTa+LayoutLMv3)	t1 T+I+L $^{+}$	**90.81**	**88.01**	**87.10**	**88.67**	**80.52**	**86.87**	91.37	**89.93**
TILFA (DeBERTa+LayoutLMv3)	t2 T+I+L $^{+}$	90.32	87.27	86.33	88.00	77.50	84.62	90.07	87.92
TILFA (DeBERTa+LayoutLMv3)	t3 T+I+L $^{+}$	88.89	84.98	84.03	86.00	79.01	85.59	**91.59**	88.59

Table 1: Performance of all frameworks on the testing set of both topics. Those below the double horizontal line use our methods, and the above are baselines. For models that have both base and large sizes, we use the large one. We abbreviate F1-score, Macro F1-score, Accuracy to F1, Ma-F1, Acc, respectively. T, I and L are short for text modality, image modality and layout modality. Three multimodal fusion methods are named t1, t2 and t3 here. Those with a superscript + use both back-translation and WordNet, while others don't use either.

of our data preprocessing and augmentation strategies. When it comes to multimodal fusion methods, the simplest Concatenation works best. We think it may because the second method is initially applied in video field (Yu et al., 2021), and the third one in pure text field (Chen et al., 2017). So, neither of them is suitable to be migrated to this task.

We merge the answers belonging to different topics together and report the Micro F1-score. With a 90.32 F1 on gun control and a 77.50 F1 on abortion, we get a Micro F1-score of 86.47, which is the top on the leaderboard, 1.41 higher than the second best team. Our score improves even further after changing the hyperparameters, up to 87.79 (90.81 on gun control and 80.52 on abortion).

Text	Image	T	W	F1 Gun	F1 Abortion
–	ResNet50	–	–	65.00	35.71
–	LayoutLMv3	–	–	56.98	39.47
DeBERTa	–	–	–	86.32	71.43
DeBERTa	ResNet50	–	–	88.04	70.59
DeBERTa	ResNet50	✓	–	88.42	71.11
DeBERTa	ResNet50	–	✓	88.77	75.61
DeBERTa	ResNet50	✓	✓	90.32	75.95
DeBERTa	LayoutLMv3	–	–	89.13	76.54
DeBERTa	LayoutLMv3	✓	–	89.73	76.92
DeBERTa	LayoutLMv3	–	✓	90.22	77.50
DeBERTa	LayoutLMv3	✓	✓	90.81	80.52

Table 2: Ablation studies in ImageArg. The first two columns illustrate text and image encoders. T and W represent back-translation and WordNet. All models use the Concatenation method for multimodal fusion.

4.3 Ablation Study

To fully understand the impact of different components, we conduct an ablation study in Table 2.

Both back-translation and WordNet do help to the improvement of model performance, with WordNet having a larger impact. Models using only text inputs outperform just image inputs. This suggests that information in the text is more effective in determining the author's stance than images. However, the best performance is achieved when both text and image inputs are used, showing that images also do contribute to stance determination.

LayoutLMv3 performs better than Resnet50 on abortion topic when based solely on image inputs, but on both topics when text inputs are added. This indicates that image encoders which can take the text and layout information in the images into account can really work better.

4.4 Case Study

We conduct a case study to better understand the behavior of our data augmentation method, with an example presented in Table 3. In the original text, we select the noun "risk". Then we find its differ-

Original Text	SCOTUS has balanced rights w/ public safety, ruling that gun safety laws essential & constitutional Rushing through a replacement to RBG could undermine that balance and put life-saving laws at risk.
Selected Noun	"risk"
Word Senses	"hazard.n.01": a source of danger; a possibility of incurring loss or misfortune "risk.n.02": a venture undertaken without regard to possible loss or injury "risk.n.03": the probability of becoming infected given that exposure to an infectious agent has occurred "risk.n.04": the probability of being exposed to an infectious agent "risk.v.01": expose to a chance of loss or damage "gamble.v.01": take a risk in the hope of a favorable outcome
Disambiguation	"hazard.n.01": a source of danger; a possibility of incurring loss or misfortune
Synonyms	"hazard.n.01" = ["peril", "jeopardy", "endangerment", "hazard"]
New Text	SCOTUS has balanced rights w/ public safety, ruling that gun safety laws essential & constitutional Rushing through a replacement to RBG could undermine that balance and put life-saving laws at peril/jeopardy/endangerment/hazard.

Table 3: An example of our data augmentation method.

ent meanings and corresponding synonym sets in WordNet. Using GlossBERT, we determine its exact meaning "hazard.n.01" and thus get the correct synonym set ["peril", "jeopardy", "endangerment", "hazard"]. Finally, we replace the noun "risk" in the original text with these synonyms to form new text.

5 Conclusion

We present **TILFA**, a new framework for multimodal argumentative stance classification. Unlike existing methods, **TILFA** considers not only the text and images in tweets but also the characters and their layout information in those images. Back-translation and WordNet also contribute to our SOTA performance. Our results reveal that better handling of images is essential to model improvement, and suggest that more effective methods for multimodal fusion are yet to be found.

Limitations

We have experimented with three multimodal fusion methods, but the simplest one, Concatenation, turned out to be the best. So the other two methods that we use are not suitable for this task actually. But we believe that there are more effective multimodal fusion methods (Liu et al., 2023a; Li et al., 2023; Yang et al., 2022) waiting to be discovered.

Also, we notice that images in the dataset vary widely, some feature only objects, but others contain significant text. Further research is needed to effectively handle these differences, and we expect that better image encoders will improve performance in future works.

Moerover, in the data augmentation part, we only explore the methods related to text, but there are also many ways to augment images. Whether these methods (Shorten and Khoshgoftaar, 2019; Xu et al., 2023) are effective for images containing lots of characters is a question worth studying.

For the text modality, we found that most instances are a piece of text containing a few events, such as the example in Table 3. With the recent advances in event understanding (Lin et al., 2023), we can incorporate different relations among events, including temporal (Fang et al., 2023), causal (Zhang et al., 2022; Wang et al., 2023c; Gao et al., 2023), sub-event (Wang et al., 2022; Zhang et al., 2020), hierarchical (Wang et al., 2023b,a).

Acknowledgements

The authors of this paper were supported by the NSFC Fund (U20B2053) from the NSFC of China, the RIF (R6020-19 and R6021-20), and the GRF (16211520 and 16205322) from RGC of Hong Kong. We also thank the support from NVIDIA AI Technology Center (NVAITC) and the UGC Research Matching Grants (RMGS20EG01-D, RMGS20CR11, RMGS20CR12, RMGS20EG19, RMGS20EG21, RMGS23CR05, RMGS23EG08).

References

Markus Bayer, Marc-André Kaufhold, and Christian Reuter. 2022. A survey on data augmentation for text classification. *ACM Comput. Surv.*, 55(7).

Winston Carlile, Nishant Gurrapadi, Zixuan Ke, and Vincent Ng. 2018. Give me more feedback: Annotating argument persuasiveness and related attributes in student essays. In *Proceedings of the 56th Annual Meeting of the Association for Computational Linguistics (Volume 1: Long Papers)*, pages 621–631, Melbourne, Australia. Association for Computational Linguistics.

Qian Chen, Xiaodan Zhu, Zhen-Hua Ling, Si Wei, Hui Jiang, and Diana Inkpen. 2017. Enhanced LSTM for natural language inference. In *Proceedings of the 55th Annual Meeting of the Association for Computational Linguistics, ACL 2017, Vancouver, Canada, July 30 - August 4, Volume 1: Long Papers*, pages 1657–1668. Association for Computational Linguistics.

Tianqing Fang, Zhaowei Wang, Wenxuan Zhou, Hongming Zhang, Yangqiu Song, and Muhao Chen. 2023. Getting sick after seeing a doctor? diagnosing and mitigating knowledge conflicts in event temporal reasoning. *CoRR*, abs/2305.14970.

Tianqing Fang, Wenxuan Zhou, Fangyu Liu, Hongming Zhang, Yangqiu Song, and Muhao Chen. 2022. On-the-fly denoising for data augmentation in natural language understanding. *CoRR*, abs/2212.10558.

Jinglong Gao, Xiao Ding, Bing Qin, and Ting Liu. 2023. Is chatgpt a good causal reasoner? A comprehensive evaluation. *CoRR*, abs/2305.07375.

Ivan Habernal and Iryna Gurevych. 2017. Argumentation mining in user-generated web discourse. *Computational Linguistics*, 43(1):125–179.

Leipeng Hao, Liangcai Gao, Xiaohan Yi, and Zhi Tang. 2016. A table detection method for pdf documents based on convolutional neural networks. In *2016 12th IAPR Workshop on Document Analysis Systems (DAS)*, pages 287–292.

Kaiming He, Xiangyu Zhang, Shaoqing Ren, and Jian Sun. 2016. Deep residual learning for image recognition. In *2016 IEEE Conference on Computer Vision and Pattern Recognition, CVPR 2016, Las Vegas, NV, USA, June 27-30, 2016*, pages 770–778. IEEE Computer Society.

Pengcheng He, Xiaodong Liu, Jianfeng Gao, and Weizhu Chen. 2021. Deberta: decoding-enhanced bert with disentangled attention. In *9th International Conference on Learning Representations, ICLR 2021, Virtual Event, Austria, May 3-7, 2021*. OpenReview.net.

Luyao Huang, Chi Sun, Xipeng Qiu, and Xuanjing Huang. 2019. GlossBERT: BERT for word sense disambiguation with gloss knowledge. In *Proceedings of the 2019 Conference on Empirical Methods in Natural Language Processing and the 9th International Joint Conference on Natural Language Processing (EMNLP-IJCNLP)*, pages 3507–3512, Hong Kong, China. Association for Computational Linguistics.

Yupan Huang, Tengchao Lv, Lei Cui, Yutong Lu, and Furu Wei. 2022. Layoutlmv3: Pre-training for document AI with unified text and image masking. In *MM '22: The 30th ACM International Conference on Multimedia, Lisboa, Portugal, October 10 - 14, 2022*, pages 4083–4091. ACM.

Yunxin Li, Baotian Hu, Xinyu Chen, Yuxin Ding, Lin Ma, and Min Zhang. 2023. A multi-modal context reasoning approach for conditional inference on joint textual and visual clues. In *Proceedings of the 61st Annual Meeting of the Association for Computational Linguistics (Volume 1: Long Papers), ACL 2023, Toronto, Canada, July 9-14, 2023*, pages 10757–10770. Association for Computational Linguistics.

Zizheng Lin, Hongming Zhang, and Yangqiu Song. 2023. Global constraints with prompting for zero-shot event argument classification. In *Findings of the Association for Computational Linguistics: EACL 2023, Dubrovnik, Croatia, May 2-6, 2023*, pages 2482–2493. Association for Computational Linguistics.

Chengliang Liu, Jie Wen, Xiaoling Luo, and Yong Xu. 2023a. Incomplete multi-view multi-label learning via label-guided masked view- and category-aware transformers. In *Thirty-Seventh AAAI Conference on Artificial Intelligence, AAAI 2023, Thirty-Fifth Conference on Innovative Applications of Artificial Intelligence, IAAI 2023, Thirteenth Symposium on Educational Advances in Artificial Intelligence, EAAI 2023, Washington, DC, USA, February 7-14, 2023*, pages 8816–8824. AAAI Press.

Xiaojing Liu, Feiyu Gao, Qiong Zhang, and Huasha Zhao. 2019. Graph convolution for multimodal information extraction from visually rich documents. In *Proceedings of the 2019 Conference of the North American Chapter of the Association for Computational Linguistics: Human Language Technologies, Volume 2 (Industry Papers)*, pages 32–39, Minneapolis, Minnesota. Association for Computational Linguistics.

Zhexiong Liu, Mohamed Elaraby, Yang Zhong, and Diane Litman. 2023b. Overview of ImageArg-2023: The first shared task in multimodal argument mining. In *Proceedings of the 10th Workshop on Argument Mining*, Online and in Singapore. Association for Computational Linguistics.

Zhexiong Liu, Meiqi Guo, Yue Dai, and Diane Litman. 2022. ImageArg: A multi-modal tweet dataset for image persuasiveness mining. In *Proceedings of the 9th Workshop on Argument Mining*, pages 1–18, Online and in Gyeongju, Republic of Korea. International Conference on Computational Linguistics.

George A. Miller. 1994. WordNet: A lexical database for English. In *Human Language Technology: Proceedings of a Workshop held at Plainsboro, New Jersey, March 8-11, 1994.*

Georgios Rizos, Konstantin Hemker, and Björn W. Schuller. 2019. Augment to prevent: Short-text data augmentation in deep learning for hate-speech classification. In *Proceedings of the 28th ACM International Conference on Information and Knowledge Management, CIKM 2019, Beijing, China, November 3-7, 2019*, pages 991–1000. ACM.

Connor Shorten and Taghi M. Khoshgoftaar. 2019. A survey on image data augmentation for deep learning. *Journal of Big Data*, 6(1):1–48.

Karen Simonyan and Andrew Zisserman. 2015. Very deep convolutional networks for large-scale image recognition. In *3rd International Conference on Learning Representations, ICLR 2015, San Diego, CA, USA, May 7-9, 2015, Conference Track Proceedings*.

Weiqi Wang, Tianqing Fang, Wenxuan Ding, Baixuan Xu, Xin Liu, Yangqiu Song, and Antoine Bosselut. 2023a. CAR: conceptualization-augmented reasoner for zero-shot commonsense question answering. *CoRR*, abs/2305.14869.

Weiqi Wang, Tianqing Fang, Baixuan Xu, Chun Yi Louis Bo, Yangqiu Song, and Lei Chen. 2023b. CAT: A contextualized conceptualization and instantiation framework for commonsense reasoning. In *Proceedings of the 61st Annual Meeting of the Association for Computational Linguistics (Volume 1: Long Papers)*, pages 13111–13140, Toronto, Canada. Association for Computational Linguistics.

X. Wang, Y. Sheng, H. Deng, and Z. Zhao. 2019. Charcnn-svm for chinese text datasets sentiment classification with data augmentation. *International Journal of Innovative Computing, Information and Control*, 15:227–246.

Zhaowei Wang, Quyet V. Do, Hongming Zhang, Jiayao Zhang, Weiqi Wang, Tianqing Fang, Yangqiu Song, Ginny Y. Wong, and Simon See. 2023c. COLA: contextualized commonsense causal reasoning from the causal inference perspective. In *Proceedings of the 61st Annual Meeting of the Association for Computational Linguistics (Volume 1: Long Papers), ACL 2023, Toronto, Canada, July 9-14, 2023*, pages 5253–5271. Association for Computational Linguistics.

Zhaowei Wang, Hongming Zhang, Tianqing Fang, Yangqiu Song, Ginny Y. Wong, and Simon See. 2022. Subeventwriter: Iterative sub-event sequence generation with coherence controller. In *Proceedings of the 2022 Conference on Empirical Methods in Natural Language Processing, EMNLP 2022, Abu Dhabi, United Arab Emirates, December 7-11, 2022*, pages 1590–1604. Association for Computational Linguistics.

John Wieting and Kevin Gimpel. 2018. Paranmt-50m: Pushing the limits of paraphrastic sentence embeddings with millions of machine translations. In *Proceedings of the 56th Annual Meeting of the Association for Computational Linguistics, ACL 2018, Melbourne, Australia, July 15-20, 2018, Volume 1: Long Papers*, pages 451–462. Association for Computational Linguistics.

Mingle Xu, Sook Yoon, Alvaro Fuentes, and Dong Sun Park. 2023. A comprehensive survey of image augmentation techniques for deep learning. *Pattern Recognition*, 137:109347.

Yang Xu, Yiheng Xu, Tengchao Lv, Lei Cui, Furu Wei, Guoxin Wang, Yijuan Lu, Dinei A. F. Florêncio, Cha Zhang, Wanxiang Che, Min Zhang, and Lidong Zhou. 2021. Layoutlmv2: Multi-modal pre-training for visually-rich document understanding. In *Proceedings of the 59th Annual Meeting of the Association for Computational Linguistics and the 11th International Joint Conference on Natural Language Processing, ACL/IJCNLP 2021, (Volume 1: Long Papers), Virtual Event, August 1-6, 2021*, pages 2579–2591. Association for Computational Linguistics.

Yiheng Xu, Minghao Li, Lei Cui, Shaohan Huang, Furu Wei, and Ming Zhou. 2020. Layoutlm: Pre-training of text and layout for document image understanding. In *KDD '20: The 26th ACM SIGKDD Conference on Knowledge Discovery and Data Mining, Virtual Event, CA, USA, August 23-27, 2020*, pages 1192–1200. ACM.

Qian Yang, Yunxin Li, Baotian Hu, Lin Ma, Yuxin Ding, and Min Zhang. 2022. Chunk-aware alignment and lexical constraint for visual entailment with natural language explanations. In *MM '22: The 30th ACM International Conference on Multimedia, Lisboa, Portugal, October 10 - 14, 2022*, pages 3587–3597. ACM.

Adams Wei Yu, David Dohan, Minh-Thang Luong, Rui Zhao, Kai Chen, Mohammad Norouzi, and Quoc V. Le. 2018. Qanet: Combining local convolution with global self-attention for reading comprehension. In *6th International Conference on Learning Representations, ICLR 2018, Vancouver, BC, Canada, April 30 - May 3, 2018, Conference Track Proceedings*. OpenReview.net.

Tiezheng Yu, Wenliang Dai, Zihan Liu, and Pascale Fung. 2021. Vision guided generative pre-trained language models for multimodal abstractive summarization. In *Proceedings of the 2021 Conference on Empirical Methods in Natural Language Processing*, pages 3995–4007, Online and Punta Cana, Dominican Republic. Association for Computational Linguistics.

Hongming Zhang, Muhao Chen, Haoyu Wang, Yangqiu Song, and Dan Roth. 2020. Analogous process structure induction for sub-event sequence prediction. In *Proceedings of the 2020 Conference on Empirical Methods in Natural Language Processing, EMNLP*

2020, Online, November 16-20, 2020, pages 1541–1550. Association for Computational Linguistics.

Jiayao Zhang, Hongming Zhang, Weijie J. Su, and Dan Roth. 2022. ROCK: causal inference principles for reasoning about commonsense causality. In *International Conference on Machine Learning, ICML 2022, 17-23 July 2022, Baltimore, Maryland, USA*, volume 162 of *Proceedings of Machine Learning Research*, pages 26750–26771. PMLR.

A Implementation Details

In this appendix, we introduce the implementation details of every component in our framework **TILFA**.

We use the dataset divisions provided in the shared task, and the dataset sizes are detailed in Table 4. Each tweet text is cut by a maximum length of 512, and each tweet image is resized to 224×224 dimension. For back-translation, we use Youdao translation API[3]. For layout information, we follow Xu et al. (2020) and use Tesseract[4], an open-source OCR engine, to get the recognized words and their 2-D positions in the images. Our models are implemented with Pytorch, and trained on a NVIDIA A6000 GPU. AdamW optimizer is used for those networks with LayoutLMv3 and Adam optimizer for others.

Topic	Train	Validation	Test
Gun control	918	96	150
Abortion	888	100	149

Table 4: Dataset scale of both topics. Following the shared task, one unavailable tweet in the abortion testing set is removed. And due to the downloading issues, our downloaded train and dev sets have little difference from the original one.

B Experimental Results

Our full experiment results are shown in Table 5.

[3]http://fanyi.youdao.com/openapi/

[4]https://github.com/tesseract-ocr/tesseract

Models	Modality	Gun Control				Abortion			
		F1	Ma-F1	AUC	Acc	F1	Ma-F1	AUC	Acc
ResNet50	I	65.00	62.50	62.90	62.67	35.71	60.42	59.55	75.84
ResNet101	I	67.43	60.91	60.86	62.00	38.89	59.71	60.44	70.47
VGG16	I	67.44	61.85	61.81	62.67	38.46	58.32	59.80	67.79
LayoutLMv3	I+L	56.98	46.67	46.92	48.67	39.47	59.38	60.66	69.13
BERT	T	81.48	74.97	74.52	76.67	64.10	75.69	79.26	81.21
RoBERTa	T	83.52	79.05	78.55	80.00	71.60	80.50	85.75	84.56
DeBERTa	T	86.32	81.34	80.54	82.67	71.43	80.11	86.40	83.89
BERT+ResNet50	T+I	81.97	76.88	76.43	78.00	65.06	75.79	81.00	80.54
RoBERTa+ResNet50	T+I	84.82	79.11	78.42	80.67	73.42	81.91	86.61	**85.91**
DeBERTa+ResNet50	T+I	**88.04**	**84.54**	**83.80**	**85.33**	70.59	79.43	85.97	83.22
BERT+ResNet101	T+I	80.63	73.34	72.99	75.33	64.52	74.21	82.52	77.85
RoBERTa+ResNet101	T+I	83.77	77.66	77.06	79.33	65.22	74.84	82.95	78.52
DeBERTa+ResNet101	T+I	87.50	82.64	81.72	84.00	73.17	81.49	87.26	85.23
BERT+VGG16	T+I	79.37	72.11	71.81	74.00	68.24	77.78	84.03	81.88
RoBERTa+VGG16	T+I	83.52	79.05	78.55	80.00	72.50	81.20	86.18	85.23
DeBERTa+VGG16	T+I	87.96	83.43	82.49	84.67	**74.07**	**82.20**	**87.70**	**85.91**
BERT+ResNet50	T+I $^+$	81.05	74.16	73.76	76.00	68.24	77.78	84.03	81.88
RoBERTa+ResNet50	T+I $^+$	84.66	79.26	78.60	80.67	71.60	80.50	85.75	84.56
DeBERTa+ResNet50	T+I $^+$	**90.32**	**87.27**	**86.33**	**88.00**	75.95	83.64	88.56	87.25
BERT+ResNet101	T+I $^+$	82.87	78.41	77.96	79.33	62.50	72.34	81.23	75.84
RoBERTa+ResNet101	T+I $^+$	84.21	78.47	77.83	80.00	68.97	78.08	85.11	81.88
DeBERTa+ResNet101	T+I $^+$	87.43	83.89	83.21	84.67	70.73	79.81	85.32	83.89
BERT+VGG16	T+I $^+$	81.03	72.89	72.62	75.33	68.97	78.08	85.11	81.88
RoBERTa+VGG16	T+I $^+$	83.24	78.14	77.60	79.33	72.50	81.20	86.18	85.23
DeBERTa+VGG16	T+I $^+$	89.73	86.60	85.75	87.33	**77.50**	**84.62**	**90.07**	**87.92**
BERT+LayoutLMv3	t1 T+I+L	81.32	76.25	75.84	77.33	65.75	77.32	79.47	83.22
RoBERTa+LayoutLMv3	t1 T+I+L	85.26	79.90	79.19	81.33	75.95	83.64	88.56	87.25
DeBERTa+LayoutLMv3	t1 T+I+L	89.13	85.94	85.16	86.67	76.54	83.89	89.64	87.25
BERT+LayoutLMv3	t1 T+I+L $^+$	81.72	75.95	75.48	77.33	69.14	78.81	83.80	83.22
RoBERTa+LayoutLMv3	t1 T+I+L $^+$	86.19	82.59	82.04	83.33	76.32	84.10	87.90	87.92
DeBERTa+LayoutLMv3	t1 T+I+L $^+$	**90.81**	**88.01**	**87.10**	**88.67**	**80.52**	**86.87**	91.37	**89.93**
BERT+LayoutLMv3	t2 T+I+L $^+$	83.52	79.05	78.55	80.00	69.88	79.13	84.89	83.22
RoBERTa+LayoutLMv3	t2 T+I+L $^+$	84.95	80.19	79.55	81.33	72.29	80.80	86.83	84.56
DeBERTa+LayoutLMv3	t2 T+I+L $^+$	90.32	87.27	86.33	88.00	77.50	84.62	90.07	87.92
BERT+LayoutLMv3	t3 T+I+L $^+$	82.16	76.73	76.24	78.00	69.05	78.45	84.46	82.55
RoBERTa+LayoutLMv3	t3 T+I+L $^+$	84.78	80.32	79.73	81.33	71.05	80.57	84.01	85.23
DeBERTa+LayoutLMv3	t3 T+I+L $^+$	88.89	84.98	84.03	86.00	79.01	85.59	**91.59**	88.59

Table 5: Experimental results of more models on both topics in ImageArg dataset. Compared to Table 1, the scores of the models which use BERT or RoBERTa as the text encoder are also listed here.

A General Framework for Multimodal Argument Persuasiveness Classification of Tweets

Mohammad Soltani and **Julia Romberg**
Heinrich Heine University Düsseldorf
{mohammad.soltani,julia.romberg}@hhu.de

Abstract

An important property of argumentation concerns the degree of its persuasiveness, which can be influenced by various modalities. On social media platforms, individuals usually have the option of supporting their textual statements with images. The goals of the *ImageArg shared task*, held with ArgMining 2023, were therefore (A) to classify tweet stances considering both modalities and (B) to predict the influence of an image on the persuasiveness of a tweet text. In this paper, we present our proposed methodology that shows strong performance on both tasks, placing 3rd team on the leaderboard in each case with F_1 scores of 0.8273 (A) and 0.5281 (B). The framework relies on pre-trained models to extract text and image features, which are then fed into a task-specific classification model. Our experiments highlighted that the multimodal vision and language model CLIP holds a specific importance in the extraction of features, in particular for task (A).

1 Introduction

How convincing are the arguments put forward in a discussion? Are these arguments effective in persuading a dissenting voice to change its opinion or behavior? Automatically answering such questions of *argument persuasiveness* holds significant importance within the field of argument mining.

There has been a growing body of research on tasks pertaining to persuasiveness (Persing and Ng, 2015; Wachsmuth et al., 2016; Chakrabarty et al., 2019). Works like Stab and Gurevych (2014, 2017) and Habernal and Gurevych (2017) have brought persuasive essays into focus. To capture the persuasiveness of arguments based on Aristotle (2007)'s idea of logos, ethos and pathos, different annotation schemes have been developed (Duthie et al., 2016; Carlile et al., 2018; Wachsmuth et al., 2018). Moreover, phenomena of argument persuasion were examined using a variety of data sources, including online debates (Lukin et al., 2017; Durmus and Cardie, 2018; Longpre et al., 2019) and news editorials (El Baff et al., 2020).

What these works have in common is their emphasis on argumentation in textual form. However, the options for persuading the counterpart of one's own view are by no means limited to written speech (Park et al., 2014). There are further means that can be employed, usually as supplements, like images or videos (Joo et al., 2014; Huang and Kovashka, 2016; Liu et al., 2022b).

In this paper, we present our solution approach to the *ImageArg shared task* (Liu et al., 2023). We propose using a general framework to solve tasks related to argument persuasiveness in multimodal settings. The framework comprises two feature extraction modules designed for processing text and image modalities, which are subsequently inputted into a classifier. In our experiments, CLIP-extracted features (Radford et al., 2021) excelled for subtask (A), and supplementing them with additional features (ConvNeXt (Liu et al., 2022c), Reformer (Kitaev et al., 2020), ELECTRA (Clark et al., 2020), LayoutLM (Xu et al., 2020), CamemBERT (Martin et al., 2020), Swin V2 (Liu et al., 2022a)) proved most beneficial for subtask (B).

We begin with a brief description of task and dataset (§2), followed by a detailed description of our methodology (§3). We then present the experimental results (§4) and analyze the errors that occur (§5). In addition, we report progress on our approach in the post-evaluation phase, which has enabled us to further improve classification performance (§6). Finally, we draw a conclusion and make recommendations for future work (§7).

2 Task Description

The shared task relies on ImageArg (Liu et al., 2022b), a multimodal dataset for argument persuasiveness. It consists of English-language argumentative tweets supported by images as provided by users. The version of the dataset used for the shared

Proceedings of the 10th Workshop on Argument Mining, pages 148–156
December 7, 2023.

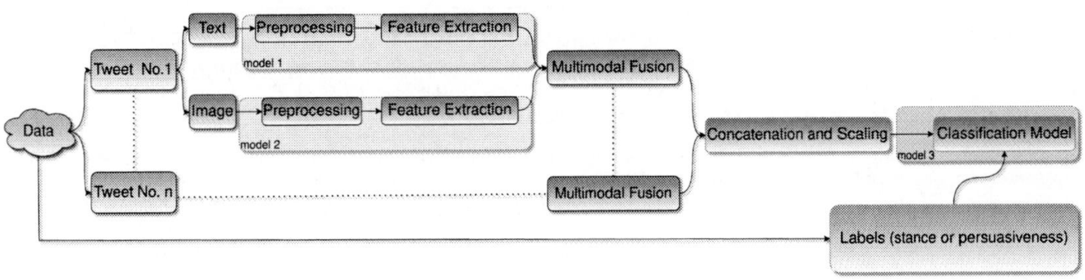

Figure 1: Framework design: model 1 and 2 extract the text and image features for each tweet as vectors of sizes a and b. Multimodal fusion combines these into a single vector of size c, with $c = a + b$. The n tweet feature vectors then jointly form a matrix $C \in \mathbb{R}^{c \times n}$. Along with the n task-specific labels, they serve as input for model 3.

task includes two subtasks: *Argumentative Stance (AS) Classification (Subtask A):* Given a tweet and an accompanying image, predict the stance (either *support* or *oppose*) that the tweet takes on a particular topic. *Image Persuasiveness (IP) Classification (Subtask B):* Given a tweet and an accompanying image, predict whether or not the image makes the tweet more persuasive (either *yes* or *no*).

Table 1 gives an overview of the dataset[1], which covers two controversial topics, *abortion* and *gun control.* Evidently, there is an imbalance in the data pertaining to both subtasks. For AS, while both stances reach a balance on gun control, opposition clearly prevails on abortion. As for IP, adding images only contributes to tweet persuasiveness in about one-third of the cases for both topics.

		AS			**IP**	
		abortion	gun control		abortion	gun control
train	total	887	914	total	887	914
	supp.	243	471	yes	278	250
	opp.	644	443	no	609	664
dev	total	100	96	total	100	96
	supp.	19	51	yes	26	31
	opp.	81	45	no	74	65
test	total	150	150	total	150	150
	supp.	33	85	yes	53	53
	opp.	117	65	no	97	97

Table 1: Overview of the data distribution among the two topics and for the different data splits.

3 Methodology

Motivated by Liu et al. (2022b), we developed a versatile framework (illustrated in Figure 1) that takes tweet texts and images as input, extracts features for both modalities, and feeds the combined features into a classification model. This framework is designed to work readily for both tasks and comprises the following stages:

3.1 Multimodal Feature Extraction & Fusion

The multimodal feature extraction consists of three steps that are iterated for every tweet in the dataset.

Feature Extraction from Text Each tweet text is first tokenized. Using some pre-trained language model (*model 1*), text features are then extracted in order to represent the semantic information.

Feature Extraction from Image In parallel, each tweet image is readied for feature extraction through transformation, resizing, normalizing, and adjusting dimensions. Subsequently, the prepared image is processed by a specified pre-trained model (*model 2*) to extract image features.

Early Multimodal Fusion We then combine features from both modalities by concatenating them along the last dimension according to the early fusion strategy suggested by Boulahia et al. (2021) for creating a unified representation that combines image and text information.

3.2 Feature Concatenation and Scaling

We retain combined features of all data instances in an array and enhance their impact during learning by scaling them (Singh and Singh, 2020). For this, we re-scale each feature by its maximum absolute value, keeping them in a range between -1 to 1.

3.3 Classification

In a final step, the tweet representation obtained by the previous process serves as input to a classification model (*model 3*). This model is trained using the given training data and the corresponding labels for the respective task (either AS or IP).

[1] Our statistics differ slightly from the organizer's data due to inconsistencies in the downloading process.

Model Type	Model Architectures
Text (model 1)	Sentence-BERT, BERT, RoBERTa, ALBERT, DistilBERT, ELECTRA, XLNet, CTRL, Longformer, DeBERTa, XLM-RoBERTa, FlauBERT, DialoGPT, LayoutLM, Funnel-Transformer, MBart, CamemBERT, Reformer, Transformer-XL, GPT3, CLIP, ALIGN
Image (model 2)	AlexNet, ConvNeXt, DenseNet, EfficientNet, EfficientNetV2, GoogLeNet, Inception v3, MaxViT, MnasNet, MobileNetV2, VGG, MobileNetV3, RegNet, ResNet, ResNeXt, ShuffleNet v2, SqueezeNet, Swin Transformer, ViT, Wide ResNet, CLIP, ALIGN
Classifier (model 3)	Logistic Regression, XGBoost, Gradient Boosting, AdaBoost, CatBoost, LightGBM, MLPClassifier, SGDClassifier, SVM (with kernels: linear, poly, rbf, sigmoid), Gaussian Naive Bayes, EasyEnsemble, KNeighborsClassifier, Random Forest, Decision Trees, Extra Trees, RUSBoostClassifier, BalancedBaggingClassifier, BalancedRandomForestClassifier, PassiveAggressiveClassifier, GaussianProcessClassifier with kernel RBF, RidgeClassifier, Linear Discriminant Analysis, Quadratic Discriminant Analysis

Table 2: Summary of the models utilized in our experiments.

		abortion			**gun control**					
	attempt	model 1	model 2	model 3	model 1	model 2	model 3	train mode	F_1 (dev)	F_1 (test)
	1	CLIP32	CLIP32	AdaBoostClassifier	CLIP32	CLIP32	AdaBoostClassifier	separate	0.9254	0.8142
	2	CLIP32	CLIP32	AdaBoostClassifier	CLIP32	CLIP32	XGboost+GradientBoosting	separate	**0.9333**	**0.8273**
AS	3	CLIP32	CLIP32	AdaBoostClassifier	CLIP32	CLIP32	RUSBoostClassifier	separate	**0.9333**	0.8000
	4	CLIP32	CLIP32	XGboost+GradientBoosting	CLIP32	CLIP32	XGboost+GradientBoosting	joint	0.9142	0.8093
	5	CLIP32	CLIP32	SVM-Poly	CLIP32	CLIP32	SVM-Poly	joint	0.9197	0.7782
	1	CLIP32	CLIP32	SVM-Poly	CLIP32	CLIP32	SVM-Poly	joint	0.6605	0.4875
	2	CLIP32	CLIP32	SGD	CLIP32	CLIP32	SGD	separate	0.6552	0.4545
IP	3	CLIP_L_14	CLIP_L_14	SVM-Poly	CLIP_L_14	CLIP_L_14	SVM-Poly	joint	0.6721	0.4762
	4	CLIP32	CLIP32	SGD	Convnext_small	REL	LogisticRegression	separate	**0.6726**	0.4778
	5	CLIP32	CLIP32	SVM-Poly	Convnext_small	REL	LogisticRegression	separate	0.6667	**0.5281**

Table 3: Selected submissions and their performance on dev and test for both tasks. Participants were free to decide whether they wanted to create a cross-topic model (train mode: joint) or topic-specific ones (train mode: separate).

4 Experiments

4.1 Model Selection for Submission

We conducted extensive experiments using our framework with a variety of pre-trained models from both PyTorch (Paszke et al., 2019) and Transformers (Wolf et al., 2020) libraries. Our Python implementation is available at https://github.com/mohsoltani/GFMAP.

In fact, we examined more than 300 different combinations of these models for each subtask and topic. For our classification approach, we experimented either with a single classifier or with ensemble learning (Dong et al., 2020), combining two or more classifiers. Table 2 provides an overview of the different models we tested.

Using CLIP as a text and image model, we conducted experiments with all of the listed classification models. Subsequently, we investigated the performance of the top classification models for other combinations of pre-trained models, where Logistic Regression was found to be the most effective classification model. The best hyperparameters of the classification model were determined by trial and error (an overview is provided in Appendix A).

Among these experiments, we identified the best-performing models, which were then candidates for further experimentation involving the joint consideration of topics within each subtask. Ultimately, our submissions for the shared task at hand consisted of the top five performing models derived from our thorough experimentation.

4.2 Results

Table 3 shows our five submissions to both tasks. In AS, attempt 2 performed best, using CLIP[2] to extract the features that are subsequently fed into the classifier (AdaBoost for abortion, an ensemble of XGBoost and GradientBoosting for gun control). While our most effective strategy utilizes models tailored to specific topics, attempt 4 demonstrates that a generalized model is only slightly inferior to customized solutions (0.8273 vs. 0.8093 F_1).

The best approach for IP shows that in this case the choice of feature extraction models is different for the topics. While CLIP is again suitable for abortion, a combination of ConvNeXt[3] and REL (a concatenation of features extracted through Reformer[4], ELECTRA[5] and LayoutLM[6]) is the best choice for gun control, leading to an F_1 score of 0.5281. Cross-topic models score significantly lower on this task, which may indicate that the role of imagery in making textual arguments more persuading is topic-dependent.

5 Error Analysis & Discussion

In the following, we analyze the outputs of our best model for AS and IP in terms of misclassifications:

[2] CLIP32: https://huggingface.co/openai/clip-vit-base-patch32; CLIP_L_14: https://huggingface.co/sentence-transformers/clip-ViT-L-14

[3] Convnext_small: https://pytorch.org/vision/stable/models/generated/torchvision.models.convnext_small.html

[4] https://huggingface.co/google/reformer-crime-and-punishment

[5] https://huggingface.co/google/electra-small-discriminator

[6] https://huggingface.co/microsoft/layoutlm-large-uncased

5.1 Argumentative Stance Classification

The main reasons behind the most prevalent mistakes are:

Sarcasm, Humor, & Lack of Information In some cases, our approach faces difficulties in discerning a tweeter's true intent. One reason for this is sarcastic tweets: If a tweet seems to express positivity, but the tweeter takes the opposite view, misclassifications occur. Likewise, very short tweets tend to be misclassified, especially when negative words dominate but the overall stance is support. However, as we have noted, indirect communication (i.e., the speaker does not explicitly express his or her intentions or feelings) using humor or sarcasm can confuse not only the model but also the human audience when it comes to understanding the author (Appendix B.1 gives further insights).

Specifics of the Gun Control Topic In the area of gun control, there are two opposing groups and one supporter group: (1) The first group of critics advocates for a world without guns. (2) The second group of critics champions personal freedom and opposes any restrictions on the sale or use of guns. (3) The supporters advocate for regulated sales and usage of firearms.

In fact, the interesting dynamic surrounding gun control is that both groups of detractors are opposed to the proponents but also hold conflicting views among themselves. This complexity can make it challenging to discern the intention behind certain words or phrases in a tweet, such as "end of gun violence". Depending on the context and tweeter's specific stance, this phrase could potentially be interpreted in two different ways: It could be seen as a call for regulations and controls on the sale and use of guns to put an end to gun violence. This interpretation aligns with the stance of supporting gun control. Alternatively, it could be interpreted as a call for complete prohibition of selling and using guns, with the aim of eliminating gun violence entirely. This interpretation aligns with the stance of opposing guns altogether. An even more complicated scenario arises when considering this phrase in the context of using firearms for defense purposes: There seems to be a shared belief among groups 2 and 3 that the presence of a firearm may occasionally reduce the likelihood of firearm-related violence when used for defense.

Facing such scenarios, it is difficult to decide definitively whether we should take the supportive group stance, since a statement may not have direct relevance to an opposing group. In certain cases, discerning between the supportive group and one of the opposing groups can be quite challenging. We are dealing with a triangular arrangement of groups that must be classified into two classes. For further insights, please refer to Appendix B.2.

Ambiguities in Labels In certain instances where there are deviations between the predicted and gold labels, we found it difficult to confirm ourselves that the predicted stance is definitely incorrect (see Appendix B.3 for more details).

5.2 Image Persuasiveness Classification

Assessing whether an image enhances the tweet's persuasiveness presents a significant challenge – even for humans. The methods for visually representing or amplifying the stance of a tweet offer a variety of options compared to pure text:

Text Within Image A common approach is to insert a repetition of the tweet text or other relevant text in the image. This also allows the text's impact to be enhanced through visual effects such as image transformations, shading, different letter styles, adding text borders, colors, and background changes. We found that our best model developed a tendency to classify images showing only text as persuasive. However, the gold standard also contains many cases where this type of image was coded as not contributing to persuasiveness. We suspect that our model's behaviour is due to the fact that it is not able to extract and understand text from images. Therefore, in these cases, the model cannot make decisions based on linguistic semantics, but only on the structure of the image.

Image Persuasion Strategies Further strategies involve illustrating cases, consequences, or outcomes related to the text argument. A more intricate approach we found in the analysis visualizes counterexamples for opposing points of view.

It is difficult to objectively determine whether these methods are compelling or not, as images provide extensive creative freedom, allowing words and phrases to take on different visual forms. In addition, image effects (see e.g. Szeliski, 2022) such as occlusion, distinct object placements, viewpoint variations, deformations, background clutter, exposure bracketing, and morphing can change the illustrating form, consequently influencing the viewer's perception in various ways. Given the multitude of phenomena, we abstain from delving into specifics within the scope of this article.

Human Label Variation Human perceptions are often subjective and influenced by emotions, personal preferences or cultural backgrounds (Pettersson, 1982). For example, depictions of scenes such as protests can evoke different reactions depending on cultural norms and personal experiences. While protests are welcome in some cultures, they can be prohibited in others, resulting in either excitement or a sense of normality. Annotators with different thinking styles, such as holistic and analytical (Li et al., 2022), may also make different judgments when considering the background context or focusing solely on the objects in an image (for examples see Appendix B.4). Liu et al. (2022b) annotated image persuasiveness by assigning an aggregate label to establish a unified scoring. To account for different valid perceptions of persuasiveness resulting from the previously listed reasons, this approach may be insufficient and deserves reconsideration.

Impact of Image In the process of constructing the dataset, when a tweet's text was rated as extremely persuasive, the supplementary persuasiveness attributed to attached images was devalued, eventually resulting in a *no* label. This may lead the machine learning approach astray since the image itself can be highly persuasive in its own right.

6 Additional Experiments

As can be seen from the results presented so far, predicting IP in particular presents a challenge. For this reason, we present additional experiments that we conducted as a follow-up to the shared task.

In our experimental efforts, we obtained notably positive results when using CamemBERT as text model, particularly for abortion in combination with ConvNeXt or Swin Transformers V2 as image model. Given the significant disparity between our dev and test scores for IP in the shared task submissions, we proceeded to conduct additional experiments with various adaptations of this model in order to find more robust models.

It turned out, that employing camembert-base[7] to extract text features and swin_v2_s[8] to extract image features for the abortion topic, while retaining the proven combination of REL and ConvNeXt for the gun control topic, resulted in promising results. The classifier was Logistic Regression. With this setup, we managed to attain an F_1 score of 0.5941 for the test set, while the F_1 score for the dev set was 0.5950. As can be seen, the approach significantly increases previous test scores (cf. Table 3) while obtaining robust results across dev and test set. Our finding suggests that model performance should generalize to further in-domain datasets.

We performed further experiments, eventually achieving test scores above 0.66. At the same time, however, the dev performance deviated strongly downwards in these cases. Despite the very encouraging results, additional investigations are needed in order to ensure reliable performance.

7 Conclusion & Future Work

On social media, users have the freedom to use informal, formal, or mixed styles of language, and to incorporate elements such as hashtags, mentions, links to websites, and emojis. In addition, images can be used to substantiate textual statements. This variety presents a challenge when trying to classify argument stances and their persuasiveness from sources such as X (formerly known as Twitter). As the analysis of our approach was able to reveal, the prevalence of sarcasm and the limited information content in tweets substantially complicates the classification. This observation underscores the need for further improvement of models tailored to the specific characteristics of social media data.

In the context of classifying the additional persuasive power of images over text, it is crucial to use models that not only extract image features or detect objects in images, but can also extract the attitude and persuasion expressed through the images themselves. This necessitates the design of visual argument extraction models. The particular difficulty of evaluating the argumentative persuasiveness of images, as well as the inherently subjective nature of the task, require special attention.

What is more, due to the training dataset's limited size, it becomes challenging to differentiate learned image features at a granular level from those in other images. A larger dataset may assist us in improving classification results, particularly to overcome the challenges outlined in Section 5.

Possible research directions also include delving into the applicability of CamemBERT to English texts and exploring the reasons why this model surpasses English models in the task at hand.

[7] https://huggingface.co/camembert/camembert-base

[8] https://pytorch.org/vision/main/models/generated/torchvision.models.swin_v2_s

Acknowledgements

Julia Romberg is funded by the Federal Ministry of Education and Research of Germany, project CIMT/Partizipationsnutzen of the funding priority Social-Ecological Research (funding no. 01UU1904). Responsibility for the content of this publication lies with the authors.

References

Aristotle. 2007. *On Rhetoric: A Theory of Civic Discourse*. Clarendon Aristotle seris. Oxford University Press. (George A. Kennedy, Translator).

Said Boulahia, Abdenour Amamra, Mohamed Madi, and Said Daikh. 2021. Early, intermediate and late fusion strategies for robust deep learning-based multimodal action recognition. *Machine Vision and Applications*, 32:121.

Winston Carlile, Nishant Gurrapadi, Zixuan Ke, and Vincent Ng. 2018. Give me more feedback: Annotating argument persuasiveness and related attributes in student essays. In *Proceedings of the 56th Annual Meeting of the Association for Computational Linguistics (Volume 1: Long Papers)*, pages 621–631. Association for Computational Linguistics.

Tuhin Chakrabarty, Christopher Hidey, Smaranda Muresan, Kathy McKeown, and Alyssa Hwang. 2019. AMPERSAND: Argument mining for PERSuAsive oNline discussions. In *Proceedings of the 2019 Conference on Empirical Methods in Natural Language Processing and the 9th International Joint Conference on Natural Language Processing (EMNLP-IJCNLP)*, pages 2933–2943. Association for Computational Linguistics.

Kevin Clark, Minh-Thang Luong, Quoc Le, and Christopher Manning. 2020. ELECTRA: Pre-training text encoders as discriminators rather than generators. In *International Conference on Learning Representations*. OpenReview.net.

Xibin Dong, Zhiwen Yu, Wenming Cao, Yifan Shi, and Qianli Ma. 2020. A survey on ensemble learning. *Frontiers of Computer Science*, 14:pages 241–258.

Esin Durmus and Claire Cardie. 2018. Exploring the role of prior beliefs for argument persuasion. In *Proceedings of the 2018 Conference of the North American Chapter of the Association for Computational Linguistics: Human Language Technologies, Volume 1 (Long Papers)*, pages 1035–1045. Association for Computational Linguistics.

Rory Duthie, Katarzyna Budzynska, and Chris Reed. 2016. Mining ethos in political debate. In *Proceedings of the Sixth International Conference on Computational Models of Argument (COMMA 2016)*, pages 299–310. IOS Press.

Roxanne El Baff, Khalid Al Khatib, Benno Stein, and Henning Wachsmuth. 2020. Persuasiveness of news editorials depending on ideology and personality. In *Proceedings of the Third Workshop on Computational Modeling of People's Opinions, Personality, and Emotion's in Social Media*, pages 29–40. Association for Computational Linguistics.

Steven Greene, Melissa Deckman, Laurel Elder, and Mary-Kate Lizotte. 2022. Do moms demand action on guns? Parenthood and gun policy attitudes. *Journal of Elections, Public Opinion and Parties*, 32(3):655–673.

Ivan Habernal and Iryna Gurevych. 2017. Argumentation mining in user-generated web discourse. *Computational Linguistics*, 43(1):125–179.

Xinyue Huang and Adriana Kovashka. 2016. Inferring visual persuasion via body language, setting, and deep features. In *Proceedings of the IEEE Conference on Computer Vision and Pattern Recognition (CVPR) Workshops*, pages 73–79. IEEE.

Jungseock Joo, Weixin Li, Francis F. Steen, and Song-Chun Zhu. 2014. Visual persuasion: Inferring communicative intents of images. In *Proceedings of the IEEE Conference on Computer Vision and Pattern Recognition (CVPR)*, pages 216–223. IEEE.

Nikita Kitaev, Lukasz Kaiser, and Anselm Levskaya. 2020. Reformer: The efficient transformer. In *International Conference on Learning Representations*. OpenReview.net.

Hao Li, Ting Wang, Yi Cao, Lili Song, Youbo Hou, and Yizhi Wang. 2022. Culture, thinking styles and investment decision. *Psychological Reports*, 125(3):1528–1555.

Ze Liu, Han Hu, Yutong Lin, Zhuliang Yao, Zhenda Xie, Yixuan Wei, Jia Ning, Yue Cao, Zheng Zhang, Li Dong, Furu Wei, and Baining Guo. 2022a. Swin Transformer V2: Scaling up capacity and resolution. In *Proceedings of the IEEE/CVF Conference on Computer Vision and Pattern Recognition (CVPR)*, pages 11999–12009. IEEE.

Zhexiong Liu, Mohamed Elaraby, Yang Zhong, and Diane Litman. 2023. Overview of ImageArg-2023: The first shared task in multimodal argument mining. In *Proceedings of the 10th Workshop on Argument Mining*. Association for Computational Linguistics.

Zhexiong Liu, Meiqi Guo, Yue Dai, and Diane Litman. 2022b. ImageArg: A multi-modal tweet dataset for image persuasiveness mining. In *Proceedings of the 9th Workshop on Argument Mining*, pages 1–18. International Conference on Computational Linguistics.

Zhuang Liu, Hanzi Mao, Chao-Yuan Wu, Christoph Feichtenhofer, Trevor Darrell, and Saining Xie. 2022c. A ConvNet for the 2020s. In *Proceedings of the IEEE/CVF Conference on Computer Vision and Pattern Recognition (CVPR)*, pages 11966–11976,. IEEE.

Liane Longpre, Esin Durmus, and Claire Cardie. 2019. Persuasion of the undecided: Language vs. the listener. In *Proceedings of the 6th Workshop on Argument Mining*, pages 167–176. Association for Computational Linguistics.

Stephanie Lukin, Pranav Anand, Marilyn Walker, and Steve Whittaker. 2017. Argument strength is in the eye of the beholder: Audience effects in persuasion. In *Proceedings of the 15th Conference of the European Chapter of the Association for Computational Linguistics: Volume 1, Long Papers*, pages 742–753. Association for Computational Linguistics.

Louis Martin, Benjamin Muller, Pedro Javier Ortiz Suárez, Yoann Dupont, Laurent Romary, Éric de la Clergerie, Djamé Seddah, and Benoît Sagot. 2020. CamemBERT: a tasty French language model. In *Proceedings of the 58th Annual Meeting of the Association for Computational Linguistics*, pages 7203–7219. Association for Computational Linguistics.

Sunghyun Park, Han Suk Shim, Moitreya Chatterjee, Kenji Sagae, and Louis-Philippe Morency. 2014. Computational analysis of persuasiveness in social multimedia: A novel dataset and multimodal prediction approach. In *Proceedings of the 16th International Conference on Multimodal Interaction*, page 50–57. Association for Computing Machinery.

Adam Paszke, Sam Gross, Francisco Massa, Adam Lerer, James Bradbury, Gregory Chanan, Trevor Killeen, Zeming Lin, Natalia Gimelshein, Luca Antiga, Alban Desmaison, Andreas Kopf, Edward Yang, Zachary DeVito, Martin Raison, Alykhan Tejani, Sasank Chilamkurthy, Benoit Steiner, Lu Fang, Junjie Bai, and Soumith Chintala. 2019. Pytorch: An imperative style, high-performance deep learning library. In *Advances in Neural Information Processing Systems*, volume 32. Curran Associates, Inc.

Isaac Persing and Vincent Ng. 2015. Modeling argument strength in student essays. In *Proceedings of the 53rd Annual Meeting of the Association for Computational Linguistics and the 7th International Joint Conference on Natural Language Processing (Volume 1: Long Papers)*, pages 543–552. Association for Computational Linguistics.

Rune Pettersson. 1982. Cultural differences in the perception of image and color in pictures. *Educational Technology Research and Development*, 30(1):43–53.

Alec Radford, Jong Wook Kim, Chris Hallacy, Aditya Ramesh, Gabriel Goh, Sandhini Agarwal, Girish Sastry, Amanda Askell, Pamela Mishkin, Jack Clark, Gretchen Krueger, and Ilya Sutskever. 2021. Learning transferable visual models from natural language supervision. In *Proceedings of the 38th International Conference on Machine Learning*, pages 8748–8763. PMLR.

Dalwinder Singh and Birmohan Singh. 2020. Investigating the impact of data normalization on classification performance. *Applied Soft Computing*, 97:105524.

Christian Stab and Iryna Gurevych. 2014. Annotating argument components and relations in persuasive essays. In *Proceedings of COLING 2014, the 25th International Conference on Computational Linguistics: Technical Papers*, pages 1501–1510. Dublin City University and Association for Computational Linguistics.

Christian Stab and Iryna Gurevych. 2017. Parsing argumentation structures in persuasive essays. *Computational Linguistics*, 43(3):619–659.

Richard Szeliski. 2022. *Computer Vision: Algorithms and Applications*. Springer Nature Switzerland AG.

Henning Wachsmuth, Khalid Al-Khatib, and Benno Stein. 2016. Using argument mining to assess the argumentation quality of essays. In *Proceedings of COLING 2016, the 26th International Conference on Computational Linguistics: Technical Papers*, pages 1680–1691. The COLING 2016 Organizing Committee.

Henning Wachsmuth, Manfred Stede, Roxanne El Baff, Khalid Al-Khatib, Maria Skeppstedt, and Benno Stein. 2018. Argumentation synthesis following rhetorical strategies. In *Proceedings of the 27th International Conference on Computational Linguistics*, pages 3753–3765. Association for Computational Linguistics.

Thomas Wolf, Lysandre Debut, Victor Sanh, Julien Chaumond, Clement Delangue, Anthony Moi, Pierric Cistac, Tim Rault, Rémi Louf, Morgan Funtowicz, Joe Davison, Sam Shleifer, Patrick von Platen, Clara Ma, Yacine Jernite, Julien Plu, Canwen Xu, Teven Le Scao, Sylvain Gugger, Mariama Drame, Quentin Lhoest, and Alexander M. Rush. 2020. Transformers: State-of-the-art natural language processing. In *Proceedings of the 2020 Conference on Empirical Methods in Natural Language Processing: System Demonstrations*, pages 38–45. Association for Computational Linguistics.

Yiheng Xu, Minghao Li, Lei Cui, Shaohan Huang, Furu Wei, and Ming Zhou. 2020. LayoutLM: Pre-training of text and layout for document image understanding. In *Proceedings of the 26th ACM SIGKDD International Conference on Knowledge Discovery & Data Mining*, pages 1192–1200. Association for Computing Machinery.

A Hyperparameter Fine-tuning

Table 4 outlines the hyperparameters used in the classification models of our submissions.

B Error Analysis: Details

B.1 Sarcasm

We have noticed that some tweets can be infused with sarcasm, such as: *Gov. Ralph 'Coonman' Northam proud to sign a slew of new 'commonsense gun safety measures' that will save lives*

	attempt	abortion classifier(s)	abortion parameters	gun control classifier(s)	gun control parameters
AS	1	AdaBoostClassifier	base_estimator= DecisionTreeClassifier(max_depth=2), n_estimators=150, learning_rate=0.2, algorithm='SAMME'	AdaBoostClassifier	base_estimator= DecisionTreeClassifier(max_depth=2), n_estimators=150, learning_rate=0.3, algorithm='SAMME'
	2	AdaBoostClassifier	base_estimator= DecisionTreeClassifier(max_depth=2), n_estimators=150, learning_rate=0.2, algorithm='SAMME'	XGboost+GradientBoosting	XGB : max_depth=3, learning_rate=0.1, subsample=0.8, colsample_bytree=0.8, reg_alpha=0.1, reg_lambda=0.1 GradientBoosting: learning_rate=0.2, n_estimators=80, random_state=42 Voting:'xgb', 'gb', voting='soft', weights=[3, 1]
	3	AdaBoostClassifier	base_estimator= DecisionTreeClassifier(max_depth=2), n_estimators=150, learning_rate=0.2, algorithm='SAMME'	RUSBoostClassifier	n_estimators=150, random_state=42, learning_rate=0.18, sampling_strategy='not majority'
	4	XGboost+GradientBoosting	XGB : max_depth=2, learning_rate=0.3, subsample=0.8, colsample_bytree=0.8, reg_alpha=0.1, reg_lambda=0.12 GradientBoosting: learning_rate=0.4, n_estimators=80, random_state=42 Voting:'xgb', 'gb', voting='soft', weights=[5, 2]	XGboost+GradientBoosting	XGB : max_depth=2, learning_rate=0.3, subsample=0.8, colsample_bytree=0.8, reg_alpha=0.1, reg_lambda=0.12 GradientBoosting: learning_rate=0.4, n_estimators=80, random_state=42 Voting:'xgb', 'gb', voting='soft', weights=[5, 2]
	5	SVM-Poly	kernel='poly', degree=2, coef0=0.6	SVM-Poly	kernel='poly', degree=2, coef0=0.6
IP	1	SVM-Poly	kernel='poly', degree=2, coef0=0.02, shrinking=False, probability=True	SVM-Poly	kernel='poly', degree=2, coef0=0.02, shrinking=False, probability=True
	2	SGD	alpha=0.0344, random_state=42	SGD	alpha=0.05, random_state=42
	3	SVM-Poly	kernel='poly', random_state=42, coef0=0.17	SVM-Poly	kernel='poly', random_state=42, coef0=0.17
	4	SGD	alpha=0.0344, random_state=42	LogisticRegression	by default
	5	SVM-Poly	kernel='poly', degree=2, coef0=0.25	LogisticRegression	by default

Table 4: Hyperparameters employed for tuning the classification models in the Python implementation.

https://t.co/3toCAPRO1b *via @twitchyteam*[9]. In the test set, this tweet has been labeled as opposing gun control. However, there is no clear evidence that the tweet explicitly expresses a contrary view, as the presence of sarcasm might be a factor to consider in this case given the particular use of quotation marks.

B.2 Specifics of the Gun Control Topic: A Triangular Perspective

The three groups in this triangular arrangement advocate for a gun policy characterized by: (1) absence of guns (opposing gun control), (2) unrestricted use of guns (opposing gun control), and (3) regulated and legally permissible use of guns (supporting gun control). Table 5 shows differences and similarities in opinion among all three groups.

Groups	Similarities in Opinion
1-2	Oppose to regulation of usage and selling guns
1-3	Safety Measures to Protect Lives from Gun Violence
2-3	Existence of guns
Groups	**Differences in Opinion**
1-2	Existence of guns
1-3	Existence of guns
2-3	Stringent Regulations for Gun Control

Table 5: Comparison of the three groups (gun control).

In certain cases, it is not straightforward to associate a sentence or tweet to one of these groups. To illustrate these challenges, we analyze the following tweet from the perspectives of all three groups: *Women are five times more likely to be killed by their abuser if there is a gun present. We can prevent tragedy. We can work together and help people. We need #gunsenselegislators. We need @JoeBiden and @KamalaHarris. #VAWA #DisarmHate #ERPO #OneThingToDo #expectUs @MomsDemand*[10].

Challenges arise in the first sentence: *Women are five times more likely to be killed by their abuser if there is a gun present.* This can be assigned to the first group that fights for the absence of guns. However, it is also conceivable that the argument could be used by the other groups. Group 3, supporters of gun control, accept the existence of guns but argue that without strict laws, the presence of guns can lead to such violence. Group 2, which criticizes gun regulation, may argue that such regulations could create situations in which women, by taking advantage of the law, might provoke abusers to use violence against them. They seem to hold the view that restrictions on gun control can lead to acts of violence.

To determine the true stance of the tweet, we analyze the following sentences. The next two sentences can align with each perspective, supporting their respective stances. The essential sentence in this tweet is as follow: *We need #gunsenselegislators.* This statement can be linked to supportive groups, as the term "gunsense" refers to individuals advocating for gun control. In addition, the tweeter

[9] 1249087853558222850: https://t.co/2KiRh4RAEA

[10] 1296267688310906880: https://t.co/ydP75LeEmQ

mentioned @MomsDemand, which reinforces the same notion (Greene et al., 2022). They are actively involved in promoting stricter gun control regulations and reducing gun violence.

This example demonstrates that the presence of a specific word or phrase can be decisive in indicating the actual stance of a tweet, even when other sentences could be associated with other or all groups. This complexity poses a major challenge for argumentation mining models.

B.3 Ambiguities in Labels

In the subsequent cases, comprehending the motivations behind the assigned stances in the test set proves to be a challenging task:

Abortion Our model has classified the following tweet as supportive, whereas in the gold standard it is labeled as opposing abortion. A closer look reveals, that it is a promotional tweet promoting clinic's abortion pills: *Abortion pills are effective, and you could have your abortion in Bethal with pills anytime at an affordable price. Contact +27727793390.* https://t.co/fj25TRLJB0[11]. This tweet emphasizes women's right to make decisions about their own bodies and, thus, seems to be in line with the positions of groups promoting abortion rights.

The following tweet criticizes the dismantling of abortion rights but has been labeled as opposing abortion, while our model predicts it as supporting abortion: *Overturning Roe v. Wade will not reduce abortions but become a contributing factor in increasing poverty, dismantling Civil Rights, and literally moving the country back decades. @mskathykhang #SCOTUS Sign the #PledgetoPause:* https://t.co/Dtf8a6SSSR[12].

Gun Control Another example of a possible misinterpretation of a tweet in the test set is: *Women are five times more likely to be killed by their abuser if there is a gun present. We can prevent tragedy. We can work together and help people. We need #gunsenselegislators. We need @JoeBiden and @KamalaHarris. #VAWA #DisarmHate #ERPO #OneThingToDo #expectUs @MomsDemand*[13]. While the gold label is oppose, the phrases "gunsenselegislators" and "MomsDemand" refer to actions advocating gun control measures. Our model has classified the aforementioned tweet as supportive of gun control.

Irrelevance to Topic *Vaccines save. Stupidity kills. #antimask #antimaskers #karensgonewild #karenmemes #trump2020 #vaccines #election2020 #prochoice #bidenharris2020 #memes #racism #covid19 #endracism #prolife #wearadamnmask #hoax #trumpvirus*[14]. This tweet refers to the topic of COVID vaccination. Although the tweet is labeled as supporting abortion in the test set (and our model predicted it as opposing abortion), there is no clear indication in the tweet to express support or opposition to abortion.

B.4 Challenging Examples in Image Persuasiveness

As noted in the discussion in subsection 5.2, a broader range of methods are available to convey the attitude of a tweet through images compared to text alone. In the test set, following tweets labeled as not persuasive were predicted as persuasive by our best model:

Abortion: *New year. New opportunities to end abortion. Are you with us? RT if you stand with preborn children. #EndAbortion #ProLife*[15]. The corresponding image mirrors the message "New Year. New opportunities to end abortion" underpinned with the illustration of a smiling pregnant woman to enhance persuasiveness (in our subjective perception).

Gun Control: *Gun stores are not essential businesses during the #COVID19 crisis. Arming the medical community with the equipment they need is. Sign this petition urging The Trump Admin to remove gun stores from that list.*[16]. The corresponding image shows a woman wearing a red shirt with a "MomsDemand" symbol to encourage signing. Again, this can be perceived to strengthen the urge for a petition to remove gun stores from the list of essential businesses during the pandemic.

[11] 1331187788096606208: https://t.co/ZFoAGRje4T
[12] 1022572268147208192: https://t.co/TS6ZNBbR8v
[13] 1296267688310906880: https://t.co/ydP75LeEmQ
[14] 1335685471205289989: https://t.co/UfJ74ayA9S
[15] 1347211895674122245: https://t.co/os3O4lwPa2
[16] 1245045552984674304: https://t.co/05vcbnrH6r

Webis @ ImageArg 2023: Embedding-based Stance and Persuasiveness Classification

Islam Torky[1] **Simon Ruth**[1] **Shashi Sharma**[1] **Mohamed Salama**[1]

Krishna Chaitanya[1] **Tim Gollub** **Johannes Kiesel** **Benno Stein**

Bauhaus-Universität Weimar, Germany

Abstract

This paper reports on the submissions of Webis to the two subtasks of ImageArg 2023. For the subtask of argumentative stance classification, we reached an F1 score of 0.84 using a BERT model for sequence classification. For the subtask of image persuasiveness classification, we reached an F1 score of 0.56 using CLIP embeddings and a neural network model, achieving the best performance for this subtask in the competition. Our analysis reveals that seemingly clear sentences (e.g., "I support gun control") are still problematic for our otherwise competitive stance classifier and that ignoring the tweet text for image persuasiveness prediction leads to a model that is similarly effective to our top-performing model.

1 Introduction

In recent years, the analysis of the argumentative stance of images and texts has gained significant attention. Several shared tasks have been conducted in this area, like the same-side stance classification (Körner et al., 2021) on texts, and the image retrieval for arguments (Bondarenko et al., 2022, 2023) on images. However, especially for images, the task of stance detection is far from being solved (Carnot et al., 2023). The ImageArg 2023 competition then provided a platform for researchers to explore this task further in the multi-modal context of tweets with images. Moreover, the competition featured a second task of predicting whether the image enhanced the persuasiveness of the text.

In this paper, we present the work conducted by our team, "feeds," for the ImageArg 2023 competition. Our efforts led to insightful findings and promising results in both tasks, shedding light on the complexities of combining visual and textual information for argumentative analysis.

For subtask A (argumentative stance classification), we employed a BERT model (Devlin et al., 2019) with stacked Transformer encoders. A separate model was trained for each of the two topics. Training encompassed tokenization, batch processing, optimizer, and learning rate optimization for F1 scores on the validation set. Our approach achieved an F1 score of 0.84 on the test set.

For subtask B (image persuasiveness classification), we employed the CLIP model (Radford et al., 2021) and a linear neural network. We integrated image and text embeddings to have multimodal features fed into the neural network. Tests with separate models and combined models for the two tasks were conducted. When removing the text features, we still get similar performance compared to using both features. Therefore image features seem more decisive for persuasiveness than the text and the multimodality of this task is hard to leverage. We achieved an F1 score of 0.56 on the test set, which is the highest among all submissions.

This paper is structured as follows: Section 2 provides a brief overview of related work. In Section 3, we detail our methodology and approaches for both subtasks. Section 4 presents our results and their implications, while Section 5 discusses the obtained results. Finally, Section 6 concludes the paper, summarizing our contributions and outlining potential directions for future research.

2 Related Work

Argumentative stance detection is still considered a major problem in NLP. Ajjour and Al-Khatib (2021) analyzed several stance classifiers for textual arguments, which achieved an accuracy between 0.50 to 0.77, and identified as challenges an inadequate topic knowledge of classifiers or when arguments only partial agree or disagree. Similarly, Carnot et al. (2023) identified several challenges for detecting the stance expressed in images when analyzing the submissions to the Touché 2022 shared task on image retrieval for argumentation (Bondarenko et al., 2022): bridging the seman-

[1]Authors contributed equally

Proceedings of the 10th Workshop on Argument Mining, pages 157–161
December 7, 2023.

Stance: Support; Persuasiveness: Yes

This has been going on since I was a kid. Guns are too easy to acquire, c'mon already. #shootings #assaultweaponsban #GunControlNow #GunReformNow #GunViolence

Figure 1: Example of tweet from the dataset, showing support for gun control and with the image increasing the persuasiveness of the text (class=yes).

tic gap for diagrams, ambiguity arising from diverse valuations leading to varied interpretations, the dependence of image understanding on background knowledge, regional relevance, the presence of both stances in one image, irony, and more. All of these also apply here, but maybe to a lesser degree as classifiers were trained for each topic. Liu et al. (2022) dealt with multi-modal analysis in persuasiveness classification. They identified an issue that the image encoder could not capture text like slogans in images. They suggested extracting and using textual features from images.

3 Task

We participated in both ImageArg subtasks:

Subtask A: Argumentative Stance Classification. Given a tweet with text and an image, predict if the tweet supports or opposes a topic.

Subtask B: Image Persuasiveness Classification. Given a tweet with text and an image, predict if the image makes the tweet text more persuasive.

For both subtasks, the organizers provide a human-annotated dataset of 2K tweets (Liu et al., 2022).[2] Submissions are evaluated using F1 score. For illustration, Figure 1 shows an example tweet for the gun control topic with associated classes: "support" for subtask A and "yes" for subtask B.

[2]The script for downloading the dataset can be found in the shared task's Git-repository: https://github.com/ImageArg/ImageArg-Shared-Task

4 Our Approach

We employed neural models on text and image embeddings for tackling the tasks. For training, we either trained two *separate* models for the two topics of the dataset ("gun control" and "abortion") to capture topic-specific characteristics, or trained a *combined model* on both topics to capture topic-independent features. We then describe data preprocessing (Section 4.1), and the models used in subtask A (Section 4.2) and B (Section 4.3). Our code is available online.[3]

4.1 Data Preprocessing

For both tasks, we tested cleaning the tweet text data and combined vs. separate models per topic.

For text cleaning, we replaced common abbreviations with their full forms, like changing "I'm" to "I am" and "won't" to "will not." We then used the 'neattext' library[4] to remove URLs, emails, phone numbers, punctuation, and special characters. The text was then converted to lowercase.

In addressing the class imbalance issue, we utilized an oversampling technique. Throughout both subtasks, we inserted random minority class examples until reaching an even distribution.

4.2 Model for Argumentative Stance Classification (Subtask A)

For stance classification, we employ a BERT model for sequence classification[5] to classify the stance based on the tweet text only.

Architecture: Figure 2 shows the employed architecture. We employed the BERT tokenizer[6] for tokenizing tweets. We feed the tokens into a pretrained 12-layer BERT model for sequence classification with 12 attention heads, 110M parameters, and 768 output nodes (CLS-Token pooled from the 768 embeddings per token), with one additional linear layer and softmax-activated classification layer.

Training: The model is trained for 8 epochs on the tweets. Tested optimizers are Adam (Kingma and Ba, 2014), AdamW (Loshchilov and Hutter, 2017), and SGD (Bottou, 2010), with learning rates between $1 \cdot 10^{-5}$ and $3 \cdot 10^{-2}$.

[3]https://github.com/webis-de/argmining23-image-arg

[4]https://github.com/Jcharis/neattext

[5]https://huggingface.co/docs/transformers/model_doc/bert

[6]https://huggingface.co/docs/transformers/model_doc/bert#transformers.BertTokenizer

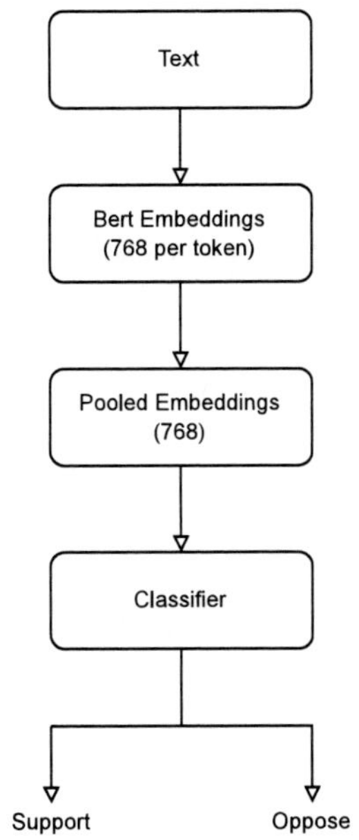

Figure 2: Our architecture for argumentative stance classification: The tweet text is tokenized, embedded through the BERT model, and then classified through a binary classification layer.

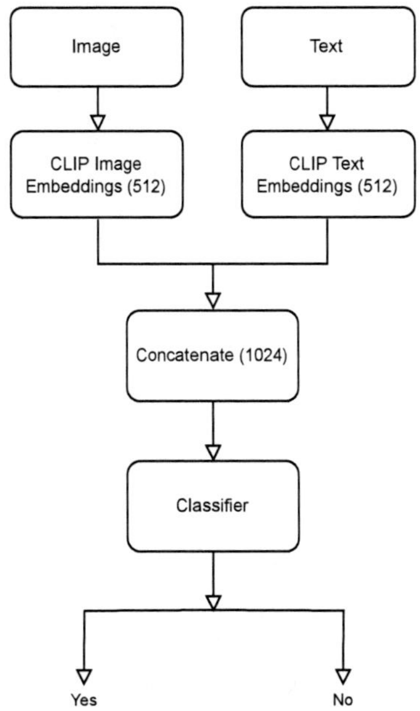

Figure 3: Our architecture for persuasiveness classification: Tweet text and image are tokenized and embedded through the CLIP model. Then features are concatenated and fed to a linear neural network, which predicts persuasiveness probability via a softmax.

Model Selection: We submitted the model with the best F1 score on the validation set, as determined by grid search, to the shared task. Namely, separate models per topic using cleaned data, the Adam optimizer with a learning rate of $3 \cdot 10^{-5}$ for the topic of "gun control", and the SGD optimizer with a learning rate of $3 \cdot 10^{-2}$ for "abortion."

4.3 Model for Image Persuasiveness Classification (Subtask B)

For image persuasiveness classification, we employ concatenated CLIP embeddings (Radford et al., 2021) of images and texts.

Architecture: Figure 3 shows the employed architecture. We used the 512-dimensional embeddings generated by CLIP for each image and text. Since CLIP can only embed texts of up to 77 word-tokens, we split longer tweets into chunks of a maximum of 77 tokens each. These chunks were then individually tokenized and stacked to a tensor to create the necessary input for CLIP's text embedding. The CLIP embeddings for text and image pairs are each represented as tensors of 512 dimensions. These embeddings are then concatenated, first the image embedding followed by the text embedding, creating a unified representation for each tweet that is 1024-dimensional. We fed the concatenated embeddings to a linear neural network, which included subsequent layers leading to a binary softmax classification layer. To investigate the influence of the features, we also tested setting all tweet texts to the empty string.

Training: The model is trained over 10 epochs for both cleaned and uncleaned tweets. We selected 10 epochs as we found that gains decreased afterward in preliminary test runs. For optimizers, we tested the same as for subtask A (Adam, AdamW, and SGD).

Model Selection: We submitted the models with the best F1 score on the validation set, determined by optimizing the learning rate and optimizer. We found that separate models per topic performed best, so we submitted those, both for cleaned and uncleaned data.

5 Results

To analyze our approach, we provide both an overview table (Table 1) and a confusion matrix (Table 2) for both subtasks.[7]

[7] Our train and dev sets have a slightly different distribution of classes compared to the original datasets, related to downloading issues.

Subtask / Model	F1 score		
	Abortion	Gun control	Overall
Subtask A: Argumentative Stance Classification			
Cleaned, separate *[7]	0.91	0.77	0.84
Uncleaned, separate	0.90	0.77	0.83
Cleaned, combined	0.89	0.72	0.81
Subtask B: Image Persuasiveness Classification			
Cleaned, separate *	0.56	0.54	0.56
Uncleaned, separate *	0.53	0.54	0.54
Image-only, separate	0.55	0.49	0.52

Table 1: Achieved best F1 scores for each Subtask on the Test Dataset. A "*" marks the submitted approaches.

A	Prediction	
Truth	Oppose	Support
Oppose	0.49	0.11
Support	0.05	0.35

B	Prediction	
Truth	Yes	No
Yes	0.18	0.14
No	0.17	0.50

Table 2: Confusion matrices for the best-performing models on both subtasks on the test set: Argumentative Stance (A) and Image Persuasiveness Classification (B).

5.1 Results for Argumentative Stance Classification (Subtask A)

As Table 1 indicates, our approach achieves an F1 score of 0.84,[8] highlighting its strong performance in stance classification based on tweet text. This score corresponds to the 3rd place in the competition. The confusion matrix (Table 2) shows that our model performs a bit better on supportive tweets ($0.05/0.40 \approx 0.13$ misclassification rate) than on opposing ones ($0.11/0.60 \approx 0.18$), but this might be an artifact from the specific topics.

Furthermore, we trained separate models on an uncleaned dataset and a combined model using the cleaned dataset that includes both topics. The results are displayed in Table 1. As the table shows, using separate models and cleaning the dataset results in slightly improved results.

5.2 Results for Image Persuasiveness Classification (Subtask B)

As Table 1 indicates, our approach achieves an F1 score of 0.56, reflecting mediocre performance despite winning the competition. From the confusion matrix (Table 2), we can observe that the model's performance is mixed. While it can relatively accurately identify images labelled as not enhancing the persuasiveness ($0.17/0.67 \approx 0.25$ false positive rate), it struggles to correctly identify images labelled as enhancing the persuasiveness ($0.14/0.32 \approx 0.44$ false negative rate). This discrepancy indicates that the model did hardly learn to recognize persuasive elements in the images. However, we assume that more features can improve the performance of our models, for example by identifying infographics or processing text from the images using on-screen character recognition.

Furthermore, we tested a model that did not consider the tweet text at all. As Table 1 shows, this approach performed nearly as good as our full approach (F1 score: 0.52 vs. 0.56), especially for the topic of abortion (F1 score: 0.55 vs. 0.56). As this result highlights, our model does currently barely take advantage of the actual text.

6 Conclusion

We presented the submissions of team "feeds" to the two subtasks of ImageArg 2023 (Liu et al., 2023) and results of further analyses we performed after the submission deadline.

Our approach for argumentative stance classification (subtask A) achieved a commendable F1 score of 0.84, but, as our analysis revealed, it, amongst other issues, struggled with classifying straightforward sentences like "I support gun control" or "I support abortion." Additionally, subtask A's model didn't incorporate image data. Future work could include images, for example using the VisualBERT[9] (Li et al., 2019) model, enabling classification using both text and images.

Our approach for image persuasiveness (subtask B) achieved the first position with an F1 score of 0.56. We observed that the model effectively classifies images that do not enhance persuasiveness, but struggles with identifying images that enhance the text's persuasiveness. This highlights the importance of advanced feature engineering to enhance the model's ability to identify nuanced persuasive elements within images. Moreover, we found that our classifiers perform nearly as good without considering the text at all. This emphasizes the influential role of CLIP image embeddings within the model's decision-making process. Further investigations are needed for understanding which role, if any, features from the tweet text could play in the classification of this task.

[8]Due to a mistake, we submitted predictions for only one topic by the ImageArg 2023 deadline. The values reported here are calculated using the evaluation script and data provided by the organizers after the deadline

[9]https://huggingface.co/docs/transformers/model_doc/visual_bert

Ethics Statement

We utilized the ImageArg dataset (Liu et al., 2023) without making substantial modifications to its content. The dataset was exclusively employed for participation in the ImageArg Shared Task, while adhering to the guidelines of the Twitter Developer Policy and the ACL Ethics Policy. Our primary objective was to perform stance and persuasiveness classification based on the provided text and images. Significantly, our experimental results underscore that our approach is presently unsuitable for product integration. Our primary focus remains on advancing research in this specific task.

References

Yamen Ajjour and Khalid Al-Khatib. 2021. Analysing the submissions to the same side stance classification task. In *Same Side Stance Classification Shared Task 2019*, volume 2921 of *CEUR Workshop Proceedings*.

Alexander Bondarenko, Maik Fröbe, Johannes Kiesel, Ferdinand Schlatt, Valentin Barriere, Brian Ravenet, Léo Hemamou, Simon Luck, Jan Heinrich Reimer, Benno Stein, Martin Potthast, and Matthias Hagen. 2023. Overview of Touché 2023: Argument and Causal Retrieval. In *Experimental IR Meets Multilinguality, Multimodality, and Interaction. 14th International Conference of the CLEF Association (CLEF 2023)*, Lecture Notes in Computer Science, Berlin Heidelberg New York. Springer.

Alexander Bondarenko, Maik Fröbe, Johannes Kiesel, Shahbaz Syed, Timon Gurcke, Meriem Beloucif, Alexander Panchenko, Chris Biemann, Benno Stein, Henning Wachsmuth, Martin Potthast, and Matthias Hagen. 2022. Overview of Touché 2022: Argument Retrieval. In *Experimental IR Meets Multilinguality, Multimodality, and Interaction. 13th International Conference of the CLEF Association (CLEF 2022)*, volume 13390 of *Lecture Notes in Computer Science*, Berlin Heidelberg New York. Springer.

Léon Bottou. 2010. Large-scale machine learning with stochastic gradient descent. *Proceedings of COMPSTAT'2010*, pages 177–186.

Miriam Louise Carnot, Lorenz Heinemann, Jan Braker, Tobias Schreieder, Johannes Kiesel, Maik Fröbe, Martin Potthast, and Benno Stein. 2023. On Stance Detection in Image Retrieval for Argumentation. In *46th International ACM SIGIR Conference on Research and Development in Information Retrieval (SIGIR 2023)*, pages 2562–2571. ACM.

Jacob Devlin, Ming-Wei Chang, Kenton Lee, and Kristina Toutanova. 2019. BERT: Pre-training of deep bidirectional transformers for language understanding. In *Proceedings of the 2019 Conference of the North American Chapter of the Association for Computational Linguistics: Human Language Technologies, Volume 1 (Long and Short Papers)*, pages 4171–4186, Minneapolis, Minnesota. Association for Computational Linguistics.

Diederik P. Kingma and Jimmy Ba. 2014. Adam: A method for stochastic optimization. *arXiv preprint arXiv:1412.6980*.

Erik Körner, Gerhard Heyer, and Martin Potthast. 2021. Same side stance classification using contextualized sentence embeddings. In *Same Side Stance Classification Shared Task 2019*, volume 2921 of *CEUR Workshop Proceedings*.

Liunian Harold Li, Mark Yatskar, Da Yin, Cho-Jui Hsieh, and Kai-Wei Chang. 2019. Visualbert: A simple and performant baseline for vision and language. *arXiv preprint arXiv:1908.03557*.

Zhexiong Liu, Mohamed Elaraby, Yang Zhong, and Diane Litman. 2023. Overview of ImageArg-2023: The first shared task in multimodal argument mining. In *Proceedings of the 10th Workshop on Argument Mining*, Online and in Singapore. Association for Computational Linguistics.

Zhexiong Liu, Meiqi Guo, Yue Dai, and Diane Litman. 2022. ImageArg: A multi-modal tweet dataset for image persuasiveness mining. In *Proceedings of the 9th Workshop on Argument Mining (ARGMINING'22)*, pages 1–18, Online and in Gyeongju, Republic of Korea. International Conference on Computational Linguistics.

Ilya Loshchilov and Frank Hutter. 2017. Decoupled weight decay regularization. *arXiv preprint arXiv:1711.05101*.

Alec Radford, Jong Wook Kim, Chris Hallacy, Aditya Ramesh, Gabriel Goh, Sandhini Agarwal, Girish Sastry, Amanda Askell, Pamela Mishkin, Jack Clark, Gretchen Krueger, and Ilya Sutskever. 2021. Learning transferable visual models from natural language supervision. In *Proceedings of the 38th International Conference on Machine Learning (ICML 2021)*, volume 139 of *Proceedings of Machine Learning Research*, pages 8748–8763. PMLR.

GC-Hunter at ImageArg Shared Task: Multi-Modal Stance and Persuasiveness Learning

Mohammad Shokri
The Graduate Center
City University of New York
mmshokri@gradcenter.cuny.edu

Sarah Ita Levitan
Hunter College
City University of New York
sarah.levitan@hunter.cuny.edu

Abstract

With the rising prominence of social media, users frequently supplement their written content with images. This trend has brought about new challenges in automatic processing of social media messages. In order to fully understand the meaning of a post, it is necessary to capture the relationship between the image and the text. In this work we address the two main objectives of the ImageArg shared task. Firstly, we aim to determine the stance of a multi-modal tweet toward a particular issue. We propose a strong baseline, fine-tuning transformer based models on concatenation of tweet text and image text. The second goal is to predict the impact of an image on the persuasiveness of the text in a multi-modal tweet. To capture the persuasiveness of an image, we train vision and language models on the data and explore other sets of features merged with the model, to enhance prediction power. Ultimately, both of these goals contribute toward the broader aim of understanding multi-modal messages on social media and how images and texts relate to each other.

1 Introduction

Argumentative stance detection is an important problem within the field of natural language processing (NLP). Its primary objective is to discern the underlying position of a text in relation to a specific topic. Accurate identification of a text's stance enhances the performance of several other NLP applications, including text summarizing, information retrieval, fact-checking, and broadly contributes to enhanced understanding of the text. In recent years, the landscape of information dissemination has evolved beyond text, and a growing number of online users express themselves on social media using multi-modal messages. This shift underscores the need for more sophisticated approaches in argumentative stance detection .

The emergence of pre-training models based on transformer architecture (Vaswani et al., 2017) has introduced new horizons for analyzing and understanding text. All areas of natural language processing have been impacted by transformers and the subsequent models derived from them. Although remarkable strides have been made in most uni-modal applications of language processing, researchers are now shifting to multi-modal problems such as vision-language learning. Similar to the uni-modal challenges, large high quality labeled datasets are needed to pre-train the multi-modal models and fine-tune them for the downstream task.

In this work, we use lightweight vision and language learning models to learn joint representations of image-text pairs to capture patterns that help us predict how an image contributes to persuasiveness of a tweet comprised of an image and text. In addition to multi-modal models, we argue that to capture the stance of a tweet toward a given topic, only processing the text modality acts as a strong baseline for any multi-modal learning models. This is because detecting the stance of the text will provide valuable insights into the overall stance of the tweet itself.

The remainder of the paper is organized as follows. We first review previous studies on argument mining and stance detection, as well as vision and language learning in Section 2. Then we introduce the dataset used in this work in Section 3. In Section 4, we detail our experiments and results obtained. Finally, we conclude in Section 5 and summarize the main findings of this work.

2 Related Work

Numerous works have studied the problem of classifying argumentative stance, focusing on developing robust and accurate models for identifying the stance expressed in text. Existing studies have explored a different approaches, such as feature based classification, structure based classification, neural networks and attention based models, and domain specific knowledge and lexicons (Li and

Proceedings of the 10th Workshop on Argument Mining, pages 162–166
December 7, 2023.

Caragea, 2019; Du et al., 2017; Rajadesingan and Liu, 2014; Habernal and Gurevych, 2017).

Earlier studies of argument mining mostly focused on learning the argumentative structure of a text document or classifying different argumentation strategies. Recently, researchers have begun to study persuasiveness-related tasks related to argument mining. Wei et al. (2016) proposed several features to capture persuasiveness in online forums. They argue that online persuasive texts contain an argument strategy that is not common in other genres. In a similar study, researchers created an annotated dataset comprised of argumentative text pairs on the same topics and performed a thorough analysis of how to quantify each argument's persuasiveness (Habernal and Gurevych, 2016). Despite these efforts to develop methods to identify persuasiveness of arguments in text, studying image persuasiveness is a largely unexplored problem.

Multi-modal learning involves joint processing of information from two or more modalities. In recent years, multi-modal learning has gained substantial attention in the machine learning community. Researchers have explored various architectures to effectively fuse information from different modalities. Some successful models use separate embeddings for image and text modalities and then capture the similarities using dot products or attention models (Faghri et al., 2017; Radford et al., 2021). Other models use deeper networks to model the image-text representations (Nguyen et al., 2020). In this work we build on prior studies to explore models and approaches for multi-modal stance detection. We use lightweight neural models for learning joint embeddings of image-text pairs in the data. We also capture similarity scores with more computationally expensive transformer embedders to gain more information about how both modalities interact with the given topic.

3 Dataset

We use the data provided for the ImageArg Shared Task 2023 (Liu et al., 2022, 2023). The data consists of a multi-modal corpus (ImageArg) of tweets on two social topics, *gun control* and *abortion*. The corpus was collected with the aim of studying the persuasiveness of a post that contains both text and an image, and also the argumentative stance of multi-modal tweets towards the topic. They develop schemes to annotate images based on their stance and persuasiveness. While stance detection is an established discipline with many resources, persuasiveness in a multimodal context is an underexplored problem without existing labeled corpora. To annotate the stance of the tweets, tweets are assumed to hold a consistent stance towards the topic in both modalities. The pipeline to annotate persuasiveness is designed in a way that only the tweets that have a clear stance towards the topic are annotated for how persuasive they are. The corpus is divided into train, validation, and test sets. The dataset details are provided in Table 1.

Topic	Train	Validaiton	Test
Abortion	891	100	150
Gun Control	923	100	150

Table 1: ImageArg dataset splits.

The train datasets are slightly imbalanced with regard to persuasiveness labels. Both datasets have more instances where the image is not making the tweet more persuasive. In terms of supporting or opposing the stance however, gun control dataset is quite balanced but in abortion dataset, "oppose" is the dominant class.

Dataset	Support	Oppose	Not Persuasive	Persuasive
Abortion	244	647	613	278
Gun Control	475	448	672	251

Table 2: Counts of labels in train datasets.

4 Experiments

4.1 Sub-task A

The aim of Subtask A of this shared task is to determine if a tweet composed of image and text supports or opposes a given topic, which is a binary classification problem. After carefully examining the data and the challenge, we hypothesized that a transformer based model fine-tuned only on text would be a solid baseline. That is because we expect users to express their attitude toward a topic in the written text and include pictures and graphics that further enhance their argument. We believe it's unlikely that a user would post an image that contradicts the message conveyed through the text. Therefore, we began our experiments by fine-tuning a BERT model (Devlin et al., 2018) on the tweet texts. We trained the model with a linear layer on top of it. We trained the model for ten epochs with a learning rate of $5e-5$, and saved the best model at the end, based on their performance on the validation set. The results of the BERT model, evaluated on both abortion and gun control datasets, are shown in Table 3. As shown in the table, the model performs slightly better on gun control validation data than abortion data. This is possibly due to the more balanced nature of the gun control data. The abortion validation data mostly contains oppose labels. The model's F1 score on the combined test sets was 0.776.

Dataset	Class	Precision	Recall	F1	Support
Abortion	Support	0.92	0.63	0.75	19
	Oppose	0.92	0.99	0.95	81
	Macro Avg	0.92	0.81	0.85	100
	Weighted Avg	0.92	0.92	0.91	100
Gun Control	Support	0.89	0.90	0.91	52
	Oppose	0.90	0.86	0.88	44
	Macro Avg	0.90	0.89	0.89	96
	Weighted Avg	0.90	0.90	0.90	96

Table 3: Bert model fine-tuned on ImageArg validation data (Subtask A).

Next, we aimed to improve the results of our text-only classification. We fine-tuned an XLM-Roberta (Conneau et al., 2019) model on the data, as its pre-trained on a lot more data and its shown to outperform BERT on the GLUE benchmark (Wang et al., 2018). We trained the model for ten epochs with learning rate of $5e-6$, and saved the model with the best performance on the validation set. The scores are depicted in Table 4. This model boosted our scores significantly on both datasets. It also scored higher on the test set with an F1 score of 0.805.

Dataset	Class	Precision	Recall	F1	Support
Abortion	Support	1.00	0.63	0.77	19
	Oppose	0.92	1.00	0.96	81
	Macro Avg	0.96	0.82	0.87	100
	Weighted Avg	0.94	0.93	0.92	100
Gun Control	Support	0.96	0.88	0.92	52
	Oppose	0.88	0.95	0.91	44
	Macro Avg	0.92	0.92	0.92	96
	Weighted Avg	0.92	0.92	0.92	96

Table 4: XLM-Roberta model fine-tuned on ImageArg validation sets (Subtask A).

After training and evaluating our baseline models, we explored using other features which could capture possible helpful information in the data. We hypothesized that if a picture accompanies text in a tweet, it should have high similarity with some aspects of the topic. We gathered text-image similarity scores with VLP (Vision and Language Pre-training) models such as CLIP(Contrastive Language-Image Pre-Training (Radford et al., 2021)). Clip is a neural model developed by OpenAI and its innovation lies in its ability to learn meaningful associations between pairs of image and their corresponding textual description through a contrastive learning approach. However, combining these scores with the logits from our text-only transformer models did not seem to improve the results in neither topics. Our best results were obtained from a random forest classifier trained on the data using ViLT (Vision and Language Transformer) classification logits (Kim et al., 2021), CLIP similarity scores, and text similarity scores between tweet text and image text. The results are depicted in table 5. ViLT has a simple architecture for joining vision-language learning and has an efficient runtime due to its lightweight and convolution-free processing of pixel-level embeddings. Figure 1 shows how a Vilt model differs from other popular multi-modal models.

Dataset	Class	Precision	Recall	F1	Support
Abortion	Support	0.44	0.95	0.60	19
	Oppose	0.98	0.72	0.83	81
	Macro Avg	0.71	0.83	0.71	100
	Weighted Avg	0.88	0.76	0.79	100
Gun Control	Support	0.79	0.85	0.81	52
	Oppose	0.80	0.73	0.76	44
	Macro Avg	0.79	0.79	0.79	96
	Weighted Avg	0.79	0.79	0.79	96

Table 5: Best Random Forest model on trained with ViLT logits, CLIP scores, and text similarity scores (Subtask A).

4.2 Sub-task B

The goal of Subtask B is to predict whether an image makes the tweet text more persuasive or not. For instance, an image that is not related to the topic will not improve the persuasiveness of the tweet. In our initial analysis of the data, we observed that many pictures have some text written in them. Therefore, for our baseline submission to Subtask B, we began by using Python's EasyOCR[1] framework with the default recognition models to extract the texts in the images. We hypothesized that if the image contributed to the persuasiveness of the post, the image text should have high similarity scores to the tweet text. We then concatenated the image text with the tweet text, using a <SEP> token to separate them for the model input.

We trained a ViLT(Vision and Language Transformer) model on our data. We trained the model

[1]`https://github.com/JaidedAI/EasyOCR.git`

separately for the two topics to maximize performance per topic. We experimented with training the Vilt on each dataset for 8 epochs and validating on the validation set. We used an Adam optimizer with a learning rate of $5e-5$. The results of our best model on the datasets are depicted in Table 6. It is clear from the results in the table that the model tends to learn better when an image does not make the tweet more persuasive. This is possibly due to the fact that it is the dominant class in the training set (Table 2).

Dataset	Class	Precision	Recall	F1	Support
Abortion	No	0.79	0.89	0.84	74
	Yes	0.50	0.31	0.38	26
	Macro Avg	0.64	0.60	0.61	100
	Weighted Avg	0.71	0.74	0.72	100
Gun Control	No	0.88	0.68	0.77	65
	Yes	0.54	0.81	0.65	31
	Macro Avg	0.71	0.74	0.71	96
	Weighted Avg	0.77	0.72	0.73	96

Table 6: Trained ViLT model performance on validation sets.

We also trained additional models with other features. For example, we ran a CLIP model on our data. The CLIP model only expects 77 tokens as text, which is the default value of the model and larger values are not supported by the model. Therefore, we passed the first 77 tokens of the text into the model and retrieved the similarity scores between the image and the tweet text. We then concatenated the image-text similarity scores with our previously extracted tweet text-image text similarity scores and passed them to a one-layered neural network along with the last hidden states of the ViLT model. We aimed to capture all the similarities among the text pairs and image-text pairs in the data. However, this model did not perform as well as our baseline on the validation set, so we did not submit it for the final evaluation.

We also trained another variation of the CLIP model on the data but passed only the context ("gun control" or "abortion") instead of the first 77 tokens of the tweet. We tested training another one-layered neural network with only the CLIP similarity scores and also merged it with the tweet text-image text similarity scores. Neither experiment outperformed our baseline scores on validation and test set. Our results on the test sets are shown in Table 7.

5 Conclusions

In this paper, we presented a strong model for multi-modal stance detection towards a given topic.

Topic	Precision	Recall	F1
Abortion	0.33	0.27	0.29
Gun Control	0.46	0.49	0.47

Table 7: Topic-wise results of our model on the test set.

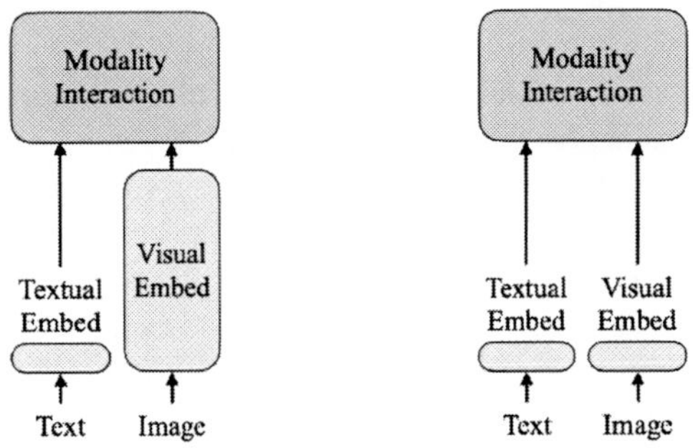

Figure 1: A ViLT model is shown on the right side, highlighting that it has fewer computations for extracting visual embeddings. It is compared with most vision language learning models that usually have an architecture more similar to the graph on the left. Figure taken from (Kim et al., 2021)

Our text-only fine-tuned models outperformed half of the participant teams, suggesting that that fine-tuning a transformer-based model only on tweet text could be a strong baseline for learning stance in multi-modal posts. To examine how an image contributes to persuasiveness of a tweet, we experimented with image-text similarity scores from a CLIP model, along with the similarity between any text in the image and the tweet text. We also extracted similarity scores between the image and the topic as another feature. Although this set of features did not produce the best results, future work could further explore these features and different ways of modeling them for improved performance.

Limitations

A limitation of our work, particularly for Subtask A, is that we did not fully explore multi-modal features. Because our text-only results outperformed our other experiments with image embeddings, we focused on those and did not explore further to extract helpful information from the image-text interaction. It is possible that a deeper exploration of both image and text modalities would yield better performance because it leverages the multimodal nature of the dataset.

Ethics Statement

This work has potential benefits that come along with potential risks. Social media platforms could benefit from a system that could perfectly detect the stance of posts towards sensitive topics that may affect the community's safety and well being, and possibly warn users or take action aligned with the guidelines of the platform. However, a system's failure to accurately identify stances or persuasive intent could inadvertently suppress genuine discourse by flagging legitimate viewpoints as misleading or manipulative, thus undermining freedom of expression. It is important for such models and systems to be interpretable and explainable so that decisions are not made based on black box systems.

References

Alexis Conneau, Kartikay Khandelwal, Naman Goyal, Vishrav Chaudhary, Guillaume Wenzek, Francisco Guzmán, Edouard Grave, Myle Ott, Luke Zettlemoyer, and Veselin Stoyanov. 2019. Unsupervised cross-lingual representation learning at scale. *CoRR*, abs/1911.02116.

Jacob Devlin, Ming-Wei Chang, Kenton Lee, and Kristina Toutanova. 2018. Bert: Pre-training of deep bidirectional transformers for language understanding. *arXiv preprint arXiv:1810.04805*.

Jiachen Du, Ruifeng Xu, Yulan He, and Lin Gui. 2017. Stance classification with target-specific neural attention networks. International Joint Conferences on Artificial Intelligence.

Fartash Faghri, David J Fleet, Jamie Ryan Kiros, and Sanja Fidler. 2017. Vse++: Improving visual-semantic embeddings with hard negatives. *arXiv preprint arXiv:1707.05612*.

Ivan Habernal and Iryna Gurevych. 2016. Which argument is more convincing? analyzing and predicting convincingness of web arguments using bidirectional lstm. In *Proceedings of the 54th Annual Meeting of the Association for Computational Linguistics (Volume 1: Long Papers)*, pages 1589–1599.

Ivan Habernal and Iryna Gurevych. 2017. Argumentation mining in user-generated web discourse. *Computational Linguistics*, 43(1):125–179.

Wonjae Kim, Bokyung Son, and Ildoo Kim. 2021. Vilt: Vision-and-language transformer without convolution or region supervision. In *International Conference on Machine Learning*, pages 5583–5594. PMLR.

Yingjie Li and Cornelia Caragea. 2019. Multi-task stance detection with sentiment and stance lexicons. In *Proceedings of the 2019 conference on empirical methods in natural language processing and the 9th international joint conference on natural language processing (EMNLP-IJCNLP)*, pages 6299–6305.

Zhexiong Liu, Mohamed Elaraby, Yang Zhong, and Diane Litman. 2023. Overview of ImageArg-2023: The first shared task in multimodal argument mining. In *Proceedings of the 10th Workshop on Argument Mining*, Online and in Singapore. Association for Computational Linguistics.

Zhexiong Liu, Meiqi Guo, Yue Dai, and Diane Litman. 2022. Imagearg: A multi-modal tweet dataset for image persuasiveness mining. *arXiv preprint arXiv:2209.06416*.

Duy-Kien Nguyen, Vedanuj Goswami, and Xinlei Chen. 2020. Movie: Revisiting modulated convolutions for visual counting and beyond. *arXiv preprint arXiv:2004.11883*.

Alec Radford, Jong Wook Kim, Chris Hallacy, Aditya Ramesh, Gabriel Goh, Sandhini Agarwal, Girish Sastry, Amanda Askell, Pamela Mishkin, Jack Clark, et al. 2021. Learning transferable visual models from natural language supervision. In *International conference on machine learning*, pages 8748–8763. PMLR.

Ashwin Rajadesingan and Huan Liu. 2014. Identifying users with opposing opinions in twitter debates. In *Social Computing, Behavioral-Cultural Modeling and Prediction: 7th International Conference, SBP 2014, Washington, DC, USA, April 1-4, 2014. Proceedings 7*, pages 153–160. Springer.

Ashish Vaswani, Noam Shazeer, Niki Parmar, Jakob Uszkoreit, Llion Jones, Aidan N Gomez, Łukasz Kaiser, and Illia Polosukhin. 2017. Attention is all you need. *Advances in neural information processing systems*, 30.

Alex Wang, Amanpreet Singh, Julian Michael, Felix Hill, Omer Levy, and Samuel R Bowman. 2018. Glue: A multi-task benchmark and analysis platform for natural language understanding. *arXiv preprint arXiv:1804.07461*.

Zhongyu Wei, Yang Liu, and Yi Li. 2016. Is this post persuasive? ranking argumentative comments in online forum. In *Proceedings of the 54th Annual Meeting of the Association for Computational Linguistics (Volume 2: Short Papers)*, pages 195–200.

Argumentative Stance Prediction: An Exploratory Study on Multimodality and Few-Shot Learning

Arushi Sharma*, **Abhibha Gupta***, **Maneesh Bilalpur***
School of Computing and Information
University of Pittsburgh
{arushi.sharma, abg96, mab623}@pitt.edu

Abstract

To advance argumentative stance prediction as a multimodal problem, the *First Shared Task in Multimodal Argument Mining* hosted stance prediction in crucial social topics of gun control and abortion. Our exploratory study attempts to evaluate the necessity of images for stance prediction in tweets and compare out-of-the-box text-based large-language models (LLM) in few-shot settings against fine-tuned unimodal and multimodal models. Our work suggests an ensemble of fine-tuned text-based language models (0.817 F1-score) outperforms both the multimodal (0.677 F1-score) and text-based few-shot prediction using a recent state-of-the-art LLM (0.550 F1-score). In addition to the differences in performance, our findings suggest that the multimodal models tend to perform better when image content is summarized as natural language over their native pixel structure and, using in-context examples improves few-shot performance of LLMs.

1 Introduction

Argumentative stance studies related to ideological topics offer valuable insights into complex dynamics of opinion, belief and discourse in various domains. These insights have far-reaching implications, extending their influence over areas including public opinion, social dynamics, and policy efficacy. By predicting the stance in real-time, policymakers and stakeholders can get immediate feedback on public reaction to new proposals or laws, allowing them to make timely and informed decisions.

Argumentative stance prediction is becoming a major endeavor in multiple research fields as the reliance on sentiment detection may be sub-optimal (Reveilhac and Schneider, 2023). While the stance prediction task appears similar to sentiment analysis, it has many theoretical differences. Sentimental analysis primarily focuses on emotions, whereas the stance prediction need not necessarily coincide with the sentiment directed towards the target. Stance prediction for sensitive and polarizing topics can be more challenging, particularly within the brief context of informal social media text (Alturayeif et al., 2023).

Previous studies have primarily concentrated on examining stance prediction in textual modalities (Alturayeif et al., 2023; Hosseinia et al., 2020). However, an increasing number of recent works are widening the focus to include other modalities, such as images. Since multimodality helps us understand language from the modalities of text, vision and acoustic, (Zadeh et al., 2018), the application of multimodal inputs in argumentative stance prediction seems promising.

Towards the perpetuation of multimodality in argumentative stance prediction as a part of the ImgArg 2023 (Liu et al., 2023) challenge, we explore the following questions using a dataset of tweets on gun control and abortion topics:

1. How well does language as a stand-alone modality perform at argumentative stance prediction?
2. Does incorporating image information improve prediction performance?
3. How do Large-Language Models (LLMs) in few-shot setting compare against fine-tuned unimodal and multimodal models?

Our work shows that an ensemble of fine-tuned language models performs the best for argumentative stance prediction from tweets. Incorporating image information into text using state-of-the-art multimodal models does not outperform the ensemble model. LLMs (particularly, LLaMA-2) in few-shot setting exhibit high recall but suffer from low precision. Though using in-context examples

* Equal contribution

Proceedings of the 10th Workshop on Argument Mining, pages 167–174
December 7, 2023.

in few-shot setting improves performance, they underperform the ensemble model.

2 Related Work

Existing work has explored the interplay between stance and sentiment to enhance stance detection. (Sobhani, 2017) investigated the relationship between stance and sentiment, utilizing SVM with N-gram, word embedding, and sentiment lexicon features. They concluded that while sentiment features offer utility, they are insufficient on their own for effective stance detection. Meanwhile, (Hosseinia et al., 2020) showcased the prowess of bidirectional transformers in achieving competitive performance without fine-tuning, harnessing sentiment and emotion lexicons. Their findings show the efficacy of sentiment information, as opposed to emotion, in discerning the stance.

(Alturayeif et al., 2023) conducted an extensive analysis of 96 primary studies spanning eight machine learning techniques for stance detection and its applications. The analysis suggests that deep learning models with self-attention mechanisms were found to be frequently outperforming the traditional machine learning models such as SVM, and emerging techniques like few-shot learning and multitask learning were increasingly applied for stance detection.

Multimodal stance detection is being increasingly used for social applications such as rumor verification (Zhang et al., 2021) and identifying public attitudes towards climate change on Twitter (Upadhyaya et al., 2023). Despite recent advancements in multimodal language models (Wang et al., 2023), the use of image modality for stance detection remains an underexplored area. Our work conducts an exploratory study to investigate the necessity of multimodal models for stance detection and compares different ways to incorporate image information into text modality.

3 Dataset and Task

The ImgArg dataset (Liu et al., 2022) is a part of the *Multimodal Argument Mining* (Liu et al., 2023) competition. Curated with the goal of expanding argumentation mining into multimodal realm, the dataset consists of Twitter texts along with their images from two topics–gun control and abortion. Each text-image pair corresponding to a tweet are annotated with a stance (support or oppose) along with its persuasiveness (no persuasiveness to extremely persuasive). In this paper, we focus on the stance prediction task. Briefly, the task can be described as given an image-text pair corresponding to a tweet, predict if it supports or opposes the topic.

It is important to note that while the gun control dataset is balanced, the abortion dataset is imbalanced by a 1:3 support:oppose stance ratio. The gun control and abortion training sets are 920[1] and 891 tweets respectively. Both datasets have an equal number of tweets in the validation (100 tweets) and test (150 tweets) sets.

4 Approach

To predict argumentative stance over multimodal tweets from gun control and abortion topics, we leverage three different ideas. We explore an ensemble of LLMs against its constituent models, incorporate image information through multimodal models as well as evaluate out-of-the-box LLMs in few-shot setting. This section describes the experimental approaches used in the process. Further details can be found in the appendix.

4.1 Ensemble Stance Prediction

Individual language models have demonstrated their superior performance across a variety of tasks. However, ensemble methods tend to perform better (Jiang et al., 2023) than their constituent models. To explore this idea, we evaluated text-based language models such as XLNet (Yang et al., 2019), XLM-RoBERTa (Conneau et al., 2019), Transformer XL (Dai et al., 2019), DeBERTa-v2 (He et al., 2020), BLOOM-560M (Scao et al., 2022). Since the dataset is a collection of tweets, conventional problems such as very long sequence length were non-existent.

Ensemble decisions were based on the weighted sum of constituent model predictions. Each model prediction was weighted by its F1-score on the validation set in order to assign a higher weight to the model that performed better on the validation set. This weighted sum is then thresholded by the F1-score averaged across models for final prediction. In our study, XLNet and BLOOM-560M received the predominant weights for attaining the highest F1 score on abortion and gun-control datasets respectively.

[1]The organizers reported 923 tweets, however, three tweets were dropped because of download issues.

4.2 Multimodal Stance Prediction

To evaluate the utility of image augmentation to text and the possible ways to achieve this, we studied models from different frameworks. The ViLT (Kim et al., 2021) is a popular vision-language transformer model with reduced computational overhead because of its convolution-free architecture. FLAVA (Singh et al., 2022), a multimodal model built to generalize to both vision tasks and language tasks. Both models were fine-tuned over the gun control and abortion datasets for the support stance prediction task.

Recent vision-language pre-trained models such as instructBLIP (Dai et al., 2023) have demonstrated solving image-centric tasks through natural language. We leverage this instruction-based summarization of image content with instructBLIP. Specifically, we summarize each image using the *briefly describe the content of the image* instruction. The resulting textual descriptions of images along with their corresponding tweets were used for stance prediction by fine-tuning a RoBERTa (Liu et al., 2019) classifier followed by early fusion. We refer to this configuration (Figure 1) as the multimodal RoBERTa.

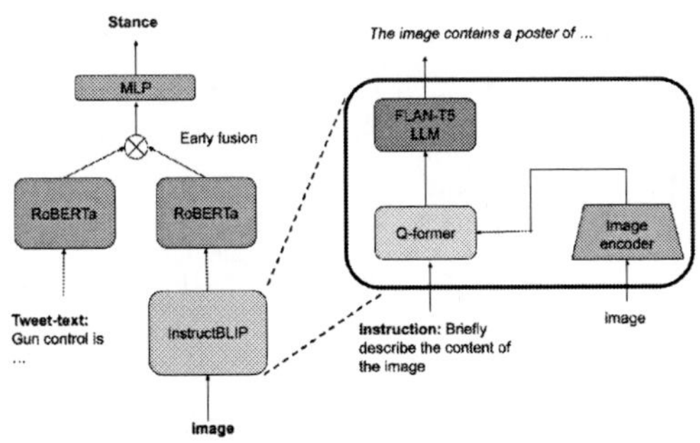

Figure 1: Multimodal RoBERTa configuration. The figure shows the input image summarized as text through instructBLIP and then used to fine-tune the RoBERTa model together with the tweet-text. Shared color between RoBERTa models indicates tied weights.

4.3 Few-Shot Stance Prediction using LLMs

Few-shot prediction typically involves using relevant examples during training to learn a new concept that was not included in pretraining. It has been a success not just in conventional language-based tasks but also in multimodal tasks (Luo et al., 2020). The large and diverse pre-training corpora used in training the foundation models is attributed as one of the reasons for their success in learning with a limited resources paradigm. Using LLaMA-2 (Touvron et al., 2023), we performed stance prediction in few-shot setting. LLaMA-2 was chosen because of its open-source implementation that outperforms commercial large-scale GPT-3 (Brown et al., 2020) with fast inference.

Choice of few-shot examples: Arguments can be made from different viewpoints or themes. For example, gun control can be referred to from ordinary themes such as the constitutionally granted *right to bear arms, governmental overreach* to targeted themes or experiences such as *school shootings*. We believe that the ImgArg dataset encompasses these diverse themes and wish to leverage the in-context examples that correspond to the same theme for few-shot experiments. We identify the themes in the training set using k-means clustering and pick examples from the same theme cluster during inference. Performance on the validation set was used as a benchmark to identify 12 clusters for the gun control dataset and 13 clusters for the abortion dataset. The manually identified cluster themes are presented as Table 8 in the Appendix A.

4.4 Experimental Setup

The imbalance in the abortion dataset is addressed using a weighted cross-entropy loss. Increased weightage was allocated to the minority category loss. The models were trained using HuggingFace (Wolf et al., 2020) on two A100 NVIDIA GPU environment[2]. Hyperparameters (learning rate, scheduler and weight decay) were optimized for the validation set and performance is reported as precision, recall and F1-score for the support stance and oppose on the test set. More experimental details are shown in Appendix A section.

5 Results

5.1 Support Stance

Table 1 compares the support class performance of individual language models against their ensemble model. The ensemble model used BLOOM-560M as it performed better than its larger counterpart on the validation set. The constituent models typically have a better recall but low precision, the ensemble model improves precision with a limited drop in the recall. Best performance was observed with the

[2]The code is available at: https://github.com/arushi-08/EMNLP-ImageArgTask-PittPixelPersuaders

Model	Precision	Recall	F1
XLNet	0.619	0.924	0.741
BLOOM-1B	0.760	0.660	0.710
BLOOM-560M	0.707	0.898	0.791
Transformer-XL	0.571	0.881	0.693
DeBERTa-v2	0.560	0.710	0.630
XLM-RoBERTa	0.650	0.880	0.750
Ensemble	**0.743**	**0.906**	**0.817**

Table 1: *Support* stance performance using text-based transformer models.

ensemble of unimodal language models with 0.817 F1-score.

Model	Precision	Recall	F1
ViLT	0.680	0.432	0.528
FLAVA	0.570	0.650	0.610
Multimodal RoBERTa	**0.531**	**0.932**	**0.677**

Table 2: *Support* stance performance using image-text multimodal transformer models.

Multimodal RoBERTa and FLAVA sacrificed precision for recall (shown in Table 2) upon fine-tuning. Both multimodal RoBERTa and FLAVA that leverage images in pixel-space achieve a recall of 0.932 and 0.650 respectively. However, their low precision (0.531 and 0.570 respectively) under-performs the ViLT model. Summarizing images to fine-tune smaller language models tends to result in improved recall albeit at the cost of precision. This approach achieves the highest among the multimodal models with an F1-score of 0.677.

Model	Precision	Recall	F1
Baseline (*support* only)	0.395	1.000	0.566
zero-shot	0.440	0.290	0.350
four-shot	0.420	0.640	0.500
four-shot w/ k-means	**0.450**	**0.700**	**0.550**

Table 3: *Support* stance performance using LLaMA-2 based few-shot experiments.

We compare our few-shot experiments with the baseline *support* only stance predictions to observe that both zero-shot and four-shot models underperform the baseline. The best performance is demonstrated using the four-shot model with k-means clustering. Clustering was found to improve the recall by 6% while precision has improved by 3%. F1-score has improved by 5% to 0.550. Few-shot LLaMA-2 underperforms the ensemble model at stance prediction.

Model	Precision	Recall	F1
ViLT	0.701	0.867	0.775
FLAVA	0.750	0.690	0.720
Multimodal RoBERTa	0.913	0.464	0.615

Table 5: *Oppose* stance performance using image-text multimodal transformer models.

5.2 Oppose Stance

Table 4 shows that the language models have higher precision than recall for the oppose class as compared to the support class (Table 1). Higher precision and lower recall shows us that the text-based language models prioritize predicting the support stance (minority class). Moreover, the ensemble approach outperforms other language models even on the oppose stance. For the multimodal models, both the ViLT and FLAVA models demonstrated superior performance for the oppose class (shown in Table 5) compared to the support class (shown in Table 2). However, the multimodal RoBERTa model follows similar pattern as text-based language models, in terms of scoring high on recall for support class vs oppose class. For LLaMa-2 experiments, The F1 scores for the support class (Table 3) across all methods are consistently higher compared to the oppose class (Table 6). This suggests that LLaMa-2 is more adept at discerning patterns associated with the support class than those of the oppose class.

Model	Precision	Recall	F1
XLNet	0.927	0.630	0.750
Bloom-1B	0.790	0.870	0.830
Bloom-560M	0.919	0.757	0.770
Transformer-XL	0.880	0.569	0.691
DeBERTa-v2	0.770	0.640	0.700
XLM-RoBERTa	0.691	0.899	0.781
Ensemble	**0.929**	**0.796**	**0.857**

Table 4: *Oppose* stance performance using text-based transformer models.

Model	Precision	Recall	F1
Baseline (*Oppose* only)	0.605	1.000	0.754
zero-shot	0.690	0.060	0.110
four-shot	0.770	0.300	0.430
four-shot w/ k-means	0.740	0.270	0.400

Table 6: *Oppose* stance performance using LLaMA-2 based few-shot experiments.

6 Discussion

Popular pre-trained language models such as XLNet, BLOOM, Transformer-XL, DeBERTa-v2 and XLM-RoBERTa were fine-tuned for stance prediction on tweets about gun control and abortion. Results demonstrate that the ensemble of these models performs better than any of the constituent models. However, the disparity is limited. XLNet achieves better recall than the ensemble model and similarly, the BLOOM-560M underperforms the ensemble by 0.026 (though precision of the ensemble is higher by 0.036). This raises the trade-off question between ensemble performance vs. the large computational requirement justified for marginal improvement in the performance.

The best performing multimodal model used the image content summarized as text, unlike its counterpart models that operate in pixel space. We believe the diversity of the images contributes to this difference. In addition to typical images containing people and objects such as guns, trucks and so on, the training set also contained propaganda-related material such as posters with statements. While vision-language models are increasingly getting better at object-centric tasks, understanding such material is closely related to problems such as optical character recognition, which are not often explored in pretraining vision-language models. Our instruction-based image summarization suggests that when explicitly prompted, vision-language models excel not just at object-centric descriptions of images but also at recognizing text from images. Attempts were made to incorporate demographic factors such as number of people in the image, their skin color and gender. However, manual inspection revealed that the resultant instructBLIP predictions were not reliable. Despite augmenting language modality with images in different ways, text-based models outperformed the multimodal models.

Out-of-the-box LLaMA-2 underperforms the baseline *support* only prediction model. However, prompting through four-shot examples greatly improves the performance. This is further enhanced by using in-context examples. This demonstrates that in-context examples that potentially share similar theme (not necessarily the stance) tend to capture the stance better than arbitrary examples from the dataset. The themes were found to include discussions along mental health, effects on children, racism, illegal acquisition, etc. for the gun control dataset; Supreme Court, birth control, religion, reproductive rights, etc. for the abortion dataset.

7 Conclusions and Future Work

Our investigation questions the necessity of images to predict stance in multimodal tweets through different ways of using image-based information in conjunction with text-based language models and investigating the inherent capabilities of LLMs for stance prediction. Results suggest that the best performance can be achieved using an ensemble of language models. Our experiments with multimodal models do not completely refute the utility of images for stance prediction, rather they merely evaluate the current state-of-the-art multimodal models. Incorporating domain knowledge (Lewis et al., 2021), and alternative prompting methods like Question Decomposition (Radhakrishnan et al., 2023) and Tree-of-Thought (Yao et al., 2023) which provide the rationale for the prediction in addition to the stance provide a future direction to address the limited performance with LLaMA-2.

References

Nora Alturayeif, Hamzah Luqman, and Moataz Ahmed. 2023. A systematic review of machine learning techniques for stance detection and its applications. *Neural Computing and Applications*, 35(7):5113–5144.

Tom B. Brown, Benjamin Mann, Nick Ryder, Melanie Subbiah, Jared Kaplan, Prafulla Dhariwal, Arvind Neelakantan, Pranav Shyam, Girish Sastry, Amanda Askell, Sandhini Agarwal, Ariel Herbert-Voss, Gretchen Krueger, Tom Henighan, Rewon Child, Aditya Ramesh, Daniel M. Ziegler, Jeffrey Wu, Clemens Winter, Christopher Hesse, Mark Chen, Eric Sigler, Mateusz Litwin, Scott Gray, Benjamin Chess, Jack Clark, Christopher Berner, Sam McCandlish, Alec Radford, Ilya Sutskever, and Dario Amodei. 2020. Language models are few-shot learners.

Alexis Conneau, Kartikay Khandelwal, Naman Goyal, Vishrav Chaudhary, Guillaume Wenzek, Francisco Guzmán, Edouard Grave, Myle Ott, Luke Zettlemoyer, and Veselin Stoyanov. 2019. Unsupervised cross-lingual representation learning at scale. *arXiv preprint arXiv:1911.02116*.

Wenliang Dai, Junnan Li, Dongxu Li, Anthony Meng Huat Tiong, Junqi Zhao, Weisheng Wang, Boyang Li, Pascale Fung, and Steven Hoi. 2023. Instructblip: Towards general-purpose vision-language models with instruction tuning.

Zihang Dai, Zhilin Yang, Yiming Yang, Jaime Carbonell, Quoc V Le, and Ruslan Salakhutdinov.

2019. Transformer-xl: Attentive language models beyond a fixed-length context. *arXiv preprint arXiv:1901.02860*.

Pengcheng He, Xiaodong Liu, Jianfeng Gao, and Weizhu Chen. 2020. Deberta: Decoding-enhanced bert with disentangled attention. *arXiv preprint arXiv:2006.03654*.

Marjan Hosseinia, Eduard Dragut, and Arjun Mukherjee. 2020. Stance prediction for contemporary issues: Data and experiments. *arXiv preprint arXiv:2006.00052*.

Dongfu Jiang, Xiang Ren, and Bill Yuchen Lin. 2023. Llm-blender: Ensembling large language models with pairwise ranking and generative fusion. *arXiv preprint arXiv:2306.02561*.

Wonjae Kim, Bokyung Son, and Ildoo Kim. 2021. Vilt: Vision-and-language transformer without convolution or region supervision. In *International Conference on Machine Learning*, pages 5583–5594. PMLR.

Patrick Lewis, Ethan Perez, Aleksandra Piktus, Fabio Petroni, Vladimir Karpukhin, Naman Goyal, Heinrich Küttler, Mike Lewis, Wen tau Yih, Tim Rocktäschel, Sebastian Riedel, and Douwe Kiela. 2021. Retrieval-augmented generation for knowledge-intensive nlp tasks.

Yinhan Liu, Myle Ott, Naman Goyal, Jingfei Du, Mandar Joshi, Danqi Chen, Omer Levy, Mike Lewis, Luke Zettlemoyer, and Veselin Stoyanov. 2019. Roberta: A robustly optimized bert pretraining approach.

Zhexiong Liu, Mohamed Elaraby, Yang Zhong, and Diane Litman. 2023. Overview of ImageArg-2023: The first shared task in multimodal argument mining. In *Proceedings of the 10th Workshop on Argument Mining*, Online and in Singapore. Association for Computational Linguistics.

Zhexiong Liu, Meiqi Guo, Yue Dai, and Diane Litman. 2022. Imagearg: A multi-modal tweet dataset for image persuasiveness mining. *arXiv preprint arXiv:2209.06416*.

Ilya Loshchilov and Frank Hutter. 2017. Fixing weight decay regularization in adam. *CoRR*, abs/1711.05101.

Huaishao Luo, Lei Ji, Botian Shi, Haoyang Huang, Nan Duan, Tianrui Li, Jason Li, Taroon Bharti, and Ming Zhou. 2020. Univl: A unified video and language pre-training model for multimodal understanding and generation. *arXiv preprint arXiv:2002.06353*.

Ansh Radhakrishnan, Karina Nguyen, Anna Chen, Carol Chen, Carson Denison, Danny Hernandez, Esin Durmus, Evan Hubinger, Jackson Kernion, Kamilė Lukošiūtė, Newton Cheng, Nicholas Joseph, Nicholas Schiefer, Oliver Rausch, Sam McCandlish, Sheer El Showk, Tamera Lanham, Tim Maxwell, Venkatesa Chandrasekaran, Zac Hatfield-Dodds, Jared Kaplan, Jan Brauner, Samuel R. Bowman, and Ethan Perez. 2023. Question decomposition improves the faithfulness of model-generated reasoning.

Maud Reveilhac and Gerold Schneider. 2023. Replicable semi-supervised approaches to state-of-the-art stance detection of tweets. *Information Processing & Management*, 60(2):103199.

Teven Le Scao, Angela Fan, Christopher Akiki, Ellie Pavlick, Suzana Ilić, Daniel Hesslow, Roman Castagné, Alexandra Sasha Luccioni, François Yvon, Matthias Gallé, et al. 2022. Bloom: A 176b-parameter open-access multilingual language model. *arXiv preprint arXiv:2211.05100*.

Amanpreet Singh, Ronghang Hu, Vedanuj Goswami, Guillaume Couairon, Wojciech Galuba, Marcus Rohrbach, and Douwe Kiela. 2022. Flava: A foundational language and vision alignment model. In *Proceedings of the IEEE/CVF Conference on Computer Vision and Pattern Recognition*, pages 15638–15650.

Parinaz Sobhani. 2017. *Stance detection and analysis in social media*. Ph.D. thesis, Universite d'Ottawa/University of Ottawa.

Thomas Wolf Philipp Schmid Zachary Mueller Sourab Mangrulkar Marc Sun Benjamin Bossan Sylvain Gugger, Lysandre Debut. 2022. Accelerate: Training and inference at scale made simple, efficient and adaptable. `https://github.com/huggingface/accelerate`.

Robert L. Thorndike. 1953. Who belongs in the family? *Psychometrika*, 18:267–276.

Hugo Touvron, Thibaut Lavril, Gautier Izacard, Xavier Martinet, Marie-Anne Lachaux, Timothée Lacroix, Baptiste Rozière, Naman Goyal, Eric Hambro, Faisal Azhar, Aurelien Rodriguez, Armand Joulin, Edouard Grave, and Guillaume Lample. 2023. Llama: Open and efficient foundation language models.

Apoorva Upadhyaya, Marco Fisichella, and Wolfgang Nejdl. 2023. A multi-task model for emotion and offensive aided stance detection of climate change tweets. *Proceedings of the ACM Web Conference 2023*.

Xiao Wang, Guangyao Chen, Guangwu Qian, Pengcheng Gao, Xiaoyong Wei, Yaowei Wang, Yonghong Tian, and Wen Gao. 2023. Large-scale multi-modal pre-trained models: A comprehensive survey. *Machine Intelligence Research*, 20:447 – 482.

Thomas Wolf, Lysandre Debut, Victor Sanh, Julien Chaumond, Clement Delangue, Anthony Moi, Pierric Cistac, Tim Rault, Rémi Louf, Morgan Funtowicz, Joe Davison, Sam Shleifer, Patrick von Platen, Clara Ma, Yacine Jernite, Julien Plu, Canwen Xu, Teven Le Scao, Sylvain Gugger, Mariama Drame, Quentin Lhoest, and Alexander M. Rush. 2020. Huggingface's transformers: State-of-the-art natural language processing.

Zhilin Yang, Zihang Dai, Yiming Yang, Jaime Carbonell, Russ R Salakhutdinov, and Quoc V Le. 2019. Xlnet: Generalized autoregressive pretraining for language understanding. *Advances in neural information processing systems*, 32.

Shunyu Yao, Dian Yu, Jeffrey Zhao, Izhak Shafran, Thomas L. Griffiths, Yuan Cao, and Karthik Narasimhan. 2023. Tree of thoughts: Deliberate problem solving with large language models.

Amir Zadeh, Paul Pu Liang, Louis-Philippe Morency, Soujanya Poria, Erik Cambria, and Stefan Scherer. 2018. Proceedings of grand challenge and workshop on human multimodal language (challenge-hml). In *Proceedings of Grand Challenge and Workshop on Human Multimodal Language (Challenge-HML)*.

Huaiwen Zhang, Shengsheng Qian, Quan Fang, and Changsheng Xu. 2021. Multi-modal meta multi-task learning for social media rumor detection. *IEEE Transactions on Multimedia*, 24:1449–1459.

A Appendix

This appendix provides details such as the number of parameters in the final classification, hyperparameters and finetuning approach for various models[3] in this work. All models used the Adam (Loshchilov and Hutter, 2017) optimizer.

Model	Size of classification head
XLNet	1024
Bloom-1B	64
Bloom-560M	64
Transformer-XL	1024
DeBERTa-v2	1536
XLM-RoBERTa	768
Multimodal RoBERTa (MLP)	1536
FLAVA	768
ViLT	768

Table 7: Table showing the size of the final classification layer for various models used in this work.

A.1 Ensemble Stance Prediction Model

We employed various pretrained language models, specifically XLNet[4], BLOOM-560M[5], Transformer-XL[6], DeBERTa-v2[7], and XLM-RoBeRTa[8]. Each model was augmented with a classification head for binary sequence classification tasks. The summary of the size of the classification head for each model is provided in Table 7. We utilized Adam optimizer with a learning rate of 1e-3. A learning rate scheduler was also incorporated into the training regimen with a patience of 3. To mitigate the risk of model overfitting, a weight decay parameter was set at 0.01. All models were trained for 10 epochs.

A.2 Multimodal Stance Prediction Model

For the multimodal RoBERTa [9], the learning rate was configured at 5e-2, and the weight decay parameter was set at 0.01 during the fine-tuning process. The training continued until the validation loss ceased to decrease for five consecutive epochs. Figure 1 presented the visualization of the Multimodal RoBERTa. For the ViLT[10] model, a low learning of 2.25e-6 was found to be optimal. The model underwent training for a total of 10 epochs. In the case of the FLAVA[11] model, an early stopping mechanism was implemented, resulting model was trained for six epochs prior to any increase in validation loss. The learning rate for this model was set at 5e-5.

A.3 Few-shot Stance Prediction Model

In this study, we employed the Hugging Face's LLaMa-2 13B[12] model for inference, leveraging the capabilities of Hugging Face Accelerate (Sylvain Gugger, 2022). The experimental design utilized Langchain[13] to formulate a tripartite template for prompt engineering. The template is segmented into three distinct components: The system prompt, which serves as a generic instructional scaffold for the language model, a set of few-shot examples to guide the model's responses, and the test set tweet that the model is tasked to analyze. While the standard convention of using no examples for zero-shot and sampling four arbitrary examples for four-shot prediction was used, in the four-shot with k-means, the training set is initially partitioned into clusters using the k-means algorithm (12 clusters for gun control and 13 for abortion). For each test example, its corresponding cluster is predicted, and four examples are randomly sampled from the clus-

[3]code used in this work would be made available after the review process to preserve the anonymity of the authors

[4]https://huggingface.co/xlnet-base-cased

[5]https://huggingface.co/bigscience/bloom-560m

[6]https://huggingface.co/transfo-xl-wt103

[7]https://huggingface.co/microsoft/deberta-v2-xlarge

[8]https://huggingface.co/facebook/xlm-roberta-xl

[9]https://huggingface.co/roberta-base

[10]https://huggingface.co/docs/transformers/model$_{d}oc/vilt$

[11]https://huggingface.co/facebook/flava-full

[12]https://huggingface.co/meta-llama/Llama-2-13b-hf

[13]https://github.com/langchain-ai/langchain

Gun control	Abortion
Gun violence as a mental health problem	Natural Law Right to Life
Effects of gun violence on children	Abortion is evil
Pro-gun control politicians	Supreme Court and abortion
Racism and gun control	Abortion is murder
Trump and guns	Birth control pills
Illegal acquisition of guns	Pro-life
Supreme Court and gun control	Religion and motherhood
Second amendment right	Reproductive rights of women
	#savethebabyhumans hashtag
	Roe v. Wade abortion case

Table 8: Themes identified using k-means clustering for few-shot examples in gun control and abortion datasets.Same theme(s) captured by multiple clusters resulted in fewer themes than reported clusters.

ter as few-shot examples. The optimal number of clusters was ascertained using the Elbow Method (Thorndike, 1953). Table 8 presents some prominent themes found using k-means clustering in gun control and abortion datasets. For LLM output generation, the temperature parameter was set to zero, and the 'top_k' parameter was configured at 30. We employed a Multinomial sampling strategy, setting the do_sample = True and num_beams parameter to 1. An exemplar of the prompt template employed is depicted in Figure 2.

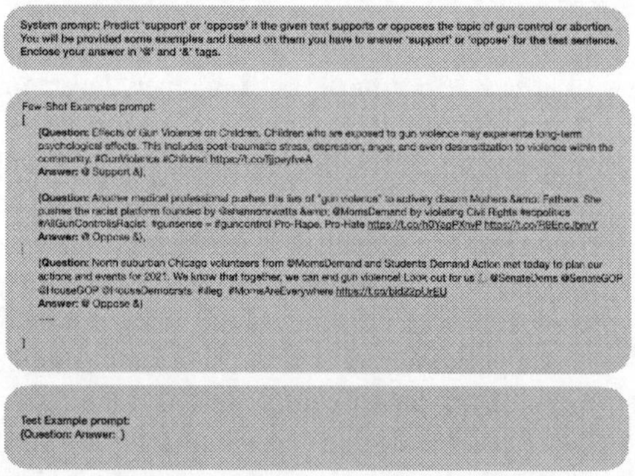

Figure 2: The provided illustration depicts a k-means few-shot prompt template employed in our experimental investigations conducted on the gun control dataset. A comparable configuration was also applied when examining the abortion dataset. For conciseness, we have omitted the inclusion of all four examples in this presentation.

SPLIT: Stance and Persuasion Prediction with Multi-modal on Image and Textual Information

Jing Zhang[1], Shaojun Yu [1], Xuan Li [2], Jia Geng[3], Zhiyuan Zheng[4], Joyce C Ho[1]
[1] Emory University [2] Carnegie Mellon University
[3] University of Miami [4] American Cancer Society
{jing.zhang2, shaojun.yu, joyce.c.ho}@emory.edu
xuanli1@andrew.cmu.edu jxg570@miami.edu jason.zheng@cancer.org

Abstract

Persuasiveness is a prominent personality trait that measures the extent to which a speaker can impact the beliefs, attitudes, intentions, motivations, and actions of their audience. The ImageArg task is a featured challenge at the 10th ArgMining Workshop during EMNLP 2023, focusing on harnessing the potential of the ImageArg dataset to advance techniques in multimodal persuasion. In this study, we investigate the utilization of dual-modality datasets and evaluate three distinct multi-modality models. By enhancing multi-modality datasets, we demonstrate both the advantages and constraints of cutting-edge models.

1 Introduction

Persuasion encompasses the art of one party endeavoring to influence another's thoughts, beliefs, or actions, and it stands as a fundamental and versatile human capability. Its significance goes far beyond the realms of business and politics, permeating numerous facets of our everyday existence. In the fast-changing realm of natural language processing (NLP) and artificial intelligence (AI), there has been a notable increase in enthusiasm for creating techniques and datasets to enhance and assess persuasiveness in natural language applications (Hunter et al., 2019; Chatterjee and Agrawal, 2006; Liu et al., 2022). The capacity to convince, sway, and captivate using language has long been a fundamental element of human communication, and with the emergence of advanced language technologies, the pursuit of leveraging persuasive capabilities in digital interactions has gained remarkable momentum. In today's digital age, the proliferation of social media platforms has ushered in a new frontier for the practice of persuasion. These platforms serve as fertile ground, affording both organizations and individuals the opportunity to engage in activities that extend beyond mere persuasion and can include disinformation campaigns.

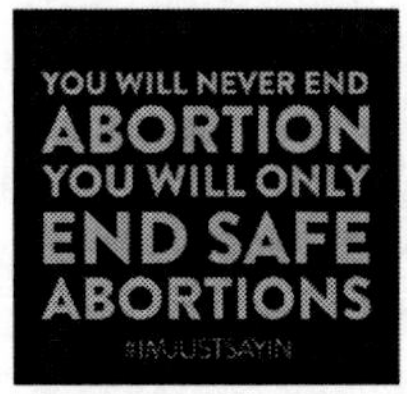

Which will only cause more harm to both the woman and the precious fetus you want to save but won't take care of. thank you for proving once again u r pro/forced birthers; hate women. #mybodymychoice #abortion #prochoice #prolife #hypocrites #childfree #abortionlaw #AbortionBan

Stance: Support
Pervasiveness: Yes

Figure 1: The abortion tweet picture (left) and its tweets (right) from Liu et al. (2023).

The pervasive reach and influence of social media amplify the potential impact of persuasive efforts, making it imperative for individuals and society as a whole to exercise discernment and critical thinking in navigating this dynamic landscape.

Most of current works in argumentation mining solely focus on textual format, such as the argumentation dialogues (Hunter et al., 2019), contextual advertising (Wen et al., 2022), and other works (Lukin et al., 2017; Persing and Ng, 2017). In their work, Nojavanasghari et al. (2016) introduced a comprehensive deep multimodal fusion approach to predict persuasiveness, incorporating three modalities: Visual, Acoustic, and Text. Nevertheless, in light of the current trend observed on Twitter, as depicted in Figure 1, it becomes evident that numerous images accompanied by text are surfacing. Mere application of computer vision (CV) techniques for object recognition proves inadequate for addressing this challenge. Liu et al. (2022) designed two tasks based on the tweets, Stance detection and Persuasion prediction. Stance detection (SD) involves the automated task of ascertaining, based on textual content, whether the author expresses a supportive, opposing, or neutral position regarding a particular proposition or subject. This subject can encompass individuals, organizations, government policies, movements, products, and more. As an illustration, considering the tweet and accompanying image in Figure 1, it is evident that the stance conveyed is one of support. Persuasion prediction (PP) determines the degree of

Proceedings of the 10th Workshop on Argument Mining, pages 175–180
December 7, 2023.

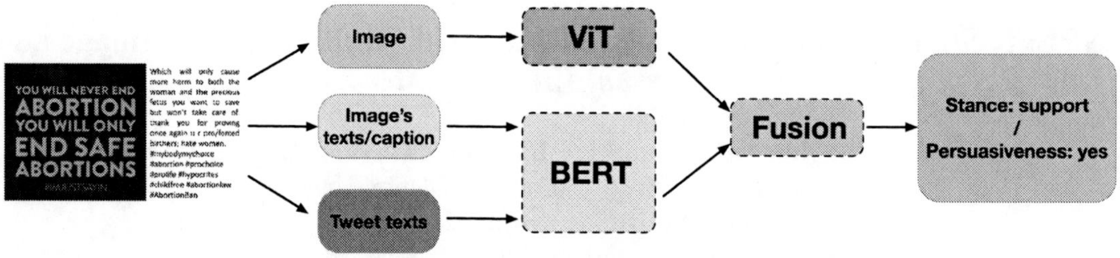

Figure 2: The overview of SPLIT framework.

persuasiveness or the potential impact that a given tweet may have on its readers or the broader audience. Given the unique characteristics of the existing Twitter data, this paper will design additional feature extraction methods, such as using Optical Character Recognition (OCR) to extract text from images, in order to enrich the feature space. This will enable a more comprehensive analysis of the stance and persuasion in the current tweets. Our code is publicly available in GitHub (`https://github.com/JZCS2018/ACT-CS`). In summary, our contributions are as follows:

- We combine current state-of-the-art (SOTA) CV and NLP models as SPLIT, to utilize the image and textual information for the SD and PP tasks.
- We align the individual tweet's text, image, and its textual information (texts in image and generated image caption), and utilize different fusion methods to show the detailed analysis.

2 Related Works

Persuasiveness Prediction Persuasiveness prediction is an under-explored topic but has attracted growing interests(Chatterjee et al., 2014; Park et al., 2016; Lukin et al., 2017; Carlile et al., 2018; Chakrabarty et al., 2020). As the majority of works (Higgins and Walker, 2012; Lukin et al., 2017; Persing and Ng, 2017; Carlile et al., 2018) utilized textual inputs - such as audience variable, report, and student essays - to analyze persuasion strategies, (Joo et al., 2014; Huang and Kovashka, 2016) pioneered the study of in persuasion in social media with visual information, including facial expression, body gesture and human portrait. Finally, Hussain et al. (2017); Guo et al. (2021) investigated sentiment, intent reasoning and persuasive strategies in advertisement context in multi-modal learning. However, a persuasive-targeted and multi-modal framework is still missing in the current NLP literatures.

Multi-modal learning Thanks to the progress in language models and alignment techniques, multi-modal learning with text and image have recently received significant attention in the CV and NLP communities. As the majority of SOTA works are built upon transformersand and its variants, different alignment strategies have been proposed and applied to fuse representations from each modality. On the one hand, many works (Radford et al., 2021; Neelakantan et al., 2022) employ modality-specific encoders and apply contrastive loss to align representations. The encoders (Dosovitskiy et al., 2020; Devlin et al., 2018) are usually pretrained to learn visual and textual representations independently and kept frozen during alignment. On the other hand, many recent works (Bao et al., 2022; Li et al., 2023a; Zhang et al., 2023; Sun et al., 2023; Koh et al., 2023) have tokenized visual representations and grounded them to unifed language model for multimodal tasks. Specifically, the visual and textual tokens are concatenated as input to the pre-trained language model, and then are aligned through various tasks such as next token prediction. However, multi-modal learning on stance and persuassive prediction are under-explored, partially due to a lack of multi-modal corpora and persuasive-specific modeling framework.

3 Approach

Let D be a tweet dataset, where each tweet d_i is represented as a tuple (I_i, T_i). I_i represents the image associated with the tweet and T_i represents the textual content of the tweet. A model f that maps the input tuples (I_i, T_i) to a predicted stance score or persuasiveness score $\hat{y}_i$, where $\hat{y}_i \in [0, 1]$. In addition, we will also extract the text in the image It_i, and generate its caption C_i as an optional feature. Then the representation of the tweet can be shown as the new tuple $(I_i, T_i, It_i/C_i)$. The framework is illustrated in Figure 2.

3.1 OCR & image captioning

Due to the limited amount of training data available, we believe that incorporating other pretrained models will significantly enhance the performance of our model. Therefore, we have incorporated two types of pretrained models in our approach: BLIP-large (Li et al., 2022), an image captioning model for generating textual descriptions, and Microsoft's TrOCR(Li et al., 2023b), an optical character recognition (OCR) model for extracting text from images. BLIP-large has been pre-trained on a vast dataset and is capable of generating textual descriptions for images. By utilizing this model, we aim to improve the understanding and contextual description of the images in our dataset. Additionally, some images contain text that is crucial to comprehend the image but the text cannot be effectively represented solely through captions especially for longer texts. To address this, we employ the OCR model to extract text from these images.

For each image I_i, we use BLIP-large model to generate the caption C_i and use TrOCR to extract the text It_i. These two features are then directly fed into our backbone model.

3.2 Backbone Models

As the fields of CV and natural NLP continue to advance, we aim to integrate SOTA models from both domains for our tasks.

The Vision Transformer (ViT) (Dosovitskiy et al., 2020) is designed for CV tasks, and it offers several compelling benefits for the image processing. Its ability to extract intricate visual patterns and characteristics from images has demonstrated remarkable effectiveness. It can seamlessly integrate with other models, especially the BERT (Devlin et al., 2018) for text, enabling the creation of powerful multi-modal models.

BERT is pre-trained on vast amounts of text data and has a deep understanding of contextual language usage. This makes it highly effective in capturing nuanced language patterns and context within tweets, which is crucial for analyzing persuasiveness.

The self-attention mechanisms in ViT and BERT models could provide insights into which parts of the image/text the model focuses on when making predictions. This interpretability can be valuable for understanding how the model assesses the stance and persuasiveness.

3.3 Fusion Methods

Multimodal fusion methods are techniques used to combine and integrate information from multiple modalities (e.g., text, images, audio) into a unified representation for analysis or decision-making (Gao et al., 2020). It can be categorised into early fusion, late fusion and intermediate fusion. Early fusion, also known as feature-level fusion, involves combining features from different modalities at the input level. For example, in text-image fusion, the features extracted from text and images are concatenated or merged before being fed into a model. This approach creates a single feature vector that represents both modalities. Late fusion, involves processing each modality separately and then combining their results at a later stage. Cross-attention was introduced in Transformers model (Vaswani et al., 2017). It often employs attention mechanisms to enable a model to selectively attend to relevant parts of one modality based on the information from another modality. This paper will apply the three methods to our experiments.

4 Experiments

We designed the experiments to answer two key questions: (1) How *accurate* is SPLIT in automating the entity matching? (2) How *important* are the different components of SPLIT?

4.1 Datasets

The benchmark dataset used in this study is sourced from the ImageArg-Shared-Task-2023, as described in Liu et al. (2023). This dataset encompasses two specific topics: abortion and gun control. In the abortion dataset, there are 891 training samples, 100 validation samples, and 150 test samples. Similarly, the gun control dataset comprises 923 training samples, 100 validation samples, and 150 test samples. For each topic, we will experiment on stance and persuasiveness prediction tasks.

4.2 Baseline models

We utilize the pretained ViT and BERT-based-uncased models for our experiments. To ensure a fair comparison, we standardize the dimensionality of both image and text embeddings to 1024 before inputting them into the classification layers. We evaluate task performance across three modalities: Image Modality (I-ViT), Text Modality (T-BERT),

Datasets	Tasks	I-ViT	T-BERT	SPLIT-IT-E	SPLIT-IT-L	SPLIT-IT	SPLIT-IET	SPLIT-IECT
Total	Stance	0.4279	0.4738	0.5863	0.6098	0.6116	0.6178	**0.6325**
	Persuasiveness	0.3968	0.3906	**0.5000**	0.4076	0.3125	0.4348	0.4432
Abortion	Stance	0.3609	0.3975	0.4337	0.4429	0.4595	0.4494	**0.4638**
	Persuasiveness	0.5438	0.4751	**0.605**	0.5982	0.3333	0.4950	0.4510
Gun control	Stance	0.4782	0.5315	0.6627	0.6689	0.6786	0.7059	**0.7030**
	Persuasiveness	0.2192	0.2908	0.3529	0.3017	0.2895	0.3614	**0.4337**

Table 1: Comparison of F1 performance for different models. The best performance is bolded.

and Multi-modality combining both text and image information. For last part, we try different configurations, such as Image + Text + Early fusion (SPLIT-IT-E), Image + Text + Late fusion (SPLIT-IT-L), Image + Text + Cross-attention (SPLIT-IT) Image + Text-extraction + Text + Cross-attention (SPLIT-IET), and Image + Text-extraction + Image-caption + Text + Cross-attention (SPLIT-IECT).

We train all models on a single NVIDIA Tesla V100 GPU with 16GB VRAM. We fix the batch size at 32 and use the Adam optimizer to train the models for 20 epochs using a linearly decaying learning rate with one epoch warmup. A learning rate sweep is done over the range [1e-5, 3e-5, 5e-5, 8e-5. 1e-4]. We also apply the early stopping strategy for the efficiency.

5 Results

5.1 Predictive Performance on Different Tasks

The Table 1 shows the results from different models on different datasets and tasks. The total datasets means we only consider the tasks instead of topics for the evaluation. For the "Stance" task in the "Total" dataset, "SPLIT-IECT" achieves the highest F1 score of 0.6325, making it the best-performing model. Among single-modality models, T-BERT outperforms I-ViT, indicating that text holds a more significant role in this Stance task. When considering the outcomes of multi-modal models, it becomes evident that incorporating text information extracted from images has a positive impact on model performance. In the context of the "Persuasiveness" task, "SPLIT-IT-E" emerges as the top-performing model, achieving an F1 score of 0.5000. Despite observing improved performance with the incorporation of additional features, it appears that the inclusion of textual information does not significantly contribute to enhancing the decision-making process. This also can be observed in the comparison between I-ViT and T-BERT.

5.2 Predictive Performance on Different Topics

In the "Abortion" topic, "SPLIT-IECT" again performs the best for the "Stance" task with an F1 score of 0.4638. However, for the "Persuasiveness" task, "SPLIT-IT-E" has the highest F1 score of 0.605. The textual content within the images is evidently more pivotal in aiding the decision-making process. Furthermore, the outcomes in the Persuasiveness task align consistently with those observed in the overall dataset for the same task.

In the context of the "Gun control" topic, "SPLIT-IECT" takes the lead in the "Stance" task, achieving an F1 score of 0.7030. Similarly, in the "Persuasiveness" task within the same topic, "SPLIT-IECT" maintains its superior performance with an F1 score of 0.4337. Notably, the results in this particular topic differ from those observed in other topics. It appears that the images within the Gun control dataset contain more valuable textual information compared to those in the Abortion dataset."

Finally, when examining fusion techniques, it becomes evident that cross-attention mechanisms can offer more potent insights for predicting outcomes.

6 Conclusion

In light of the recent advancements in persuasiveness and stance prediction research, this study combines state-of-the-art computer vision (CV) and natural language processing (NLP) models under the name SPLIT, and explores various fusion approaches. The findings indicate that the cross-attention mechanism outperforms other methods. In the future, we will focus on how to visualize and interpret the predictions from the model, which could provide more comprehensive analysis to the researchers.

Acknowledgements. This work was supported by the National Science Foundation award IIS-2145411.

References

Hangbo Bao, Wenhui Wang, Li Dong, Qiang Liu, Owais Khan Mohammed, Kriti Aggarwal, Subhojit Som, Songhao Piao, and Furu Wei. 2022. Vlmo: Unified vision-language pre-training with mixture-of-modality-experts. *Advances in Neural Information Processing Systems*, 35:32897–32912.

Winston Carlile, Nishant Gurrapadi, Zixuan Ke, and Vincent Ng. 2018. Give me more feedback: Annotating argument persuasiveness and related attributes in student essays. In *Proceedings of the 56th Annual Meeting of the Association for Computational Linguistics (Volume 1: Long Papers)*, pages 621–631.

Tuhin Chakrabarty, Christopher Hidey, Smaranda Muresan, Kathy McKeown, and Alyssa Hwang. 2020. Ampersand: Argument mining for persuasive online discussions. *arXiv preprint arXiv:2004.14677*.

Moitreya Chatterjee, Sunghyun Park, Han Suk Shim, Kenji Sagae, and Louis-Philippe Morency. 2014. Verbal behaviors and persuasiveness in online multimedia content. In *Proceedings of the Second Workshop on Natural Language Processing for Social Media (SocialNLP)*, pages 50–58.

Niladri Chatterjee and Saumya Agrawal. 2006. Word alignment in english-hindi parallel corpus using recency-vector approach: some studies. In *Proceedings of the 21st International Conference on Computational Linguistics and 44th Annual Meeting of the Association for Computational Linguistics*, pages 649–656.

Jacob Devlin, Ming-Wei Chang, Kenton Lee, and Kristina Toutanova. 2018. Bert: Pre-training of deep bidirectional transformers for language understanding. *arXiv preprint arXiv:1810.04805*.

Alexey Dosovitskiy, Lucas Beyer, Alexander Kolesnikov, Dirk Weissenborn, Xiaohua Zhai, Thomas Unterthiner, Mostafa Dehghani, Matthias Minderer, Georg Heigold, Sylvain Gelly, et al. 2020. An image is worth 16x16 words: Transformers for image recognition at scale. *arXiv preprint arXiv:2010.11929*.

Jing Gao, Peng Li, Zhikui Chen, and Jianing Zhang. 2020. A survey on deep learning for multimodal data fusion. *Neural Computation*, 32(5):829–864.

Meiqi Guo, Rebecca Hwa, and Adriana Kovashka. 2021. Detecting persuasive atypicality by modeling contextual compatibility. In *Proceedings of the IEEE/CVF International Conference on Computer Vision*, pages 972–982.

Colin Higgins and Robyn Walker. 2012. Ethos, logos, pathos: Strategies of persuasion in social/environmental reports. In *Accounting forum*, volume 36, pages 194–208. Elsevier.

Xinyue Huang and Adriana Kovashka. 2016. Inferring visual persuasion via body language, setting, and deep features. In *Proceedings of the IEEE Conference on Computer Vision and Pattern Recognition Workshops*, pages 73–79.

Anthony Hunter, Lisa Chalaguine, Tomasz Czernuszenko, Emmanuel Hadoux, and Sylwia Polberg. 2019. Towards computational persuasion via natural language argumentation dialogues. In *KI 2019: Advances in Artificial Intelligence: 42nd German Conference on AI, Kassel, Germany, September 23–26, 2019, Proceedings 42*, pages 18–33. Springer.

Zaeem Hussain, Mingda Zhang, Xiaozhong Zhang, Keren Ye, Christopher Thomas, Zuha Agha, Nathan Ong, and Adriana Kovashka. 2017. Automatic understanding of image and video advertisements. In *Proceedings of the IEEE conference on computer vision and pattern recognition*, pages 1705–1715.

Jungseock Joo, Weixin Li, Francis F Steen, and Song-Chun Zhu. 2014. Visual persuasion: Inferring communicative intents of images. In *Proceedings of the IEEE conference on computer vision and pattern recognition*, pages 216–223.

Jing Yu Koh, Ruslan Salakhutdinov, and Daniel Fried. 2023. Grounding language models to images for multimodal inputs and outputs. *ICML*.

Junnan Li, Dongxu Li, Silvio Savarese, and Steven Hoi. 2023a. Blip-2: Bootstrapping language-image pre-training with frozen image encoders and large language models. *arXiv preprint arXiv:2301.12597*.

Junnan Li, Dongxu Li, Caiming Xiong, and Steven Hoi. 2022. Blip: Bootstrapping language-image pre-training for unified vision-language understanding and generation. In *International Conference on Machine Learning*, pages 12888–12900. PMLR.

Minghao Li, Tengchao Lv, Jingye Chen, Lei Cui, Yijuan Lu, Dinei Florencio, Cha Zhang, Zhoujun Li, and Furu Wei. 2023b. Trocr: Transformer-based optical character recognition with pre-trained models. In *Proceedings of the AAAI Conference on Artificial Intelligence*, volume 37, pages 13094–13102.

Zhexiong Liu, Mohamed Elaraby, Yang Zhong, and Diane Litman. 2023. Overview of ImageArg-2023: The first shared task in multimodal argument mining. In *Proceedings of the 10th Workshop on Argument Mining*, Online and in Singapore. Association for Computational Linguistics.

Zhexiong Liu, Meiqi Guo, Yue Dai, and Diane Litman. 2022. ImageArg: A multi-modal tweet dataset for image persuasiveness mining. In *Proceedings of the 9th Workshop on Argument Mining*, pages 1–18, Online and in Gyeongju, Republic of Korea. International Conference on Computational Linguistics.

Stephanie M Lukin, Pranav Anand, Marilyn Walker, and Steve Whittaker. 2017. Argument strength is in the eye of the beholder: Audience effects in persuasion. *arXiv preprint arXiv:1708.09085*.

Arvind Neelakantan, Tao Xu, Raul Puri, Alec Radford, Jesse Michael Han, Jerry Tworek, Qiming Yuan, Nikolas Tezak, Jong Wook Kim, Chris Hallacy, et al. 2022. Text and code embeddings by contrastive pretraining. *arXiv preprint arXiv:2201.10005*.

Behnaz Nojavanasghari, Deepak Gopinath, Jayanth Koushik, Tadas Baltrušaitis, and Louis-Philippe Morency. 2016. Deep multimodal fusion for persuasiveness prediction. In *Proceedings of the 18th ACM International Conference on Multimodal Interaction*, pages 284–288.

Sunghyun Park, Han Suk Shim, Moitreya Chatterjee, Kenji Sagae, and Louis-Philippe Morency. 2016. Multimodal analysis and prediction of persuasiveness in online social multimedia. *ACM Transactions on Interactive Intelligent Systems (TiiS)*, 6(3):1–25.

Isaac Persing and Vincent Ng. 2017. Why can't you convince me? modeling weaknesses in unpersuasive arguments. In *IJCAI*, pages 4082–4088.

Alec Radford, Jong Wook Kim, Chris Hallacy, Aditya Ramesh, Gabriel Goh, Sandhini Agarwal, Girish Sastry, Amanda Askell, Pamela Mishkin, Jack Clark, et al. 2021. Learning transferable visual models from natural language supervision. In *International conference on machine learning*, pages 8748–8763. PMLR.

Quan Sun, Qiying Yu, Yufeng Cui, Fan Zhang, Xiaosong Zhang, Yueze Wang, Hongcheng Gao, Jingjing Liu, Tiejun Huang, and Xinlong Wang. 2023. Generative pretraining in multimodality. *arXiv preprint arXiv:2307.05222*.

Ashish Vaswani, Noam Shazeer, Niki Parmar, Jakob Uszkoreit, Llion Jones, Aidan N Gomez, Łukasz Kaiser, and Illia Polosukhin. 2017. Attention is all you need. *Advances in neural information processing systems*, 30.

Taylor Jing Wen, Ching-Hua Chuan, Jing Yang, and Wanhsiu Sunny Tsai. 2022. Predicting advertising persuasiveness: A decision tree method for understanding emotional (in) congruence of ad placement on youtube. *Journal of Current Issues & Research in Advertising*, 43(2):200–218.

Yiyuan Zhang, Kaixiong Gong, Kaipeng Zhang, Hongsheng Li, Yu Qiao, Wanli Ouyang, and Xiangyu Yue. 2023. Meta-transformer: A unified framework for multimodal learning. *arXiv preprint arXiv:2307.10802*.

Semantists at ImageArg-2023: Exploring Cross-modal Contrastive and Ensemble Models for Multimodal Stance and Persuasiveness Classification

Rajaraman Kanagasabai[1], Saravanan Rajamanickam[1], Hariram Veeramani[2], Adam Westerski[1], and Kim Jung Jae[1]

[1]Agency for Science, Technology and Research (A*STAR)
Institute for Infocomm Research, Singapore,
[2]University of California Los Angeles (UCLA), USA
[1]{kanagasa,saravananr,adam-westerski,jjkim}@i2r.a-star.edu.sg
[2]hariram@ucla.edu

Abstract

In this paper, we describe our system for ImageArg-2023 Shared Task that aims to identify an image's stance towards a tweet and determine its persuasiveness score concerning a specific topic. In particular, the Shared Task proposes two subtasks viz. subtask (A) Multimodal Argument Stance (AS) Classification, and subtask (B) Multimodal Image Persuasiveness (IP) Classification, using a dataset composed of tweets (images and text) from controversial topics, namely gun control and abortion. For subtask A, we employ multiple transformer models using a text based approach to classify the argumentative stance of the tweet. For sub task B we adopted text based as well as multimodal learning methods to classify image persuasiveness of the tweet. Surprisingly, the text-based approach of the tweet overall performed better than the multimodal approaches considered. In summary, our best system achieved a F1 score of 0.85 for sub task (A) and 0.50 for subtask (B), and ranked 2nd in subtask (A) and 4th in subtask (B), among all teams submissions.

1 Introduction

Persuasiveness mining is an important task within Argument Mining(Green, 2014; Stede et al., 2019), that is aimed at detecting and analyzing the ability to influence one's beliefs, attitude, intentions, motivation, and behavior (Lawrence and Reed, 2019). It has gained increased attention recently (Carlile et al., 2018; Chakrabarty et al., 2020) though most of the research focused on texts.

Persuasion, however, may depend not only on natural language but on other modalities (eg. visual means) as well. ImageArg is an initiative that attempts to capture this opportunity and expand persuasiveness mining into a multi-modal realm (Liu et al., 2022, 2023). It presents a multi-modal dataset consisting of annotations on tweets along with associated images, that supports benchmarking of state-of-the-art models on multiple argumentative classification tasks. ImageArg Shared Task 2023 proposes two subtasks viz. subtask (A) Multimodal Argument Stance (AS) Classification: Given a tweet composed of a text and image, predict whether the given tweet supports or opposes the topic, and subtask (B) Multimodal Image Persuasiveness (IP) Classification: given a tweet composed of text and image, predict whether the image makes the tweet more persuasive or not. In this paper, we report our systems for addressing both the subtasks.

Transformer based Multimodal text-embedded classification has been a promising approach recently (Sun et al., 2021; Liang et al., 2022b; Li et al., 2019; Radford et al., 2021; Li et al., 2019; Jia et al., 2021; Dosovitskiy et al., 2020). Taking inspiration from this, we explore multiple transformer models using text as well as multimodal learning methods, for both subtasks (A) and (B). Surprisingly, the text-based approach of the tweet performed better than the multimodal approaches considered. In particular, our best text based model achieved a F1 score of 0.85 for sub task (A) and 0.50 for subtask (B), and ranked 2nd in subtask (A) and 4th in subtask (B), among all teams submissions. Also, our benchmark results highlight the challenge of these tasks and indicate there is ample of room for model improvement. We demonstrate the limitation of these general multi-modal methods and discuss possible future work.

2 Related works

2.1 Stance Classification:

Stance Detection has been extensively studied in the literature ranging from detecting the stance of authors towards a single topic or different aspects of heterogeneous topics/entities (Küçük and Can, 2020). Some of the earlier contributions (Augenstein et al., 2016; Riedel et al., 2017; Thorne

Proceedings of the 10th Workshop on Argument Mining, pages 181–186
December 7, 2023. ©2023 Association for Computational Linguistics

et al., 2017) to stance detection involved the usage of basic ML algorithms, bag-of-words(BOW) as features, TF-IDF feature based dense MLPs, sequence models such as LSTM by processing temporal and linguistic sequence information. Recently, several approaches have emerged adopting transformer based architectures. While stance detection is being actively pursued (Liang et al., 2022a), challenges such as the following remain: i) Learning with less data ii) Learning contrastive representations robust enough for complex stance features jointly by reusing the encoder representations to directly classify the stance based on extracted features as opposed to using a dedicated classifier, iii) Identifying right modality combination for the anchor, reference subspaces.

2.2 Persuasiveness Classification:

Past works have addressed several persuasiveness related tasks (Carlile et al., 2018; Chakrabarty et al., 2020), and in particular, ranking debate arguments (Wei et al., 2016), how audience variables (e.g., personality) influence persuasiveness through different argument styles (Lukin et al., 2017; Persing and Ng, 2017), but mainly focused on texts. (Nojavanasghari et al., 2016) explored coarse-grained fusion ideas such as concatenation for persuasiveness mining. In the area of vision-language, tasks are mainly designed for evaluating models' ability to understand visual information as well as expressing the reasoning in language (Antol et al., 2015; Goyal et al., 2017; Hudson and Manning, 2019). In addition to the main stream, a few works study the relationship between image and text: (Alikhani et al., 2019) annotates the discourse relations between text and accompanying imagery in recipe instructions; and (Kruk et al., 2019) investigates the multi-modal document intent in instagram posts. However, multimodal learning for AM has been under-explored due to a lack of multi-modal corpora.

3 Task and Dataset Description

ImageArg dataset is composed of tweets (images and text) from controversial topics, namely gun control and abortion. ImageArg shared task is divided into two subtasks.

Subtask A: *Argumentative Stance (AS) Classification* Given a tweet composed of a text and image, predict whether the given tweet Supports or Opposes the given topic, which is a binary classification task.

Subtask B: *Image Persuasiveness (IP) Classification* Given a tweet composed of text and image, predict whether the image makes the tweet text more Persuasive or Not, which is also a binary classification task.

For convenience, below we refer to the subtasks (A) and (B) simply as Tasks A and B.

4 Our approach

4.1 Task A - Stance Classification:

For Task A, as the training data is not large, we ventured to explore a predominantly text-based approach, with tweet text and tweet image contents extracted from OCR fed as the inputs to the system. Our idea was to build a model capable of learning their corresponding unified representations which could be sufficiently discriminative in the stance detection classifier space. We considered multiple candidate models that satisfy this criteria and evaluated them on the ImageArg dataset. For all our approaches, we randomly split the instances into 80/20 percent and performed 5-fold cross-validation on the validation(dev) set to select the best model.

Approach 1: (T5 NLI) We used pretrained T5(Text-to-Text Transformer) to fine tune the model for the given dataset and also adjusted the hyper-parameters based on the best performance. During T5 training, we set the number of beams as 50 and the number of returned sequences as 5.

Approach 2: (BERTweet-based model) Sentiment based classifier using BERTweet(Nguyen et al., 2020), a large-scale language model pretrained for English Tweets using RoBERTa model and cross-entropy loss with custom linear layers. The positive and negative labels of the classifier corresponds to support and oppose labels of stance classification task. We have used the pretrained BERTweet model and fine-tuned the model for its best performance.

Approach 3: (Contrastive BERT model) : We adopt a multi-task contrastive learning framework with a two step representation learning paradigm, similar to (Chen et al., 2022). Firstly, stance label prefixed textual sequences were fed as inputs to a transformer encoder as the target Input anchor. Second, the corresponding positive and negative reference input samples were fed as inputs to a shared BERT encoder in the parameter space. Then, the final hidden state classifier token [CLS] is used as the

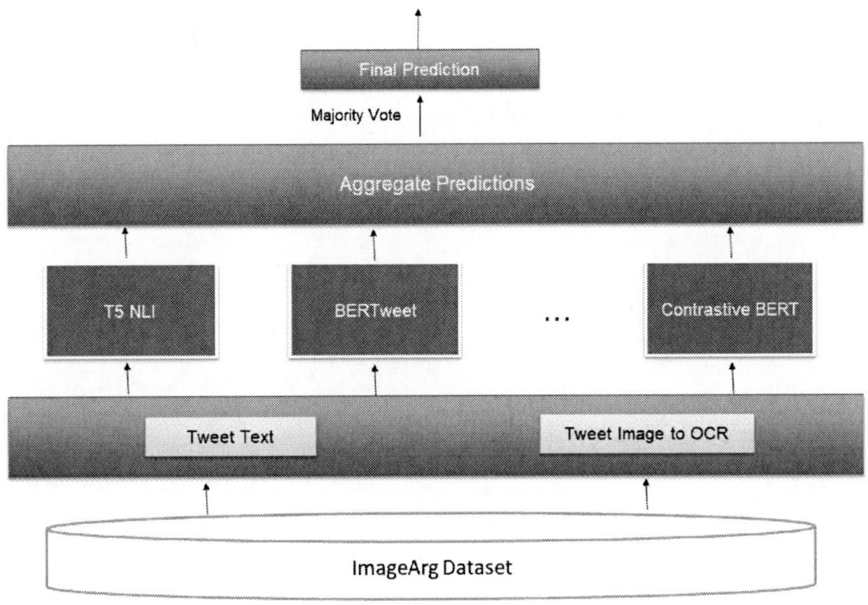

Figure 1: Illustration of Our Approach - Ensemble model of multiple classifiers such as T5 NLI, BERTWeet model, Contrastive BERT

standalone output label representation of the input sequence and the remaining hidden layer outputs served as sequence representation with labels encoded. Among the different variants of contrastive learning available, we used dual stance aware supervised contrastive learning technique with linear classifier. We also evaluate several candidate groups to serve as the anchor, positive, negative reference triplets in the proposed Dual Stance Aware Supervised Contrastive Learning space and found the more straightforward tweet text to act as efficient anchors in this space.

Approach 4: (Ensemble model) : We also considered a final model that uses an ensemble approach. In this model, we classify new data points by first applying the above 3 models, and then taking a majority vote of the predictions. In other words, the final prediction is determined by the class predicted by at least two models.

We have experimented a few other approaches, but as we observed on validation set, Contrastive BERT performed the best, followed by T5 and BERTweet based model. The ensemble model was marginally better in comparison. Thus we considered only these four models.

4.2 Task B - Image Persuasiveness:

For Task B, given the previously studied limitations in literature of projecting the claim and the evidence separately, it becomes imperative to utilize both the tweet text and the tweet image to assess the persuasiveness of the input sample. Hence, we propose separate models for Task B which can jointly deal with both the input modalities or the corresponding input sequences and understand their representations. Thus, as in Task A, we explored multiple candidate models and evaluated them on the ImageArg dataset.

Approach 1: (T5 NLI model) We adopted a sentence pair classification approach with T5 model. The tweet text and tweet image (OCR to Text) were passed as the two sentences, and fine tuned the model for the image persuasiveness dataset. We adjusted the hyper-parameters based on the best performance, as in the case of Task A.

Approach 2: (Stancy BERT) We use a BERT-base model which is fine-tuned with the standard Cross-Entropy Loss and the proposed consistency loss based on sequence similarity based on the tweet text evidence and supporting tweet image based texts/captions/expressions. This joint loss helps the model to acquire classifying features in addition to features central to stance similarity between two sequences.

Approach 3:(Multimodal ALBEF model) In addition to the text only model, we also experimented with multimodal fusion techniques using pretrained models of image encoder ResNet50 (He et al., 2016), VGG and ViT, ALBEF model (aligning the image and text representations before fusing them through cross-modal attention with contrastive loss) and fine-tune them with linear classifiers. During validation, multimodal learning for Image Persuasiveness for Task B (Image and Text only) using ALBEF model performs better than the other variants of image encoders.

Approach 4: (Ensemble model) As in Task A, we considered an ensemble model that adopts a majority vote of the predictions by the 3 models above.

5 Experiments & Results:

For both Task A and Task B, we used tweet text, tweet image-text (OCR to text, using EasyOCR tool[1]) and custom pre-processing techniques to refine and clean up the textual sequences. For the latter, we used the BERTweet preprocessing scripts[2]. All the images are resized to (224*224) dimension and minor data augmentation(i.e., horizontal-flipped, rotation) was performed during training.Subsequently, we trained and performed experiments as outlined in Section 4.

To measure performance, we employ Precision, Recall and F1-score as metrics. In addition, we also consider class-weighted F1-score to account for class imbalance.

The experiments were executed on NVIDIA-GeForce Tesla V100 series SXM2-32GB with 5 cores of GPU machines. Models were trained for 10 epochs, and the pretrained weights for the transformers prior to fine-tuning were downloaded from the HuggingFace Library.

5.1 Task A - Stance Classification:

For stance classification, we adopted the four approaches described in Section 4.1. We used hyperparameters which were previously found to be optimum for Textual Entailment tasks including a Contrastive System Loss, AdamW optimizer, learning rate of 2e-5/5e-5.

The results of Task A on test set are shown in Tables 1 and 2.

Expectedly, the ensemble model achieved the best performance on the test also, but the ranking of the other models was slightly different. We argue that this could be because of the variance and the size of the dataset being on the smaller side.

[1]https://github.com/JaidedAI/EasyOCR

[2]https://github.com/VinAIResearch/BERTweet

Table 4 shows two examples where most of the models misclassified. In the first example, the summary text is inclusive but unfortunately requires the full text from the URL to classify correctly. The second example is expressed in a supportive tone, but the facepalm expression presumably misleads model to classify this as a sarcastic/opposing tweet.

5.2 Task B - Image Persuasiveness:

The Task B results on test are presented in Tables 1 and 3. We observe that, on test set, T5 NLI performed the best, followed by the ensemble model. The multimodal approach (ALBEF) had a surprisingly poor score, which could mean that larger datasets are required to deal with multimodal classification. Also, the results imply that Image Persuasiveness classification is a far more challenging problem and there is significant room for improvement.

6 Conclusion

This paper described our system for ImageArg-2023 Shared Task consisting of two subtasks viz. Subtask (A) Multimodal Argument Stance (AS) Classification, and Subtask (B) Multimodal Image Persuasiveness (IP) Classifi- cation. The tasks used a dataset composed of tweets (images and text) from controversial topics, namely gun control and abortion.

For subtask (A), we employ multiple transformer models using a text based approach to classify the argumentative stance of the tweet. For sub task (B) we adopted text based as well as multimodal learning methods to classify image persuasiveness of the tweet. Surprisingly, the text-based approach of the tweet overall performed better than the multimodal approaches considered. In summary, our best system achieved a F1 score of 0.85 for sub task (A) and 0.50 for subtask (B), and ranked 2nd in subtask (A) and 4th in subtask (B), among all teams submissions.

The results imply that image persuasiveness classification is a far more challenging problem and there is a significant room for improvement. However, it might require larger datasets to deal with the multimodal classification challenges.

References

Malihe Alikhani, Sreyasi Nag Chowdhury, Gerard de Melo, and Matthew Stone. 2019. Cite: A cor-

Task	Model name	F1 Positive(test)	F1 Weighted(test)
Stance Classification	T5 (NLI based)	0.8333	0.8533
	BERTweet+Linear layer+CE Loss	0.8429	0.8633
	BERT+Dual Contrastive Loss	0.8473	0.8604
	Simple Ensemble	**0.8504**	0.8504
Image Persuasiveness	T5 (NLI based)	**0.5022**	0.6300
	Stancy BERT	0.4123	0.5533
	Multimodal ALBEF model	0.2839	0.6466
	Simple Ensemble	0.4633	0.6833

Table 1: Task A: Stance Classification - F1 scores of submitted models and Task B: Image Persuasiveness - F1 scores of submitted models

Topic	F1 +ve	Precision	Recall
Abortion	0.7532	0.8788	0.6591
GunControl	0.8865	0.9647	0.8200

Table 2: Topicwise Results for Task A- Best Performing Model

Topic	F1 +ve	Precision	Recall
Abortion	0.4644	0.4603	0.4733
GunControl	0.5020	0.5233	0.5267

Table 3: Topicwise Results for Task B- Best Performing Model

Example	Incorrect Label
Poland 's anti-abortion push highlights pandemic risks to democracy HTTPURL HTTPURL. HTTPURL	Support
This packaging could be a useful form of gun control. Put all guns in these and no one will ever be able to get them out. **FACEPALM**. HTTPURL	Oppose

Table 4: Misclassified Examples- Sentences vs Incorrect Labels

pus of image-text discourse relations. *arXiv preprint arXiv:1904.06286*.

Stanislaw Antol, Aishwarya Agrawal, Jiasen Lu, Margaret Mitchell, Dhruv Batra, C Lawrence Zitnick, and Devi Parikh. 2015. Vqa: Visual question answering. In *Proceedings of the IEEE international conference on computer vision*, pages 2425–2433.

Isabelle Augenstein, Tim Rocktäschel, Andreas Vlachos, and Kalina Bontcheva. 2016. Stance detection with bidirectional conditional encoding. *arXiv preprint arXiv:1606.05464*.

Winston Carlile, Nishant Gurrapadi, Zixuan Ke, and Vincent Ng. 2018. Give me more feedback: Annotating argument persuasiveness and related attributes in student essays. In *Proceedings of the 56th Annual Meeting of the Association for Computational Linguistics (Volume 1: Long Papers)*, pages 621–631.

Tuhin Chakrabarty, Christopher Hidey, Smaranda Muresan, Kathy McKeown, and Alyssa Hwang. 2020. Ampersand: Argument mining for persuasive online discussions. *arXiv preprint arXiv:2004.14677*.

Qianben Chen, Richong Zhang, Yaowei Zheng, and Yongyi Mao. 2022. Dual contrastive learning: Text classification via label-aware data augmentation. *arXiv preprint arXiv:2201.08702*.

Alexey Dosovitskiy, Lucas Beyer, Alexander Kolesnikov, Dirk Weissenborn, Xiaohua Zhai, Thomas Unterthiner, Mostafa Dehghani, Matthias Minderer, Georg Heigold, Sylvain Gelly, et al. 2020. An image is worth 16x16 words: Transformers for image recognition at scale. *arXiv preprint arXiv:2010.11929*.

Yash Goyal, Tejas Khot, Douglas Summers-Stay, Dhruv Batra, and Devi Parikh. 2017. Making the v in vqa matter: Elevating the role of image understanding in visual question answering. In *Proceedings of the IEEE conference on computer vision and pattern recognition*, pages 6904–6913.

Nancy Green. 2014. Towards creation of a corpus for argumentation mining the biomedical genetics research literature. In *Proceedings of the First Work-*

shop on Argumentation Mining, pages 11–18, Baltimore, Maryland. Association for Computational Linguistics.

Drew A Hudson and Christopher D Manning. 2019. Gqa: A new dataset for real-world visual reasoning and compositional question answering. In *Proceedings of the IEEE/CVF conference on computer vision and pattern recognition*, pages 6700–6709.

Chao Jia, Yinfei Yang, Ye Xia, Yi-Ting Chen, Zarana Parekh, Hieu Pham, Quoc Le, Yun-Hsuan Sung, Zhen Li, and Tom Duerig. 2021. Scaling up visual and vision-language representation learning with noisy text supervision. In *International conference on machine learning*, pages 4904–4916. PMLR.

Julia Kruk, Jonah Lubin, Karan Sikka, Xiao Lin, Dan Jurafsky, and Ajay Divakaran. 2019. Integrating text and image: Determining multimodal document intent in instagram posts. *arXiv preprint arXiv:1904.09073*.

Dilek Küçük and Fazli Can. 2020. Stance detection: A survey. *ACM Computing Surveys (CSUR)*, 53(1):1–37.

John Lawrence and Chris Reed. 2019. Argument mining: A survey. *Computational Linguistics*, 45(4):765–818.

Liunian Harold Li, Mark Yatskar, Da Yin, Cho-Jui Hsieh, and Kai-Wei Chang. 2019. Visualbert: A simple and performant baseline for vision and language.

Bin Liang, Zixiao Chen, Lin Gui, Yulan He, Min Yang, and Ruifeng Xu. 2022a. Zero-shot stance detection via contrastive learning. In *Proceedings of the ACM Web Conference 2022*, pages 2738–2747.

Tao Liang, Guosheng Lin, Mingyang Wan, Tianrui Li, Guojun Ma, and Fengmao Lv. 2022b. Expanding large pre-trained unimodal models with multimodal information injection for image-text multimodal classification. In *Proceedings of the IEEE/CVF Conference on Computer Vision and Pattern Recognition*, pages 15492–15501.

Zhexiong Liu, Mohamed Elaraby, Yang Zhong, and Diane Litman. 2023. Overview of ImageArg-2023: The first shared task in multimodal argument mining. In *Proceedings of the 10th Workshop on Argument Mining*, Online and in Singapore. Association for Computational Linguistics.

Zhexiong Liu, Meiqi Guo, Yue Dai, and Diane Litman. 2022. Imagearg: A multi-modal tweet dataset for image persuasiveness mining. *arXiv preprint arXiv:2209.06416*.

Stephanie M Lukin, Pranav Anand, Marilyn Walker, and Steve Whittaker. 2017. Argument strength is in the eye of the beholder: Audience effects in persuasion. *arXiv preprint arXiv:1708.09085*.

Dat Quoc Nguyen, Thanh Vu, and Anh Tuan Nguyen. 2020. BERTweet: A pre-trained language model for English Tweets. In *Proceedings of the 2020 Conference on Empirical Methods in Natural Language Processing: System Demonstrations*, pages 9–14.

Behnaz Nojavanasghari, Deepak Gopinath, Jayanth Koushik, Tadas Baltrušaitis, and Louis-Philippe Morency. 2016. Deep multimodal fusion for persuasiveness prediction. In *Proceedings of the 18th ACM International Conference on Multimodal Interaction*, pages 284–288.

Isaac Persing and Vincent Ng. 2017. Why can't you convince me? modeling weaknesses in unpersuasive arguments. In *IJCAI*, pages 4082–4088.

Alec Radford, Jong Wook Kim, Chris Hallacy, Aditya Ramesh, Gabriel Goh, Sandhini Agarwal, Girish Sastry, Amanda Askell, Pamela Mishkin, Jack Clark, et al. 2021. Learning transferable visual models from natural language supervision. In *International conference on machine learning*, pages 8748–8763. PMLR.

Benjamin Riedel, Isabelle Augenstein, Georgios P Spithourakis, and Sebastian Riedel. 2017. A simple but tough-to-beat baseline for the fake news challenge stance detection task. *arXiv preprint arXiv:1707.03264*.

Manfred Stede, Jodi Schneider, and Graeme Hirst. 2019. *Argumentation mining*. Springer.

Lin Sun, Jiquan Wang, Kai Zhang, Yindu Su, and Fangsheng Weng. 2021. Rpbert: a text-image relation propagation-based bert model for multimodal ner. In *Proceedings of the AAAI conference on artificial intelligence*, volume 35, pages 13860–13868.

James Thorne, Mingjie Chen, Giorgos Myrianthous, Jiashu Pu, Xiaoxuan Wang, and Andreas Vlachos. 2017. Fake news stance detection using stacked ensemble of classifiers. In *Proceedings of the 2017 EMNLP workshop: natural language processing meets journalism*, pages 80–83.

Zhongyu Wei, Yang Liu, and Yi Li. 2016. Is this post persuasive? ranking argumentative comments in online forum. In *Proceedings of the 54th Annual Meeting of the Association for Computational Linguistics (Volume 2: Short Papers)*, pages 195–200.

Overview of PragTag-2023: Low-Resource Multi-Domain Pragmatic Tagging of Peer Reviews

Nils Dycke, Ilia Kuznetsov, Iryna Gurevych
Ubiquitous Knowledge Processing Lab (UKP Lab)
Department of Computer Science and Hessian Center for AI (hessian.AI)
Technical University of Darmstadt
ukp.informatik.tu-darmstadt.de

Abstract

Peer review is the key quality control mechanism in science. The core component of peer review are the review reports – argumentative texts where the reviewers evaluate the work and make suggestions to the authors. Reviewing is a demanding expert task prone to bias. An active line of research in NLP aims to support peer review via automatic analysis of review reports. This research meets two key challenges. First, NLP to date has focused on peer reviews from machine learning conferences. Yet, NLP models are prone to domain shift and might underperform when applied to reviews from a new research community. Second, while some venues make their reviewing processes public, peer reviewing data is generally hard to obtain and expensive to label. Approaches to low-data NLP processing for peer review remain under-investigated. Enabled by the recent release of open multi-domain corpora of peer reviews, the PragTag-2023 Shared Task explored the ways to increase domain robustness and address data scarcity in pragmatic tagging – a sentence tagging task where review statements are classified by their argumentative function. This paper describes the shared task, outlines the participating systems, and summarizes the results.

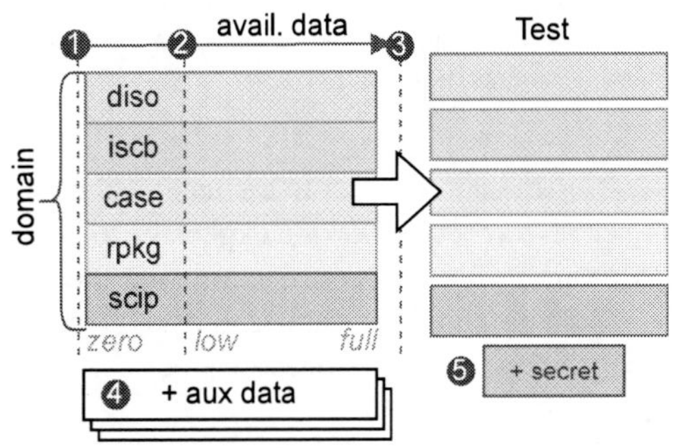

Figure 1: PragTag-2023 Overview. Given a mixed-domain corpus of peer reviews annotated with pragmatic tags, the participants submit systems trained with varying amounts of training data (1-3) with optional use of unlabeled auxiliary data (4). The systems are evaluated in each of the five domains (Section 3.1), as well as on a previously unseen secret domain (5).

1 Introduction

Scholarly communication lies at the heart of scientific discovery (Johnson et al., 2018) and is argumentative by nature. Scientific publications present results, interpret them, justify the experimental setup, and substantiate the claim for new knowledge (Teufel et al., 2009). Peer review reports, in turn, assess the validity, novelty and impact of the underlying publication and argue for or against its acceptance. Peer review is a key component of scientific quality assurance. It is a complex process prone to heuristic behavior (Rogers and Augenstein, 2020) and bias (e.g. Stelmakh et al., 2020; Wang and Shah, 2018). A growing area of NLP for peer review analysis aims to investigate those issues by analyzing argumentation in peer review reports (e.g. Kang et al., 2018; Cheng et al., 2020; Hua et al., 2019; Kuznetsov et al., 2022; Dycke et al., 2023). The resulting systems have numerous potential applications, incl. facilitating meta-scientific analysis of reviewing practices, helping authors and program chairs aggregate information from multiple reviews, and supporting junior reviewers in giving thorough, objective and helpful feedback.

Standards and practices of scholarly communication vary across research communities. Yet, to date, NLP for peer review has focused on data from machine learning conferences (Kang et al., 2018; Hua et al., 2019; Cheng et al., 2020; Kennard et al., 2022), and the applications outside of this domain remain under-investigated. This over-focus on one domain can be attributed to data scarcity – while some communities make their reviewing public, peer reviews are generally hard to obtain and legally clear for research use (Dycke et al.,

Proceedings of the 10th Workshop on Argument Mining, pages 187–196
December 7, 2023. ©2023 Association for Computational Linguistics

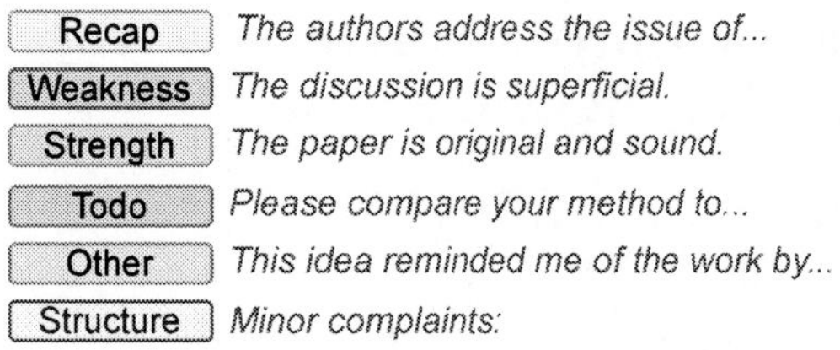

Figure 2: Pragmatic tags. `Recap` neutrally summarizes the paper; `Weakness` and `Strength` outline the negative and positive aspects of the work; `Todo` covers explicit requests to the paper authors; `Other` marks non-argumentative statements; `Structure` denotes structural elements of the review text.

Figure 3: Number of sentences by domain (left) and label (right) in the F1000RD core data (train and test).

2022). In addition, due to the technical nature of peer review texts, they are expensive to annotate. Measuring the effects and mitigating the impact of domain shift and data scarcity are important and under-researched questions in NLP for peer reviews.

The introduction of open multi-domain corpora of peer reviews (Dycke et al., 2023) and domain-neutral review analysis tasks (Kuznetsov et al., 2022) makes it possible to investigate these questions empirically. The PragTag-2023 Shared Task[1] collaboratively explored multi-domain NLP for peer reviews under data scarcity. As an exemplary task we took pragmatic tagging – a sentence-level argumentation labeling task that classifies peer review statements by their communicative purpose (Section 2). PragTag-2023 has received five diverse submissions that provide new insights into multi-domain low-data pragmatic tagging, and propose a wide spectrum of methods to increase model robustness under four increasingly challenging conditions. This paper describes the shared task setup, summarizes the submissions, and aggregates the main insights from the competition. To support further investigation of multi-domain low-data NLP for peer review, we archive the code and data of the shared task and make them publicly available[2].

2 Pragmatic tagging

Task. Pragmatic tagging is a sentence classification problem where given the sequence of sentences $s_1^r, ..., s_n^r$ from a review report r, a model should predict the pragmatic label for each sentence $l_1^r, ..., l_n^r$ from the label set L. We adopt the label set proposed by Kuznetsov et al. (2022), illustrated in Figure 2. The label set was evaluated in an annotation study and shown to be well-applicable across different research fields and communities while yielding good inter-annotator agreement of approx. 0.7 Krippendorff's α. The core sources of disagreement are the coarse granularity of the schema (necessary for generalization), sentence-level analysis (necessary to avoid discrepancies due to differences in sub-sentence splitting), and the natural ambiguity of the classes (e.g. `Weakness` vs `Todo`).

Evaluation. Kuznetsov et al. (2022) provide the data, but do not specify metrics for evaluating NLP systems for pragmatic tagging. In PragTag-2023, we evaluate system performance via the F1 score. Since the label distribution is skewed, we opt for the macro-averaged F1 within each domain for evaluation. We then compute scores for each domain individually and use the mean across all domains as the final leaderboard score (Section 4).

Baselines. To contextualize the submission scores, we implemented two baselines. The supervised **RoBERTa** baseline is a `roberta-base` model (Liu et al., 2019) fine-tuned for 20 epochs on the training data available for a given experimental condition (Section 4.2). The **majority** baseline directly assigns the most frequent pragmatic tag from the training data to the input sentence.

3 Data

The participants of the shared task were given two types of data (Figure 4). The smaller-scale *core data* contains peer review texts labeled with pragmatic tags on the sentence level. Core data is used for training and evaluating the systems. The large-scale *auxiliary data* consists of two unlabeled text collections. It can be used to enhance the systems' robustness to low-data conditions in the

[1] `https://codalab.lisn.upsaclay.fr/competitions/13334`

[2] `https://github.com/UKPLab/pragtag2023`

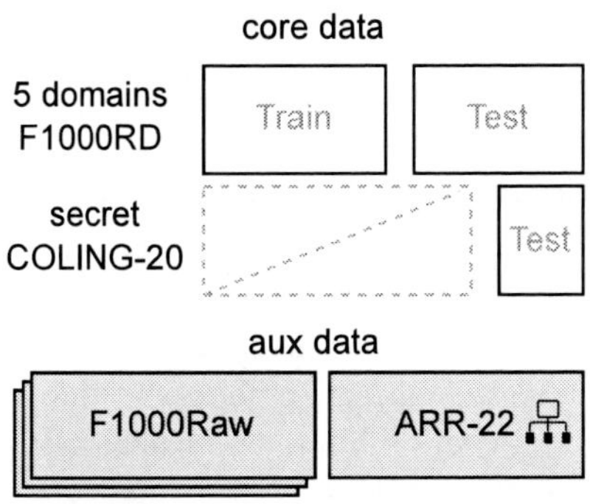

Figure 4: PragTag-2023 data overview. In addition to labeled core data from F1000RD and COLING-20, the parcitipants are provided with two unlabeled collections: a large multi-domain corpus of unstructured peer reviews (F1000Raw), and smaller collection of *semi-structured* peer reviews in the NLP domain (ARR-22).

multi-domain setting.

3.1 Core Data

The core data originates from the F1000RD corpus (Kuznetsov et al., 2022), and contains review reports with manually annotated pragmatic tag labels for each sentence. Each review report belongs to one of the five domains:

- Disease outbreaks (`diso`)
- Computational biology (`iscb`)
- Medical case studies (`case`)
- R Packages (`rpkg`)
- Scientific policy research (`scip`).

The core data from F1000RD covers 4911 sentences from 224 peer review reports. Figure 3 shows the label and domain distribution in the F1000RD data. The instances are unequally distributed both across domains (slightly) and across pragmatic tags (substantially). The skewed pragmatic tag distribution reflects a natural distribution in peer review texts, with most sentences dedicated to critically assessing the work and suggesting improvements. The differences in the number of instances across domains stem from the per-review data sampling procedure in the F1000RD corpus and the review length variation across domains. To account for the uneven distribution, PragTag-2023 employed macro-averaging by label and by domain during evaluation (Section 2).

We split the core data into training set (2326 sentences) and test set (2585 sentences), at random, on review basis, per domain. We did not provide a fixed development set – instead, the participants were free to derive it from the training set by themselves. We note that the training data is a *mixed* collection with instances from all domains; per-instance domain identifier is provided. The test data, on the other hand, is split *by domain*, and evaluation is performed on *each* of the domains separately. The rather uncommon $50/50$ training-test split is thus necessary to ensure sufficient amount of test data in each domain.

In addition to the five F1000RD domains listed above, the final phase of the competition evaluated the systems on a previously unpublished *secret* test set. This collection includes 255 sentences from 10 peer reviews in computational linguistics taken from the COLING-20 portion of the NLPeer corpus and annotated with pragmatic tags following the F1000RD tagset. Labeling was performed by two annotators proficient in the NLP domain, reaching an agreement of 0.65 Krippendorff's α – slightly lower than in the original study. The labels were adjudicated by an expert annotator closely familiar with the F1000RD labeling schema. The domain and composition of this new data were unknown to the participants until the start of the final evaluation.

3.2 Auxiliary data

Using unlabeled or partially-labeled auxiliary data is a common way to mitigate domain shift and to address the lack of labeled data. To enable application of such techniques, the shared task provided the participants with two additional auxiliary datasets.

F1000Raw is a large multi-domain collection of papers and peer reviews from a wide range of domains. The data originates from the F1000Research platform – same source as the non-secret core data. F1000Raw corresponds to the F1000-22 subsection of the NLPeer corpus (Dycke et al., 2023), excluding the instances that appear in the core shared task data, and covers approx. 10k reviews for 4.8k papers, 3.8M review words in total (Dycke et al., 2023). Like the core data, F1000Raw contains full-text, unstructured peer reviews. Unlike the core data, F1000Raw does not contain explicit domain identifiers or pragmatic tag labels.

ARR-22 is a corpus of papers and peer reviews in the NLP domain from the data collection campaigns at ACL Rolling Review (Dycke et al., 2022). It covers 684 reviews for 476 papers, approx. 266k review words in total (Dycke et al., 2023). The reviews are semi-structured, and each review is

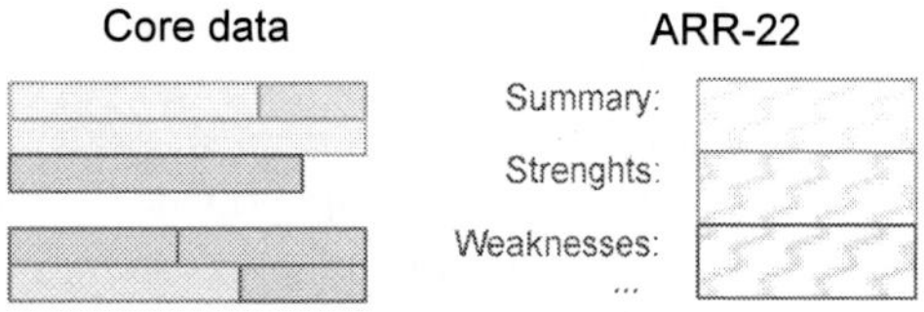

Figure 5: Difference between sentence-level unstructured core data and section-level semi-structured ARR-22 data from peer reviews that use review forms. Colors correspond to different pragmatic tags (see Figure 2).

split into free-text fields: "*Summary*", "*Strengths*", "*Weaknesses*", "*Suggestions*" and "*Ethical concerns*". The similarity between the review form fields and the pragmatic tags is not coincidental: both reflect review pragmatics, implicitly (pragmatic tags) or explicitly (form fields). Yet, unlike the core data, ARR-22 does not contain sentence-level pragmatic tags, and not every sentence in a review section corresponds to its overall pragmatics (Figure 5). Finding a solution to bridge this gap is left to the participants.

We envisioned F1000Raw as a valuable source of data for increasing cross-domain robustness of the participating systems. We envisioned ARR-22 as a potential distant supervision source for low-data scenarios explored in PragTag-2023.

4 Setup

4.1 Implementation

The shared task was run via CodaLab (Pavao et al., 2023). The competition website provided necessary information about the task, the core and auxiliary data, as well as a starting kit including an evaluation script and a baseline implementation. The participants would apply their system to the test set inputs and submit the predictions via CodaLab, where they would be compared to the gold outputs. The score would be stored in the participants' dashboard and could be submitted to the publicly available leaderboard.

4.2 Conditions and Rules

The participants submitted systems to one of the following conditions, simulating different training data availability scenarios:

- **No-data**: The system observed no instances of the core data neither at training time nor at inference time.
- **Low-data**: The system is trained on 20% of the core training data (33 reviews, 739 sentences). The exact 20% split is provided by the shared task organizers and is identical among all participants.
- **Full-data**: the system has access to 100% of the core training data (117 reviews, 2326 sentences).

The test data was identical across these three conditions. At the end of the competition, the participants could submit *any* of their systems to a special **Final** condition, which included the core test data as well as the secret test data, as detailed in Section 3.1.

To promote reproducibility of the results and fair competition, we imposed a few restrictive **rules** on the submissions. The teams were allowed to use PragTag-2023 auxiliary data without restrictions. However, pre-training or fine-tuning the submissions on *any* other data was not allowed. We imposed no requirements upon the system architecture. However, in case of large language models, the participants were requested to only use non-commercial models with publicly available weights, e.g. Llama (Touvron et al., 2023). Submissions built on top of commercial models like ChatGPT and GPT-4 (OpenAI, 2023), etc. were not considered for the evaluation. To prevent optimization on the hidden test data, each team was allowed up to five submissions to each of the conditions. A special **Sandbox** condition with no submission limit was provided for troubleshooting purposes.

5 Submissions

Out of over 20 teams that signed up for the competition, five teams have made it to the final submission. The submitted systems explore a wide range of techniques and architectures for multi-domain pragmatic tagging in low-resource scenarios. We summarize the main ideas behind each submission below and refer to the system papers for details.

CATALPA_EduNLP (Ding et al., 2023) investigated a wide array of approaches. For the full- and low-data setting, this includes supervised sentence labeling via RoBERTa (Liu et al., 2019) augmented with additional features (domain, position, context, word normalization), as well as IOB-style sequence tagging using long-document Transformers and nearest-neighbor-based labeling using SBERT (Reimers and Gurevych, 2019). In the zero-shot setting, the team experimented with labeling test instances based on their similarity to class defini-

	mean	case	diso	iscb	rpkg	scip	secret
DeepBlueAI	**84.1**	82.9	84.1	82.8	**86.0**	**89.0**	**80.1**
NUS-IDS	83.2	83.8	**85.4**	**83.3**	84.8	87.8	74.1
MILAB	82.4	**84.0**	83.7	80.1	85.4	86.5	74.9
SuryaKiran	82.3	82.0	82.8	81.8	82.8	86.5	77.9
CATALPA	81.3	80.8	82.0	81.1	82.5	82.5	78.8
Ensemble	84.4	84.0	85.2	83.3	87.3	88.7	78.0
RoBERTa	80.3	80.3	80.8	79.9	83.1	83.8	73.7
Majority	8.0	9.3	7.3	7.5	8.6	7.9	7.3

Table 1: Final evaluation leaderboard, mean F1-macro score across domains and scores per domain, converted to percentage points for readability. Top: submissions, Middle: majority-vote ensemble of system predictions (Section 7), Bottom: baselines. Bold: best score per column (w/o ensembling).

tions from the shared task description, as well as with prompting via GPT3.5. The participants used the ARR-22 auxiliary data, addressing the gap in label distribution between ARR and the core data via subsampling, and explored data augmentation based on F1000raw auxiliary data. By ensembling best per-domain configurations selected on the validation set, they found that a BERT-based model with additional features outperforms sequence tagging and nearest-neighbor labeling on the full data, while a BERT-based model augmented with additional data performs best in the low-data setting. Prompting GPT3.5 in the zero-shot setting was shown vastly superior to SBERT-based classification based on task definitions – yet, following the PragTag rules, GPT3.5 result was not used for the leaderboard submission.

DeepBlueAI (Luo et al., 2023) focused their approach on increasing the robustness of pre-trained models in the sentence labeling setting. The experiments were conducted using three models – RoBERTa, DeBERTa (He et al., 2023) and XLM-RoBERTa (Conneau et al., 2020). The participants augmented the model via max pooling and attention pooling, introduced adversarial training via fast gradient method, and reported comparative performance of the models trained under different settings via cross-fold validation, showing that the modifications lead to variable performance gains. The authors report that the DeBERTa model consistently outperforms the other two models on the task. To tackle the secret test set in the final phase of the competition, the authors used a voting approach combining a range of models trained in different configurations and selecting the label with the maximum vote, stressing the benefits of fusing different types of models for prediction.

NUS-IDS (Gollapalli et al., 2023) explored multiple approaches to the task for each experimental condition. In the zero-shot no-data condition, the participants proposed two methods: a question-answering model that selects passages from the peer review based on a set of questions derived from peer reviewing guidelines of NLP conferences, and a prompting-based approach based on the Flan-T5 (Chung et al., 2022) model. For the low- and full-data setting, the participants experimented with fine-tuning pre-trained language models, additionally exploring ensembling and data augmentation techniques by tentatively labeling the auxiliary shared task data. The results indicate that prompting via Flan-T5 outperforms question-answering based approach in the no-data setting; in low- and full-data data, fine-tuning a T5 model (Raffel et al., 2019) on tentatively labeled auxiliary data followed by fine-tuning on the core task data performs best.

MILAB (Lee et al., 2023) approached the problem of data scarcity and domain shift via data augmentation. In particular, to compensate for the lack of data, the team applied an ensemble of RoBERTa-based classifiers to label auxiliary data from F1000raw and ARR-22. Apart from majority labeling, the authors explored a novel recall labeling technique: the models assign tentative labels to the unlabeled instances in the decreasing order of recall on a validation set, while labeling the residual instances as Other. Additionally, the authors experimented with diversifying the data by applying off-the-shelf synonym generation followed by BERTScore filtering (Zhang et al., 2020). The results indicate that the proposed data augmentation techniques combined with ensembling improve the model performance on the task, especially in the no-data condition.

SuryaKiran (Suri et al., 2023) explored the use of unsupervised pre-training on F1000raw auxiliary data to increase domain robustness of the pragmatic tag classifier. In particular, the participants pre-trained the DeBERTa model on F1000raw using masked language modeling objective (Devlin et al., 2019), and later used an ensemble of five models further fine-tuned on different training data splits to make the test set prediction. Their results demonstrate that pre-training via masked language modeling leads to improved performance only in some cases; the authors attribute this to the vocabulary discrepancies between the domains. The team submitted their system only to the final evaluation.

6 Main results

The final leaderboard of PragTag-2023 is shown in Table 1. The participants were invited to submit their best system trained under *any* condition to the leaderboard – expectedly, the best-performing systems trained on full data were submitted. As we can see, on average, all systems outperform the RoBERTa baseline fine-tuned on full training data, and the majority baseline scores poorly due to the macro-averaging of F1 across labels. The submission by DeepBlueAI achieves the highest F1-score both on average, and on the secret test domain. However, this superior performance is not absolute, and on per-domain basis we observe variation in the system rankings: the CATALPA system performs second-best on the `secret` test set, NUS-IDS achieves best performance in the `diso` and `iscb` domains, and the best score in the `case` domain is taken by MILAB. We note consistent and substantial performance degradation on the secret domain across all submissions and baselines. We attribute this to domain shift: while the systems could observe *some* data from *each* of the other domains during training, the secret data is truly out-of-distribution, originating from an entirely different research community and reviewing platform. This gap in performance highlights the importance of cross-domain study of NLP for peer reviews.

Turning to the data scarcity, Table 2 summarizes mean submission scores for various data conditions, from no-data zero-shot learning to full-data fine-tuning. Here, too, all submissions have outperformed the RoBERTa baselines, albeit by a smaller

	no-data	low-data	full-data
MILAB	**51.6**	77.1	83.9
NUS-IDS	40.2	**81.3**	**85.0**
CATALPA	22.2	74.5	81.8
DeepBlueAI	-	80.8	**85.0**
RoBERTa	-	74.4	80.3

Table 2: Mean F1-macro score across domains for different data scarcity conditions, without secret domain.

margin in the low-data setting. The no-data and low-data results show great variation both in terms of absolute scores and in terms of leaderboard rankings. Especially in the no-data setting, the highest- and lowest-scoring submission differ by almost 30 percent F1-measure, compared to the 3 percent gap on full data. The submission by MILAB scores best in the no-data scenario, while the system by NUS-IDF performed best on low data. Secret test set not taken into account, DeepBlueAI and NUS-IDS share the first place in the full-data condition. These observations demonstrate the value of evaluating NLP systems for pragmatic tagging in varying data availability conditions.

7 Analysis

Access to all the participating system's predictions at once allows additional insights into the task. Given the broad range of approaches proposed by the PragTag-2023 participants, a natural question arises if these approaches are complementary. We investigate this by combining the predictions of the best-performing submissions via majority vote. The results show that a majority ensemble indeed outperforms every individual system on average (Table 1, middle). Considering per-domain results reveals more nuance: the ensemble maintains the best systems' performance for the domains `case` and `iscb`, slightly lagging behind on `diso` and `scip`, substantially improving the best result in `rpkg`, and showing average performance on the `secret` test set. This variation demonstrates the importance of fine-graned evaluation of pragmatic tagging in multi-domain setting, and we deem the use of alternative, e.g. weighted, ensembling methods for the task promising.

Analysis of the confusion matrix between the true labels and the majority ensemble predictions allows us to see which labels are particularly hard for the systems to handle. Figure 6 presents the

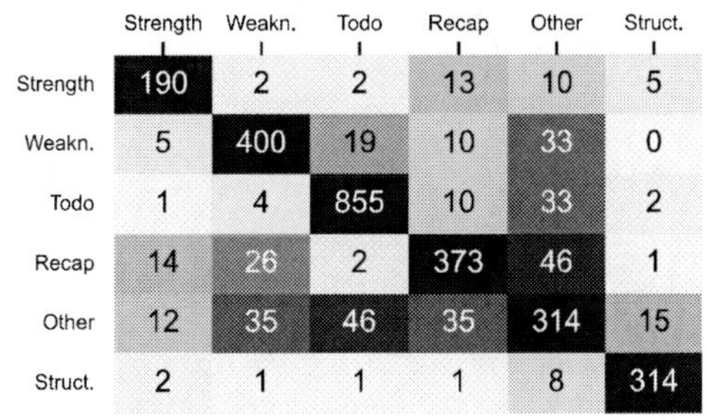

Figure 6: Confusion matrix of PragTag-2023 submission majority ensemble on the final test data: true label (rows) vs predicted label (columns).

results. We observe that, in aggregate, the systems are successfully able to distinguish between *Strengths*, *Weaknesses*, *Todo* and *Structure*, while the *Recap* and especially the open *Other* class constitute frequent sources of confusion, in line with the annotation study observations by Kuznetsov et al. (2022). This result suggests that future labeling schemata for pragmatic tagging might consider refining the *Recap* and *Other* class definitions, or, alternatively, merging these classes into a general *Other* class, eliminating the hard distinction and resulting in more robust systems, at the loss of granularity. We leave this exploration to the future.

8 Discussion

A high-level picture of the submissions to the PragTag competition reveals several trends. Despite the advances in LLM development, fine-tuning of BERT-family LMs was still used by most participants, although some have experimented with prompting. While our rules prohibited the use of commercial LLMs, new open LLMs like Llama (Touvron et al., 2023) have been released. Investigating the performance of these models for our task is a promising avenue for future studies.

While some submissions focused on modifying the model architecture and pre-training regime, others explored data augmentation and creative adaptations of the task, e.g. by casting it as a question-answering task or labeling the instances based on the similarity to guideline class definitions. Most participants used auxiliary data as an unlabeled substrate for pseudo-labeling or language model pre-training. We note the wide use of model ensembling across the submissions, and believe that such techniques will remain relevant in the age of LLMs. PragTag-2023 was designed to accommodate various approaches to the task: pragmatic tagging can be cast as sentence labeling and as sequence labeling, and can can be approached via prompting. While the participants have experimented with many of these options, in-context learning (Dong et al., 2023) remained under-explored. We deem such exploration promising.

The ongoing adaptation of the field to the last-generation LLMs presents new challenges to the benchmarking and shared task methodology. The technical requirements of pre-training and fine-tuning LLMs put the teams without access to massive data and compute at disadvantage. The opaqueness of the LLM pre-training for commercial models introduces the risk of model exposure to the test data or related datasets. PragTag-2023 attempted to mitigate these issues by explicitly limiting the competition to the models for which open weights are available and pre-training procedure is known, and by prohibiting the use of any additional pre-training sources apart from the core and auxiliary data provided with the task. An alternative solution could be to limit the competition to several open LLM instances, inference-only. This, however, would limit the scope of methods the participants can explore to prompting-based approaches. We leave the search for flexible, fair and reproducible benchmarking methodology in the age of LLMs to future work.

9 Conclusion

This paper has introduced PragTag-2023: the shared task in low-resource multi-domain pragmatic tagging of peer reviews. We have described the rationale behind the task, introduced the data and outlined a range of experimental conditions under which the competition took place. The shared task participants proposed a wide range of techniques for increasing the robustness of pragmatic tagging across domains and data availability scenarios. The results of the competition underline the importance of evaluating pragmatic tagging systems across different domains and in different data availability conditions. The arguably most important gain from an organized competition is not finding the best-performing system for the task, but the accompanying exploration of approaches to solving the problem at hand. To this end, we hope that the ideas and observations from the PragTag-2023 submissions foster future progress in pragmatic tagging, and in cross-domain and low-data processing of peer reviews in general.

Limitations

Few limitations of our setup can be addressed by future work. As common in scholarly NLP, our study is limited to English. Once available, the future multilingual datasets of research papers and peer reviews would enable the study of NLP for peer review across languages *and* domains. A coarse-grained pragmatic tagging schema could eliminate the hard `Recap` vs `Other` distinction (Section 7) and increase the robustness of the evaluation. Obtaining more labeled data per domain would enable the study of data scarcity on *per-domain basis* as well as *across individual training-test domain pairs*, e.g. training on `case` and evaluating on `rpkg`. Alternatively, shifting the focus to zero-shot learning with instruction-following LLMs would allow using all available data for evaluation – yet it would be methodologically limiting (Section 8). Incorporating other peer review analysis tasks into the setup would provide additional insights into the low-data and cross-domain NLP for peer reviews.

Ethics Statement

Increasing the domain robustness and sample efficiency of NLP systems are key steps towards sustainabile and widely applicable NLP. Pragmatic tagging is a basic argumentation analysis task with many potential applications that would increase the transparency, fairness and efficiency of scholarly peer review. We believe that the potential for misuse of this technology is low. The data used in the shared task was obtained according to strict licensing and data management procedures, and is open and freely available for research use.

Acknowledgements

PragTag-2023 is part of the InterText initiative at UKP Lab.[3]. We thank the shared task participants and the organizers of the 10th Workshop on Argument Mining[4] for making this shared task possible. The work was funded by the German Research Foundation (DFG) as part of the PEER project (grant GU 798/28-1), and by the European Union as part of the InterText ERC project (101054961). Views and opinions expressed here are, however, those of the author(s) only, and do not necessarily reflect those of the European Union or the European Research Council. Neither the European Union nor the granting authority can be held responsible for them.

[3]`https://intertext.ukp-lab.de`

[4]`https://argmining-org.github.io/2023/index.html`

References

Liying Cheng, Lidong Bing, Qian Yu, Wei Lu, and Luo Si. 2020. APE: Argument pair extraction from peer review and rebuttal via multi-task learning. In *Proceedings of the 2020 Conference on Empirical Methods in Natural Language Processing (EMNLP)*, pages 7000–7011, Online. Association for Computational Linguistics.

Hyung Won Chung, Le Hou, Shayne Longpre, Barret Zoph, Yi Tay, William Fedus, Yunxuan Li, Xuezhi Wang, Mostafa Dehghani, Siddhartha Brahma, Albert Webson, Shixiang Shane Gu, Zhuyun Dai, Mirac Suzgun, Xinyun Chen, Aakanksha Chowdhery, Alex Castro-Ros, Marie Pellat, Kevin Robinson, Dasha Valter, Sharan Narang, Gaurav Mishra, Adams Yu, Vincent Zhao, Yanping Huang, Andrew Dai, Hongkun Yu, Slav Petrov, Ed H. Chi, Jeff Dean, Jacob Devlin, Adam Roberts, Denny Zhou, Quoc V. Le, and Jason Wei. 2022. Scaling instruction-finetuned language models. *arXiv:2210.11416*.

Alexis Conneau, Kartikay Khandelwal, Naman Goyal, Vishrav Chaudhary, Guillaume Wenzek, Francisco Guzmán, Edouard Grave, Myle Ott, Luke Zettlemoyer, and Veselin Stoyanov. 2020. Unsupervised cross-lingual representation learning at scale. In *Proceedings of the 58th Annual Meeting of the Association for Computational Linguistics*, pages 8440–8451, Online. Association for Computational Linguistics.

Jacob Devlin, Ming-Wei Chang, Kenton Lee, and Kristina Toutanova. 2019. BERT: Pre-training of deep bidirectional transformers for language understanding. In *Proceedings of the 2019 Conference of the North American Chapter of the Association for Computational Linguistics: Human Language Technologies, Volume 1 (Long and Short Papers)*, pages 4171–4186, Minneapolis, Minnesota. Association for Computational Linguistics.

Yuning Ding, Marie Bexte, and Andrea Horbach. 2023. CATALPA_EduNLP at PragTag-2023. In *Proceedings of the 10th Workshop on Argument Mining*, Singapore. Association for Computational Linguistics.

Qingxiu Dong, Lei Li, Damai Dai, Ce Zheng, Zhiyong Wu, Baobao Chang, Xu Sun, Jingjing Xu, Lei Li, and Zhifang Sui. 2023. A survey on in-context learning. *arXiv:2301.00234*.

Nils Dycke, Ilia Kuznetsov, and Iryna Gurevych. 2022. Yes-yes-yes: Proactive data collection for acl rolling review and beyond. In *Findings of the Association for Computational Linguistics: EMNLP 2022*, pages 300–318.

Nils Dycke, Ilia Kuznetsov, and Iryna Gurevych. 2023. NLPeer: A unified resource for the computational study of peer review. In *Proceedings of the 61st Annual Meeting of the Association for Computational Linguistics (Volume 1: Long Papers)*, pages 5049–5073, Toronto, Canada. Association for Computational Linguistics.

Sujatha Das Gollapalli, Yixin Huang, and See-Kiong Ng. 2023. NUS-IDS at PragTag-2023: Improving pragmatic tagging of peer reviews through unlabeled data. In *Proceedings of the 10th Workshop on Argument Mining*, Singapore. Association for Computational Linguistics.

Pengcheng He, Jianfeng Gao, and Weizhu Chen. 2023. Debertav3: Improving deberta using electra-style pretraining with gradient-disentangled embedding sharing. *arXiv:2111.09543*.

Xinyu Hua, Mitko Nikolov, Nikhil Badugu, and Lu Wang. 2019. Argument mining for understanding peer reviews. In *Proceedings of the 2019 Conference of the North American Chapter of the Association for Computational Linguistics: Human Language Technologies, Volume 1 (Long and Short Papers)*, pages 2131–2137, Minneapolis, Minnesota. Association for Computational Linguistics.

Rob Johnson, Anthony Watkinson, and Michael Mabe. 2018. *The STM Report: An overview of scientific and scholarly publishing*. International Association of Scientific, Technical and Medical Publishers, The Hague, Netherlands.

Dongyeop Kang, Waleed Ammar, Bhavana Dalvi, Madeleine van Zuylen, Sebastian Kohlmeier, Eduard Hovy, and Roy Schwartz. 2018. A dataset of peer reviews (PeerRead): Collection, insights and NLP applications. In *Proceedings of the 2018 Conference of the North American Chapter of the Association for Computational Linguistics: Human Language Technologies, Volume 1 (Long Papers)*, pages 1647–1661, New Orleans, Louisiana. Association for Computational Linguistics.

Neha Kennard, Tim O'Gorman, Rajarshi Das, Akshay Sharma, Chhandak Bagchi, Matthew Clinton, Pranay Kumar Yelugam, Hamed Zamani, and Andrew McCallum. 2022. DISAPERE: A dataset for discourse structure in peer review discussions. In *Proceedings of the 2022 Conference of the North American Chapter of the Association for Computational Linguistics: Human Language Technologies*, pages 1234–1249, Seattle, United States. Association for Computational Linguistics.

Ilia Kuznetsov, Jan Buchmann, Max Eichler, and Iryna Gurevych. 2022. Revise and resubmit: an intertextual model of text-based collaboration in peer review. *Computational Linguistics*, 48(4):949–986.

Yoonsang Lee, Dongryeol Lee, and Kyomin Jung. 2023. MILAB at PragTag-2023: Enhancing cross-domain generalization through data augmentation with reduced uncertainty. In *Proceedings of the 10th Workshop on Argument Mining*, Singapore. Association for Computational Linguistics.

Yinhan Liu, Myle Ott, Naman Goyal, Jingfei Du, Mandar Joshi, Danqi Chen, Omer Levy, Mike Lewis, Luke Zettlemoyer, and Veselin Stoyanov. 2019. Roberta: A robustly optimized bert pretraining approach. *arXiv:1907.11692*.

Zhipeng Luo, Jiahui Wang, and Yihao Guo. 2023. DeepBlueAI at PragTag-2023: Ensemble-based text classification approaches under limited data resources. In *Proceedings of the 10th Workshop on Argument Mining*, Singapore. Association for Computational Linguistics.

OpenAI. 2023. GPT-4 technical report. *arXiv:2303.08774*.

Adrien Pavao, Isabelle Guyon, Anne-Catherine Letournel, Dinh-Tuan Tran, Xavier Baro, Hugo Jair Escalante, Sergio Escalera, Tyler Thomas, and Zhen Xu. 2023. Codalab competitions: An open source platform to organize scientific challenges. *Journal of Machine Learning Research*, 24(198):1–6.

Colin Raffel, Noam Shazeer, Adam Roberts, Katherine Lee, Sharan Narang, Michael Matena, Yanqi Zhou, Wei Li, and Peter J. Liu. 2019. Exploring the limits of transfer learning with a unified text-to-text transformer. *arXiv:1910.10683v1*.

Nils Reimers and Iryna Gurevych. 2019. Sentence-BERT: Sentence embeddings using Siamese BERT-networks. In *Proceedings of the 2019 Conference on Empirical Methods in Natural Language Processing and the 9th International Joint Conference on Natural Language Processing (EMNLP-IJCNLP)*, pages 3982–3992, Hong Kong, China. Association for Computational Linguistics.

Anna Rogers and Isabelle Augenstein. 2020. What can we do to improve peer review in NLP? In *Findings of the Association for Computational Linguistics: EMNLP 2020*, pages 1256–1262, Online. ACL.

Ivan Stelmakh, Nihar B Shah, and Aarti Singh. 2020. Catch me if i can: Detecting strategic behaviour in peer assessment. In *ICML Workshop on Incentives in Machine Learning*.

Kunal Suri, Prakhar Mishra, and Albert Nanda. 2023. SuryaKiran at PragTag 2023 - benchmarking domain adaptation using masked language modeling in natural language processing for specialized data. In *Proceedings of the 10th Workshop on Argument Mining*, Singapore. Association for Computational Linguistics.

Simone Teufel, Advaith Siddharthan, and Colin Batchelor. 2009. Towards domain-independent argumentative zoning: Evidence from chemistry and computational linguistics. In *Proceedings of the 2009 conference on empirical methods in natural language processing*, pages 1493–1502.

Hugo Touvron, Thibaut Lavril, Gautier Izacard, Xavier Martinet, Marie-Anne Lachaux, Timothée Lacroix, Baptiste Rozière, Naman Goyal, Eric Hambro, Faisal

Azhar, Aurelien Rodriguez, Armand Joulin, Edouard Grave, and Guillaume Lample. 2023. Llama: Open and efficient foundation language models. *arXiv:2302.13971*.

Jingyan Wang and Nihar B Shah. 2018. Your 2 is my 1, your 3 is my 9: Handling arbitrary miscalibrations in ratings. *arXiv:1806.05085*.

Tianyi Zhang, Varsha Kishore, Felix Wu, Kilian Q. Weinberger, and Yoav Artzi. 2020. Bertscore: Evaluating text generation with bert. *arXiv:1904.09675*.

CATALPA_EduNLP at PragTag-2023

Yuning Ding[1], Marie Bexte[1], and Andrea Horbach[1,2]
[1]CATALPA, FernUniversität in Hagen, Germany
[2]Hildesheim University, Germany

Abstract

This paper describes our contribution to the PragTag-2023 Shared Task. We describe and compare different approaches based on sentence classification, sentence similarity, and sequence tagging. We find that a BERT-based sentence labeling approach integrating positional information outperforms both sequence tagging and SBERT-based sentence classification. We further provide analyses highlighting the potential of combining different approaches.

1 Introduction

This paper describes the CATALPA_EduNLP entry to the First Shared Task on Pragmatic Tagging of Peer Reviews (Dycke et al., 2023). In this task, sentences within peer-reviews for academic articles from various domains are assigned a label expressing the pragmatic function of that sentence, namely *Recap*, *Strength*, *Weakness*, *Todo*, *Structure* or *Other* (Kuznetsov et al., 2022).

We experiment with various approaches presented in Section 3 and 4. As there is no clear winner among them (see results in Section 5), we further focus on comparing them to see under which conditions each setting works best (Section 6).

2 Datasets

We participated in all three evaluation setups of the Shared Task, which provided different amounts of training data. In the **full-data** setting, 117 reviews with 2326 sentences are provided, from which we split ten reviews to serve as our internal validation data. In the **low-data** setting, 33 reviews with 739 sentences are used (we take five of these reviews as our internal testing data or perform four-fold cross-validation). In the **no-data** setting, we use our internal test data from the **full-data** setting for evaluation.

The Shared Task provides two additional data sets: **F1000raw** contains unlabeled data (7423 reviews from the same domains as the training data. To use this data, we first extract the domain for each article via a lookup of the respective gateway on `https://f1000research.com`. Since a large number of articles cannot be assigned any domain, we only use articles for which we can assign a domain, yielding 269 additional *iscb*, 144 *rpkg*, 445 *diso*, 525 *case* and 227 *scip* reviews. The **ARR-22** dataset consists of 684 labeled reviews coming from a different domain and using a different annotation scheme (Dycke et al., 2022). While some of the mappings are straightforward (*paper summary* to *Recap*, *summary of strengths* to *Strength*, *summary of weaknesses* to *Weakness*), we mapped *comments, suggestions and typos* to *Todo* and found no correspondences for *Structure* and *Other*.

3 Approaches with Training Data

We explore three complementary approaches, following similar tasks of identifying sections in scientific articles or abstracts that cast the problem as one of sentence classification (Mullen et al., 2005; Teufel and Kan, 2009) or sequence labeling (Hirohata et al., 2008): A BERT-based sentence classification model (Liu et al., 2019), a Longformer-based sequence tagging model (Beltagy et al., 2020), and a SBERT-based model (Reimers and Gurevych, 2019) to compute semantic similarity between sentences. The total training and inference time was about 22 hours on a single GPU.

3.1 BERT-Based Sentence Classification

This set of approaches are extensions of the Roberta-based baseline released with the Shared Task training data. In the **full-data** setting, apart from experimenting with a different variant of pretrained models (*roberta-large*) (Liu et al., 2019), we also included positional information (**+ Pos.**), by providing either the absolute position of the respective sentence within a review and the relative position by normalizing the former by the number of sentences in that review. Besides, the

Proceedings of the 10th Workshop on Argument Mining, pages 197–201
December 7, 2023. ©2023 Association for Computational Linguistics

one-hot-encoded review domain is also used as an additional feature (**+ Domain**). These additional features are concatenated to the sentence embedding as an array. The combined representation was used to train the classification layer. To provide contextual information, we append the full review text after the sentence to be classified after a special separator token in the **+ Context** setting.

Reviews often contain domain-specific words occurring mainly in one domain, but not the others such as "malaria" in the "diso" domain or "cytobrowser" in "iscb". To improve the cross-domain generalizability of the model, we compute for each word (in its original form) a metric inspired by tf-idf where we set the frequency in the domain (using the F1000raw dataset to have a broader data basis) in relation to its general frequency provided by the wordfreq Python package[1] in its default setting. We replaced words exceeding a certain threshold (Equation 1) with a special <term> token. In addition, tokens containing the string "http" were replaced by a special <link> token and tokens without any letters by a <non_letter> token. We named this approach as **+ Word Normalization**.

$$\frac{domain\ frequency}{general\ frequency + 0.5} > 1 \qquad (1)$$

Combining the approaches above, we made a domain-specific model selection where sentences from a certain domain are scored by the model that performed best on this domain during validation. The result is reported as **Best**.

Using the Additional ARR-22 data We experimented with the **ARR-22** dataset as additional training data (**+ ARR**), but found the label distribution to be very different from the main training data. (The majority class in ARR-22 is "weakness", while "Todo" is the dominant class in the **full data**.) Therefore, we sampled the mapped elements in ARR-22 dataset according to the class distribution in the full-data. No further filtering or normalization was applied to this dataset.

3.2 Longformer-based Sequence Tagging

This approach follows Ding et al. (2022) to inherently integrate a sentence's context into the prediction. We applied it on the **full data** setting. Since it shows no advantage compared to the other sentence classification approaches, we didn't apply it to other settings. It utilizes tokens with gold-standard annotation represented by Inside-Outside-Beginning (IOB) tags. For example, the gold-standard annotation ***Recap***: *"The paper proposes ..."* will be represented as ***B-Recap***: *The,* ***I-Recap***: *paper,* ***I-Recap***: *proposes, ...* These labeled tokens are input into a pretrained Longformer language model (longformer-large-4096) for token classification. We trained for 10 epochs and then used the model with the best performance on the validation data to predict a label for each token in the test data. Each sentence got the most frequent token label assigned. We also tested the **+ Word Normalization** approach from the sentence classification in this setting.

3.3 SBERT-Based Sentence Classification

In this approach, we follow the similarity-based content scoring methodology described in Bexte et al. (2022) and Bexte et al. (2023), making predictions based on the most similar reference examples and fine-tuning an SBERT model (Reimers and Gurevych, 2019) for 10 epochs with a batch size of 8, otherwise sticking to default values.

In the **full-data** setting, we train eight separate models and take their majority vote to obtain predictions on the test data. Five of these models are experts for one of the five domains in the dataset. These are therefore trained on the respective subset of the training data (fine-tuning the *All-MiniLM-L6-v2* base model). The remaining three models are trained across all domains: An **overall** model builds training pairs across all training instances, while the training instances of two **within-domain** models (one based on *All-Mini-LM-L6-v2*, the other on *All-MiniLM-L12-v2*) are restricted to pairs of sentences from the same domain.

We pursue the same similarity-based approach in the **low-data** setting: First, we train a single model on our internal split of the limited training data. We then further pursue a 4-fold cross-validation. We found it beneficial to augment the training data using the auxiliary data from F1000Research. For each of our models from the cross-validation, we select additional reference sentences in the following way: For each target label, we include the 15 nearest neighbors, i.e., those we find the highest similarity to an existing reference answer to. This is done for three rounds, after which the resulting extended set of reference data is used to make predictions on the test data by taking the label of

[1] https://pypi.org/project/wordfreq/

the most similar reference element[2] To prepare our submission to the challenge, we again perform a majority voting, taking the four votes of the augmented models from our cross-validation and that of the model trained on our internal train-test split.

4 Zero-Shot Approaches

This section describes our **no-data** approaches.

4.1 Clustering

Using a pretrained SBERT model (*All-MiniLM-L12-v2*), we encode representations of the target labels to serve as the centroids of clusters. These representations are derived from the label descriptions the challenge organizers gave and a set of at most three keywords per label (see Appendix A.1). Each answer from the testing data is then assigned to the label representation with the highest cosine similarity, thus predicting the respective label for this test instance.

4.2 GPT

We also explore using large commercial language models in a zero-shot setting. We prompt the GPT3.5 through the openai API by providing label definitions in the Shared Task description. As a post-processing step, we replace labels not corresponding to one of the six categories provided with *Other*.

5 Results

Following the evaluation scheme in the Shared Task, we report macro-averaged F1-scores per domain for our own data split and only an overall F1-score for the challenge test set.

Table 1 shows the results of our internal splits of the data. For the **full-data** setup, we see that adding additional information like position, domain, or context to the BERT-based model does only improve the results for individual domains but leads to performance drops on others, so there is no substantial improvement overall (column *mean*). However, if we select per domain the setup performing best on the training data, we see an overall improvement on the test data (.88 vs .82 for the baseline model.) Adding the ARR data as additional training data led to decreased performance, although sampling the ARR data to a similar distribution to the main training data helped somewhat. Both the SBERT-based model and the sequence tagging approach did not reach the performance of the BERT-based model in the full-data setup (.62 and .79 vs .88 in the best configuration).

However, the situation changes drastically when the amount of available training data is reduced (**low-data**). In this scenario, the BERT-based model could hardly learn anything while the SBERT-based model reached a performance close to the **full-data** setup. Note that the results are not directly comparable across the different dataset variants, as the test data is not identical. Performance in the **no-data** setting is unsurprisingly again reduced, with GPT outperforming our SBERT-based clustering method.

Table 2 shows the methods that led to the best

	Domain					
	case	diso	iscb	rpkg	scip	mean
	Full-data					
BERT-based						
Roberta-large	.80	.87	.88	.75	.77	.82
+ Word Normalization	.87	**.88**	.94	.68	.56	.79
+ Pos.	.76	.85	.92	.74	.77	.81
+ Domain	**.89**	.79	.82	.69	.81	.80
+ Context	.87	.83	.83	.75	.76	.81
+ Pos., Context	.87	.82	**.94**	**.83**	.70	.83
+ Pos., Context, Domain	.83	.81	.88	.72	**.85**	.82
Best	.89	.88	.94	.83	.85	**.88**
+ ARR	.60	.72	.78	.61	.67	.68
+ ARR Sampled	.68	.66	.78	.60	.78	.70
Sequence Tagging	.67	.65	.72	.56	.51	.62
+ Word Normalization	.59	.65	.77	.56	.53	.62
SBERT-based						
ALL	.82	.78	.83	.64	.85	.78
ALL_large	.71	.74	.86	.67	.70	.74
ALL_cross	.84	.74	.77	.67	.77	.76
Domains	.75	.76	.66	.74	.80	.74
Voting	.88	.81	.84	.67	.77	.79
	Low-data					
BERT-based						
Roberta-large	.10	.17	.19	.11	.24	.16
SBERT-based						
Train-test split	.52	1.0	.70	.91	.68	.76
4-fold CV	.71	.71	.77	.66	.69	.71
4-fold CV + aux	.74	.72	.80	.65	.74	.73
	No-data					
SBERT-based	.19	.33	.17	.22	.15	.21
GPT	.53	.54	.46	.24	.42	.44

Table 1: F1 results on our internal validation split.

Setting	Submission	mean
Final	Roberta large + Pos., Text	.81
Full-data	Roberta large + Pos., Text	.82
Low-data	SBERT 4-fold voting	.75
No-data	SBERT clustering	.22

Table 2: F1 results on challenge test data.

[2]We also experimented with additional fine-tuning using this augmented training set but found this not helpful.

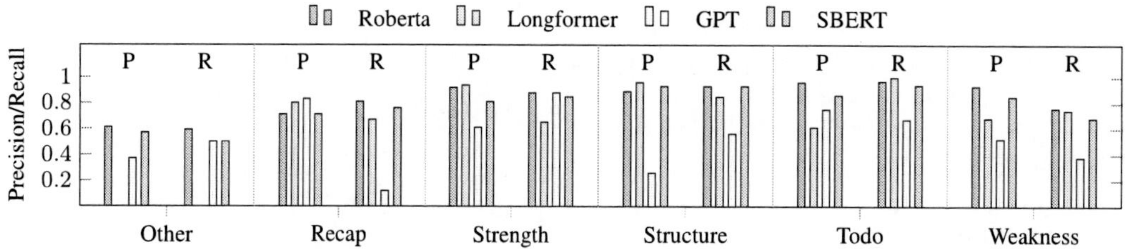

Figure 1: Per-label precision and recall of our different methods on our internal test data of the full-data setting.

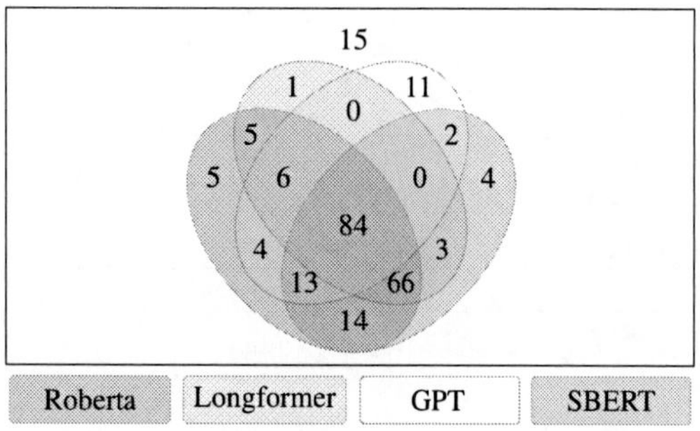

Figure 2: Venn diagram of how many sentences are classified correctly by which methods.

performance on the challenge test data in the different settings. Unfortunately, our **Best** approach on the validation set did not beat the **+Pos., Context** approach on the test data in the **full-data** setting. Therefore, we only submit the **+Pos., Context** approach in the final round.

The test data in the **final** setting contains unseen data from a "secret" domain, which might explain the slight performance drop (.82 vs. .81). But our approach reaches the second-best performance on the data from the "secret" domain with an F1-score of 0.79 on the leaderboard, indicating its good generalization ability.

In the **low-data** setting, our SBERT-based method performs better than the BERT-based methods, which consists of the results observed on the validation set. The **no-data** performance of our SBERT-based method is slightly better on the test set than the average on our validation splits. (Following the competition rules regarding reproducibility, we did not submit our GPT results since the model requires a paid API.)

6 Analysis

The different approaches produce results in the same ballpark so that one may wonder if they can be used interchangeably. To investigate this we compare the results by checking four conditions: The percentage of sentences that **all** four models judge correctly, the percentage that **none** of the models classified correctly, which proportion is classified correctly in a **majority** setting and the percentage of correctly classified sentences that could be reached in an **oracle** condition if we knew to which model a sentence should be passed, i.e. the percentage of sentences judged correctly by at least one model.

For this analysis, we use the respective best-performing model variant on our internal split of the data provided for the full data setting. We analyze all four approaches we took: Sentence classification using Roberta, similarity-based classification with SBERT, sequence tagging using the longformer architecture, and zero-shot application of GPT. Figure 2 gives an overview of how many sentences are correctly classified by which method. The **oracle** condition sums up to 94% of test instances being assigned the correct label, meaning that the remaining six percent are classified correctly by **none** of the methods. About a third (36%) of the data is correctly solved by **all** four models, and a **majority** voting over their predictions comes up to 83% accuracy, which is 1% lower than what Roberta achieves on its own.

Overall, GPT seems the most distinct from the other methods: It has the highest number of 11 sentences that none of the other methods can classify correctly. Such sentences often have the label *Other*, for example "Dear Authors". However, there are 66 sentences for which all other methods except GPT predict the correct label. GPT rarely labeled instances of "Recap" correctly and often mislabeled "Structure" as "Other", such as "Reviewer response for version 1". Figure 1 breaks down performance for the individual labels, revealing GPT to be much worse in both precision and recall when it comes to *Structure*, and showing especially low recall for *Recap*. All methods have the most difficulty with sentences labeled *Other*, with our sequence tagging approach having both precision and recall of zero. The overall best-performing Roberta method especially shows superiority in terms of high and balanced precision and recall values for the labels *Strength*, *Todo*, and *Weakness*.

7 Conclusion

We have presented experiments using a variety of very different approaches. The comparison shows that they behave quite differently and that a sensible combination of approaches yields further improvements. Future work therefore has to determine which approach is most suitable for a given item to be classified.

Acknowledgements

This work was partially conducted at "CATALPA - Center of Advanced Technology for Assisted Learning and Predictive Analytics" of the FernUniversität in Hagen, Germany.

References

Iz Beltagy, Matthew E Peters, and Arman Cohan. 2020. Longformer: The long-document transformer. *arXiv preprint arXiv:2004.05150*.

Marie Bexte, Andrea Horbach, and Torsten Zesch. 2022. Similarity-based content scoring - How to make S-BERT keep up with BERT. In *Proceedings of the 17th Workshop on Innovative Use of NLP for Building Educational Applications (BEA 2022)*, pages 118–123.

Marie Bexte, Andrea Horbach, and Torsten Zesch. 2023. Similarity-based content scoring-a more classroom-suitable alternative to instance-based scoring? In *Findings of the Association for Computational Linguistics: ACL 2023*, pages 1892–1903.

Yuning Ding, Marie Bexte, and Andrea Horbach. 2022. Don't drop the topic - the role of the prompt in argument identification in student writing. In *Proceedings of the 17th Workshop on Innovative Use of NLP for Building Educational Applications (BEA 2022)*, pages 124–133, Seattle, Washington. Association for Computational Linguistics.

Nils Dycke, Ilia Kuznetsov, and Iryna Gurevych. 2022. NLPEER: A unified resource for the computational study of peer review. *arXiv preprint arXiv:2211.06651*.

Nils Dycke, Ilia Kuznetsov, and Iryna Gurevych. 2023. Overview of PragTag-2023: Low-resource multi-domain pragmatic tagging of peer reviews. In *Proceedings of the 10th Workshop on Argument Mining*, Singapore. Association for Computational Linguistics.

Kenji Hirohata, Naoaki Okazaki, Sophia Ananiadou, and Mitsuru Ishizuka. 2008. Identifying sections in scientific abstracts using conditional random fields. In *Proceedings of the Third International Joint Conference on Natural Language Processing: Volume-I*.

Ilia Kuznetsov, Jan Buchmann, Max Eichler, and Iryna Gurevych. 2022. Revise and resubmit: An intertextual model of text-based collaboration in peer review. *Computational Linguistics*, 48(4):949–986.

Yinhan Liu, Myle Ott, Naman Goyal, Jingfei Du, Mandar Joshi, Danqi Chen, Omer Levy, Mike Lewis, Luke Zettlemoyer, and Veselin Stoyanov. 2019. RoBERTa: A robustly optimized BERT pretraining approach. *arXiv preprint arXiv:1907.11692*.

Tony Mullen, Yoko Mizuta, and Nigel Collier. 2005. A baseline feature set for learning rhetorical zones using full articles in the biomedical domain. *ACM SIGKDD Explorations Newsletter*, 7(1):52–58.

Nils Reimers and Iryna Gurevych. 2019. Sentence-bert: Sentence embeddings using siamese bert-networks. In *Proceedings of the 2019 Conference on Empirical Methods in Natural Language Processing and the 9th International Joint Conference on Natural Language Processing (EMNLP-IJCNLP)*. Association for Computational Linguistics.

Simone Teufel and Min-Yen Kan. 2009. Robust argumentative zoning for sensemaking in scholarly documents. In *Natural Language Processing for Digital Libraries Workshop*, pages 154–170. Springer.

A Appendix

A.1 Keywords for Zero-Shot Clustering Label Assignment

'Todo': ['should', 'could', 'need'], 'Strength': ['good', 'strength', 'clear'], 'Weakness': ['weakness', 'shortcoming', 'flaw'], 'Structure': ['reviewer'], 'Recap': ['authors', 'describe', 'article'], 'Other': ['other']

DeepBlueAI at PragTag-2023:Ensemble-based Text Classification Approaches under Limited Data Resources

Zhipeng Luo **Jiahui Wang** **Yihao Guo**
DeepBlue Artificial Intelligence Technology (Shanghai) Co., Ltd, Shanghai, China
{luozp, wangjh, guoyh}@deepblueai.com

Abstract

Due to the scarcity of review data and the high annotation cost, in this paper, we primarily delve into the fine-tuning of pretrained models using limited data. To enhance the robustness of the model, we employ adversarial training techniques. By introducing subtle perturbations, we compel the model to better cope with adversarial attacks, thereby increasing the stability of the model in input data. We utilize pooling techniques to aid the model in extracting critical information, reducing computational complexity, and improving the model's generalization capability. Experimental results demonstrate the effectiveness of our proposed approach on a review paper dataset with limited data volume.

1 Introduction

Peer review stands as a fundamental pillar of the scientific process, yet it presents formidable challenges that could greatly benefit from automation and support. At the heart of peer review are review reports – concise, argumentative documents in which reviewers assess research papers and offer recommendations for improvement. Automating the analysis of argumentation within peer reviews (Dycke et al., 2023) holds vast potential, ranging from facilitating meta-scientific investigations into review practices to consolidating insights from multiple reviews and aiding less experienced reviewers.

Text classification is a significant and challenging task. However, when relying on relatively small datasets, traditional machine learning methods may encounter issues such as overfitting and poor generalization performance. In such cases, pre-trained models serve as powerful tools that offer robust solutions for addressing data scarcity. Pre-trained models, particularly those based on the deep learning Transformer (Vaswani et al., 2017) architecture, have demonstrated significant success in natural language processing tasks.

RoBERTa (A Robustly Optimized BERT Pretraining Approach) (Liu et al., 2019), XLM-RoBERTa (Conneau et al., 2019) and DeBERTa (Deep BERT with Disentangled Attention) (He et al., 2023) are pre-trained models based on the Transformer architecture that have garnered widespread attention in the field of NLP. Through fine-tuning these pre-trained models, exceptional performance can be achieved on smaller datasets, mitigating overfitting issues and improving generalization performance.

This paper focuses on the application of RoBERTa, XLM-RoBERTa and DeBERTa to address text classification problems within a peer review dataset.

2 Related work

Pragmatic tagging of peer reviews is, in fact, a classification task, and in common classification tasks. In the field of text classification, models like Recurrent Neural Networks (RNN) (Jordan, 1997), and Long Short-Term Memory networks (LSTM) (Hochreiter and Schmidhuber, 1997) introduced more nonlinear factors, enabling them to automatically learn feature representations from data and achieving remarkable results.

However, deep learning methods may face overfitting issues on small datasets and require a substantial amount of labeled data for training. To address these issues, the development of pre-trained models has become a groundbreaking direction. Pre-trained models are trained on large-scale unlabeled corpora, learning rich language representations that enable them to better capture semantic relationships between words, as seen in models like BERT (Devlin et al., 2018). Subsequently, these pre-trained models can be fine-tuned for specific tasks to exhibit exceptional performance.

Among these models, RoBERTa (Liu et al., 2019) and DeBERTa (He et al., 2023) are representatives of pre-trained models based on the Trans-

Proceedings of the 10th Workshop on Argument Mining, pages 202–206
December 7, 2023.

	Recap	Strength	Weakness	Todo	Other	Structure
Count	87	62	130	245	106	109
Percentage(%)	11.77	8.39	17.59	33.15	14.34	14.75

Table 1: Number and percentage of each category in low_data

former architecture. RoBERTa achieved significant performance improvement across various NLP tasks by adjusting pre-training strategies and hyperparameters. On the other hand, DeBERTa enhanced the model's generalization capability and performance on different tasks by introducing disentangled attention mechanisms. In small dataset text classification tasks, models like RoBERTa and DeBERTa demonstrate remarkable capabilities. Their learned rich semantic representations from extensive corpora enable them to effectively extract features and capture relationships between sentences even in data-limited scenarios.

In the application of pre-trained models, researchers have introduced various techniques to further optimize model performance. Techniques such as k-fold cross-validation better evaluate the model's stability and generalization ability. Adversarial training methods like Fast Gradient Method (FGM)(Miyato et al., 2016) enhance the model's robustness, preventing it from being disrupted by adversarial attacks. Pooling techniques such as max pooling, min pooling and attention pooling allow models to understand text information at different levels. Additionally, model ensemble techniques combine predictions from multiple models, improving overall classification performance.

3 Task description

The goal of this task is to perform automatic analysis of argumentation in peer review. Our input data consists of each sentence in the argumentation, and the output results are the corresponding label categories for each sentence. The competition is divided into multiple stages, each providing two datasets(Kuznetsov et al., 2022)(Dycke et al., 2022): "low_data" and "full_data".

The training set provided in the "low_data" comprises a total of 34 review articles, 793 sentences in total. The objective is to classify each sentence into one of the six categories. We have conducted a statistical analysis for each category in the dataset, and the results are presented in Table 1.

The training set provided in the "full_data" consists of a total of 118 review articles, 2324 sentences in total. The objective remains the classification of each sentence into one of the six categories. Similar to the previous dataset, we conducted a statistical analysis for each category in the dataset, and the results are presented in Table 2.

4 Methodology

4.1 Model architecture

In this task, we primarily utilized three architecture-based pre-trained models: DeBERTa-v3-large, RoBERTa-large and XLM-RoBERTa-large, as our benchmark models. We incorporated a pooling layer to project features into lower dimensions, effectively reducing the number of parameters and computational load in the network while preserving essential information. Moreover, specific linear layers were added based on the number of task categories, yielding probabilities for each category. Ultimately, the highest predicted probability was selected to determine the final classification outcome of the model.

4.2 Pooling

In this section, we mainly used 2 types of pooling, attention pooling and maximum pooling, and ensembled the two different pooling models obtained when calculating the final result.

Attention Pooling: Attention pooling is a technique that enhances critical information while capturing local features in text. We calculate the weight for each token and effectively model relationships between different words. Specifically, the input word embedding sequence is weightedly aggregated and normalized, yielding a weight vector. This weight vector indicates the higher significance of specific words within the text. By element-wise multiplication of this weight vector with the word embedding sequence, we obtain the text representation after attention pooling.

Max Pooling: Max pooling is a common pooling technique employed to extract crucial features from local regions. In our approach, we apply max pooling to text representations to emphasize significant information within the text. Specifically, we perform max pooling operations on each window, se-

	Recap	Strength	Weakness	Todo	Other	Structure
Count	346	220	377	681	401	301
Percentage(%)	14.875	9.458	16.208	29.278	17.240	12.941

Table 2: Number and percentage of each category in full_data

lecting the maximum value within the window as the representation for that window. This technique aids in capturing key features in the text.

4.3 Adversarial Training

To enhance the model's robustness, we introduced adversarial training, specifically utilizing the Fast Gradient Method (FGM). FGM is an adversarial attack technique that we applied during the training process by injecting slight perturbations into the embedding layer. This compels the model to better handle adversarial attacks. Adversarial training in our approach involves computing the gradient of the loss function with respect to the input at each training iteration and slightly updating the input. By incorporating adversarial training, our approach elevates the model's robustness, enabling it to better handle interference within input data.

K-fold	bs = 2	bs = 4	bs = 4
P0(%)	83.538	82.384	80.533
P1(%)	80.711	82.431	82.29
P2(%)	78.298	83.859	91.789
P3(%)	88.55	90.106	73.363
P4(%)	85.141	81.899	79.638
P5(%)	-	-	87.8
P6(%)	-	-	84.755
P7(%)	-	-	79.021
P8(%)	-	-	82.161
Avg(%)	83.2476	84.1358	82.372

Table 3: Multifold cross-validation results for different models on low_data

4.4 K-Fold Cross Validation:

Model ensemble is a widely employed technique in machine learning competitions, while k-fold cross-validation serves as a common method to assess and enhance model performance during the training process. In k-fold cross-validation, the dataset is partitioned into k mutually exclusive subsets. Among these, k-1 subsets are utilized as training data, and the remaining subset serves as validation data. We iterate through k-fold cross-validation multiple times, each time selecting a different subset as the validation data. This ensures that each sample gets an opportunity to be used for validation. This way, we obtain k performance evaluation metrics, enabling a comprehensive understanding of the model's performance.

5 Experiments

5.1 Setting

On the "low_data" dataset, we fine-tuned various parameter values and selected the parameter combination that yielded the best experimental results. Specifically, the batch size was set to different values, namely 2 and 4, while the initial learning rate was set to 1×10^{-4}. Other configurations remained consistent with those used on the "full_data" dataset. For the "full_data" dataset, during the training process of all models, we set the batch size to 8 and the initial learning rate to 1×5^{-4}. Subsequently, a learning rate decay was applied, with a decay rate of 0.5 and a minimum of 1×10^{-7}. The models were trained for 10 epochs, with the early stopping strategy in place. Training would be stopped if the performance did not improve after 3 consecutive epochs. All training was conducted on V100-32G GPUs.

5.2 Training results on low_data

We recorded the results of k-fold cross-validation during the training process of the single DeBERTa-v3-large model on the "low_data" dataset. The batch size for the first experimental group was set to 2, while the subsequent two groups used a batch size of 4. For the first two groups of experiments, the dataset was divided into 5 subsets for training. In the third group, the dataset was split into 9 subsets for training. The interim results of training, as well as the average across folds, are presented in Table 3. Since the same model was employed, the first row of the table distinguishes solely based on the batch size used.

5.3 Training results on full_data

As depicted in Table 4, we have documented the k-fold cross-validation outcomes of model training on the "full_data" dataset. The models em-

K-fold	RoBERTa	RoBERTa(MaxPooling)	DeBERTa	DeBERTa	XLM-R	XLM-R(FGM)
P0(%)	86.116	86.452	86.846	87.037	86.920	84.518
P1(%)	83.246	85.259	86.379	85.024	80.433	86.149
P2(%)	87.273	90.455	90.991	91.699	90.519	89.422
P3(%)	81.627	84.676	84.919	82.878	81.76	81.183
P4(%)	83.13	84.020	85.513	83.994	81.852	83.624
P5(%)	81.005	85.078	87.435	87.106	84.208	81.121
P6(%)	85.932	85.915	88.821	86.818	85.833	86.397
P7(%)	83.861	85.112	84.617	82.779	84.290	85.753
P8(%)	82.959	82.026	84.044	82.713	82.863	80.679
P9(%)	81.775	83.326	82.336	-	82.722	84.827
Avg(%)	83.6924	85.232	86.190	85.561	84.14	84.3673

Table 4: Presentation of results at various stages

ployed in this study are RoBERTa-large, XLM-RoBERTa-large and DeBERT-v3-large. For the fine-tuning of RoBERTa-large, we adopted the max pooling approach, after applying the max pooling technique during fine-tuning, the avg_f1_mean score increased from 83.6924 to 85.2319. When fine-tuning with XLM-RoBERTa-large, we experimented with the inclusion of FGM. Compared to not using FGM, the avg_f1_mean score improved from 84.14 to 84.3673. When fine-tuning DeBERT-v3-large, we conducted two sets of experiments, both utilizing attention pooling techniques. The primary distinction between the first and second experiments lay in the use of 10-fold and 9-fold cross-validation, respectively. Across multiple trials, the experimental outcomes of the DeBERTa model consistently surpassed those of RoBERTa, underscoring the robust performance of the DeBERTa model.

In the final stage of the competition, a secret test dataset was introduced to assess the models' generalization performance. The experimental outcomes are presented in Table 5. We used a total of 19 models for voting, including 9-fold DeBERTa and 10-fold DeBERTa models, and selected the class with the highest frequency as the final result. The final F1_mean score was 0.8383. Using a combination of 9-fold DeBERTa, 10-fold DeBERTa, and 10-fold RoBERTa models, we used a total of 29 models for voting, and the final F1_mean was 0.8413. By further incorporating 10-fold XLM-RoBERTa models alongside the previous ones, totaling 39 models for voting, the final F1_mean was 0.8411. It can be observed that the fusion of different types of models is beneficial to the results. Although there was a slight decrease on the XLM-RoBERTa model, the diverse feature extraction capabilities among multiple models contribute significantly to the improvement of results.

6 Conclusion

In this paper, we have presented a comprehensive approach for text classification tasks on small-scale peer review datasets. By combining attention pooling, max pooling, and adversarial training (FGM), we achieved significant performance improvements. Through experimental validation, we have demonstrated the superiority of our method on small datasets. In the evolving era of deep learning, our approach amalgamates various techniques, providing an effective solution for text classification on small datasets. It overcomes the challenges posed by data scarcity, enhancing both model performance and robustness, offering novel insights and methodologies for addressing text classification challenges on small datasets.

	f1_mean	f1_case	f1_diso	f1_iscb	f1_rpkg	f1_scip	f1_secret
submission1	0.8383	0.829	0.842	0.836	0.854	0.889	0.779
submission2	0.8413	0.829	0.841	0.828	0.860	0.890	0.801
submission3	0.8411	0.831	0.847	0.828	0.860	0.882	0.798

Table 5: Final leaderboard scores for our submission

References

Alexis Conneau, Kartikay Khandelwal, Naman Goyal, Vishrav Chaudhary, Guillaume Wenzek, Francisco Guzmán, Edouard Grave, Myle Ott, Luke Zettlemoyer, and Veselin Stoyanov. 2019. Unsupervised cross-lingual representation learning at scale. *arXiv preprint arXiv:1911.02116*.

Jacob Devlin, Ming-Wei Chang, Kenton Lee, and Kristina Toutanova. 2018. Bert: Pre-training of deep bidirectional transformers for language understanding. *arXiv preprint arXiv:1810.04805*.

Nils Dycke, Ilia Kuznetsov, and Iryna Gurevych. 2022. Nlpeer: A unified resource for the computational study of peer review. *arXiv preprint arXiv:2211.06651*.

Nils Dycke, Ilia Kuznetsov, and Iryna Gurevych. 2023. Argmining 2023 shared task - pragtag: Low-resource multi-domain pragmatic tagging of peer reviews. In *Proceedings of the 10th Workshop on Argument Mining*, Singapore. Association for Computational Linguistics.

Pengcheng He, Jianfeng Gao, and Weizhu Chen. 2023. DeBERTav3: Improving deBERTa using ELECTRA-style pre-training with gradient-disentangled embedding sharing. In *The Eleventh International Conference on Learning Representations*.

Sepp Hochreiter and Jürgen Schmidhuber. 1997. Long short-term memory. *Neural computation*, 9(8):1735–1780.

Michael I Jordan. 1997. Serial order: A parallel distributed processing approach. In *Advances in psychology*, volume 121, pages 471–495. Elsevier.

Ilia Kuznetsov, Jan Buchmann, Max Eichler, and Iryna Gurevych. 2022. Revise and resubmit: An intertextual model of text-based collaboration in peer review. *Computational Linguistics*, 48(4):949–986.

Yinhan Liu, Myle Ott, Naman Goyal, Jingfei Du, Mandar Joshi, Danqi Chen, Omer Levy, Mike Lewis, Luke Zettlemoyer, and Veselin Stoyanov. 2019. Roberta: A robustly optimized bert pretraining approach. *arXiv preprint arXiv:1907.11692*.

Takeru Miyato, Andrew M Dai, and Ian Goodfellow. 2016. Adversarial training methods for semi-supervised text classification. In *International Conference on Learning Representations*.

Ashish Vaswani, Noam Shazeer, Niki Parmar, Jakob Uszkoreit, Llion Jones, Aidan N Gomez, Łukasz Kaiser, and Illia Polosukhin. 2017. Attention is all you need. *Advances in neural information processing systems*, 30.

MILAB at PragTag-2023: Enhancing Cross-Domain Generalization through Data Augmentation with Reduced Uncertainty

Yoonsang Lee[1*], Dongryeol Lee[2*], Kyomin Jung[2, 3†]
[1]College of Liberal Studies, Seoul National University
[2]Dept. of Electrical and Computer Engineering, Seoul National University
[3]ASRI, Seoul National University
`{lysianthus, drl123, kjung}@snu.ac.kr`

Abstract

This paper describes our submission to the PragTag task, which aims to categorize each sentence from peer reviews into one of the six distinct pragmatic tags. The task consists of three conditions: `full`, `low`, and `zero`, each distinguished by the number of training data and further categorized into five distinct domains. The main challenge of this task is the domain shift, which is exacerbated by non-uniform distribution and the limited availability of data across the six pragmatic tags and their respective domains. To address this issue, we predominantly employ two data augmentation techniques designed to mitigate data imbalance and scarcity: *pseudo-labeling and synonym generation.* We experimentally demonstrate the effectiveness of our approaches, achieving the *first* rank under the `zero condition` and the *third* in the `full and low conditions`.[1]

1 Introduction

Peer review is a fundamental procedure for assessing the quality of academic manuscripts (Ware and Mabe, 2015). Most reviews are characterized by concise argumentative feedback, wherein reviewers highlight both strengths and weaknesses while offering suggestions for revision. This observation has led researchers to frame the structures of peer reviews as a subset of argument mining (Lawrence and Reed, 2020; Lauscher et al., 2018; Hua et al., 2019). Parallel to these insights, efforts have been made to automate the peer review process (Yuan et al., 2022; Wang et al., 2020). The automation of this process yields two primary advantages: it facilitates authors by distilling the main feedback from reviews and helps reviewers by aggregating information from multiple reviews.

Recently, Dycke et al. (2023) introduced a novel task, pragmatic tagging for peer review, wherein each sentence of a scientific review is classified into one of six predefined pragmatic categories. The proposed task is tailored for a multi-domain scientific corpus, where certain domains might employ specific terminologies that are not prevalent in others or require a unique evaluative perspective during the review process (Rogers and Augenstein, 2020). Furthermore, the nature of scientific review necessitates profound domain knowledge and careful examination by the reviewer, thereby posing challenges in large-scale data collection. Such challenges, referred to as cross-domain generalization (Caciularu et al., 2021; Du et al., 2020), have been the subject of intensive investigation within natural language processing.

To address these challenges, we propose two approaches to enhancing the generalization of the model over multiple domains: pseudo-labeling and synonym generation. Under `full` and `low conditions`, we finetune BERT (Devlin et al., 2018) based classifiers using the training data and pseudo-label auxiliary data through an ensemble approach to ensure label quality. In the `zero condition`, we exploit the existing sections of the ARR dataset and inject intrinsic characteristics of pragmatic tags without utilizing any large language models. Our method accomplished the *highest* performance in the `zero condition` as well as the *third* in the `full` and `low conditions`.

2 Related Works

Multi-class Classification The task of categorizing input sentences into multiple labels has seen extensive development across various domains (Soleimani and Miller, 2016; Dang et al., 2020). Among the readily available models for text classification, RoBERTa (Liu et al., 2019) stands out, characterized by its incorporation of a classification layer with a transformer encoder. Notably,

* Equal contribution.

† Corresponding authors.

[1]The codes are available at `https://github.com/lilys012/pragtag`

Proceedings of the 10th Workshop on Argument Mining, pages 207–211
December 7, 2023. ©2023 Association for Computational Linguistics

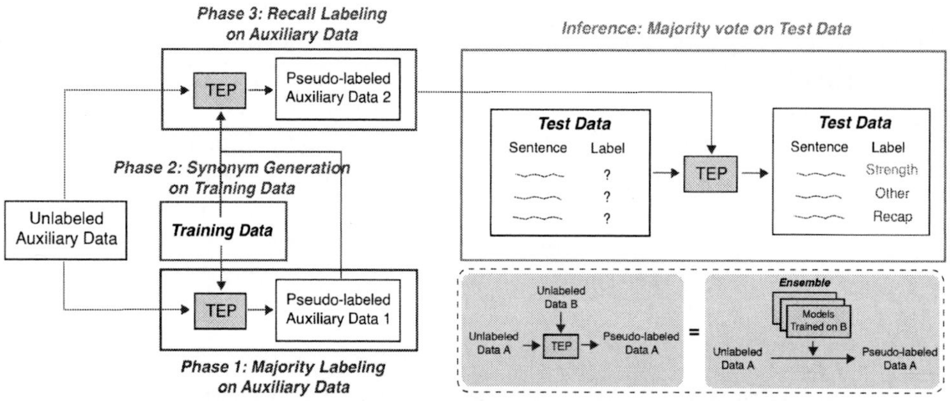

Figure 1: Overview of our proposed approach to pragmatic tagging in the full condition. Phase 1: pseudo-labeler models are trained using provided training data and subsequently utilized to label unlabeled auxiliary data. Phase 2: Training data are augmented by a synonym generator. Phase 3: Augmented data from Phase 1 and 2 are used to finetune the labeler. Models reapply tagging to the auxiliary data with increased certainty. Phase 4: Classifier trained with the labeled data from Phase 3 are ensembled to predict the labels of the test data.

this model is acclaimed for its capability to generalize across diverse domains. However, for datasets tailored to specific domains, models such as SciBERT (Beltagy et al., 2019) and BioBERT (Lee et al., 2020) have been proposed. Additionally, existing research illustrates that the performance of these models can be further enhanced through the employment of ensemble techniques (Saha and Srihari, 2023).

Data augmentation Data augmentation is widely exploited to enrich and generalize datasets (Chen et al., 2023). A sentence can be expanded through the utilization of rule-based techniques and interpolation (Feng et al., 2021). Furthermore, in the case of unlabeled datasets, a trained model can assign pseudo-labels to the unlabeled data, thereby facilitating supplementary training (Lee et al., 2013).

3 Dataset

Task Data The data for the task is sourced from F1000RD (Kuznetsov et al., 2022), which is a comprehensive multi-domain collection of both reviews and their pragmatic labels. Under the `low condition`, only 20% of the full task dataset is employed. Detailed statistics of the six tags across five distinct domains are described in Table 1.

Auxiliary Data The auxiliary data is comprised of two datasets: F1000raw and ARR-22 (Dycke et al., 2022). The former, F1000raw, is an extensive, unlabeled corpus originating from the same source as F1000RD. Conversely, ARR-22 represents a collection of peer reviews from the ACL community. Each review within ARR-22 is segmented into sections designated as Paper Summary, Comments / Suggestions / Typos, Summary of Strengths, and Summary of Weaknesses. It is important to note that the utilization of any external datasets beyond these is strictly prohibited for our task.

	Full						
Domain	**Strg.**	**Weak.**	**Strc.**	**Rec.**	**Td.**	**Oth.**	**Total**
scip	46	73	70	52	115	105	461
iscb	30	93	53	77	173	70	496
rpkg	67	85	64	69	132	89	506
diso	43	81	61	76	135	79	475
case	34	45	53	72	126	58	388
Total	220	377	301	346	681	401	2326

Table 1: Task data statistics based on full conditions and five domains: science policy research (scip), bioinformatics (iscb), R package (rpkg), disease outbreak (diso), and medical case reports (case). Within each domain, the count of sentences is categorized by six labels: Strength (Strg.), Weakness (Weak.), Structure (Strc.), Recap (Rec.), Todo (Td.), and Other (Oth.).

4 Methodology

The efficacy of an individual model can be influenced by various hyperparameters throughout the training process, which could potentially lead to inaccurate predictions. Therefore, we opt for an ensemble approach for our task, as depicted in Figure 1. From the entire training data, we set aside 18 reviews to constitute a validation subset. This subset excludes reviews that belong to the `low condition` dataset. The validation subset is consistently applied across all scenarios for the selection of hyperparameters and models.

	Majority	Consensus
F1000raw	**0.8454**	0.8333
F1000raw+ARR	0.8263	0.8251

Table 2: F1-mean score for auxiliary data labeling. Models are trained using the F1000raw dataset or in conjunction with the ARR dataset. Validation data is labeled by majority and consensus methods.

seed	model	learning rate	score
42	RoBERTa-base	1e-5	**0.7498**
142	RoBERTa-base	2e-5	**0.7667**
242	SciBERT	3e-5	0.7260
342	BioBERT	1e-5	**0.7534**
442	RoBERTa-base	3e-5	0.7306

Table 3: Classifier performance under the low condition. Bold score indicates the selection for majority labeling.

4.1 Pseudo-labeling

To overcome the scarcity of training data, we devise a strategy involving pseudo-labeling (Lee et al., 2013) for the auxiliary data. We train five RoBERTa-base classifiers (Liu et al., 2019) with the training data, each instantiated with varying random seeds. Subsequently, the F1000raw and ARR datasets (Dycke et al., 2022) are partitioned [2] and labeled via each of the aforementioned classifiers. We now introduce two distinct ensemble methodologies as shown in Figure 1: 1) Majority labeling for Phase 1 and Phase 4. 2) Recall labeling for Phase 3.

Majority labeling Majority labeling selects the tag that receives the majority vote among the classifiers. We also compare it with consensus labeling, which retains only the reviews labeled identically. Table 2 indicates that the combination of majority labeling and only utilizing the F1000raw dataset outperforms other combinations. In scenarios of `low condition`, different random seeds, pretrained models, and learning rates are employed for training initial classifiers. F1000raw dataset is then majority labeled across four distinct models: three distinguished by their performance on the validation set (bold in Table 3), and an additional model trained on synonym-augmented data.

Recall labeling We propose a novel approach named Recall labeling to minimize the uncertainty of each label. For each pragmatic tag, we select the model with the highest recall. In descending order of their recall scores in Table 4, models label the sentences. Notably, *Other* tag consistently registered the lowest recall across all experiments. After labeling the distinct tags, any residual sentences are designated as "*Other.*" To further avoid the noise from arbitrary segmentation, we intentionally omit the sentences consisting of a singular word.

[2] Using NLTK, https://www.nltk.org

Strength	Weakness	Structure
0.936	0.892	1.0
Recap	**Todo**	**Other**
0.928	0.990	0.685

Table 4: Recall scores of the best model selected for each pragmatic tag.

4.2 Synonym generation

The disparities in data quantities across domains and classes are evident in Table 1. Such class imbalances have been documented to foster biases towards the majority class, subsequently leading to diminished classification performance (Ali et al., 2013; Johnson and Khoshgoftaar, 2019). To address this prevalent issue of class imbalance, we employ data augmentation techniques to harmonize the distribution of labels in each domain. Specifically, we utilize the NLPaug[3] package to substitute nouns in each sentence with their synonymous counterparts. To ensure the quality of augmented sentences, we compute BERTSCORE (Zhang et al., 2019) between augmented and original sentences, and only add top-k augmented sentences into the training dataset.[4]

5 Results

Experiment results over different conditions and domains are presented in Table 5.

5.1 Full-data

Test data is labeled in a majority-vote manner using the best-performing models from Phase 3. The F1-score for each specific model is depicted in Figure 2. Through this methodology, the classifier achieved an F1-score of 0.838. We trained an extra model using the entire task data, including the validation set. The performance in Table 5 is derived from the inclusion of this auxiliary model within the majority labeling paradigm.

[3] https://github.com/makcedward/nlpaug

[4] The selection of k varied across domains.

	f1_mean	f1_case	f1_diso	f1_iscb	f1_rpkg	f1_scip	f1_secret
full	0.839	0.840	0.837	0.801	0.854	0.865	-
low	0.771	0.778	0.746	0.754	0.777	0.800	-
zero	0.516	0.502	0.518	0.551	0.492	0.516	-
final (full)	0.824	0.844	0.840	0.798	0.843	0.864	0.755
final (zero)	0.517	0.502	0.520	0.557	0.508	0.489	0.528

Table 5: Best model performances across the following conditions: full, low, zero, and final phases of both full and zero settings. F1 scores are computed across six distinct domains in a macro average.

5.2 Low-data

As expounded in Section 4.1, a classifier is trained utilizing the F1000raw dataset, subject to majority labeling encompassing four distinct models. We train over 25 epochs with a batch size of 8 and a learning rate of 2e-5.

5.3 Zero-data

We segment the ARR dataset into sentences and label them into 4 categories following Dycke et al. (2022): *Strength*, *Weakness*, *Recap*, and *Todo*. *Structure* tends to encompass short instructions that end with ":", in following the examples such as "Typos:" and "However a few queries:". Hence, we label all sentences that end with ":", as well as sentences of five or fewer words as *Structrue*. Lastly, *Weakness* and *Recap* are commonly mislabeled as *Other*, thus we randomly transform 15% of them into *Other*. Surprisingly, synonym generation seems to have introduced perturbations that have led to a disruption in the intended context of the original sentences, thereby slightly decreasing the performance. This could potentially be attributed to the notably lower volume of the ARR dataset compared to F1000raw.

5.4 Secret-data

We further evaluate our best models in the secret domain. In the full data setting, the exclusion of the auxiliary model mentioned in section 5.1 results in a minor decrease of 0.0003 in the F1-mean score, while the F1-secret score increases by 0.006. Notably, there exists a subtle variation in the F1-scores within the same domain under the `zero condition`, as detailed in Table 5. This variance arises due to the random allocation of *Other* tag.

5.5 Discussion

Models tend to exhibit proficiency in classifying examples that are apparent, yet encounter challenges when confronted with ambiguous reviews. Recall labeling assists the classifier, as each model specializes in distinguishing different tags. The cumulative effect of this approach is a reduction in uncertainty during the pragmatic labeling process.

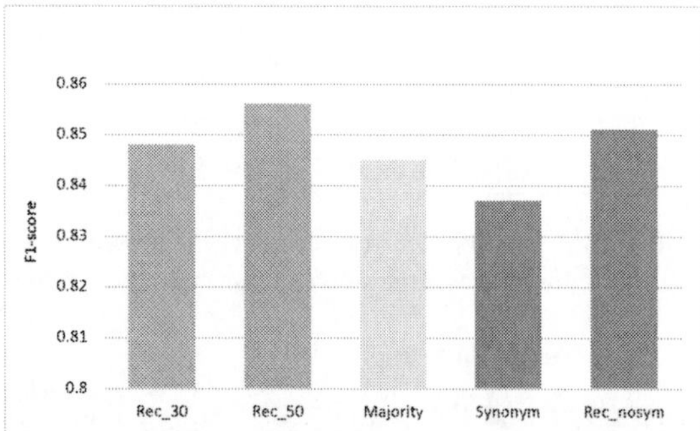

Figure 2: F1-scores of models employed for majority labeling under the full condition. Classifiers are trained using the following methods in the order from left to right: recall labeling over 30 and 50 epochs, majority labeling, synonym generation, and recall labeling among models trained without synonym generation.

6 Conclusion

In this study, we have empirically demonstrated the effectiveness of data augmentation methodologies, particularly in scenarios characterized by limited data availability. Our findings pinpoint that strategies such as pseudo-labeling and synonym generation are instrumental in leveraging unlabeled auxiliary data, therefore amplifying the generalization capacity of the classifier. Furthermore, our exploration of an ensemble approach for pseudo-labeling, aimed at maximizing certainty, suggests promising avenues for enhancing the efficacy of pragmatic tagging processes.

Acknowledgements

This work was supported by the National Research Foundation of Korea (NRF) grant funded by the Korea government (No. 2021R1A2C2008855). This work was partly supported by Institute of Information & communications Technology Planning & Evaluation (IITP) grant funded by the Korea government(MSIT) [NO.2021-0- 02068, Artificial Intelligence Innovation Hub (Artificial Intelligence Institute, Seoul National University) & NO.2021-0-01343, Artificial Intelligence Graduate School Program (Seoul National University)]. K. Jung is with ASRI, Seoul National University, Korea.

References

Aida Ali, Siti Mariyam Shamsuddin, and Anca L Ralescu. 2013. Classification with class imbalance problem. *Int. J. Advance Soft Compu. Appl*, 5(3):176–204.

Iz Beltagy, Kyle Lo, and Arman Cohan. 2019. Scibert: A pretrained language model for scientific text. *arXiv preprint arXiv:1903.10676*.

Avi Caciularu, Arman Cohan, Iz Beltagy, Matthew E Peters, Arie Cattan, and Ido Dagan. 2021. Cdlm: Cross-document language modeling. *arXiv preprint arXiv:2101.00406*.

Jiaao Chen, Derek Tam, Colin Raffel, Mohit Bansal, and Diyi Yang. 2023. An empirical survey of data augmentation for limited data learning in nlp. *Transactions of the Association for Computational Linguistics*, 11:191–211.

Nhan Cach Dang, María N Moreno-García, and Fernando De la Prieta. 2020. Sentiment analysis based on deep learning: A comparative study. *Electronics*, 9(3):483.

Jacob Devlin, Ming-Wei Chang, Kenton Lee, and Kristina Toutanova. 2018. Bert: Pre-training of deep bidirectional transformers for language understanding. *arXiv preprint arXiv:1810.04805*.

Chunning Du, Haifeng Sun, Jingyu Wang, Qi Qi, and Jianxin Liao. 2020. Adversarial and domain-aware bert for cross-domain sentiment analysis. In *Proceedings of the 58th annual meeting of the Association for Computational Linguistics*, pages 4019–4028.

Nils Dycke, Ilia Kuznetsov, and Iryna Gurevych. 2022. Nlpeer: A unified resource for the computational study of peer review. *arXiv preprint arXiv:2211.06651*.

Nils Dycke, Ilia Kuznetsov, and Iryna Gurevych. 2023. Overview of PragTag-2023: Low-resource multi-domain pragmatic tagging of peer reviews. In *Proceedings of the 10th Workshop on Argument Mining*, Singapore. Association for Computational Linguistics.

Steven Y Feng, Varun Gangal, Jason Wei, Sarath Chandar, Soroush Vosoughi, Teruko Mitamura, and Eduard Hovy. 2021. A survey of data augmentation approaches for nlp. *arXiv preprint arXiv:2105.03075*.

Xinyu Hua, Mitko Nikolov, Nikhil Badugu, and Lu Wang. 2019. Argument mining for understanding peer reviews. *arXiv preprint arXiv:1903.10104*.

Justin M Johnson and Taghi M Khoshgoftaar. 2019. Survey on deep learning with class imbalance. *Journal of Big Data*, 6(1):1–54.

Ilia Kuznetsov, Jan Buchmann, Max Eichler, and Iryna Gurevych. 2022. Revise and resubmit: An intertextual model of text-based collaboration in peer review. *Computational Linguistics*, 48(4):949–986.

Anne Lauscher, Goran Glavaš, and Simone Paolo Ponzetto. 2018. An argument-annotated corpus of scientific publications. Association for Computational Linguistics.

John Lawrence and Chris Reed. 2020. Argument mining: A survey. *Computational Linguistics*, 45(4):765–818.

Dong-Hyun Lee et al. 2013. Pseudo-label: The simple and efficient semi-supervised learning method for deep neural networks.

Jinhyuk Lee, Wonjin Yoon, Sungdong Kim, Donghyeon Kim, Sunkyu Kim, Chan Ho So, and Jaewoo Kang. 2020. Biobert: a pre-trained biomedical language representation model for biomedical text mining. *Bioinformatics*, 36(4):1234–1240.

Yinhan Liu, Myle Ott, Naman Goyal, Jingfei Du, Mandar Joshi, Danqi Chen, Omer Levy, Mike Lewis, Luke Zettlemoyer, and Veselin Stoyanov. 2019. Roberta: A robustly optimized bert pretraining approach. *arXiv preprint arXiv:1907.11692*.

Anna Rogers and Isabelle Augenstein. 2020. What can we do to improve peer review in nlp? *arXiv preprint arXiv:2010.03863*.

Sougata Saha and Rohini Srihari. 2023. Rudolf christoph eucken at semeval-2023 task 4: An ensemble approach for identifying human values from arguments. *arXiv preprint arXiv:2305.05335*.

Hossein Soleimani and David J Miller. 2016. Semi-supervised multi-label topic models for document classification and sentence labeling. In *Proceedings of the 25th ACM international on conference on information and knowledge management*, pages 105–114.

Qingyun Wang, Qi Zeng, Lifu Huang, Kevin Knight, Heng Ji, and Nazneen Fatema Rajani. 2020. Reviewrobot: Explainable paper review generation based on knowledge synthesis. *arXiv preprint arXiv:2010.06119*.

Mark Ware and Michael Mabe. 2015. The stm report: An overview of scientific and scholarly journal publishing.

Weizhe Yuan, Pengfei Liu, and Graham Neubig. 2022. Can we automate scientific reviewing? *Journal of Artificial Intelligence Research*, 75:171–212.

Tianyi Zhang, Varsha Kishore, Felix Wu, Kilian Q Weinberger, and Yoav Artzi. 2019. Bertscore: Evaluating text generation with bert. *arXiv preprint arXiv:1904.09675*.

NUS-IDS at PragTag-2023: Improving Pragmatic Tagging of Peer Reviews through Unlabeled Data

Sujatha Das Gollapalli
Institute of Data Science
National University of Singapore
Singapore
idssdg@nus.edu.sg

Yixin Huang*
Télécom Paris
Institut Polytechnique
de Paris, France
yixin.huang@ip-paris.fr

See-Kiong Ng
Institute of Data Science
National University of Singapore
Singapore
seekiong@nus.edu.sg

Abstract

We describe our models for the *Pragmatic Tagging of Peer Reviews* Shared Task at the 10th Workshop on Argument Mining at EMNLP-2023. We trained multiple sentence classification models for the above competition task by employing various state-of-the-art transformer models that can be fine-tuned either in the traditional way or through instruction-based fine-tuning. Multiple model predictions on unlabeled data are combined to tentatively label unlabeled instances and augment the dataset to further improve performance on the prediction task. In particular, on the F1000RD corpus, we perform on-par with models trained on 100% of the training data while using only 10% of the data. Overall, on the competition datasets, we rank among the top-2 performers for the different *data conditions*.

1 Introduction

Peer Review is employed across various subject domains to assess the quality of research documents such as grant proposals, journal manuscripts, and conference proceedings. Peer reviews are performed by independent researchers with expertise on the relevant topic for purposes such as awarding grants or publishing latest research for the advancement of Science. Review text reports, the result of these peer assessments, are brief summaries describing the document's main contributions, its strengths and weaknesses, along with other revision related comments and constructive feedback (Griessenauer and Roach, 2019).

Though standards and practices may vary across different subject domains and even across venues within the same domain, the main objective of the peer review process is to ensure the advancement of quality research (Glonti et al., 2019). To this end, alleviating the reviewing burden and supporting the diverse nature of reviewer expertise becomes vital (Huisman and Smits, 2017) and motivates the on-going research on developing tools to assist and improve the peer reviewing process (Walker and Rocha da Silva, 2015; Checco et al., 2021; Yuan et al., 2022; Schulz et al., 2022). In particular, a significant direction towards developing AI-assisted peer reviewing models involves the compilation of relevant datasets to support the meta-analyses of reviews (Kang et al., 2018; Ghosal et al., 2022; Dycke et al., 2023a).

From the perspective of language and NLP research, review reports provide a rich ground for investigation for various argument mining problems (Hua et al., 2019) including classification tasks such as paper acceptance prediction and sentence labeling (Bao et al., 2021; Kuznetsov et al., 2022). The PragTag Shared Task[1] at the 10th Workshop on Argument Mining at EMNLP-2023 comprises one such sentence labeling task in which every sentence from a review report is assigned a label from one of the pragmatic categories: { `Recap`, `Strength`, `Weakness`, `Todo`, `Other`, `Structure`}. Due to space constraints, we refer our readers to Kuznetsov, et al. (2022) and Dycke, et al. (2023b) for the precise definitions of the pragmatic categories and the F1000RD Corpus which forms the basis for the datasets used in the PragTag-2023 competition.

1.1 Task Description and Evaluation

In PragTag-2023, the pragmatic tagging task is presented in a cross-domain, low-resource setting using data from the F1000RD Corpus. The F1000RD is a multi-domain collection of free-text peer reviews annotated with pragmatic labels at the sentence level. Each peer review is associated with a domain (related to Medicine, Computer Science, or Scientific Policy Research). Additionally, recently released unlabeled review corpora from Dycke, et

*Work done during internship at the Institute of Data Science, NUS, Singapore

[1]https://codalab.lisn.upsaclay.fr/competitions/13334

Proceedings of the 10th Workshop on Argument Mining, pages 212–217
December 7, 2023. ©2023 Association for Computational Linguistics

al. (2023a) were made available as auxiliary data sources. The following three **data conditions** were proposed for the competition:

1. No-data: where no labeled instances are available for the task–zero-shot setting (Radford et al., 2019).

2. Low-data: where about 20% of the labeled data for the task can be used for training models–few-shot setting (Brown et al., 2020).

3. Full-data: which is the standard machine-learning setting where the entire training split of the labeled data can be used to train models.

For measuring model performance on this sentence classification task, the average performance across domains is used in each of the above conditions where the performance in a domain is simply measured by the macro-F1 computed across all review sentences of that domain. For the final evaluation, the test data comes from a "secret" domain, different from those covered in the training data, thus measuring cross-domain model performance.

Consider the definitions of labels: *Recap: summarizes the manuscript, For e.g. "The paper proposes a new method for..."*; ... Question: Which of the above labels most applies to the following sentence? Sentence: []

Table 1: Prompt for LLM Models

2 Proposed Methods

In this section, we briefly describe the various models we employed for the Pragmatic Tagging task under the three data conditions.

No-data setting: We studied two approaches for predicting pragmatic tags under the no-data condition. In the first "*Semantic Search*" approach, we simply use a list of "questions" to find sentences in the review texts that best answer the question. This list was curated based on the typical questions employed during the peer review process of NLP conferences and augmented to cover labels such as "Recap".[2] Example questions include "How original are the results described in the paper?" and "What is the main finding of this paper?". We used the state-of-the-art Sentence Transformer models trained for Semantic Search for this method (Wang et al., 2020; Nassiri and Akhloufi, 2023).[3]

Recent breakthrough research has shown that large language models (LLMs) can be trained "to act in accordance with the user's intentions" and as a consequence be "prompted" to perform a range of NLP tasks (Radford et al., 2019; Brown et al., 2020; Christiano et al., 2017). For our second approach, in keeping with this recent direction, we designed a multiple-choice question prompt along with the task description provided in the competition for use in Instruction Fine-tuned Language Models (Ouyang et al., 2022; Chung et al., 2022). Our prompt is listed in Table 1 and we refer to the use of this approach as "*MC-Prompt*" in Section 3.[4]

Low-data/Full-data setting: In current practice, fine-tuning large pre-trained language models (PLMs) for a new task has become the standard approach for training models (Howard and Ruder, 2018). We therefore adopt the state-of-the-art transformer-based models and directly train supervised models on the available labeled data for the low/full data conditions.

With the objective to utilize the unlabeled data provided in the competition as means to overcome the scarcity of labeled data in the low-data settings, we employed traditional semi-supervised approaches–self-training and voting, to combine predictions from multiple learners[5] and obtain tentative labels for the unlabeled data (Li et al., 2019; Sosea and Caragea, 2022). The "tentatively labeled" unlabeled data is incorporated via two methods in our models. In the pretraining approach (*PT*), we simply pretrain our classifier on the tentatively-labeled unlabeled data before fine-tuning on the labeled data whereas in the *Combined* approach, the augmented dataset is used to train a model.

3 Experiments

Datasets: We used the datasets from previous works (Kuznetsov et al., 2022; Dycke et al., 2023a) for showcasing our proposed methods on this task.

[2]Complete list shared as part of the code distribution

[3]https://huggingface.co/sentence-transformers/multi-qa-mpnet-base-dot-v1

[4]We experimented with slight variations and paraphrases of the label descriptions, prompts with and without examples, as well as a yes/no prompt that uses a yes/no question with each label. Our best prompt based on validation performance is listed in Table 1.

[5]In addition to the provided RoBERTa-based competition baseline, we also fine-tuned models based on T5 and FlanT5 models from Google. These details are provided in Section 3.

Setting	#Labeled Sentences	Model	Accuracy	Macro-F1
No data	0	QA-MPNet (*Semantic Search*)	0.31	0.32
	0	FlanT5-XL (*MC-Prompt*)	**0.53**	**0.42**
Low data (10%)	338	RoBERTa	0.75	0.71
	338	FlanT5-large	0.70	0.68
	338	T5-large	0.78	0.74
	14673/338	T5-large (*PT*)	**0.81**	**0.80**
	15011	T5-large (*Combined*)	0.77	0.76
Full-data	2691	Roberta	0.83	0.82
	2691	FlanT5-large	0.82	0.80
	2691	T5-large	0.84	0.82
	15844/2691	T5-large (*PT*)	**0.86**	**0.85**
	18535	T5-large (*Combined*)	0.85	0.83

Table 2: Performance of various models is shown on the test split of the F1000RD corpus. The best performance in each setting is highlighted in bold. For the "X/Y" values shown in the #Labeled Sentences column of PT rows, X is the number of tentatively-labeled unlabeled instances and Y, the number of labeled instances from the training data.

In particular, we used the F1000RD Corpus[6] for presenting our observations in this section. For the competition, in accordance with the competition rules, we only used the provided main and auxiliary datasets (Dycke et al., 2023b).

Implementation Details: We fine-tuned the Text-to-Text Transfer Transformer (T5) model for our classification task. T5 incorporates various tasks such as translation, question answering, and classification uniformly as text-to-text learning tasks, thereby harnessing the power of transfer learning across multiple tasks, and has been shown to obtain state-of-the-art performance across a range of tasks (Raffel et al., 2020). The T5 models were extended to incorporate instruction-based fine-tuning into the FlanT5-family of models (Chung et al., 2022). For T5 and FlanT5 experiments, we used latest implementations available from HuggingFace (Wolf et al., 2019). In total, for the low/full data conditions, three classifiers were trained using T5, FlanT5, and the RoBERTa baseline provided in the competition.

All experiments were performed on a single GPU of an Nvidia Tesla cluster machine with 32GB RAM. On this machine, based on the size of the datasets and the specific models, training time ranges between 0.5-24 hours. On our available infrastructure, the biggest models we were able to train were the "large" variants (T5-large and FlanT5-large) from the T5 and FlanT5 model families. The performance on the development/validation split of the dataset was used to set the number of epochs for the final models.[7]

3.1 Results and Observations

We illustrate the performance of our models under the three data conditions on the F1000RD dataset.[6] For the *low-data* condition shown in Table 2, we used a randomly-selected 10% subset of the training data. In this table, we see that, not surprisingly, the accuracy and macro-F1 scores of models in the full-data condition are significantly higher than those in the low-data condition. However, in absolute terms, even with 10% of the labeled data the performance is reasonably high on this dataset. Moreover, using appropriate prompts in the FlanT5-XL model, we are able to obtain almost half of the Macro-F1 score obtained with full-data models even in the no-data condition.

Based on the competitive validation performance afforded by the T5-large models in both *low-data* and *full-data* conditions, we selected this model for exploring the improvements with unlabeled data. For these two data conditions, we used the three models (RoBERTa, FlanT5-large, T5-large) to obtain predictions for the auxiliary (unlabeled) data made available in the competition. We incorporate those examples for which there is agreement between RoBERTa and FlanT5-large model predictions but no agreement with T5-large model

[6]https://github.com/UKPLab/f1000rd

[7]https://github.com/NUS-IDS/PragTag2023

Setting	Model	F1-case	F1-diso	F1-rpkg	F1-iscb	F1-scip	F1-mean
No-data	QA-MPNet	0.352	0.310	0.354	0.326	0.291	0.326
	FlanT5-large	0.420	0.396	0.413	0.424	0.357	0.402*
Rank-1	Unknown	0.502	0.518	0.492	0.551	0.516	0.516
Low-data	T5-large	0.764	0.792	0.789	0.796	0.827	0.794
(**Rank-1**=Us)	FlanT5-large	0.804	0.835	0.803	0.803	0.820	0.813*
Full-data	T5-large	0.813	0.853	0.829	0.806	0.861	0.832
	T5-large (*PT*)	0.843	0.834	0.827	0.821	0.854	0.836
	T5-large (*Combined*)	0.838	0.854	0.848	0.833	0.878	0.850*
Rank-1	Unknown	0.829	0.842	0.854	0.836	0.889	0.850

Table 3: Phase-1 Results from the competition. We indicate the performance of the best system in the **Rank-1** row and highlight our best F1-mean score with a *

Setting	Model	F1-secret	F1-mean
No	FlanT5-large	0.425	0.406
Low	FlanT5-large	0.759	0.804
Full	T5-large (*Combined*)	0.741	0.832
Rank-1	Unknown	0.801	0.841

Table 4: Phase-2 Results. The Rank-1 row shows the performance of the best model from the competition.

Class Label	Default	PT	Combined
Other	0.63	**0.70**	0.62
Recap	0.74	**0.80**	*0.77
Strength	0.83	**0.87**	*0.85
Structure	**0.95**	0.92	**0.95**
Todo	0.94	**0.95**	0.94
Weakness	0.84	**0.85**	***0.85**
Macro Average	0.82	**0.85**	0.83

Table 5: Test F1 performance for each class label is shown for the three T5-large models from Table 2. The best performances are **bolded**. We also highlight the cases where the *Combined* setting outperforms the default setting with a *.

predictions as the subset of "weakly-labeled" data for training new T5 models in *PT* and *Combined* settings described in Section 2.

That is, during data augmentation, we add the "hard" cases for which the T5-large model predictions do not match the labels predicted by both RoBERTa and Flan-T5. This step cuts down the amount of unlabeled data added back to the dataset by excluding "uninformative" samples for which the original T5 model predictions already conform to the other models. In our early experiments, we observed that adding all examples for which we have majority labels significantly increases the training time with no significant improvements in the validation performance.

As can be seen in Table 2, both *PT* and *Combined* settings result in improved test performance for *low-data* as well as the *full-data* conditions. In particular, the improvement is significantly higher in the macro F1 score in the *low-data* condition. Indeed, with pretraining (*PT*), the test performance in low-data conditions is comparable to those of models trained on full data.

In Table 5, the per-class F1 scores on the test split for the three models: T5-large, T5-large (PT), T5-large (Combined) from Table 2 are shown. The improved F1 scores across classes in both *PT* and *Combined* settings are indicative of a significant reduction in the number of erroneous predictions over the baseline setting. As such, F1 improvements are seen for five out of the six classes in the *PT* setting, and three out of the six classes in the *Combined* setting.

3.2 Competition Performance and Ranking

The results with our models in the competition are showcased for the two phases in Tables 3 and 4. Within the competition timeframe and limits on number of submissions, we were unable to test all our models on the final dataset. We highlight our best-performing models among those we submitted and also the overall best submission in the competition (Rank 1) for each condition. During the competition, for the *PT* and *Combined* runs, we used all unlabeled examples with majority labels (different from the settings used in Table 2).

Overall, we ranked among the top-2 performing of the four-six submitted systems for the various data conditions. Compared to the performances highlighted in Tables 2 and 3, our models underperform on the data from the secret domain (Table 4) indicating that they may not be generalizing well for new/unseen domains.

4 Related Work

Sentence classification tasks are well-studied in NLP research with deep learning models comprising the state-of-the-art (Cohan et al., 2019). Some recent sentence-level classification tasks include identification of complex linguistic phenomena in texts such as emotions, empathy, humor, sarcasm, and dialog acts (Song et al., 2022; He et al., 2021; Wang et al., 2022; Bunescu and Uduehi, 2022).

Recently, efforts are underway for collecting relevant datasets for designing assistive automation aids for peer review (Yuan et al., 2022; Checco et al., 2021; Kang et al., 2018; Ghosal et al., 2022; Dycke et al., 2023a). In this context, Kuznetsov, et al. (2022) introduced pragmatic tagging for labeling sentences of peer reviews using a schema that applies across different research fields and communities. We borrow from the latest NLP advances such as prompt-based models and combine them with unlabeled data on precisely this task.

5 Conclusions and Future Work

We presented our approaches for the pragmatic tag prediction task for peer reviews as part of the PragTag Shared Task @ ArgMining Workshop 2023. In particular, we studied prompt-based fine-tuning as a viable alternative to traditional learning methods for this task and showcased how unlabeled data may be utilized via multiple learners to improve performance in the low-data settings. In future, we would like to address the generalizability of our proposed models across various subject domains as well as extend our approaches to related tasks such as paper acceptance prediction (Bao et al., 2021; Yuan et al., 2022).

Acknowledgments

This research/project is supported by the National Research Foundation, Singapore under its Industry Alignment Fund–Pre-positioning (IAF-PP) Funding Initiative. Any opinions, findings and conclusions or recommendations expressed in this material are those of the author(s) and do not reflect the views of National Research Foundation, Singapore.

References

Peng Bao, Weihui Hong, and Xuanya Li. 2021. Predicting paper acceptance via interpretable decision sets. In *Companion Proceedings of the Web Conference 2021*, WWW '21, page 461–467, New York, NY, USA. Association for Computing Machinery.

Tom Brown, Benjamin Mann, Nick Ryder, Melanie Subbiah, Jared D Kaplan, Prafulla Dhariwal, Arvind Neelakantan, Pranav Shyam, Girish Sastry, Amanda Askell, et al. 2020. Language models are few-shot learners. *Advances in neural information processing systems*, 33:1877–1901.

Razvan C. Bunescu and Oseremen O. Uduehi. 2022. Distribution-based measures of surprise for creative language: Experiments with humor and metaphor. In *Proceedings of the 3rd Workshop on Figurative Language Processing (FLP)*, pages 68–78, Abu Dhabi, United Arab Emirates (Hybrid). Association for Computational Linguistics.

Alessandro Checco, Lorenzo Bracciale, Pierpaolo Loreti, Stephen Pinfield, and Giuseppe Bianchi. 2021. Ai-assisted peer review. *Humanities and Social Sciences Communications*, 8.

Paul F. Christiano, Jan Leike, Tom B. Brown, Miljan Martic, Shane Legg, and Dario Amodei. 2017. Deep reinforcement learning from human preferences. In *Advances in Neural Information Processing Systems 30: Annual Conference on Neural Information Processing Systems 2017, December 4-9, 2017, Long Beach, CA, USA*, pages 4299–4307.

Hyung Won Chung, Le Hou, Shayne Longpre, Barret Zoph, Yi Tay, William Fedus, Eric Li, Xuezhi Wang, Mostafa Dehghani, Siddhartha Brahma, et al. 2022. Scaling instruction-finetuned language models. *arXiv preprint arXiv:2210.11416*.

Arman Cohan, Iz Beltagy, Daniel King, Bhavana Dalvi, and Dan Weld. 2019. Pretrained language models for sequential sentence classification. In *Proceedings of the 2019 Conference on Empirical Methods in Natural Language Processing and the 9th International Joint Conference on Natural Language Processing (EMNLP-IJCNLP)*, pages 3693–3699, Hong Kong, China. Association for Computational Linguistics.

Nils Dycke, Ilia Kuznetsov, and Iryna Gurevych. 2023a. NLPeer: A unified resource for the computational study of peer review. In *Proceedings of the 61st Annual Meeting of the Association for Computational Linguistics (Volume 1: Long Papers)*, pages 5049–5073, Toronto, Canada. Association for Computational Linguistics.

Nils Dycke, Ilia Kuznetsov, and Iryna Gurevych. 2023b. Overview of PragTag-2023: Low-resource multi-domain pragmatic tagging of peer reviews. In *Proceedings of the 10th Workshop on Argument Mining*, Singapore. Association for Computational Linguistics.

Tirthankar Ghosal, Kamal Kaushik Varanasi, and Valia Kordoni. 2022. Hedgepeer: A dataset for uncertainty detection in peer reviews. In *Proceedings of the 22nd ACM/IEEE Joint Conference on Digital Libraries*, JCDL '22, New York, NY, USA. Association for Computing Machinery.

Ketevan Glonti, Daniel Cauchi, Erik Cobo, Isabelle Boutron, David Moher, and Darko Hren. 2019. A scoping review on the roles and tasks of peer reviewers in the manuscript review process in biomedical journals. *BMC medicine*, 17:1–14.

Christoph J Griessenauer and Michelle K Roach. 2019. Scientific peer review. *A Guide to the Scientific Career: Virtues, Communication, Research and Academic Writing*, pages 403–406.

Zihao He, Leili Tavabi, Kristina Lerman, and Mohammad Soleymani. 2021. Speaker turn modeling for dialogue act classification. In *Findings of the Association for Computational Linguistics: EMNLP 2021*, pages 2150–2157, Punta Cana, Dominican Republic. Association for Computational Linguistics.

Jeremy Howard and Sebastian Ruder. 2018. Universal language model fine-tuning for text classification. In *ACL*, pages 328–339.

Xinyu Hua, Mitko Nikolov, Nikhil Badugu, and Lu Wang. 2019. Argument mining for understanding peer reviews. In *Proceedings of the 2019 Conference of the North American Chapter of the Association for Computational Linguistics: Human Language Technologies, Volume 1 (Long and Short Papers)*, pages 2131–2137, Minneapolis, Minnesota. Association for Computational Linguistics.

Janine Huisman and Jeroen Smits. 2017. Duration and quality of the peer review process: the author's perspective. *Scientometrics*, 113(1):633–650.

Dongyeop Kang, Waleed Ammar, Bhavana Dalvi, Madeleine van Zuylen, Sebastian Kohlmeier, Eduard Hovy, and Roy Schwartz. 2018. A dataset of peer reviews (PeerRead): Collection, insights and NLP applications. In *Proceedings of the 2018 Conference of the North American Chapter of the Association for Computational Linguistics: Human Language Technologies, Volume 1 (Long Papers)*, pages 1647–1661, New Orleans, Louisiana. Association for Computational Linguistics.

Ilia Kuznetsov, Jan Buchmann, Max Eichler, and Iryna Gurevych. 2022. Revise and resubmit: An intertextual model of text-based collaboration in peer review. *Computational Linguistics*, 48(4):949–986.

Xinzhe Li, Qianru Sun, Yaoyao Liu, Shibao Zheng, Qin Zhou, Tat-Seng Chua, and Bernt Schiele. 2019. *Learning to Self-Train for Semi-Supervised Few-Shot Classification*.

Khalid Nassiri and Moulay Akhloufi. 2023. Transformer models used for text-based question answering systems. *Applied Intelligence*, 53(9):10602–10635.

Long Ouyang, Jeffrey Wu, Xu Jiang, Diogo Almeida, Carroll Wainwright, Pamela Mishkin, Chong Zhang, Sandhini Agarwal, Katarina Slama, Alex Ray, et al. 2022. Training language models to follow instructions with human feedback. *Advances in Neural Information Processing Systems*, 35:27730–27744.

Alec Radford, Jeffrey Wu, Rewon Child, David Luan, Dario Amodei, Ilya Sutskever, et al. 2019. Language models are unsupervised multitask learners. *OpenAI blog*, 1(8):9.

Colin Raffel, Noam Shazeer, Adam Roberts, Katherine Lee, Sharan Narang, Michael Matena, Yanqi Zhou, Wei Li, and Peter J. Liu. 2020. Exploring the limits of transfer learning with a unified text-to-text transformer. *JMLR*, 21(140):1–67.

Robert Schulz, Adrian Barnett, René Bernard, Nicholas J.L. Brown, Jennifer A. Byrne, Peter Eckmann, Małgorzata A. Gazda, Halil Kilicoglu, Eric M. Prager, Maia Salholz-Hillel, Gerben ter Riet, Timothy Vines, Colby J. Vorland, Han Zhuang, Anita Bandrowski, and Tracey L. Weissgerber. 2022. Is the future of peer review automated? *BMC Research Notes*, 15(1).

Xiaohui Song, Longtao Huang, Hui Xue, and Songlin Hu. 2022. Supervised prototypical contrastive learning for emotion recognition in conversation. In *Proceedings of the 2022 Conference on Empirical Methods in Natural Language Processing*, pages 5197–5206, Abu Dhabi, United Arab Emirates. Association for Computational Linguistics.

Tiberiu Sosea and Cornelia Caragea. 2022. Leveraging training dynamics and self-training for text classification. In *Findings of the Association for Computational Linguistics: EMNLP 2022*, pages 4750–4762, Abu Dhabi, United Arab Emirates. Association for Computational Linguistics.

Richard Walker and Pascal Rocha da Silva. 2015. Emerging trends in peer review—a survey. *Frontiers in Neuroscience*, 9.

Jiquan Wang, Lin Sun, Yi Liu, Meizhi Shao, and Zengwei Zheng. 2022. Multimodal sarcasm target identification in tweets. In *Proceedings of the 60th Annual Meeting of the Association for Computational Linguistics (Volume 1: Long Papers)*, pages 8164–8175, Dublin, Ireland. Association for Computational Linguistics.

Wenhui Wang, Furu Wei, Li Dong, Hangbo Bao, Nan Yang, and Ming Zhou. 2020. Minilm: Deep self-attention distillation for task-agnostic compression of pre-trained transformers. In *Proceedings of the 34th International Conference on Neural Information Processing Systems*, NIPS'20, Red Hook, NY, USA. Curran Associates Inc.

Thomas Wolf, Lysandre Debut, Victor Sanh, Julien Chaumond, Clement Delangue, Anthony Moi, Pierric Cistac, Tim Rault, Rémi Louf, Morgan Funtowicz, and Jamie Brew. 2019. Huggingface's transformers: State-of-the-art natural language processing. *CoRR*, abs/1910.03771.

Weizhe Yuan, Pengfei Liu, and Graham Neubig. 2022. Can we automate scientific reviewing? *J. Artif. Int. Res.*, 75.

SuryaKiran at PragTag 2023 - Benchmarking Domain Adaptation using Masked Language Modeling in Natural Language Processing For Specialized Data

Kunal Suri
Optum
kunal_suri@optum.com

Prakhar Mishra
Optum
prakhar_mishra29@optum.com

Albert Nanda
Optum
albert_nanda@optum.com

Abstract

Most transformer models are trained on English language corpus that contain text from forums like Wikipedia and Reddit. While these models are being used in many specialized domains such as scientific peer review, legal, and healthcare, their performance is subpar because they do not contain the information present in data relevant to such specialized domains. To help these models perform as well as possible on specialized domains, one of the approaches is to collect labeled data of that particular domain and fine-tune the transformer model of choice on such data. While a good approach, it suffers from the challenge of collecting a lot of labeled data which requires significant manual effort. Another way is to use unlabeled domain-specific data to pre-train these transformer model and then fine-tune this model on labeled data. We evaluate how transformer models perform when fine-tuned on labeled data after initial pre-training with unlabeled data. We compare their performance with a transformer model fine-tuned on labeled data without initial pre-training with unlabeled data. We perform this comparison on a dataset of Scientific Peer Reviews provided by organizers of PragTag-2023 Shared Task[1] and observe that a transformer model fine-tuned on labeled data after initial pre-training on unlabeled data using Masked Language Modelling outperforms a transformer model fine-tuned only on labeled data without initial pre-training with unlabeled data using Masked Language Modelling.

1 Introduction

Transformer based models like BERT Devlin et al. (2019), RoBERTa Liu et al. (2019), and DeBERTa He et al. (2020) have become de-facto models for Natural Language Processing (NLP) tasks outperforming all past techniques by significant margins. However, most of these models are originally trained on English corpus such as BookCorpus Yao and Huang (2018), English Wikipedia, and OpenWebText Liu et al. (2019). This becomes an issue when dealing with data from specialized domains such as medicine, healthcare, law, scientific peer reviews, etc. because these models are not aware of the specialized vocabulary in the domains due to which their performance is is generally subpar. This can be seen in Lee et al. (2019) where BERT performs poorly as compare to a model initialized with BERT weights and pre-trained on medical data. Training Transformer based models on data of specialized domain from the ground up poses significant challenges due to the scarcity of extensive datasets within these domains. So we resort to the practice of refining models originally trained on the English corpus by incorporating data sourced from such domains. Traditionally, this refinement process entails acquiring labeled data, structured according to well-defined formats pertinent to a task within the domain of interest. Subsequently, the model undergoes fine-tuning using this collected data. This approach is not efficient due to the labor-intensive and expensive nature of gathering substantial volume of labeled data. An alternative strategy – when we have a lot of unlabeled data and only a handful of labeled data - is domain adaptation (DA). In this paper we benchmark Masked Language Modelling (MLM) Devlin et al. (2019) as a DA strategy and see how it performs on PragTag-2023 Shared Task Dycke et al. (2023a). Although it is one of the strategies used to pre-train BERT, it has shown promise as a DA technique as can be seen in Ladkat et al. (2022), Karouzos et al. (2021).

2 Related Work

According to V7 Labs [2], Domain Adaptation (DA) is a technique to improve the performance of a model on a target domain containing insufficient

[1]https://www.aclweb.org/portal/content/pragtag-shared-task-argmining-workshop-2023

[2]https://www.v7labs.com/blog/domain-adaptation-guide

Proceedings of the 10th Workshop on Argument Mining, pages 218–222
December 7, 2023.

annotated data by using the knowledge learned by the model from another related domain with adequate labeled data. Source Domain is the data distribution on which the model is trained using labeled examples. Target domain is the data distribution on which a model pre-trained on a different domain is used to perform a similar task. In this paper, Source Domain is the data distribution present in english corpus such as BookCorpus, English Wikipedia, and OpenWebText and Target Domain is the data distribution present in the data of this shared task.

There are primarily four types of DA techniques - Supervised DA, Semi-Supervised DA, Weakly Supervised DA, and Unsupervised DA. For this paper, we will primarily focus on Supervised and Unsupervised DA. In Supervised Domain Adaptation (SDA), target domain data is completely labeled. In Unsupervised Domain Adaptation (UDA), any kind of labels for the target domain data are entirely missing.

Lee et al. (2019) initialize BioBERT with weights from BERT, which was pre-trained on general domain corpora. Then, BioBERT is pre-trained on biomedical domain corpora. To show the effectiveness of our approach in biomedical text mining, BioBERT is fine-tuned and evaluated on three popular biomedical text mining tasks - NER, RE, and QA. The authors show that pre-training BERT on biomedical corpora largely improves its performance on these three tasks.

Karouzos et al. (2021) start from a model that is pretrained on general corpora, keep pretraining it on target domain data using the MLM task. On the final fine-tuning step, the update the model weights using both a classification loss on the labeled source data and Masked Language Modeling loss on the unlabeled target data.

Ladkat et al. (2022) use BERT-base model for MLM and finetune it for text classification on the target dataset. They freeze the encoder layer while training only the embedding and final task-specific dense layers. By doing so, they specialise the general domain word representations according to the target tasks and show that the performance of the resultant model is better than only BERT-base model.

In this paper, we will focus on Masked Language Modelling (MLM) which is a type of pre-training method that was introduced in BERT.

3 Task Description

In this task, we are given two datasets extracted from Kuznetsov et al. (2022). Both of these datasets contain a multi-domain collection of free-text peer reviews labeled with pragmatic labels on the sentence level. In the first dataset, each peer review can belong to medical articles, computer science, and scientific policy research. It has two parts parts - training dataset and test dataset. Training dataset is used to train the model and test dataset is used to evaluate the performance of the model trained on the training dataset. Going forward, we refer to these two datasets as *Train Dataset* and *Full Dataset* respectively. The second dataset is a secret test set *Secret Dataset*. Train, Full, and Secret Dataset contain same domains with Secret Dataset containing one additional domain not present in Train or Full Datasets. Every sentence in these datasets has one of the following pragmatic labels: Recap, Strength, Weakness, Todo, Other, and Structure. Our goal in this task is to correctly classify each peer review sentence into one of these categories.

In addition to these datasets, we use an auxiliary dataset, F1000raw, extracted from Dycke et al. (2023b) which is used for pre-training. This is a large unlabeled collection of peer reviews.

4 Methodology

For our experiments, we use DeBERTa-Base since it has been shown to perform better than models like BERT and RoBERTa. We first pre-train DeBERTa-Base on F1000raw using Masked Language Model (MLM) as shown in Fig.1. We then fine-tune this model using Train Dataset. We also fine-tune a DeBERTa-Base model using only Train Dataset without the pre-train step. We can see this workflow in Fig.2. We then pass each review from Full and Secret Datasets, take an average of the logits for all the classes and output the class with the highest logit score as shown in Fig.3. We then compare the performance of these two models and show that MLM helps improve the performance of the model on this classification task.

5 Implementation Details

Our solution comprises of two steps -

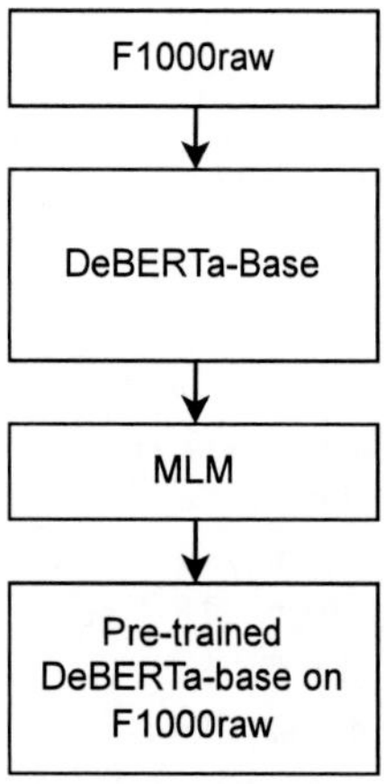

Figure 1: Pre-training on DeBERTa-base by using MLM Objective

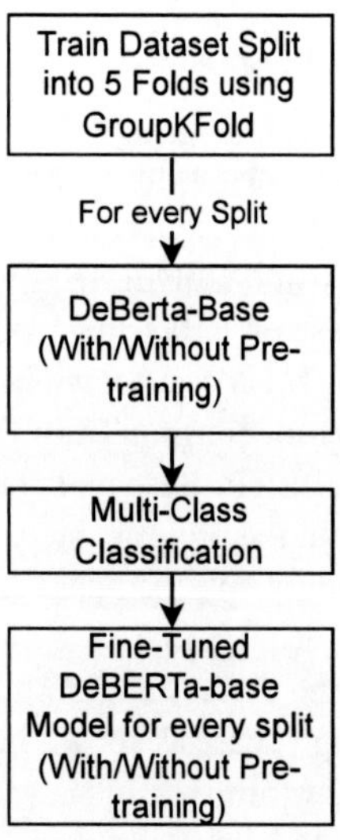

Figure 2: Finetuning DeBERTa-Base

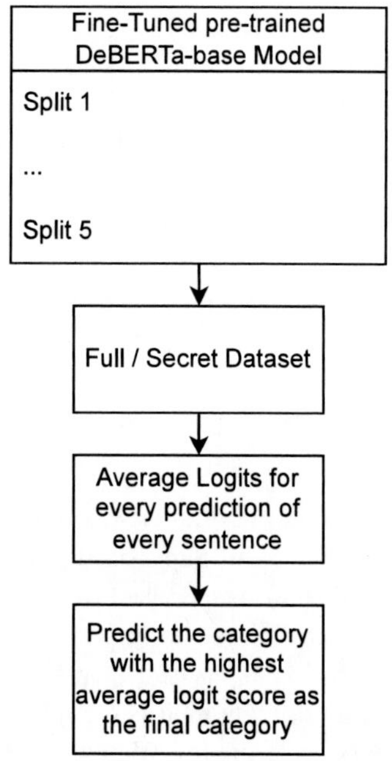

Figure 3: Inference on Fine-Tuned DeBERTA-base

5.1 Masked Language Modelling using F1000raw

As part of this step, we use all reviews in F1000raw. We combine these reviews and randomly split them into train, validation, and test datasets with 50%, 25%, and 25% share of data. We tokenize each of these datasets using a tokenizer created from the DeBERTa-base model. After tokenization, we concatenate all the sequences and split the concatenated sequences into shorter chunks of block_size of 512. We used this block_size because it covers all reviews and also it is short enough for T4 GPU.

5.2 Fine-tuning on Train Dataset

In this step, we use train a multi-class classification model on the Train Dataset. Since our objective is to compare performance of fine-tuning a multi-class classification model on a domain adapated model vs fine-tuning a multi-class classification model on a base model without domain adaptation, we perform the below steps twice - first for the domain adapted DeBERTa-Base obtained from above step and second for DeBERTa-Base without domain adaptation.

We use GroupKFold Cross Validation Strategy from scikit-learn Pedregosa et al. (2011) in order to ensure that each domain belongs to either train or validation or test split. We perform a 5 Group-KFold to create 5 Train-Validation splits of the

Domain	Split 1		Split 2		Split 3		Split 4		Split 5	
	W	WO	W	WO	W	WO	W	WO	W	WO
RPKG	-	-	**84.75**	80.79	**73.89**	66.76	**76.33**	74.13	**79.90**	70.06
CASE	69.17	**76.13**	**87.66**	82.57	**82.07**	81.27	**90.55**	88.27	**68.58**	63.96
SCIP	**84.97**	73.44	**75.73**	72.13	**62.05**	59.89	**91.01**	68.18	**75.**	61.32
ISCB	**93.27**	83.46	75.27	**77.58**	-	-	**84.04**	81.48	**79.84**	78.91
DISO	68.35	**80.98**	38.18	**50.**	86.28	**88.73**	**80.63**	72.04	**97.13**	91.11
Mean	**78.94**	78.50	72.32	**72.62**	**76.10**	74.16	**84.51**	76.82	**80.09**	73.07

Table 1: Comparison of F1 Scores for With (W) and Without (WO) MLM for all 5 Splits

Domain	With MLM	Without MLM
RPKG	82.75%	**84.06%**
CASE	81.97%	**82.94%**
SCIP	**86.45%**	85.04%
ISCB	**81.81%**	80.75%
DISO	**82.76%**	81.42%
Mean	**83.15%**	82.84%

Table 2: F1 Score for Full Dataset

Domain	With MLM	Without MLM
RPKG	82.75%	**84.06%**
CASE	81.97%	**82.94%**
SCIP	**86.45%**	85.04%
ISCB	**81.81%**	80.75%
DISO	**82.76%**	81.42%
SECRET	**77.93%**	73.21%
Mean	**82.28%**	81.24%

Table 3: F1 Score for Secret Dataset

training data. Within every split, we perform another GroupKFold split to divide the Validation into Validation and Test datasets. This ensures that we get Test score for every fold and use validation set exclusively for getting the best model.

6 Results and Discussion

We evaluate results on three datasets - 1) *Train Dataset*, 2) *Full Dataset*, and 3) *Secret Dataset*. For evaluating performance using Train Dataset, we use test dataset created in 5.2 of every split and pass it through the model trained using training data from that split. For evaluating performance on Full and Secret Datasets, we pass each review from these datasets through all five models, take an average of the logits for all the classes and output the class with the highest logit score.

Train Dataset gives us an idea about how both of the models compare across different splits and if one model is consistently better than the other model. Full Dataset contains similar domains as we have in Train Dataset but doesn't contain target variable. In Secret Dataset we have a new domain in addition to domains present in Full Dataset. The scores for every split of Train Dataset can be found Table 1, scores for Full Dataset can be found in Table 2, and the scores for Secret Dataset can be found in Table 3.

One interesting observation from Table 1, 2, and 3 is that the domain adaptation seems to be working on only for some domains and not others. This might be discouraging as it suggest that MLM only works sporadically but it is actually not the case. The reason why MLM works for some domains and not for others is due to difference in word distributions in different domains. Interested readers can refer to the analysis in the Supplementary Materials Section for detailed analysis of word frequencies of various domains in full and secret dataset and different splits of training data. The analysis shows us that domain adaptation is very effective in domains where the distribution has more words about Peer Reviews (which is the theme of this task) viz. SCIP, ISCB as compared to splits which have more health related terms viz. CASE and DISO.

7 Conclusion and future work

As we can see in the results, domain adapted DeBERTa-base beat DeBERTa-base without domain adaptation. While this is an encouraging result, how is this performance difference impacted by the scale of models and architecture of the model remains to be studied. We also need to study this problem on datasets from other niche domains as well. In addition to this, we can also study how domain adaptation impacts LLMs which are orders of magnitude larger than architectures such as BERT, RoBERTa, and DeBERTa.

Limitations

One of the biggest limitations of this analysis would be utilization of GPUs with more RAM as the size of the models scale. For example - We had to settle for DeBERTa-base because DeBERTa-large wouldn't fit in a GPU with 24 GB RAM. So, as we analyse models with more parameters, we might have use GPUs with more RAM which might be a financial constraint to some teams.

References

Jacob Devlin, Ming-Wei Chang, Kenton Lee, and Kristina Toutanova. 2019. BERT: Pre-training of deep bidirectional transformers for language understanding. In *Proceedings of the 2019 Conference of the North American Chapter of the Association for Computational Linguistics: Human Language Technologies, Volume 1 (Long and Short Papers)*, pages 4171–4186, Minneapolis, Minnesota. Association for Computational Linguistics.

Nils Dycke, Ilia Kuznetsov, and Iryna Gurevych. 2023a. Argmining 2023 shared task - pragtag: Low-resource multi-domain pragmatic tagging of peer reviews. In *Proceedings of the 10th Workshop on Argument Mining*, Singapore. Association for Computational Linguistics.

Nils Dycke, Ilia Kuznetsov, and Iryna Gurevych. 2023b. NLPeer: A unified resource for the computational study of peer review. In *Proceedings of the 61st Annual Meeting of the Association for Computational Linguistics (Volume 1: Long Papers)*, pages 5049–5073, Toronto, Canada. Association for Computational Linguistics.

Pengcheng He, Xiaodong Liu, Jianfeng Gao, and Weizhu Chen. 2020. Deberta: Decoding-enhanced BERT with disentangled attention. *CoRR*, abs/2006.03654.

Constantinos Karouzos, Georgios Paraskevopoulos, and Alexandros Potamianos. 2021. UDALM: Unsupervised domain adaptation through language modeling. In *Proceedings of the 2021 Conference of the North American Chapter of the Association for Computational Linguistics: Human Language Technologies*, pages 2579–2590, Online. Association for Computational Linguistics.

Ilia Kuznetsov, Jan Buchmann, Max Eichler, and Iryna Gurevych. 2022. Revise and Resubmit: An Intertextual Model of Text-based Collaboration in Peer Review. *Computational Linguistics*, 48(4):949–986.

Arnav Ladkat, Aamir Miyajiwala, Samiksha Jagadale, Rekha A. Kulkarni, and Raviraj Joshi. 2022. Towards simple and efficient task-adaptive pre-training for text classification. In *Proceedings of the 2nd Conference of the Asia-Pacific Chapter of the Association for Computational Linguistics and the 12th International Joint Conference on Natural Language Processing (Volume 2: Short Papers)*, pages 320–325, Online only. Association for Computational Linguistics.

Jinhyuk Lee, Wonjin Yoon, Sungdong Kim, Donghyeon Kim, Sunkyu Kim, Chan Ho So, and Jaewoo Kang. 2019. BioBERT: a pre-trained biomedical language representation model for biomedical text mining. *Bioinformatics*, 36(4):1234–1240.

Yinhan Liu, Myle Ott, Naman Goyal, Jingfei Du, Mandar Joshi, Danqi Chen, Omer Levy, Mike Lewis, Luke Zettlemoyer, and Veselin Stoyanov. 2019. Roberta: A robustly optimized BERT pretraining approach. *CoRR*, abs/1907.11692.

F. Pedregosa, G. Varoquaux, A. Gramfort, V. Michel, B. Thirion, O. Grisel, M. Blondel, P. Prettenhofer, R. Weiss, V. Dubourg, J. Vanderplas, A. Passos, D. Cournapeau, M. Brucher, M. Perrot, and E. Duchesnay. 2011. Scikit-learn: Machine learning in Python. *Journal of Machine Learning Research*, 12:2825–2830.

Wenlin Yao and Ruihong Huang. 2018. Temporal event knowledge acquisition via identifying narratives. In *Proceedings of the 56th Annual Meeting of the Association for Computational Linguistics (Volume 1: Long Papers)*, pages 537–547, Melbourne, Australia. Association for Computational Linguistics.

Author Index

Association for Computational Linguistics
209 N. Eighth Street
Stroudsburg, Pennsylvania 18360

ISBN 978-1-7138-8595-5

9 781713 885955

CURRAN ASSOCIATES INC.
proceedings.com